THE TRADER'S BOOK OF VOLUME

THE TRADER'S BOOK OF VOLUME

The Definitive Guide to Volume Trading

Mark Leibovit

McGraw Hill

New York Chicago San Francisco Lisbon London
Madrid Mexico City Milan New Delhi San Juan
Seoul Singapore Sydney Toronto

The McGraw-Hill Companies

1 2 3 4 5 6 7 8 9 0 DOC/DOC 1 5 4 3 2 1

ISBN-13: 978-0-07-175375-3
ISBN-10: 0-07-175375-3

This book is printed on acid-free paper.

To my mom, Geraldine (Gilada) Leibovit, who passed in her 94th year when I was heading to Israel, where she now eternally rests, and who could never understand how I ended up in the stock market.

To Louis Rukeyser, who took a Jewish cowboy from Sedona, Arizona, and placed him in the midst of Wall Street big shots, confirming his belief that research from the canyons of the west can equal or outdo research from the canyons of Wall Street.

To Yale Hirsch, whose *Stock Traders Almanac* (my first read book on the stock market in 1967) provided infinite encouragement to stay with the stock market.

CONTENTS

FOREWORD

I have been actively involved in the markets for over 35 years; my financial market education came solely from reading every technical book I could get my hands on. Being educated as an aerospace engineer is probably what attracted me to technical analysis in the first place. I have some concern of late. Many who are new to the art of technical analysis seem to have lost sight of the basics. I don't think many have spent the time required to prepare properly, as in my case, by reading and studying extensively. One missing component I have noticed is that volume is sorely overlooked by many. Why is this? I believe the use of ever-present technical analysis software has caused many to forget a key ingredient of market analysis, that is, they have forgotten to thoroughly study the markets and learn their history. This is easy to do, since just clicking on a button many times can yield charts with a variety of technical indicators and analysis.

Back in the 1980s, I remember helping Mark create charts of his work for his newsletter. He was insistent upon accuracy and clearly defining not only the process, but also the message. This was the beginning of a long relationship of respect and admiration. To put all that into perspective, you have to remember that computer software in the early 1980s was fairly basic and required a considerable amount of work on the part of the user to obtain the desired results. I don't want to even think about the difficulty of obtaining reliable data using a 300-baud modem. That was all back when I was in the technical analysis software business. The good news is that things have really changed today in the technical analysis software business for the positive. However, the bad news is that newcomers to this field seem to ignore the steep learning curve that is necessary for good market analysis. Experience is a critical element in all endeavors, and certainly in technical analysis.

I see analysts talking about head-and-shoulders chart patterns, and they seem excited that they have been able to identify the pattern, but in most cases, their lack of technical education causes them to see only the pattern, and woefully, in isolation. Edwards and Magee's text *Technical Analysis of Stock Trends*, first published in 1948 (my edition, is from 1973), clearly includes volume as an essential component of the head-and-shoulders pattern. For example, they say that a head-and-shoulders pattern is developing because the volume at the head is somewhat less than the volume that occurred on the left shoulder. They spend pages discussing how the pattern evolves and its effectiveness coupled with the volume action. Oh, how many times I have witnessed young analysts who are excited about discovering a head-and-shoulders pattern without any mention of the volume action! This is sad, very sad, indeed. Patterns in isolation are just not adequate analysis. When I wrote the third edition of my *Candlestick Charting Explained*, I provided a number of pages just to discuss that candle patterns in isolation rarely mean anything.

I could spend pages writing about the other component of chart patterns (both classic and candle) that seems to be missing these days, and that is the underlying trend that precedes it. If you are identifying a reversal pattern, doesn't it have to reverse something? Of course it does. So identifying a pattern is only a small part of the analysis process. Do not forget the volume and the trend. It takes all three components to make it successful.

Very few technical analysis books are devoted to volume alone; in fact, many have only a single chapter devoted to the subject, and none are as reference-oriented as *The Trader's Book of Volume*. Mark's Volume Reversal measures have been in use by him for 30 years, and he is still at it—that says something, doesn't it? I could delve into all the various uses of volume in market analysis, the hoards of technical indicators that use volume, but it isn't necessary here, because you are reading a book that covers the subject exceptionally well. I'll just let Mark tell the volume story form here. Enjoy the trip.

—Greg Morris, Big Canoe, GA, 2010

Greg Morris is the author of *Candlestick Charting Explained* and *Complete Guide to Market Breadth Indicators* and is Chief Technical Analyst, and Chairman of the Investment Committee, Stadion Money Management.

ACKNOWLEDGMENTS

We stand on the shoulders of giants. I am humbled by all the insight, genius, and pragmatism of my peers, both current and past. Though my own volume work has its unique aspects, it still all comes down to the fact that other very thoughtful and innovative technicians spent countless hours pondering the volume/price relationship, and they, too, laid the groundwork for what you will read herein.

Closer to home, I have to thank my business partner, Laura Reiben, who conceptualized this project with me and insisted that I write this book on volume. Laura is an attorney who is passionate about the contribution of Volume Analysis to technical analysis, and she helped orchestrate this book as one does a symphony from the proposal stage through final edits of the manuscript.

Particular recognition and thanks goes to my friend and colleague Wayne Corbitt, CMT of Market Perspectives LLC, without whose support in research, technical analysis, charting, and programming this book would not have happened.

I want to thank Curt Renz, author of *The Investor's Guide to Technical Analysis,* for introducing me to McGraw-Hill; Jake Bernstein, every technical writer's inspiration, for encouraging me to write a "long overdue" book on volume analysis; Mary Glenn, Morgan Ertel, and Leah Spiro from McGraw-Hill, for recognizing that a comprehensive book on volume was necessary; Peter Sander, my editor, for helping to organize the manuscript and keeping us to a deadline; Ruth Mannino at McGraw-Hill for her patience during the production process; Robert Deadman, of Trading Systems Analysis Group, for programming our Volume Reversal trading software add-on for Metastock; Jeff Gibby from MetaStock for the use of MetaStock charts in this book; my assistant, Michael E. Newton, author of *The Path to Tyranny*, for his many hours providing research to our newsletter; Rick Imperiale, of Forward Uniplan Advisors, for his input regarding tactical overlays; and Bill Brower, of Inside Edge Systems, for his Volume Reversal (VR) programming using TradeStation.

I want to acknowledge my stock market and health food mentor, Roger Cole, who so graciously appeared in 1974 and then left my life all too quickly. His candor and perspective left an indelible mark and a moral compass from which to conduct myself.

A special thank-you to my children, who suffered through countless hours of time I spent away from them at work in the markets. They are always there despite my irascible nature, and I am eternally grateful to them for allowing me to pursue my obsession, though they probably wouldn't have allowed it if they were asked.

THE TRADER'S BOOK OF VOLUME

INTRODUCTION

In April 2010, my proverbial ducks were lined up. I called the sharp stock market reversal, which started with the painful "flash crash" of May 6, 2010, and ended up in the worst May stock market performance in 70 years.

I've also called many other serious market reversals, as I'll describe shortly. These downturns may have been precipitated by the events and news headlines of the time, but they were also foretold by observable indications of vulnerability before the crises struck.

How was I able to accomplish this? What's so special about the methodology I employ? How is it different from all the other trading strategies out there, all those crystal balls that work—until they don't? In a word, my methodology is based on a key component that few comprehend or have taken the time to truly examine. My methodology—upon which *The Trader's Book of Volume* is based—reflects my more than 30 years in the financial industry exploring and analyzing how volume affects the markets.

The Volume/Price Relationship

The stock market adage that "volume precedes price" is really more than just an adage or a memorable saying. It is my contention that volume is a determining factor in market strength and trend direction. As I have stated so often in my seminars—and as you will read in depth in this book—without a proper Volume Analysis, you are essentially trading in "the land of the blind." Using volume indicators and oscillators (in my own work, I rely heavily on my proprietary Leibovit Volume Reversal™ indicator), a trader can generate indisputable signals concerning the future direction of the markets.

In my career, I have *never* been caught in a stock market crash. I'm on record as having called the 1987 crash on Louis Rukeyser's *Wall Street Week* on PBS. I also called the bear market in February 2000 at the height of the Internet bubble and the decline ahead of the horrific attacks on September 11, 2001. Most recently, I provided my clients with a "Sell" signal weeks ahead of the "flash crash" of May 6, 2010.

Calling the Shots

So how did I come to anticipate this latest broad market trend reversal? A good place to start was with the "shot across the bow" fired on April 16, 2010, when the Securities and Exchange Commission charged Goldman, Sachs & Company and one of its vice presidents with fraud tied to a subprime mortgage financial product. Nearly 8.1 billion shares traded to the downside that day, generating a technical sell signal in the Leibovit Volume Reversal indicator. There are many factors I consider in my Volume Analysis; the sharp increase in volume—signaling a sudden shift in the marketplace from buyers to sellers on that date—was one of them.

Several other pieces of dramatic news rocked the markets over the next few days. The first was on April 27, 2010, when the stock market sold off on heavy volume amid increased speculation that Greece would be forced to restructure its debt. The second occurred amid growing rumors that Chinese regulators might try to slow their country's robust economy. Regardless of the news, or the trading events around it, I rely on Volume Analysis for my timing signals. In my volume methodology, a second negative Leibovit Volume Reversal raised a red warning flag that market internals were deteriorating.

In Charts I.1 and I.2, a trader using Volume Analysis would be able to spot the negative divergences warning that "something is rotten in the state of Denmark." Chart I.1 reveals that despite rising prices in the Standard & Poor's 500 Index (S&P 500) during March and April, the Money Flow Index was declining and the Volume Price Trend was not in sync with price. In Chapters 8 through 10 of *The Trader's Book of Volume*, we will be looking in depth at these and other volume-based indicators and oscillators and how they're used in Volume Analysis.

In Chart I.2, the Leibovit Volume Reversal indicator generated numerous Negative Volume Reversal patterns in the weeks prior to the flash crash. It clearly demonstrated that "smart money" was exiting the market and provided footprints of a shift in trend direction (in this case, lower) in the markets. As a result of Volume Analysis and my volume tactical overlays (see Chapter 11), we flashed a sell signal to our financial newsletter subscribers at VRTrader.com in the weeks and days prior to

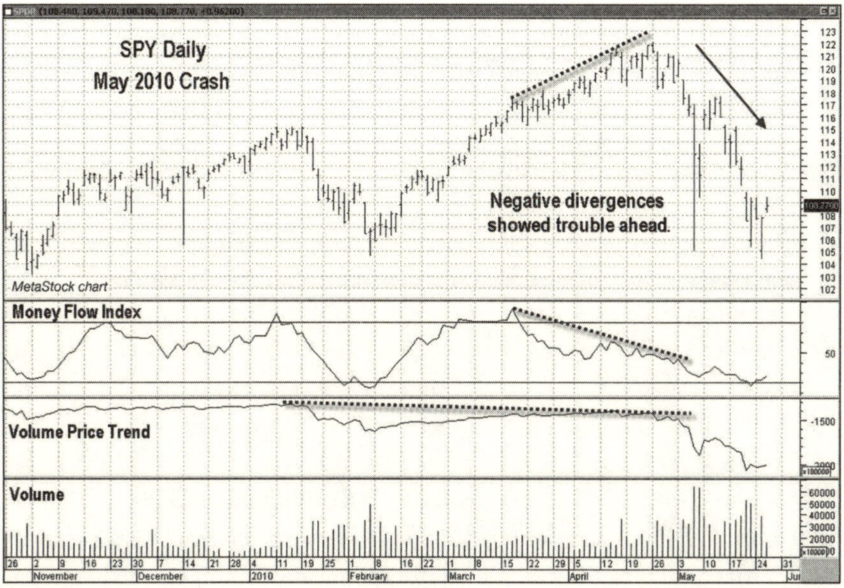

Chart I.1 SPY: S&P 500 Depository Receipt ("Spyder"—SPY), May 2010 Crash

Source: MetaStock

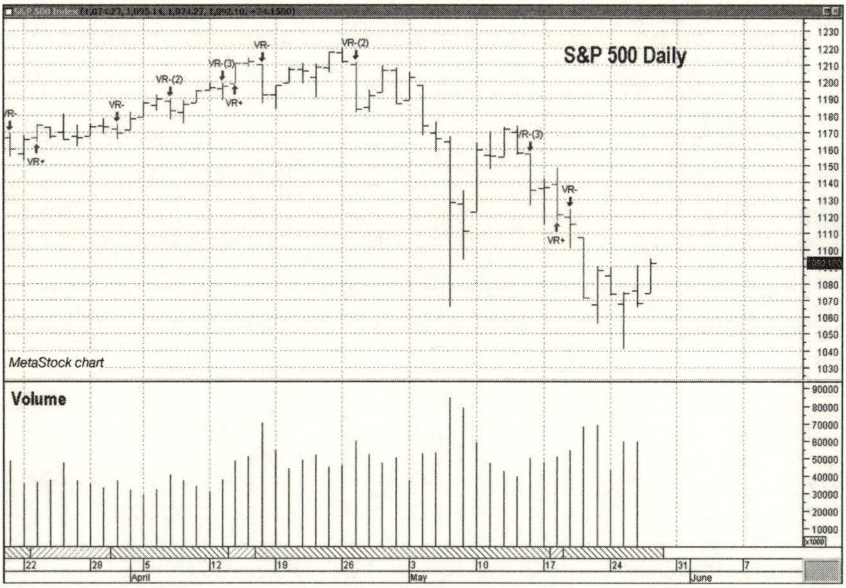

Chart I.2 S&P 500 Daily, Volume Reversal® Indicator, May 2010 Crash

Source: MetaStock

the event. In effect, a trader using Volume Analysis would not have viewed the events of May 6, 2010 and the market's 1,000-point decline as a random event; rather, it should have been technically anticipated.

This market call comes on the heels of numerous other such calls I've made in recent years, all coming as a result of a sudden shift from buyers to sellers. For instance, before the attacks on the World Trade Center on September 11, 2001 (9/11), the broad market was setting up for a reversal. In Chart I.3, note the sequence of Negative Volume Reversals in the weeks prior to the attack, which in my approach was a clear sign of market "distribution" (or selling). There was no way of predicting the tragedy of 9/11 or the market crash that was around the corner, but volume clearly signaled traders to step aside, sell, and take profits—or even to go short.

In Chart I.4, the Nasdaq 100 Index (NDX), and Chart I.5, the exchange-traded fund (ETF) equivalent (QQQQ), it was abundantly clear that during 2007 a market top was forming by virtue of negative divergences (i.e., rising price and declining volume), warning of potential trouble. In addition, my

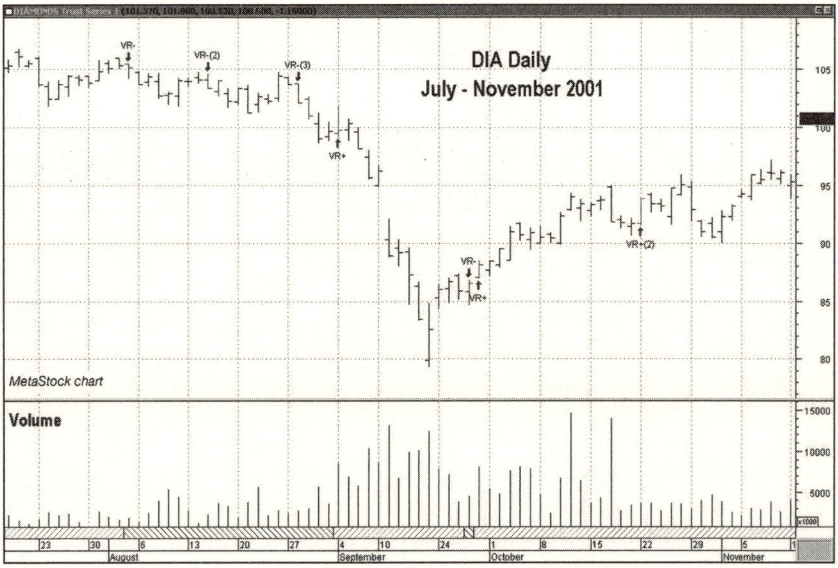

Chart I.3 Dow Jones Industrial Average (DIA) Daily, Volume Reversals, July to November 2001

Source: MetaStock

Chart I.4 2007 Market Top and Negative Volume Reversals, Nasdaq 100 Futures

Source: MetaStock

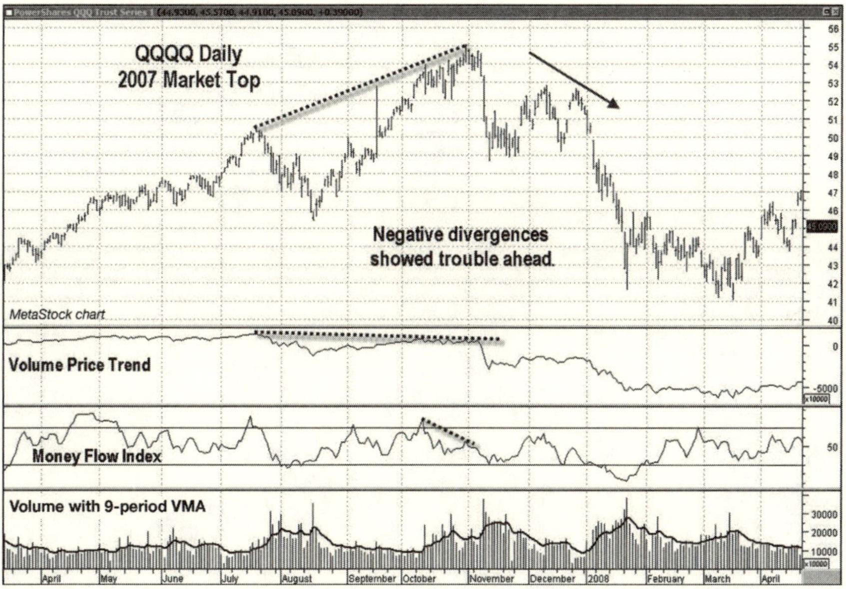

Chart I.5 2007 Market Top, Multiple Indicator Divergence, Nasdaq PowerShares ETF

Source: MetaStock

Leibovit Volume kicked in during the fall of 2007 with Negative Volume Reversals, or "–VRs" (Chart I.4), as sellers were getting more and more aggressive. The end result, of course, was the huge decline during the fall of 2008 and into March 2009.

The pattern was even clearer when observing the divergence between price, Volume Price Trend, and Money Flow Index in the Nasdaq PowerShares ETF (QQQQ).

Many recall the brief 1998 market panic caused by Russia's debt crisis, and for those who don't, Sergei Ulatov offers a great summary in the *Brookings Papers on Economic Activity*: "On August 17, 1998, about a little more than a month after an international package of emergency financing and economic reforms was announced, Russia was forced to devalue the ruble. Russia also declared its intention to restructure all official domestic currency debt obligations falling due to the end of 1999. . ."

Looking at the Volume Reversals in the "E-Mini" S&P 500 futures contract (see Chart I.6), the signs were there in the market prior to both stages of the decline.

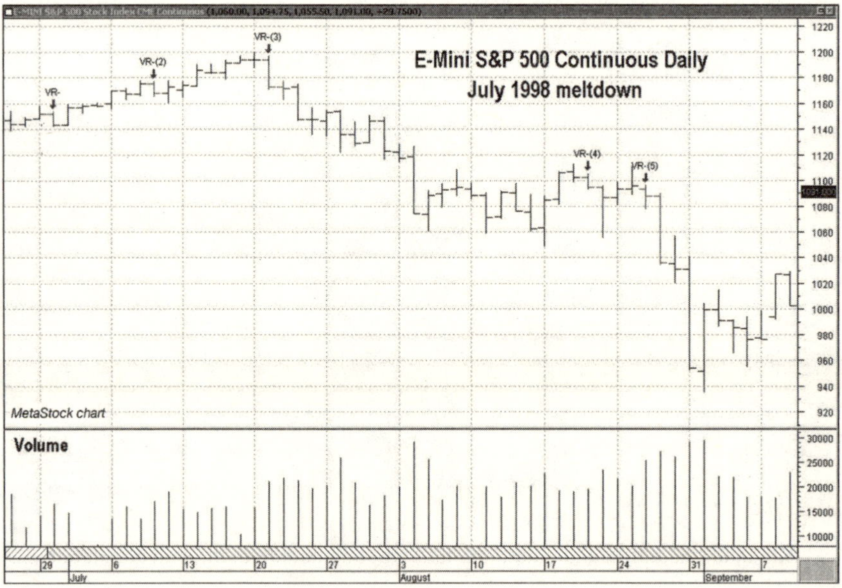

Chart I.6 The 1998 Russian Debt Crisis, Volume Reversals, E-Mini S&P 500 Futures

Source: MetaStock

It's worth taking another look at the top in March 2000, which led to a two-year bear market. The exact day of the top for the Nasdaq was March 10, 2000, and as can be seen in Chart I.7, sellers were active all through the spring and summer of 2000. Volume was again telling us that trouble was on the horizon—specifically, the volume on the upswings was weak, indicating that traders, especially large buy-side traders, were running out of gas.

Many of you may not have been in the market during 1987 or experienced the hair-raising crash on Monday, October 19, of that year, but Volume Analysis warned that there were problems ahead, and the crash was truly no surprise. Using IBM as a surrogate for the Dow Jones Industrials, note in Chart I.8 the heavy distribution (negative Volume Reversals) beginning in mid-August 1987. As in all the previous examples, the charts were warning of problems ahead, enough so that you should have been looking to exit long positions or consider playing the short side. As we have often experienced, selling can lead to panics, and if volume is telling us that "smart money" is getting out of the market, aren't we best advised to head for higher ground?

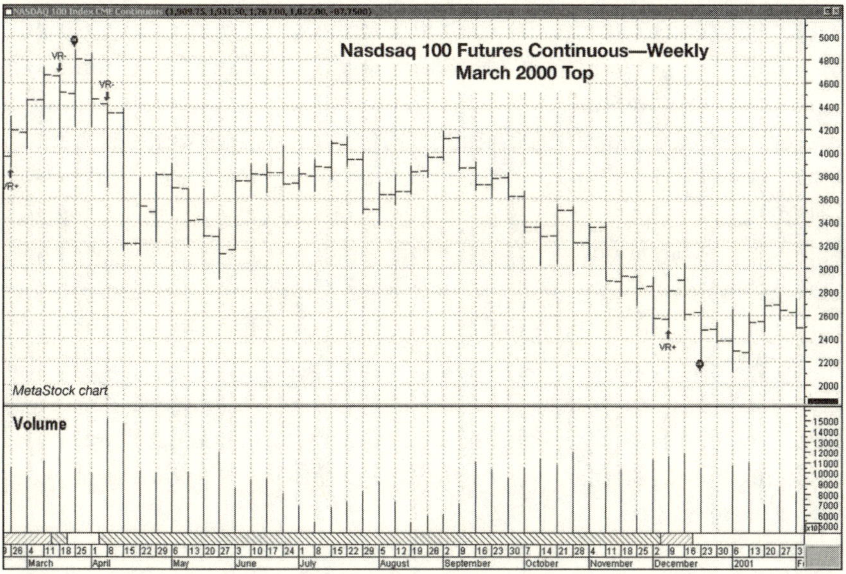

Chart I.7 March 2000 Market Top, Negative Volume Reversals, Nasdaq 100 Futures

Source: MetaStock

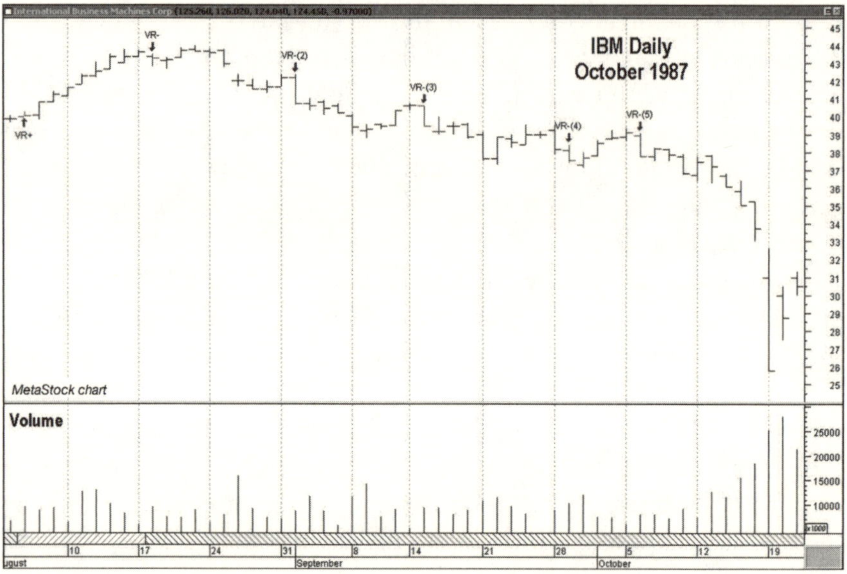

Chart I.8 The 1987 Crash, Negative Volume Reversals, IBM Stock

Source: MetaStock

A Picture Is Worth a Thousand Words

Truth be told, I can't really look at a price chart and tell you what's happening without viewing an accompanying volume chart. Volume is what really tells me how much conviction, or strength, there is behind a move. There are many analogies for this, and I explore some of them in Chapter 1. In short, volume tells me the strength—or the weakness—behind a price move. It gives me a more complete view, a more dependable, reliable, and consistent picture of market trends. As traders, we know that, when price rises or falls on increasing volume, there is strength and validity to the trend. When price rises or falls on diminishing volume, it's a sign that the trend is tired, buyers and sellers are tired, and the trend is vulnerable to a reversal. In *The Trader's Book of Volume*, we take these basic concepts further, examining, in depth, factors affecting volume and exploring how to ultimately translate the information that volume provides into trading profits.

Volume Technical Analysis

If it were only so simple, we'd all be traders right off the bat. The truth is, while many volume signals are clear and strong, most are far more subtle and require translation. Putting your preconceived notions of trading aside, I contend that it is the combination of volume and price—the relationship, the patterns, the divergences, the strengths and weaknesses—that really form the basis for Volume Analysis. But that said, I'll stand clearly in the camp that with volume and price together, it's a "one-plus-one-equals-three" story; that is, price and volume, taken together, tell far more to a trader about market trends, reversals, and tactical timing than either can separately.

The Leibovit Volume Reversal

Here's headline news from my *VRTRADER.COM Platinum Newsletter*, June 4, 2010:

> The stock market is getting hit after declines in Europe and following a smaller than expected increase in payrolls. The Dow is down 212, S&P down 22, and NASDAQ down 41. VRTrader did it again. We bought inverse ETFs yesterday and this morning we took profits. That's the third time in a row we profitably bet on a falling market.

Indeed, I've been making such calls for years based on the Leibovit Volume Reversal indicator. In fact a Leibovit VR™ was the basis for my call of most of the major market turns and crashes outlined in the beginning of this introduction.

The Leibovit Volume Reversal indicator has been remarkably accurate in its ability to produce high-performance trades in both stocks and indexes based on the combined behaviors of price and volume. Because disclosing the details of the formula might compromise its effectiveness, I can't share too much of what happens inside this "black box," but suffice it to say that it has been a remarkably successful trading system and application of volume technical analysis. I cover the Volume Reversal in greater detail in Chapter 9.

Why a Trader's Book of Volume?

As I mentioned earlier, there seems to be a plethora of books on trading, but there are few that pursue volume-based technical analysis in depth. *The Trader's Book of Volume* provides a comprehensive treatment that will allow traders to gain access to Volume Analysis–centric tools and methods and to develop their own Tactical Volume Overlay Strategies.

The Trader's Book of Volume focuses exclusively on volume analysis: of patterns and trends based on the volume/price relationship. It doesn't advance a methodology or trading strategy, but rather is constructed to provide a trader's eye toward exploring and using volume-based technical indicators and oscillators as a component in trading strategy.

A Brief Word about Tools

It's worth taking a minute to describe the charting and software tools that I use and that were used to develop the 300-plus examples illustrating the indicators and oscillators presented in this book.

One of my favorites is MetaStock, which is a proprietary computer program created by Equis International and is used for charting and technical analysis of stock prices. It has both real-time and end-of-day versions. The newest version (MetaStock 11) is 27 years in the making. The Web site is www.equis.com/.

MetaStock enables you to scan a database of thousands of securities looking for prime trading opportunities. Among the 200 built-in indicators for individual stocks and 80 built-in indicators for broad market analysis are most of the volume indicators and oscillators discussed in this book. MetaStock also provides a subscription-based add-on for traders using my Volume Reversal indicators for the equity and commodities markets in the United States, Canada, and abroad.

In addition, many other charting and trading packages contain volume-based indicators and oscillators.

About My Newsletters

My technical expertise lies in Volume Analysis, and that subfield of technical analysis is what *The Trader's Book of Volume* is all about. Beyond this book, and preceding it, I have applied my technical experience and expertise toward the publication of four newsletters to provide short-term, high-performance stock trades and market timing based upon the Leibovit Volume Reversal indicators and trading strategy. By tracking positive and negative Volume Reversal signals, I have been able to call market moves and to flash buy or sell signals and profitably exploit the momentum and volatility of short- and midterm moves in stocks, indexes, and commodities with clearly defined risk management guidelines.

Currently I publish four newsletters:

- *VR Platinum* is targeted to high-performance traders; offers specific recommendations, entry points, targets, and stops for individual stocks and stock indexes and ETFs; and provides subscribers with a daily list of all monitored Positive and Negative Volume Reversals. *VR Platinum* is published premarket, postmarket, and on an "as needed" basis intraday. The premarket update provides an "Action Alert" section for the stock market, the Dow Transportation Average, gold and metals, bonds, crude oil, and the U.S. dollar.
- *VR Silver* offers some of the *VR Platinum* material, but in a premarket and postmarket edition only, and is targeted to less active traders, as no specific recommendations are made.
- *VR Forecaster* is an annual forecast published between mid-January and early February and contains my cyclical forecast for the major markets for the year.
- *VR Gold Letter* is a weekly newsletter that provides traders, portfolio managers, and investors with unique insights, opinions, and recommendations for the gold, silver, and platinum markets utilizing the Leibovit Volume Reversal and cyclical (Annual Forecast Model) strategies.

These newsletters are based on, and will expand your knowledge of, Volume Analysis–based trading. You can find out more about the newsletters at www.VRtrader.com and about our consulting group at www.VRstrategic.com.

Road Map

The Trader's Book of Volume, Part One, explores the concepts of volume technical analysis from a trading perspective. Chapter 1, "Volume Basics: A Trader's View," discusses the importance of Volume Analysis in analyzing market behavior. In Chapter 2, "The Trader's Mantra: Volume Precedes Price," Volume Analysis is shown to provide traders with a multidimensional view of the trading terrain and greater depth and understanding of the volume/price relationship. Chapter 3, "Navigating the Volume Trading Terrain," describes the six basic volume/price relationships of which every trader should be aware.

Chapter 4, "Spotting Volume/Price Patterns and Market Trends," uses Volume Analysis and various volume overlay tools to explain market trends. In Chapter 5, "The Volume Alert: Identifying Trend Reversal Patterns," the focus shifts to identifying volume patterns that signal a potential for a trend reversal. Chapter 6, "News, Noise, and Volume," examines some of the factors and dynamics that affect volume patterns, such as daily market internals, seasonality, earnings announcements, and internal and external news events. Chapter 7, "Trading Time Frames and Indicator Selection," explains the ways to understand and select the right indicators, oscillators, and time frames to fit the market condition, the securities being traded, and your own trading style; there's no "one size fits all" solution.

Part Two is a compilation of volume-based indicators and oscillators with trading examples and offers guidance on developing tactical volume overlays. Chapter 8, "Broad Market Volume Indicators," covers 13 major volume indicators and oscillators that are used to assess trend direction, trend strength, and reversals across the broader markets. Chapter 9, "The Volume Indicators," comprises a description and detailed examples of 10 new volume *indicators* and their behavior under a variety of trading conditions.

Chapter 10, "The Volume Oscillators," describes and gives detailed examples of 10 volume oscillators and their behavior under a variety of trading conditions. Chapter 11, "Developing Tactical Volume Overlays," serves as a guide for traders in developing tactical volume overlays for trend identification, short-term trading opportunities, and sector and broad market timing. The Conclusion, "Keeping a Trader's Eye on Volume," delivers parting comments on the volume trading terrain.

• • •

One ongoing frustration of mine has been that Volume Analysis has never been presented in a comprehensive format. In this book, I try to include the most widely available volume indicators and oscillators that were developed by the many very talented and creative market technicians who preceded me. As we all know, we stand on the shoulders of giants. Throughout this book, I express opinions based on my 30-plus years of market experience studying volume. *The Trader's Book of Volume* should help fill a void and hopefully inspire you while generating some creative discourse surrounding the volume/price trend relationship.

Relevant equations and supplementary material can be found at www.mhprofessional.com/tradersbookofvolume.

PART ONE

THE IMPORTANCE OF VOLUME IN TECHNICAL ANALYSIS AND HOW BASIC VOLUME ANALYSIS WORKS

Chapter 1

VOLUME BASICS: A TRADER'S VIEW

Is it volume which causes price changes, or do price changes cause volume—the hen or the egg, which came first?

—H. M. Gartley, *Profits in the Stock Market*

Back in 1934, R. W. Schabacker commented in *Stock Market Profits,* his 300-page treatise on trading: "In our entire study of Plate V we have given no consideration to the factor of volume of trading, though this is another highly important and valuable angle of the technical approach to short-swing trading."

Having recognized the value of volume, he spent only three paragraphs discussing this highly important and valuable tool. Why was so little consideration given to volume? One explanation is that the data required for Volume Analysis were largely unavailable at the time and reserved only for the eyes of an elite group of market participants, an "insiders' club" comprising floor traders, market makers, and institutions.

Today, with the development of sophisticated desktop trading interfaces along with more readily available market data, traders can access information that was previously in the exclusive realm of insiders. This more accessible data flow has opened the door into the realm of Volume Analysis and the strategic deployment of volume-based indicators, oscillators, and overlays to enhance trading performance.

In this chapter, we challenge you to rethink any preconceived notions of price and volume as they relate to your trading strategy and offer you a short primer on the basics of volume.

The Case for Volume

Volume Analysis provides a trader with a clear and focused view of the collective behavior of financial market participants. Overwhelmingly, we traders have been indoctrinated with price-based indicators, but what if what is lying under the hood staring us in the face has eluded us? What if, at the end of the day, the behavior revealed by volume is the high-octane fuel that creates, accelerates, or decelerates market conditions?

We've been told that market trends are created by market participants agreeing in aggregate that a fair price for a stock or commodity can be found and that price moves accordingly to higher or lower levels. In Volume Analysis, we view the development of market trends as a dynamic process that cannot simply be explained based upon price movement alone. Our standard for identifying and predicting trend changes incorporates the volume action accompanying these price movements. Throughout our exploration of volume, our guiding principle will remain arguably simple.

Volume Action Is Linked to Price Movement

Most traders have a minimal understanding that a price move accompanied by strong or heavy volume is likely to continue in its current direction, and, conversely, if volume is lighter than "normal," the trend may be suspect. These concepts are about as in-depth an understanding as most traders will ever develop about volume. So what of the behavior of volume in technical chart patterns, in trend continuation and reversals, and in volume overlays?

It is our belief that volume is an essential component of every price move and pattern. If a trader is unable to read or translate volume information, if his understanding of it remains limited, then he is forced into the trading strategies and routine guidance more commonly serving the interests of the institutional crowd. By taking our trading off-road and examining the complexities of volume, we are taking a detour from trading based on price-driven data alone. It is our hope that as you explore the pages of this book on volume, you will gain predictive insight into trend direction and reversals and ultimately develop your own set of defensive tactical strategies.

A Dynamic Volume Analogy

There are many analogies to describe the dynamic effects of volume on price trends. Most commonly, it is compared to fuel in a car engine. If the tank is low on gas (i.e., weak volume), the car engine eventually will falter and stall. Had the tank been full (i.e., strong volume), the car would have just cruised on down the road. Just as too much fuel can flood an engine, too much volume, in the form of spikes and surges (indicates an emotionally charged trading environment), can signal that the "engine" might stop heading in its current direction (i.e., a change in trend is near).

> Remember: Volume action is inextricably linked to price trend movement.

In *The Trader's Book of Volume,* our focus will be to translate the meaning of volume information into trading strategies and ultimately into tactical volume overlays. How to begin to do this is to understand some *volume basics;* the coordinates we are measuring will act as our guide. We begin by understanding what information is embedded within and represented by volume.

Volume as a Measure of Supply and Demand

On any given day, both volume and price in the markets are constantly readjusting to accurately reflect the current market environment. If there is an imbalance of buyers in the market, price may adjust to higher levels to entice existing holders to sell their positions to offset demand or buying pressure. If there is an imbalance of sellers, price may adjust to lower levels to entice new buying to offset supply or selling pressure.

As more traders line up and execute their intentions on either the buy side or the sell side, the increased activity shows up in the form of volume. How volume interacts with price on any trading day reveals the level of supply and demand in the market for that security or commodity. The behavior of volume during the trading day represents hard evidence that the imbalance between buyers and sellers is being resolved. Ultimately, it is the *volume* action, not the price action, as most of us have been taught, that signals the first indication of the direction of that resolution.

Volume as a Gauge of Trader Sentiment and Interest

When we look at a fuel gauge, we get a sense of our ability to go the distance. Similarly, we can take a volume measurement to represent how much bullish or bearish sentiment there is in trading a particular market, index, or issue. Elevated interest in the form of higher-than-*normal* volume gives clarity as to when and at what level the next potential price move *may* occur. "Normal" volume will depend on our trading time frame and the unique volume characteristics of the index or issue being traded, but once normal is determined, any departure from that is significant.

A case in point: Using a volume moving average, a trader can identify higher-than-normal volume with small price swings, which may indicate that shares are being either *accumulated* or *distributed* in a sideways market. Below-normal volume on larger price swings, especially in trending markets, may signal to a trader that a shift in trend is imminent. Volume Analysis thus serves to improve a trader's predictive ability as to the timing and direction of trends and reversals.

Using Volume to Track the Major Market Players

A major strength of Volume Analysis is its ability to track the trading activity of the largest market participants: that is, mutual funds, large hedge funds, and institutional players. These elite players often intentionally camouflage their positions. By using Volume Analysis, a trader has the ability to recognize their volume patterns and uncover their tracks. Traders with volume expertise are in the enviable position of being able to take the lead or tailgate their positions.

Measuring and Charting Volume Data

Much as drivers assess coordinates before taking their vehicles off-road, we will be taking a preliminary look at how volume data are measured and charted.

Volume is very versatile in that it can be used in its "raw" form (which is expressed and read simply as volume bars plotted at the bottom of a chart) or in "smoothed" form (which uses a calculated overlay such as a moving average). These pure volume measurements can in turn be used alone, as components of other volume indicators, and in combinations, ultimately allowing us to gauge our trading terrain.

Volume has been defined for charting purposes as the number of units traded during a given period of time. These units are typically represented by either shares or contracts. Volume is plotted with price to determine the strength or conviction behind price movement. There are several variations in the way this volume information can be displayed on stock and commodities charts. These different methods of display have their own strengths and weaknesses. Our trading time frame generally dictates our display preferences. This section explores some of the more common ways to exhibit and interpret volume information on common stock or other security charts.

Bar Plots

The most common method for plotting volume is the standard *bar plot*. The bar plot allows for quick analysis between price points to measure the strength or conviction behind a move. Chart 1.1 shows a simple bar plot of volume.

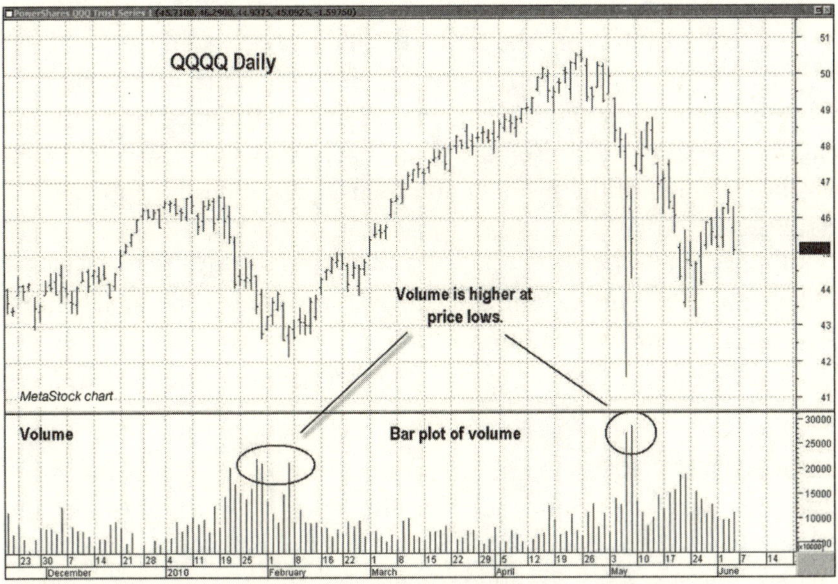

Chart 1.1 Bar Plot, Nasdaq 100 Trust ETF Daily

Source: MetaStock

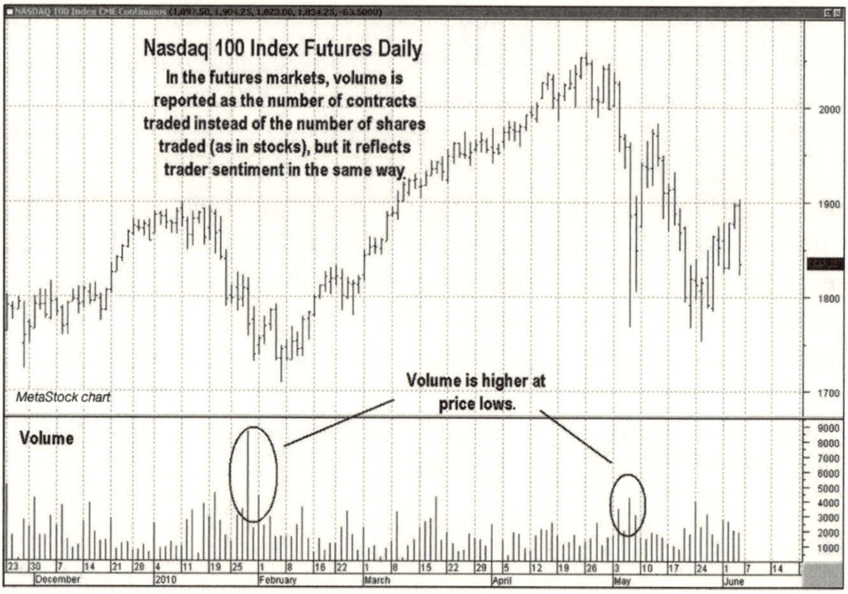

Chart 1.2 Futures Contract Volume, Nasdaq 100 Index Futures

Source: MetaStock

Bar plots of volume can be either zero-based or based on the lowest volume total in a data or time series. In either case, a good bar plot gives the bars a consistent, uniform starting point, which makes comparisons between values easier. For instance, in Chart 1.1, notice how volume spikes higher at price lows on the chart. Later in the book, we will examine the meaning of these spikes and their implications for future price movements.

Although the example in Chart 1.1 shows the trading of an exchange-traded fund (ETF) in the form of shares, we should note that such volume depictions also work for futures, which are sold as contracts, not shares. Chart 1.2 shows an example of volume expressed in contracts traded.

Colored Bar Plots

One preferred way to enhance the display of volume is to color the volume bars. Many charting packages allow for the coloring of volume bars, making it easier to distinguish between days in which price closed higher and days in which price closed lower. Chart 1.3 has volume bars colored in black on days when price closed higher than the previous day,

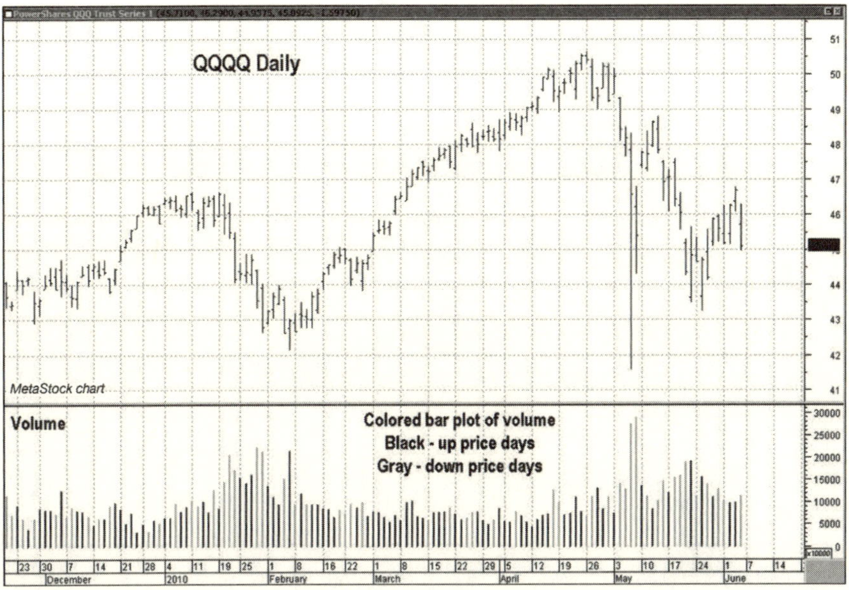

Chart 1.3 Colored Volume Bar Plot (Grayscale), QQQQ Daily, Nasdaq 100 Trust ETF Daily

Source: MetaStock

while days that closed lower than the previous day are colored in gray. Although our color choices in this book are limited to shades of black and white, other colors, most commonly red and green, can be used in most charting software. These color differentiations allow for quicker identification of positive versus negative volume.

Simple Line Plot

The simple line plot is another method that is less commonly used for displaying volume. Rather than displaying volume bars, volume is shown as a line. Chart 1.4 shows a simple line plot for volume. Showing volume in this way can allow for a quick analysis of volume spikes and surge patterns. It will not work on more thinly traded (lower-volume) securities, as the line plot can be very erratic. Unlike the bar plot, smaller-scale shorter-term volume comparisons are more difficult to measure.

Volume Moving Averages

The selection of a volume plotting methodology increases in importance when adding overlays to volume. One of the most widely used methods

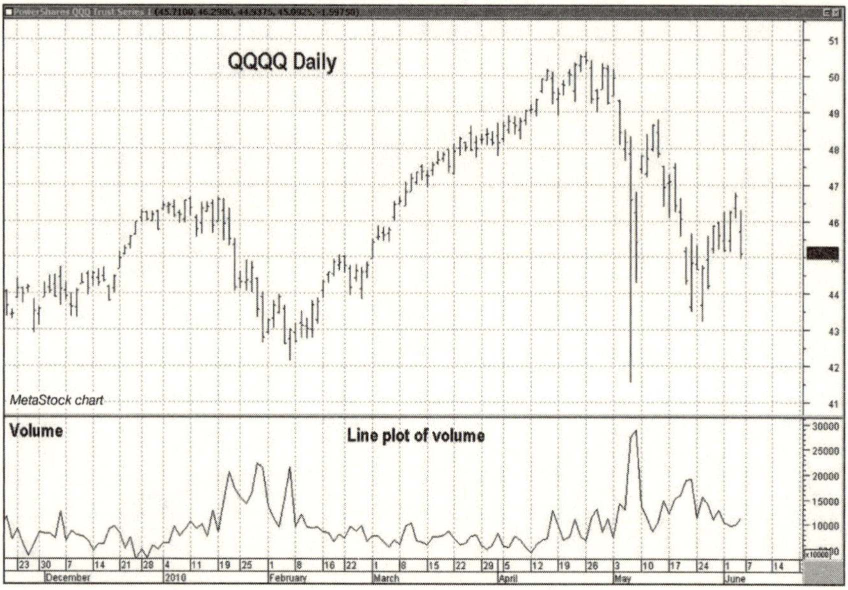

Chart 1.4 Simple Line Plot, Nasdaq 100 Trust ETF Daily

Source: MetaStock

of analyzing volume data is with a calculated volume moving average, more commonly known as a "VMA."

A volume moving average shows the average number of shares or contracts that have been traded over a set period of time. In the Nasdaq 100 Trust ETF (QQQQ), Chart 1.5, a bar plot of volume also contains a 9-period moving average of volume, a common volume moving average setting for shorter-term traders. (We'll discuss time frames in more detail in Chapter 7.) Note how the volume moving average plots make it easy to spot the days where the daily volume jumped above the average.

We've examined some of the different ways that volume data, the basic building blocks of Volume Analysis, can be displayed to accommodate a trader's charting preferences. Placing pure volume (bars) below price on a trading chart establishes that first reference point for Volume Analysis. In the remainder of this book, we will be taking a new perspective on the volume window and focusing on translating these volume bars, indicators, oscillators, and overlays into profitable trading signals and strategies.

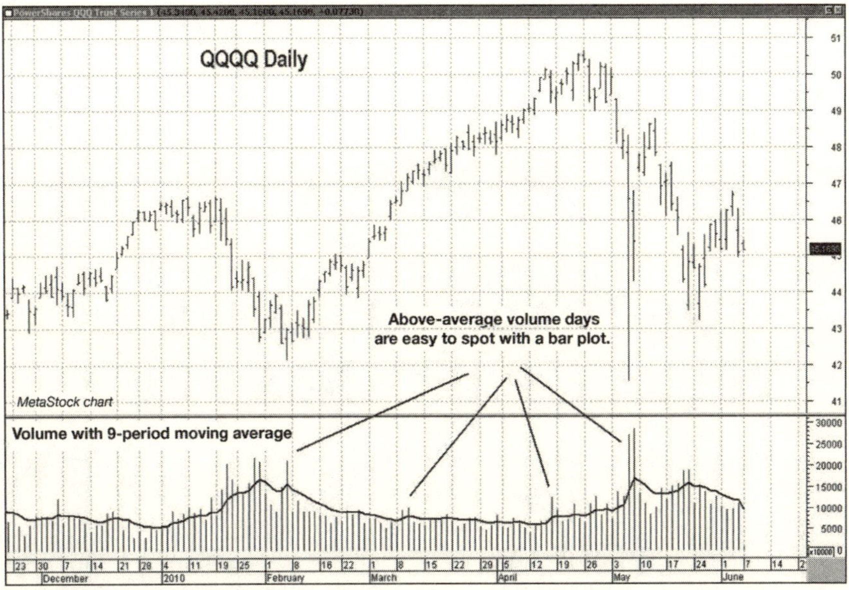

Chart 1.5 A 9-Period Volume Moving Average with Bar Plot, Nasdaq 100 Trust ETF Daily

Source: MetaStock

Summary

- Volume has the ability to uncover the movements of larger market participants and track their "footprints in the sand."
- Volume serves as a gauge of supply and demand and overall trading conviction, and is inextricably linked with price movement. Volume can be used to predict the direction, strength, and timing of those trends.
- Volume data, in conjunction with price information, may be charted in a variety of ways. The basic volume bar plot with a volume moving average (VMA) overlay is one of the most effective ways to chart the volume/price relationship.

Chapter 2

THE TRADER'S MANTRA: VOLUME PRECEDES PRICE

The mantra that volume precedes price has served many a trader well and remains as much a fundamental truth today as it was when I first heard it more than 35 years ago. Price movements occur daily in the financial markets. Using Volume Analysis, we turn our focus on the volume action behind these movements and look for insight into the strength and intensity of the crowd that fueled the move. Although not all market participants are equivalent, the volume numbers continually reveal their collective sentiment.

Market price trends do not happen in a vacuum; rather, it is the behavioral or programmed responses of traders and managers that result in the volume shifts that precede a price move. As the crowd mobilizes, as reflected in the volume numbers, its size and conviction will determine the direction and strength of the price movement. As the conviction of the crowd falters and the volume numbers pull back and diminish, so too will this impact the timing and direction of the trend. This chapter displays some visual examples of this truth at work.

Viewing the Market in Three Dimensions

One of the major reasons for using Volume Analysis is to capture volume's ability to signal *changes* in trading sentiment to traders, which ultimately cause changes in trend or price direction. It helps to think of Volume Analysis as a multidimensional map of the trading environment. While price action looks at two dimensions, the inclusion of volume gives a visual look behind price movement, providing greater detail as to what the driving forces are and how they can be anticipated to behave.

One way to think of this combination is to consider the situation of a mountain biker traveling through rugged terrain. Our biker can pack a simple flat map or one showing topographical features. A biker with a map of the technical features of the course will have considerably more information and be able to make qualitatively different decisions from a rider using a flat map. Our biker relying on a topographical map will be able to gauge the level of difficulty of the incline, the ruggedness of the course, and ultimately the time frame for completion. He will be able to access the amount of energy he needs to reserve for certain portions of the course. Sure, our biker might get from point A to point B with a flat map, but lacking information about the technical terrain could be both costly and life threatening.

Volume as a Third Dimension: A Brief Example

The incorporation of a volume component into your trading strategy can be illustrated by a simple exercise. While sitting down, focus your eyes on a point in front of you in the room. Now cover one of your eyes. You should notice two things. First, your field of vision is cut in half, as the peripheral vision on one side is completely gone. Second, covering one eye compromises depth perception. You've just seen how adding volume gives you a broader read on market activity (peripheral vision) while also allowing you to see intensity and conviction behind price movements (depth perception). Now let's consider the example of the iShares Dow Jones Real Estate Trust ETF (IYR) shown in Chart 2.1. The top frame shows a flat, two-dimensional price momentum analysis. The bottom frame shows the Relative Strength Index, or RSI, a price-based momentum oscillator that is essentially a calculated figure representing the cumulative number of incrementally higher and lower closes in a given period. Even though the RSI is quite a sophisticated tool, the only input for its calculation is price data.

Notice how, as price moves into the vicinity of its previous low, the 14-period RSI breaks down to a new low, which could be interpreted as an indication that the downside price action will continue.

Now, let's examine the same price plot of IYR, only this time with volume bars plotted beneath price. The goal with this type of chart is to concentrate on the synergy between volume and price. In Chart 2.2, note how, as the iShares Dow Jones Real Estate Trust ETF (IYR) approached the same price point shown in Chart 2.1, the volume action, which heretofore had been low,

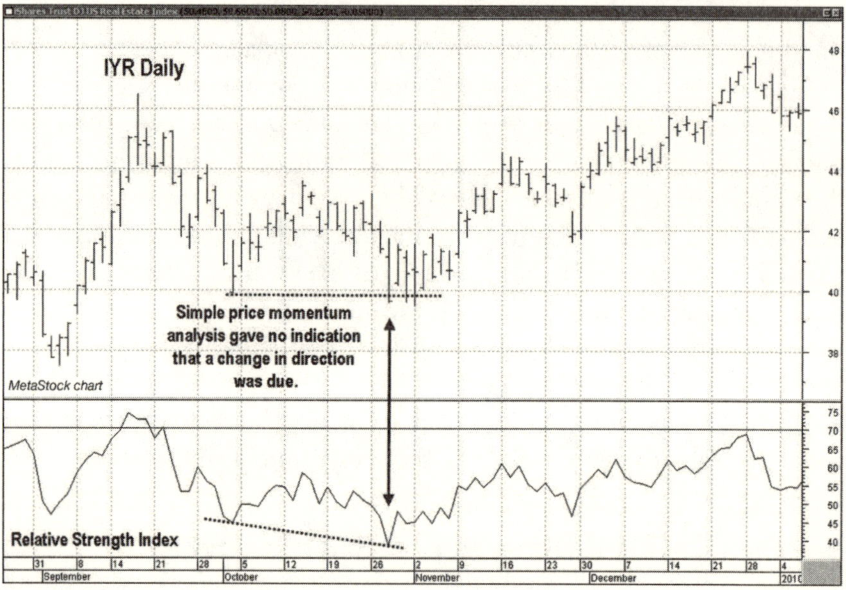

Chart 2.1 Price and Relative Strength Index, DJ Real Estate Trust ETF

Source: MetaStock

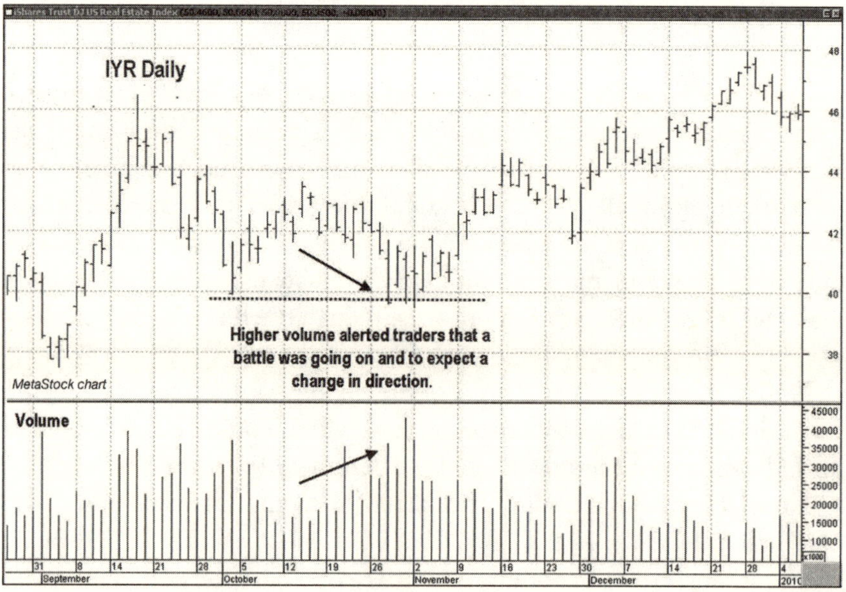

Chart 2.2 Price Movement with Volume, DJ Real Estate Trust

Source: MetaStock

noticeably increased. Using Volume Analysis, a sharp-eyed trader would translate this as a battle for near-term direction. This type of increased volume action would be recognized as a signal that a change in direction was due.

Rather than confirming the trend using RSI (erroneously, as it turns out), this multidimensional focus on both price trend and volume action suggests more correctly that a *change* in price direction was in the offing. It was only with the addition of volume that we were able to uncover the intensity and conviction of buying and selling pressure, and ultimately the money flowing into or out of the IYR index. This sort of multidimensional view reveals the power of Volume Analysis—and the potential limitations of relying on price-based technical analysis alone.

The Three-Dimensional View: A Second Example

This second example displays the S&P Select SPDR Financial Trust ETF (XLF) in its January to February 2010 decline. Equities were getting hit with a spirited pullback, but the buildup in volume on XLF as it made its January and February lows showed heightened activity that alerted traders that a change in trend was coming.

First, in Chart 2.3, a price plot of XLF is shown using a one-dimensional price momentum study. The chart shows the price of XLF plotted

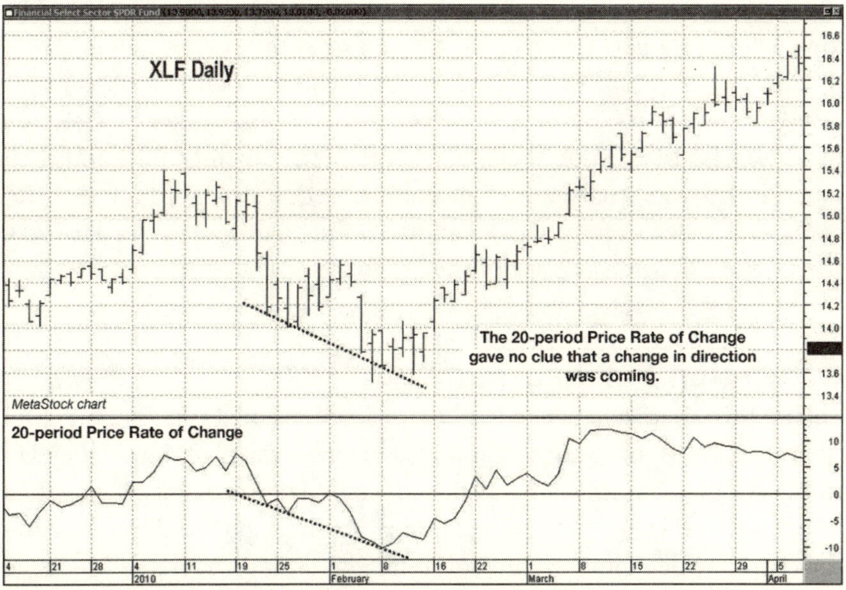

Chart 2.3 Price and 20-Period Rate of Change, S&P Financial SPDR (XLF)

Source: MetaStock

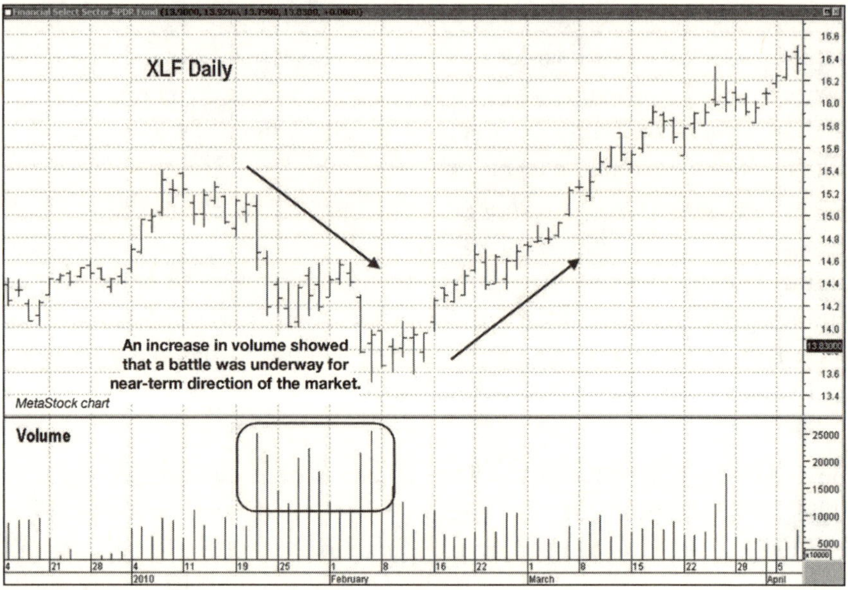

Chart 2.4 Price with Daily Volume, S&P Financial SPDR (XLF)

Source: MetaStock

with its 20-period Price Rate of Change, measuring the momentum, or strength of price movement. Note how the price indicator tumbled to new lows without signaling a potential reversal in trend.

Contrast Chart 2.3 of XLF with a chart with its volume plotted below price, as shown in Chart 2.4. This added frame now shows that volume increased as price made its January 2010 low, rallied briefly, and then made its final February low. This volume action displayed a tug-of-war going on for near-term price direction. As the chart reveals, buyers eventually won the battle as price pushed higher into the spring.

Conviction Is What Counts

Taking this discussion a step further, two-dimensional price momentum indicators can show overbought and oversold levels, but where they fall short is in their ability to display the conviction of the traders that pushed price to these levels. In classic technical analysis, one of the most commonly used price momentum tools is the Stochastic Oscillator developed by George Lane. The Stochastic is an excellent and much-relied-upon banded oscillator that works well with volume indicators. However, many traders attempt to perform their complete trading analysis based upon its relationship to price movement. The following example shows how adding volume to this banded oscillator gives a trader a multidimensional and more accurate representation of a market trend.

Chart 2.5, the Nasdaq 100 Trust ETF (QQQQ), shows the Stochastic Oscillator and its behavior during the 2008 market meltdown. It reached the oversold level many times throughout the decline, but it really did not show the conviction behind each push into oversold territory. With a two-dimensional price oscillator, it is difficult to see any difference from one oversold instance to another. Analyzing the market using price alone did not provide essential trading information as to the sentiment behind these overbought or oversold market conditions. This is where volume comes into play, improving a trader's ability to interpret those conditions and ultimately to trade more efficiently and profitably.

When volume and a volume-based indicator are added to the chart, it gives a visual display of the conviction behind the selling pressure during the 2008 price decline (see Chart 2.6 for QQQQ); we added the Force Index, a volume-based oscillator developed by Dr. Alexander Elder that is discussed in greater detail in Chapter 10.

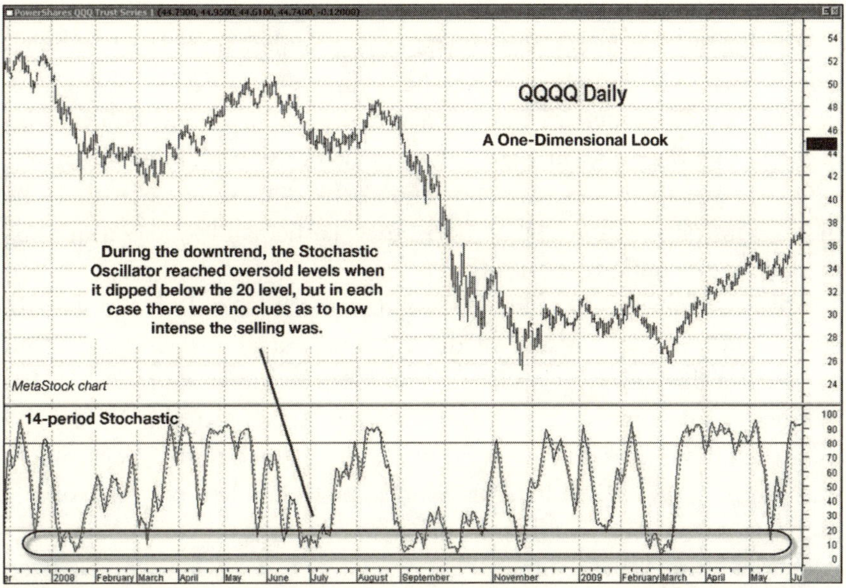

Chart 2.5 Stochastic Oscillator without Volume Component, Nasdaq 100 Trust ETF

Source: MetaStock

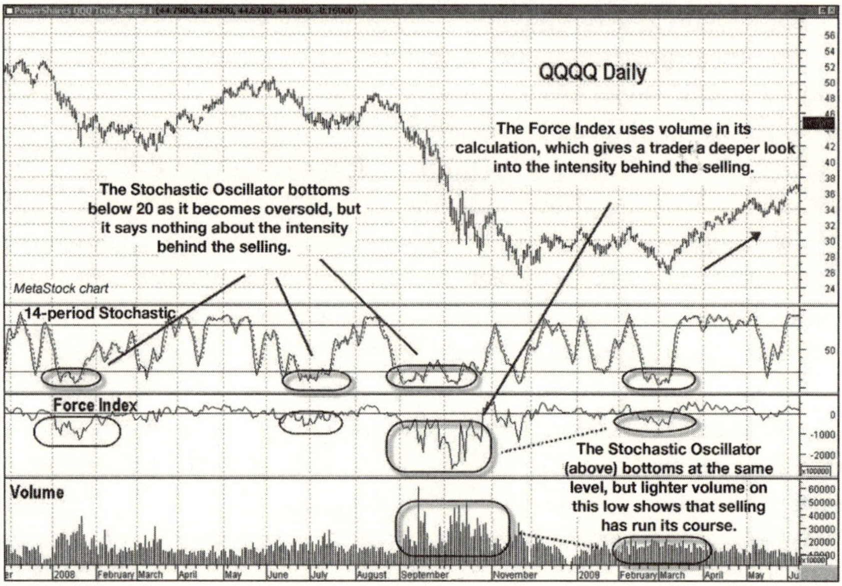

Chart 2.6 Stochastic Oscillator with Force Index (Volume-Based), Nasdaq 100 Trust ETF

Source: MetaStock

The Force Index uses volume data in its calculation and is able to provide a more accurate assessment of the trading terrain. While the Stochastic indicator bottomed in the same range each time, the Force Index plunged to a deep low in September 2008 (in the middle of the chart), which showed the intensity or conviction behind the selling pressure. The increase in volume showed that more crowd participants were contributing to the intensity of this decline.

The depth of the September 2008 plunge in the Force Index could have been used as a comparison for determining that the second sell-off in March 2009 had less conviction. This provided an important piece of information for interpreting the March 2009 low. It signaled that sellers had exhausted themselves as compared to what happened during September's push lower. The fact that the Force Index made a higher low (and volume itself was much lower) while price bottomed at the same level (November 2008 and March 2009) showed that a change in trend should have been anticipated. The price-based Stochastic Oscillator indicated that the ETF was oversold. It was the added volume component, however, that revealed the crowds lagging conviction and a strong probability of a reversal.

Flash Crash: A Preliminary Look at Volume Analysis

Here's another look at how Volume Analysis and a volume-based oscillator could have alerted traders that a change of trend was on the way. This example uses both price- and volume-based oscillators leading up to the May 6, 2010 "flash crash." (See Chapter 6 for more details.) Chart 2.7 once again displays the Stochastic Oscillator plotted just below price. This time the volume-based *Klinger Oscillator* (see Chapter 10) is added to a plot of daily volume in the bottom frame. This oscillator is often used to spot long-term trends in money flow as well as short-term reversals. Note how the Stochastic indicator topped at over 80 (the overbought zone) several times, signaling that a short-term pullback could be expected. However, the Stochastic indicator alone was unable to gauge the conviction of traders behind the move.

The Klinger Oscillator, on the other hand, painted a much different picture. While the Stochastic Oscillator was topping in the same area over 80 as price made its final top on April 26, 2010, the Klinger Oscillator made a much lower peak. This served as a red flag that there was very little conviction behind the push to the new price high. This situation is

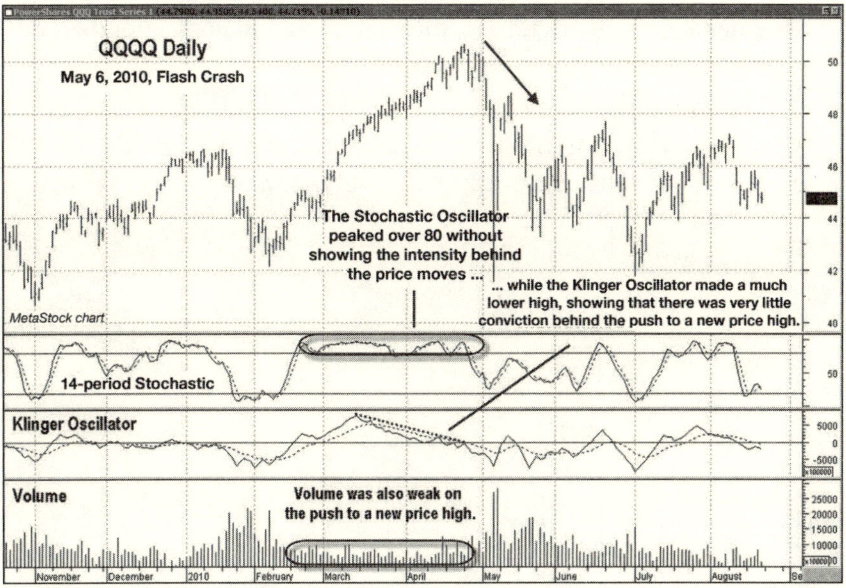

Chart 2.7 Stochastic with Klinger Oscillator, May 2010 Flash Crash, Nasdaq 100 Trust ETF

Source: MetaStock

known as a *negative divergence* between price and volume, a condition alerting a trader that a change in trend may be near. Such signals tell a trader at the very least to lighten up on equity exposure, as a pullback in price is expected. Also note the lighter volume in the bottom frame of Chart 2.7, confirming a diminished conviction behind the push into the April 26, 2010, high. This negative divergence displayed by the Klinger Oscillator served as an early warning signal as price collapsed in the wake of the May 6, 2010, flash crash less than two weeks later.

We've just seen how adding volume serves to complement more traditional price-based indicators and analysis. Volume Analysis works well in a layered format; we will cover such "overlays" throughout the book and, in particular, in Chapter 11.

Summary

- Volume Analysis respects the relationship between volume and price.
- Adding volume is equivalent to adding a third dimension to your trading strategy. By using volume, we gain insight into the topography of the trend and the sentiment and conviction behind the price movement.
- Volume Analysis can enhance trading profits substantially when utilized to assess trend strength, direction, and timing. The omission of volume can cause oversights and formidable errors.

Chapter 3

NAVIGATING THE VOLUME TRADING TERRAIN

Developing a trader's eye for market direction requires recognizing the behavior of volume in price charting patterns. These volume patterns provide us with our first true snapshot of the trading terrain. In this chapter, we explore some basic and then more complex relationships between volume and price.

Volume Analysis requires the ability to identify how volume interacts with simple price charting patterns, specifically, how volume patterns precede and confirm price movement in trending and nontrending markets.

Volume, when interpreted accurately, acts as a trader's navigation system, a daily amplifier of price movements revealing the strength and conviction of buyers or sellers that move price invariably into one of these charting configurations. Once we recognize the trading terrain, we will take these volume price patterns off-road, apply them to volume indicators and oscillators, and use them to discern a tradeworthy trend.

Six Basic Volume/Price Relationships

Recognizing the basic relationship patterns between volume and price provides traders coordinates with which to predict future market movements and trends. Here are six such basic volume/price relationship patterns that

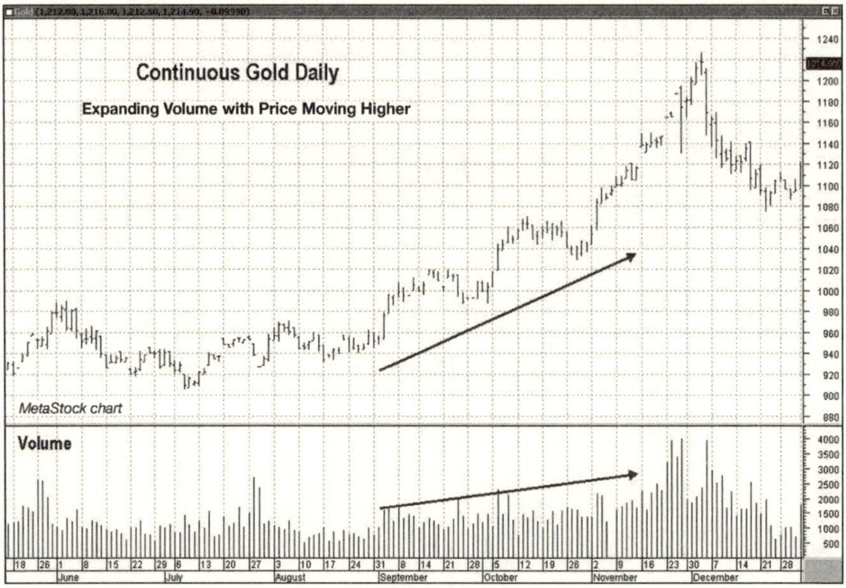

Chart 3.1 Expanding Volume with Price Moving Higher, Continuous Gold Daily

Source: MetaStock

every trader should know. The first two involve expanding volume, the second two deal with contracting volume, and the final two are concerned with static or constant volume.

Expanding Volume with Price Moving Higher or Lower

When the market is in an uptrend (characterized by higher highs and higher lows) or in a downtrend (characterized by lower highs and lower lows), we see consistent conviction among traders, which displays itself as expanding volume in the direction of the trend. This increases the odds that price movement in the direction of the trend will continue. Chart 3.1 shows the price/volume relationship in an uptrending market.

Expanding Volume with Minimal or No Price Movement

Lack of price movement on expanding volume, such as exemplified in Chart 3.2, shows that buyers and sellers are struggling for control of market direction. We see this short-term sideways pattern in a trending market. It is an indication that countertrend forces are building and that the movement

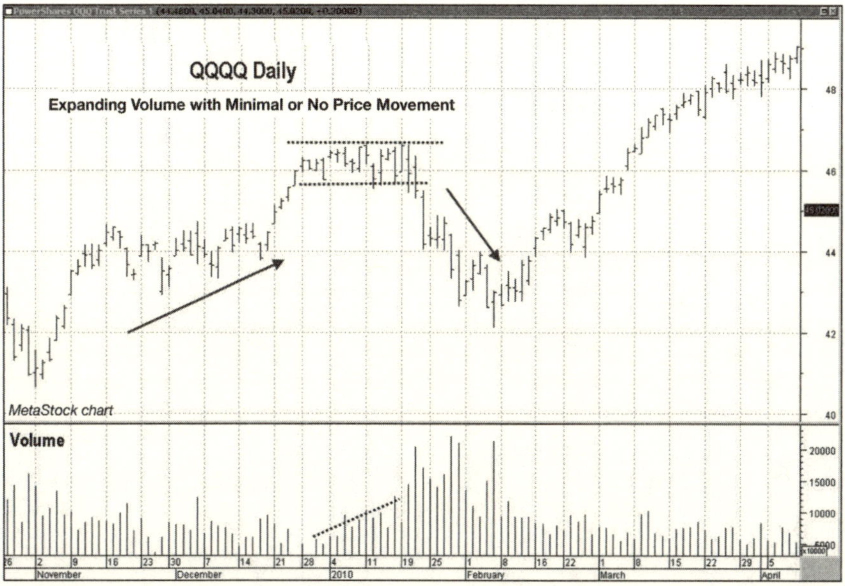

Chart 3.2 Expanding Volume with Minimal or No Price Movement, Nasdaq 100 Trust ETF

Source: MetaStock

of the trend is becoming labored, which puts the continuation of the trend in jeopardy. Typically, price trades in a range for a number of days in this type of pattern.

Contracting Volume with Price Moving Higher or Lower

When volume contracts as the price moves higher (see Chart 3.3), the volume pattern is not confirming the price trend. This means that the conviction behind the trend is not strong enough to attract new participants. The absence of new participants decreases the odds that the existing trend will continue; a reversal is possible.

Contracting Volume with Minimal or No Price Movement

Lack of price movement on a pattern of contracting volume, as in Chart 3.4, shows that both buyers and sellers lack conviction that the price trend will continue. We see this trend in a consolidation phase. New participants are required to initiate a new trend.

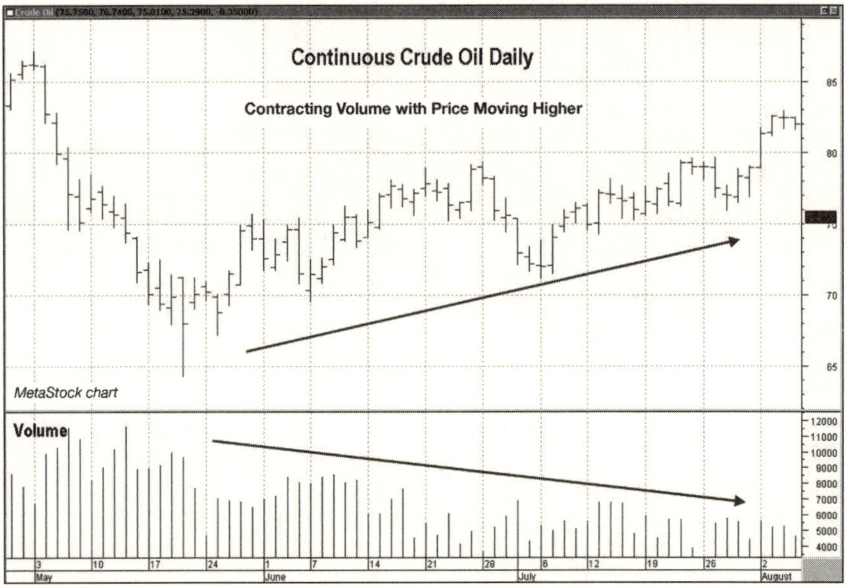

Chart 3.3 Contracting Volume with Price Moving Higher or Lower, Continuous Crude Oil Daily

Source: MetaStock

Chart 3.4 Contracting Volume with Little or No Price Movement, S&P SPDR Trust ETF

Source: MetaStock

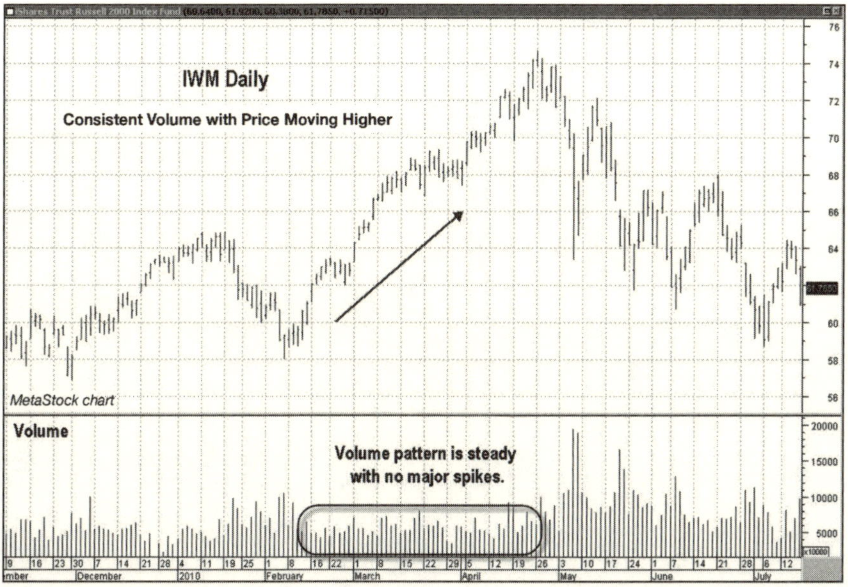

Chart 3.5 Consistent Volume with Price Moving Higher, iShares Russell 2000 Index ETF

Source: MetaStock

Consistent Volume with Price Moving Higher or Lower

Price movement with a consistent volume pattern shows that buyers and sellers are in agreement that the trend should continue. Any transactions against the trend (sells in an uptrend or short covering on a downtrend) are a product of profit-taking decisions, not necessarily changes in sentiment. Chart 3.5 shows consistent volume as the price moves higher.

Consistent Volume with Minimal or No Price Movement

Buyers and sellers are in agreement that a stock, index, or commodity is fairly valued at its current price range. This is an example of a trendless market. Chart 3.6 shows consistent volume and little to no price movement.

These six basic volume relationships can be used to gauge the market environment and increase the odds of a successful trading strategy. We will use them as a preliminary guidance mechanism upon which to interpret complex patterns. Traders choosing to employ volume methods should familiarize themselves with these volume/price relationships and their corresponding volume patterns.

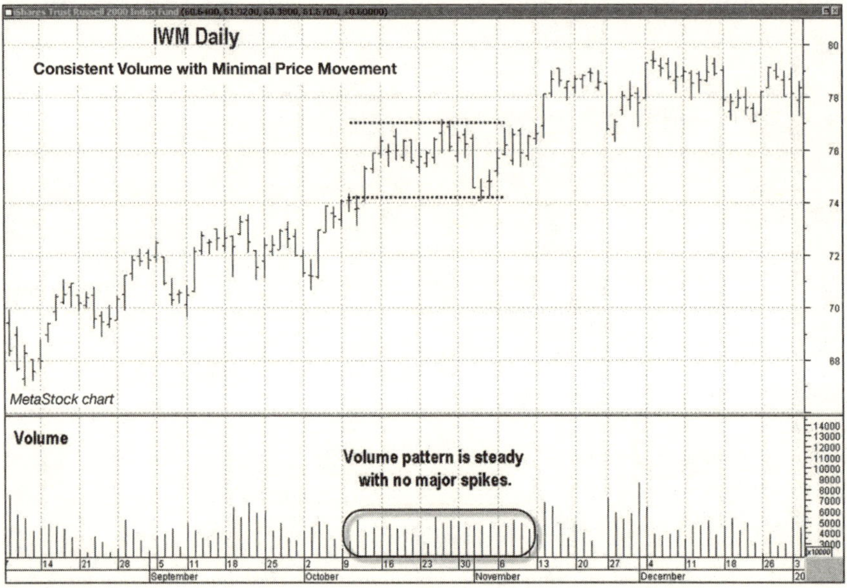

Chart 3.6 Consistent Volume with Minimal or No Price Movement, iShares Russell 2000 Index ET

Source: MetaStock

Patterns in a Trending Market: Trend Continuation Patterns

The first task in our Volume Analysis is to identify the direction of the price trend. A plot of price or an indicator that includes price is a requirement. Once we make this determination, we can use an assortment of tools to determine how this trend will behave and how best to trade using it. One of the ways we go about this is to look toward traditional technical price chart patterns and their corresponding volume patterns. To accomplish our analysis, we place volume bars below price on our charts. Interpreting trend direction will provide insight as to whether the trend is bullish or bearish and whether volume is expanding in the direction of the trend. Initially, these corresponding volume patterns can be used to confirm trends. Later, using volume overlays, we will examine these patterns in more depth and begin to predict how these trends will behave in the future.

How Volume Confirms an Uptrend

In a healthy uptrend, volume expands in the direction of positive price movement. There is a normal ebb and flow of higher highs and higher lows. This pattern is caused by traders selling profitable positions in the direction of the trend to new buyers. We can usually see profit-taking pullbacks, characterized by generally small decreases in volume as price drifts lower. Once the profit taking has run its course, new buyers enter the market, creating a demand imbalance (i.e., more buyers than sellers) and driving prices higher.

A volume increase on trend resumption shows that the prevailing trend is in good health and is likely to continue. There are a number of trend continuation patterns that can give a trader a chance to jump on existing trends. More complex patterns are discussed in Chapter 4. For now, we will show an example of how volume confirms a simple bullish trend continuation based on a "flag" pattern.

Chart 3.7 for IBM shows the characteristics of a series of bullish flag patterns that occur in strongly trending markets. The flag represents the shape of the pattern. Notice how volume dries up during the pullback, then explodes higher once the uptrend resumes. This is often the point at which traders trading in anticipation of the trend will enter their positions. It shows that buyers are in control, and higher prices can be expected.

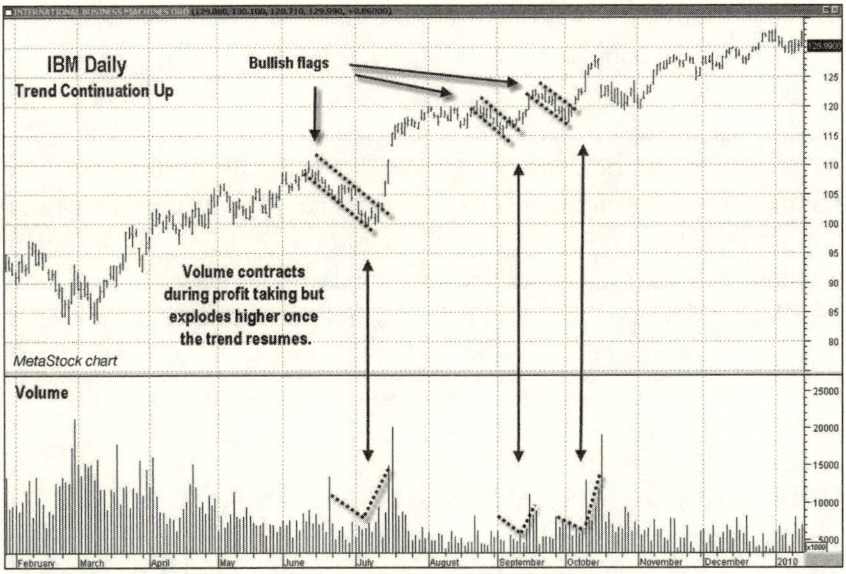

Chart 3.7 Trend Continuation, Uptrend, IBM

Source: MetaStock

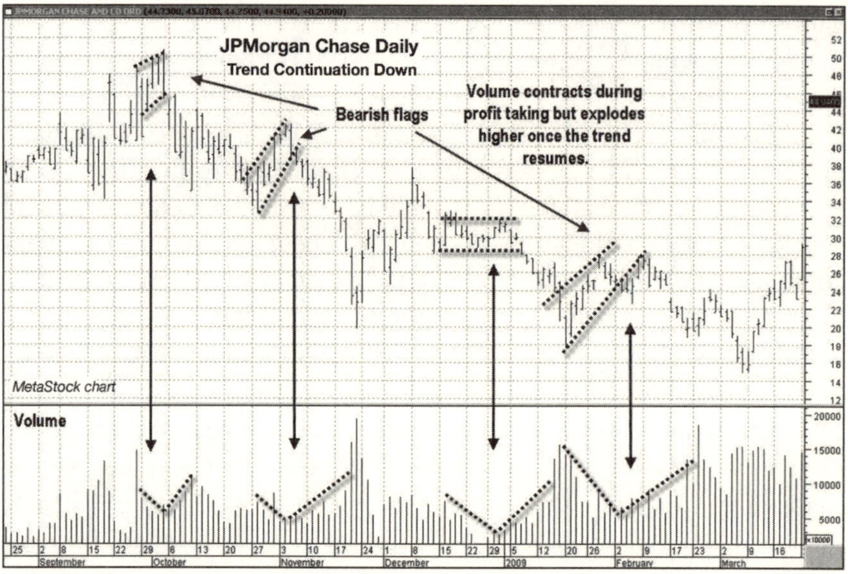

Chart 3.8 Trend Continuation, Downtrend, JPMorgan Chase

Source: MetaStock

How Volume Confirms a Downtrend

The characteristics of trend continuation patterns in a downtrend are similar to those in an uptrend, the only difference being that *volume expands on decreasing price movement*, and the roles of buyers and sellers are reversed. Note in the example from JPMorgan Chase (JPM) in Chart 3.8 how volume contracts as price moves higher, then accelerates as the downtrend resumes. The low volume on moves higher can be thought of as a combination of short sellers locking in profits and some buying in anticipation of a bottom. Volume spikes—sudden aberrations in volume—are much more prevalent in downtrends than in uptrends. Sell-offs are typically more emotional events as traders unload their shares, either by decision or through stop-loss orders, in an attempt to avoid further pain in a losing position.

Indecision or Rest: Consolidation Patterns

The basic premise behind consolidation patterns is that traders are entering a period of indecision or resting, which can be translated into a lack of price direction. This pattern consists of a well-defined pattern of price containment known as support and resistance. The consolidation period ends when price breaks out over either the support or the resistance level. Volume plays a key role in validating or refuting the breakout.

This type of price pattern will occur with a simultaneous pattern of volume contraction. It appears that traders who have participated in the trend up to the consolidation point are content to hold their positions; at the same time, there isn't enough excitement or energy among new participants to resume the trend. This results in some interesting patterns or shapes, the most common of which are the triangle and flag patterns.

Triangle Consolidation

The triangle is probably the most widely recognizable consolidation pattern. Chart 3.9 for the iShares COMEX Gold Trust ETF (IAU) is a classic example of a triangle pattern and trader indecision. Notice how price in the early part of the chart exhibited a strong uptrend, then took a breather as it was compressed into a triangle pattern on declining volume. That showed a lack of conviction among buyers in the direction of the trend, yet at the same time selling pressure was weak. Volume continued to contract as the triangle formed, then exploded higher on the breakout, which signaled a resumption of the uptrend.

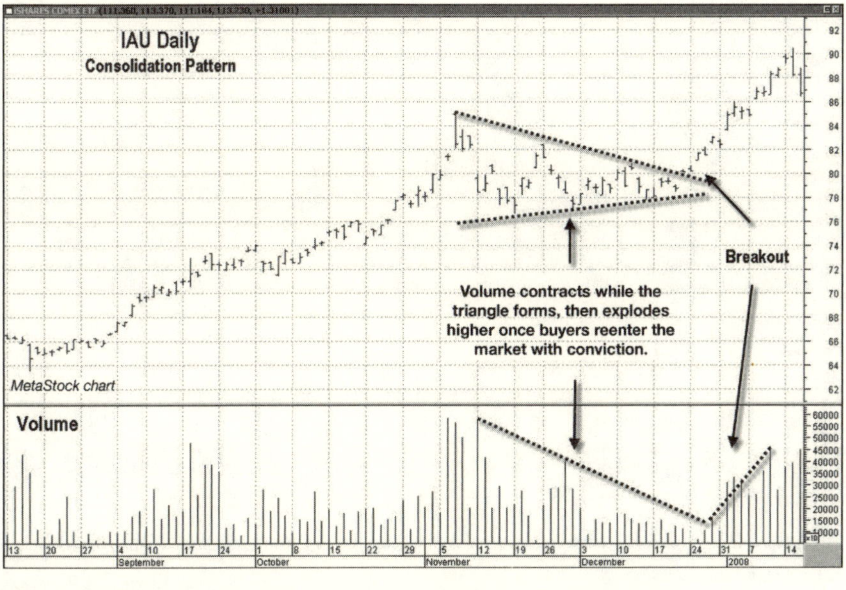

Chart 3.9 Triangle Consolidation Pattern, COMEX Gold Trust ETF

Source: MetaStock

Flag Consolidation

Consolidation patterns in both uptrends and downtrends have similar characteristics. In most cases, consolidation patterns are resting phases before the previous price trend resumes. In Chart 3.10 for iShares Cohen & Steers Realty Trust ETF (ICF), we see a bearish flag consolidation during a weak countertrend push higher before the downtrend resumed with a vengeance. Notice how as each flag formation developed, price labored to push higher in a choppy, low-volume pattern. Once the weak buying action concluded, sellers reestablished their dominance and the downtrend resumed.

Note that in Chart 3.10, if you weren't specifically looking at volume, you would have no idea whether the price would continue in the upward direction indicated by the flag or in some other direction. The volume bars provide an additional dimension in this case. Declining volume shows the lack of conviction and thus a weakness in the push higher. Volume tells us that we're in a consolidation phase, and it may also signal how prices will emerge from that pattern.

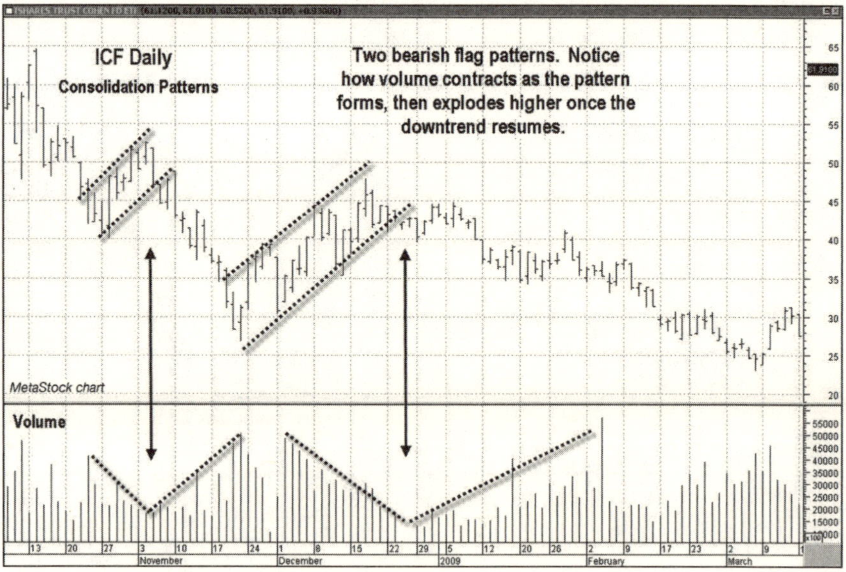

Chart 3.10 Bearish Consolidation, Flag Pattern, Cohen & Steers Realty Trust ETF (ICF)

Source: MetaStock

Volume Patterns in Sideways Markets

When a market is trending upward (i.e., making higher highs and higher lows) or downward (i.e., making lower highs and lower lows), it is easy to glance at a chart to see whether buyers or sellers are in control of the market. What about trendless markets, those moving sideways or within a trading range? Volume can give important clues as to who is winning the supply/demand battles, which can help us anticipate the direction of breakouts from the range.

A range-bound market (i.e., a market trading in a fairly definable range) is a great place for larger entities, such as mutual funds and hedge funds, to accumulate shares. Securities become range bound for a reason. The upper boundary is seen as the most that traders are willing to pay, which encourages selling, while the bottom end of the range is seen as a good value, which brings in buyers. The behavior of price and volume at these levels gives insight as to the activity of these larger players. Here you can observe their "footprints in the sand" as a function of the flow of money into and out of the security, with an accumulation of shares in anticipation of breakouts in the trend. Also, it is within these boundaries that the high-frequency trading players and swing traders make consistent and profitable trades.

Bullish Accumulation Pattern

In Chart 3.11 for Cisco Systems (CSCO), note how price moved higher out of its July 2009 low to establish a new range. The volume pattern in this range shows that shares were being accumulated as volume picked up while price moved higher off of the lower end of the range. This accumulation pattern, repeated three times, preceded an upside breakout of the range in March 2010.

Bearish Distribution Pattern

The pattern just described can happen in reverse: Price and volume behavior in the range takes on a more bearish tone as sellers apply more pressure than buyers. This shows that the security is being distributed—that is, sold off, especially by large players—rather than accumulated.

These types of distribution patterns are typical after strong up moves, while less sophisticated traders are still excited and willing to buy the

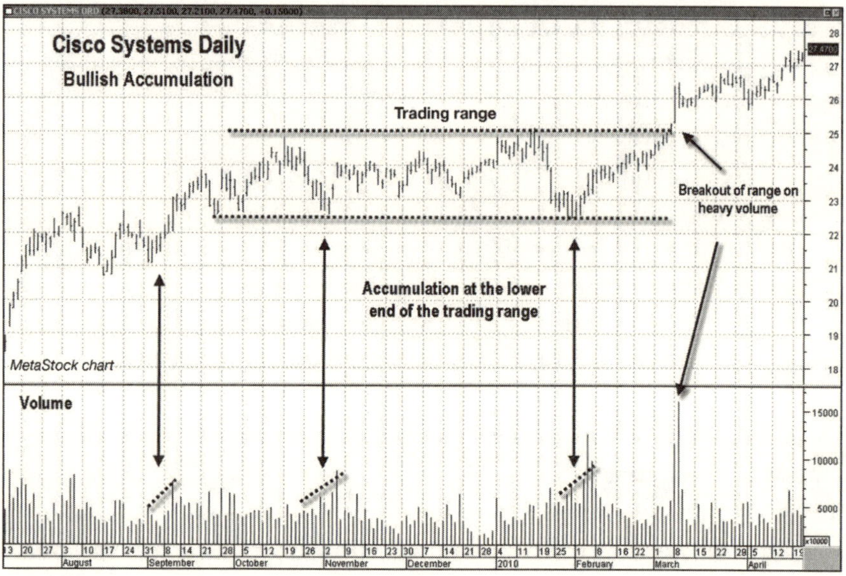

Chart 3.11 Bullish Accumulation Pattern, Cisco Systems

Source: MetaStock

security being distributed by the larger players (mutual funds, hedge funds, etc.). Chart 3.12 for the Euro FX Composite shows how volume picked up at the peaks as price turned lower within the range. This volume pickup was an indication that there was more overhead supply than the market could bear, so from a simple supply and demand viewpoint, price had to adjust lower to compensate for the supply/demand imbalance. Note also in Chart 3.12 how volume exploded when price broke down out of its range. That was a sure signal that sellers had assumed control and that the euro was headed lower.

Patterns in a Trend Reversal

A reversal pattern is a price and volume pattern that can alert a trader that a change in price direction is imminent. These patterns take time to form, and volume plays a very important role in their identification and validation. An example of a reversal at a top or a bottom is the spike pattern. We will be examining the many reversal patterns in greater detail in Chapter 5.

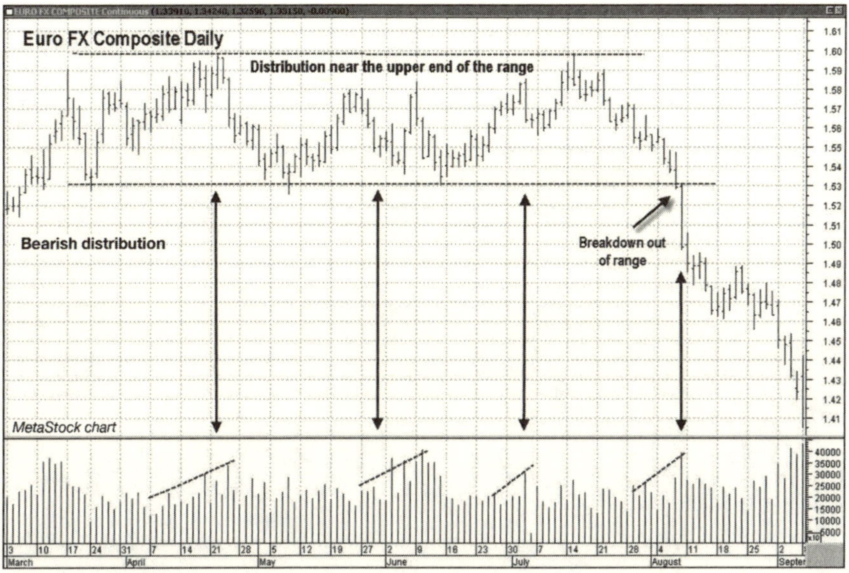

Chart 3.12 Bearish distribution, Euro FX Currency

Source: MetaStock

Volume Spike Pattern at Market Highs and Lows

Volume spikes are emotion-driven events that signify that buyers or sellers may have exhausted themselves in one direction or another after an extended move. Depending upon where in the trend a volume spike occurs, a trader may be able to either reaffirm the existing trend or be alerted to a potential change of direction in the market. While rising volume is good for the strength and sustainability of trends, too much volume in a strongly trending market can be a warning sign that a change is about to occur.

In order for trends to continue, there needs to be a *constant* (a key word) supply of new participants who want to take positions in the direction of the trend. An abundance of new participants shows up in expanding volume totals in trending markets. If, however, volume spikes to levels much higher than anything seen during the uptrend, it is a sign that buyers have exhausted themselves or that a larger-than-normal number of buyers rushed in to purchase shares, leaving fewer new buyers willing to support the trend. This makes markets vulnerable and can cause them to correct, as the selling pressure created by profit takers is not met with an equal or greater number of new buyers willing to participate. The Nasdaq Composite example in Chart 3.13 shows volume spikes that led to short-term tops in the market.

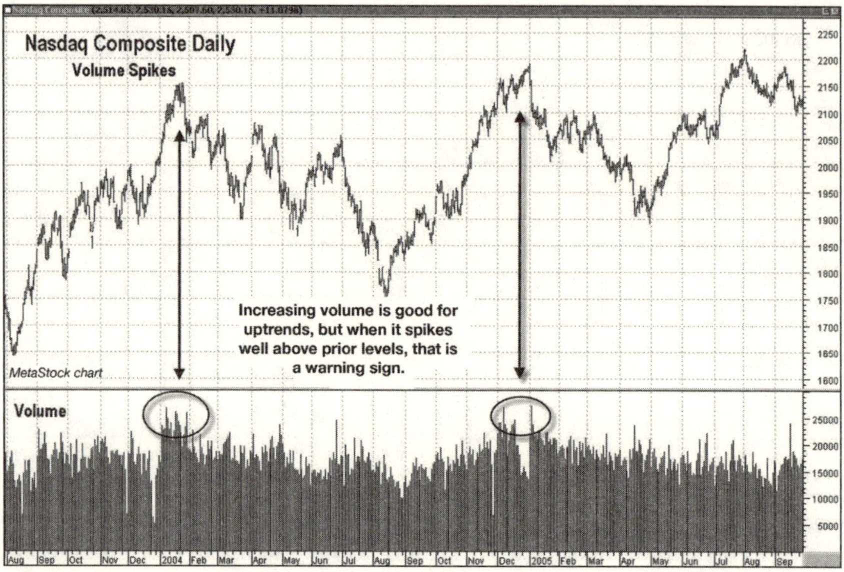

Chart 3.13 Volume Spikes at Market Tops, Nasdaq Composite

Source: MetaStock

Volume spikes are also good for identifying short-term market lows, particularly after extended moves. Increasing volume on pullbacks can be an early sign of a trend change, but patience in reacting can be the key to jumping on a great buying opportunity. Steadily increasing volume on sell-offs is typically a bearish sign, while spikes on sell-offs can be an indication that sellers have exhausted themselves to the downside.

In either case, price movement can be expected as volume settles back to normal levels and the market resets. In Chapters 8 to 10, we will look at some other volume indicators that are used to identify changes in volume behavior. For an example of price bottoms indicated by volume spikes, see Chart 3.14 for the Energy Select SPDR Trust ETF (XLE).

Divergences between Volume and Price

Divergences between price and volume occur when price is trending upward or downward but volume is decreasing. This behavior shows that volume is not confirming the trend. Divergences show traders that conviction behind price movement is lacking, which means that the odds of a trend reversal increase. Including volume in chart analysis can

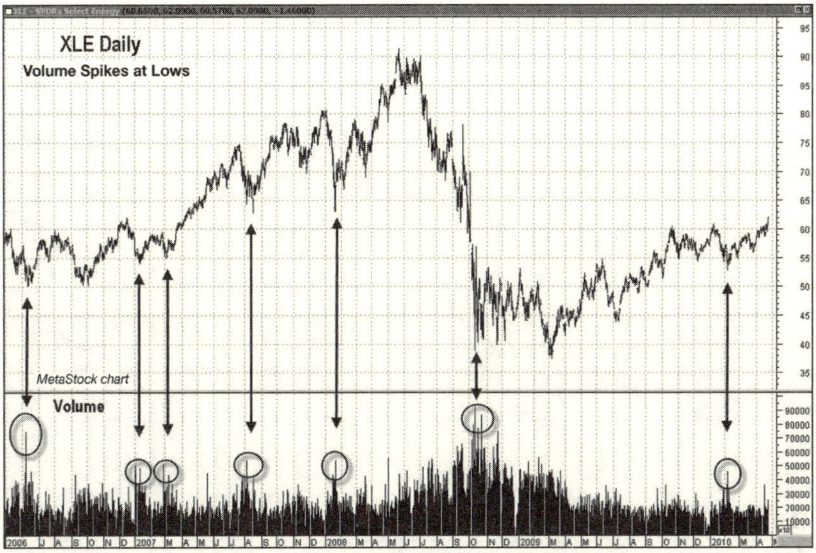

Chart 3.14 Volume Spikes at Market Bottoms, Energy Select SPDR Trust ETF

Source: MetaStock

give a trader a quick, clear snapshot of the extent of buying or selling pressure in trending markets. As price trends higher or lower, volume should also be expanding, showing a higher level of participation among traders. If volume is contracting while price is trending upward or downward, it is a signal that either a price correction or an all-out trend change may be imminent.

Since volume is the "fuel" needed to sustain price direction, think of falling volume as moving closer to empty on the gas gauge for that price movement. For instance, volume helps to discern the lessening conviction behind a downtrend. The Consumer Staples Select Sector Trust ETF (XLP) example in Chart 3.15 shows how volume contracted during its 2008 downtrend. That was an indication that there were fewer and fewer sellers as price declined, thus opening the door in March 2009 for buyers to assume control and take XLP higher.

Up to this point, we have explored the six basic volume/price relationships and seen some simple examples of the types of price patterns that traders encounter in trending and nontrending markets. Watching volume patterns in action, we see how they serve to affirm continuation, consolidation, range-bound, and trend-reversal patterns.

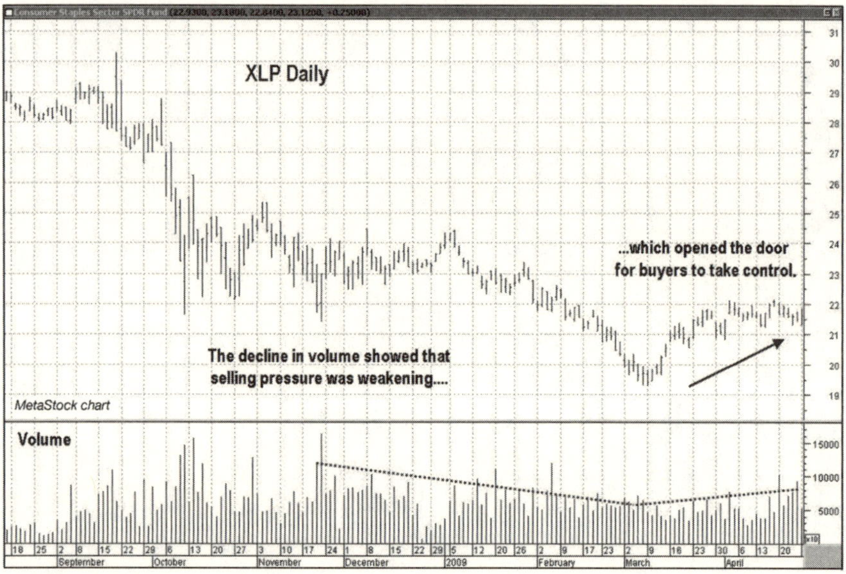

Chart 3.15 Volume/Price Trend Divergence, Consumer Staples Select Sector Trust ETF

Source: MetaStock

Summary

- There are six basic volume/price relationships. These basic relationships form all or part of more complex volume/price patterns.
- Essentially, volume action can confirm or refute price patterns in trending and trendless markets. Volume can be anticipated to behave in certain ways under specific trading conditions. If a corresponding volume pattern does not confirm the price trend pattern, the sustainability of the trend is in doubt.
- Divergences between volume and price can give traders some of the clearest signals of possible trend changes and reversals.
- Not all increases or expansions in volume indicate price trend changes in the same way. Depending upon where in the trend a volume spike occurs, a trader may be able to either reaffirm the existing trend or be alerted to a potential change of direction in the market.

Chapter 4

SPOTTING VOLUME/PRICE PATTERNS AND MARKET TRENDS

Volume shows how many shares or contracts changed hands between buyers and sellers over a set period of time (e.g., an hour, a day, or a week) and provides insight as to the strength and sustainability of the trend.

While the actions of market traders can be summed up in daily price movements, volume reflects the conviction behind the move. Volume can be thought of as the collective sentiment of the market. In Volume Analysis we see a graphical representation of the supply and demand relationship displayed in our volume measurements. If price is trending with less conviction (i.e., declining volume), a change in sentiment may be under way that favors the odds for a change in direction. In contrast, if price is trending with stable or higher conviction (i.e., steady or increasing volume), the trend can be viewed as healthy and sustainable. Leaving volume out of the picture does not provide the depth of analysis necessary to make informed trading decisions.

All that said, just as with price, the signals provided by volume aren't always easily observable. Many textbook examples of volume confirming price trends shown in the last several chapters occur in real life and are easy to find for traders doing their homework. But that would be too easy. If all volume signals were obvious, all traders would recognize them and trade with them, and in the end they would no longer work. So it becomes important to deploy more sophisticated ways to detect trends in volume and translate volume/price behavior. This chapter begins to describe some of the more complex volume behaviors, those of consolidation/continuation patterns, and how to spot them over time.

We also focus on using volume *overlays* (supplemental volume indicators) to more clearly display the volume trend in conjunction with price. Chapter 5 gives the other side of the coin: identifying trend changes, or *reversals*, using similar tools.

Using Overlays to Spot and Assess Volume Trends

While a normal daily bar plot of volume can seem erratic and without pattern or trend, there are methods that can be used to detect trends in volume that are not readily apparent to the naked eye. This type of volume trend analysis is best accomplished through the use of *overlays*.

Overlays are indicators plotted over the top of price or volume bars with the same value scale. Such overlays are more commonly used with price plots, but using them with volume can display the corresponding volume activity for a given market trend. As volume precedes price, confirmation of a price trend (expanding volume in the direction of the trend) means that the trend is likely to continue, while nonconfirmation of a price trend means that the trend is suspect and likely to reverse.

In this section, we take a look at three types of volume overlays: volume moving averages (VMAs), linear regression lines, and volume Moving Average Convergence/Divergence (MACD of volume).

Volume Moving Averages

A volume moving average shows the average volume (number of shares or contracts that have been traded) over a set period of time. The purpose of a moving average is to smooth out volatility or "noise," which can be confusing and can compromise proper market analysis. This allows traders working within a preferred time frame to see if volume for a price move has been heavier or lighter than normal—which, in turn, can result in different interpretations of that price movement. Since higher volume totals show more conviction behind a price movement, days that have above-average volume are more meaningful than days that have below-average volume.

Moving averages come in many different types, such as simple, exponential, weighted, time series, and triangular. For the purpose of this first example, we will use a *simple volume moving average (SMA)*. A moving average is constructed by summing the past n periods of volume and dividing by n. For example, if an intermediate time frame setting using a 20-day-period moving average of volume is desired, add up the last $n = 20$ days of volume and divide by 20 $[(V_1 + V_2 + \cdots + V_{20})/20]$. This gives an average volume total of the last 20 days that provides a much smoother graphical representation of volume than the sometimes erratic readings that can occur from day-to-day bar plots.

Such a moving average allows a trader to see whether volume is increasing (the sign of a healthy trend) or decreasing (the sign of a suspect trend). Any competent charting package will let you overlay volume with a moving average in a couple of mouse clicks.

One of the most commonly used moving averages for Volume Analysis is the 50-day *volume moving average (VMA)*, which is good for a higher-degree trend analysis. There is one disadvantage to using this longer-term moving average: It tends to be slower to respond to changes in volume trends. For this reason, it's important that the time frame settings for the VMA match your time horizon as a trader. Chart 4.1 for JPMorgan Chase (JPM) shows how a 50-day VMA is used to confirm a downtrend, showing that sellers are clearly in control.

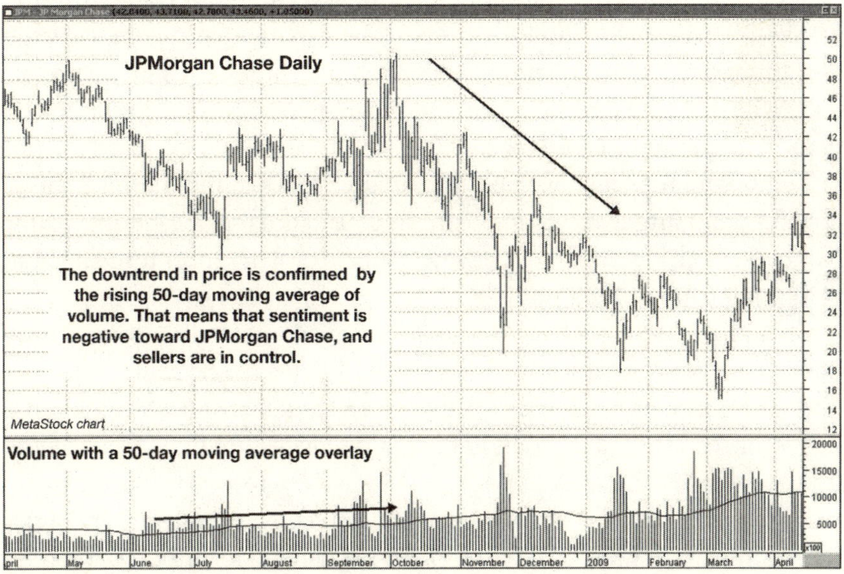

Chart 4.1 Long-Term Volume Moving Average Overlay, JPMorgan Chase

Source: MetaStock

Chart 4.1 shows a rising pattern of volume bars, but the 50-day VMA overlay displays the volume trend more clearly. Note that as the 50-day VMA drops older and adds newer periods, it is still less responsive to current changes in volume. This was demonstrated by the 50-day VMA rising while volume tailed off in April. The longer the averaging period of the VMA, the slower the moving average is to respond to change and the greater the lag effect. This means that shorter time periods for the VMA (5 to 10 days) are much more sensitive to volume fluctuations than the longer-term VMA (50 days). The trade-off, thus, when setting *n* is between its sensitivity to most recent volume data and the timeliness of its signal. Longer *n* periods mean a smoother trendline but also more lag.

The VMA is an excellent tool for capturing the patterns of greater than "normal" or escalating periods of volume. These patterns of increased volume activity typically precede a reversal in price, depending upon where they occur in the price trend movement and on what side of the trend they occur. Ultimately, the time frame setting you choose for your VMA will determine its sensitivity to the volume trend. Depending on the length of the settings, the VMA can detect escalated activity in volume above the norm over the short term (up to 10 days), intermediate term (up to 50 days), and long term (50 days and more). This allows a trader to determine the volume norm and detect these surges in volume within a preferred trading time frame. The exponential moving average of volume gives more weight to recent volume values, thus increasing its sensitivity as compared to the simple moving average. (This is discussed in more depth in Chapters 5 and 7.)

The 60-minute view of Apple Inc. trading (AAPL) in Chart 4.2 shows how intraday surges in volume can be detected using a 7-period VMA. Notice how the volume surges and coincides with short-term turning points that can last for a number of days.

Escalating periods of volume that occur over a slightly longer time frame have more of an impact on price direction. The daily record of Apple Inc. in Chart 4.3 uses a 5-day VMA to detect short-term volume surges that can lead to reversals in the intermediate term that last anywhere from 1 week to 3 months.

Higher-degree trend changes can be detected by using an even longer VMA to detect volume surges. In Chart 4.4, a daily record of Apple Inc., a 20-day VMA is used to detect intermediate-term volume surges. These surges can affect price for periods up to 3 months or longer. Note how the October 2008 surge tipped off traders that a bottom was near. It took the

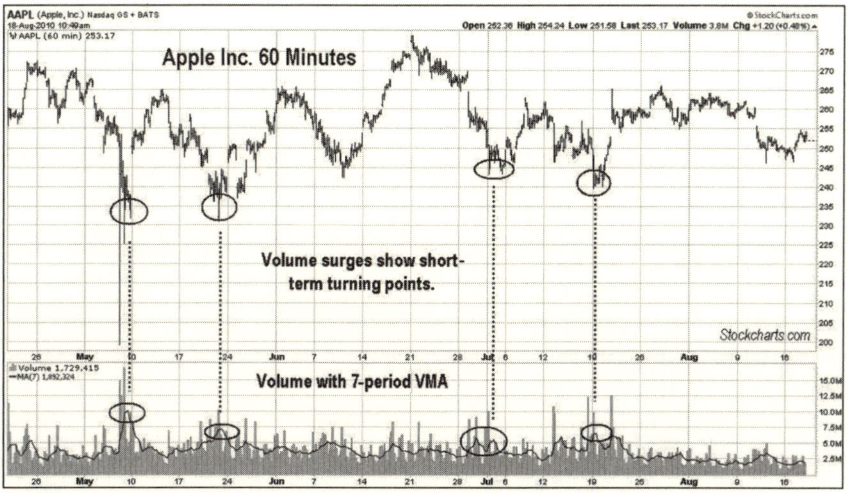

Chart 4.2 Detecting Intraday Volume Surges Using a 7-period VMA, Apple Inc., 60 Minutes

Source: StockCharts

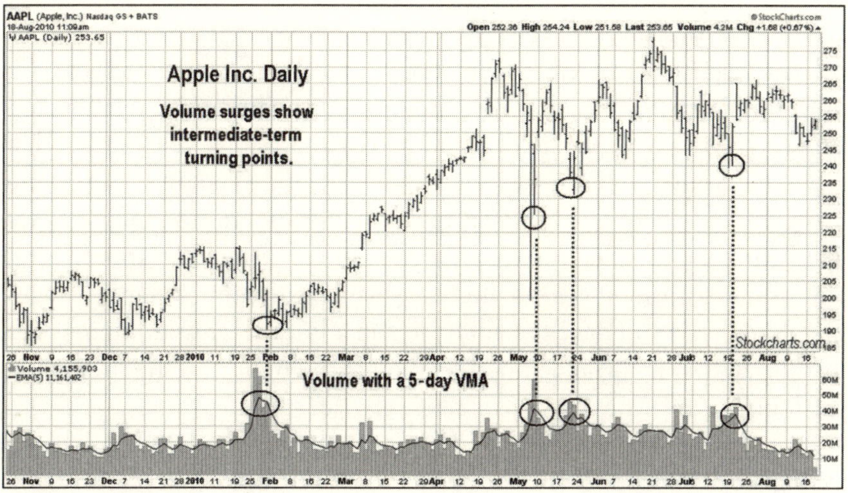

Chart 4.3 Detecting Short-Term Volume Surges Using a 5-day VMA, Apple Inc., Daily

Source: StockCharts

bottom 5 months to form because of the extraordinary market events unfolding at that time. The October 2008 volume surge alerted traders that buyers were stepping up to defend the $80 level, which provided support until the broader market turned in March 2009, allowing Apple to begin its strong uptrend.

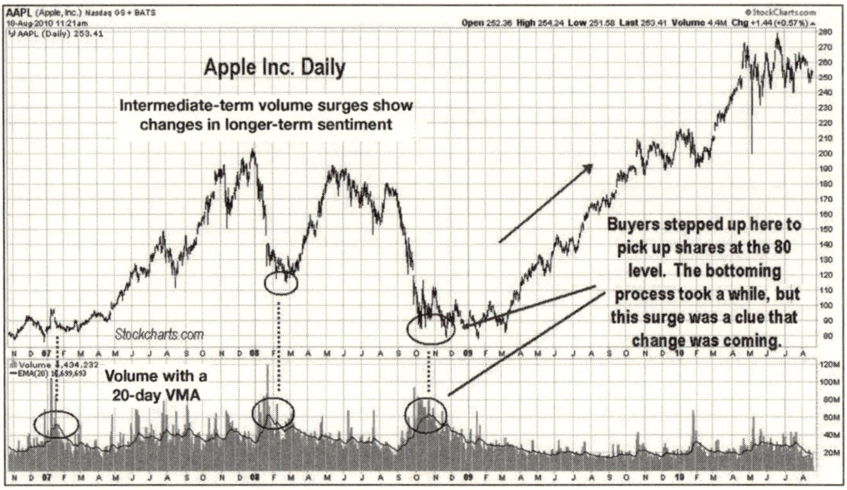

Chart 4.4 Detecting Intermediate-Term Volume Surges Using a 20-Day VMA, Apple Inc., Daily

Source: StockCharts

Linear Regression Overlay

A *linear regression line* can also be used as a volume overlay to show volume trends more clearly. Linear regression analyzes the relationship between two separate variables in order to define a single relationship that is plotted as a straight line—in this instance, volume and time. As volume totals can be very erratic from day to day, a linear regression line provides a straight trend line that can easily be interpreted, if a trend is indeed present. Linear regression is a tool that is available with more advanced charting packages. If you have the ability to add a linear regression line, it can provide an easy at-a-glance interpretation of the trend and the strength of the trend.

The *linear regression overlay (LRO)* is interpreted similarly to a moving average, but it has two distinct advantages over moving averages. First, unlike a moving average, a *linear regression indicator (LRI)* does not exhibit much lag. Second, since the indicator is not averaging volume, but rather "fitting" a line to the data points, the linear regression line is more responsive to volume changes.

Chart 4.5 for JPMorgan Chase shows a daily time frame from April 2007 through April 2008. In this instance, a linear regression line instead of a moving average has been plotted. Notice how straight and clear the linear regression line is compared to the previous moving average example.

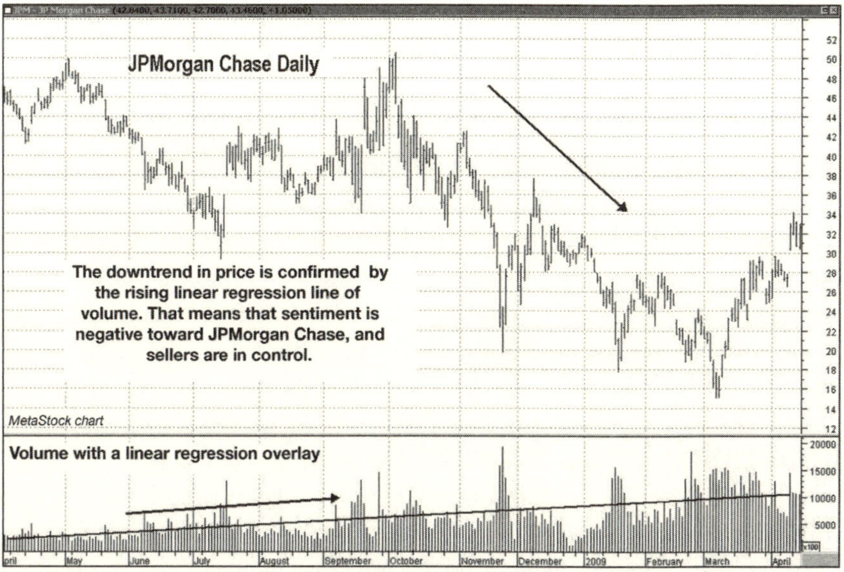

Chart 4.5 Linear Regression Overlay, Downtrend, JPMorgan Chase

Source: MetaStock

Moving Average Convergence/Divergence Using Volume

The MACD price momentum indicator was developed by noted technical analyst Gerald Appel. Unlike the previous two overlay examples, the MACD of volume uses its own volume scale rather than sharing the volume scale used for individual volume bars. It is included in this overlay section, however, because its plot not only closely mirrors that of the volume bars, but also can give insights into volume momentum that are useful to traders employing a shorter time frame for their analysis.

The MACD is a trend-following momentum indicator using the difference between a 12-day exponential moving average and a 26-day exponential moving average to compute a singular daily value. An *exponential moving average (EMA)* is a technique for weighting more recent data more heavily in the averaging calculation; a 12-day EMA gets more weight from the most recent values and thus is more sensitive than a 26-day EMA. The difference between the two numbers indicates direction and strength.

The raw MACD figure, in turn, is normally plotted with its own 9-day exponential moving average, which is known as the *signal line*. Crosses above the signal line on the MACD show that volume momentum is building, while crosses below show that volume momentum is slowing.

Also, MACD values above zero are viewed as having positive momentum, while values below the zero line are viewed as having negative momentum.

The volume MACD can be used to pinpoint where volume momentum is peaking in relation to price. For JPMorgan Chase (JPM) in Chart 4.6, note how the MACD peaks at price lows (the solid black lines) and troughs at price highs (the dotted lines). This showed that volume momentum was building on sell-offs and diminishing on rallies or consolidations. This is another method of showing that sellers were in control during this time frame and that the downtrend was likely to continue.

Confirming Trend Strength: Robust Trends

In Chapter 3, we presented a brief overview of the market trends and volume/price patterns you will encounter as a trader. In this chapter, by using Volume Analysis we will take a more in-depth look at the trading terrain with a focus on consolidation/continuation patterns in trending and sideways markets. In Chapter 5, we will focus on reversal patterns. Once we've determined the price-trend direction, we will take a "read" on that trend. Price-trend direction can be determined using the price plot,

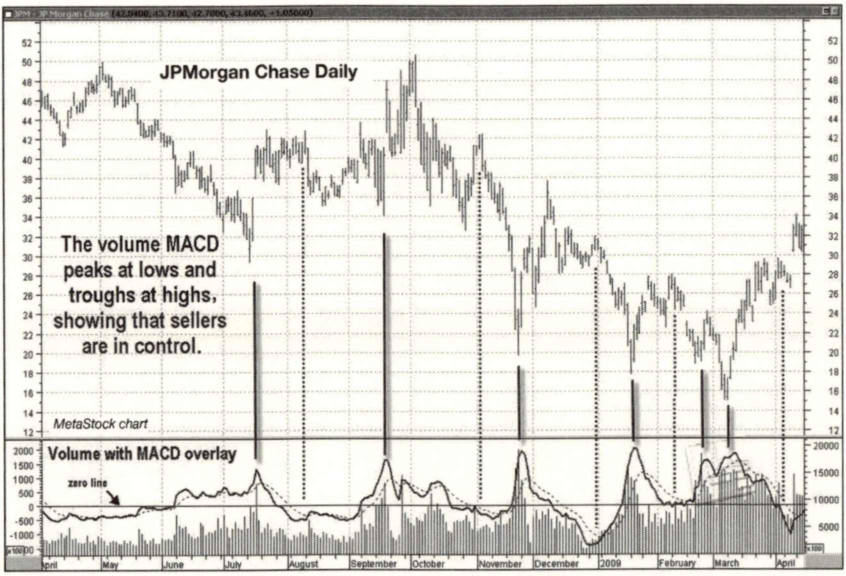

Chart 4.6 Volume MACD Confirms Downtrend, JPMorgan Chase

Source: MetaStock

price bar, price indicators, or a moving average. Our Volume Analysis here will focus on the volume that precedes and confirms that trend. A robust trend is one that is showing a discernible trend in price (whether up or down), along with a simultaneous expansion in volume. Volume levels show how strongly market participants feel (intensity, sentiment, and conviction) about the future value of a security, whether the perceived value is higher or lower.

Confirming Robust Trends with VMA, Linear Regression, and MACD

Chart 4.7 for Newmont Mining (NEM) shows how the rising 50-day VMA confirmed the strong uptrend in price, signaling that this was a robust, healthy trend. This is a classic example of demand overwhelming supply, which is shown by the rising price and rising volume trend.

Chart 4.8 shows a linear regression plot line of volume for Newmont Mining. The rising slope of the line is an indication that more buyers are entering over the entire period, reinforcing the upward price movement. Note again how straight the regression line is and how easy it is to interpret.

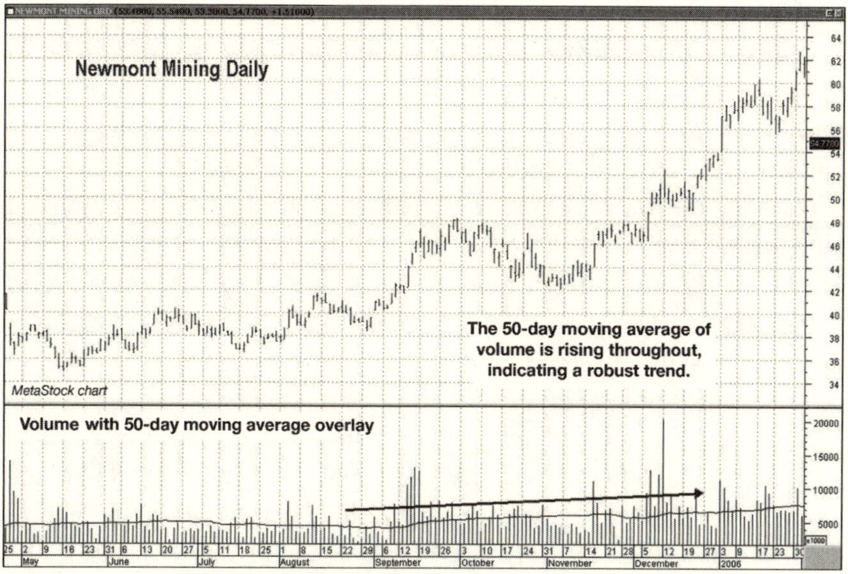

Chart 4.7 Robust Uptrend Confirmed by 50-Day VMA, Newmont Mining

Source: MetaStock

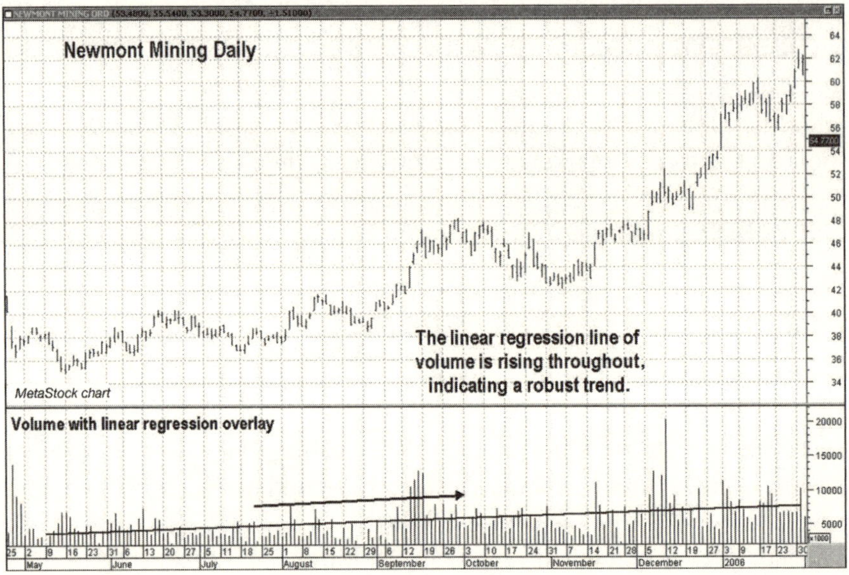

Chart 4.8 Robust Uptrend Confirmed by Linear Regression, Newmont Mining

Source: MetaStock

Finally, we show how a volume MACD can be used to confirm robust trends, in this case an uptrend. NEM in Chart 4.9 is an example of the MACD of volume during the same uptrend. Note how the MACD peaks at short-term market tops (the dashed lines) and crosses below the MACD zero line during corrections (the solid lines). This shows strong buying pressure on rallies and weak selling pressure on pullbacks.

Carrying the example further, everything seems fine with the uptrend until NEM breaks out to even higher highs in early 2006. Notice how the MACD of volume is much weaker on its pushes higher as price moves sharply higher. This was an indication that the uptrend was in its latter stages and that there were fewer buyers to support the trend. It would have been a prudent time to lock in profits.

If we view the end of Chart 4.9 and move forward (see Chart 4.10), we can see what followed the MACD of volume warning just described. Price pushed to new highs, but the MACD of volume failed to confirm the price action, indicating that buying pressure was slowing. NEM then corrected over 22 percent, demonstrating the value of the MACD warning given.

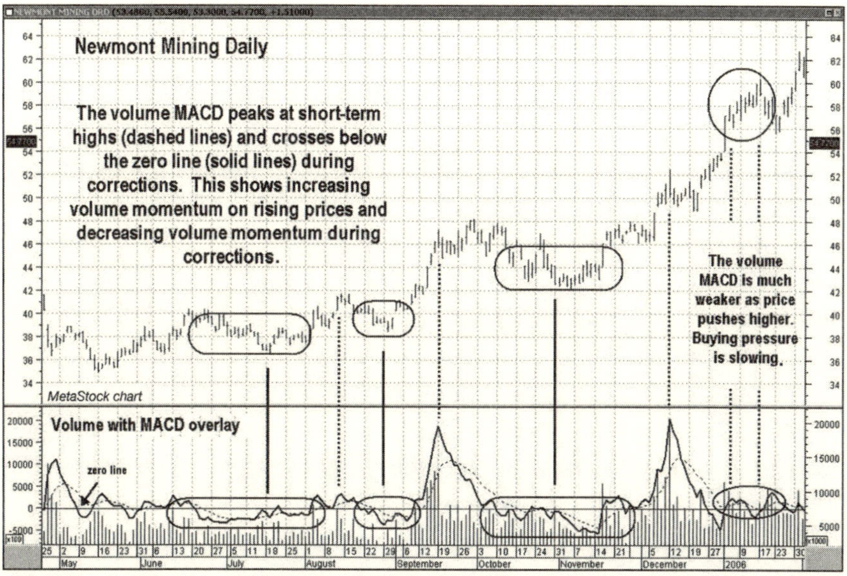

Chart 4.9 Robust Trend Confirmed Followed by Nonconfirmation, Volume MACD, Newmont Mining

Source: MetaStock

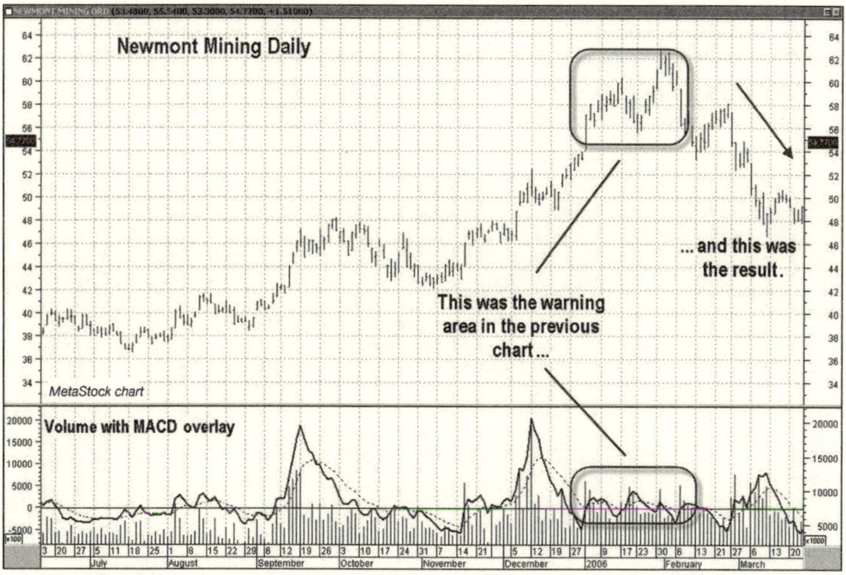

Chart 4.10 Robust Uptrend and Reversal Following MACD Nonconfirmation, Newmont Mining

Source: MetaStock

Confirming Trend Weakness: Lagging Trends

Since volume most often precedes price, weakening volume during a trend shows that traders lack the conviction necessary to keep the trend moving. This lack of conviction eventually shows up in reduced buying or selling pressure, which can spell doom for the continuation of a trend. This type of divergence is especially noticeable in uptrends. In an uptrend, as price climbs higher, more buying pressure is needed to sustain the move. Consistent or increasing volume is the signature of a robust trend. But if a security reaches a point at which those who planned to buy have already purchased their shares, the volume begins to weaken (or lag), and simple profit taking can cause the beginning of a serious correction.

Johnson & Johnson (JNJ) in Chart 4.11 is an example of a lagging uptrend, as volume is weakening throughout the trend. Notice how the 50-day moving average of volume is drifting lower as price rises. The declining volume during the uptrend indicates that fewer buyers are participating as prices appreciate. That situation leaves the door open for a nasty decline, as the chart illustrates.

As evidenced in Chart 4.12, a MACD overlay of volume can be a great short-term momentum tool to show the strength of volume pushes at various stages of a trend. Volume MACD can also be used to show lagging

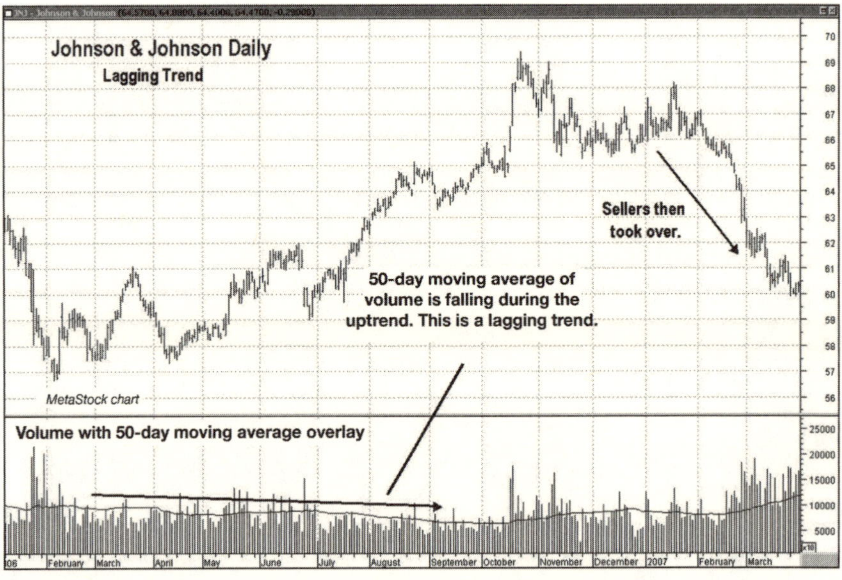

Chart 4.11 Lagging Uptrend, VMA Overlay, Johnson & Johnson

Source: MetaStock

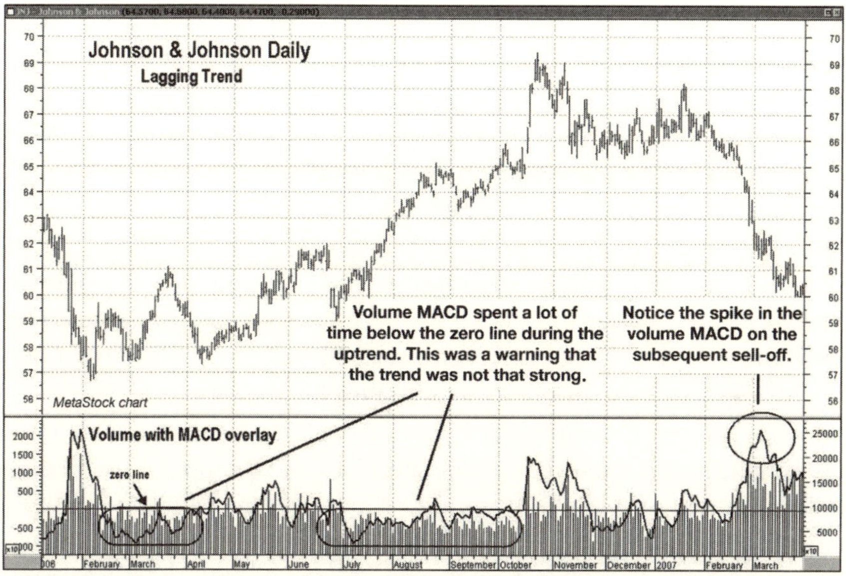

Chart 4.12 Lagging Uptrend, Volume MACD Overlay, Johnson & Johnson

Source: MetaStock

trends. Remember: When the MACD is below the zero line, it is in a weak position, and, when it is above the zero line, it is in a position of strength. In Chart 4.12 for Johnson & Johnson, note how the MACD of volume showed weakness (below the zero line) as price pushed higher. Then, note how the volume MACD spiked once sellers took over.

Trendless Markets: Volume Patterns at Support and Resistance Levels

As we discussed previously, a trendless or sideways market usually moves between upper and lower price boundaries. These boundaries are known as support (the lower boundary) and resistance (the upper boundary). Volume characteristics around areas of support and resistance help to predict the future direction of the trend.

Volume Accumulation at Support

Support can be thought of as the lower boundary of what is perceived as good value for the security between buyers and sellers. As price approaches the lower boundary support level, either buyers accumulate shares or selling pressure diminishes. In either case, prices are prevented from falling any further because of value that is perceived for the time being at that price level. Support levels can be easily identified on a chart by simply connecting the daily price lows during a particular time period. The level at which buyers enter is usually more of a tight price range near the support level than a specific price target.

Even though the dynamics of support zones are such that good value is seen at that price, there is no guarantee that the support level will hold. If it is broken, that is a sign that the sellers have won the battle by bringing more supply than the market can bear, causing price to adjust, sometimes sharply, to lower levels. As price approaches the support area, volume behavior can give clues as to the actions of the larger players, such as institutions and hedge funds. If volume increases and the price support area holds, this demonstrates buying interest at that level, which is usually a clue that the larger players are accumulating shares or contracts.

Chart 4.13 for Barrick Gold (ABX) shows how volume increased repeatedly as price approached the support area. The fact that volume increased and price reversed higher off support showed that the buying pressure at support was enough to create an imbalance on the side of demand over

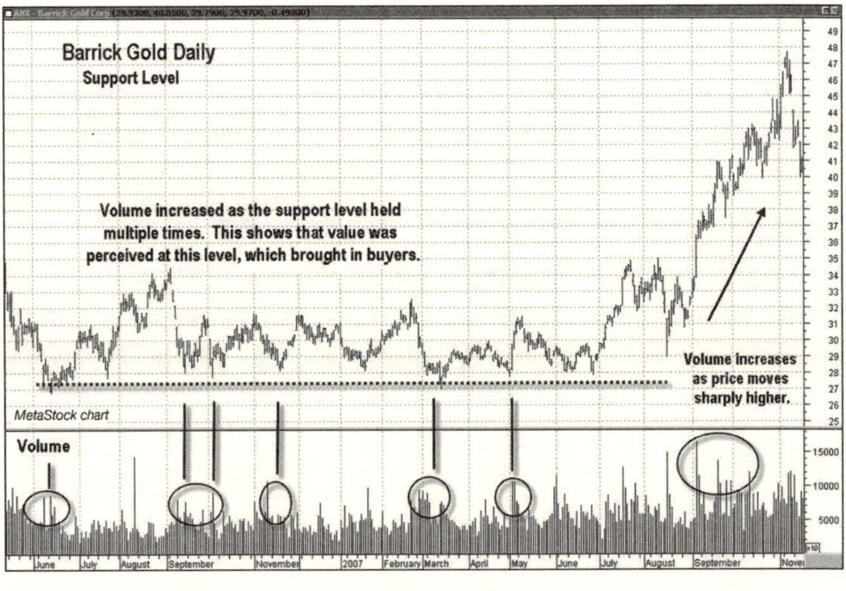

Chart 4.13 Trendless Market, Support Level Accumulation, Barrick Gold

Source: MetaStock

supply, which then pushed prices higher. Instead of continuing to purchase shares, however, buyers were content to let the price drift back down to accumulate shares again at a price level seen as a good value. After repeating this relatively bullish accumulation, the trendless pattern was broken as volume increased sharply with a strong price move to $48 after the period of accumulation in the $27–$28 range.

When Accumulation at Support Fails

While Chart 4.13 for Barrick Gold shows how shares are being accumulated as price bounces higher off of support on increased volume, there are other times where there is no evidence of buying at the support level. These situations can lead to breaks below support, or sharper price breakdowns.

Citigroup (C) in Chart 4.14 is an example of a price support around the $45 area. Notice how, as price moves lower and approaches the support line, the action (volume) is much more subdued than in the previous example. There are some minor pops higher in Citigroup's volume, but nothing that shows that a real battle between buyers and sellers is taking place. Finally, notice how volume picks up in mid-October as price falls, indicating a new supply of shares entering the market. Since

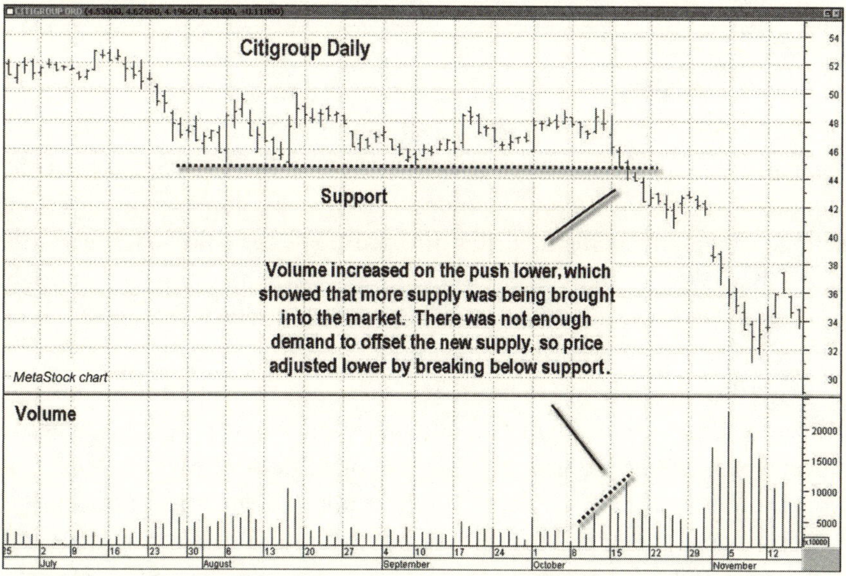

Chart 4.14 Trendless Market, Lack of Accumulation at Support, Citigroup

Source: MetaStock

there was not enough demand to absorb this new supply, price adjusted lower by breaking down through support.

Volume Distribution at Resistance

Resistance is a price boundary where supply levels prevent price from rising any further. The price at resistance is seen as the upper boundary of what is perceived as good value by traders. The most common method for determining the boundary range for resistance is to draw a line through an equity's respective highs during the time frame under analysis. A second method is to compare the amount of volume at a given price point with the amount of volume that was traded the last time it reached that same price point. If volume was greater on a previous attempt, then the resistance may be inferred as holding. Conversely, if volume was less on a previous attempt, then resistance may be failing, and a breakout could be imminent. As price reaches a resistance level or zone, either sellers take profits or buying pressure diminishes. Distribution at resistance is accompanied by an increase in volume over the previous day without price appreciation. If price is to get through a resistance area, a large enough increase in volume is needed to absorb the overhead supply. If volume does not increase to provide the fuel necessary to push through resistance, then either price will remain in a trading range or sellers will take over and drive the price lower.

IBM in Chart 4.15 gives a great example of a resistance area that needed an increase in volume to push through. Notice how volume was weak throughout the time that resistance held in the \$77– \$78 area. That signified that there was not much conviction or passion among buyers or sellers. Once buyers decided that the prospects for IBM made it worth more than \$78 per share, they entered the market and provided enough buying power (volume) to absorb the overhead supply of shares, which in turn allowed IBM to move significantly higher.

The IBM example in Chart 4.15 was a happy ending for those buying IBM stock, but what about the other side, or when sellers overwhelm buyers? Remember, a resistance level is in place because there is more supply than demand at that price. If there is not enough conviction among buyers to push the price higher, then prices will ultimately move lower.

Chart 4.16 for KLA Tencor (KLAC) shows how the dynamics of price and volume around a resistance area can give clues to whether or not that resistance area is likely to hold. Notice how in October 2009 KLA

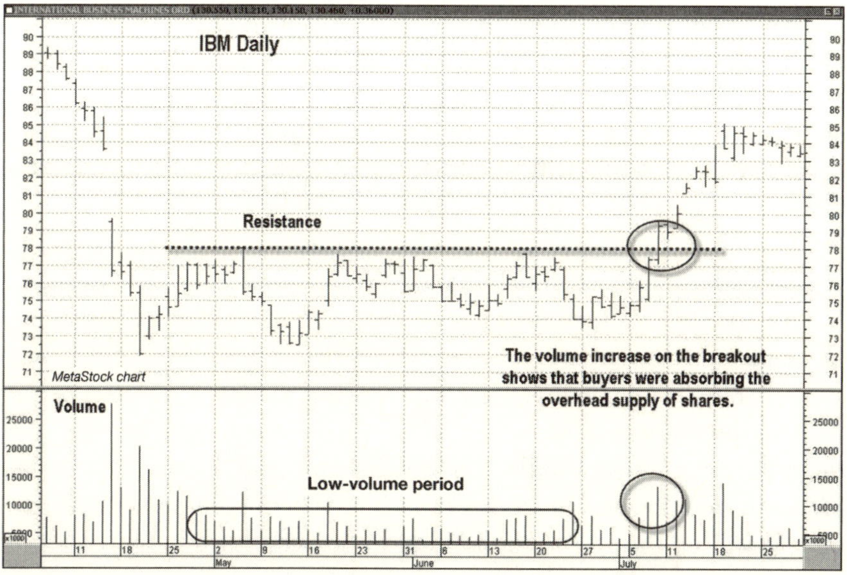

Chart 4.15 IBM Breakout over Resistance

Source: MetaStock

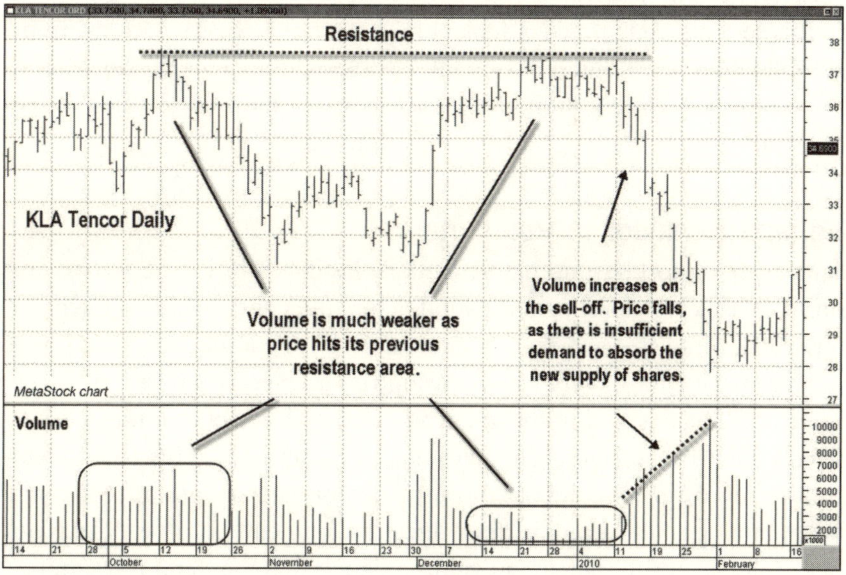

Chart 4.16 Resistance in Trendless Market with Downside Breakout Volume Support, KLA Tencor

Source: MetaStock

Tencor made a price high on solid volume in the 37.50 area. After a good sell-off, price once again approached the 37.50 level in December, but this time volume was much lighter. If nothing had materially changed for KLA Tencor over the previous couple of months, chances were that 37.50 would still be viewed as the upper end of fair value for the stock. If sellers were going to emerge at that level, the lighter volume in December was a clue that there may not have been enough demand at 37.50 to push price through that level.

Sure enough, after churning sideways for about three weeks in December at resistance, volume picked up as price fell. There was already some evidence that there was not much demand interest at this level, as demonstrated by the low volume. That opened the door for selling pressure or a new supply of shares coming onto the market to drive prices sharply lower. Notice how the increase in volume showed that change was on the way in the form of increased selling activity. This is a good example of how volume precedes price.

Volume in Action: Trend Consolidation/ Continuation Chart Patterns

In this section we will take a look at how volume behaves during a trend consolidation phase and breaks out in a continuation of the previous trend. We explore the corresponding volume patterns of some of the more widely recognized price chart patterns used in trading today.

Volume Behavior in Pennants

A *pennant* is short term in nature (usually lasting from 1 to 12 weeks) and normally reflects a brief consolidation before the continuation of the previous trend. Since this pattern represents short-term consolidation and trader indecision, it can on very rare occasions be a reversal pattern (as will be shown in Chapter 5), but the overwhelming majority of the time it represents a short pause before the prevailing trend resumes. This pattern typically forms at the midpoint of a move and occurs after a sharp price advance or decline, depending on the trend direction, on heavy volume. A breakout of the pattern on an increase in volume signals that the trend is resuming.

Chart 4.17 shows an example of a pennant pattern for Cisco Systems (CSCO). The pennant pattern is formed by price fluctuations within a range, and it needs at least two touches each on the resistance line and the support line to be valid. The pennant formation is recognized by its

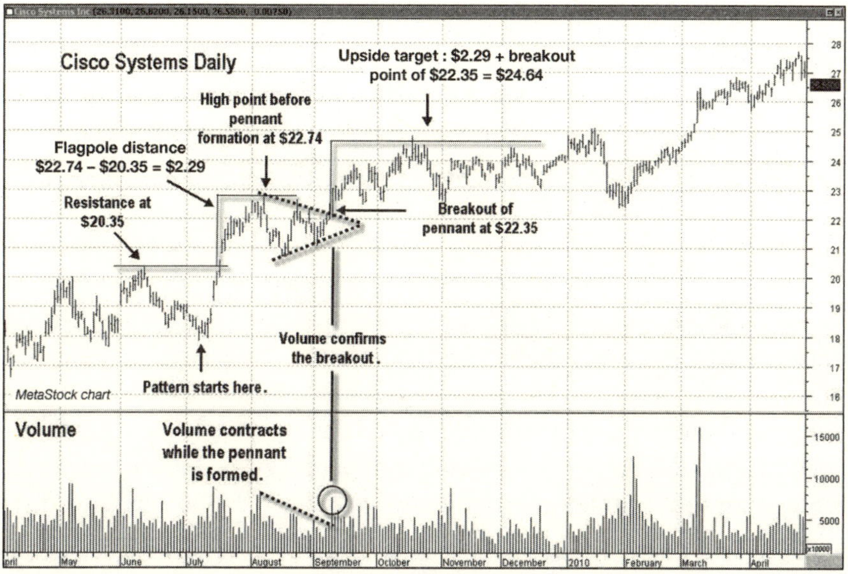

Chart 4.17 Bullish Pennant Pattern Confirming Uptrend, Cisco Systems

Source: MetaStock

symmetrical triangle shape, with price action being compressed as the pattern matures.

Note that the "flagpole" is an important component of the pennant formation. It is the distance from the break of either support or resistance, depending on trend direction, to the high or low of the pennant. The flagpole must be formed on heavy volume to validate the pattern. Once the pattern is validated, the length of the flagpole is used to compute a price target for the move. Chart 4.17 shows a bullish pennant formation, its characteristics, and how to compute a price target:

1. The price move starts at the $18 price level in July 2009.
2. Price rallies sharply, breaking through resistance at $20.35 and hitting a high of $22.74 before the consolidation begins.
3. Once a valid pennant forms, with at least two touches on each boundary line on contracting volume, a calculation of the length of the flagpole can be done as follows in order to set a trading price target:
   a. Measure from the point of the breakout over resistance ($20.35) to the top of the initial rally ($22.74) and subtract the breakout level from the high ($22.74 – 20.35 = $2.29). The computed

value ($2.29) is used on the breakout of the pennant formation to project the price target.

b. Once price breaks out of the pennant formation on heavy volume, add the length of the flagpole ($2.29) to the price at the point it broke out of the pennant, in this case $22.35, to get the trading price target of $24.64.

Volume Behavior in Flags

Flags are also short term in nature, lasting from 1 to 12 weeks. A flag is a small rectangular pattern that develops against the prevailing trend. For example, if the trend is up, the flag forms in a downward-sloping manner (a bull flag), and vice versa for downtrends (a bear flag). As with pennants, the pattern develops between a support and a resistance line. The flag differs from the pennant in that the flag is defined and contained by two *parallel* lines, while the pennant features two *converging* lines.

Volume is a key component in the development of the flag pattern. The flag formation also needs a flagpole, which must be formed on an increase in volume. Next, volume must contract as the flag pattern forms and matures. Finally, volume must confirm a breakout of the pattern by increasing noticeably at the point of the breakout. Chart 4.18 for iShares Barclays 20+ Year Treasury Bond Trust ETF (TLT) shows a bearish flag formation, its characteristics, and how to compute a price target:

1. The price decline starts in the $106 area in early April 2009.
2. Price breaks down through support at $100.38 on an increase in volume before finding support at $94.33, which is where the price consolidation begins.
3. Price then rises between two parallel lines, forming a channel, or bearish flag, against the trend.
4. Once the bearish flag formation is realized, you can compute the length of the flagpole by subtracting the low point of the flag ($94.33) from the support line that was broken ($100.38), which gives a flagpole length of $6.05.
5. Price breaks down out of the flag formation at $96.70 on increasing volume, which validates the breakdown.
6. The length of the flagpole ($6.05) is subtracted from the breakdown point ($96.70) to project a price target of $90.65.

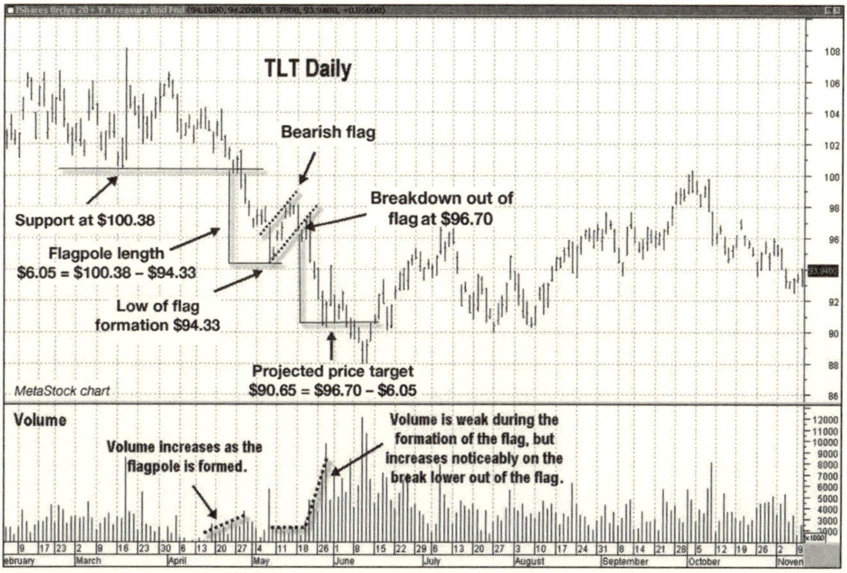

Chart 4.18 Bearish Flag Pattern Confirming Downtrend, iShares 20+ Year Bond Trust ETF

Source: MetaStock

Using Flags and Pennants in Practice

As with other patterns, suspected flag and pennant formations can be misleading if you don't carefully follow a few rules. Here are a few key points to remember about flag and pennant formations:

1. The price action before the flag or pennant forms must be a strong move with healthy volume. This action forms the flagpole.
2. The pennant forms a symmetrical triangle pattern, while the flag forms against the trend in a channel between two parallel lines. Volume contracts as the patterns are formed.
3. The pattern becomes valid when there are at least two touches on the upper and the lower boundary lines.
4. A breakout of the pattern is validated or confirmed by an increase in volume.
5. The length of the flagpole is projected from a break of either support or resistance to either the high or low point of the formation, depending on the direction of the trend.
6. The length of the flagpole is projected from the breakout point of the pattern to generate a price target.

Volume Behavior in Triangles

Triangles are patterns created during consolidation phases, representing a pause in the prevailing trend before continuing in the trend direction. They form in a horizontal consolidation that reflects diminishing interest in trading a particular security. In order for any triangle pattern to qualify as a continuation pattern, there must be a pre-existing trend in place. A triangle is formed with at least two touches on each of the converging support and resistance lines.

As with the previous consolidation/continuation patterns, volume is lackluster while the triangle forms. An increase in volume is used to confirm, or validate, the breakout of the pattern. Triangles come in three forms:

1. Ascending
2. Descending
3. Symmetrical

Ascending Triangles

An *ascending triangle* is a bullish pattern that has a flat top line (representing resistance) and an upward-sloping bottom line (representing support). The pattern consists of at least two highs at or near the same price level, with higher lows made on each rally attempt. The higher lows on each decline show diminishing supply or selling pressure on each push lower, which causes the upward-sloping support line. *Volume should be lower than average and/or be decreasing as the pattern develops and the price action is compressed.*

Chart 4.19 for Euro FX Composite illustrates the ascending triangle. Notice the flat resistance line and the upward-sloping support line. The resistance level was set at $1.2359 on the January 2006 high. Price declined after that, and the consolidation process started as price made a series of higher lows with each decline. Price then made another attempt to break through resistance at $1.2359, but was temporarily turned away, resulting in one final touch of the support line. The next attempt to break out was successful, as volume increased, showing an increase in demand, which caused price to reset to a new, higher level as the trend resumed.

Descending Triangles

A *descending triangle* is a bearish pattern because it appears primarily in downtrending markets. In contrast to the ascending triangle, it consists of a flat lower line (support) and a downward-sloping top line (resistance).

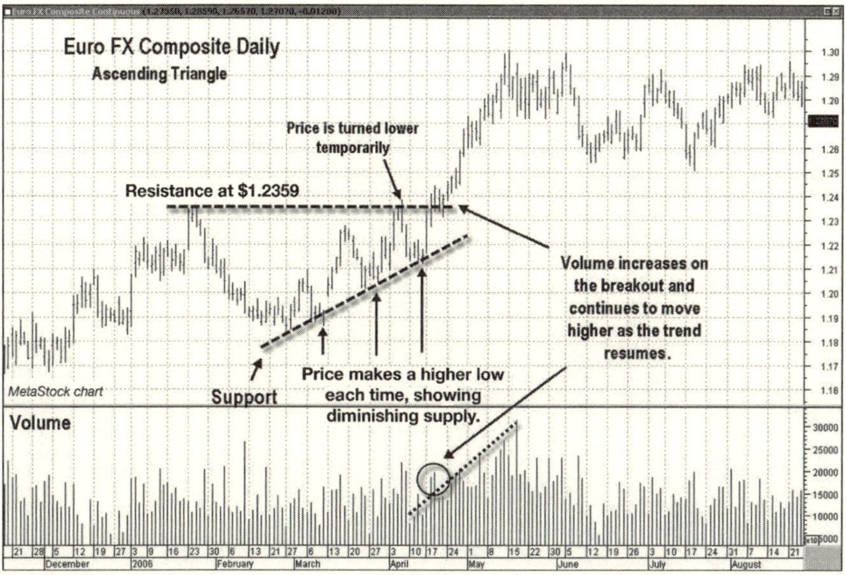

Chart 4.19 Bullish Ascending Triangle Pattern, Euro FX Composite

Source: MetaStock

The pattern consists of at least two lows at or near the same price level, with lower highs made on each rally attempt. The lower highs on each rally attempt indicate diminishing demand on each push higher, thus causing the downward-sloping resistance line. *Volume should be lower than average and/or be decreasing as the pattern develops and the price action is compressed.*

Chart 4.20 for AMR Corp. shows a descending triangle. The initial low of the pattern was made at $10 in March 2004, with a test of that low coming later that year in May. That formed the flat support line in the $10 area, which was the level to watch for a break lower. Notice how, as the pattern formed, price made a lower high on each rally attempt, which allowed a downward-sloping resistance line to be drawn by connecting the highs. Volume was rather lackluster as the pattern developed before price finally broke lower with increased volume in July as the downtrend resumed.

Symmetrical Triangles

A *symmetrical triangle* is very similar to a pennant formation because it involves the same basic shape. Symmetrical triangles, however, are longer in duration, since they represent a longer-term period of trader

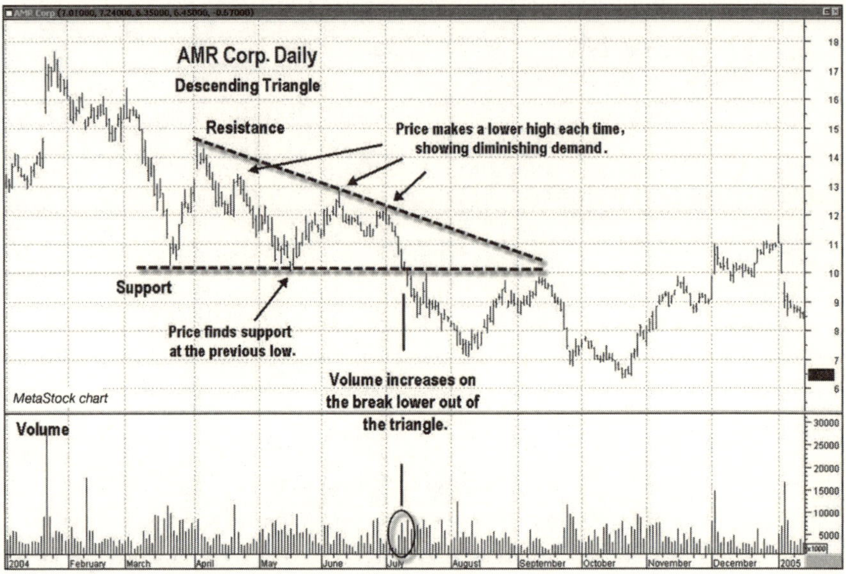

Chart 4.20 Bearish Descending Triangle, AMR Corp.

Source: MetaStock

indecision. The consolidation period shows an absence of conviction from both buyers and sellers, thus allowing supply and demand to appear virtually equal as price consolidates sideways. *Volume should be lower than average and/or be decreasing as the pattern develops and price action is compressed.*

Chart 4.21 for Google (GOOG) shows a symmetrical triangle pattern that formed following a sharp rally. The pattern lasted for eight months, however, as lack of demand was matched by a lack of supply. Notice the pattern of lower highs and higher lows as the support and resistance lines converge. Volume moved higher as demand for Google shares finally forced the price higher to break out of the triangle. The breakout was upward in continuation of the previous trend, and the increased volume validated the breakout direction.

Volume Confirmation of Trend Continuation Patterns

These patterns can appear both in trending markets and following consolidation patterns. They reflect the resumption or continuation of a trend in its most recent direction.

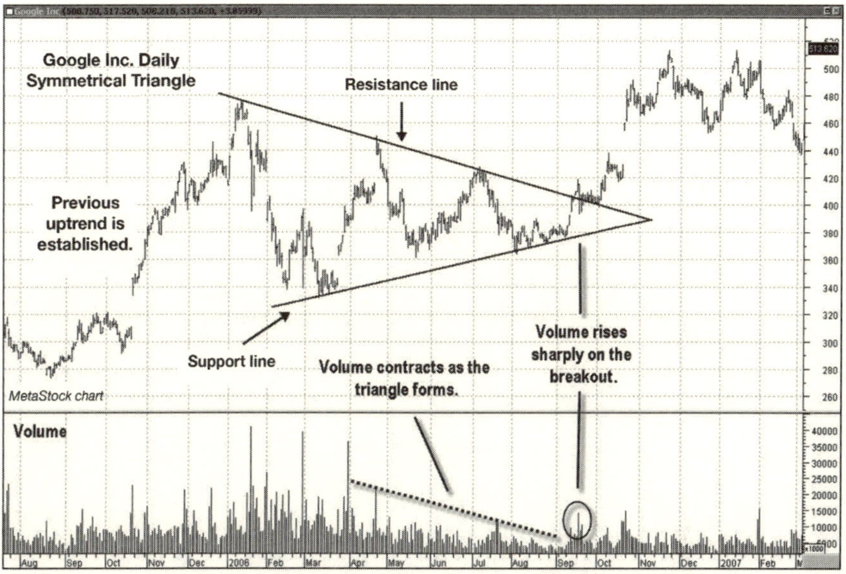

Chart 4.21 Bullish Breakout from Symmetrical Triangle Pattern, Google Inc.

Source: MetaStock

Continuation Gaps

Gaps are just what the name implies—a large step up or down in price, forming a "gap" from the previous position on the chart. Most commonly, the term is used in the context of a "gap open," where the price opens substantially above or below the previous closing price.

A *continuation gap* occurs in the middle of a move and in the same direction as the existing trend. Unlike *exhaustion gaps*, continuation gaps make good trade entry points in the existing trend, as these patterns are a signal that buying or selling interest has accelerated. These gaps are also known as *measuring gaps* or *runaway gaps*.

Chart 4.22 for Amazon.com (AMZN) shows a continuation gap in an uptrend. Notice how price moved higher off the November 2008 low before forming a bullish flag pattern as price consolidated. On January 30, 2009, price gapped higher on huge volume, signaling that the newly formed uptrend was ready to continue.

Candlestick Continuation Patterns

Candlestick charts have become one of the more popular tools of both the trader and the serious technician. The candlestick charting method was developed in Japan in the seventeenth century. Greg L. Morris introduced the software methodology to traders in the United States back in the

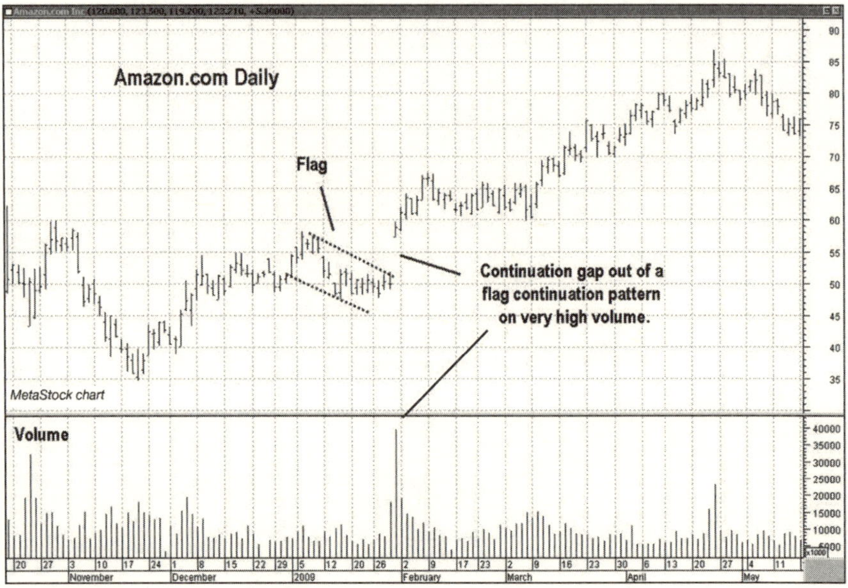

Chart 4.22 Bullish Continuation Gap, Amazon.com

Source: MetaStock

early 1990s. As the story unfolds, a Japanese rice futures trader noticed that in addition to supply and demand, trader emotion played a large part in market behavior. This emotion could sometimes cause a disconnect between the price and the actual value of the rice market. The candlestick methodology was developed in an attempt to graphically represent intraday price relationships that were driven by trader sentiment. Candlestick charting is very popular among active traders because it reflects short-term outlooks (usually less than two weeks in duration). Chart 4.23 shows the components of a candlestick.

The difference between standard bar charting and candlestick charting is that the "real body" of the candlestick shows the relationship between the open and close for the period. If the close is higher than the open, the real body is hollow or white. If the close is below the open, the real body is darkened, whether it is black, red, or whatever color the chartist chooses. That is a very simplistic overview of how candlesticks are constructed. Candlestick charting is a very complex topic and beyond the scope of this book.

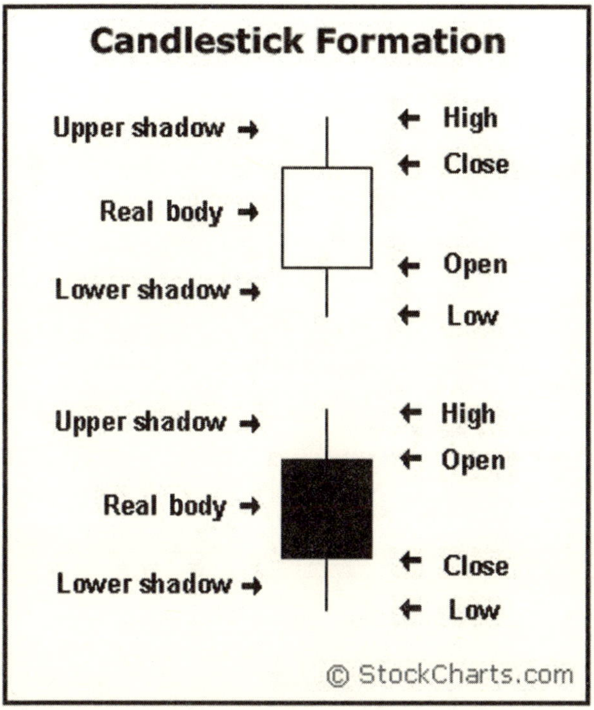

Chart 4.23 Components of a Candlestick

One example of a common candlestick continuation pattern that is especially common in the foreign exchange (FX) market is interestingly named the *in-neck thrusting pattern*. The example of the E-Mini Euro FX futures contract in Chart 4.24 shows the in-neck thrusting pattern as it unfolds during a downward move. Note that most candlestick patterns are short term in nature, so they develop quickly. Chart 4.24 illustrates the pattern in a downtrend, but this pattern is also valid in uptrends as well. In the downtrend example in Chart 4.24, the pattern unfolds as follows:

- Day 1. Consists of a long black candle signaling the conviction among sellers.
- Day 2. The candle has a white body (which means that the closing price is above the opening price) as buyers step in to try to stem the decline. This candle usually has a long tail, which signals that there was a strong battle to push price lower, but for this day the buyers prevailed.

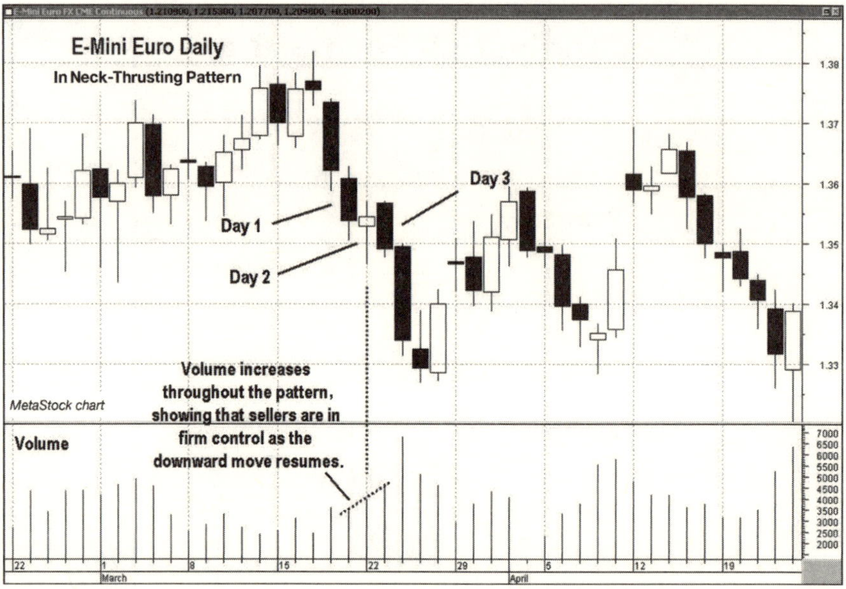

Chart 4.24 Candlestick Continuation Pattern, E-Mini Euro Futures

Source: MetaStock

- Day 3. On the third day, buyers attempt to push price higher but fail, and the sellers resume control, which results in another large black candle resuming the downtrend.

Volume increases throughout the pattern, showing a definite battle for control of the market. In this case, it was ultimately won by sellers.

This chapter has presented volume overlays as a way to detect and assess trend strength. We have also learned to identify and confirm price chart formations using their corresponding volume patterns to predict continuation in trend direction.

Summary

- Volume allows traders the opportunity to see how much intensity or conviction is behind price movements of individual stocks or the market as a whole. In a sense, volume "validates" price movements and can also give insight as to whether a trend is likely to continue or change direction. Keep in mind the trader's mantra: *Volume precedes price.*

- As such, volume will show changes in its characteristics that will alert traders to the end of an uptrend or a downtrend before the price actually reverses. For example, in a downtrending market, the volume should expand during the down moves (confirmation of trend) and contract during countertrend bounces. When the volume patterns begin to change, they serve to alert a trader to shifts in trend.
- Trends, and the strength of those trends, can be assessed and confirmed through the use of *overlays* to determine volume strength and the conviction behind price movement. Such overlays can confirm robust or lagging trends.
- Popular overlays include volume moving averages, linear regression, and Moving Average Convergence/Divergence (MACD) of volume.
- Price formation patterns, when used in conjunction with their corresponding volume patterns, can also give strong confirmation as to the direction of a tradeworthy trend. Spotting the price patterns and corresponding volume patterns of pennants, flags, triangles, and gaps helps to predict a continuation in trend direction.

Chapter 5

THE VOLUME ALERT: IDENTIFYING TREND REVERSAL PATTERNS

So far in our Volume Analysis, we have explored a variety of trading tools and methods to identify chart patterns and assess trends. A trend reversal pattern can occur intraday, lasting a few hours; short term, lasting a few days to a few weeks; or long term, lasting several months. The recognition of reversals is a critical skill in the trader's toolbox; it is typically easier to spot and follow trends, but also easier to "get burned" when a reversal signal is missed. A great degree of analysis and insight is required to spot reversal patterns, and the ability to do so can set you apart from the average trader. Chapter 5 focuses specifically on identifying trend reversal patterns.

These chart patterns contain volume behavior that provides insight into the conviction of the trend and can alert us to perhaps the most critically important patterns in the market for traders. In our Volume Analysis, we will examine examples of broad-market trend reversals, index reversals, and the reversals of individual issues. We will look at longer-term "macro" trend reversals and shorter-trend reversals, of interest only to an intraday trader. What to keep in mind when examining these charts is the trader's mantra: volume precedes price. The intensity of a reversal may come as a surprise, but the reversal itself never should. The market flashes warning signals, and the volume behavior within these patterns is an early alert that a change in sentiment and trend is underway.

Macro, or Longer-Term, Trend Reversals

Using Volume Analysis, we identified the price trend and assessed under what circumstances we might anticipate a reversal. In this section, we focus our attention on actual trend reversal patterns. All the reversal patterns that we will be discussing can occur in the broad market, in an index or commodity, or in an individual issue. Our first three examples display simple trend reversal patterns in the macro, or longer-term, prevailing trend.

Chart 5.1 for the iShares Russell 2000 Trust ETF (IWM) shows how the volume pattern tipped traders off that a change in price direction was coming in the summer of 2007. Price had been in an uptrend (a pattern of higher highs and higher lows) since March 2003 (the full trend duration is not shown, in order to scale recent events properly).

As price made new highs in May and June 2007, seen in area A, the price pattern became choppy. Looking at price alone would tell you that IWM was in a consolidation phase, but that's about it. When volume is included in the analysis, however, the picture becomes clearer. Notice how volume activity increased during this choppy phase. Following a trend, choppy price action combined with an increase in volume is a sign of distribution. Every time eager buyers entered the market, there were

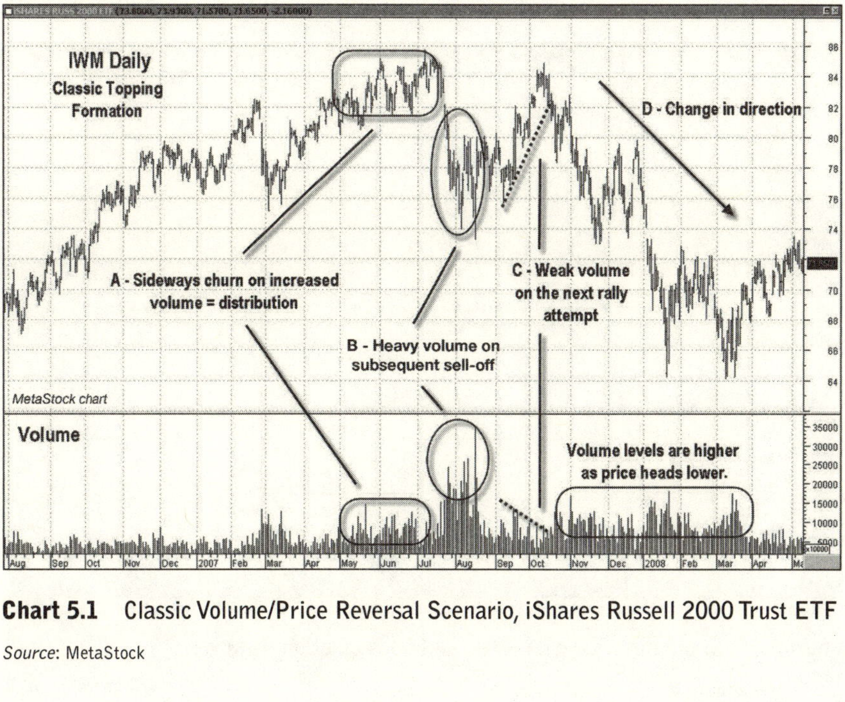

Chart 5.1 Classic Volume/Price Reversal Scenario, iShares Russell 2000 Trust ETF

Source: MetaStock

sellers willing to take profits and give up their shares. The elevated supply held price in check, which prevented any further upward push in price.

In area B, the overhead supply proved too much for the market to bear, which prompted sharp selling into August. At that point, a trend reversal was definitely taking shape, but we needed one more piece of evidence before making that call. That piece of evidence was the behavior of volume on the next rally attempt in area C.

Note how, on the rally attempt following the August sell-off, the volume contracted as price moved higher and approached the summer 2007 highs. This was a definite sign that there was not enough fuel in the tank (volume) to push prices significantly higher, which opened the door for a sell-off (area D). Notice the consistently higher level of volume during the sell-off as compared to the previous rally attempt in area C. That showed a definite shift in trader sentiment and that sellers were firmly in control.

Just as a volume spike in a strong uptrend can alert traders that buying pressure has exhausted itself in the market, a spike in volume following a steep downtrend can also alert traders that sellers have exhausted themselves in a fit of panic selling.

Note in Chart 5.2 for IBM that the volume pattern is rather consistent throughout the three-month downtrend from December 2004 through

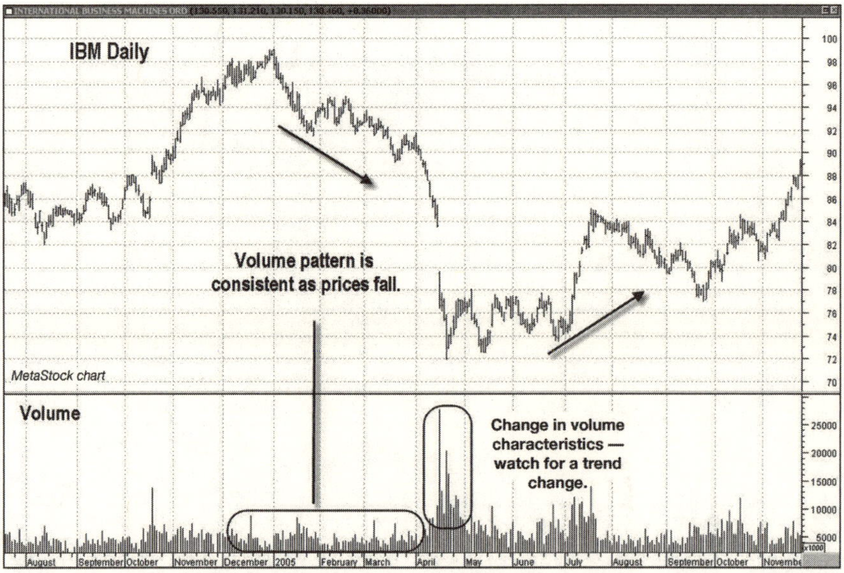

Chart 5.2 Trend Reversal with Spike and Consolidation, IBM

Source: MetaStock

April 2005. In mid-April, however, volume spiked higher as price dropped sharply to a new low. The sharp increase in volume showed that sellers wanted out so bad that they were willing to dump shares on the market in order to protect themselves from further losses. This type of seller behavior usually marks a low point in sentiment. Note also how price chopped sideways in a three-month consolidation pattern before reversing and moving higher.

Reversal Off an Intense Downtrend

Intense downtrend reversals are characterized by falling prices with noticeably rising volume. While the previous example in IBM showed steady selling with a consistent volume pattern, the intense downtrend shows true and strong negative sentiment.

Chart 5.3 for the S&P Industrial Select SPDR ETF (XLI) shows a new downtrend developing in May 2008. Note how volume increased throughout the sell-off as price was making a series of lower lows and highs. This type of intensity reflected increasing negative sentiment, as traders looked to eliminate further loss.

The consistently high volume in October and November 2008 confirmed that negative sentiment toward XLI was still very strong. After a brief

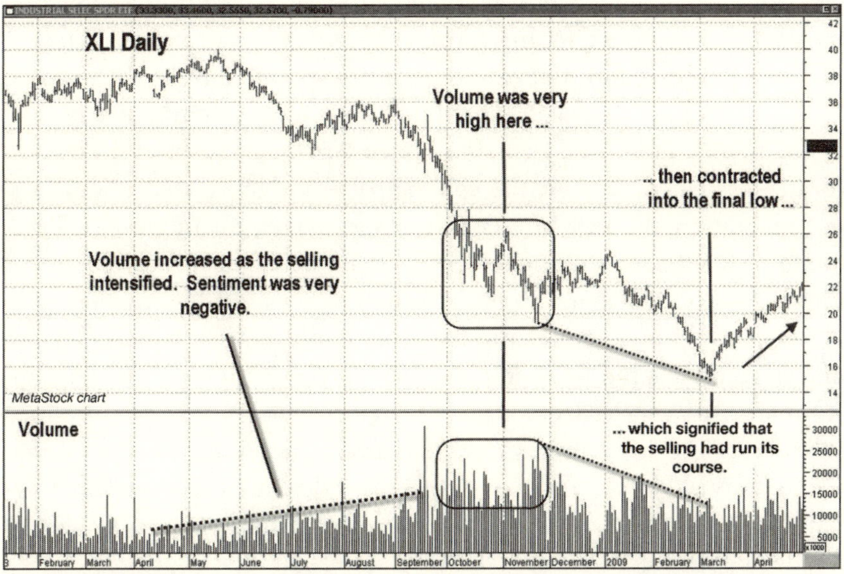

Chart 5.3 Reversal Off Intense Downtrend, S&P Select Industrial SPDR ETF

Source: MetaStock

rally from late November into early January 2009, price once again headed lower, this time making a new low. As the new low was made, notice how volume decreased as price pushed lower. This change in the volume pattern showed that negative sentiment was waning. This meant selling pressure had weakened, indicating that a trend change was imminent.

Short-Term Reversals and Overlays

In the previous three examples, we concentrated on long-term macro trend changes based on our Volume Analysis over a period of months. What about changes in volume patterns for the more active trader wishing to capitalize on short-term price movements? One solution lies in the use of volume overlays. In this section, we will concentrate on the use of volume moving averages (VMAs), first introduced and explained in Chapter 4.

Shorter-period VMA parameters show changes in volume patterns useful for the active trader to spot short-term trends. The key to selecting the proper time frame for your VMA is to pick a length that is neither too short (which can lead to trading whipsaws) nor too long (which can lead to "indicator lag," or the generation of late signals).

In our Volume Analysis of short-term reversals, we chose a 9-period exponential moving average (EMA) to use with our daily charts. An EMA, which weights more recent data more heavily, is favored over a simple, or linear, moving average for this purpose because of its sensitivity to recent data and thus its ability to reveal more recent volume shifts.

When examining the behavior of the VMA, traders should note its dual ability to both confirm a trend and signal a potential reversal. In the following discussion, we note the volume pattern of the VMA under different market conditions. In an uptrending market, an increasing VMA confirms that trader sentiment is positive, as buying pressure forces prices higher. A VMA that peaks and begins to turn lower in an uptrending market signals that buying pressure has temporarily peaked, which provides an early alert to a pullback or to a potential reversal in trend. In a declining market, a rising VMA indicates that trader sentiment is negative, since selling pressure drives price movement lower, confirming the downtrend. Once the VMA peaks and moves lower in a downtrending market, it signals that selling pressure has diminished, thus providing an early alert to a rally or potential reversal.

Chart 5.4 for the S&P 500 SPDR ETF (SPY) shows how the 9-day VMA can be used to pinpoint short-term lows in the market. Note how

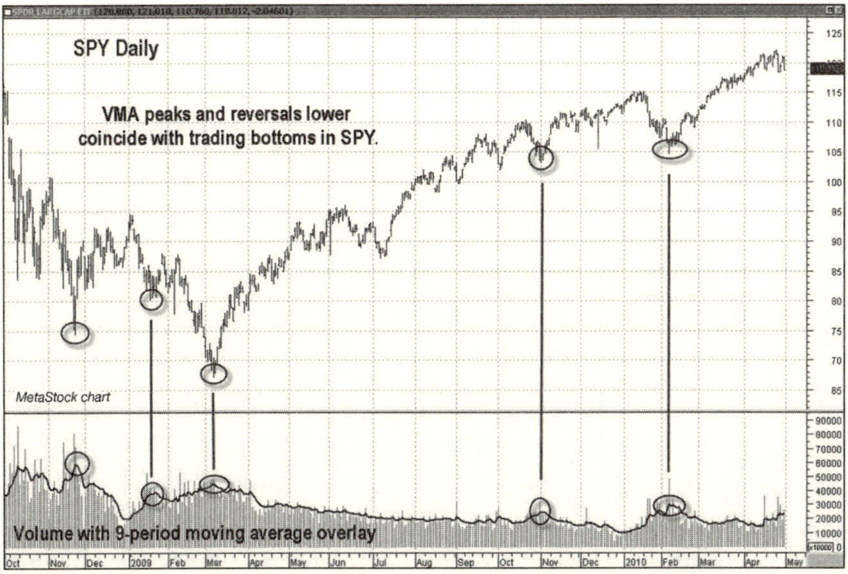

Chart 5.4 Reversals Signaled by 9-Day VMA Overlay, S&P 500 SPDR ETF

Source: MetaStock

each time the VMA peaked after moving higher, a short-term trading bottom was formed in the market.

Chart 5.5 of the Nasdaq 100 Trust ETF (QQQQ) shows the 9-day exponential moving average at work there also. This overlay tends to show more bottoms than tops because of the more emotional nature of market participants (elevated volume) during sell-offs, but notice in the QQQQ chart how the 9-day VMA caught a couple of swing highs in QQQQ in March and June 2009.

Reversals Signaled by MACD Volume Overlay

It's worth looking at the same chart of QQQQ using the same volume principle, only this time using the Moving Average Convergence/Divergence (MACD) volume overlay (see Chart 5.6). This is a more sensitive overlay, as it shows more frequent and more clearly defined peaks. Notice how each time the MACD of volume peaked well above the zero line and turned lower, price changed short-term direction. This alerted the active trader to short-term changes in direction, which could be used for taking profits or initiating new positions.

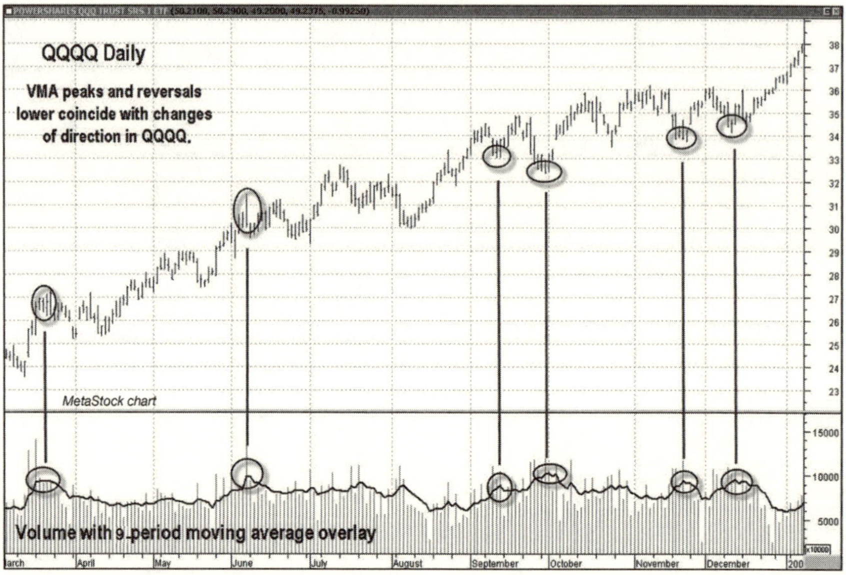

Chart 5.5 Reversals Signaled with 9-Day VMA Overlay, Nasdaq 100 Trust ETF

Source: MetaStock

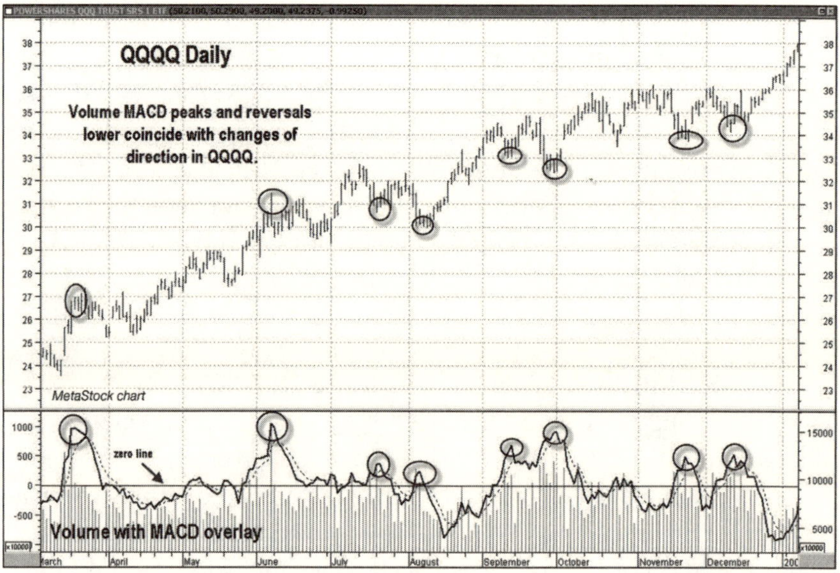

Chart 5.6 Reversals Signaled with MACD Overlay, Nasdaq 100 Trust ETF

Source: MetaStock

Volume Behavior in Trend Reversal Patterns

Every *trend reversal pattern* requires some pattern of volume in its development. In Volume Analysis, we interpret this volume pattern to either confirm the reversal pattern or refute it. The identification of these patterns can help a trader who trades with the trend to lock in profits and step aside, while a short-term trader may choose to catch the reversal. Either way, the goal here is not to get "caught" in a reversal, and volume patterns give plenty of warning signals to avoid them. In this section we will look at several widely identified reversal patterns.

The Wedge

A *wedge* is a chart pattern constructed by two converging lines connecting a series of price peaks (resistance) and price lows (support). It is like a pennant or symmetrical triangle pattern (discussed in Chapter 4), except that it usually occurs in a rising or falling, not a horizontal, direction. The wedge reversal pattern is typically longer term in nature, lasting anywhere from three to six months. In order for a wedge pattern to be a valid reversal pattern, however, there must be a prior trend in place to reverse. There are two types of wedge patterns, rising and falling.

Falling Wedges

The falling wedge has bullish implications, as it normally breaks up out of the wedge to begin an uptrend. The boundary lines of this pattern converge, with each slanting downward as the pattern forms. Another characteristic of a falling wedge is that the upper boundary line (or resistance line) normally has a sharper slope than the lower boundary line (or support line) in the pattern. A flatter support line shows that selling pressure is diminishing, as sellers are unable to push the price down much farther with each new round of selling.

Price should touch each line (support and resistance) at least twice during the formation of the pattern. The more times the boundary lines are touched, the more reliable the pattern is thought to be. During the formation of the pattern, volume generally lightens as the wedge develops, showing a lack of conviction among both buyers and sellers.

A buy signal is given when price breaks through the upper resistance line. The breakout should be confirmed by heavier volume, but price must also confirm the breakout by posting successive closes above the upper resistance line. Chart 5.7 for Starbucks (SBUX) shows how volume drops

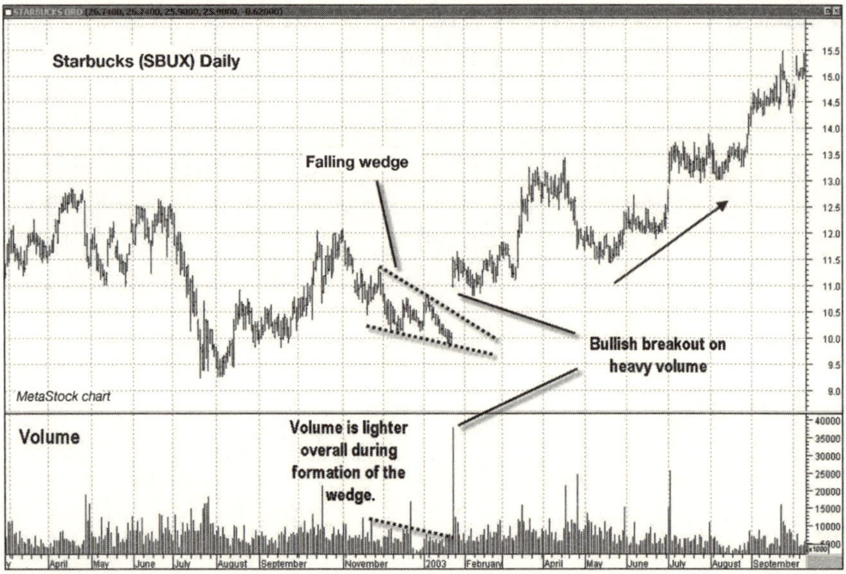

Chart 5.7 Bullish Reversal, Falling Wedge Pattern, Starbucks Corporation

Source: MetaStock

as the pattern is formed and then explodes on the bullish breakout, sending prices sharply higher.

Rising Wedges

A *rising wedge* has bearish implications, as price normally breaks out to the downside to resolve the pattern and begin a downtrend. Price movement contracts (i.e., narrows) as the pattern develops, showing that upside momentum is slowing. The top line (resistance) typically has a flatter slope than the bottom line as it pushes higher, showing diminishing buying pressure as the pattern progresses.

A sell signal is given when price breaks below the support line. As with the falling wedge, the breakout should be confirmed by heavier volume. The breakout must also be confirmed by price posting two successive closes below the support line. Cisco Systems (CSCO) in Chart 5.8 shows the low-volume pattern as the rising wedge forms, followed by the volume explosion on the downside breakout.

The Head-and-Shoulders Reversal Pattern

The standard *head-and-shoulders reversal pattern* forms after an uptrend; it signals a bearish reversal. It consists of three peaks, with the middle peak

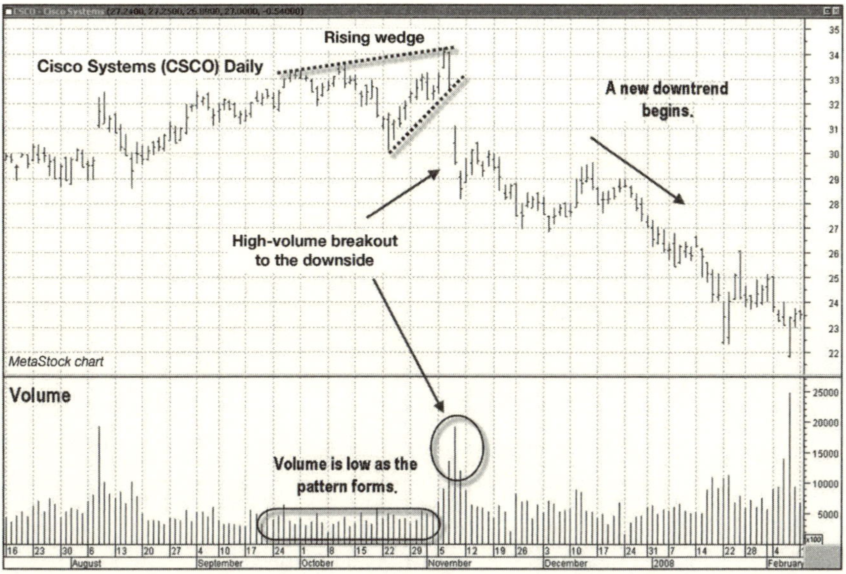

Chart 5.8 Bearish Reversal, Rising Wedge Pattern, Cisco Systems

Source: MetaStock

(the head) being higher than the other two (the shoulders). The shoulders are typically (but not always) equal in height. The reaction lows of the first two peaks (i.e., the left shoulder and the head) can be connected to form the "neckline," or signal line. Chart 5.9 illustrates the pattern. The head-and-shoulders pattern signals a top as the last bits of buying energy come into a stock or contract. The "head" is the final upsurge, with the right shoulder representing a smaller surge of "late" buyers coming to the party, only to be eventually disappointed. Buyers may make more than one weak attempt to push prices higher, as is described shortly.

Volume plays a very important role in confirming the head-and-shoulders pattern as it develops. Volume should be lighter on the head than on the left shoulder, and volume should be lighter on the right shoulder than on the head. The most critical of the three peaks, however, is the right shoulder. Volume should contract noticeably, signaling that buying interest in the security is weakening, which indicates that a change in sentiment is underway. Volume should increase on the downside break of the neckline, showing that selling pressure is building. Following the neckline break, there is usually one more rally back up to the neckline, which should act as resistance. The rally to "test" the neckline should be on lighter

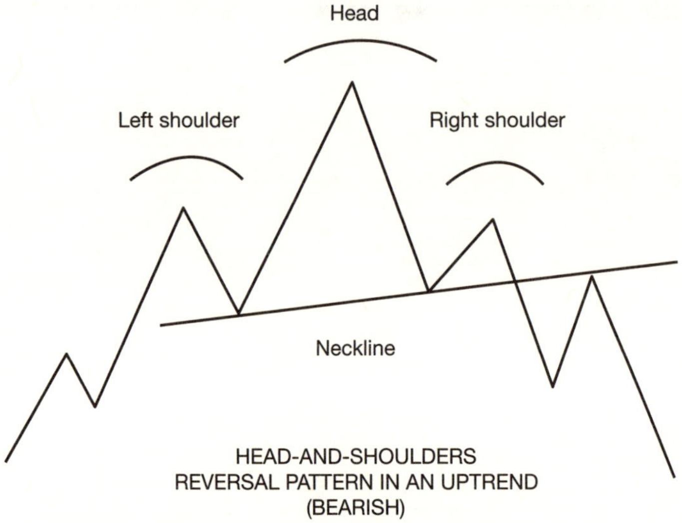

Chart 5.9 Standard Head-and-Shoulders Reversal Pattern

volume than the downside break of the neckline. Prices should then roll over one more time on expanding volume to indicate that a new downtrend is underway.

The chart of the Dow Jones Industrial Average Diamonds Series Trust ETF (DIA) in Chart 5.10 shows a typical head-and-shoulders reversal pattern. Notice the distinct peaks at the top of the chart that form the left shoulder, head, and right shoulder. A head-and-shoulders reversal pattern is not readily apparent until the pattern corrects from the head and begins to form the right shoulder. At this point, the pattern should be watched, but nothing more. Notice that as the right shoulder formed, volume dropped, signifying that there was insufficient demand to push price back to the high (the head).

As price pushed lower from the right shoulder, it broke down through the neckline as volume increased dramatically. This shows that sentiment had changed and that sellers were in control. Price then consolidated for two months before rallying up to test the neckline in March into May 2008. As price approached the neckline, volume decreased, confirming the negative sentiment. Once price touched the neckline and was unable to break through, volume picked up again as price resumed its downtrend.

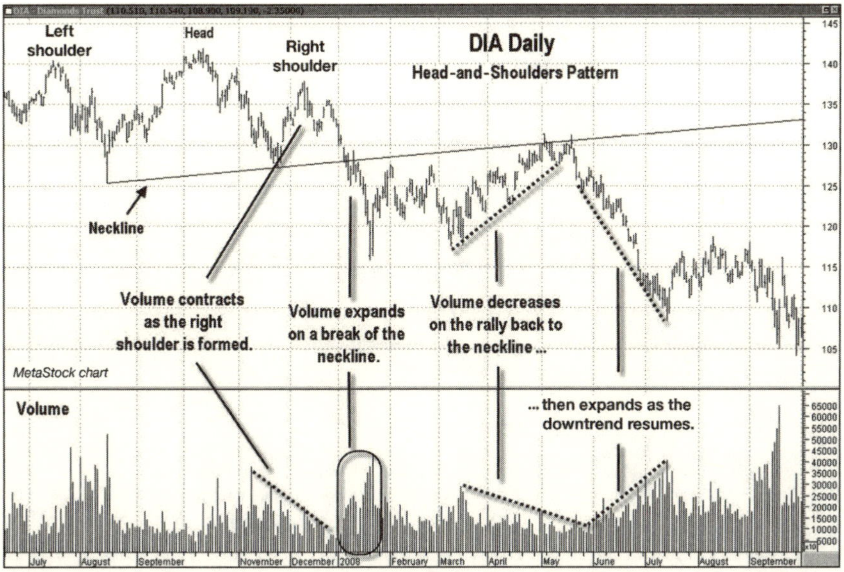

Chart 5.10 Bearish Reversal, Head-and-Shoulders Pattern, DJ Diamonds Trust ETF

Source: MetaStock

Calculating Price Targets with Head-and-Shoulders Patterns

The head-and-shoulders reversal pattern allows accurate price targets to be generated. Price targets are computed by measuring the distance between the head and the neckline. That amount is projected lower from the point of penetration of the neckline after the right shoulder is formed. Projections from these formations can give a trader a price area to look for support and possible long entry, depending on other confirmatory indicators. Chart 5.11 shows the price target projection methodology.

Using the DIA chart from Chart 5.12, we can examine the price projection that could be generated by the head-and-shoulders formation noted previously. The price calculation is as follows:

1. Project straight down from the high point of the head ($141.95) to the value of the neckline ($126.40) on that particular day.
2. Subtract the value of the neckline from the high: $141.95 – $126.40 = $15.55.
3. When the neckline is broken (after the right shoulder is formed), subtract $15.55 from the value of the neckline on the day it was broken: $128.15 – $15.55 = $112.60.

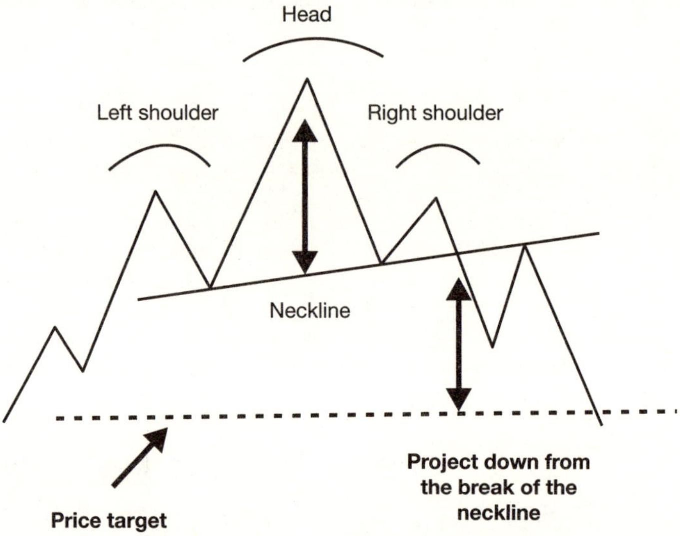

Chart 5.11 Projecting Price Targets with Head-and-Shoulders Patterns

Source: MetaStock

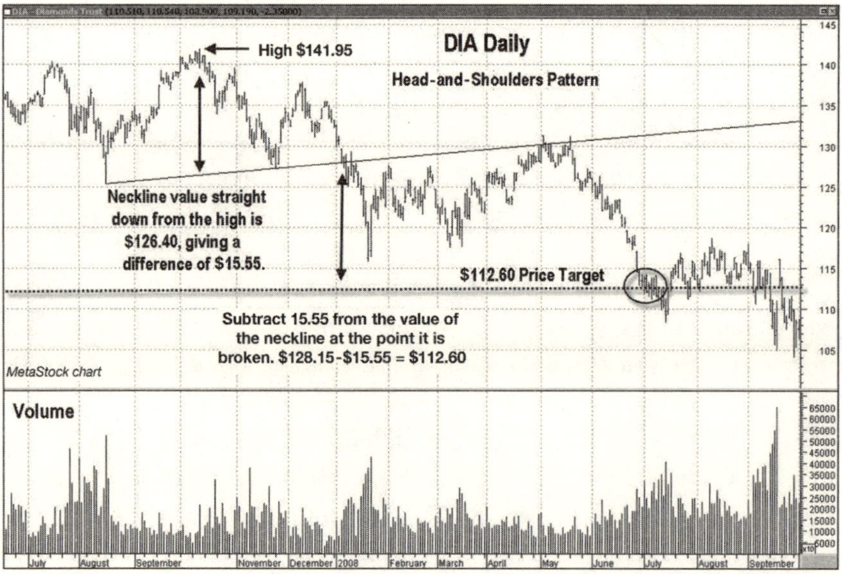

Chart 5.12 Projecting Price Targets, Head-and-Shoulders Pattern, DJ Diamonds Trust ETF

Source: MetaStock

Once the price target is reached, it is more of a signal to take profits on short positions than a blind buy signal for those looking to get long. Whenever looking to initiate a new position, always make sure that other indicators confirm the fact that a bottom may be in place. Notice how after a brief period of consolidation, the price for DIA turned lower yet again, as sentiment toward it remained negative.

Inverse Head-and-Shoulders Pattern

The *inverse head-and-shoulders* is a bullish pattern, essentially the "upside-down" version of the standard head-and-shoulders reversal pattern, and it is formed at price lows. It is just as reliable as the head-and-shoulders formations at highs, only the chart pattern is inverted. The same volume characteristics apply during the formation of the pattern, as it should be weakest at the formation of the right shoulder and explode higher on an upside break of the neckline.

In Chart 5.13 for Amazon.com (AMZN), notice how volume is subsequently weaker from the left shoulder to the head and from the head to the right shoulder. As price gaps up through the neckline, volume explodes higher, showing that sentiment is positive and a new uptrend is beginning.

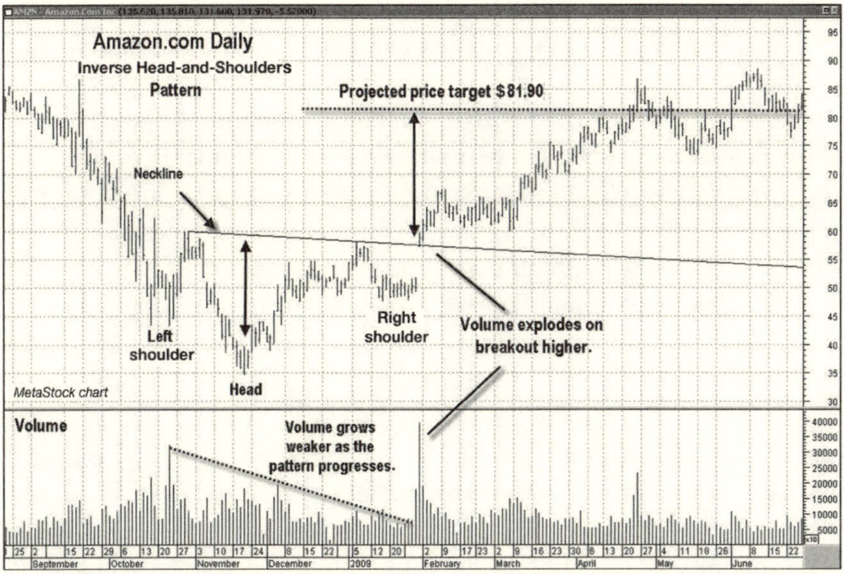

Chart 5.13 Bullish Reversal, Inverse Head-and-Shoulders Pattern, Amazon.com

Source: MetaStock

The inverse head-and-shoulders pattern projects price targets in the same manner as the head-and-shoulders reversal pattern at tops:

1. Project straight up from the low of the head ($34.68) to the value of the neckline ($59.33) on that particular day.
2. Subtract the low from the value of the neckline: $59.33 – $34.68 = $24.65.
3. When the neckline is broken (after the right shoulder is formed), add $24.65 to the value of the neckline on the day it was broken: $57.25 + $24.65 = $81.90.

Candlestick Reversal Patterns

We introduced candlesticks as a popular charting tool in Chapter 4, and gave one example of a candlestick pattern that signaled trend continuation. Here we switch the subject to reversals, where several well-known candlestick patterns can play a valuable part in their identification.

Spinning-Top Reversal

A *spinning top* is a classic candlestick pattern showing trader indecision following an advance or a decline. The small real body shows little difference between the opening and closing prices, yet the long shadows show that there was considerable intraday action on the part of both buyers and sellers.

The spinning-top formation is a sign that sentiment may be changing, as the day's trading activity essentially ends in a stalemate. Volume can also give clues as to the validity of such patterns, showing the sentiment of traders. Chart 5.14 for Citigroup (C) shows two examples of spinning tops, one following an uptrend and one a downtrend.

After the uptrend through late April, the spinning top, looking somewhat like an elongated plus sign, formed on very low volume, signifying that there was not much positive sentiment or buying power left to prolong the advance. Price reversed the next day, beginning a six-week decline. At the end of the decline in mid-July, another spinning top formed. This time it was on a noticeable increase in volume, signifying that buyers were stepping up to meet the sellers and putting the brakes on the decline. The elevated volume with the spinning-top pattern showed a short-term change in sentiment that led to a furious six-day rally. As Chart 5.14 shows, it is the *change* in volume along with the shape of the candlestick and the prior price

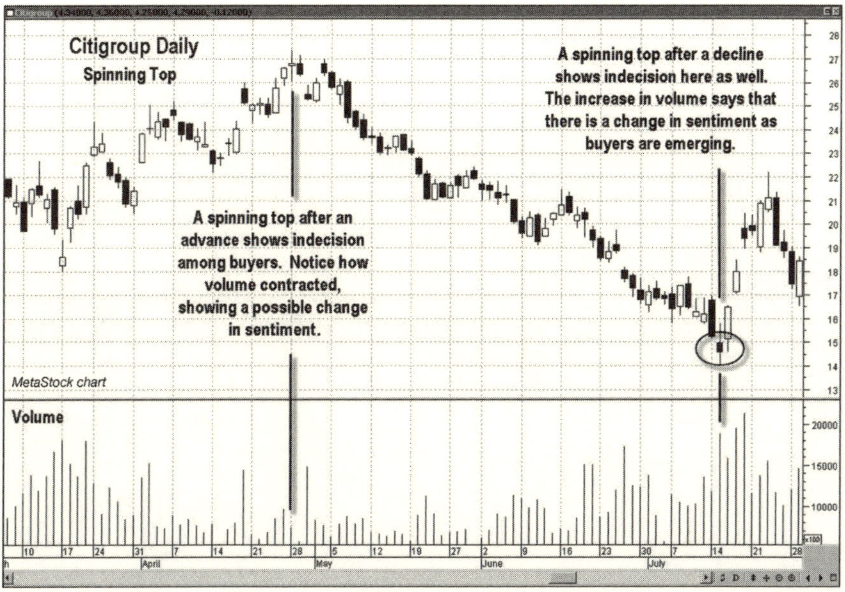

Chart 5.14 Spinning-Top Candlestick Reversals, Citigroup

Source: MetaStock

behavior that indicates a reversal. A weakening of volume indicates a weakening of the prevailing sentiment, while a significant strengthening shows a greater struggle emerging between buyers and sellers.

Doji Reversal

A *doji* is formed when the day's opening and closing prices are virtually equal, causing the real body to look like a dash or a straight line. A doji is like a spinning top, except with much shorter upper and lower legs—that is, much less intraday price fluctuation. It is also an indication of indecision, signaling that the forces behind the prevailing trend may be weakening. Lower volume on a doji is an indication that those who have wanted to participate in the trend have done so for the time being, while an increase in volume shows that there may be a struggle for near-term direction underway between buyers and sellers. It either case, a doji can represent a short-term change in sentiment and thus price direction.

In Chart 5.15 for Freeport-McMoRan (FCX), note how the doji formed after a move higher through virtually the entire month of November 2004. The two white candles before the doji occurred on decreasing volume; that was a sign of trouble. The formation of the doji on increasing volume was

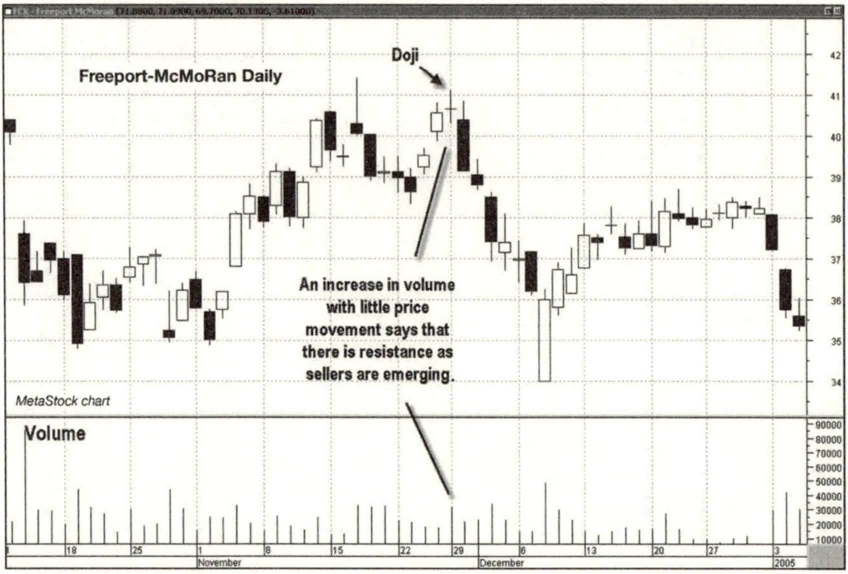

Chart 5.15 Doji Candlestick Reversal, Freeport-McMoRan

Source: MetaStock

a sign that a reversal—in this case, a correction—was near. Price reversed lower the very next day, leading to a decline of 17 percent over the next seven trading days. This is a fairly basic doji reversal pattern, and there are many others beyond the scope of this book.

Hammer Reversal

A *hammer* is a bullish reversal pattern that forms after a decline. The pattern consists of a small real body at the top of the candle with a long shadow or tail, a bit like a piston in an automotive engine. The pattern shows that sellers drove the price lower earlier in the session, but then buyers saw value and came in to provide support to prices. This is a form of climax selling that is validated by heavy volume. The reversal is confirmed by either a gap up or a large white candle the following day on heavy volume.

In Chart 5.16, the S&P 500 shows a classic bullish hammer reversal. Note how price had declined prior to the formation of the hammer, so there was prior negative price action to reverse. The day following the hammer formation was a large white candle (bullish) on even heavier volume, confirming the start of a new uptrend.

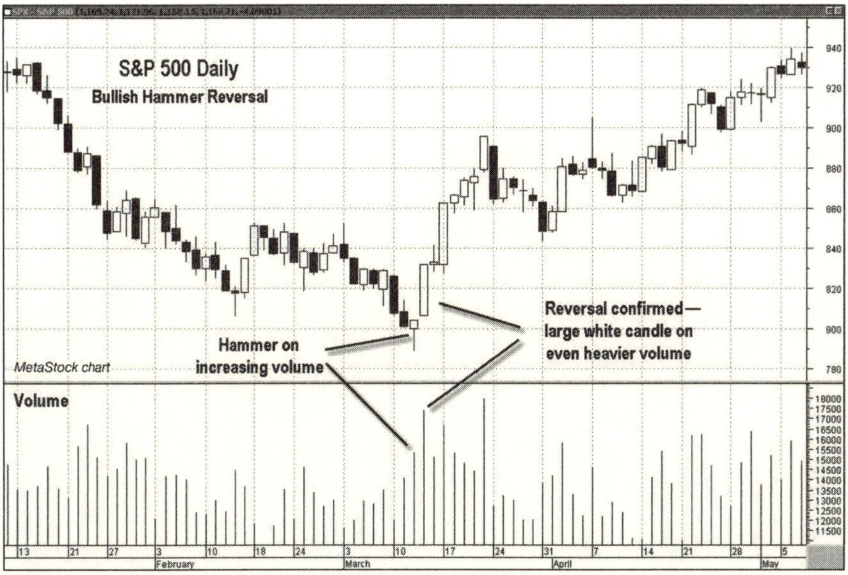

Chart 5.16 Bullish Hammer Candlestick Reversal, S&P 500

Source: MetaStock

Note that the same pattern inverted, with an upside-down hammer, indicates a bearish reversal. The long tail above the hammer body reflects a stronger buying interest that failed intraday, giving way to weakness to follow. To interpret such candlesticks, it also helps to look at intraday volume: That is, where the higher volume occurred on the formation of the tail—on the way up, or on the way down. Weak volume on the up-leg with stronger volume on the downward intraday move, of course, would show weakness.

Exhaustion Gaps

A *gap* is caused by a break in the price pattern—or a "blank spot" on the chart where no trading occurs at specific price levels. Gaps most commonly occur on opening prices following a specific news event that causes a large number of either buy or sell orders to accumulate prior to the open. That accumulation causes a large adjustment in price relative to the prior close.

We first described gaps in Chapter 4 in the context of "continuation gaps"; here they come up again as part of a reversal pattern called an *exhaustion gap*. Exhaustion gaps occur following a strong move in the price of a security as demand overwhelms supply, or vice versa. The large

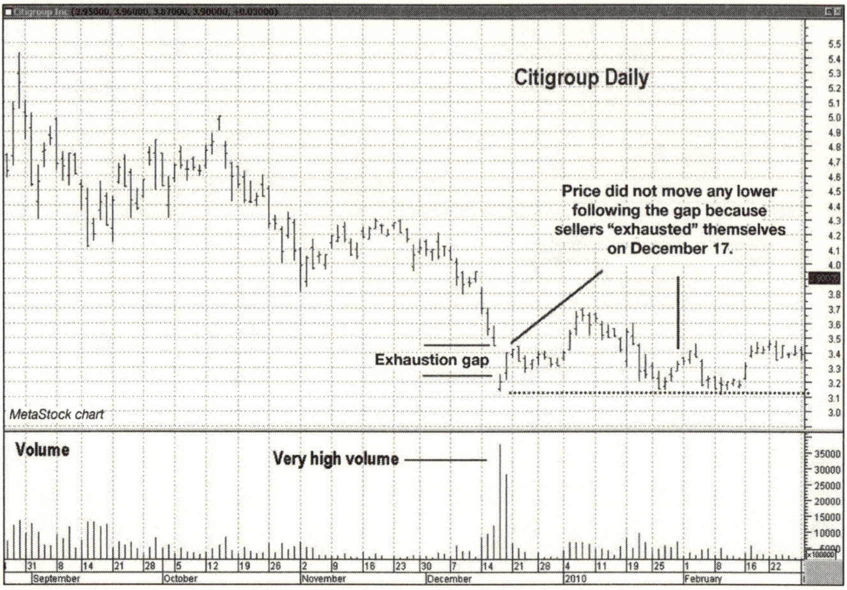

Chart 5.17 Exhaustion Gap, Citigroup

Source: MetaStock

gap in the direction of the trend along with a spike in volume suggests that trader conviction may have exhausted itself. While a gap higher on strong volume can look very bullish, and a gap lower on strong volume can look very bearish, recognizing these reversal patterns can help a trader lock in profits and preserve capital.

Chart 5.17 for Citigroup shows an exhaustion gap on December 17, 2009, following a long downtrend. Notice how price gapped strongly to the downside on a huge spike in volume. That was a sign that the selling had reached a crescendo there and that a bottom could be expected in that price area. Gaps are not always an indication of a quick turn in the other direction, but at the very least there should be little or no pressure left to continue the previous trend. The continuation gap (see Chapter 4) occurs after a period of indecision; the exhaustion gap acts more like a crescendo at the end of a definable trend.

Blow-Off Tops

Blow-off reversals are associated with tops and are similar in psychology to exhaustion gaps in that they occur at the end of trends and are characterized by one last thrust higher, giving a sharp peak on the price chart.

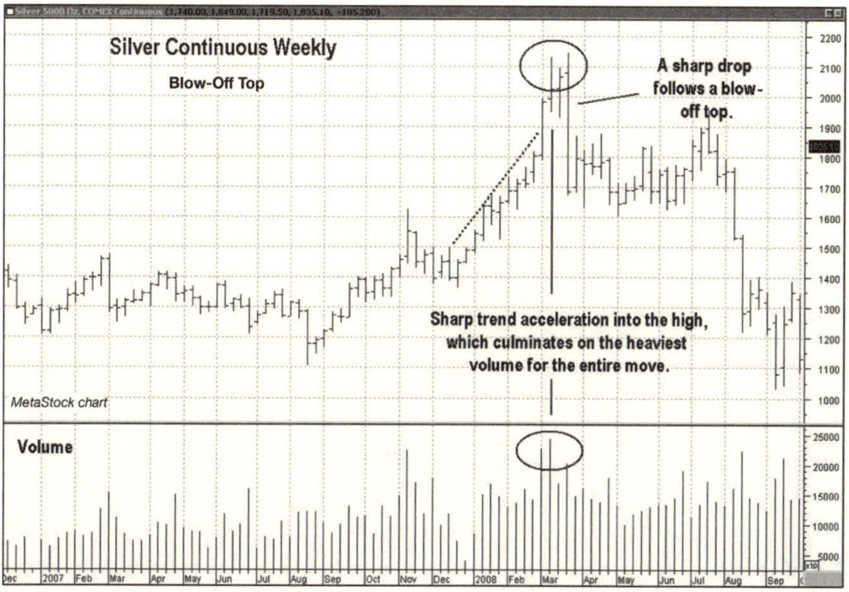

Chart 5.18 Blow-Off Top, Silver

Source: MetaStock

Following the final thrust of an uptrend, price usually reverses sharply lower, as all of the buying pressure has been exhausted during the final push into the high. That leaves a vacuum, which allows price to fall very rapidly as the profit takers and late buyers sell their shares.

The weekly chart of silver in Chart 5.18 shows how the uptrend accelerated in early 2008. Notice how, as price reached what would turn out to be the top, volume accelerated very rapidly, signaling that a change in direction was imminent. Notice also the sharp reversal in price, which makes this a textbook example of a blow-off top.

It is also possible to have blow-off bottoms, which are simply the inverse of the blow-off top pattern.

Parabolas

Parabolas are reversal patterns showing a sharp acceleration in buying; they are most frequently associated with tops. The parabolic move begins with an acceleration that moves higher off an established trendline, often in a parabolic or curved fashion. As price accelerates higher, it no longer moves in a normal, linear uptrending manner. The advance takes on the shape of a curve or parabola. This pattern shows very strong,

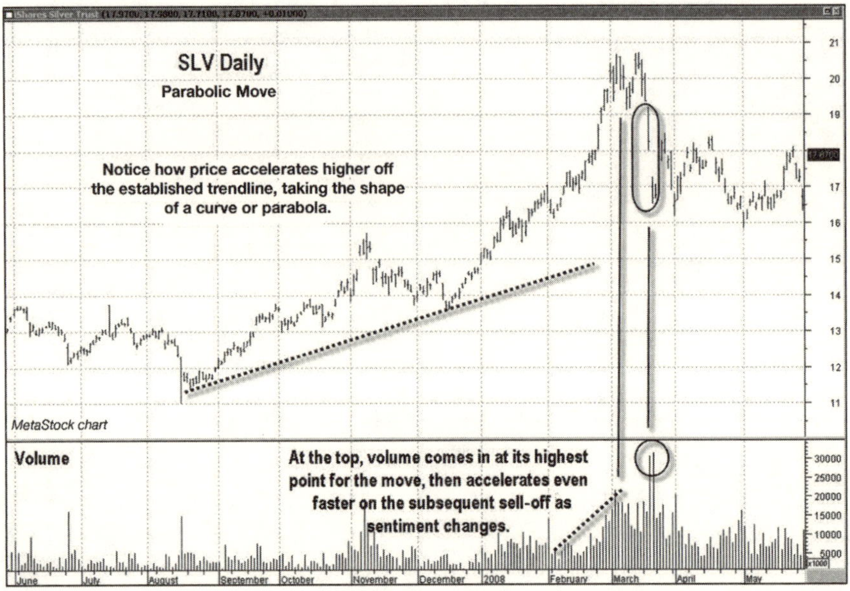

Chart 5.19 Parabolic Reversal, iShares Silver Trust ETF (SLV)

Source: MetaStock

almost frenzied activity among buyers. Parabolas have a pronounced increase in volume as they come into the high, typically the highest point of volume for the move. If a trader stays too long, these patterns end badly, with sharp increases in volume as price falls rapidly.

Chart 5.19 for the iShares Silver Trust ETF (SLV) is a classic example of how a parabolic move begins with an acceleration that launches off an established trend line. Once the move is complete on the highest volume to date for the move, SLV reverses sharply on even larger volume, signaling that the up move is definitely over.

Double and Triple Reversals

We conclude this chapter with a description of double and triple reversals, a commonly used set of patterns indicating exhaustion prior to reversal after a long uptrend or downtrend.

Double Bottom Reversal

A *double bottom reversal* is a pattern formed off of a long uptrend. The pattern consists of two consecutive lows at relatively the same level with a moderate "swing peak" formed in between them. It signifies that selling has run its course for the trend and that trader sentiment is changing. The pattern takes the shape of a W, with volume typically lower on the second low point than on the first. Double bottoms are typically a long-term signal; that is, they occur over the course of several days or even weeks.

Chart 5.20 for Hewlett-Packard (HPQ) shows how a double bottom is formed. Price had been in a prolonged downtrend prior to the formation of the double bottom in the summer and fall of 2002. The double bottom reversal developed as follows:

1. Price came down and made a new low at point A, which was the first line in the W pattern.
2. Price then rallied to set a moderately higher peak at point B, which formed the next line in the W pattern.
3. Following the peak at point B, price went back down to a point very similar to the first low, point C, which formed the third line of the W. Notice how volume coming into the low at point C was very light as compared to the low at point A.
4. Price then moved higher from the low at point C on accelerating volume, indicating a change in sentiment and forming the final line in the W pattern.

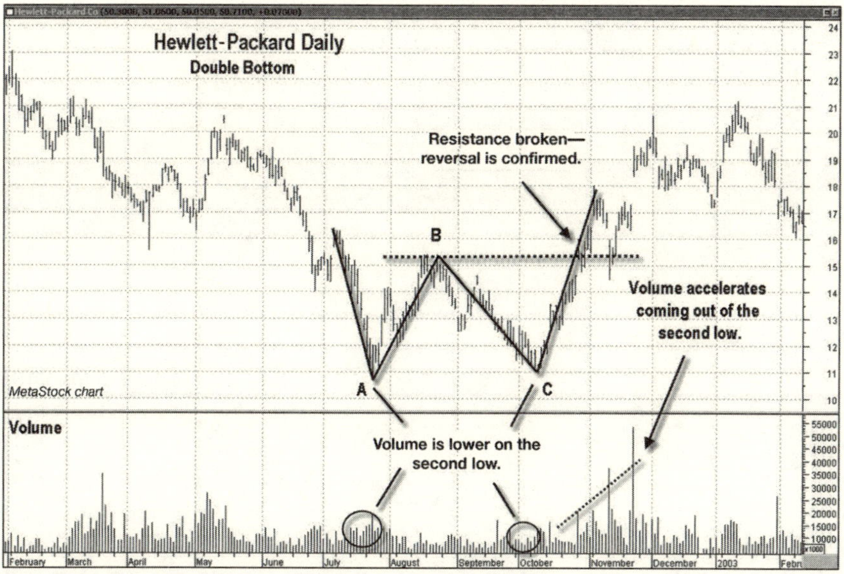

Chart 5.20 Double Bottom Reversal, Hewlett-Packard

Source: MetaStock

5. The reversal and a new uptrend were not confirmed until price moved above resistance at point B. After price moved above point B, long trades should have been considered.

Double Top Reversal

A *double top reversal* is the opposite of a double bottom. It is formed following a long uptrend and consists of two consecutive highs at relatively the same level, with a moderate swing low formed in between. It signifies that demand for the stock or contract is weakening, which leaves the door open for a change in direction as sentiment is changing. This pattern takes the shape of an M, with volume typically lower on the second high. Generally, this also is a long-term signal.

We'll use Hewlett-Packard as an example again. Chart 5.21 shows how a double top is formed. Price had been in a prolonged uptrend prior to the formation of the double top in the summer and fall of 2002. The double top reversal developed as follows:

1. Price made a new high at point A, which was the first line in the M pattern.
2. Price then declined to set a moderately lower trough at point B, which formed the next line in the M pattern.

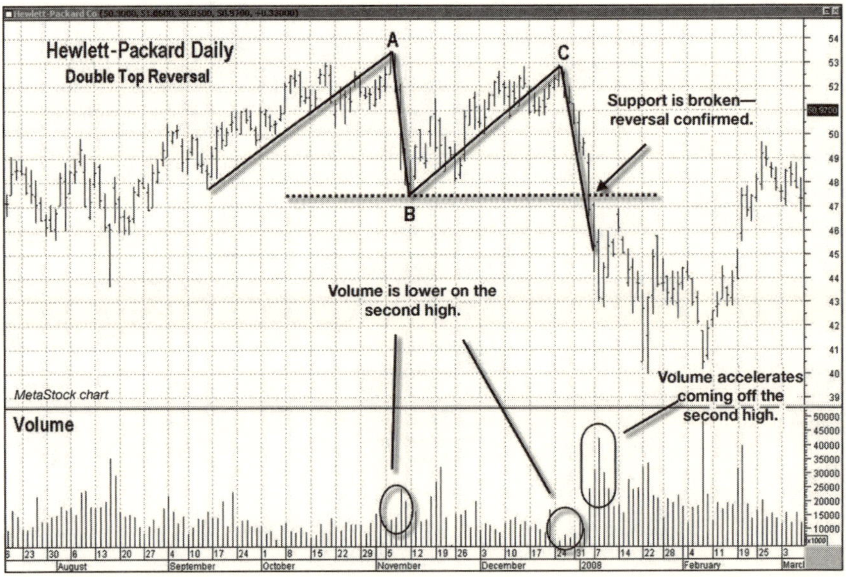

Chart 5.21 Double Top Reversal, Hewlett-Packard

Source: MetaStock

3. Following the low at point B, price went back up to a point similar to the first high, point C, forming the third line of the M. Notice how volume coming into the high at point C was very light as compared to the high at point A.
4. Price then moved lower from the low at point C on accelerating volume, indicating a change in sentiment, which formed the final line in the M pattern.
5. The reversal and a new downtrend were not confirmed until price moved below support at point B. After price moved below point B, long trades should have been exited, and short trades could have been considered.

Triple Top Reversal

The *triple top reversal* pattern consists of three peaks at relatively the same price level with two intervening swing lows, or troughs. The pattern is resolved by breaking down through the support line drawn connecting the two trough points in the pattern. As with the double top pattern, volume plays a key role in both identifying the pattern and then confirming the reversal in the triple top. The triple top is, of course, similar to the double top, except that the confirming break through support doesn't occur until after the third top.

Oracle (ORCL) in Chart 5.22 shows how a triple top is formed. Price had been in a prolonged uptrend prior to late 2007, when this chart begins. The triple top reversal formed as follows:

1. Price made a new high at point A.
2. Price then declined down to point B. At the time, this looked like nothing more than a normal swing low in an uptrend.
3. Price then moved higher to a price almost equal to point A. This formed point C. At point C, this could have been a double top in the process of forming. But remember, the swing low at point B would have to be taken out to confirm a reversal.
4. Price then declined to point D, which was higher than point B, so no reversal signal was given.
5. Price rallied and stopped at point E, which was virtually equal to point C at the $23.50 level. Notice how, at point E, volume contracted after price hit resistance at $23.50. That showed a lack of demand at that level, which indicated that a change in sentiment

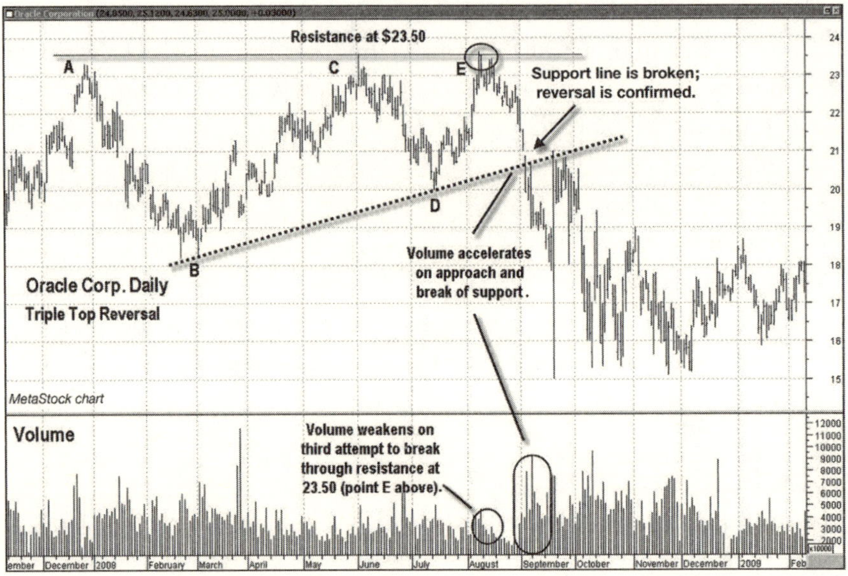

Chart 5.22 Triple Top Reversal Pattern, Oracle Corporation

Source: MetaStock

was beginning to take hold as the third attempt to get through $23.50 was faltering.

6. Price declined from the high at point E on accelerating volume.
7. Price broke through the support line (point B to point D) on increasing volume, which confirmed the reversal in sentiment and trend.

It should be obvious that if the double top reversal isn't confirmed in a chart, there is still a chance for a triple top, and it should continue to be tracked for such. Again, the key is to watch price and volume behavior as the price approaches the support level.

Triple Bottom Reversal

The *triple bottom reversal* pattern consists of three lows, or troughs, at relatively the same price level, with two intervening swing highs or peaks. The pattern is resolved by breaking up through the resistance line drawn connecting the two high points in the pattern. As with the double bottom pattern, volume plays a key role in both identifying the pattern and confirming the reversal.

Chart 5.23 for Yahoo! (YHOO) shows how a triple bottom is formed. Price had been in a prolonged downtrend prior to the formation of the pattern. The triple bottom reversal formed as follows:

1. Price hit a low at point A. This low actually consists of two points: the first high-volume push down and then the low-volume drift back down to the low area once emotions settled down.
2. Price then advanced up to point B. *Volume on the advance was weak*, signaling that investor sentiment had not yet changed.
3. Price then moved lower to a price almost equal to point A. This formed point C, which could be the second low in a double bottom; but that it was the second low could not be verified unless price broke through the high at point B.
4. Price then advanced to point D, which was lower than point B, so no double bottom reversal signal was given.
5. Price declined and stopped at point E, which was virtually equal to point C. Notice how volume contracted to almost nothing at point E. That showed a lack of supply at that level, which indicated that a change in sentiment was beginning to take hold as the third trip down to the low area was faltering.

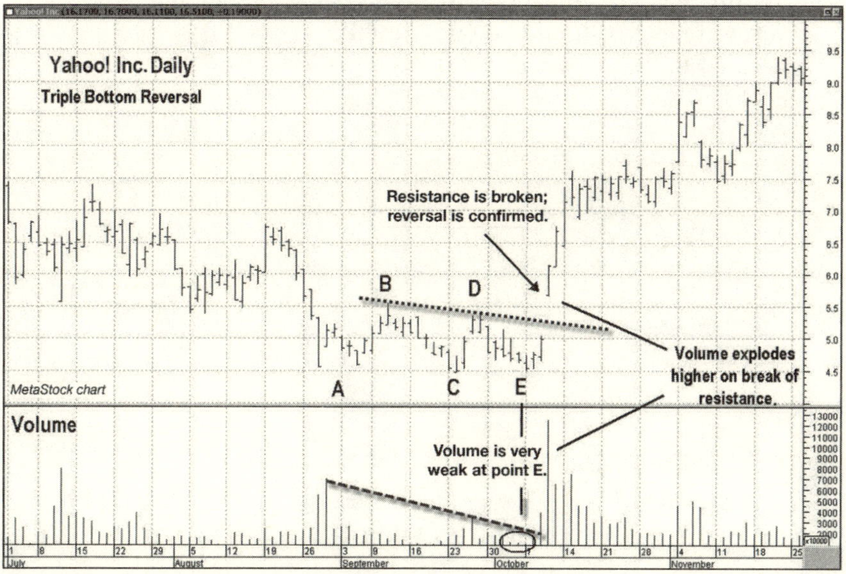

Chart 5.23 Triple Bottom Reversal Pattern, Yahoo! Inc.

Source: MetaStock

6. Price advanced from the low at point E *on accelerating volume.*
7. Price broke through the resistance line (B to D) as volume exploded, confirming the reversal in sentiment and trend.

Summary

- A combination of price and volume patterns can signal and confirm a trend reversal, whether they occur in the broad market or in an individual security, and whether they be longer-term macro or shorter term. Throughout our Volume Analysis of these reversal patterns, the trader's mantra continues to hold true: volume precedes price.
- Important reversal patterns include wedges, head-and-shoulders, certain candlestick patterns, double and triple tops and bottoms, exhaustion gaps, blow-off tops, and parabolas. A trader should recognize the pattern and confirm it with volume behavior.
- Every technical price reversal pattern has a volume pattern component; this volume component can be used to verify a trader's translation of the reversal pattern. In the absence of volume pattern confirmation, a trader's translation of a trend reversal pattern should be questioned.

Chapter 6

NEWS, NOISE, AND VOLUME

The central theme of our Volume Analysis thus far has been to identify how volume affects price trends and reversals. In this chapter, we "dial in" to how external events, including news items, market events, time factors, and the seasonal characteristics of markets themselves, can influence volume patterns. We also seek to distinguish the normal and anticipated fluctuations in volume patterns (noise) from meaningful changes in volume patterns that signal a shift in trend direction.

We'll start by describing the effects of news, both "external" news that is relevant to the business, financial, or political climate in general and "internal" news, or news that is pertinent to the company or particular security in mind. We'll continue with a description of other time- and event-related factors that affect volume, including options expiration, dividend payments, and seasonality. Finally, we'll touch on the latest phenomenon affecting market volume and liquidity (but, to the surprise of many, in our view it doesn't significantly affect volume patterns or trend direction), that is, the advent and growth of computer-driven high-frequency trading.

Read All about It: How News Affects Volume and Trading

The market price for an equity, bond, index, or commodity is affected by a constant flow of external and internal news and data. Whether it is company earnings, crop reports, a change in corporate structure, or any other piece of news, traders are constantly adjusting their opinion of fair market value. The important thing to remember is this: The impact of any given news event or corporate announcement is reflected in volume.

In many cases, volume spikes occur at these important junctures because of the availability of news to all market participants simultaneously. A volume spike is best defined as a sudden, dramatic increase in volume from one trading day to the next. Volume spikes have become more prevalent recently for two main reasons:

1. The SEC enforcement of Regulation FD on October 23, 2000
2. The advent and development of the Internet and electronic news media

Regulation FD (Fair Disclosure) was introduced to "level the playing field" with regard to dissemination of pertinent company information and its availability to individual investors. It states that firms must disclose all relevant information to everyone at once and without delay, whether that information is favorable or unfavorable. The introduction of Regulation FD came about to alleviate concerns surrounding the fact that individual investors did not receive corporate disclosures as quickly as brokers, major market players, and large institutional clients. Regulation FD attempts to eliminate the advantage enjoyed by the better-connected players, who could use early releases of information to front-run expected reactions by the crowd. The regulation and its intents were aimed more at internal information gathered by brokers and fund managers in direct conversations with companies, such as their outlook on earnings, or even hints as to good or bad future expectations.

The effect of Regulation FD has been to suppress conversations on many topics that once were discussed in meetings between major Wall Street players and company management. Passage of the regulation has led to a more uniform reporting procedure, which limits the ability of brokers and money managers to receive pertinent information ahead of the general investing public. The net effect of this regulation has been to create huge spikes in market activity surrounding newsworthy events, as all market participants receive and act on the same piece of information simultaneously.

Regulation FD was developed with the Internet in mind. The advent and development of the Internet has provided the perfect conduit for the distribution of company news releases. In contrast, in years past, analyst reports were mailed to clients, who may have taken their time reading and acting on the reports. Also, for most traders, stock prices were not readily available until either a late evening or early morning edition of the local newspaper. Now there are countless news sites and organizations that are capable of relaying company news. The ability of cell phones to receive e-mail, tweets, brokerage alerts, and the like contributes to a massive, instantaneous, and simultaneous flow of information that can cause thousands, if not millions, of traders to input their orders at once. Regulation FD makes sure that companies do not prerelease any important information to specific individuals, but when the information is released according to Regulation FD guidelines, the effect is an almost instantaneous spike in volume.

The following items can cause volume spikes:

- Earnings announcements and company conference calls
- Revised earnings outlooks
- Analyst upgrades and downgrades
- Mergers and acquisitions
- Changes in company leadership
- Legal action and settlements
- News of a product defect or liability issue (injuries, recalls, etc.)
- Failure or success of a developmental drug in trial stages
- Granting or denial of approval by the U.S. Food and Drug Administration (FDA)
- Marketwide phenomena, such as elections, interest rate adjustments, and geopolitical events

Most of the previous examples apply to individual stocks, bonds, and indexes, but macroeconomic events have equally far-reaching effects on worldwide markets, such as the currency, commodities, and interest rate markets. For example, crop and commodity supply/demand reports and geopolitical events can have enormous impact on commodity prices and currency markets.

Earnings Announcements

Traders understand that the price of a given stock reflects the sum of all knowledge regarding that stock at a given time. Applying this principle, quarterly earnings announcements provide a perfect opportunity to surprise traders or provide a catalyst for a move to sharply higher or lower prices. The presence of a volume spike provides confirmation that the conviction of the masses has decided that price must move higher or lower to reflect the newly released information.

On April 15, 2010, Google announced earnings that easily beat Wall Street expectations. However, once the news was digested, there were two perceived problems with the announcement. First, traders had become accustomed to Google beating earnings estimates by a wider margin. Second, there was a simmering dispute with China that threatened to reduce Google's exposure and market presence in that country. Those two pieces of information caused trading sentiment to change quickly, leading to an increase in selling pressure. Google's share price moved lower on a large volume spike.

In Chart 6.1 for Google (GOOG), note first a fairly common volume pattern in which volume tends to dry up in the weeks prior to an earnings release. As is typical with such a pattern, volume picked up a few days ahead of the announcement as traders either exited because of uncertainty or entered new positions in optimistic anticipation of the release. During the day following the announcement, volume spiked, revealing that the report had been poorly received, and leading to a change in trader sentiment.

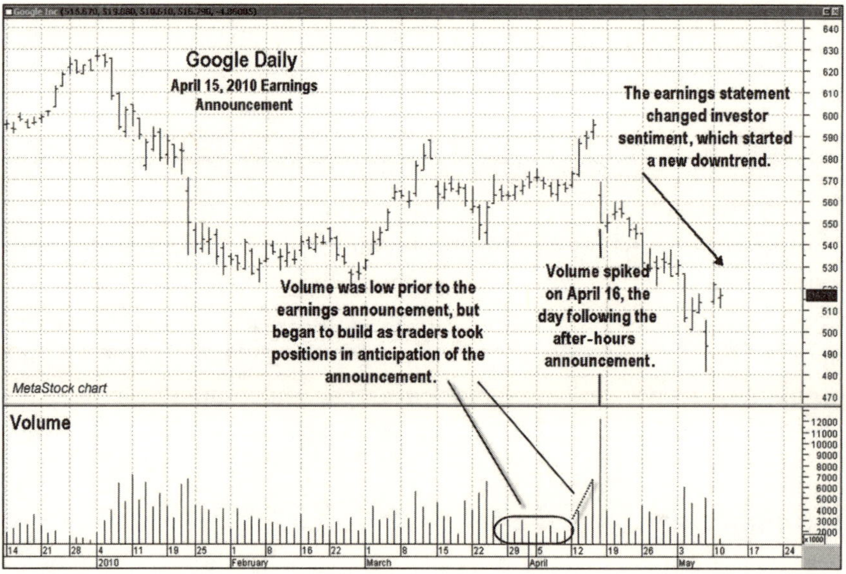

Chart 6.1 Volume Spike in Response to Earnings Announcement, Negative Price Response, Google Inc.

Source: MetaStock

Earnings announcements do not always cause a change in price direction. Chart 6.2 for Apple Inc. (AAPL) shows volume spiking intraday as buyers and sellers wrestled for control over price direction, but at the end of the day, sentiment remained close to where it had been prior to the announcement.

Unlike the Google example in Chart 6.1, where there was a clear change in sentiment, the Apple Inc. earnings announcements validated the current market sentiment toward the company. As a result, the price trend continued in the direction and pattern exhibited prior to the announcement. Note again how volume began to increase prior to the announcement. Since earnings were released after hours, price reactions occurred on the next trading day.

Notice that the far right-hand side of Chart 6.2, following the April 21, 2010 price reaction, exhibited a brutal sell-off. That was in reaction to external news, the European debt crisis, which affected the market as a whole. Worldwide—or macro—events can affect stocks as a group and supersede any company-specific information. Volume plays an important role in identifying these situations as well.

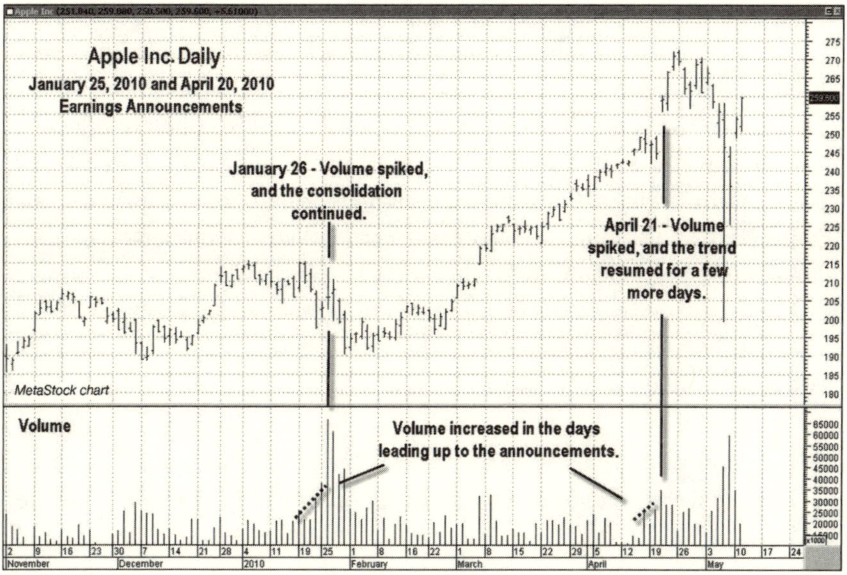

Chart 6.2 Volume Spike in Response to Earnings Announcement, Neutral Price Response, Apple Inc.

Source: MetaStock

Marketwide Events

The types of news events mentioned previously often cause volume spikes and sentiment changes for individual equities. Most of these events are "internal," that is, about and generally initiated by the company.

External marketwide events that cause volume spikes and surges typically take weeks and in some cases months to unfold before sentiment culminates in a change in price and trend direction. One of the best examples of volume spikes culminating in dramatic shifts in trader sentiment can be seen during the Russian financial crisis and the subsequent Long-Term Capital Management bailout in the fall of 1998. The Russian financial crisis (also called the "ruble crisis") followed on the heels of the Asian financial crisis, which started in July 1997; both were related to declining commodity prices. Decline in productivity, fiscal deficits, and a high fixed exchange rate of the ruble led to the meltdown.

The Russian financial crisis first became evident in the news as early as May 1998, but its effects were not felt in U.S. markets until July of that year. It was only at that point that traders became concerned that it could mushroom into a worldwide economic event.

On top of the potential Russian debt default, a major U.S. hedge fund, Long-Term Capital Management (LTCM), had significant exposure to Russian assets and was suffering heavy losses. LTCM's failure led to a coordinated and substantial bailout of banks and investment firms by the Federal Reserve. The markets plunged in early September 1998, rallied briefly, then plunged again in early October despite a government bailout of LTCM; traders continued to panic that not enough was being done to avert a global financial crisis. Each plunge lower in the early fall was accompanied by sharp increases in volume. One week after the October low, the Fed announced its second rate cut in two weeks. That, in turn, helped the equity market to recover and begin the journey up to the 2000 highs.

Chart 6.3 shows the strong and emotionally driven volume spikes and selling. Note the double bottom price pattern (see Chapter 5) generated on large, emotion-driven volume spikes. Once the selling pressure eased, the markets were in a good position to rebound in the absence of further bad news.

Calendar- and Time-Driven Events

Time-dependent fluctuations in volume play a role in shaping volume behavior and volume patterns over a day, a week, a month, or a year. Failure to understand these time-dependent volume patterns can expose

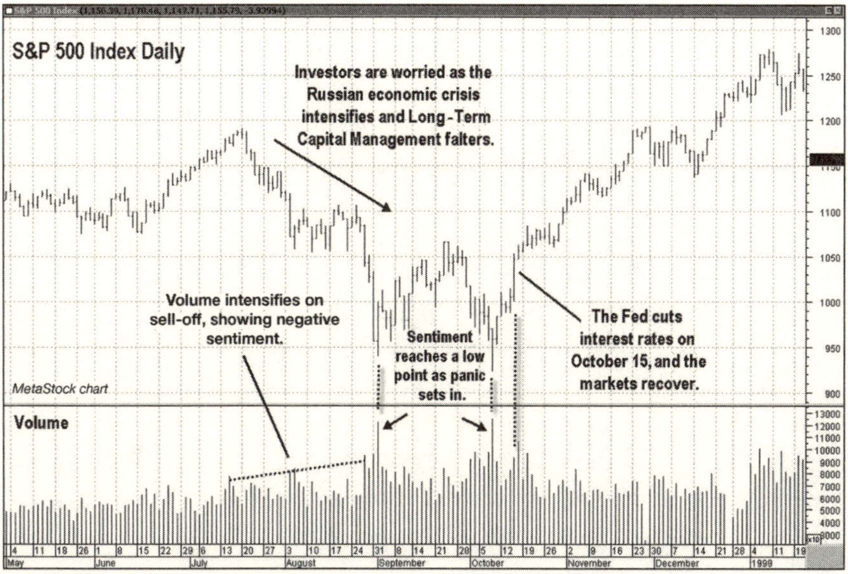

Chart 6.3 Volume Spikes from External News Events, S&P 500 Index

Source: MetaStock

you to poor decisions in response to perceived changes in volume driven less by buying and selling pressure than simply by the timing of their occurrence. Such calendar- and time-dependent normal volume patterns include options expiration, intraday volume (the pattern of volume through the course of an ordinary trading day), dividend payment schedules, and normal seasonality patterns.

Options Expiration

An option contract is a derivative, meaning that its value is derived from the value of an underlying asset. Option contracts exist for futures contracts, commodities, stocks, stock indexes, bonds, and interest rates, among others. Options expiration is a day when the holders of option contracts must either "exercise" them—that is, initiate a transaction to acquire or dispose of the underlying security—or let them expire worthless.

Options expiration occurs on different days in different markets. The best-known and most reported expiration dates occur monthly ("triple witching" expirations), which are related to options on individual stocks, index futures, and stock indexes expiring concurrently. Quarterly expirations, or "quadruple witching" expirations, occur with the concurrent expiration of options on individual stocks, index futures, stock indexes, and single stock futures. Both occur on the third Friday of the month. There is typically, but not always, a noticeable rise in volume on these days, depending on what security or index is examined. Expiration days that produce very heavy volume may not necessarily be meaningful as far as trend or even supply/demand analysis is concerned. On these days there are many crosscurrents flowing beneath the market as traders exercise their contracts to fulfill contractual obligations, which tends to add "noise" to meaningful volume analysis.

In Chart 6.4, showing the E-Mini S&P 500 futures, the options expiration dates for the first five months of 2010 are marked. Notice how expiration days on higher volume did not translate into any appreciable change in trend direction.

Next is a look at the S&P 500 Cash Index (see Chart 6.5), the most widely quoted benchmark for equity or broader stock market performance. The same pattern appears in the broader market. Notice how, in both Charts 6.4 and 6.5, the higher volume totals in the March and April expirations did not lead to immediate trend changes. In fact, the strength of the March trend continued following the March expiration. A case could be made for April, however, as the price trend reversed and headed lower

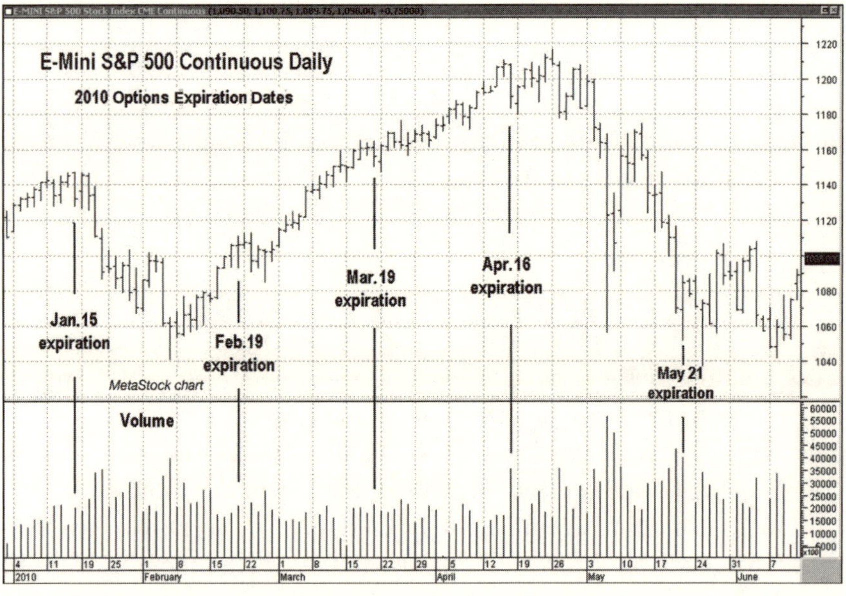

Chart 6.4 Volume Increases at Option Expiration, S&P 500 E-Mini Futures Contract

Source: MetaStock

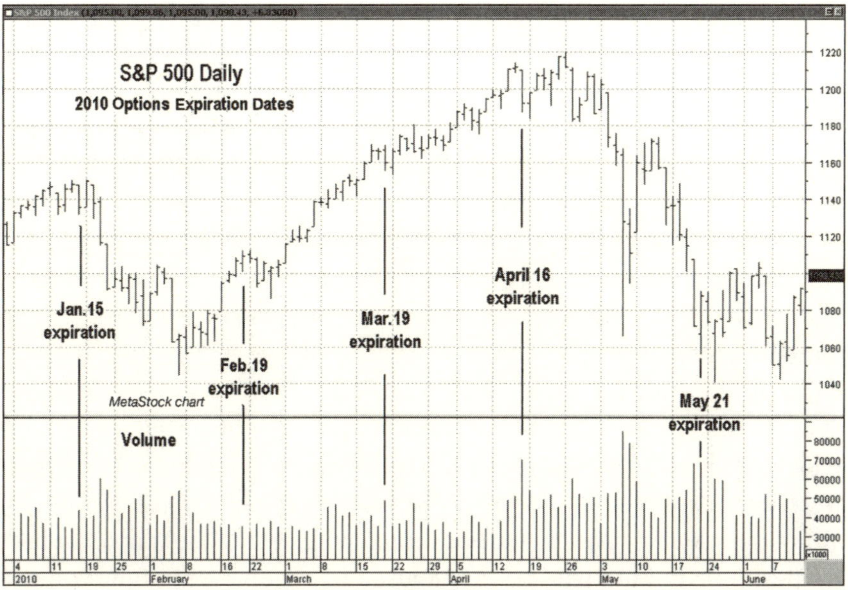

Chart 6.5 Volume Surges at Options Expiration, S&P 500 Cash Index

Source: MetaStock

two weeks later. At best, the increase in volume could be described as the beginning of a two-week distribution pattern; notice that more higher-volume days were seen on pullbacks than on advances.

Intraday Volume Patterns: Optimum Liquidity

Markets tend to exhibit increased volume near the open and often at the end of the market day, in the two hours prior to the close. Intraday volume patterns are predictable. They typically show a U-shaped structure, with higher volume totals coming at the open and the close, while volume slows dramatically at midday, typically 11 a.m. to 2 p.m. U.S. Eastern Time for equities.

Volume is typically higher at the open as traders, managers, and institutions place their buy, sell, and market orders. Traders have had 17.5 hours from the market close to digest the previous day's market activity and prepare to enter their trades. They have an even longer period of time from a Friday close to a Monday open. Trading volume is also higher at the end of the day as traders who trade only during open-market hours (day traders) square up their positions before the market close.

Optimum liquidity or tighter bid/ask spreads typically occur within 90 minutes of the open and two hours before the close, as volume steadily increases after 2 p.m. Eastern time. The 15-minute chart of SPY (Chart 6.6) showing the volume patterns of June 7 and 8, 2010, is typical of the daily volume pattern in equities.

The "normal" intraday volume patterns in Chart 6.6 reveal when the most liquid times of day occur for the most favorable bid/ask spreads. Midday news events can disrupt these normal volume trading patterns and cause volume spikes, such as in our Federal Reserve (Fed) policy announcement example, Chart 6.7, which shows a 15-minute interval chart of SPY on March 15 and 16, 2010. The Fed statement came out at 2:15 p.m. Eastern time on March 16. Notice how price movement (volatility) contracted sharply with volume during the middle of the trading session on both days, but even more so on March 16, just before the announcement. At 2 p.m., traders started wading into the market to take up positions in anticipation of the announcement. Note how volume and price volatility both explode higher following the announcement. The price bars grow as many more traders enter the market, causing wider price swings.

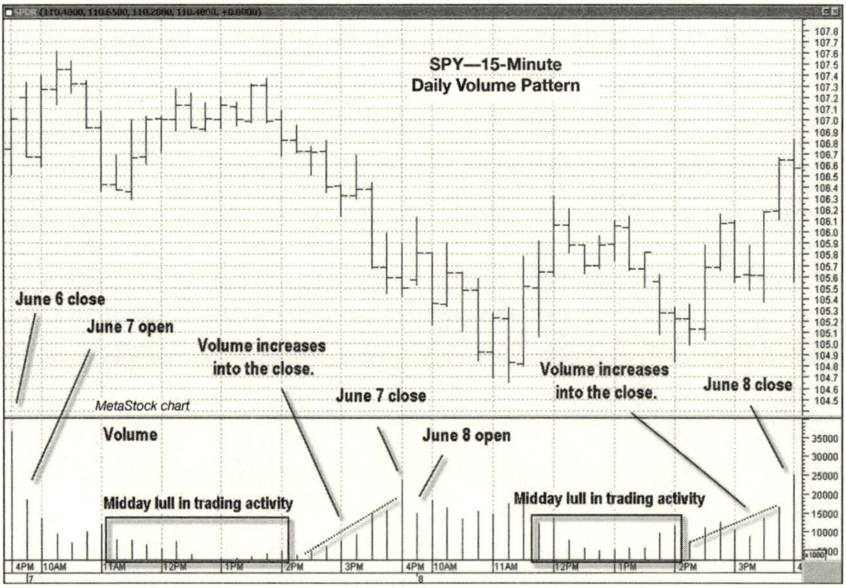

Chart 6.6 Intraday Volume Pattern, iShares S&P 500 Trust ETF (SPDR)

Source: MetaStock

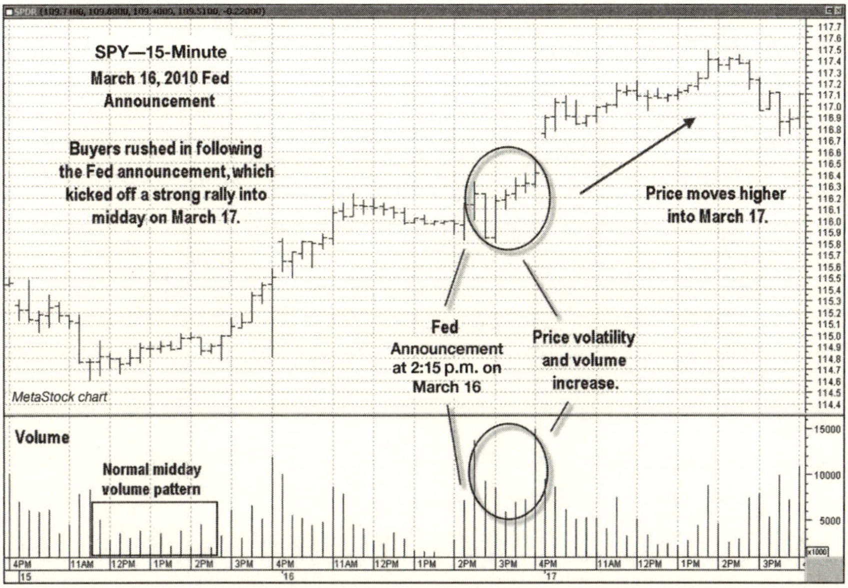

Chart 6.7 Intraday Volume Swings, 15-Minute Intervals, Fed, March 16, 2010 Announcement, iShares S&P 500 Trust ETF (SPDR)

Source: MetaStock

Now if we step back and examine how March 16, 2010 looked in a normal daily time frame (one bar per day), we can see that the intraday "explosion" of volume was really a nonevent, just an intraday distortion of an otherwise normal daily volume level. In Chart 6.8, note how low the volume total was for March 16, and that the upward swing experienced by the market lasted for only a day before retracting.

This example displays the importance of choosing your trading time frame correctly. The rally following the Fed announcement on March 16 and into March 17 might signal a nice uptrend for an intraday or swing trader, while the reaction following the Fed announcement would be nothing more than noise to a longer time frame position trader.

Dividends and Ex-Dividend Dates

The topic of dividends is more complex than simply buying a stock and collecting the dividend. While many trading strategies include dividend-paying stocks to generate income, traders and managers must also factor in the tax consequences of those strategies. This can create buy, sell, and hold trading activity around ex-dividend dates. The many decision points made

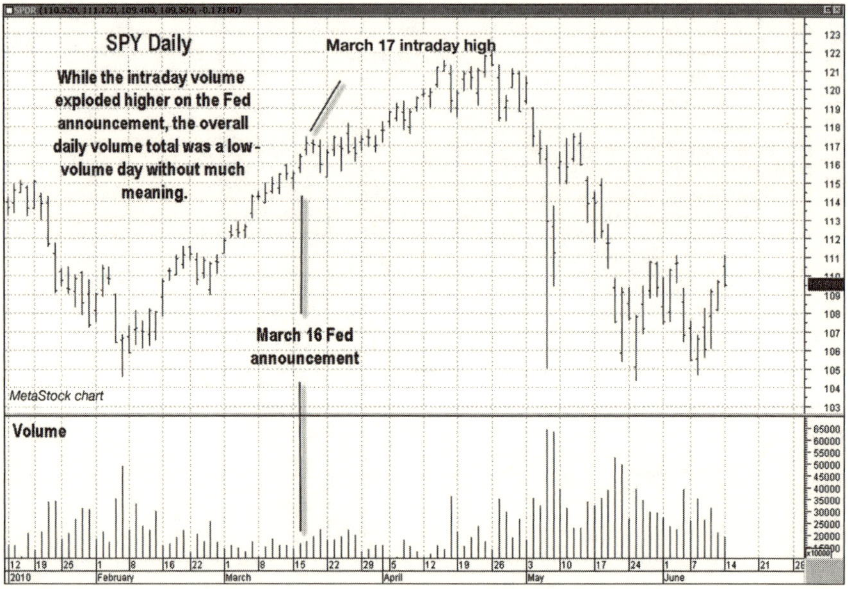

Chart 6.8 Daily Volume, Including Fed March 16, 2010 Announcement, iShares S&P 500 Trust ETF (SPDR)

Source: MetaStock

around these key dates can cause slight increases in volume behavior. Again, this volume action is not necessarily related to trader sentiment toward a particular stock or ETF, but rather to the tax implications of a trader or manager's actions. The ex-dividend dates—that is, the dates of share ownership for dividend eligibility—of stocks are published in advance; this allows for planning by those who trade around the payout date. The price of the stock is adjusted to remove the dividend so that traders cannot simply buy the shares, collect the dividend, and sell the stock.

Ex-dividend dates allow those planning to purchase a stock to wait until after the dividend is paid to avoid the taxable event of the dividend payout. While these strategies are valid and are used, we note that their execution has little effect on price trend movements outside of the normal flow of orders throughout the trading day. The example of 3M Company (MMM) in Chart 6.9 shows that planned quarterly dividend payouts do not create much in the way of abnormal trading activity or volume levels. This is the case with just about any dividend-paying stock that pays on a regularly scheduled basis.

There are times, however, when "special" dividends can create quite a stir. The example of Scotts Miracle-Gro (SMG; see Chart 6.10) shows the

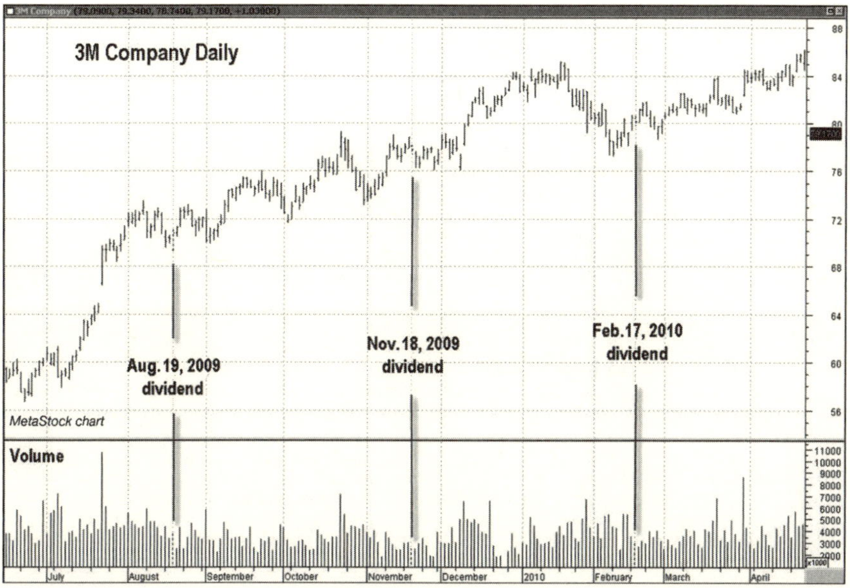

contrast between a known dividend event of $0.125 per share on February 6, 2007, and a one-time dividend payout of $8.00 per share announced on February 16, 2007, with an ex-dividend date of February 22, 2007.

Chart 6.10 shows how volume action surrounding a quarterly scheduled dividend payout is typically noneventful as compared to a special dividend payment. On February 6, 2007, while some traders collected their dividends and exited their positions, other traders interested in avoiding the dividend tax waited on the sidelines for entry, as demonstrated by average volume totals for the stock. On February 16, Scotts Miracle-Gro announced a special one-time dividend of $8 per share to accomplish a financial restructuring. Note how buyers rushed in on February 20 to take advantage of the one-time payout; then on February 21 volume remained above normal as others locked in profits from the run-up on February 20. Volume remained elevated for the next week, as those who purchased shares strictly for the dividend exited their positions while those who waited to avoid the dividend payout purchased new positions.

Although substantial volume effects resulted from this rather unusual occurrence, dividends and dividend timing are usually "noise" in the markets so far as volume is concerned; but for savvy traders they are still worth observing.

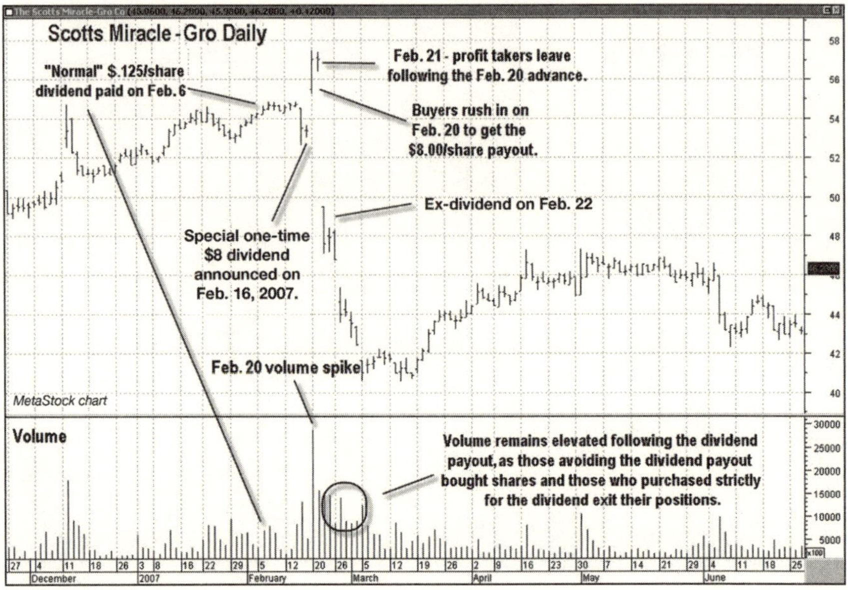

Chart 6.10 Special Dividend Effect on Volume, Scotts Miracle-Gro

Source: MetaStock

Seasonal Volume

While volume can be affected at any time by news and world events throughout the year, broader market volume tends to show predictable seasonal and holiday patterns. Factoring these patterns into Volume Analysis allows a trader to identify when the broad market will be more heavily traded and anticipate normally lighter volume periods.

"Sell in May and Go Away" has become a truism in the marketplace, as history points to the likelihood that trading markets tend to decline between May and mid-September. This tends to lead to lower volume during the summer months. Following Labor Day, positive seasonality begins to return, with volume increases in early fall; the increased volume pattern usually carries through until the following May. Volume also tends to decline just prior to long holiday weekends. Pick your holiday, Memorial Day, the Fourth of July, Easter, Thanksgiving, Christmas, President's Day, or Labor Day: The light volume pattern is generally the same. However, lower volume does not necessarily equate to lower market volatility. In fact, because of lower volume, the markets are more thinly traded, and buy or sell orders can translate into disproportionately greater movements in both the up and down directions. During these holiday

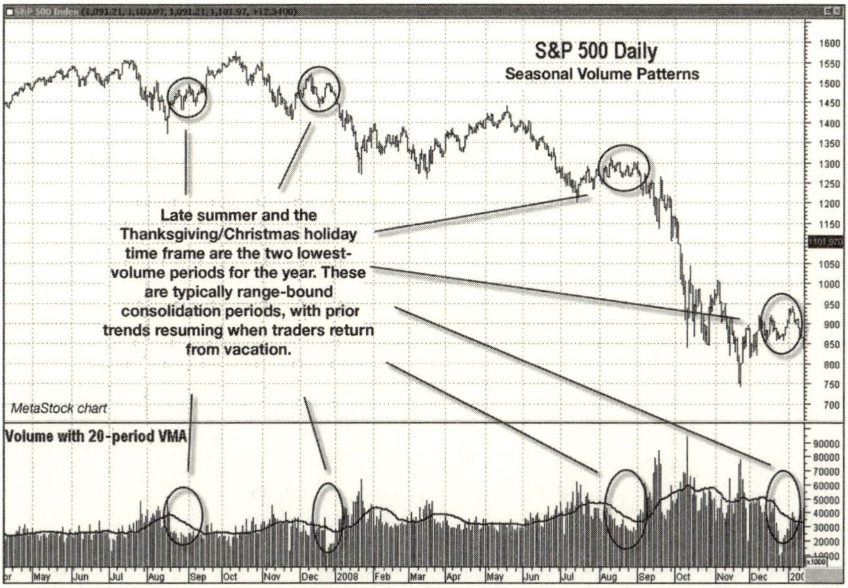

Chart 6.11 Volume Seasonality, S&P 500 Index

Source: MetaStock

periods, we also see price action tending to follow a choppy, range-bound pattern as the lighter volumes lack sufficient energy to push prices in one direction or the other.

Chart 6.11 shows the S&P 500 for years 2007 and 2008. Volume is plotted with its 20-day volume moving average (VMA) to make it easier to spot times when volume contracts below normal levels. Note how late August and mid- to late December show declining volume with little price movement. Once these low-volume time frames pass, the previous trend usually resumes.

Does High-Frequency Trading Affect Volume Analysis?

In part as a result of the so-called flash crash of May 6, 2010, high-frequency trading (HFT) has become mainstream news. The flash crash refers to the intraday sell-off that drove the Dow Industrials down as much as 1000 points before it recovered to –300 points. Human error and computer-generated trades have been the scapegoats to date. Although this phenomenon of extremely rapid computerized trading strategies has gone on for as many as 10 years, it has come to account for a vastly larger portion of overall stock market activity in the past two to three years. By many accounts, it makes up as much as 75 percent of all trading on certain high-profile, large-cap stocks, although only a handful of trading firms actually engage in it.

What is HFT? It is a set of trading strategies, mostly undertaken by large Wall Street firms and a few specialized hedge funds with access to the right technologies, to buy and sell in very rapid trades to capture very small price increments on each trade. Trading time intervals are measured in microseconds; trading increments can be fractions of pennies. The overall strategy is to capture as many small price increments as possible repeatedly throughout the trading day and, in some strategies, to "front-run" larger orders before other players can act. Often this is done through sheer physical proximity to the exchange floors; the New York Stock Exchange (NYSE) has created special leased spaces next to its own computers for trading firms to locate their servers, shaving tiny increments off the physical speed of connectivity to the exchange.

The technical details and specific strategies of HFT are beyond the scope of this book. But the obvious question is: What effect does HFT have on volume? And since our technical models are based on volume, doesn't HFT disrupt the very foundation of Volume Analysis?

These are questions we've pondered—and tested—for some time. One issue, of course, is whether the incremental volume generated by computers flinging orders rapid-fire back and forth with each other truly represents supply and demand, which is, of course, the "pressure" behind the volume we look for. The answer is "probably not"; much of this activity is just what it is—trades going back and forth, back and forth throughout the day. So does that actually distort our models?

At this point in time, through backtesting and observation of the effects of increased volume, we think the answer is no. Sure, volumes have increased dramatically in the past few years. But our observations are for the most part that the volume increase is simply scalar; that is, volumes have increased, but the underlying behavior of volume, and the interpretation of volume shifts, has not. Although so-called quote stuffing, placing unusually large numbers of electronic orders to buy or sell stocks and then canceling them, can have an effect on intraday pricing, we believe Volume Analysis may actually reveal these marketplace shenanigans. We see higher daily volumes, and larger spikes in some cases, as occurred during the flash crash, but overall volume patterns have not changed in such a way as to negate the volume indicators and oscillators you will read about in upcoming chapters.

One side note: High-frequency trading is often confused with so-called algorithmic trading, where large institutional orders are systematically taken apart into smaller increments to hide their size in the market. Currently, the SEC is exploring one such type of order that is placed in increments as small as one-tenth of a cent and at a distance from the actual price. This type of "subpenny pricing" may be used to make it appear that more volume actually exists and that demand is actually elevated, thus benefiting sellers. Such order partitioning spreads demand and supply throughout the day, which has had an effect on some of the oscillators mentioned in Chapter 10 that depend on intraday volume. For the most part, however, our Volume Analysis already takes such patterns into account. As a result, at the time of this writing, we do not believe traders using Volume Analysis should be overly concerned about high-frequency trading.

Summary

- Volume and volume patterns can be affected by an assortment of factors. They can be market-intrinsic factors like options expirations, ex-dividend dates, and even time of day within the trading day. They can be exogenous factors like scheduled and unscheduled company news releases, earnings announcements, and so forth.
- These "news and noise" items can have varying influences on trading patterns, depending on the normal volume and pattern of the market or security being traded. Traders should understand these influences and take them into account when charting or modeling any given security.
- Thus far, so-called high-frequency trading influences total volume but not volume patterns in a way sufficient to change volume models. This assessment bears watching in the future, however.

Chapter 7

TRADING TIME FRAMES AND INDICATOR SELECTION

Up to this point in our Volume Analysis, we have developed our ability to recognize technical volume trends and technical volume/price patterns with the help of volume overlays. We have explored the charts of simple and complex trading environments and provided some basic illustrations of how volume plays into the analysis of trend continuation, reversal, and sideways patterns. Now we shift our attention to how best to use Volume Analysis to navigate the trading terrain.

In order to navigate successfully, a trader is faced with several strategic choices. One of the most critical, in our view, is, "Which volume indicators and oscillators should I select to best support my trading time frame?" This chapter examines the parameters a trader should consider in making this decision, provides a detailed explanation of the nature of indicators and oscillators and the combinations thereof, and offers guidance in the process of indicator selection.

Trading Time Frames and Signal Frequency

It's worth our noting briefly that the selection of a trading time frame will determine, to a greater or lesser degree, the number of trading signals generated, interpreted, and acted upon over a given time period. The best way to illustrate this signal frequency is by example: A trader working within five-minute time frames will have to deal with many more signals in a trading day than someone trading in daily or weekly time frames. Trading in shorter time frames is a demanding and more time-intensive approach, while longer time frame traders generally have fewer and less frequent signals to interpret. Although a longer time frame may appear simpler, trading off fewer signals has its own inherent risks. Often, a shorter time frame with increased signal frequency can yield more trading opportunities.

Selecting Volume Indicators and Oscillators for Your Volume Analysis

As every trader knows, the selection of trading tools can feel overwhelming. There are dozens, perhaps hundreds, of technical tools to choose from. The indicators we have chosen to discuss are those that can supply an additional volume dimension to your trading strategy. Although there is no such thing as one size fits all in trading, we do have some parameters that can help in navigating the volume terrain. Indicators perform differently under different trading conditions, so seek to utilize a volume component that will be versatile and provide signals to complement your existing strategy. Consider including the following in your Volume Analysis:

- A bar plot of volume so that you can quickly refer to current volume patterns. As price is inextricably tied to volume, every technical price charting formation will have a confirming volume pattern.
- A VMA or other volume overlay to act as a leading or confirmatory indicator. (Use settings that complement your trading time frame.) Depending upon your VMA time setting and its sensitivity to change points, the VMA will provide you the conviction behind the price trend, tops and bottoms, and turning points.
- A macro, or longer-term, indicator to identify the direction of the prevailing trend. Trades in the direction of the larger-degree trend have a higher chance of success. One such indicator is On-Balance Volume, which gives a trader a good read on the longer trend and provides a basic framework from which trades in the direction of the trend can be favored.
- A volume indicator or oscillator complementary to your trading time frame. Having both volume- and price-based components, these tools are able to identify not only the direction of the prevailing trend, but the conviction as well.

When using and combining indicators, it is wise not to combine indicators that are redundant or that measure and display the same technical patterns.

Longer-Term versus Mid- to Short-Term Volume Indicators and Oscillators

The volume indicators and oscillators listed here are discussed in more depth in Chapters 8, 9, and 10. We've placed these technical tools in their most user-friendly time frames; as such, these placements are intended to act only as preliminary guidance.

Longer Time Frame Volume Indicators

The following indicators and oscillators work best at displaying a more accurate picture of the longer-term or prevailing trend. Longer time frame indicators generate fewer trading signals Please note that all of these are examined in more detail in Part Two.

- Accumulation/Distribution
- Cumulative Volume Index (broad market indicator)
- Intraday Intensity
- Negative Volume Index
- On-Balance Volume
- Positive Volume Index
- Volume Accumulation Oscillator
- Volume Price Trend
- Volume moving average (settings: 60 days or longer)

Mid to Short Time Frame Volume Indicators

This set of indicators works best at detecting shifts in price and/or volume momentum over a short to intermediate time frame. Mid and short time frame indicators generate more frequent buy/sell signals, depending upon the sensitivity of their settings.

- 10-Day Open ARMS (broad market indicator)
- 30-Day Open ARMS (broad market indicator)
- Chaikin Advance/Decline Oscillator

- Chaikin Money Flow
- Demand Index
- Ease of Movement
- Force Index
- Money Flow Index
- 10-Day Up/Down Volume Oscillator (broad market indicator)
- ARMS Index (broad market indicator)
- Volume Oscillator
- Volume Rate of Change
- Leibovit Volume Reversal
- Volume moving average (settings: short, up to 5 days; mid, 5 to 60 days)

Broad Market or Individual Security Indicator

The indicators mentioned previously that are marked "broad market indicator" use price and volume data from the major exchanges. These are required for broader market analysis and may not be suited to analyzing an individual security. However, if that security does track equivalently with a broad market indicator, then these tools can be used. Doing a simple price overlay of the security against the broad market indicator will answer this question. Any of the other indicators/oscillators listed previously, however, could be applied directly to an equity, index, or commodity, if so desired.

Indicators versus Oscillators

Volume Analysis provides traders with visual tactics to discern trends and patterns. Our charts contain volume indicators and oscillators designed to represent variations on the volume/price relationship. These mathematical formulas, which include volume, may reflect these aspects of price and volume in various weightings, as a single variable or set of numbers. When charted, these formulations can help spot trend strength, divergences, reversals, and other useful characteristics of price and volume over a given time period. As you read more about these trading tools, you'll soon discover that they fall into two categories: *indicators* and *oscillators*. Most traders will deploy an assortment of indicators and oscillators to fit their particular market and trading style.

One way to understand indicators and oscillators is to understand the difference between the two.

Indicators

A technical trading indicator is derived by applying a formula to a series of data points of price and/or volume. This produces a series of resulting calculated values that are usually graphically shown above or below the price chart. Creating a series of calculations and plotting them over time allows for analysis of where today's value is in relation to past values.

Volume indicators are used to provide an extra level of analysis in addition to simple price and volume action alone. This type of analysis is used to either confirm a trend or show where the price trend may be ready to change (i.e., a divergence). Indicators often provide buy and sell signals based on their patterns. It is important, however, to use a weight-of-the-evidence approach by confirming indicator signals with price and volume patterns to validate that signal. For example, it is normally unwise to execute a sell signal flashed by an indicator without confirmation when the behavior patterns of both price and volume indicate that a robust uptrend is in place.

Oscillators

An oscillator is a technical tool that applies a formula to a series of data points that move above and below a center line or between upper and lower boundary levels on a set scale as its value changes with each time period. Oscillators are most commonly used to track momentum—the rate at which price or volume rises or falls. As price or volume rises in a healthy uptrend, momentum also increases. If price or volume continues to rise, but at a slower rate, then momentum will not keep pace, showing a divergence in the oscillator. A divergence shows that a trend is weakening and may be ready for a reversal.

Oscillators come in two types. *Banded oscillators* use "overbought" and "oversold" lines that give signals when crossed, while centered oscillators generate signals when they cross above or below a central line (usually with a value of zero). *Centered oscillators* are best for identifying the strength and/or direction of the trend, with readings above the center line showing positive momentum and readings below the center line showing negative momentum. Banded oscillators, in contrast, can identify when the trend has become overextended, such as overbought

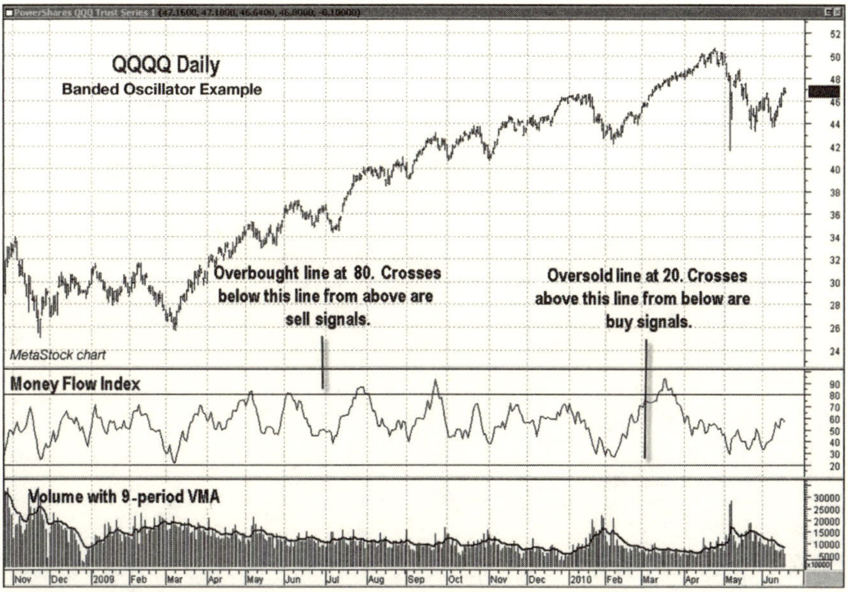

Chart 7.1 Banded Oscillator Example, QQQQ, Nasdaq 100 Trust ETF

Source: MetaStock

readings in a downtrend or oversold readings in an uptrend, which can provide great trade setups. Centered oscillators can show extreme readings above or below the center line, but they are not best suited for that purpose.

Chart 7.1, the daily record of the Nasdaq 100 Trust ETF (QQQQ) shows the Money Flow Index (MFI), which is further defined in Chapter 10 as an example of a banded oscillator. You can see one of the drawbacks of using a banded oscillator in a trending market. Notice how the MFI did not reach the oversold zone (a reading below 20) during the 2009 bottom and for the entire uptrend.

It is important to know the characteristics of any indicator that you use and how it behaves in trending and nontrending markets. As with any indicator or indicator combination, select the ones you find most user friendly and learn how they work—both independently and together.

Chart 7.2 shows the Demand Index as an example of a centered oscillator using zero-line crossovers to generate buy and sell signals. Crosses above the zero line from below are buy signals, while crosses down below the zero line from above are sell signals.

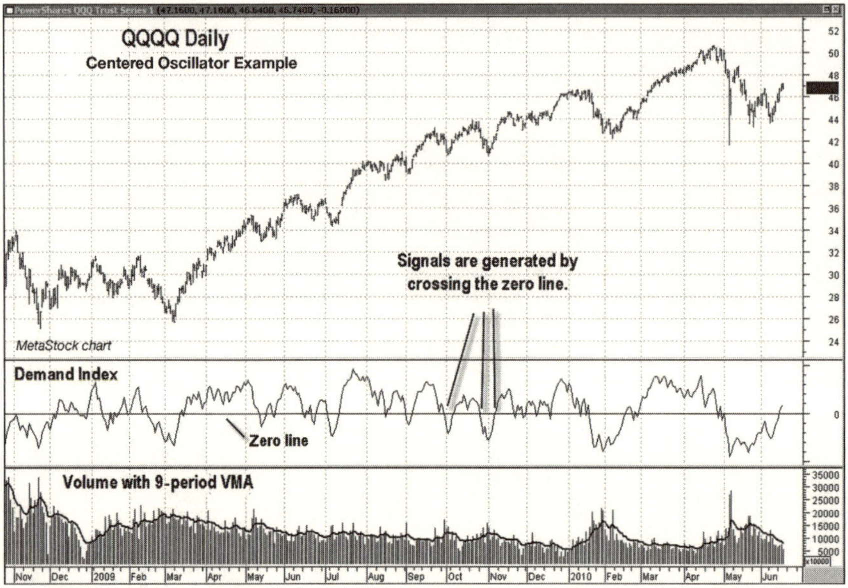

Chart 7.2 Centered Oscillator Example, Money Flow Index, Nasdaq 100 Trust ETF

Source: MetaStock

Oscillators as Predictive Tools

One of the main concepts behind the use of oscillators is their ability to show *divergences*, or a weakening of the current price trend, which some say makes them "leading" indicators. There really is no such thing as a leading indicator, only a leading technical pattern, since all indicators are constructed using past data.

Divergences reveal that a trend is weakening, but such divergences can last for weeks. This means that exiting a trade prematurely merely on the existence of a divergence can cost a trader much in the way of profits. There are two types of divergences. A *positive divergence* occurs when price makes a new low but the oscillator does not, while a *negative divergence* occurs when price makes a new high but the oscillator does not.

In either case, the divergence is viewed as a *nonconfirmation* of price action, which serves as a warning that a change in trend direction may be near. But traders shouldn't stop their Volume Analysis at this point: Trading divergences should always include some form of confirmation by at least one additional source before making a trade. For example, a divergence shown by the Money Flow Index would need confirmation from a separate indicator, such as the Leibovit Volume Reversal. (For more on this specific indicator, see Chapter 9.)

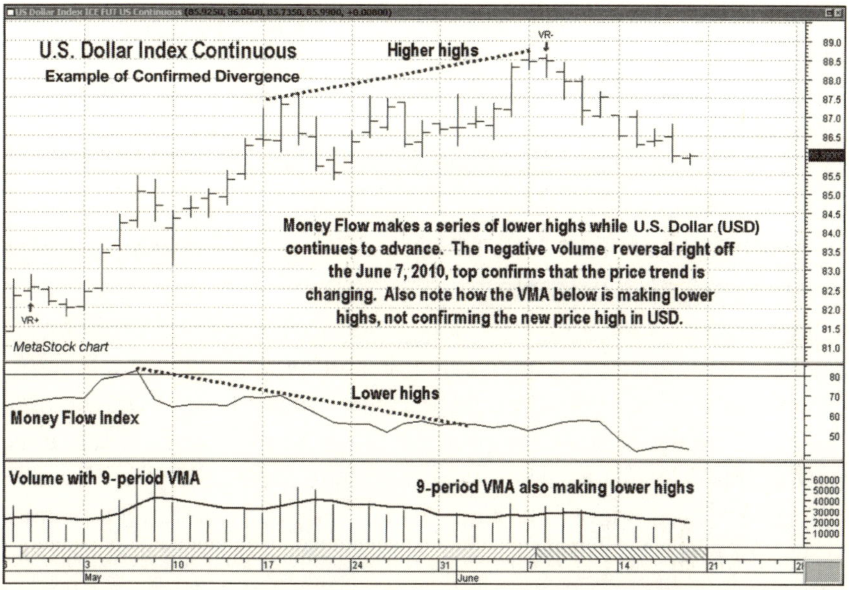

Chart 7.3 Confirmed Divergences, VR Money Flow Index, with VMA, U.S. Dollar Index
Source: MetaStock

The example of the U.S. Dollar Index in Chart 7.3 shows how the MFI was showing a clear negative divergence as price made new highs. Naturally, such a divergence calls into question whether an aggressive trader should go short or take profits on the long side. As discussed previously, when a divergence occurs, it is unwise to exit prematurely or jump in with a position against the trend, as divergences can last for days or even weeks. This example also shows the use of a second indicator to confirm the divergence. In this case, it is a volume indicator, the 9-day volume moving average (VMA) plotted at the bottom of the chart.

The Leibovit VR is a very good indicator for showing when control of the market is shifting from sellers to buyers, or in this case, from buyers to sellers. Notice in Chart 7.3 how the VR pinpointed the best time to act on the negative divergence in the MFI.

Using Oscillators with Other Indicators

Oscillators are most effective when used in conjunction with other Volume Analysis methods, such as overlays and volume patterns, to determine support/resistance, trendlines, and so forth. It always helps to look at oscillator signals in the proper context as they relate to other methods of analysis.

One of the drawbacks of oscillators is that they can give false or whipsaw signals. That is another reason to use oscillators with other trading tools. Doing so helps reduce the number of false signals that may be generated.

Matching Volume Indicators and Oscillators with Market Conditions

Often a trader must choose the trading indicator that best suits the current market environment. Is one indicator or another more useful in trending markets or in range-bound markets? How should a trader view the indicator and oscillator selection process? For example, banded oscillators, such as the Volume Oscillator described at the end of Chapter 10, which fluctuate between upper and lower bands, are widely believed to be best suited for range-bound markets, as they show overbought and oversold situations.

To use oscillators for this purpose alone, however, takes away from another valuable use of oscillators—their ability to show the strength and sustainability of an existing trend. In general, assigning different indicators to different market conditions presents a host of issues regarding trading analysis, including timely identification of range-bound versus trending markets and frequent changes in strategies. In our experience, simple is better.

One option we highly recommend is to use a trending or longer-term volume indicator with a short- to intermediate-term indicator or oscillator that covers most market conditions. In Part Two, where specific indicators and oscillators are discussed, we do suggest combinations of indicators and oscillators that make sense in specific trading environments, but for the most part we prefer designing a strategy that works across trading environments.

Still, it is important to learn the characteristics of your preferred indicators and how they actually behave under different market conditions. Once you get comfortable with your chosen indicators and the signals they send, you will know at a glance what type of market trend is prevalent. For example, if a longer-term trending indicator such as On-Balance Volume (see Chapter 9) is moving higher (higher highs and higher lows), you know that the market or security is in a recognizable uptrend. The same reading can also be made by looking at an oscillator, because in uptrends oscillators tend to top and bottom at different levels, that is, to move in a different range from what they do in downtrends. It is also important to know where support and resistance levels are and to watch how price, volume, and your indicators behave as these support and resistance areas are encountered. Doing so can keep you one step ahead of the crowd in knowing whether a trend will continue or whether a trading range or reversal is forming.

As an example of how oscillators perform differently in uptrends versus downtrends, note in Chart 7.4 how the Money Flow Index (MFI; further described in Chapter 10) tends to top and bottom at lower levels in a downtrend versus higher levels in an uptrend. Since the MFI is a banded oscillator, it uses the level of 80 for overbought and 20 for oversold. Blindly using and accepting only these levels can cause a trader to miss out on some great trading opportunities, as the MFI, when used with its common default setting of 14 periods, rarely reaches 80 (overbought) in downtrends and likewise rarely reaches 20 (oversold) in uptrends. It is important to plot the indicator and note its characteristics on any market or security you trade so that you can know where to expect range shifts and turning points based on the trend.

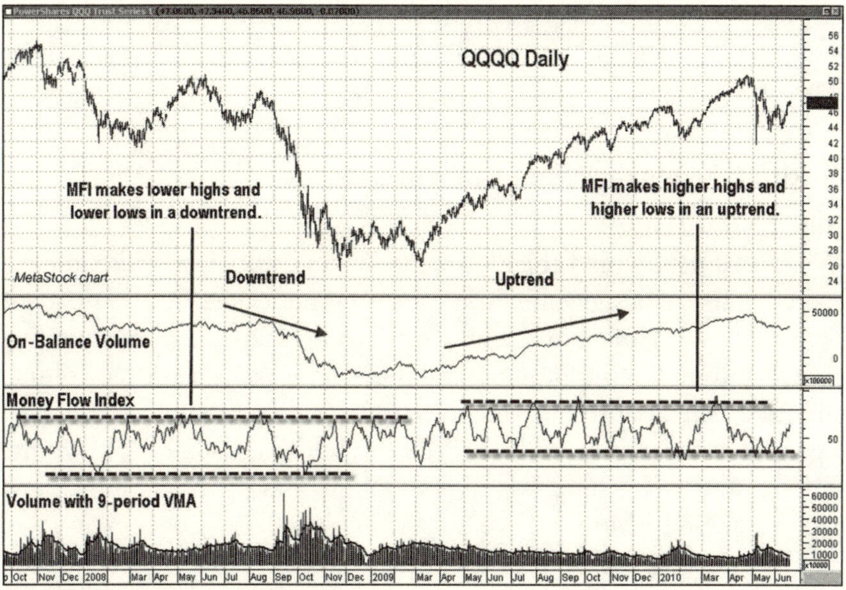

Chart 7.4 Money Flow Index Oscillator, Contrasting Behavior in Uptrend versus Downtrend, Nasdaq 100 Trust ETF

Source: MetaStock

Indicators versus Volume and VMA

While volume is a tremendous tool for measuring trader sentiment, it is only one dimension of the analysis process, much like using price action alone. For this reason, in our Volume Analysis we never lose sight of the fact that volume and price movement are inextricably linked. The key is to look at both volume and price together—or to use indicators that combine volume and price components.

Volume and the volume moving average (VMA; see Chapter 3) are great for spotting trends and turning points in sentiment. They fall short, however, as they are unable to identify the direction of the price trend or the proper price points at which trades should be entered and exited.

Longer-term trending indicators such as On-Balance Volume (Chapter 9), in contrast, use the daily change in closing price to determine whether the volume for the day has been positive or negative. Short-term to mid-term oscillators such as the Money Flow Index use price data before volume data are applied to their calculation. Both of these indicators have the ability to give a sense of both direction and strength of price movement, which are the most critical components of trend determination. Volume measures the strength or conviction behind the identified price trend, giving a trader clues to whether the trend is likely to continue or deteriorate. Essentially, it is our view that both types of Volume Analysis are complementary and serve to confirm each other.

Position Traders: When to Exit and Stand Aside

When trading the market and using indicators, it is always wise to heed the warning signals given by your preferred indicators. Position traders, who are less interested in catching turning points than they are in riding trends and protecting profits, should consider using multiple volume indicator combinations to signal when there is real trouble ahead. The example of the Nasdaq 100 Trust ETF (QQQQ) in Chart 7.5 uses the combination of Volume Price Trend (VPT) and the MFI and volume with a 9-period VMA.

The example given by the steady uptrend followed by the volatile reversal in the first half of 2010 (punctuated by the "flash crash") is telling. Notice in the move higher off the March 2009 low through January 2010 that VPT continues to make higher highs as price pushes higher. Even though these increments were marginal, they were higher just the same,

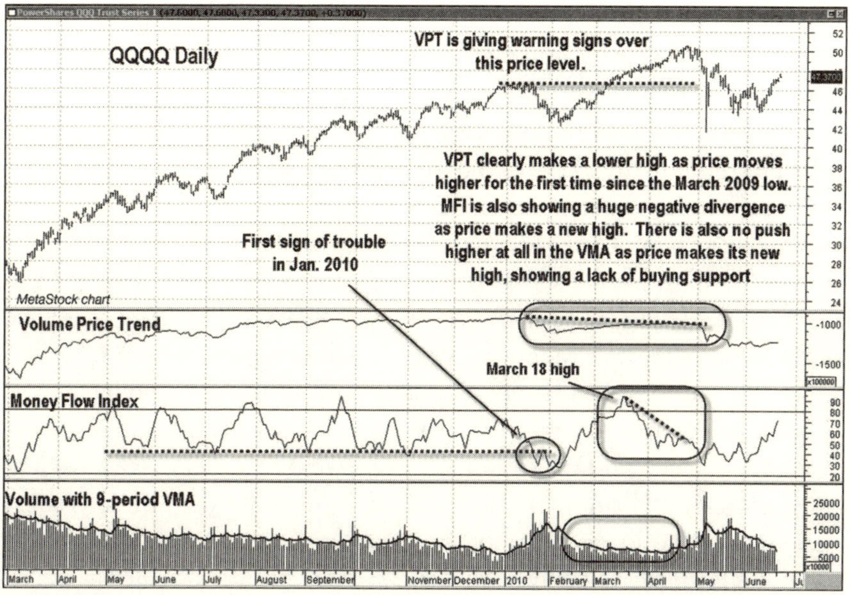

Chart 7.5 Multiple Indicators Signal a Downturn, 2010 1H, Nasdaq 100 Trust ETF

Source: MetaStock

thus validating the rally. Now take a look at MFI just below VPT in Chart 7.5. This is an example of knowing the characteristics of your selected indicators. MFI bottomed at the 37 to 40 level throughout the uptrend. Each time MFI moved down to that level, a momentum bottom was formed as MFI reversed higher, giving an indication that prices were ready to resume their uptrend.

The first sign of trouble for the uptrend was in January 2010 as MFI made the lowest low along the way, clearly breaking down through the 40 level, all the way down to 27. This was a sign that, during this pullback, sellers were applying more pressure than in any other previous pullback, during the rally. That didn't signal that the uptrend was over; it merely showed that the uptrend was losing its strength.

The uptrend resumed following the pullback as price pushed out to new highs in March, grinding higher into May. As price continued higher, note how MFI made its final high on March 18 and began to decline as price continued higher. That shows an obvious loss of momentum, but what about the major trend? What is VPT showing? Notice how VPT never eclipsed its January high, even as price moved considerably higher into May. That was a major sign that the uptrend was laboring.

Finally, take a look at the VMA in the very bottom frame of Chart 7.5. Note how it never increased during the final push higher into May. Other rallies lacked impressive volume to that point, but there were at least periodic surges in volume that managed to push the VMA higher. There were no such surges in the March–May 2010 period, showing that buying pressure was waning.

Now let's zoom in on the final rally from the February 2010 low to the May 2010 high to see where risk or equity exposure could have been reduced (see Chart 7.6). Of course, as with any trading strategy, you need to have a plan for how much risk you are willing to take off the table and when, but the combination of indicators in this situation would have given ample warning to allow for the execution of such a plan.

Chart 7.6 shows how a trendline was drawn off the February 2010 low. Even though VPT and MFI are showing signs of trouble, there is still a definite uptrend in prices supporting the plot of a trendline. When that trendline is violated, it is time to move to cash and stand aside.

Prior to the trendline being violated, however, the new high made in March is not validated by either VPT or MFI. That signaled that equity exposure should be reduced. That wasn't necessarily a signal to exit and stand aside because divergences can last for weeks—as was the case here.

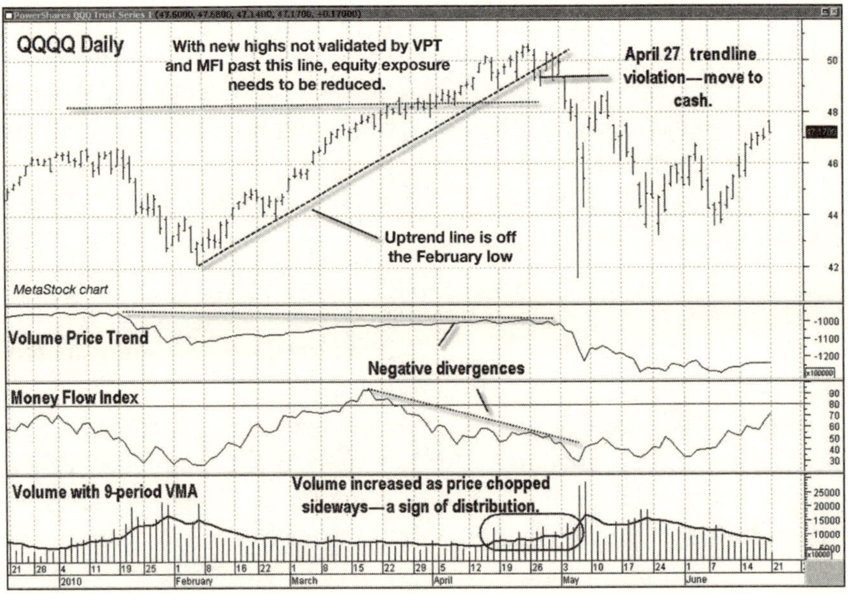

Chart 7.6 Seeing a Downturn before It Happens, 2010 1H, Nasdaq 100 Trust ETF

Source: MetaStock

Selling into rallies was the best plan, as price continued to grind higher with an obvious loss of momentum.

One final piece of the warning puzzle: Volume finally began to pick up in late April 2010 as price chopped sideways. Again, this was another change in the characteristics of the rally. Volume had been uninspiring to that point, and when it increased with difficult upward price movement, that was a sign that sellers were putting solid overhead supply on the market. On April 27, the uptrend line off the February low was violated, which gave plenty of time to move to cash before the May 6 flash crash occurred.

Indicator and Oscillator Sensitivity

When incorporating indicators into your volume Analysis, it is important to select the proper trading time frame parameters. For example, when using MFI on a daily chart, the most commonly used setting is 14 days, as used in the previous examples. A time frame of 5 days gives more overbought/oversold readings, while a time frame of 21 days gives fewer—but perhaps stronger—overbought/oversold readings. The long-term example from August 2008 of the Nasdaq 100 Trust ETF (QQQQ) in Chart 7.7

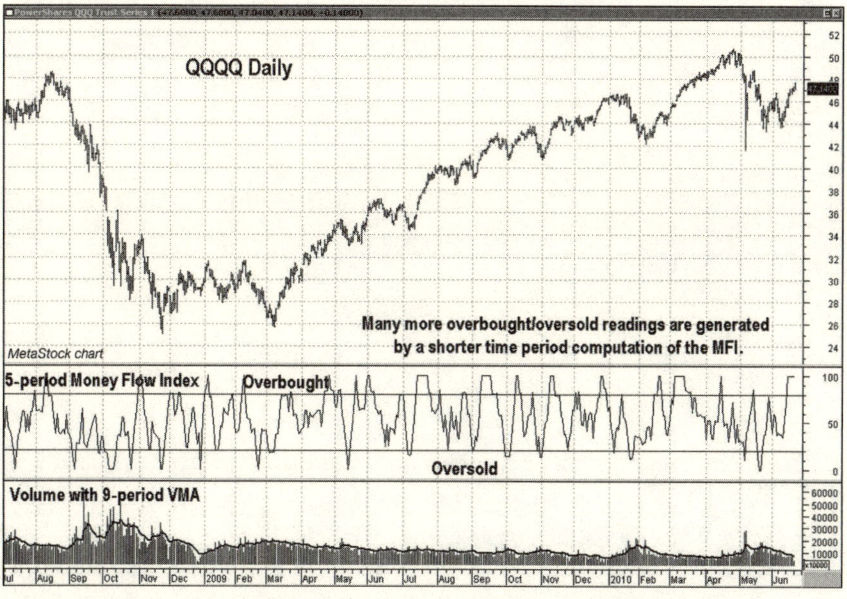

Chart 7.7 Five-Day Money Flow Index, Nasdaq 100 Trust ETF (QQQQ)

Source: MetaStock

shows the number of overbought/oversold reading generated with the 5-day versus the 21-day setting.

Notice on the 5-day setting how MFI reached the overbought/oversold levels many times throughout the 22 months shown. Settings this sensitive give many false signals, so care must be taken to find the right balance between quantity and quality of signals.

As for the 21-day setting (see Chart 7.8), note how it never quite reached the oversold level in the 22 months shown, while it reached the overbought level only once, in March 2010. When it did reach that level, however, the signal was strong and important, given what followed.

These are simple examples of how the time frame settings can affect the performance and frequency of signals in an indicator or oscillator.

Chart 7.9 displays a 30-minute view of the U.S. Dollar Index continuous contract with the combination of VPT and MFI. Even though the 30-minute time frame is considered very short by less active traders, a true sense of trend can be determined by both price action and VPT. As VPT makes a series of lower highs and lower lows, it shows real intraday weakness in the U.S. Dollar Index. That means that since the trend is down, MFI can be used as a trade filter to identify potentially profitable short positions as it rises to overbought levels (above 80) and crosses back below 80.

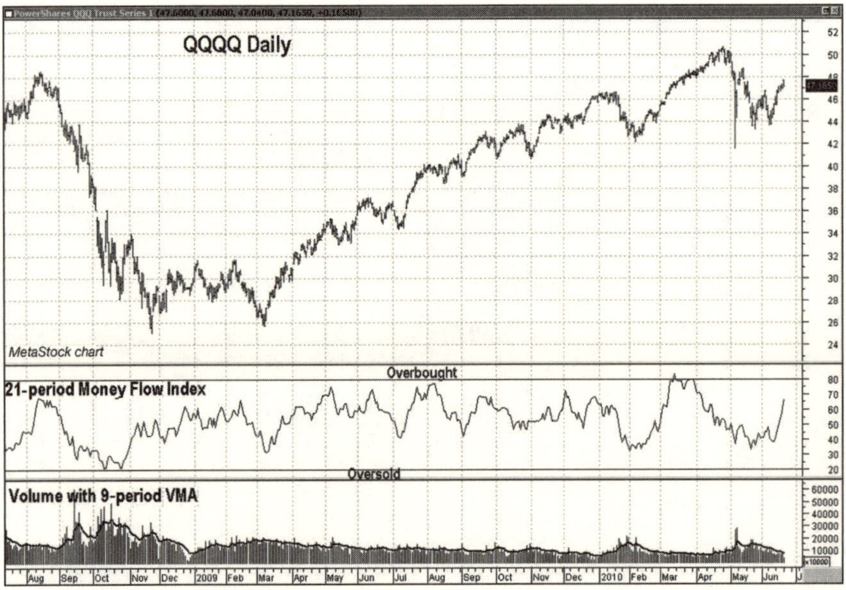

Chart 7.8 Twenty-One-Day Money Flow Index, Nasdaq 100 Trust ETF

Source: MetaStock

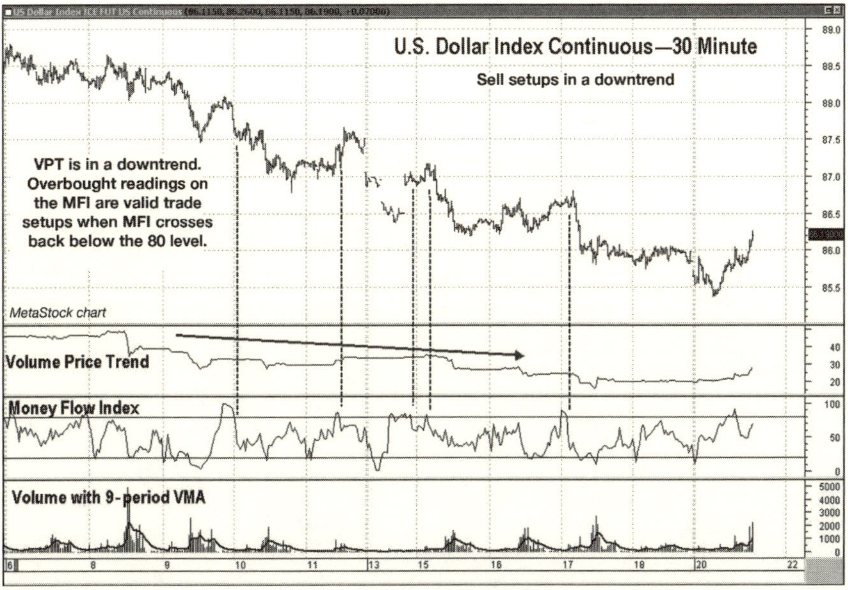

Chart 7.9 Money Flow Index, Sell Setups in a Downtrend, U.S. Dollar Index

Source: MetaStock

However, the trade should not be executed without a trigger such as a move that takes out a prior low. One reason for this is that the MFI reflects momentum and requires some other form of confirmation to determine that the downtrend is indeed resuming. Note how the downtrend from June 9 through June 17, 2010 yielded some great intraday shorting opportunities.

The next example shows how combining indicators at the opposite end of the time spectrum can also be effective. Chart 7.10 is a weekly frame of the SPDR Gold Shares ETF (GLD). The indicators paired in this example are Accumulation/Distribution and Ease of Movement. Accumulation/Distribution is a cumulative trending indicator, while Ease of Movement is a centered oscillator, meaning that it generates signals when it crosses above or below its center line—which has a value of zero. The Ease of Movement indicator tends to bottom very close to the zero line in uptrends and top very close to the zero line in downtrends. In this example we are only interested in those crossovers that push decisively above or below the zero line.

Note in Chart 7.10 how Accumulation/Distribution shows a solid uptrend since the 2004 low with the exception of one corrective period in the second half of 2008. By pairing Accumulation/Distribution with Ease

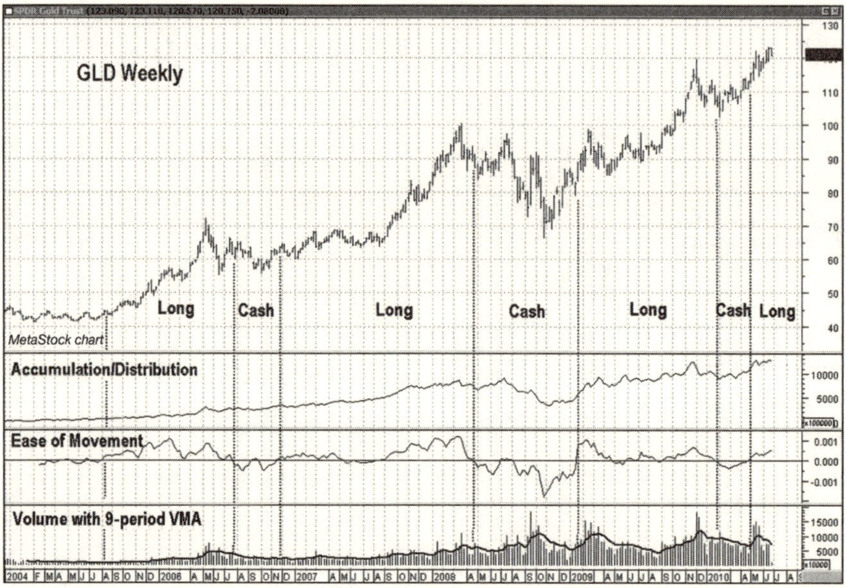

Chart 7.10 Weekly Chart of the SPDR Gold Shares ETF (GLD)

Source: MetaStock

of Movement, an effective trend-following strategy can be developed. Blindly buying and holding during this period would have ultimately worked out for the buyer, but no doubt he or she would have developed stomach ulcers along the way. Using a Volume Analysis strategy combining these indicators would have helped a gold trader sleep better at night, especially during the 2008 meltdown when GLD lost over 30 percent.

The GLD example in Chart 7.10 has the zero line marked in Ease of Movement. Crossovers of this line provide signals to either take long positions or move to cash. This strategy doesn't catch every ounce of upside, but it allows a trader to catch the meat of each trend while sitting out the sharp selloffs.

Up until now we have looked at some of the more conventional volume indicator pairings. In this final example, we will add another layer to take the guesswork out of the timing of our entry. The U.S. Dollar Index example in Chart 7.11 shows how a combination of indicators in a five-minute time frame can yield great results.

The plot follows the MFI and VPT on June 20, 2010. First, note that the VPT is making higher lows while the MFI is bottoming at around the 40 level even as price has pulled back. Both are bullish characteristics.

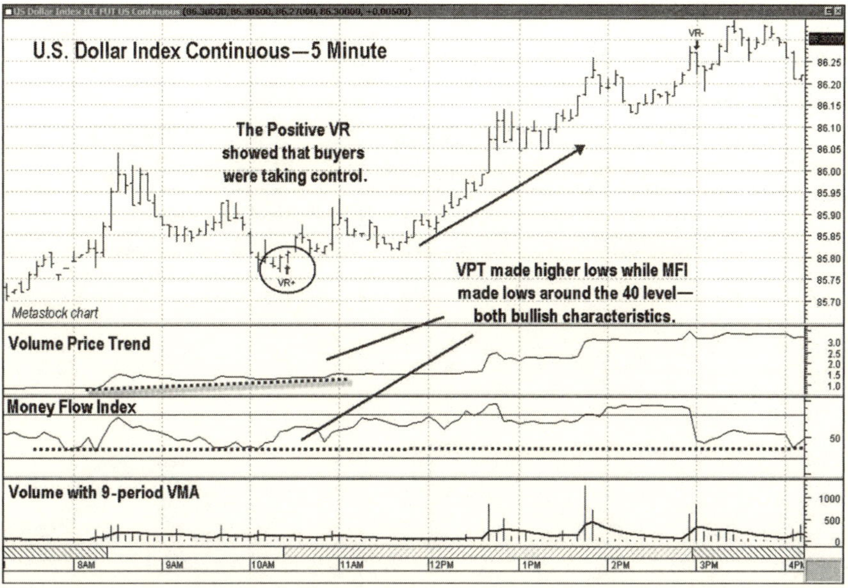

Chart 7.11 Money Flow Index and Volume Price Trend, Combined in Short Intervals, U.S. Dollar Index, Continuous 5-Minute

Source: MetaStock

With a setup like this, it is time to look for a long trade entry. The question is: What will be the trigger to execute the trade?

A conservative solution would be to wait for the previous resistance level to be taken out. A more aggressive solution would be to simply buy here with a price stop just below the previous lows. Since the first option would leave precious profits on the table and the second would be more of a exercise in blind faith, let's add one more piece to our analysis, the Leibovit Volume Reversal.

Notice in Chart 7.11 how the Positive VR between 10 a.m. and 11 a.m. signaled that buyers were taking control of the market. In this case, the Positive VR is backed up by the positive setups in both VPT and MFI, and it led to a very successful trade.

Summary

- Volume Analysis requires understanding volume technical indicators and oscillators and how they perform and apply to the market conditions and securities being traded.

- To a large degree, finding the right indicators among multiple combinations of indicators takes practice and experience; there is no "one size fits all" solution.
- One of the more challenging tasks in an analysis is designing combinations of indicators to support a trading time frame. It isn't just about selecting the indicators; it's also about selecting complementary time frames and setting trading parameters.

PART TWO

VOLUME-BASED INDICATORS, OSCILLATORS, AND TACTICAL VOLUME OVERLAYS

There is no "perfect" way to categorize all technical tools that incorporate volume. Some are designed as broad market indicators, while others are used more often to analyze and trade individual securities. Some work better in long time frames, others work better in short or intermediate time frames, and some work in multiple time frames. Some are indicators—mathematically calculated formulations of actual price or volume data points. Some are oscillators, capturing the movement of price or volume in relation to a center line or upper and lower boundaries. *All* of these tools have an underlying volume component and are not based on price action alone.

We've chosen to break down these sets of technical tools into three chapters. Chapter 8 covers broad market volume indicators and oscillators designed to capture the aggregate market trend: direction, strength, and change. Chapter 9 discusses volume-based indicators, and Chapter 10 covers volume-based oscillators, as applied to both individual stocks and commodities. All three chapters present these technical volume tools in alphabetical order. Commentary and trade setups are generally accepted best practices; however, some are based on the experiences and opinions of this author. Chapter 11 discusses how to utilize these tools to build tactical volume overlays.

Chapter 8

BROAD MARKET VOLUME INDICATORS AND OSCILLATORS

Chapter 8 explores the details of the most widely used broad market volume indicators and oscillators in trading today. The selection of one or more of these indicators and oscillators as a Volume Analysis component is based on its fit to your trading strategy, trading time frame, and the security or market involved. Thirteen of the most widely used volume-based broad market indicators and oscillators are

1. Advance/Decline Volume Ratio
2. ARMS (TRIN) Index
3. 10-Day Open ARMS (TRIN) Index
4. 30-Day Open ARMS (TRIN) Index
5. Cumulative Volume Index
6. Exchange Volume
7. 5-Day Up/Down Volume Oscillator
8. Index Volume
9. Nasdaq/NYSE Volume Ratio
10. 10-Day Up/Down Volume Oscillator
11. Upside/Downside Volume
12. Upside/Downside Volume Oscillator
13. Yo-Yo indicator

Each indicator and oscillator is described and accompanied by a chart example, descriptions of how the indicator or oscillator behaves in uptrending or downtrending markets, and corresponding discussions. To help explain how these tools are put into practice, there is a sample trade setup and execution for each indicator or oscillator, followed by a brief assessment of its strengths, weaknesses, and overall applicability.

Advance/Decline Volume Ratio

Advancing and declining volume and the relationship between the two are valuable pieces of information that can tell a trader whether buyers or sellers are in control of the market. Advancing and declining volume data capture the collective volume of stocks that advanced as well as the collective volume of stocks that declined. Advancing and declining data can be found in any reputable financial publication or on numerous Internet sites.

Formulation

Two main methods are used to analyze advancing and declining data. One is to subtract down volume from up volume and plot a cumulative total. That method creates the *Cumulative Volume Index*, described later in this chapter. The second method is simply to divide each day's up volume by down volume to compute a daily ratio—the Advance/Decline Volume Ratio. This method produces a spiked appearance, but the data are still useful for identifying periods of bullish or bearish control. Additionally, if the data series is smoothed with a moving average, it can provide valuable insights into long-term buying and selling forces in the market. We will examine both the raw and smoothed plots and show the value of each.

Raw Advance/Decline Volume Ratio

Chart 8.1 is a daily record of the S&P 500 from November 2008 through January 2010 with the "raw" value of the Advance/Decline Volume Ratio plotted. The line is erratic but does show spikes in positive versus negative volume.

Displaying the indicator in its raw state provides clues as to the *strength* of the trend as well. Note in Chart 8.2 how the volume spikes coincide with the initiation of new rally phases. The size of the spike correlates to the strength of the uptrend. This type of behavior shows that buyers are in control and further confirms the uptrend.

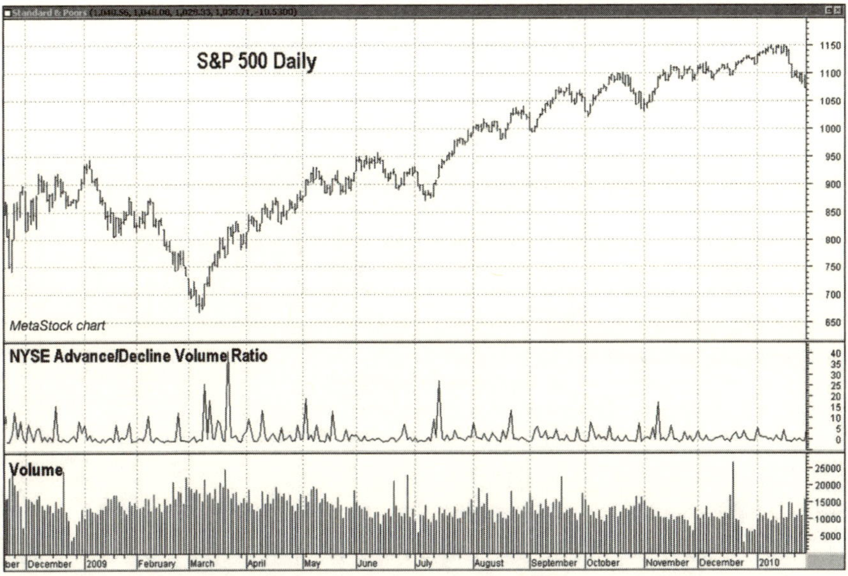

Chart 8.1 Advance/Decline Volume Ratio, S&P 500 Daily

Source: MetaStock

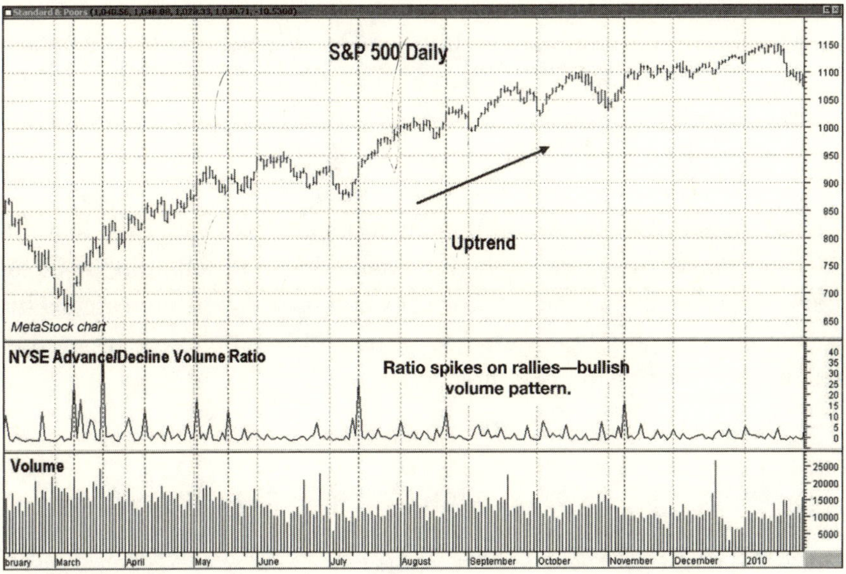

Chart 8.2 Advance/Decline Volume Ratio Confirming Uptrend Strength, S&P 500 Daily

Source: MetaStock

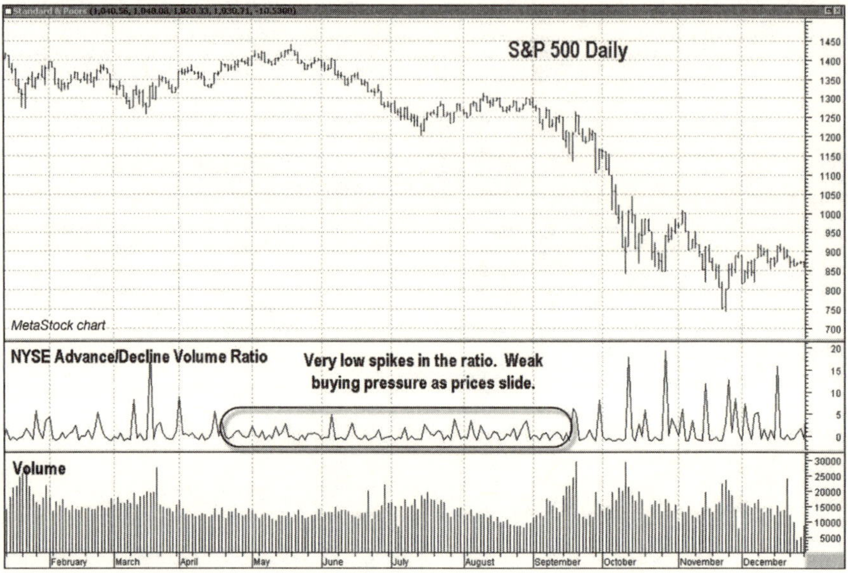

Chart 8.3 Advance/Decline Volume Ratio in a Downturn, S&P 500 Daily

Source: MetaStock

It's also worth examining the Advance/Decline Volume Ratio's behavior in a downtrend. Recall in Chart 8.2 how the ratio spiked on new rally phases. Chart 8.3 shows that the ratio is rather tame as it remains range bound throughout the September 2008 decline phase. With no real change in advancing versus declining volume, low buying pressure was indicated, and the downtrend remained intact. Note, however, that the indicator spikes increased on the right-hand side of the chart in the October–December 2008 period as volatility and trader angst increased. This increase was a clue that a change in market psychology was coming, leading to a change in price direction at the March 2009 low.

Don't Fight—or Forget About—the Prevailing Trend

Whenever interpreting indicators, always be mindful of the higher-degree or prevailing trend. The 2008 volume spikes showed that volatility was increasing along with brief bouts of strong buying pressure, whether it was short covering or accumulation. The main point is that the indicator pattern was changing, alerting us that trader sentiment was beginning to change. Always remember that volume reflects the degree of trader sentiment or conviction in the market. In the uptrend example in Chart 8.4 of the April 2009 to January 2010 S&P 500, the intensity and trend direction were pointing higher, as indicator spikes kicked off a new rally phase in July. These indicator spikes revealed that buyers were reentering the market to push prices higher.

Smoothed Advance/Decline Volume Ratio

Next we will take a look at smoothing the Advance/Decline data series with a 10-day simple moving average. This method gives a slightly longer-term look to the data stream and allows the trader to spot short-term trends and divergences. In Chart 8.4, note how the 10-day moving average of the ratio declined from April into July 2009 while price pushed higher into June. This created a negative divergence in which prices made higher highs while the indicator made lower highs. This divergence warned of a potentially serious correction unfolding, which occurred in June and July 2009. Following the correction, note how the 10-day moving average spiked higher on the resumption of the uptrend. The July spike in the indicator was a signal that a new rally phase was unfolding.

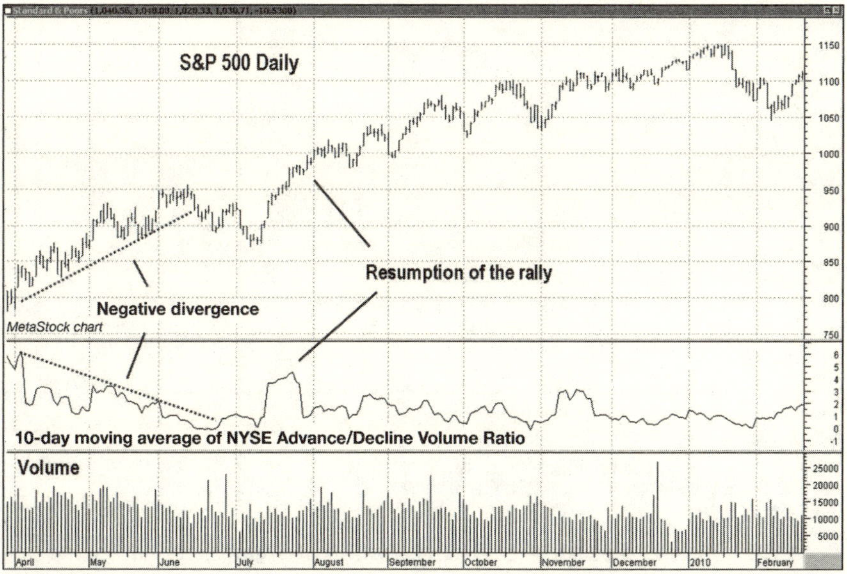

Chart 8.4 Advance/Decline Volume Ratio, 10-Day Moving Average, S&P 500 Daily

Source: MetaStock

Remember: Divergence Is Not Death

The example on Chart 8.4 is a great reminder not to place a trade or abandon positions too quickly simply because of the divergence of an indicator. The divergence warns of a weakening trend, but taking drastic action on the divergence would have been a bad decision, as the market continued higher into June. It is always best to wait for a violation of the price trend (trendline, moving average, etc.) as confirmation before trading on divergences. Be patient.

Chart 8.5 is an example of the behavior of an indicator in a positive divergence shown by the 10-day moving average of the ratio. The chart shows the S&P 500 during the steep decline from May through November of 2008. Notice how the indicator is making higher highs from September through December 2008—an indication that positive volume is building and that a change in trader psychology is occurring. The market bottomed just a few months later, in March 2009, but the action in the

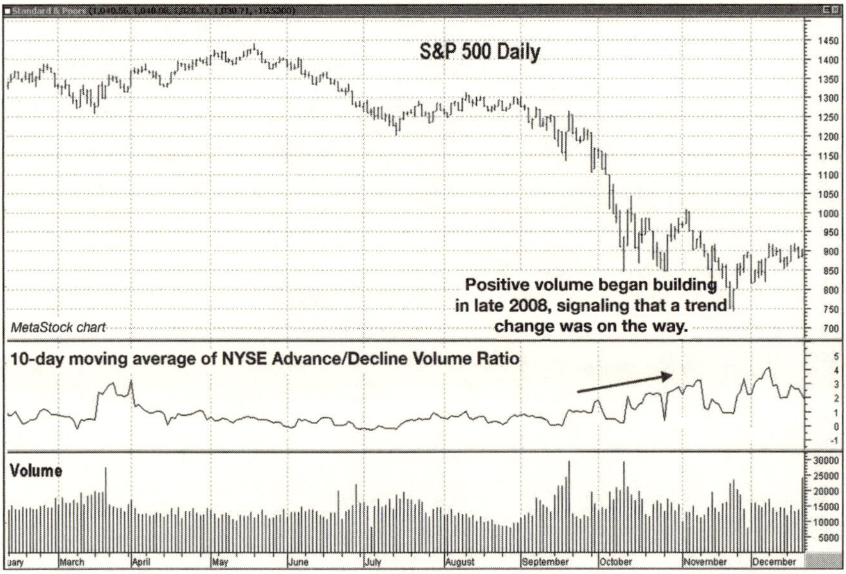

Chart 8.5 Advance/Decline Volume Ratio, Positive Divergence, 10-Day Moving Average, S&P 500 Daily

Source: MetaStock

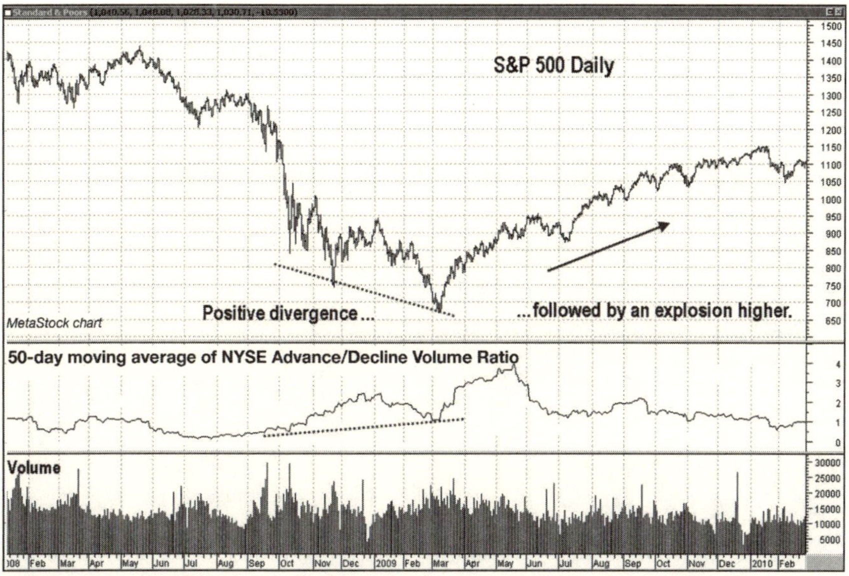

Chart 8.6 50-Day Moving Average of the Advance/Decline Volume Ratio, Positive Divergence, S&P 500 Daily

Source: MetaStock

10-day moving average of the Advance/Decline Volume Ratio showed that a change in trend was coming.

A long-term use of this indicator is given by smoothing it with a 50-day simple moving average. This long-term look can show long-term trends and divergences. In Chart 8.6, note the size of the positive divergence at the March 2009 low as price continued to make lower lows from September 2008 through March 2009 while the indicator made a higher low in March. This showed that selling pressure had weakened considerably compared to six months earlier and was a sign that a trend change was imminent.

Since the Advance/Decline Volume Ratio is good for alerting traders when sentiment is changing, it can be used in its smoothed form for broad market trading entry points. The following example shows the trade setup on the S&P 500, but a surrogate such as the iShares S&P 500 Trust ETF, or "SPDR," could be used in its place for trading purposes.

Trade Setup

In Chart 8.7, a 30-day moving average of the NYSE Advance/Decline Volume Ratio is plotted in the pane below price. This indicator will be displayed and used in conjunction with a 30-day simple moving average

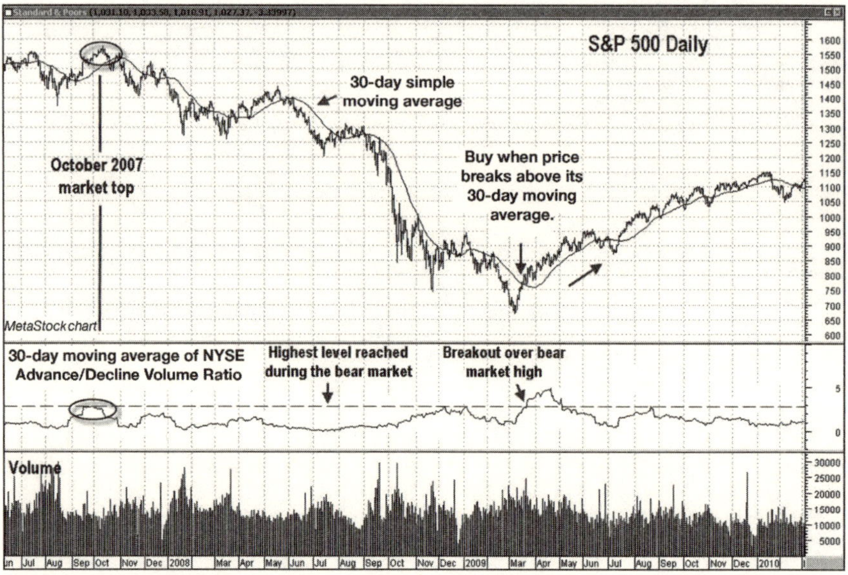

Chart 8.7 Trade Setup, Upside Breakout, Advance/Decline Volume Ratio, 30-Day Moving Average, S&P 500 Daily

Source: MetaStock

of price to time our entry. Note in Chart 8.7 how the 30-day moving average of the NYSE Advance/Decline Volume Ratio has an upper limit that had acted as resistance since the October 2007 market top. The breach of that resistance line was a signal that trader sentiment was changing toward the market. Simply buying on that breach without price confirmation would be risky, however. A confirmatory price close above its own 30-day moving average would confirm that there is sufficient strength in the move to warrant a trade. Chart 8.7 gives a long-term look at the setup.

Trade Entry

Chart 8.8 shows a close-up of the March 2009 time frame when the Advance/Decline Volume Ratio broke up through its overhead resistance line. At the same time, note how price was trading firmly above its 30-day moving average, which was a sign of strength. A buy could have been executed on March 23, 2009, with the initial stop placed below the March 20 reactionary low. The trade can be managed from here by moving the stop higher along the 30-day moving average, by moving the stop higher to more recent swing lows, or by any other method with which a trader is comfortable.

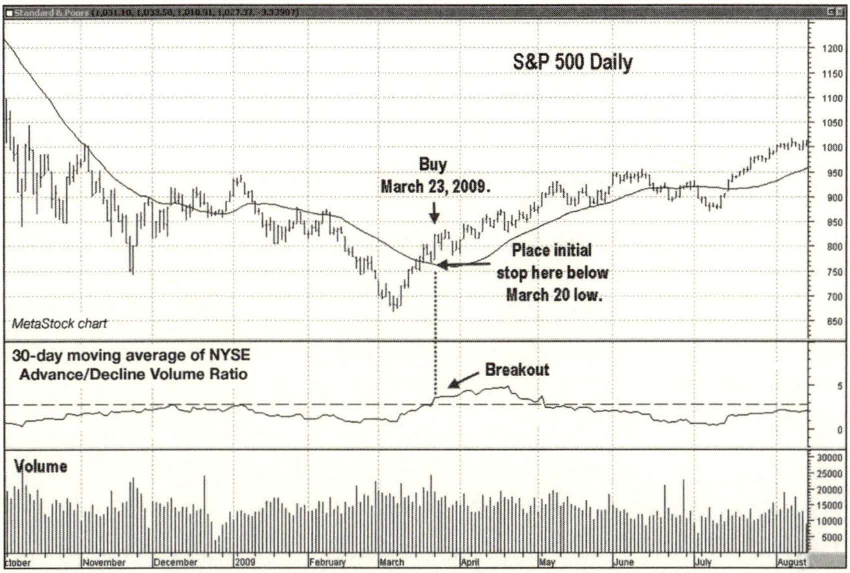

Chart 8.8 Trade Execution, Upside Breakout, Advance/Decline Volume Ratio, 30-Day Moving Average, S&P 500 Daily

Source: MetaStock

The Advance/Decline Volume Ratio is a valuable tool to give a deeper look into market action beyond the daily headlines. Each method (raw or smoothed) has its advantages.

Trader Tips

The Advance/Decline Volume indicator is a simple and useful tool to show the presence and extent of broad market buying or selling pressure. Specific advantages include the following:

1. Raw method
   - Daily spikes in positive, or upside, volume confirm uptrends.
   - The absence of upside volume confirms downtrends.
2. Smoothed method
   - The 10-day moving average smoothed ratio is valuable for spotting shorter-term trends and divergences.
   - The 50-day moving average smoothed ratio is good for longer-term trends and divergences.

One disadvantage is that it isn't good for finding exact turning points; however, it can alert traders to changes in volume patterns that lead to trend change.

ARMS Index/TRIN

The ARMS Index, also known as the TRIN (Traders' Index), owes its name to its developer and one of the most original and creative of all market technicians, Richard Arms Jr., who developed it in 1967. He developed it as a contrarian indicator to detect overbought and oversold conditions in the market. Because of its calculation, it has an inverse relationship to the direction of the market.

Formulation

The ARMS Index is calculated as follows:

$$\frac{\text{(Advancing issues/Declining issues)}}{\text{(Advancing volume/Declining volume)}}$$

The indicator starts out by identifying the ratio of advancing to declining issues but confirms the strength of that simple price-based ratio by relating it to advancing and declining volume. Typically the indicator is bullish when it reads below 1.0 (i.e., positive volume is strong in relationship to the current positive price activity) and is bearish when it is above 1.0 (i.e., positive volume isn't strong enough to confirm current positive price activity).

Extreme oversold readings (exceeding 1.25, as explained later) can show buying opportunities, and extreme overbought readings (below 0.80) can reveal selling or short-selling opportunities. ARMS is generally thought of as a shorter-term indicator, which in many cases is plotted on an inverse scale so that the indicator appears to move in sync with the market. In the examples below, its versatility as a reliable indicator over different time frames will be revealed.

Here we will cover three versions: the standard ARMS Index plus two variations, the 10-Day Open ARMS and the 30-Day Open ARMS (which will be explained in later paragraphs).

Because of its inverse relationship with the market, ARMS can be challenging to interpret for those who are used to seeing indicators move in the same direction as price. Spikes *higher* in the ARMS usually coincide

Chart 8.9 ARMS/TRIN Confirming Short-Term Lows, S&P 500 Daily

Source: StockCharts.com

with short-term market *lows*. Note in the example of the S&P 500 in Chart 8.9 that spikes in the ARMS coincide with short-term lows.

Chart 8.10 of the Dow Jones Industrial Average from July 2009 to March 2010 shows spikes in the ARMS occurring at or near short-term lows in an uptrend. These spikes can mark solid buying opportunities.

Fear and Complacency

The ARMS can also be a useful tool for identifying the trading sentiment, or "mood," of the market. Extreme high readings show excessive bearishness or fear as sellers overwhelm buyers. These "fear spikes" can cause short-term buying opportunities, as strong bounces usually follow. The ARMS can also show periods of relative calm as markets trend and traders accept the trend. Chart 8.11 shows the Dow Jones Industrial Average in a period of relative complacency from February 2008 through early October 2008 as compared to the periods of fear earlier and later that same year.

Inverted ARMS

Another way to display the ARMS is to invert the scale so that the ARMS appears to move in conjunction with the market index that is being tracked. Remember, the indicator is inverted now, so lower spikes

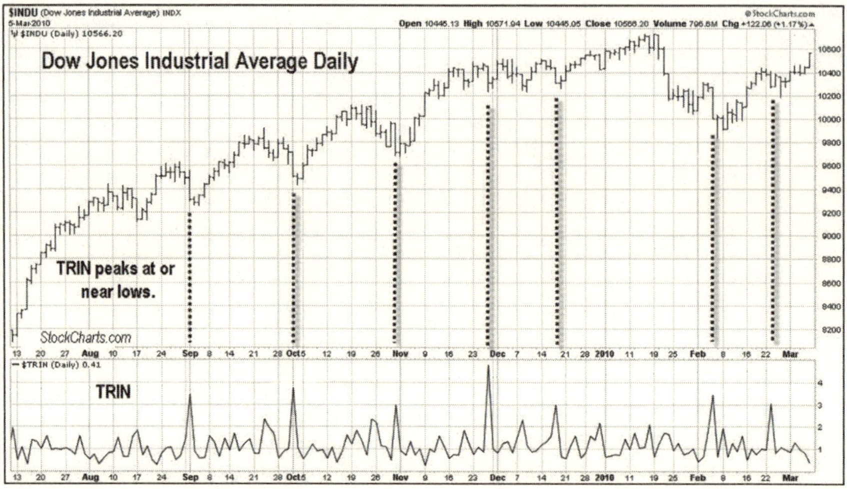

Chart 8.10 ARMS/TRIN Confirming Short-Term Lows in an Uptrend, DJIA Daily

Source: StockCharts.com

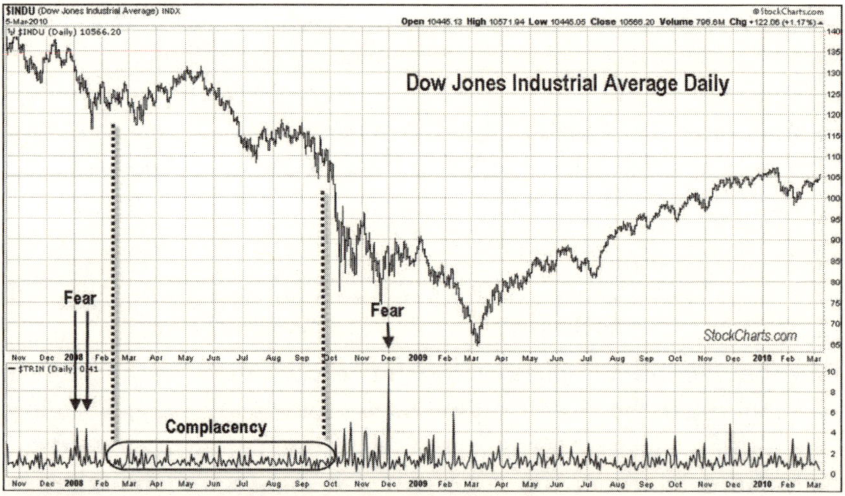

Chart 8.11 ARMS/TRIN as a Measure of Complacency and Fear, DJIA Daily

Source: StockCharts.com

denote selling pressure. In Chart 8.12, the Dow Jones Industrial Average shows a positive divergence, as price made lower lows while the inverted ARMS made higher lows. This showed that selling pressure weakened heading into the March 2009 low. The inverted indicator makes it easier to spot the divergence caused by weakening selling pressure.

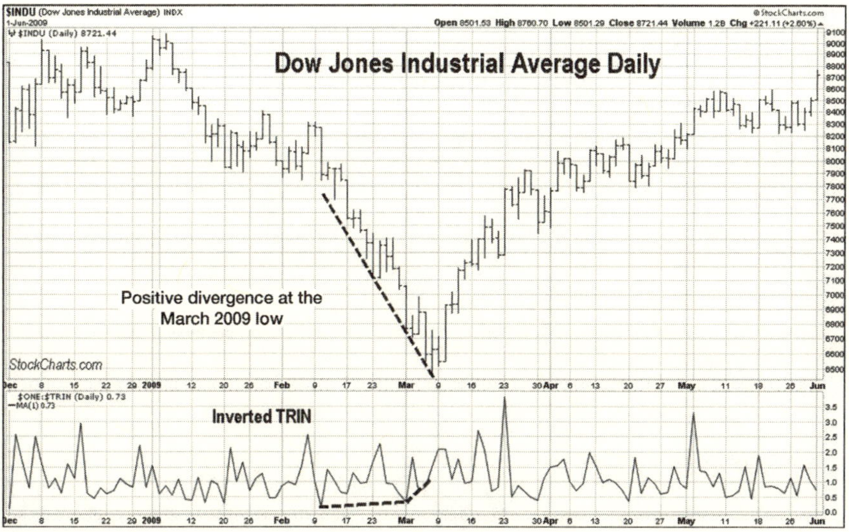

Chart 8.12 Inverted ARMS/TRIN Divergence, DJIA Daily

Source: StockCharts.com

Smoothing the ARMS

Another way to plot the inverted ARMS (or a standard ARMS) is by smoothing it with a 10-day simple moving average. Using the 10-day moving average shows trends and divergences and allows the ARMS to display more as a shorter-term indicator. Chart 8.13 shows the NYSE Composite Index plotted with the 10-day moving average of an inverted ARMS. Note how it smoothed the data and more clearly showed divergences and trends.

It's worth zeroing in on a section of the NYSE Composite Index in Chart 8.13. Chart 8.14 looks at the September 2009–March 2010 period. Notice the negative divergence shown by the 10-period moving average. Price made a higher high, while the 10-day moving average of the inverted ARMS made a much lower high. This was a warning that a correction was imminent. Following the negative divergence, the NYSE Composite Index corrected more than 10 percent during the next two weeks.

Detecting Overbought and Oversold Conditions

Another way to use the ARMS is to show overbought and oversold levels. ARMS considers the market overbought when the 21-day moving average of ARMS is below 0.8 and oversold when it is above 1.2. Chart 8.15, which uses a normal (not inverted) ARMS, illustrates those levels.

Chart 8.13 Inverted ARMS/TRIN, Moving Average, NYSE Composite Daily

Source: StockCharts.com

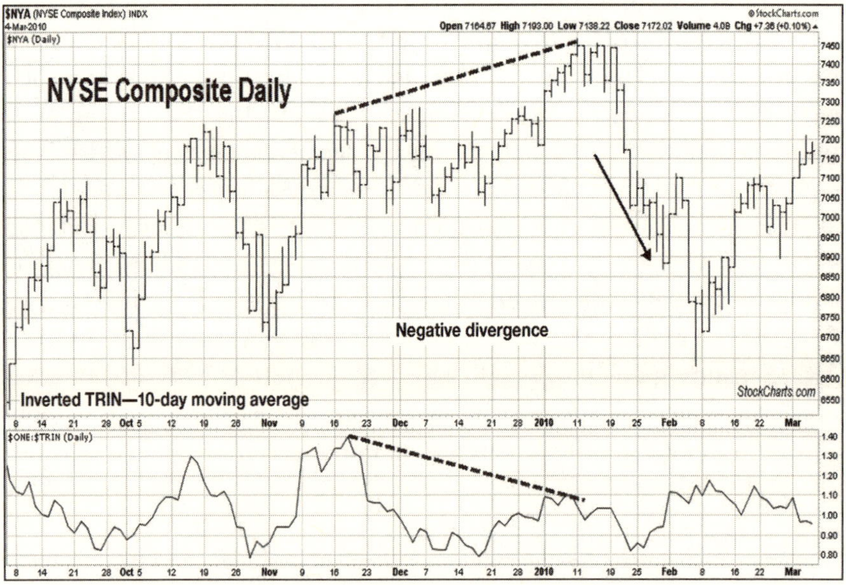

Chart 8.14 Inverted ARMS/TRIN, 10-Day Moving Average, Negative Divergence, Signaling Correction, NYSE Composite Daily

Source: StockCharts.com

Chart 8.15 ARMS/TRIN Illustrating Overbought and Oversold Levels, S&P 500 Daily

Source: StockCharts.com

TRIN with Longer-Term Moving Averages

Another common use for the ARMS indicator is to smooth it with either a 21-period or a 55-period simple moving average. This gives the ARMS a longer-term look and is good for spotting longer-term trends and divergences. Chart 8.16 shows a 21-day moving average of an inverted ARMS. Inverting the indicator when plotting with a longer-term moving average is often preferred in order to more easily spot trends and divergences.

Note on the right side of the chart how ARMS had not confirmed the advance from September 2009 through March 2010 as price moved higher while the indicator trended lower. This strong divergence didn't bode well for the market.

Chart 8.17 shows the 55-day moving average of the inverted ARMS. Notice how the extra smoothing caused it to show peaks in May and September 2009 in contrast to peaks in March and September 2009 for the 21-day moving average. It also showed the same troubling divergence from September 2009 through March 2010. This long divergence showed that buying pressure was weakening, leading to the April 2010 top.

Trade Setup

While ARMS is often used for broader market analysis, it can be used for shorter-term trading signals. The 10-day moving average of an inverted

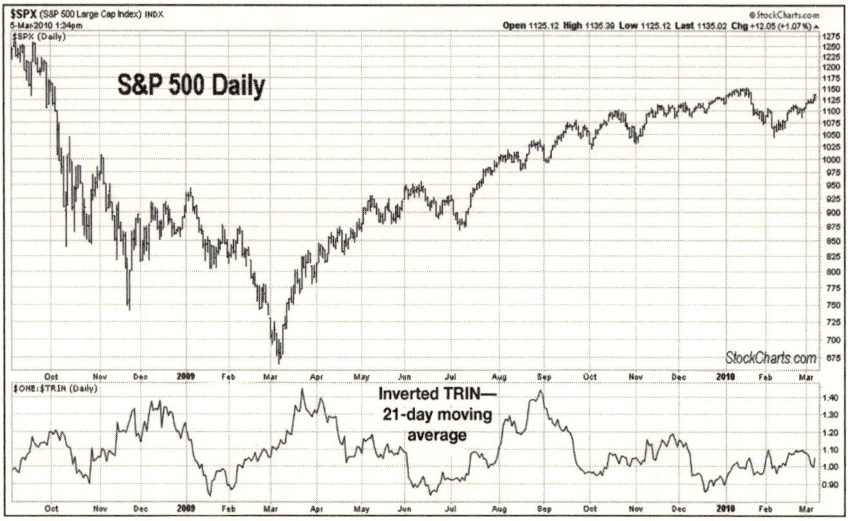

Chart 8.16 Inverted ARMS/TRIN, 21-Day Moving Average, Nonconfirming Divergence, S&P 500 Daily

Source: StockCharts.com

Chart 8.17 Inverted ARMS/TRIN, 55-Day Moving Average, S&P 500 Daily

Source: StockCharts.com

ARMS shows excellent divergences to alert a short-term trader when buying or selling pressure is weakening. Chart 8.18 uses the iShares S&P 500 Trust ETF (SPY) broad market ETF with a 10-day moving average of the inverted ARMS Index.

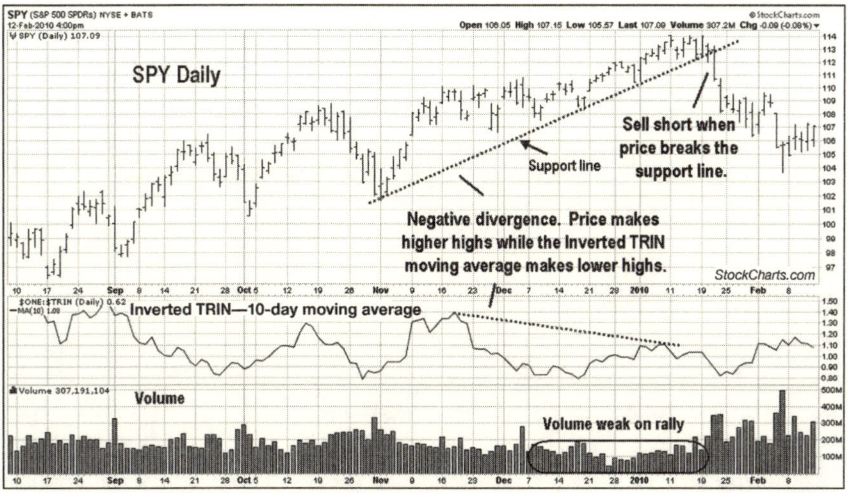

Chart 8.18 Trade Setup, Inverted ARMS/TRIN with Divergence, S&P 500 Trust ETF

Source: StockCharts.com

Note how as price continued higher in the November 2009–January 2010 period, the 10-day moving average of the inverted ARMS made lower highs, creating a negative divergence with price. Remember that divergences are warnings that the trend is weakening, but in order to enter a trade based on the divergence, some sort of "trade trigger" is needed. The trigger in this case will be a violation of the support line that connects the November, December, and early January lows. One more piece of evidence building the case for a short trade was the weak volume on the rally. Note also how volume failed to show a resounding endorsement of the rally from new buyers.

Trade Entry

Next is a close-up look of the time frame in which a trade could have been executed. The negative divergence between price and the ARMS moving average had been in place for almost two months, showing a pronounced weakening of buying pressure. Once the support line was broken, permission was given to initiate a short position with a stop just over the recent high. The January 21, 2010, break of the support line triggered a short trade, with an initial protective stop placed over the January 19 high of 115.13. Note also how volume confirmed that the short-term trend was changing as it increased on the sell-off. Chart 8.19 illustrates this entry scenario.

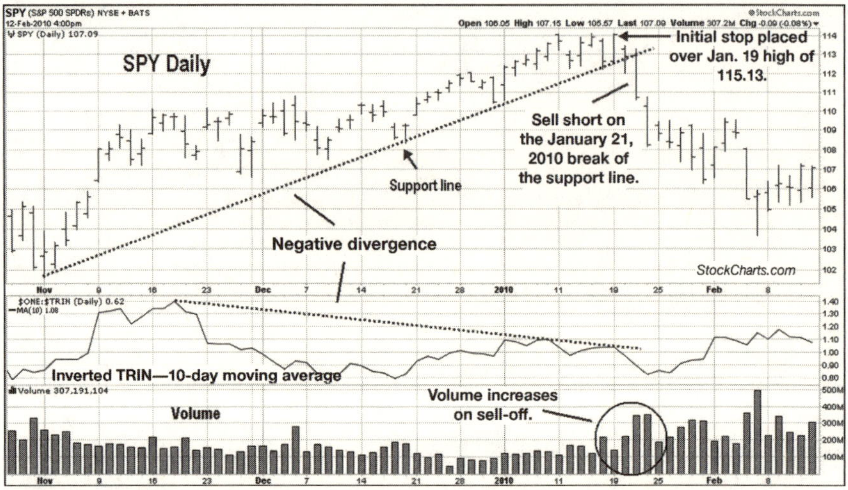

Chart 8.19 Trade Entry, Inverted ARMS/TRIN with Negative Divergence and Signal, S&P 500 Trust ETF

Source: StockCharts.com

Trader Tips

The ARMS is an extremely versatile indicator with short-term trading roots. The use of moving averages and inversion help it to give an accurate picture of market health.

The ARMS can be used to identify a range of market conditions, including

- Overbought and oversold conditions
- Periods of fear and complacency in the market
- Market trends through inversion and moving averages, including longer-term trends using longer-term moving averages
- Trend divergences through inversion and moving averages

The 10-Day Open ARMS

The 10-Day Open ARMS is a variation of the ARMS Index. It provides a smoother data stream in its raw form than the ARMS because it is constructed using 10 days of data instead of just one.

Formulation

The formula for the 10-Day Open ARMS is as follows:

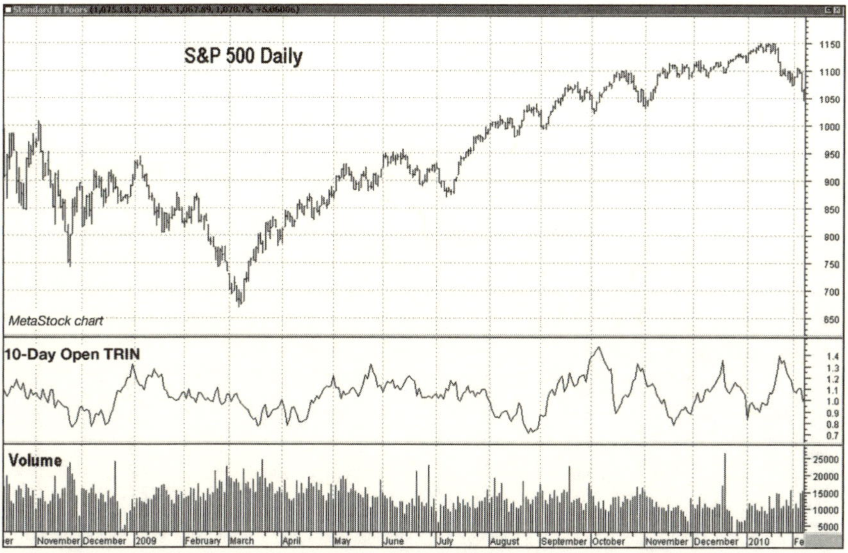

Chart 8.20 10-Day Open ARMS/TRIN, S&P 500 Daily

Source: MetaStock

$$\frac{\text{Last 10 days' advances/Last 10 days' declines}}{\text{Last 10 days' advancing volume/Last 10 days' declining volume}}$$

This method computes the 10-day summation of each component before computing the ratio, in contrast to applying a moving average to the daily ARMS ratio, as was shown earlier. Just as with the ARMS, the 10-Day Open ARMS is used to analyze the relationship of volume in advancing issues to volume in declining issues.

Intermediate is the key word with the 10-Day Open ARMS. This indicator is an excellent tool for gauging intermediate-term overbought and oversold market conditions, short to intermediate trends, and trend divergences. Chart 8.20 contains a plot for the S&P 500 of the 10-Day Open ARMS. Remember that in its normal form, the 10-Day Open ARMS moves inversely to price, which means that spikes in the ARMS coincide with price lows, and troughs in the ARMS coincide with price highs.

Spikes at Lows

Like the ARMS Index, the 10-Day Open ARMS is excellent at spotting shorter-term market lows. The Dow Jones Industrial Average in Chart 8.21 shows how the 10-Day Open ARMS spikes higher at short-term lows in an uptrend. These spikes provide excellent buying opportunities in the uptrend.

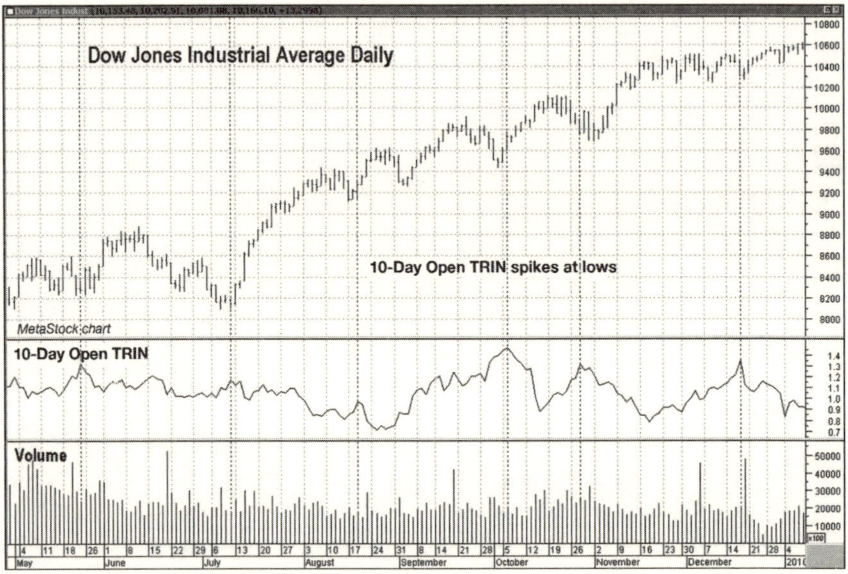

Chart 8.21 10-Day Open ARMS/TRIN, Low Spikes on Uptrend, DJIA Daily

Source: MetaStock

Inverted 10-Day Open ARMS

Like the normal ARMS, the 10-Day Open ARMS moves inversely to the market, and it is sometimes easier to interpret when the scale is inverted. We find that inversion makes it easier to spot overbought and oversold conditions as well as divergences. Chart 8.22 for the Dow Jones Industrial Average shows how the inverted 10-Day Open ARMS is used to spot overbought and oversold conditions in the market. Readings <0.8 are considered overbought, and readings >1.2 are considered oversold.

Inversion also allows for easier identification of divergences, signaling potential market turning points. The DJIA in Chart 8.23 shows a brief countertrend rally in the spring of 2008. Note that as prices pushed higher, the inverted 10-Day Open ARMS made a lower high, indicating that the downtrend was ready to resume. The inverted 10-Day Open ARMS (see Chart 8.24) is also useful in showing positive divergences when price moves lower but the indicator moves higher, making higher lows. This identifies situations of latent strength, showing that buyers are accumulating shares even as price moves lower. Such situations during uptrends can be great buying opportunities.

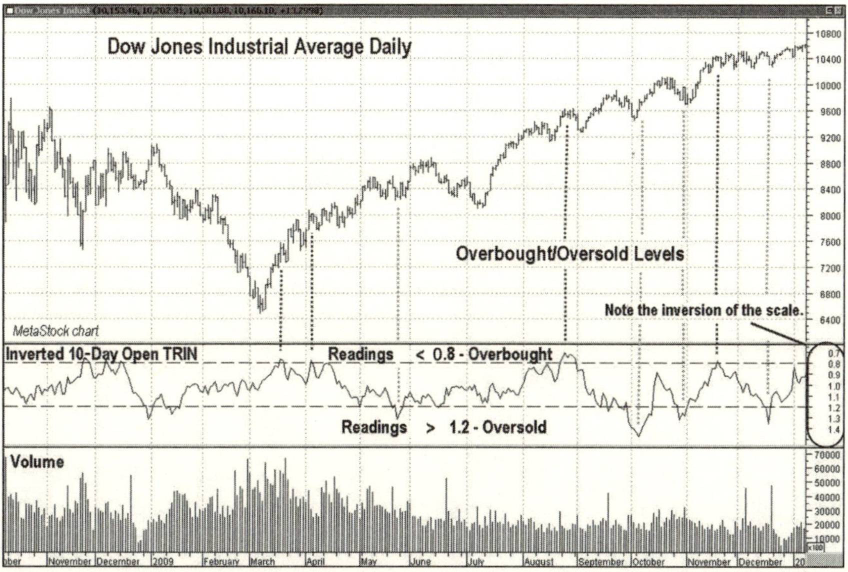

Chart 8.22 Inverted 10-day Open ARMS/TRIN, Overbought/Oversold Levels, DJIA Daily

Source: MetaStock

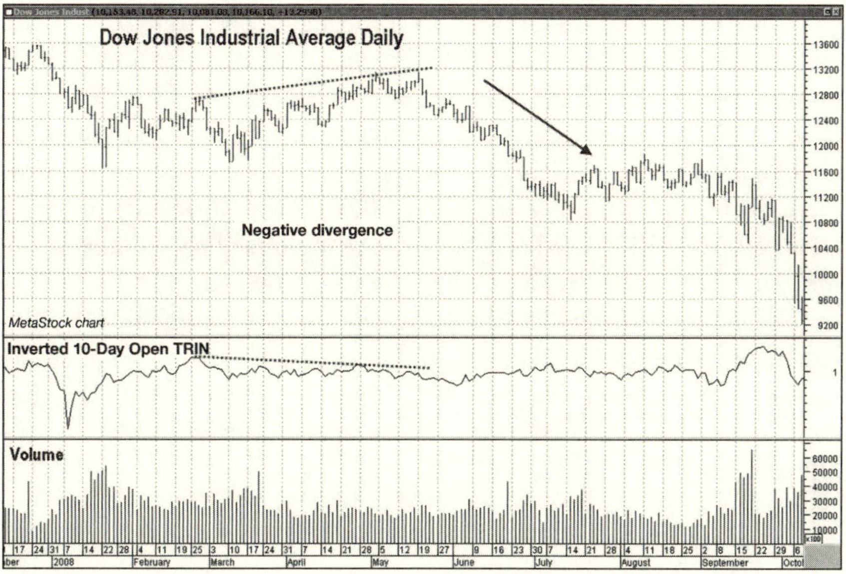

Chart 8.23 The 10-Day Open ARMS/TRIN, Negative Divergence, DJIA Daily

Source: MetaStock

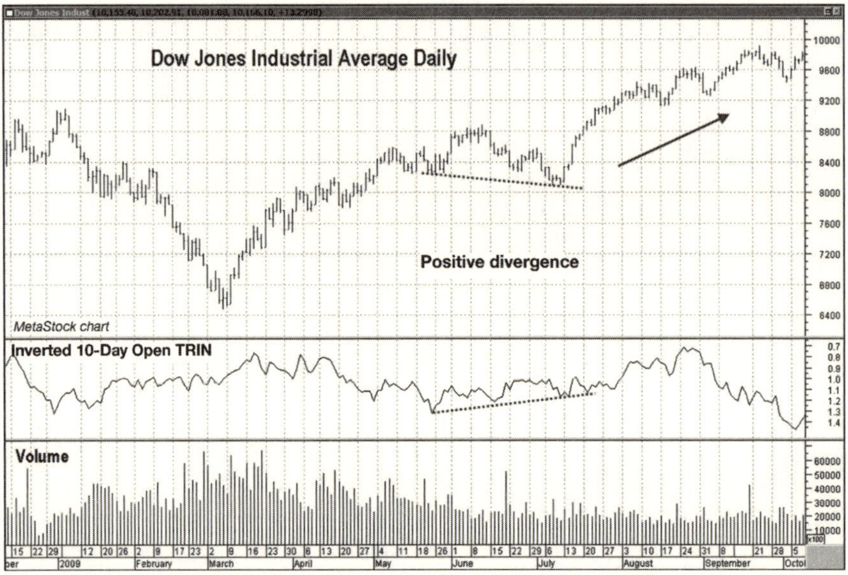

Chart 8.24 Inverted 10-Day Open ARMS/TRIN, Positive Divergence, DJIA Daily

Source: MetaStock

Trade Setup

The inverted 10-Day Open ARMS can be a great tool to look for trend continuation trades, as it shows divergences—that is, reduced selling pressure—during corrections in uptrends. This setup turns the previous chart (Chart 8.24) into a trend continuation trading opportunity. In Chart 8.25, the inverted 10-Day Open ARMS is plotted in the pane below price. Note that during the June–July 2009 price pullback, the inverted 10-Day Open ARMS made higher lows. Also notice how volume in the lower pane did not increase on the sell-off—a good sign that the selling wouldn't last. Making trades based solely on indicator divergences is risky, so a trade would not be executed until we received confirmation that the prevailing price trend was ready to continue. That confirmation would come in the form of a break over the resistance line drawn across the tops of the June–July pullback.

Trade Entry

Chart 8.26 zooms in on the April–October 2009 time frame to give a closer look at executing the trade. Recall in the setup that a trade would not be executed due solely to the positive divergence shown by the 10-Day

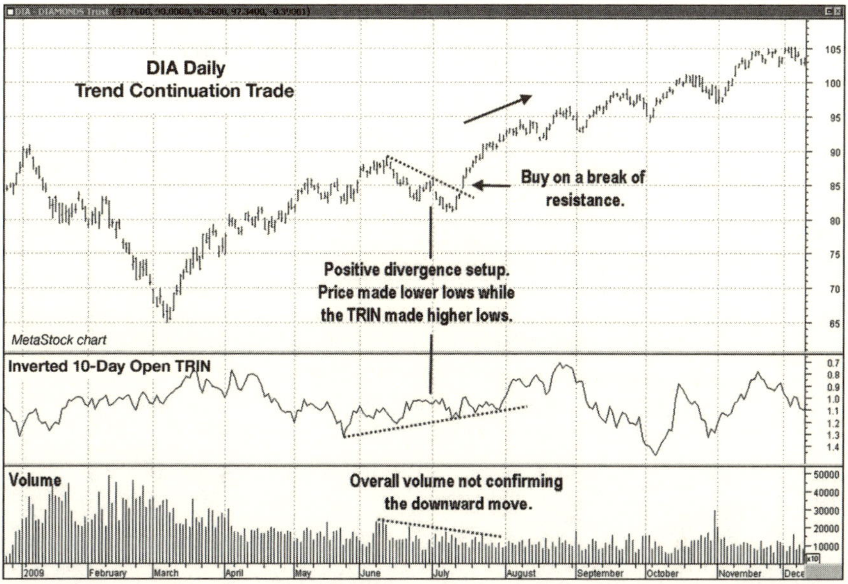

Chart 8.25 Trade Setup, Inverted 10-Day Open ARMS/TRIN, DJ Diamonds Trust ETF

Source: MetaStock

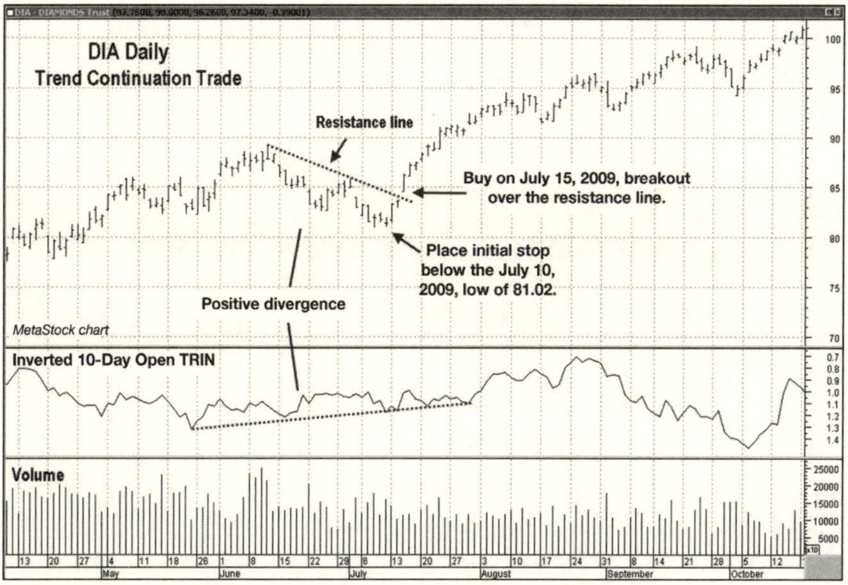

Chart 8.26 Trade Entry, Inverted 10-Day Open ARMS/TRIN, DJ Diamonds Trust ETF

Source: MetaStock

Open ARMS. A breakout over the resistance line of the pullback would be required. That breakout occurred on July 15, 2009, which was a signal to take a long position, as the correction against the trend was over. A protective stop could have been placed below the July 10 low of 81.02.

Trader Tips

The 10-Day Open ARMS is a great indicator to use for the following:

- Identifying short-term to intermediate-term overbought and oversold situations
- Recognizing short-term to intermediate-term trend divergences
- Pinpointing short-term to intermediate-term highs and lows

The 10-Day Open ARMS is just as versatile as the ARMS Index but adds a smoother appearance and a slightly longer-term time frame.

The 30-Day Open ARMS

The 30-Day Open ARMS is another variation of the ARMS indicator. It is used in the same way as the ARMS and the 10- Day Open ARMS, but the calculation smooths the indicator even further, making this version of ARMS better suited for longer-term analysis.

Formulation

The following is the formula for the 30-Day Open ARMS:

$$\frac{\text{Last 30 days' advances/Last 30 days' declines}}{\text{Last 30 days' advancing volume/Last 30 days' declining volume}}$$

The 30-Day Open ARMS gives a longer-term perspective on market lows, trend confirmation, and trend divergences. However, the 30-Day Open ARMS is not as accurate at pinpointing market bottoms as the shorter-term versions. Chart 8.27 shows how the 30-Day Open ARMS for the DJIA spikes in the vicinity of market lows, but not always coincidentally with the lows.

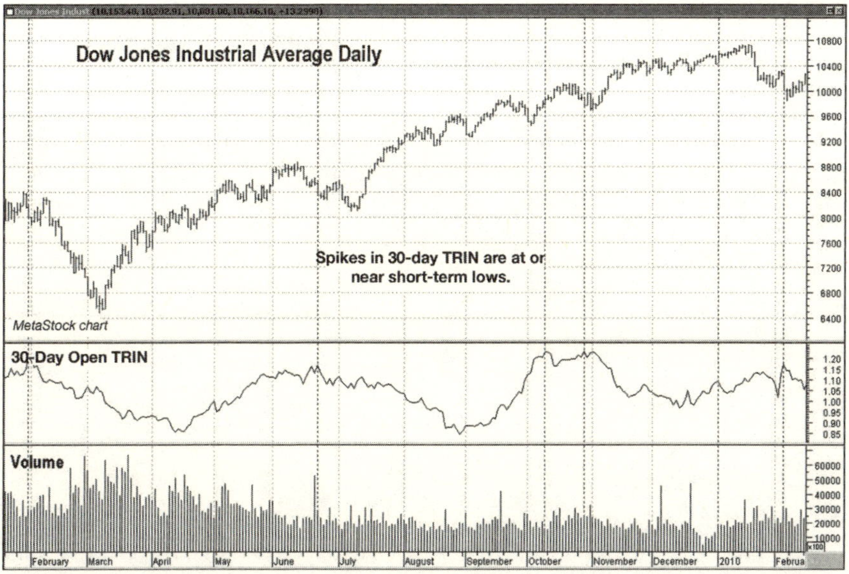

Chart 8.27 30-Day Open ARMS/TRIN, DJIA Daily

Source: MetaStock

Inverted 30-Day Open ARMS

Just as with other versions of ARMS, inversion of the price scale is common to allow the indicator to track with market prices. The smoother look of the 30-Day Open ARMS has advantages in catching long-term divergences that can show corrections or trend changes before they materialize.

In Chart 8.28, note how the 30-day Open ARMS actually started a downtrend before price topped in October 2007. The negative divergence (i.e., higher prices, lower indicator) gave traders an indication that a pullback was due. The downtrend that followed was very strong, as the indicator maintained its downtrend even during subsequent market rallies. Positive divergences (i.e., lower prices, higher indicator) can also give powerful signals. In Chart 8.29, note how positive divergences of the S&P 500 developed heading into the March 2009 low and also during the first major correction of that rally in June–July 2009.

Determining Overbought and Oversold Conditions

The 30-Day Open ARMS can also be used for overbought and oversold conditions. However, its long-term nature makes it less volatile, so it tends

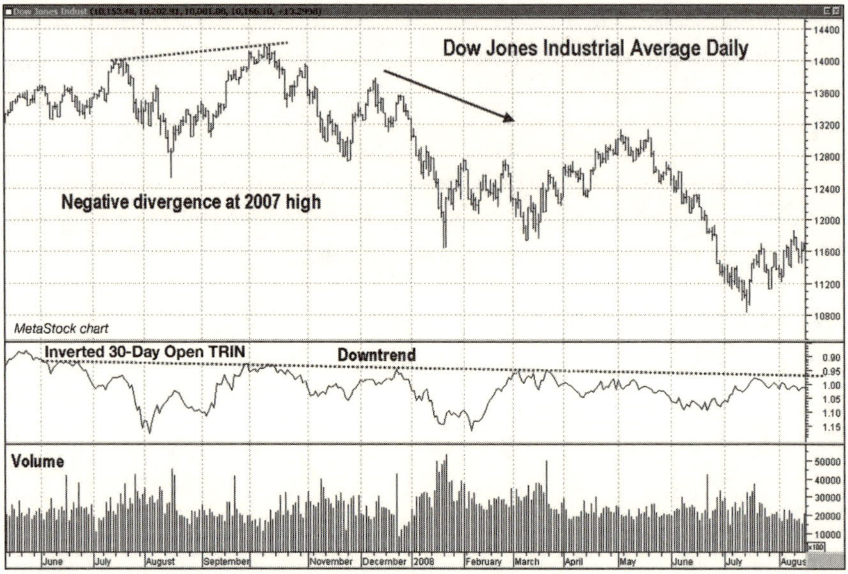

Chart 8.28 Negative Divergence and Downtrend, 30-Day Open ARMS/TRIN, DJIA Daily

Source: MetaStock

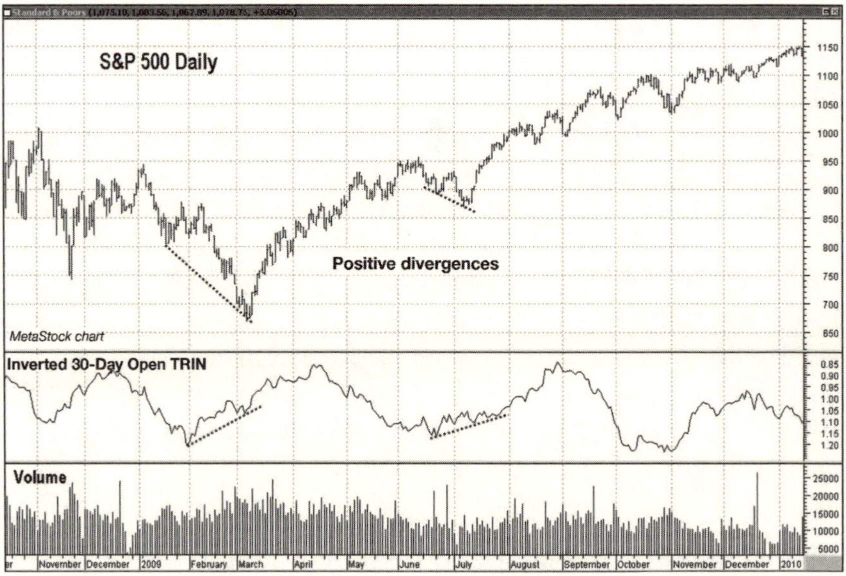

Chart 8.29 Positive Divergences, 30-Day Open ARMS/TRIN, S&P 500 Daily

Source: MetaStock

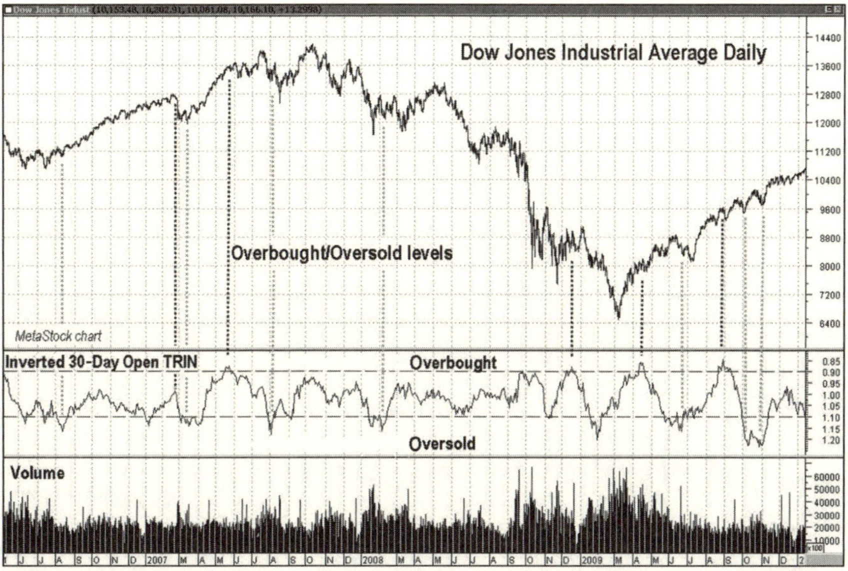

Chart 8.30 Overbought/Oversold, Inverted 30-Day Open ARMS/TRIN, DJIA Daily

Source: MetaStock

to move in a slightly narrower range. Shorter versions of the ARMS may be more timely for this type of application.

In Chart 8.30 of the DJIA, the overbought and oversold boundaries were moved closer together to 0.9 and 1.1, as the indicator does not travel below 0.8 or above 1.2 (i.e., the shorter ARMS boundaries) very often. Also note that overbought/oversold readings don't necessarily occur at optimal times in relation to price action.

Trade Setup

The 30-Day Inverted ARMS is a good tool to show divergences with price that can signal an imminent price reversal. This is especially true when the divergence forecasts a continuation of the larger-degree trend. In a downtrend, look for the Inverted 30-Day Open ARMS to show weakening buying pressure on corrective rallies. This can lead to profitable shorting opportunities.

Chart 8.31 for the DJ Diamonds Trust shows price in a downtrend since topping in October 2007 (top not shown). The corrective rally that unfolded from March to May 2008 was weak from a buying pressure

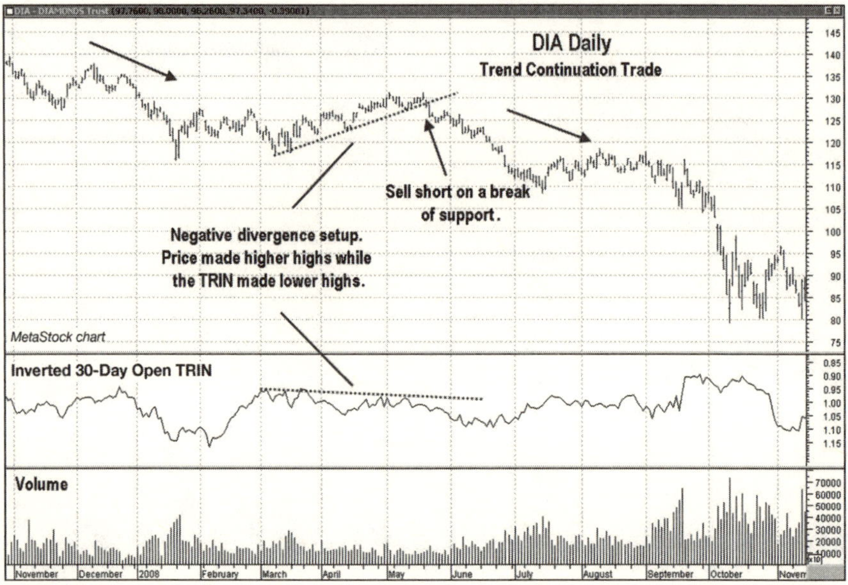

Chart 8.31 Trade Setup, Inverted 30-Day Open ARMS/TRIN, DJ Diamonds Trust ETF

Source: MetaStock

standpoint, as the 30-Day Open ARMS demonstrated. Note the negative divergence as the DJIA made a series of higher highs while the ARMS made a series of lower highs. When the lows of the corrective pattern were connected, a support line was drawn that would trigger a short sale when broken.

Trade Entry

Chart 8.32 for the DIA zooms in on the January to August 2008 time frame to give a closer look at executing the trade. Remember, it is very risky to trade divergences on their own without some form of price confirmation that the trend is indeed changing direction.

The price action provided that confirmation on May 20, 2008, as price broke down through the support line that had been in effect since March. An initial protective stop should have been placed over the May 19 reactionary high of 131.26. Price broke down from there, which would have made this a very successful trade. Also notice how volume (in the bottom pane) increased as price fell—a sure sign that sellers were in control.

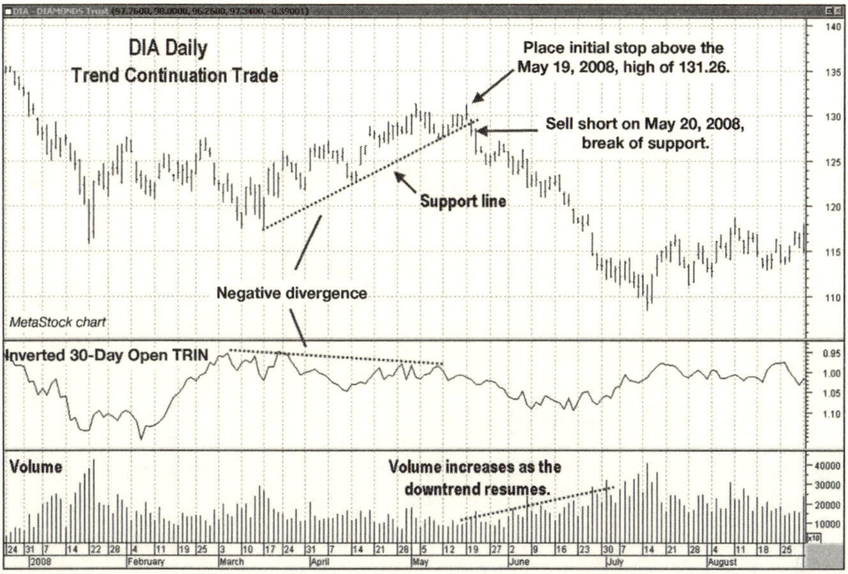

Chart 8.32 Trade Entry, Inverted 30-Day Open ARMS/TRIN, DJ Diamonds Trust ETF

Source: MetaStock

Trader Tips

The 30-Day Open ARMS is a long-range version of the ARMS designed to give an intermediate- to long-term perspective. The 30-Day Open ARMS is useful for the following:

- Spotting intermediate- to long-term trend divergences
- Confirming intermediate- to long- term trends
- Giving long-term overbought/oversold signals in the general vicinity of reversals

The 30-Day Open ARMS is less sensitive than its 10-day counterpart, making it less useful for timing market swings in shorter time frames.

The 5-Day Warning

Note that while using the ARMS index is best known for measuring fear in the market and pinpointing bottoms, using it to identify tops is much more challenging. Complacency can be prevalent for long periods in uptrends, which can camouflage subtle messages that the ARMS Index may be sending. The astute market technician Terry Laundry applies the ARMS Index to identify impending market tops in what he calls his *5-day warning*. Laundry's premise is that when the ARMS Index posts readings below 1 (overbought) in an uptrend for five consecutive days, with the 5-day average ARMS reading falling to or below 0.80, this very overbought condition constitutes an early warning that a reversal in trend is imminent. The 5-day warning does not indicate the exact timing of the reversal. It is rather a caution signal alerting traders that it is time to lighten up on long positions.

Cumulative Volume Index

The Cumulative Volume Index (CVI) gauges buying and selling pressure in the entire stock market by subtracting the combined volume of all declining issues from the combined volume of all advancing issues and adding this to the previous value of the indicator.

Formulation

The following is the formula for the CVI:

$$\text{CVI} = \text{yesterday's CVI} + (\text{advancing volume} - \text{declining volume})$$

Since CVI is a cumulative indicator, the actual value itself is less relevant than the slope and direction of the time series of calculations and the resulting trendline. The CVI is a great tool to either confirm trends or show divergences with price action.

Trend Confirmation

CVI is an important tool for the confirmation of trends. The CVI will show if there are sufficient inflows into the market to support an uptrend, or if there are sufficient outflows to continue a downtrend. A confirmed uptrend is one in which both the index and the CVI make higher highs and higher lows. A confirmed downtrend is one in which both the index and the CVI make lower highs and lower lows.

The NYSE Composite Index in Chart 8.33 (from June 2006 through July 2007) shows uptrend confirmation from the CVI. Notice how both the index price and the CVI each made higher highs and higher lows.

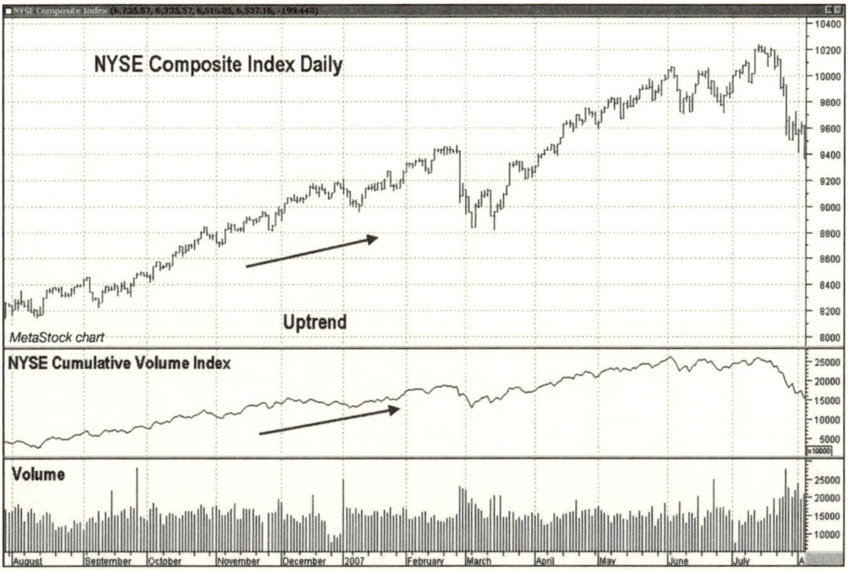

Chart 8.33 Cumulative Volume Index, Uptrend Confirmation, NYSE Composite Daily

Source: MetaStock

Next is a look at the chart of the NYSE Composite Index from August 2007 through September 2008 (see Chart 8.34). The CVI provided confirmation that the market was in an established downtrend. Note the lower highs and lower lows posted by both the price of the index and the indicator.

Divergences

While the CVI is a great indicator for trend confirmation, it can also alert the trader when a correction or all-out trend change is imminent. Divergences occur when price continues in its original direction while the CVI diverges, or goes in the opposite direction. Divergences come in two types, positive or negative. Positive divergences (i.e., lower index prices with a rising CVI) or negative divergences (i.e., higher index prices with a falling CVI) can give clues as to whether or not control is changing from buyers to sellers, or vice versa.

Chart 8.35 shows a positive divergence at the July 2009 low in the NYSE Composite Index. While the selling at that time was the most intense since the March 2009 low, the CVI was showing that the selling pressure was not very strong and that the uptrend was ready to resume.

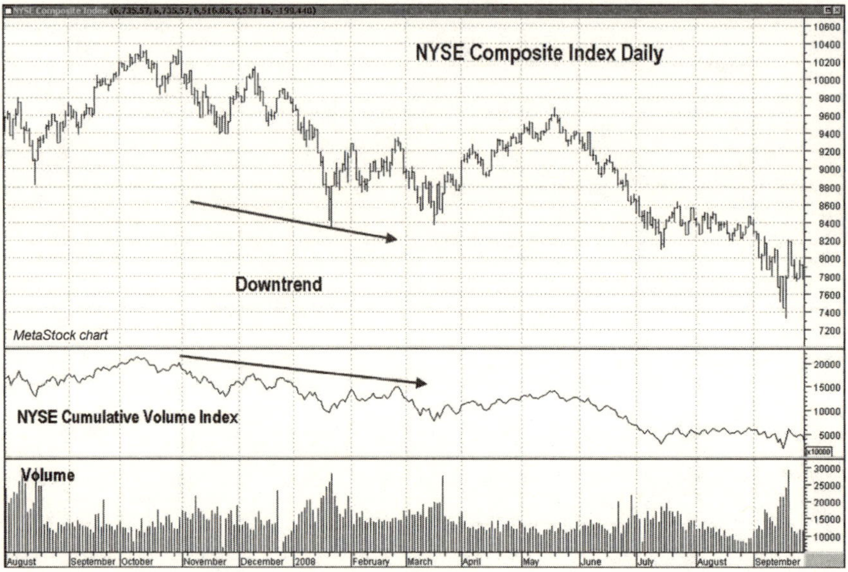

Chart 8.34 Cumulative Volume Index, Downtrend Confirmation, NYSE Composite Daily

Source: MetaStock

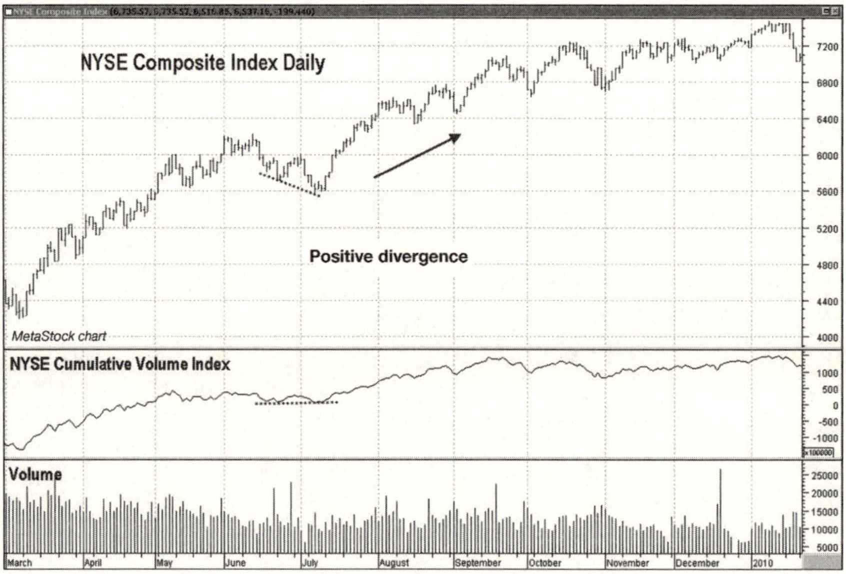

Chart 8.35 Cumulative Volume Index, Positive Divergence, NYSE Composite Index Daily

Source: MetaStock

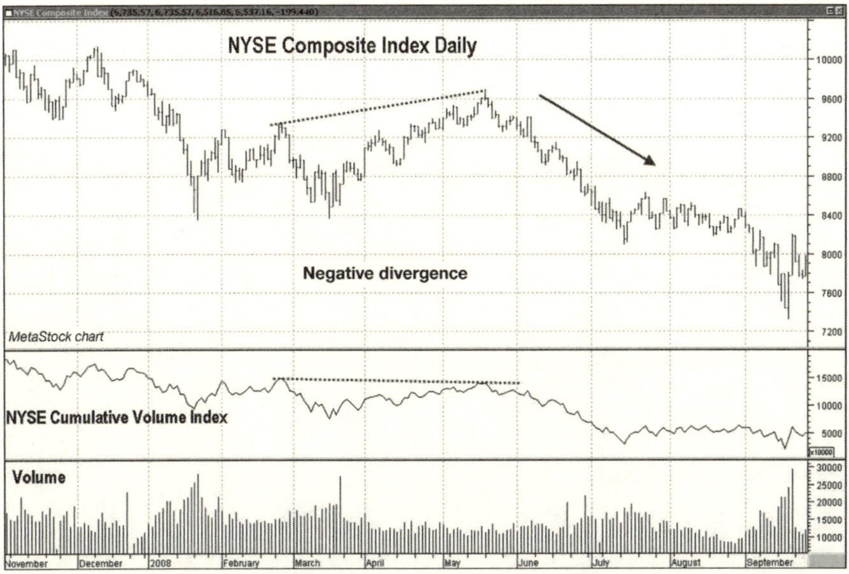

Chart 8.36 Cumulative Volume Index, Negative Divergence, NYSE Composite Index Daily

Source: MetaStock

Negative divergences are good warning signs that at the very least a correction is imminent, which gives traders time to get more defensive or to cash out winners. In Chart 8.36 for the NYSE Composite, notice how the index price made a higher high while the CVI made a lower high. This gave a clue that a resumption of the downtrend was just around the corner.

Pairing the CVI with a Moving Average

Given the fact that the CVI tends to trend with prices, it is well suited for use with a moving average. In Chart 8.37 of the NYSE Composite Index, note how crossovers of its 50-day simple moving average can be used to keep a trader on the right side of the market and to allow more aggressive traders to spot countertrend moves. By experimenting with different moving average lengths, you can use the 50-day moving average as a starting point from which to adjust to a preferred trading time frame.

Trade Setup

Like many other broad market indicators, the CVI shows when buying or selling pressure is weakening against the prevailing trend. The trade example in Chart 8.38 shows how the CVI could have been used to short the

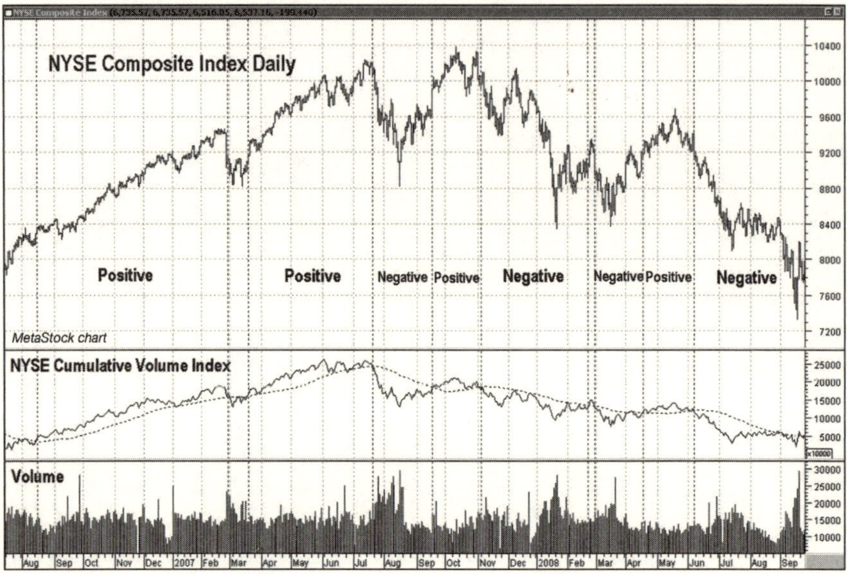

Chart 8.37 CVI with 50-Day Moving Average Crossovers, NYSE Composite Daily Index

Source: MetaStock

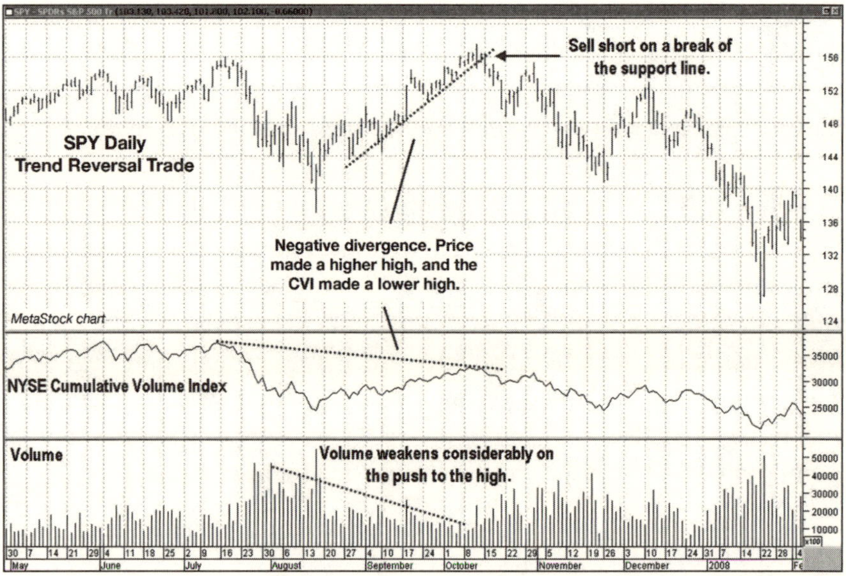

Chart 8.38 CVI and Volume Trade Setup, S&P 500 Trust ETF

Source: MetaStock

market against the October 2007 top. Chart 8.38 for the S&P 500 Trust ETF ("SPDR," or SPY) has the CVI plotted in the middle pane, and regular volume is plotted in the bottom pane. On the final push to the October 2007 market top, volume was noticeably weak, as demonstrated by the negative divergence in the CVI versus price, and also by the obvious decline in volume as price moved higher. Divergence alone is no reason to short the market here, as some sort of price confirmation that a trend change is occurring is necessary. By connecting the price lows on the final weak-volume push to the high, a support line is created. A violation of that line would be the trigger to enter a short trade.

Trade Entry

The SPY example in Chart 8.39 zooms in on the July–December 2007 time frame to give a closer look at executing the trade. Since price had been in an uptrend, it is very important to wait for some form of price confirmation before entering a trend reversal trade. The price action gave that confirmation when it violated the support line on October 15, 2007. That line was drawn by connecting the lows in the low-volume rally from mid-August through mid-October. An initial protective stop should have

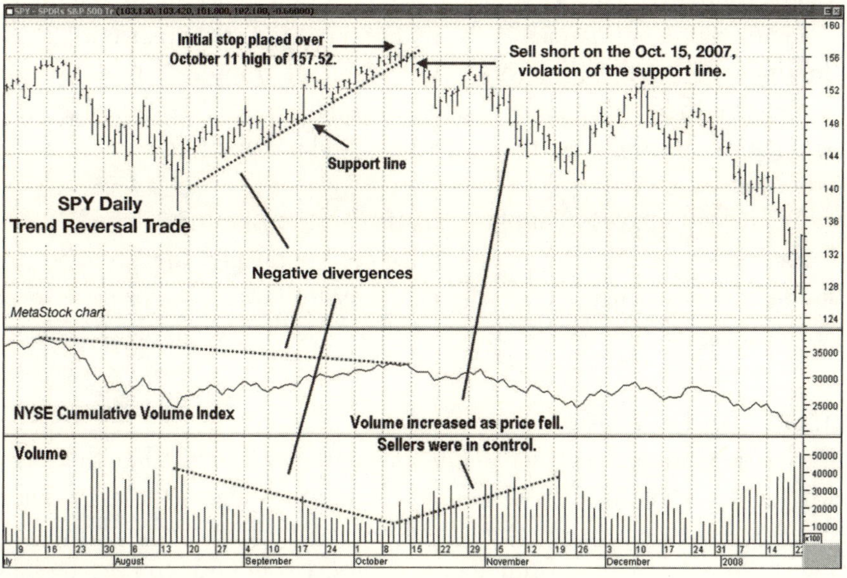

Chart 8.39 CVI and Volume Trade Entry, S&P 500 Trust ETF

Source: MetaStock

been placed over the October 11 high of 157.52. This methodology allowed a short trade entry just off a major market top. Notice how volume (in the bottom pane) increased as price fell—a sure sign that the uptrend was reversing.

Trader Tips

The CVI is a great tool for doing the following:

- Confirming market trends
- Spotting divergences that warn of corrections or full trend changes
- Pairing with moving averages to measure the strength and direction of the trend

One CVI drawback is that it tends to lag the broader market at turning points, which causes less timely entries and exits. Overall, however, the CVI as an indicator should be part of every technician's basic tool set.

Exchange Volume

Exchange Volume is simply the total number of shares traded in a day at a stock exchange. This information can be found in any reputable financial publication or financial Web site. For our purposes here, we will limit our discussion to the New York Stock Exchange volume and the Nasdaq Composite Index volume. Exchange Volume can be a useful tool to confirm trends, spot short-term turning points, and reveal divergences between price and volume.

Chart 8.40 shows a plot of the Nasdaq Composite Index with Nasdaq Exchange Volume. Exchange Volume is commonly plotted with its 50-day simple moving average. If the volume bar extends over the moving average line, that day's volume is above average. If it closes below, it is below average.

Trend Confirmation

Exchange Volume is a great tool for confirming price trends. In either case, whether the trend is up or down, expanding volume is necessary to keep trends going as buyers or sellers assume control. In an uptrend, expanding volume is proof that sufficient support exists to push equities higher. Chart 8.41 shows the Nasdaq Composite Index with above-average spikes in volume on up moves. This is bullish behavior.

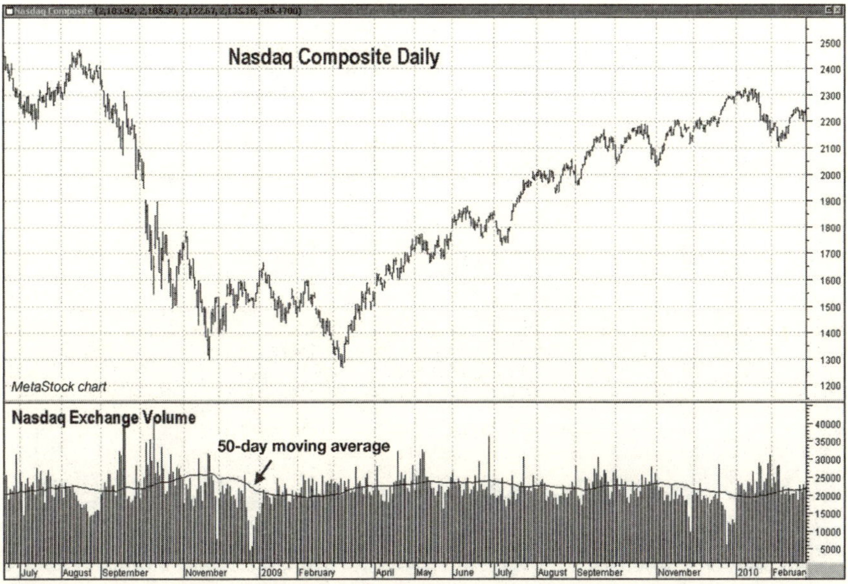

Chart 8.40 Nasdaq Exchange Volume with 50-Day Moving Average

Source: MetaStock

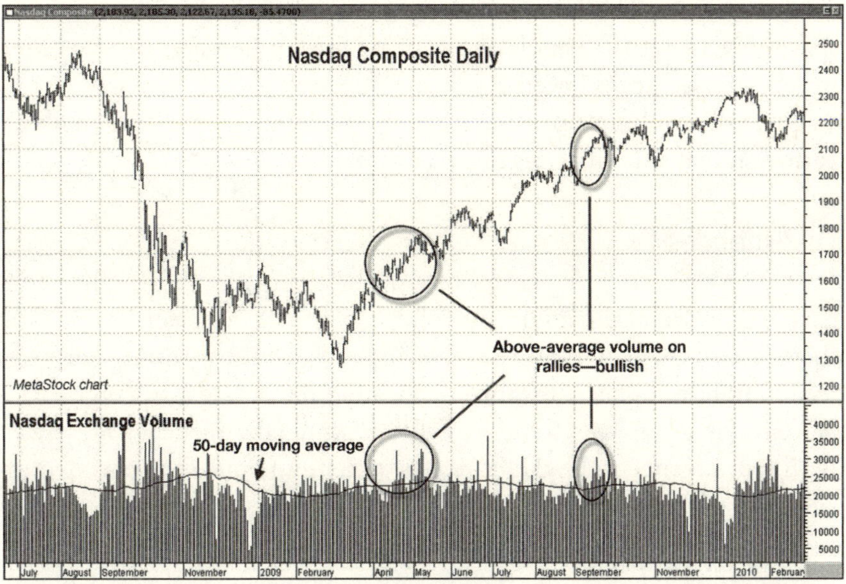

Chart 8.41 Exchange Volume, Bullish Confirmation, Nasdaq Composite Daily

Source: MetaStock

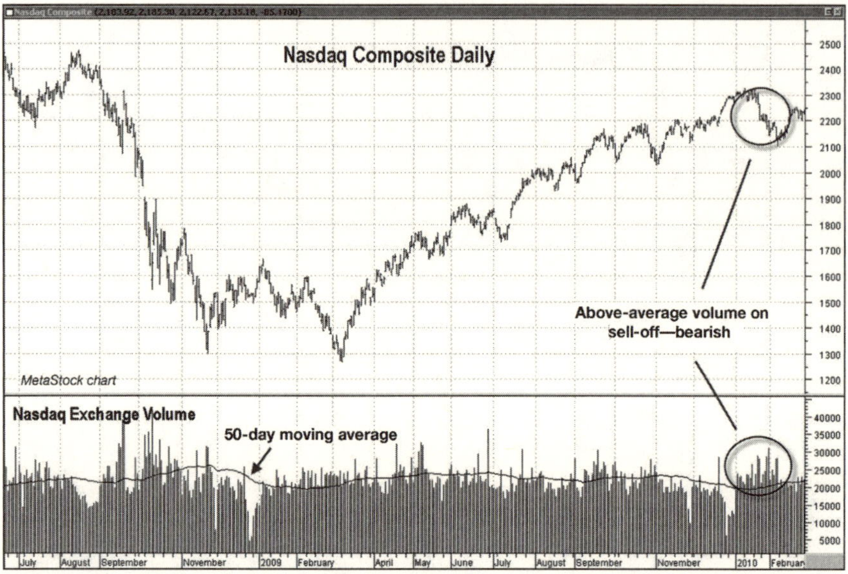

Chart 8.42 Exchange Volume, Bearish Pattern, Nasdaq Composite Daily

Source: MetaStock

Now look at the same chart for an example of a bearish exchange volume pattern. Note on the far right side of Chart 8.42 how volume spiked in early 2010. That is a bearish sign that sellers are overwhelming buyers as price heads lower.

Expanding volume on sell-offs following a long uptrend is normally an early sign that a trend change is developing.

Divergences

Exchange Volume is also useful in showing divergences when price continues in its trend direction but volume contracts to lower levels. That shows a weakening of support for the current trend. These divergences can lead to minor pullbacks, or they can lead to much larger trend changes. Never trade against the trend based on a simple divergence. Always wait for the divergence to be confirmed by a trendline break, a moving average line violation, or an additional indicator.

In Chart 8.43, notice the sharp drop in volume of the Nasdaq Composite Index heading into the March 2009 low (as compared to volume in the fall of 2008), followed by a push higher in volume in the period following the low. This showed a renewed interest on the part of buyers, which was the fuel necessary to push the market higher.

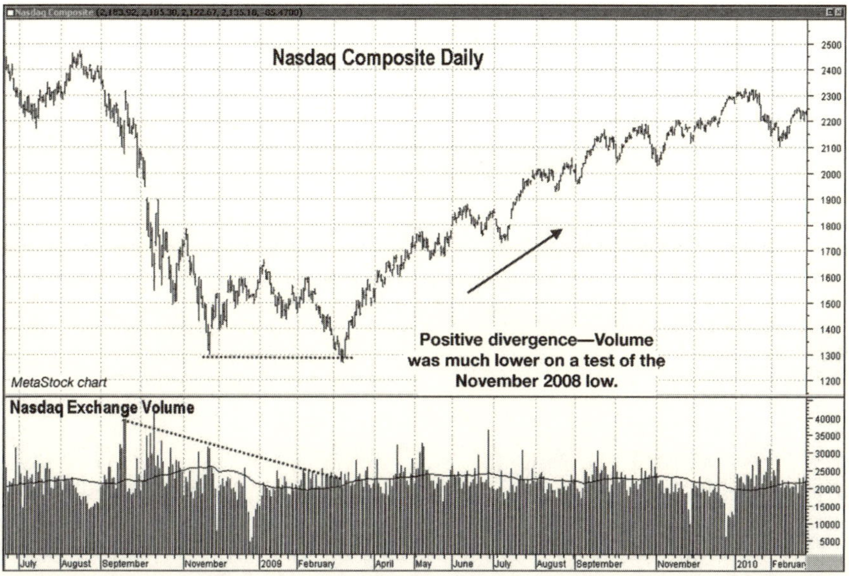

Chart 8.43 Exchange Volume, Positive Divergence at the March 2009 Low, Nasdaq Composite Daily

Source: MetaStock

Chart 8.44 shows a short-term negative divergence of the NYSE Composite Index, which led to a correction. Notice how as price pushed higher in May and June of 2009 volume contracted, unable to push prices higher in the near term. The index then corrected over the next four weeks before resuming the uptrend in July.

Exchange Volume and Short-Term Lows

Exchange Volume is also a tool used by aggressive traders to spot short-term lows in downtrends. Chart 8.45 of the NYSE Composite from June 2007 through February 2009 identifies volume spikes at short-term lows, which become short-term reversal points. These lows may hold for only a day or two, or they may last for weeks. The point here is that during downtrends, selling comes in waves. As each wave crests (i.e., the volume spikes), there is a chance for profits to be made on price reversals. Again, this is a methodology recommended for aggressive traders.

Note that this strategy is not used in uptrends because volume usually contracts at lows before a fresh wave of buying pushes the index higher.

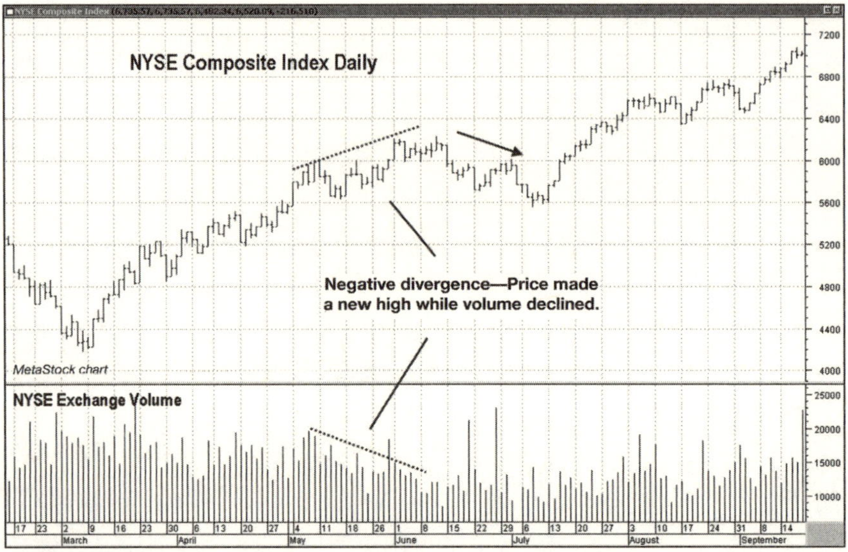

Chart 8.44 Exchange Volume, Negative Divergence, NYSE Composite Daily

Source: MetaStock

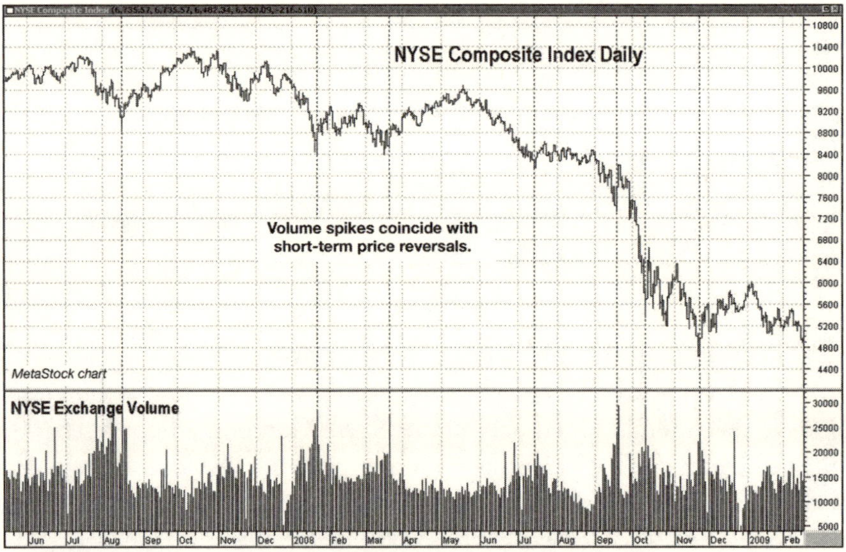

Chart 8.45 Volume Spikes, Short-Term Reversal Points, NYSE Composite Index Daily

Source: MetaStock

Trade Setup

While Exchange Volume is not necessarily used for trade setups and entries, it can be utilized in certain situations to alert a trader when a tradable

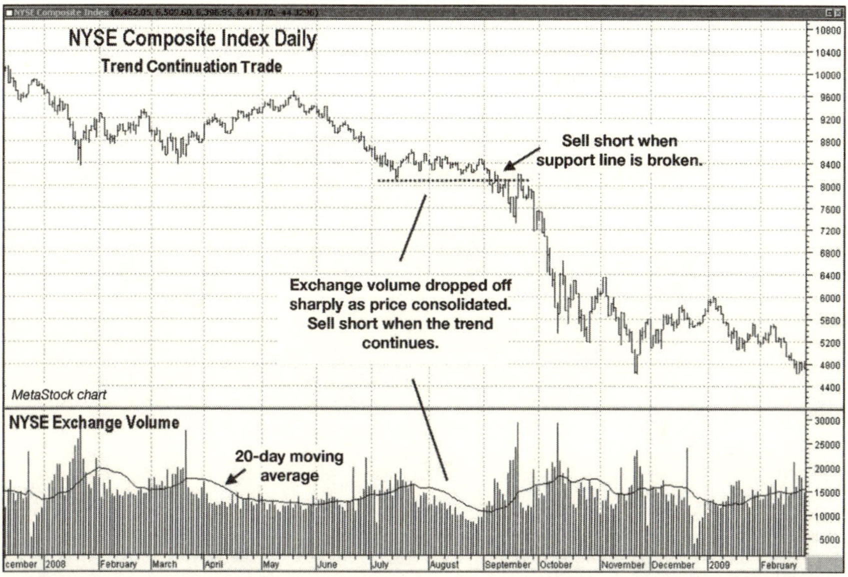

Chart 8.46 NYSE Exchange Volume, Trend Continuation Setup, NYSE Composite Daily

Source: MetaStock

situation is developing. Chart 8.46 shows the NYSE Composite Index with its daily exchange volume. When executing this trade, an index surrogate such as SPY or DIA (or inverse ETFs for short trades such as DOG, the Inverse Dow ETF, or SH, the inverse S&P 500 ETF) may be used.

The period to focus on in the example is the sideways consolidation pattern that formed in July and August 2008. Notice how volume dropped sharply as the consolidation continued. Up to that point, the trend had been down since the NYSE Composite topped in October 2007, so odds favored a continuation of the downtrend. This particular pattern was a great trade setup because of the flat support line that developed during the period. A violation of that line would be a signal that sellers were once again ready to assume control of the market and drive it lower.

Trade Entry

This trade could have been tracked and managed using NYSE Composite Index price levels. A breach of an important level (such as a stop) on the NYSE Composite Index would force liquidation of a trader's preferred ETF, such as the SPY, DIA, SH, or DOG. Notice in Chart 8.46 that on September 4, 2008, price closed below the support line, triggering a

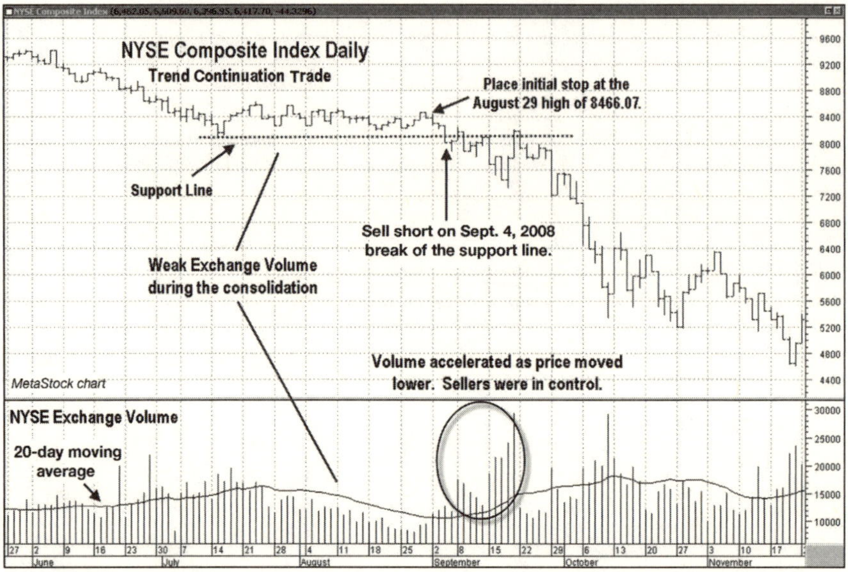

Chart 8.47 NYSE Exchange Volume, Trend Confirmation Trade Entry, NYSE Composite Index Daily

Source: MetaStock

short entry. The initial protective stop should have been placed over the August 29 high price of 8466.07.

Confirmation of trend continuation was given by the sharp increase in volume once the support level was breached on and after September 4, as shown in Chart 8.47. That showed that market participants were heading for the exits in a big way, which preceded a very steep drop in price. The trade could have been managed either by sliding the stop lower via a trendline or by placing the stop just above recent highs as price moved lower. That is a great example of volume reflecting trader sentiment, which alerted traders to a probable trend continuation.

Trader Tips

Exchange Volume is a big-picture tool useful for quick assessments of market direction and trend. It can be used for the following:

- Confirming price trends
- Spotting divergences against the trend
- Locating short-term turning points in downtrends for the most aggressive traders

The 5-Day Up/Down Volume Oscillator

The 5-Day Up/Down Volume Oscillator measures the internal strength or weakness of market trends by calculating a short-term oscillator based on daily advancing/declining exchange volume figures.

Formulation

The 5-Day Up/Down Volume Oscillator is formulated as follows:

Sum of last 5 days' advancing volume – sum of last 5 days' declining volume

This trading tool is plotted as a centered oscillator, with crosses of the zero line giving either positive (cross up) or negative (cross down) signals. A rallying market should see up volume exceed down volume, and a falling market should show down volume exceeding up volume.

When price action and the indicator are in sync, market internals confirm price action; however, if price is moving in one direction but the 5-Day Up/Down Volume Oscillator is diverging, market internals show that either a trend correction or a trend reversal is likely to occur. This is a short-term oscillator and is not recommended for longer-term trading decisions. Chart 8.48 shows the plot of the 5-Day Up/Down

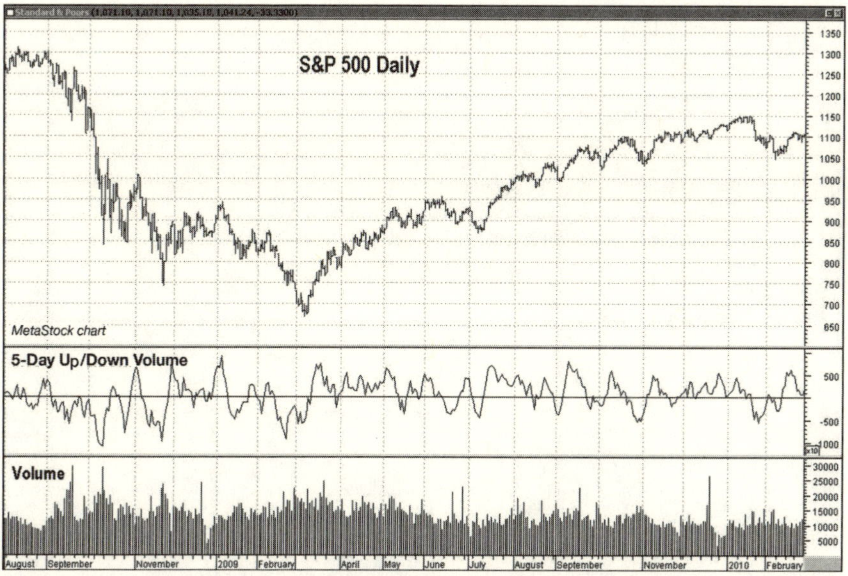

Chart 8.48 The 5-Day Up/Down Volume Oscillator, S&P 500 Daily

Source: MetaStock

Volume Oscillator for the S&P 500. The movement of the oscillator back and forth across the zero line shows changes, albeit short term, in market sentiment. Consecutive periods above or below the line—and the strength and direction of those periods (as will be shown next)—reflect somewhat longer-term sentiment changes.

Divergences

Divergences occur when price is moving higher, but the indicator is moving lower (i.e., negative divergence) or when price is moving lower and the indicator is moving higher (i.e., positive divergence). These divergences alert the trader that a potential correction against the trend is ready to unfold. Chart 8.49 shows a negative divergence in the S&P 500 between price and the 5-Day Up/Down Volume Oscillator from March through May 2008, which preceded a sell-off in the index.

Because of the short-term nature of the 5-Day Up/Down Volume Oscillator, it can also be used to spot short-term trading opportunities, such as the negative divergences that developed in the S&P 500 (Chart 8.50) over the August–October 2009 period. Note that these were countertrend trades, as the trend was higher during that time. Positive divergences can

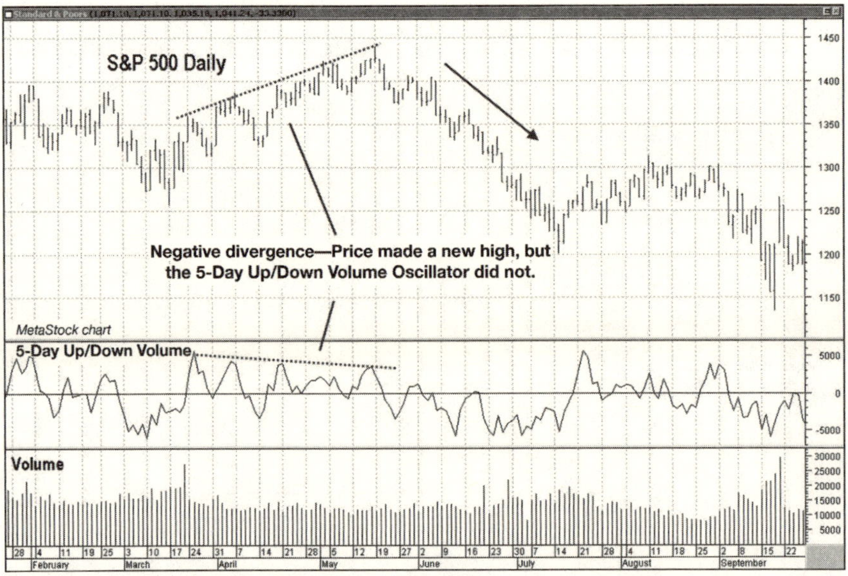

Chart 8.49 The 5-Day Up/Down Volume Oscillator, Negative Divergence, S&P 500 Daily

Source: MetaStock

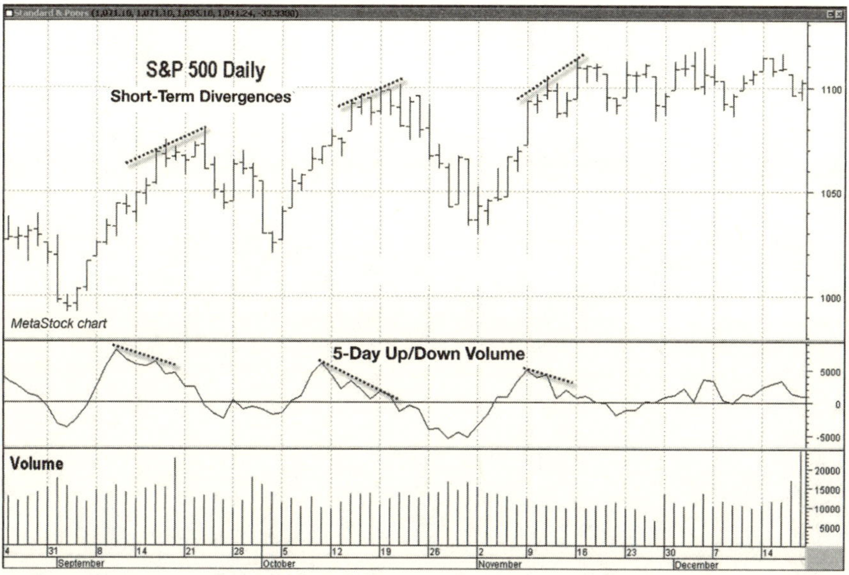

Chart 8.50 The 5-Day Up/Down Volume Oscillator, Short-Term Negative Divergences, S&P 500 Daily

Source: MetaStock

create great buying opportunities as well. A positive divergence occurs when price is making lower lows, but the indicator is making higher lows.

Zero-Line Crossovers

Oscillators such as the 5-Day Up/Down Volume Oscillator generate buy and sell signals by crossovers of the zero line. When the indicator crosses from below to above the zero line, a buy signal is generated. When the indicator crosses from above the zero line to below, a sell signal is generated. A word of caution: Signals in this oscillator should be taken only in the direction of the larger-degree trend. For example, sell signals may be false in an uptrend, and buy signals may be false in a downtrend. Chart 8.51 for the S&P 500 shows zero-line cross-up buys in an uptrend. Note that the crossovers come right after pullback lows.

Chart 8.52 of the S&P 500 shows zero-line crossover sell signals in a downtrend. Most of these signals preceded a continuation of the downtrend, which resulted in profitable shorting opportunities. Chart 8.52 also shows the difference in trader psychology in downtrends in the form of increased volatility as opposed to the relatively tame volatility in the uptrend shown in Chart 8.51. Remember: Zero-line crossover signals

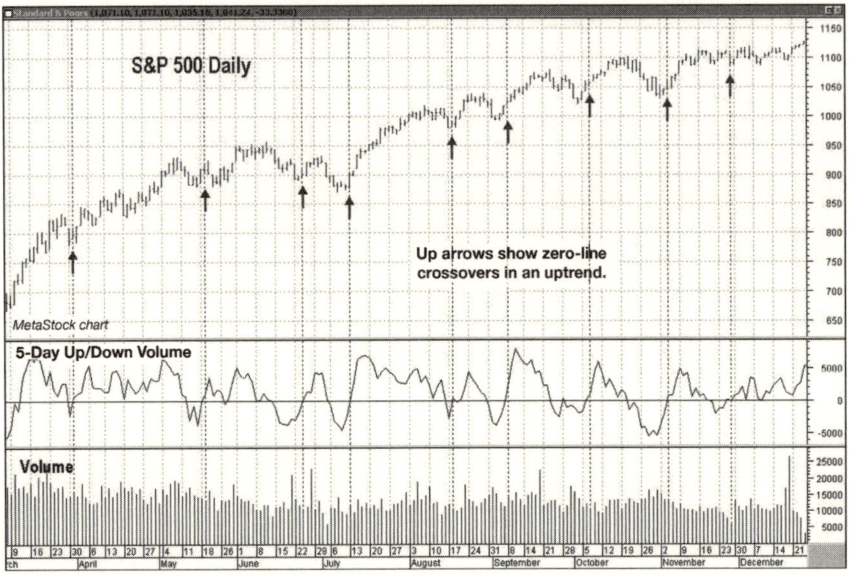

Chart 8.51 The 5-Day Up/Down Volume Oscillator, Zero-Line Crossovers in an Uptrend, S&P 500 Daily

Source: MetaStock

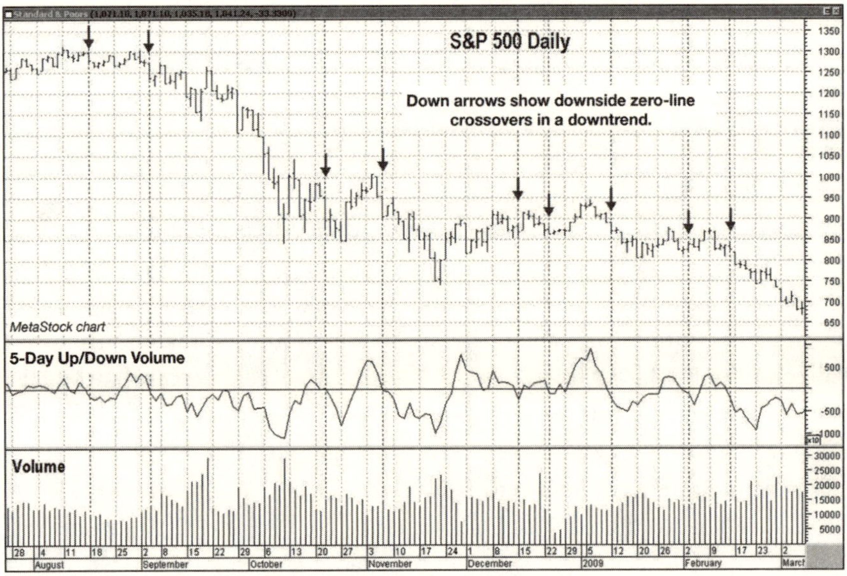

Chart 8.52 The 5-Day Up/Down Volume Oscillator, Zero-Line Crossovers in a Downtrend, S&P 500 Daily

Source: MetaStock

using the 5-Day Up/Down Volume Oscillator are best used in the direction of the larger-degree trend.

Trade Setup

Since the 5-Day Up/Down Volume Oscillator is best used in the direction of the larger-degree trend, we will look for a trade setup that develops during a countertrend move. In this example, we will exploit the weak countertrend rally that developed in the March–May 2008 period following the October 2007 market top.

Since the 5-Day Up/Down Volume Oscillator is a broad market indicator, a broad market index ETF (the S&P 500 Trust ETF SPDR, or SPY) will be used for trading purposes. In Chart 8.53 for SPY, notice how a downtrend started following the October 2007 market top. That was followed by a weak countertrend rally in March 2008 to May 2008. The weakness of the rally is shown by the negative divergence in the 5-Day Up/Down Volume Oscillator as well as the low volume level during the push higher.

A short trade should be entered when the support line connecting the March-to-May lows is broken and the 5-Day Up/Down Volume Oscillator crosses below zero, as shown in Chart 8.53.

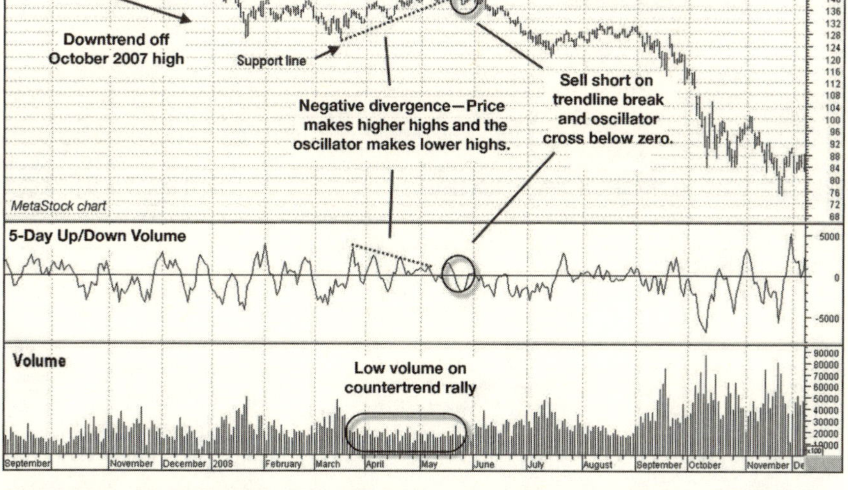

Chart 8.53 The 5-Day Up/Down Volume Oscillator, Trend Continuation Trade Setup, S&P 500 Trust SPDR ETF

Source: MetaStock

Trade Entry

Next let's zoom in on the time period in which a short or inverse trading position could be entered. Note in Chart 8.54 how price broke the upward-sloping support line on May 21, 2008, as the 5-Day Up/Down Volume Oscillator crossed down through the zero line. This was the signal to enter a short position as the downtrend resumed. The initial stop would have been placed over the May 19 high of $144.30. Volume also played an important role in this trade, as its increase confirmed the resumption of the downtrend.

Trader Tips

The 5-Day Up/Down Volume Oscillator is a great tool for doing the following:

- Showing the relationship between up and down volume
- Showing short- to intermediate-term trend divergences
- Providing indications of near-term market strength or weakness in the direction of the trend

One drawback of this oscillator is that it is short term in nature; its volatility can give whipsaw trading signals.

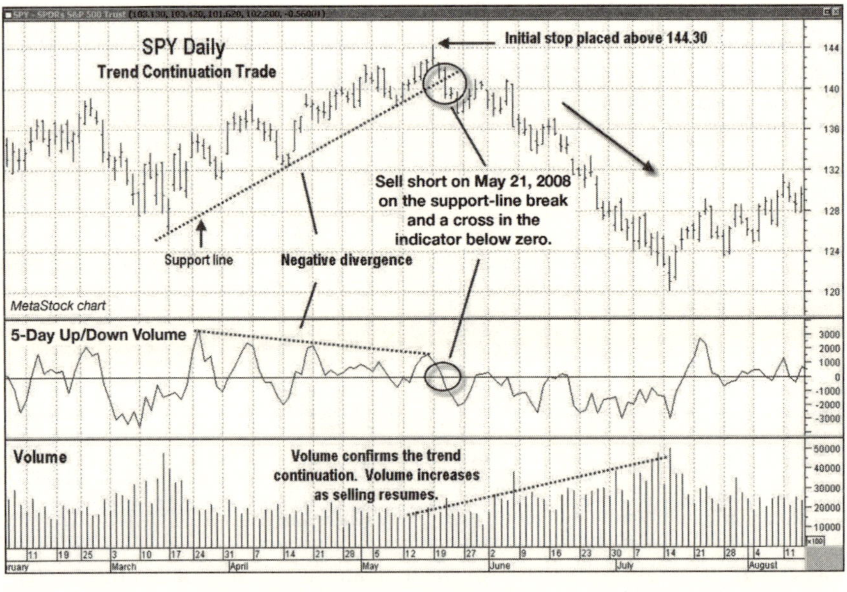

Chart 8.54 The 5-Day Up/Down Volume Oscillator, Trend Continuation Trade Entry, S&P 500 Trust SPDR ETF

Source: MetaStock

Index Volume

Index Volume is similar to Exchange Volume in that each reports the total volume of a collection of stocks. As the name implies, Index Volume is the cumulative volume of stocks that make up an index, such as the S&P 500, the Dow Jones Industrial Average, and the Nasdaq 100. In many cases, the major indexes are used as proxies for the broader market, which makes analysis of their volume patterns very important. Analysis of Index Volume is the same as analysis of Exchange Volume, as trend confirmations and trend divergences occur in the same manner.

Trend Confirmation

Rising volume confirms the trend, whether that trend is up or down. It shows conviction on the part of buyers (uptrend) or sellers (downtrend) and increases the odds of a continuation of the trend being analyzed. In Chart 8.55 for the S&P 500, volume accelerated on each push lower in the downtrend from September 2007 through November 2008. This behavior should have prompted traders to assume a more defensive posture. Chart 8.56 shows the S&P 500 in an uptrend from March 2009 through January 2010. Each time the uptrend resumed following pullbacks or corrections, note how volume accelerated, providing the necessary fuel to push prices higher.

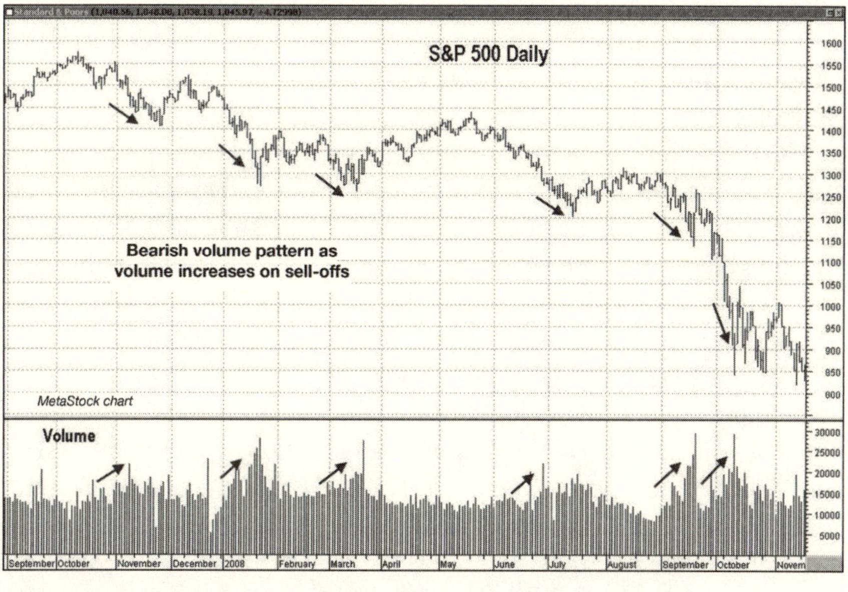

Chart 8.55 Index Volume, Bearish Volume Pattern, S&P 500 Daily

Source: MetaStock

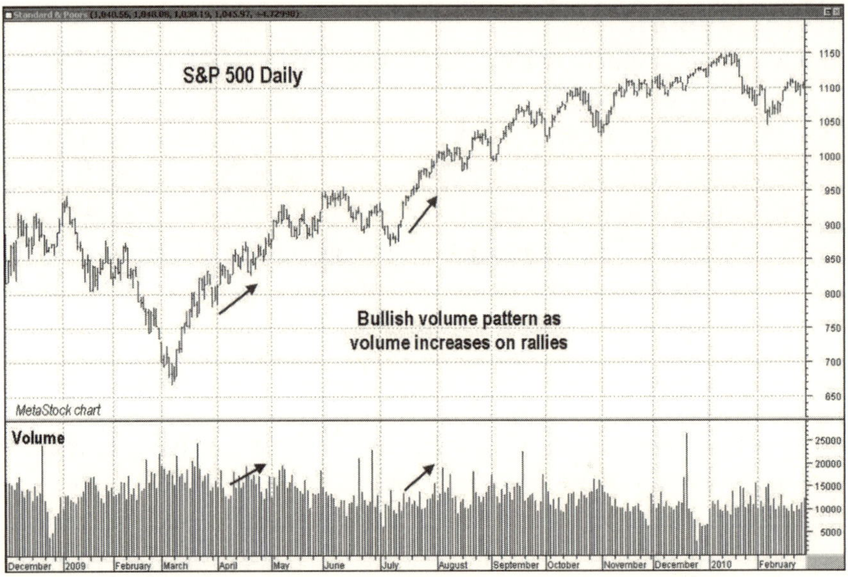

Chart 8.56 Index Volume, Bullish Volume Pattern, S&P 500 Daily

Source: MetaStock

Divergences

Index Volume also shows trend divergences in the index being analyzed. When price moves in either direction but volume drops during that time, that is a *non*confirmation of that period's movement. Nonconfirmation can range from a period of minutes (for intraday traders) to a period of weeks.

Chart 8.57 for the Nasdaq 100 shows a positive divergence. Notice the huge volume spikes as price traded into the November 2008 low. Next, look at volume in March 2009 as it tested the November low. Volume was much lighter on the test, which was evidence of much lighter selling pressure. That was a strong indication that the November low would hold, which ultimately led to one of the best buying opportunities of the decade.

Index Volume can also show negative divergences that occur when price moves higher but volume decreases. The S&P 500 in Chart 8.58 shows a weak rally period in July and August 2008, where prices moved higher but volume was very anemic. This weak rally was a huge clue that a resumption of the downtrend was imminent. September 2008 was the beginning of the fall meltdown, in which the S&P 500 lost 43 percent of its value over the next 13 weeks.

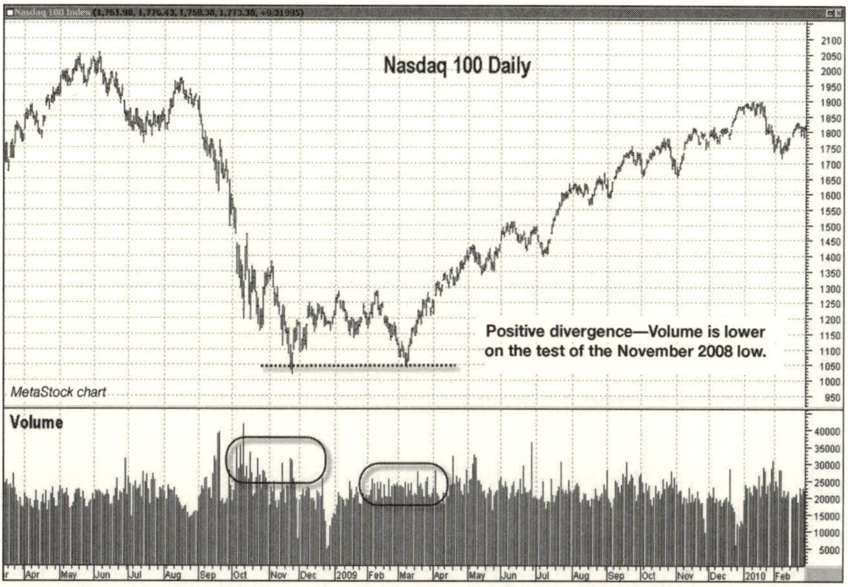

Chart 8.57 Index Volume, Positive Divergence, Nasdaq 100 Daily

Source: MetaStock

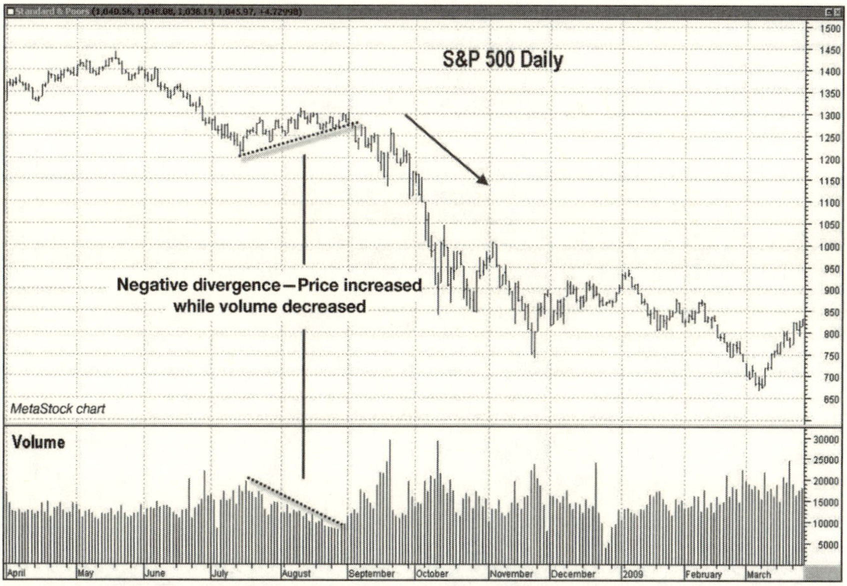

Chart 8.58 Index Volume, Negative Divergence, S&P 500 Daily

Source: MetaStock

Trend Changes

Index Volume can also be used to alert traders that a trend change may be imminent. Recall in the previous example that the Nasdaq 100 showed a positive volume divergence at the March 2009 low. The Dow Jones Industrial Average showed no such divergence, but the heightened level of volume at the March low was an indication that change was imminent.

Note in Chart 8.59 how volume really picked up in mid-February but stayed elevated through the entire bottoming period. There were volume spikes in September, October, and November 2008, but the spikes were not sustained. The sustained elevation of volume around the March low showed that the bulls were digging in their heels and there was a real battle for control of the trend. This activity should have alerted traders that they could increase risk, as a trend change was imminent.

While trend reversals at market lows are usually volatile and emotional events, trend changes at market tops are usually rather calm, with downside volume building as the trend develops. Chart 8.60 of the October 2007 top in the S&P 500 illustrates that point. Notice on the final push higher in October 2007 that volume is weak as price makes its final high. The initial sell-off from that high showed a marked increase in volume, which was

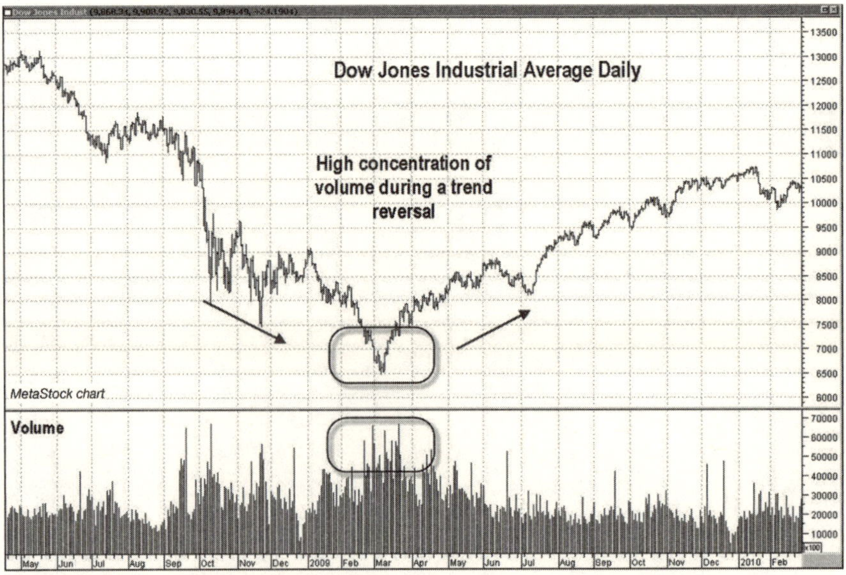

Chart 8.59 Index Volume, Volume Concentration on Reversal, DJIA Daily

Source: MetaStock

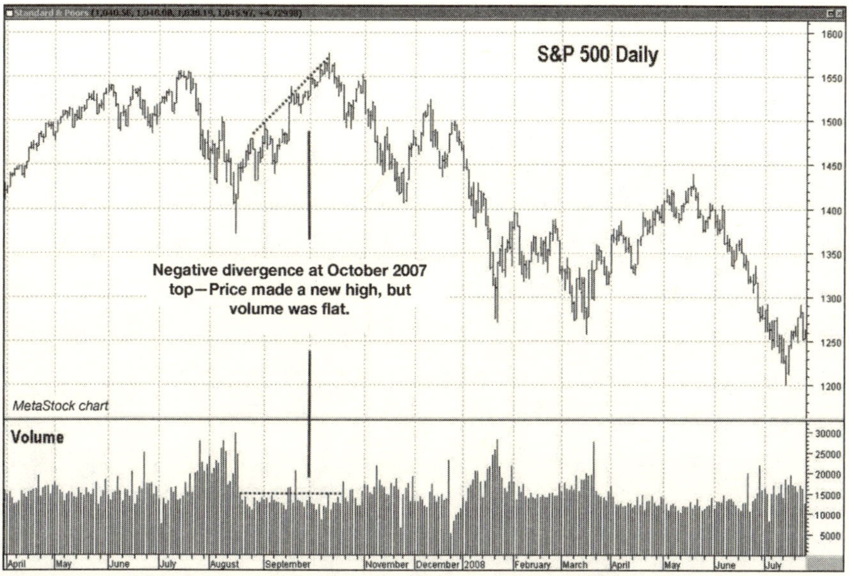

Chart 8.60 Index Volume, Negative Divergence, S&P 500 Daily

Source: MetaStock

a clue that at the very least a spirited correction might have been unfolding. It was a signal for traders to get more defensive and take some risk off the table.

Trade Setup

Making trading decisions based solely on Index Volume levels and price action is not common, but it can be done. Typically there is another trigger indicator or oscillator involved.

In this example, we will use a pair of volume moving averages (VMAs) in conjunction with the breach of a support level to enter a trend continuation trade. A cross of the 5-day VMA up through the 20-day VMA would signal increased volume activity. Note in Chart 8.61 for the S&P 500 that price has been in a very strong downtrend throughout most of 2008. After price bottomed in November 2008, a corrective countertrend rally developed. The rally was not very strong, as indicated by the declining tops in the 5-day VMA in the bottom pane. Price was also chopping modestly higher, which showed a lack of buying conviction. A trade should be considered once price breaks down through its support line and the 5-day VMA crosses up through the 20-day VMA.

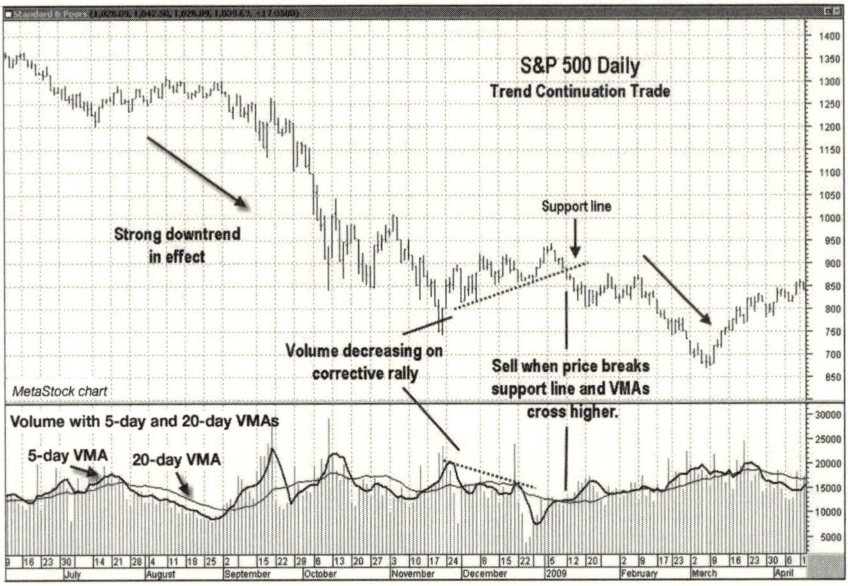

Chart 8.61 Index Volume with VMAs, Trend Continuation Trade Setup, S&P 500 Daily

Source: MetaStock

Trade Entry

Chart 8.62 takes a close-up look at the November 2008–March 2009 period in which the trade was triggered. Notice the negative divergence on the rally, as shown by the declining tops on the 5-day VMA while price advanced. Also note that the 5-day VMA spent most of its time below the 20-day VMA even as price pushed higher during the countertrend rally. That VMA configuration showed that near-term volume pressure was not strong enough to ignite a more serious rally.

A trade was triggered when price broke down through the support line *and* when the 5-day VMA crossed above the 20-day VMA. This was a signal that the larger-degree downtrend was resuming. The initial stop should have been placed over the January 6 high level of 943.85. The S&P 500 Index values could have been used to track the trade, whether futures or ETFs were used as the trading vehicle. This means that theoretical stops could have been placed using S&P 500 price levels. When the stop level is breached on the S&P 500, the trade should be exited.

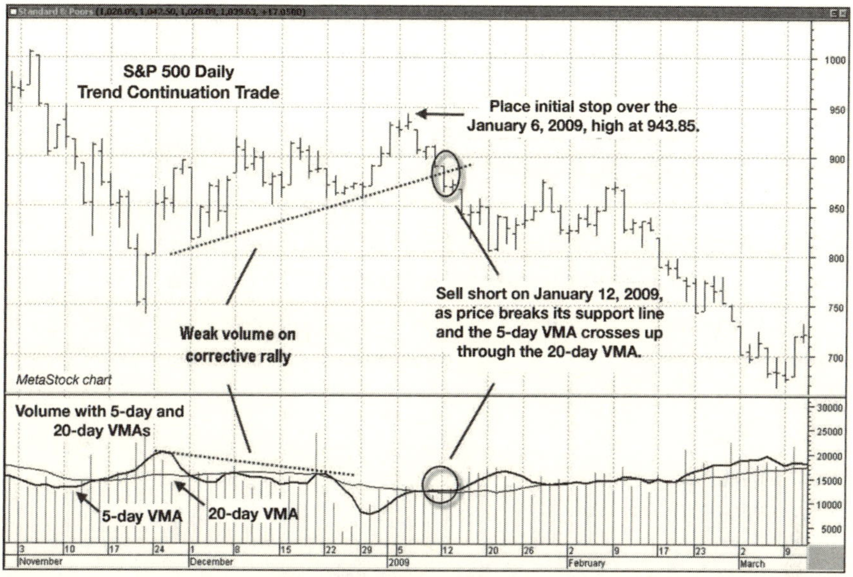

Chart 8.62 Index Volume with VMAs, Trend Continuation Trade Entry, S&P 500 Daily

Source: MetaStock

Trader Tips

Index Volume is another broad market tool that is very good for doing the following:

- Confirming trends
- Showing trend divergences
- Alerting traders to imminent trend reversals

Index Volume is a great tool to study groups of stocks in aggregate, as the major indices are used as proxies for the entire market.

Nasdaq/NYSE Volume Ratio

Measuring the volume ratio of the Nasdaq and the New York Stock Exchange (NYSE) was an early method of intermarket analysis that was used to attempt to measure trader appetite for risk.

In its infancy, the Nasdaq was seen as the minor leagues of the exchanges, where smaller, younger, and riskier companies were listed.

The NYSE was the place all of these smaller companies wanted to be once they met the listing requirements. This comparison showed whether or not traders were willing to "bet," or take on higher risk by buying the shares of these younger companies, or whether they were pulling back from risk by investing more in the established NYSE stocks.

The Nasdaq is no longer seen as the minor leagues compared to the NYSE, and it is now seen as the proper place for innovative technology companies. In spite of the improved image of the Nasdaq, it is still seen as the riskier of the two exchanges, which means that analyzing the volume flows between these two exchanges can still give analysts a deeper look into trader appetite for risk.

Formulation

The formula for the Nasdaq/NYSE Volume Ratio is very simple:

$$\frac{\text{Today's Nasdaq volume}}{\text{Today's NYSE volume}}$$

Chart 8.63 for the Nasdaq Composite shows the plot of the ratio, which seems to be very volatile and of little use in its "raw" form.

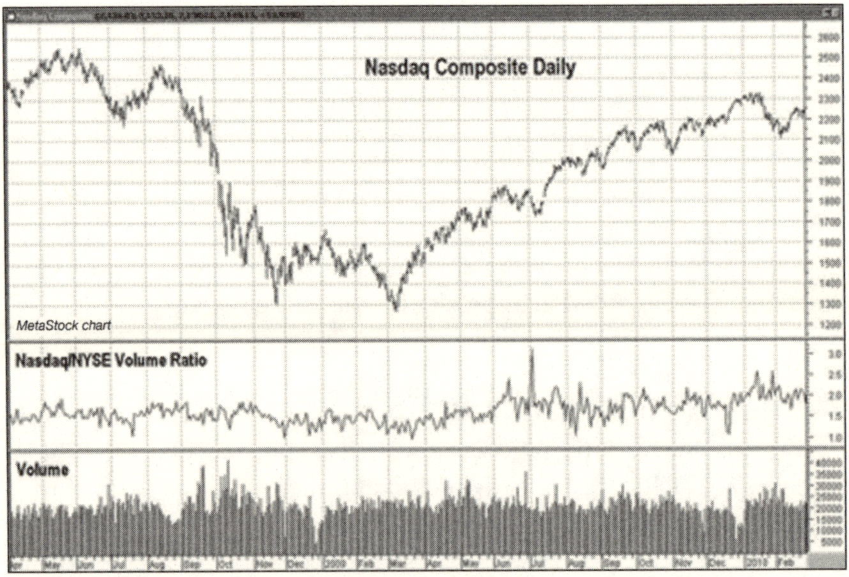

Chart 8.63 Nasdaq/NYSE Volume Ratio, Nasdaq Composite Daily

Source: MetaStock

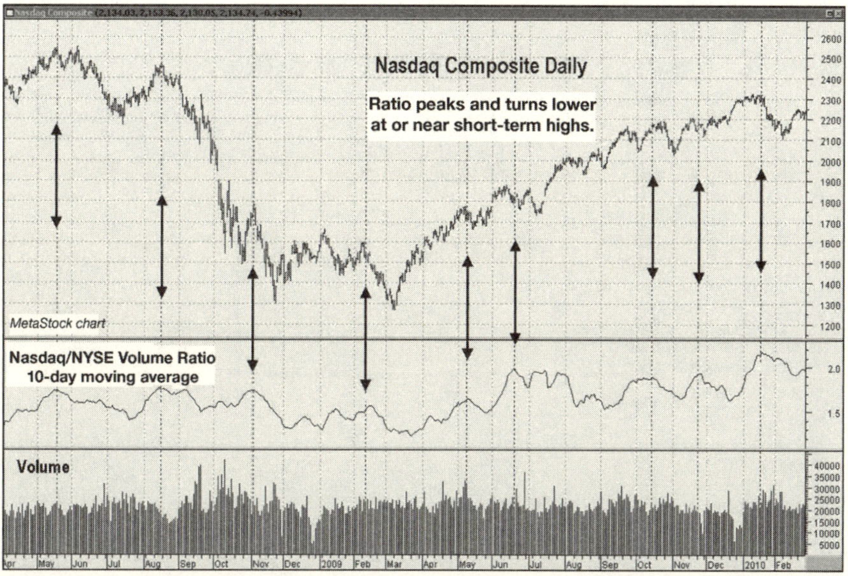

Chart 8.64 Nasdaq/NYSE Volume Ratio, 10-Day Moving Average, Nasdaq Composite Daily

Source: MetaStock

Smoothing the Ratio

Now if we take the same data stream for the ratio and smooth it with a 10-day simple moving average, it becomes more useful. Note in the same record of the Nasdaq Composite how the 10-day moving average of the ratio tends to peak and reverse at or near short-term changes in price direction (Chart 8.64). The 10-day simple moving average of the Nasdaq/NYSE Volume Ratio is also useful in confirming short-term market lows. Note in Chart 8.65 how the indicator troughs and turns higher just after a short-term low in price has been made. The turn higher in the indicator shows an increased appetite for risk among traders, which is necessary to fuel market advances. Some of the short-term lows shown in Chart 8.65 were very short lived, however, so it is always necessary to be mindful of the overall market trend before taking any action.

Volume Ratio as an Oversold Indicator

Historically, the Nasdaq/NYSE Volume Ratio has provided positive signals when it reverses higher off lows. The plot of the S&P 500 in Chart 8.66 shows a 10-day simple moving average of the Nasdaq/NYSE Volume Ratio.

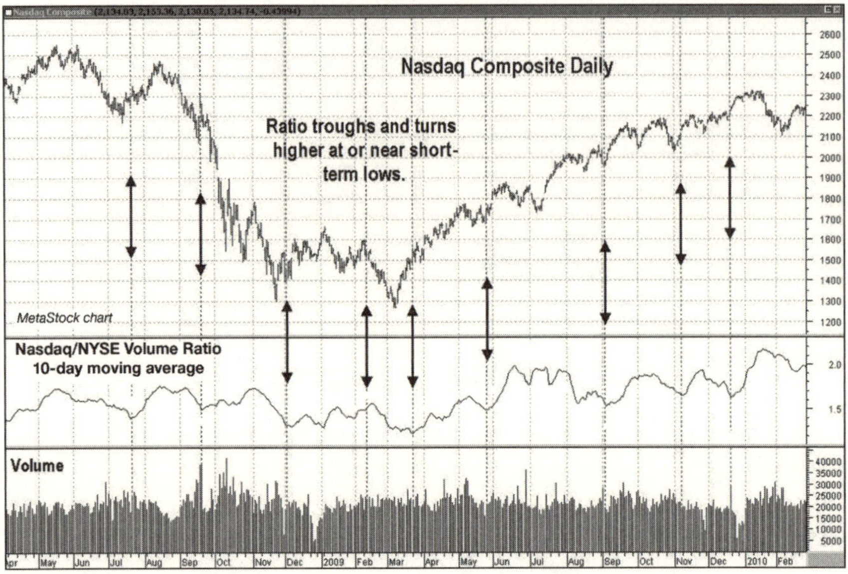

Chart 8.65 Nasdaq/NYSE Volume Ratio, 10-Day Moving Average, Nasdaq Composite Daily

Source: MetaStock

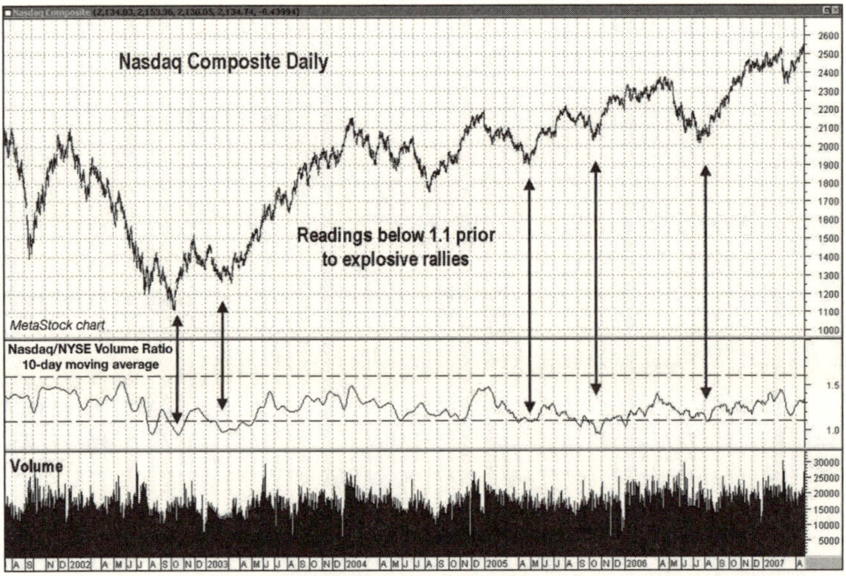

Chart 8.66 Nasdaq/NYSE Volume Ratio, 10-Day Moving Average Set Up as an Oscillator, Nasdaq Composite Daily

Source: MetaStock

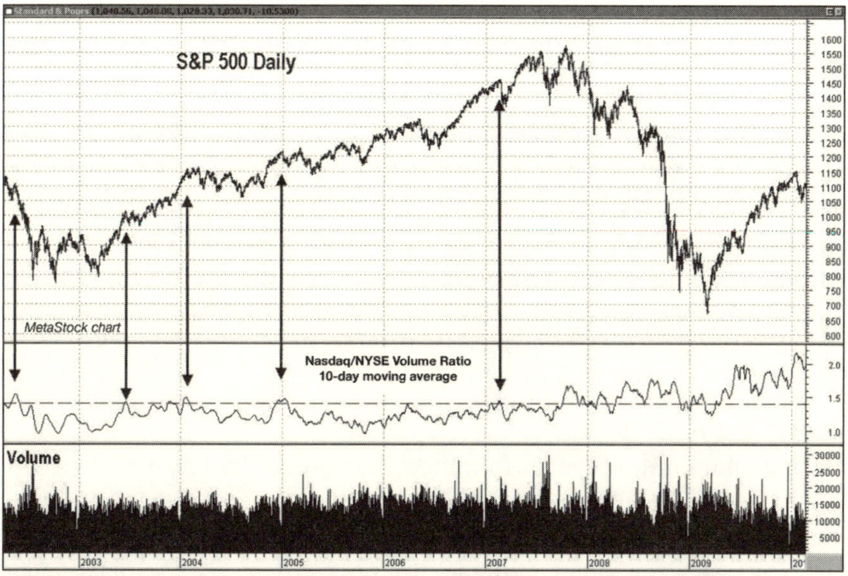

Chart 8.67 Nasdaq/NYSE Volume Ratio, 10-Day Moving Average Set Up as an Oscillator, Nasdaq Composite Daily

Source: MetaStock

Note how in years past when the 10-day moving average dipped below 1.1 and turned higher, that marked a low in the market. Unfortunately, though, Nasdaq volume has come in at a much higher pace than NYSE volume over the last couple of years, so the ratio has risen over the years and has failed to some degree to establish a predictable range. This is a great example of how indicator performance can be affected by intrinsic changes in the market. The period shown in Chart 8.66 is 2002 through early 2007.

In the past, peaks over a ratio of 1.4 on the 10-day simple moving average have preceded market corrections. Now that the Nasdaq volume is regularly higher than NYSE volume, each peak in the indicator marks a short-term top, even as it heads higher, well above the 1.4 level. For the S&P 500 (Chart 8.67), notice how well peaks over 1.4 worked in the 2002–2007 period, before the ratio really began to climb. Prior to 2008, whenever the ratio climbed above 1.4, at the very least a sideways corrective phase followed.

Trade Setup

We find that the Nasdaq/NYSE Volume Ratio is an indicator that does not lend itself well to making near-term trading decisions. It can be used, however, as an indicator to inform a trader as to when to lighten up on long or short positions due to changes in sentiment.

When the ratio is moving higher, it's a sign of higher activity in more speculative tech stocks, as opposed to the more conservative NYSE stocks. This shows a healthy appetite for risk, which is necessary to fuel rallies. The longer-term view of the Nasdaq 100 Trust ETF (QQQQ) in Chart 8.68 has the 10-day moving average of the ratio plotted in the middle window, which shows bullish characteristics as it bottoms in the same vicinity as the uptrend continues. Notice, however, how volume (plotted in the bottom window) is lackluster on the push to the final highs in April 2010. This was a sign that the trend might have been losing steam.

Speculation, however, was increasing among the fewer participants who were pushing the price higher, as demonstrated by the increase in the 10-day moving average of the volume ratio. This gave traders something to watch as a clue that the final speculators were running out of gas and the trend was likely to reverse. It would have provided an excellent opportunity for traders to avoid the May 6 "flash crash."

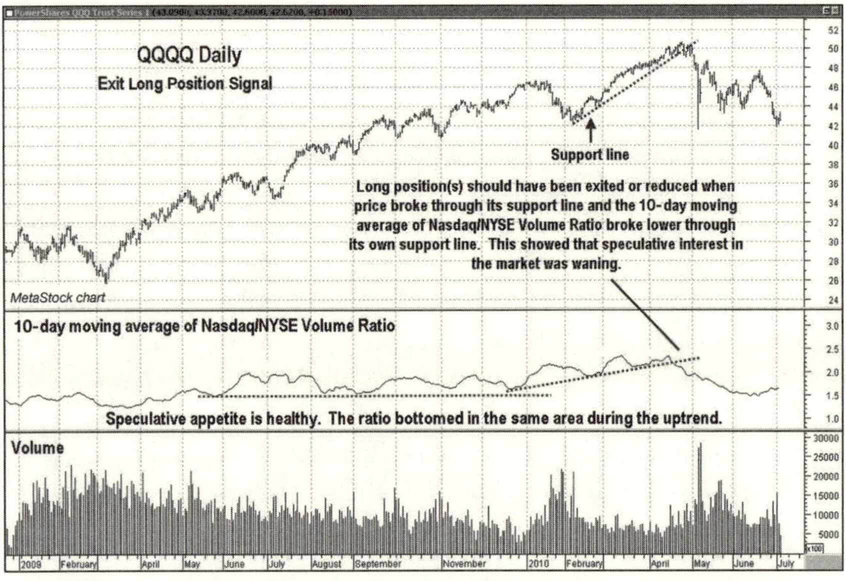

Chart 8.68 Nasdaq/NYSE Volume Ratio, Exit Long Position Signal, Nasdaq 100 Trust ETF

Source: MetaStock

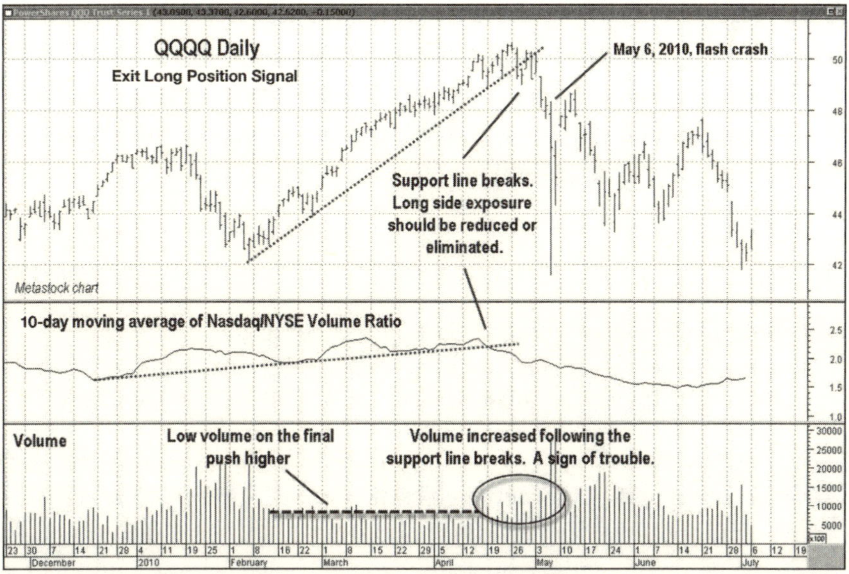

Chart 8.69 Nasdaq/NYSE Volume Ratio, Exit Long Position Signal, Nasdaq 100 Trust ETF

Source: MetaStock

Trade Entry

In this case, a "trade entry" was more like a "trade exit," as the concurrent violation of support lines by both price and the 10-day moving average of the Nasdaq/NYSE Volume Ratio provided a warning that the speculative mood that fueled the final push higher was leaving the market. Remember also that the final push higher occurred on tepid volume, another sign that the trend was in trouble. The view of QQQQ in Chart 8.69 shows how the concurrent violation of support lines in price and the Nasdaq/NYSE Volume Ratio, along with the increase in volume activity on the breakdown of support, was a solid signal to take profits and step aside.

Trader Tips

- The Nasdaq/NYSE Volume Ratio has been a reliable indicator in the past, but recent changes in market volume patterns have changed overbought and oversold levels that were reliable thresholds in the past.
- Especially in its smoothed form, it can show short-term market turning points with its peaks and troughs.

The 10-Day Up/Down Volume Oscillator

The 10-Day Up/Down Volume Oscillator is a longer version of the 5-Day Up/Down Volume Oscillator. Like the 5-Day Up/Down Volume Oscillator, the 10-Day Up/Down Volume Oscillator measures the internal strength or weakness of market trends by using daily advancing/declining exchange volume numbers.

Formulation

The 10-Day Up/Down Volume Oscillator is computed as follows:

Sum of last 10 days' advancing volume – sum of last 10 days' declining volume

The result is plotted as a centered oscillator, with crosses of the zero line giving either positive (i.e., cross up) or negative (i.e., cross down) signals. A rallying market should see up volume exceed down volume, and a falling market should exhibit down volume exceeding up volume.

When price action and the indicator are in sync, market internals confirm price action; however, if price is moving in one direction but the 10-Day Up/Down Volume Oscillator is diverging, it shows that either a trend correction or a trend reversal is likely. Chart 8.70 for the S&P 500

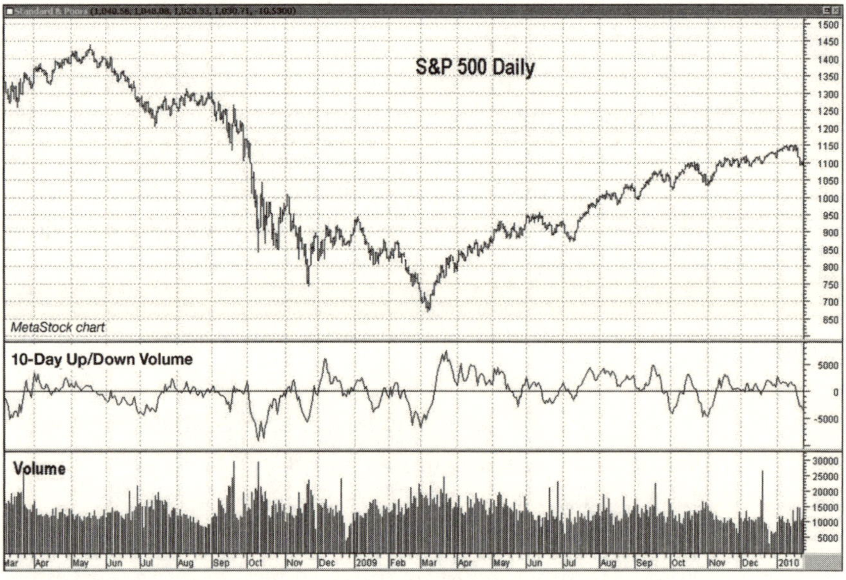

Chart 8.70 The 10-Day Up/Down Volume Oscillator, S&P 500 Daily

Source: MetaStock

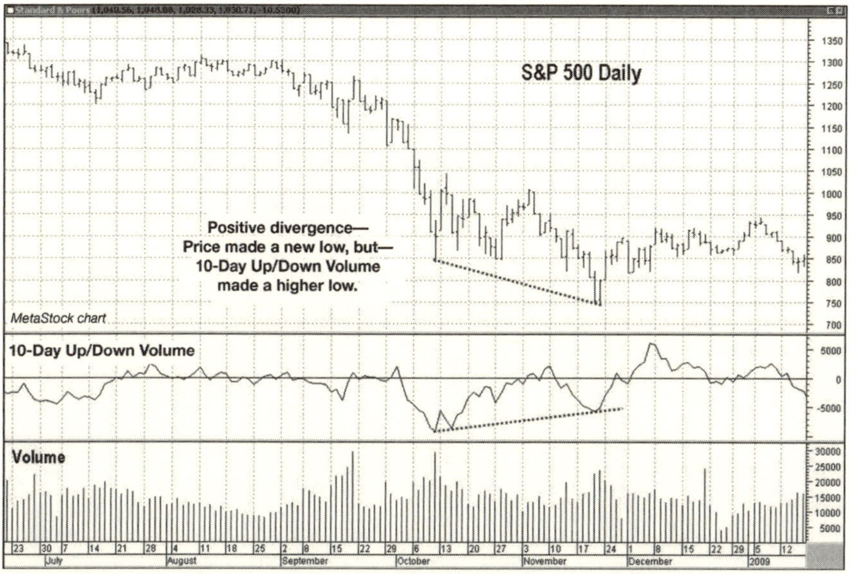

Chart 8.71 The 10-Day Up/Down Volume Oscillator, Positive Divergence, S&P 500 Daily

Source: MetaStock

shows the plot of the 10-Day Up/Down Volume Oscillator. Note the spikes in the indicator as its short-term nature produces sharp moves in either direction.

Divergences

The 10-Day Up/Down Volume Oscillator is great for showing either positive trend divergences (i.e., a falling price with a rising indicator) or negative trend divergences (i.e., a rising price with a falling indicator).

The S&P 500 as shown in Chart 8.71 shows a positive divergence in October and November of 2008. As prices crashed down, losing over 40 percent of their value from the August high, an initial low was made in October, followed by a bounce in prices. That bounce eventually gave way to more selling as price made an even lower low in November. Notice how the 10-Day Up/Down Volume Oscillator made a higher low from October to November. This was a sign that sellers were out of gas temporarily and a bounce was due.

The S&P 500 in Chart 8.72 shows a negative divergence between price and the oscillator. This is the time period immediately following the example in Chart 8.71. Note in Chart 8.72 how price rallied and made a higher

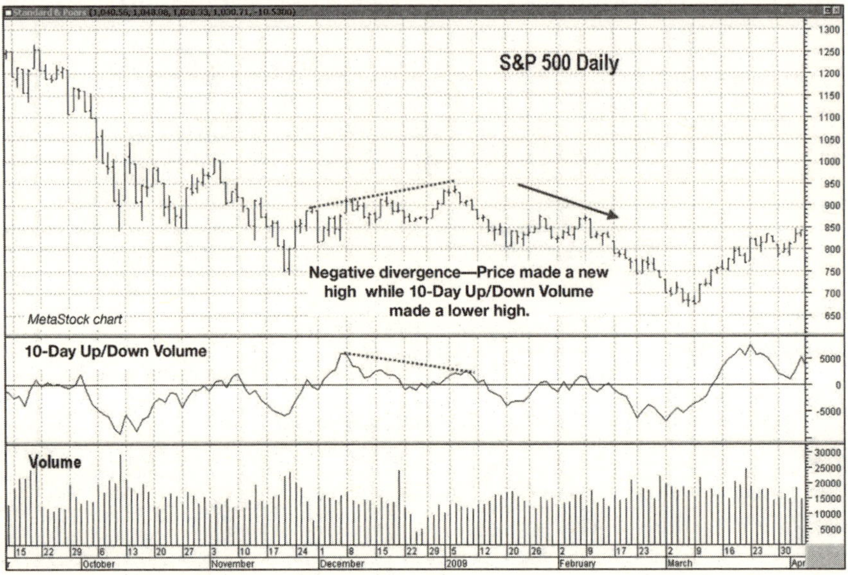

Chart 8.72 The 10-Day Up/Down Volume Oscillator, Negative Divergence, S&P 500 Daily

Source: MetaStock

high from December 2008 into January 2009 while the oscillator made a lower high. That was a signal that the reversal off of the November low was losing steam. The market then rolled over and plunged into the March 2009 low.

Zero-Line Crossovers

The 10-Day Up/Down Volume Oscillator also generates positive or negative market signals by crossing above or below the zero line. These signals should be heeded only when they are in the direction of the larger-degree trend. For example, crosses up (positive) should be viewed as predicting near-term market strength in uptrends, and crosses down (negative) should be viewed as predicting near-term market weakness in downtrends. Crosses above the zero line in downtrends and crosses below the zero line in uptrends should not be given the same consideration because they are against the prevailing trend. The S&P 500 as shown in Chart 8.73 shows crosses up above the zero line in an uptrend, predicting periods of near-term market strength from May to December 2009.

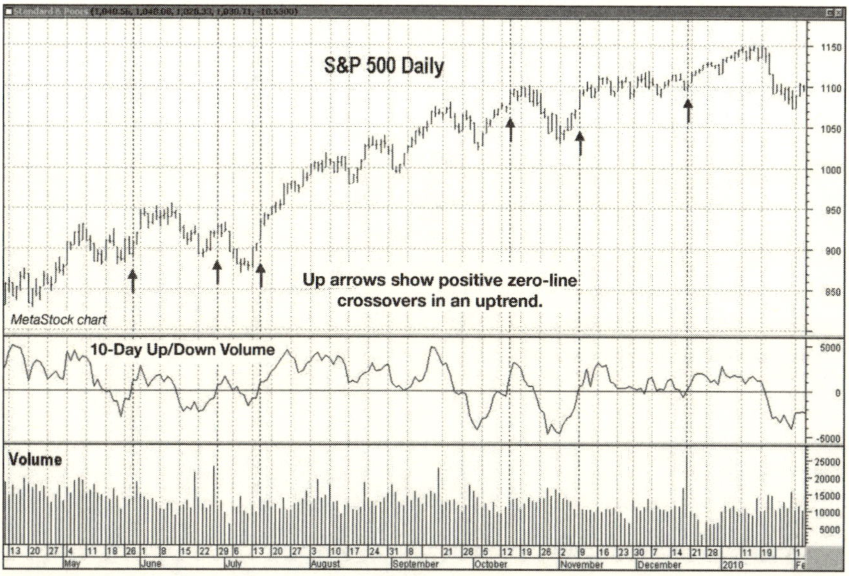

Chart 8.73 The 10-Day Up/Down Volume Oscillator, Positive Zero-Line Crossovers, S&P 500 Daily

Source: MetaStock

Next is an example of negative zero-line crossover action, again with the S&P 500. Chart 8.74 crosses below the zero line in a downtrend, which predicts near-term market weakness. The different psychology in downtrending markets versus uptrending markets can cause premature signals. Note how some of the signals occurred before brief rallies or consolidation periods, followed by resumptions of the downtrend.

Again, always remember that zero-line crossover signals are most meaningful when they occur in the direction of the prevailing trend.

Trade Setup

The 10-Day Up/Down Volume Oscillator is a great tool to spot divergences with price that can alert a trader that the larger-degree trend is ready to resume after a corrective phase. In this example, an index ETF is used, since 10-Day Up/Down Volume is created with broad market data.

The plot of the DJ Diamonds Trust ETF (DIA) in Chart 8.75 shows a positive divergence as price corrects in January and February 2010.

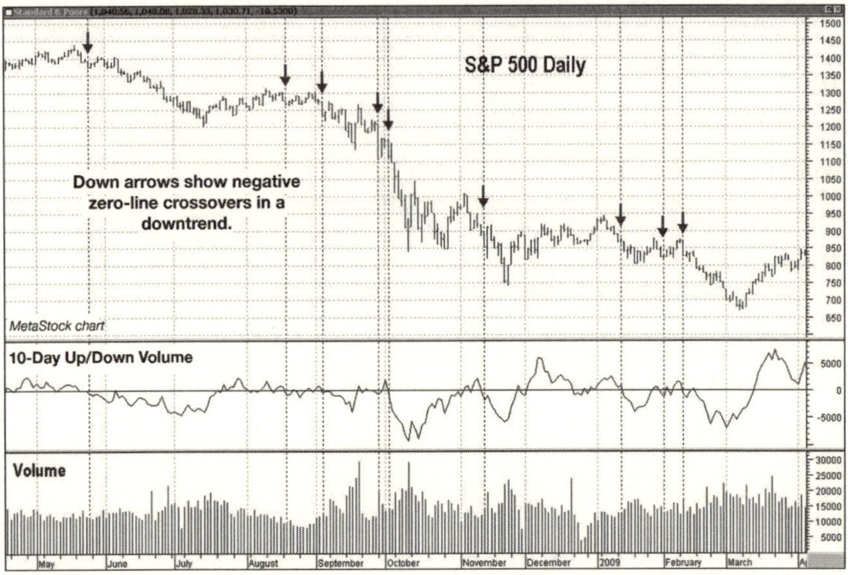

Chart 8.74 The 10-Day Up/Down Volume Oscillator, Negative Zero-Line Crossovers, S&P 500 Daily

Source: MetaStock

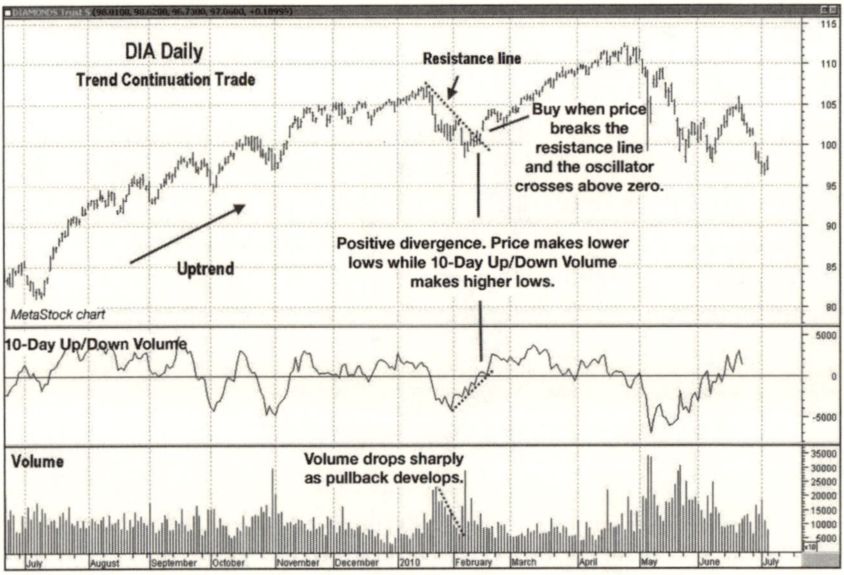

Chart 8.75 The 10-Day Up/Down Volume Oscillator, Trend Continuation Trade Setup, DJ Diamonds Trust ETF Daily

Source: MetaStock

As price continues to fall, 10-Day Up/Down Volume makes higher lows, showing that buying pressure is building. Also note once again the value of simple volume as plotted in the bottom window. There is a sharp drop in volume as the correction proceeds, showing that selling pressure is diminishing. This is a great sign that a continuation of the larger-degree uptrend is imminent. A buy can be executed once price breaks up through its resistance line and the 10-Day Up/Down Volume crosses back above zero.

Trade Entry

Chart 8.76 of the DIA gives a close-up view of the time period in which a trade would have been executed. Note how the 10-Day Up/Down Volume Oscillator crossed up through its zero line the same day that price broke up through its resistance line. This was a clear-cut signal that the trend was resuming. The initial stop should have been placed at the February 5 low of 98.36. It would have been a beautiful trade, as price moved steadily higher into its April 26, 2010, top.

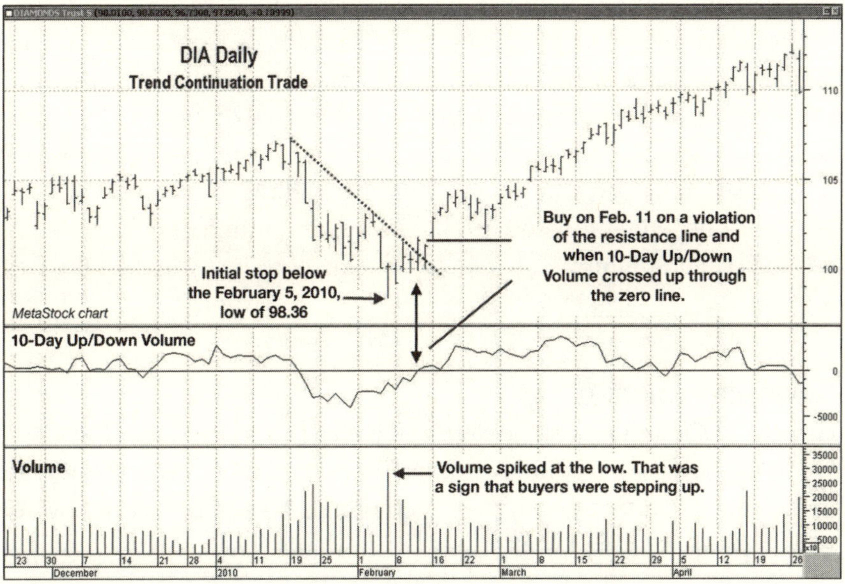

Chart 8.76 The 10-Day Up/Down Volume Oscillator, Trend Continuation Trade Entry, DJ Diamonds Trust ETF Daily

Source: MetaStock

Trader Tips

The 10-Day Up/Down Volume Oscillator is a great tool for doing the following:

- Illustrating the relationship between advancing and declining volume
- Showing trend divergences
- Providing indications of near-term market strength or weakness in the direction of the trend

Because of its short-term nature, the 10-Day Up/Down Volume Oscillator should not be considered for longer-term market analysis. This versatile tool can, however, give an accurate short-term reading of market conditions.

Upside/Downside Volume

Upside/Downside Volume can tell the "story within the story" of the market as trends develop and mature. In uptrends, Upside Volume should be greater than Downside Volume, while the opposite is true in downtrends. If Upside Volume slows in an uptrend, it can be a negative divergence that can warn of a possible trend correction or reversal. The same principle applies to the slowing of Downside Volume in a downtrend, which creates a positive divergence and also warns of a possible trend correction or reversal. In this section we will look at Upside Volume and Downside Volume independently. An Upside/Downside Volume Oscillator can be created by combining the two data sets; this tool is covered in the next section.

Downside Volume

Chart 8.77 shows a plot of the S&P 500 with a line plot of New York Stock Exchange Downside Volume. Notice how volatile the volume data are. Spikes in the data line up with short-term market bottoms, however, which gives a good indication that sellers have exhausted themselves, opening the door for a short-term bounce higher in the market.

In its raw form, Downside Volume can also give clues to when a trend change may be developing. In Chart 8.78 of the S&P 500, a brutal downtrend is shown in force from March 2008 through March 2009. The dashed

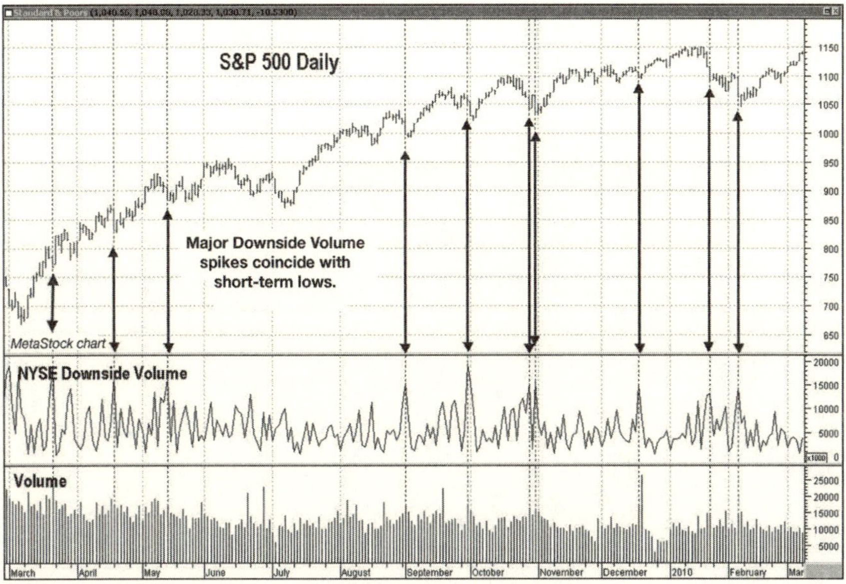

Chart 8.77 Downside Volume Indicator, S&P 500 Daily

Source: MetaStock

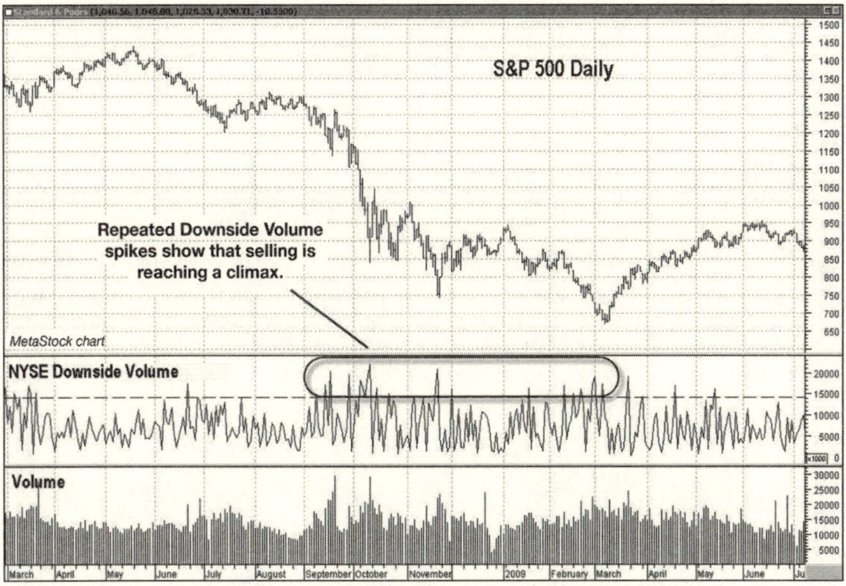

Chart 8.78 Downside Volume Indicator as a Trend Change Indicator, S&P 500 Daily

Source: MetaStock

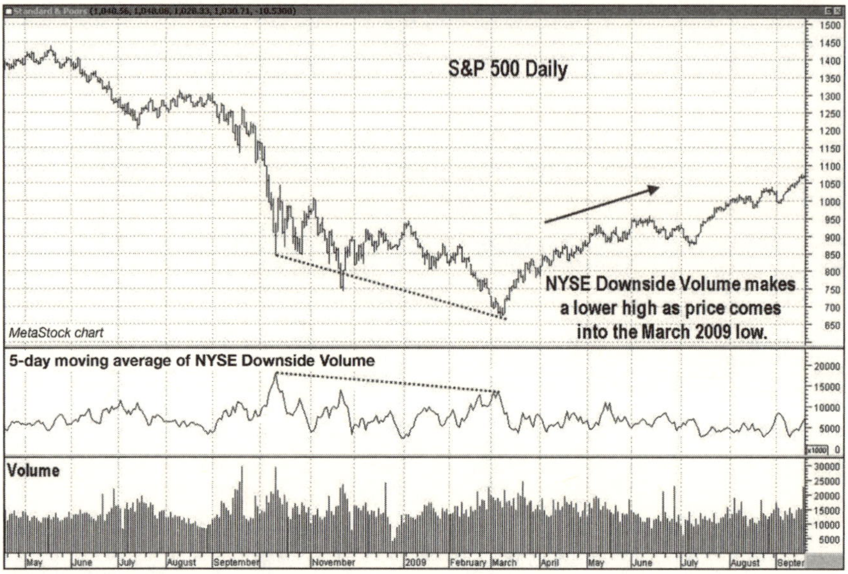

Chart 8.79 Downside Volume Indicator, 5-Day Moving Average, S&P 500 Daily

Source: MetaStock

line in the NYSE Downside Volume plot is simply to illustrate where most of the prior downside volume spikes had stopped earlier in the downtrend. Note how Downside Volume really picked up in the fall of 2008 as there were repeated spikes over the dashed line. This showed building pessimism, which in turn revealed that selling was reaching a climax.

Smoothing the Downside Volume with a 5-day simple moving average gives it a different look, allowing it to better show divergences. For the S&P 5000 as shown in Chart 8.79, note how the Downside Volume made a lower high as price came into its March 2009 low. This showed that selling pressure was lighter than at the September low, which was an indication that a low was near. The indicator was easier to interpret in its moving average form.

Upside Volume

Upside Volume is typically tamer than Downside Volume simply because the psychology is different in uptrends from that in downtrends. It can provide clues to trend changes, however, especially coming into climactic, emotional lows such as the one that occurred in March 2009.

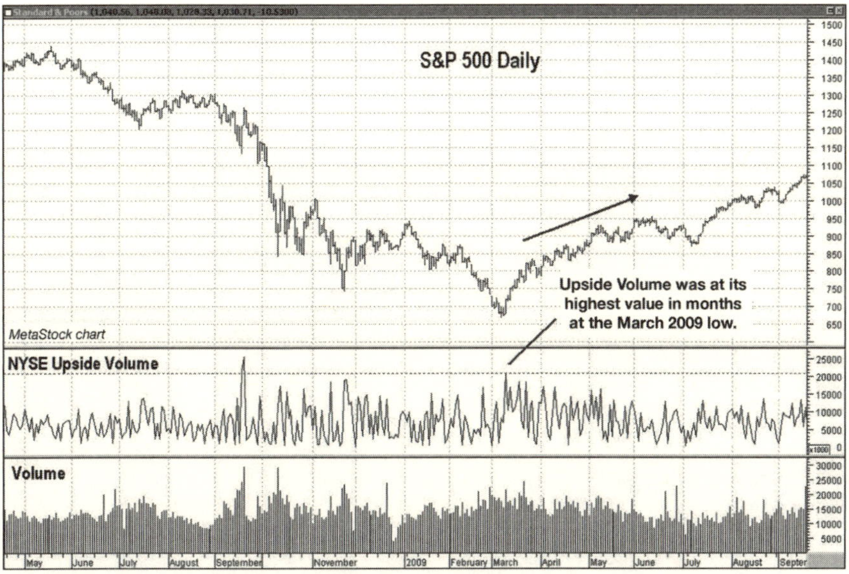

Chart 8.80 Upside Volume Indicator, S&P 500 Daily

Source: MetaStock

Chart 8.80 shows that the Upside Volume of the S&P 500 was rather tame during the downtrend, with the exception of the massive spike in September 2008, when the real meltdown began. A line has been drawn across the top of the March 2009 spike to demonstrate how much higher that spike was compared to the spikes that followed the previous September 2008 spike high. Earlier we discussed the behavior of Downside Volume coming into the March 2009 low. Now with Upside Volume spiking and prices reversing, chances were good that this would at the very least lead to a solid recovery rally.

Smoothing Upside Volume with a moving average is good for showing divergences with price. In Chart 8.81, Upside Volume of the S&P 500 has been smoothed with a 5-day simple moving average. Note how in March 2010 price makes a lower low while Upside Volume makes a higher low, showing that shares were being accumulated as price worked lower.

The S&P 500 as shown in Chart 8.82 shows a negative divergence in December 2008 through January 2009 with the 5-day simple moving average of Upside Volume. Price worked its way higher through December and into January, while Upside Volume dropped noticeably. This preceded the sharp, final drop into the March 2009 low.

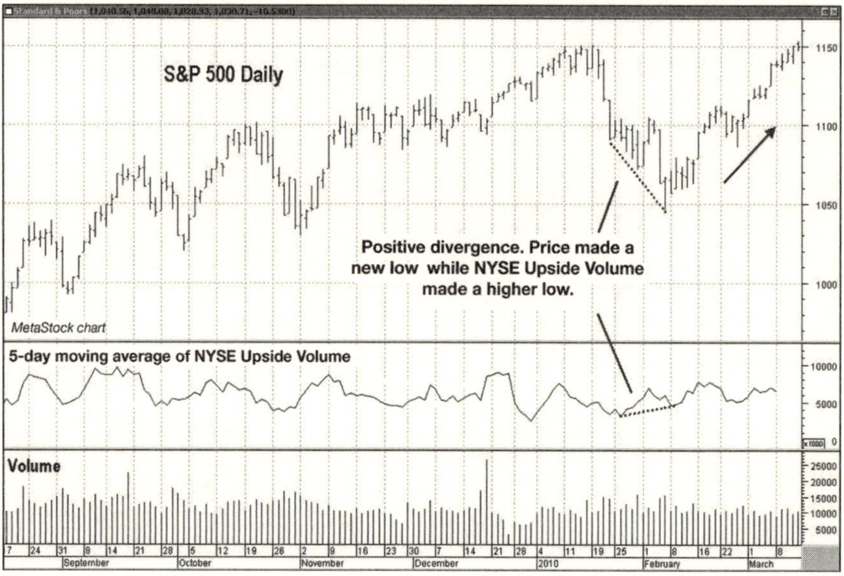

Chart 8.81 Upside Volume Indicator, 5-Day Moving Average, Positive Divergence, S&P 500 Daily

Source: MetaStock

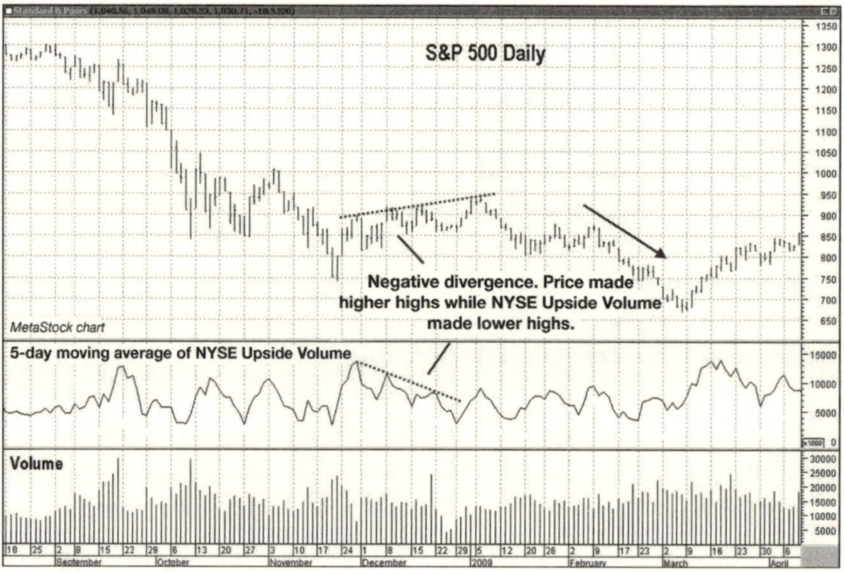

Chart 8.82 Upside Volume Indicator, 5-Day Moving Average, Negative Divergence, S&P 500 Daily

Source: MetaStock

Trade Setup

This trade setup example of the DJ Diamonds Trust ETF (DIA) will use a 5-day moving average of NYSE Upside Volume in conjunction with price action to initiate a short trade.

In Chart 8.83, note how price formed a top in October 2007 in what turned out to be the major top prior to the 2008 bear market. At the time, however, it simply looked like a solid trend continuation trading opportunity was developing. The short-term corrective rally that began in November was rather sharp from a price perspective, but the 5-day moving average of NYSE Upside Volume was showing a negative divergence with price. Overall volume (in the bottom window) was lackluster on the push higher, which was also a clue that there was more selling to come. Those two divergences made a compelling case for a short trade. The trade entry trigger would be a violation of the support line drawn that connected the November and December lows.

Trade Entry

Chart 8.84 takes a closer look at the time frame in which a trade could have been initiated. Once price penetrated the support line to the downside on

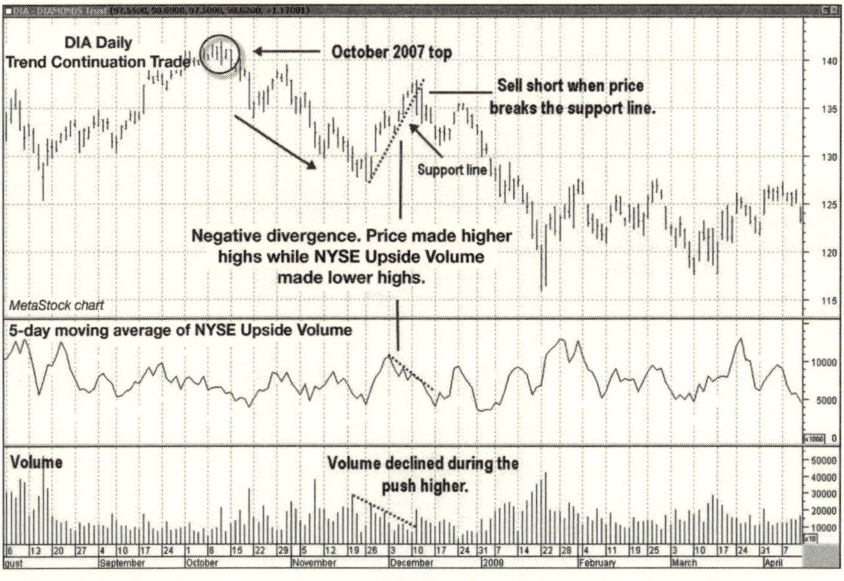

Chart 8.83 Upside Volume Indicator, Negative Divergence Trade Setup, DJ Diamonds Trust ETF

Source: MetaStock

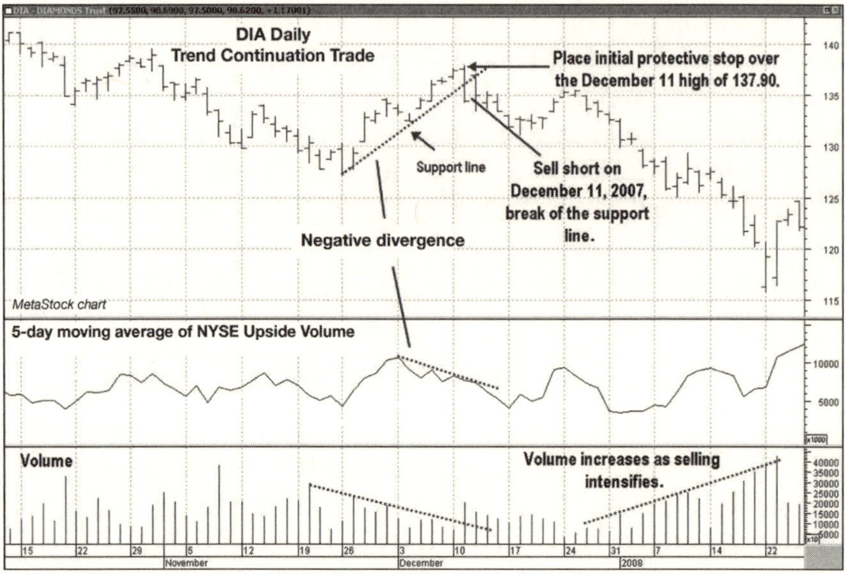

Chart 8.84 Upside Volume Indicator, Negative Divergence Trade Entry, DJ Diamonds Trust ETF

Source: MetaStock

December 11, 2007, a short position could have been initiated. The initial protective stop should have been placed over the December 11 high of 137.90. The tight stop on this trade opened the door for solid profit potential with a very small amount of risk.

Trader Tips

Upside and Downside Volume can be analyzed separately and are good for the following:

- Showing changes in volume patterns, giving clues to potential trend changes
- Spotting divergences between price and volume

One drawback of using Upside/Downside Volume indicators is that they are short term in nature and not well suited for intermediate- and longer-term trading decisions. Many useful oscillators and ratios are made by combining up and down volume, and analyzing them separately can give a slightly different perspective on trends and their strength. The next section carries this idea further.

Upside/Downside Volume Oscillator

Upside Volume and Downside Volume can be a valuable analysis tool when they are examined separately, but combining these pieces of data into an oscillator creates a versatile technical tool that can be used for overbought/oversold conditions, showing divergences and giving positive or negative market signals on zero-line crossovers.

Formulation

The computation of this oscillator is very simple:

Current day's advancing volume – current day's declining volume

This computation is identical to the cumulative volume, except that the daily results are not added to a running total. That creates a volatile data stream good for identifying short-term overbought or oversold conditions as well as divergences. This oscillator can be created with either NYSE or Nasdaq exchange data.

Identifying Overbought/Oversold Conditions

In the S&P 500 plot in Chart 8.85, note how earlier in the uptrend spikes above 1.2 billion shares in the oscillator usually resulted in consolidations

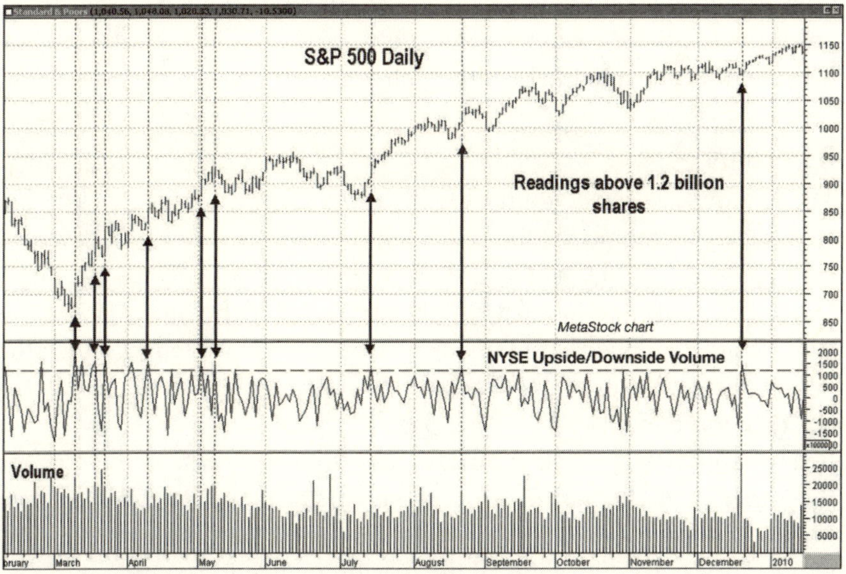

Chart 8.85 Upside/Downside Volume Oscillator, Overbought Conditions, S&P 500 Daily

Source: MetaStock

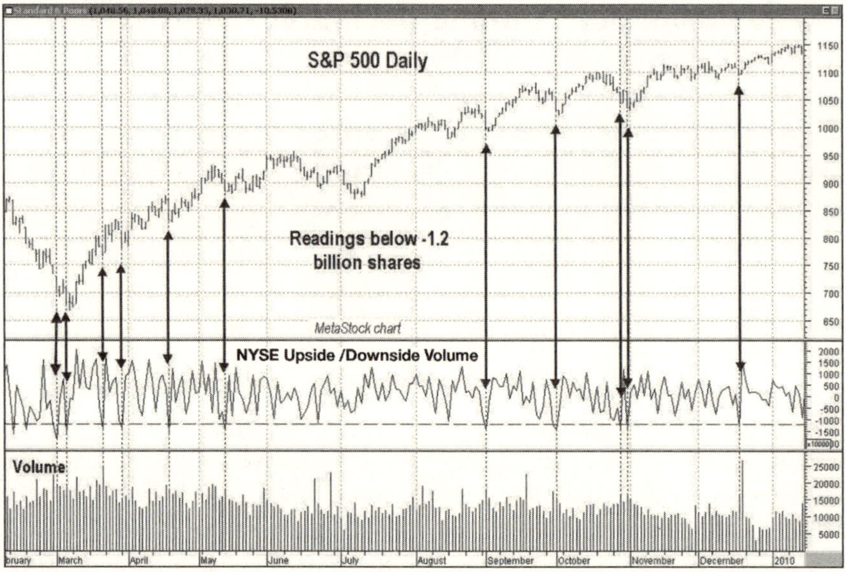

Chart 8.86 Upside/Downside Volume Oscillator, Oversold Conditions, S&P 500 Daily

Source: MetaStock

or pullbacks, but as the trend regained strength, they signaled continuation moves. The way the oscillator reacts to overbought levels can give insight as to the strength of the trend being analyzed. The oscillator also reflects oversold conditions in the market. In Chart 8.86 of the S&P 500, note how oscillator readings below negative 1.2 billion shares coincide with short-term market lows in the uptrend.

Divergences

The Upside/Downside Volume Oscillator also shows divergences that can alert traders to trend corrections that may be ready to unfold. The Nasdaq Composite shown in Chart 8.87 shows a positive divergence, as price continues lower while the oscillator makes a series of higher lows. This shows latent market strength, as buyers are more active than sellers. Once the divergence was resolved, the Nasdaq Composite rose almost 20 percent in less than three months.

The S&P 500 plotted in Chart 8.88 shows a negative divergence (i.e., price made higher highs but the oscillator made lower highs) from March through May 2008. This gave traders a warning that the brief uptrend was corrective and that the downtrend would resume.

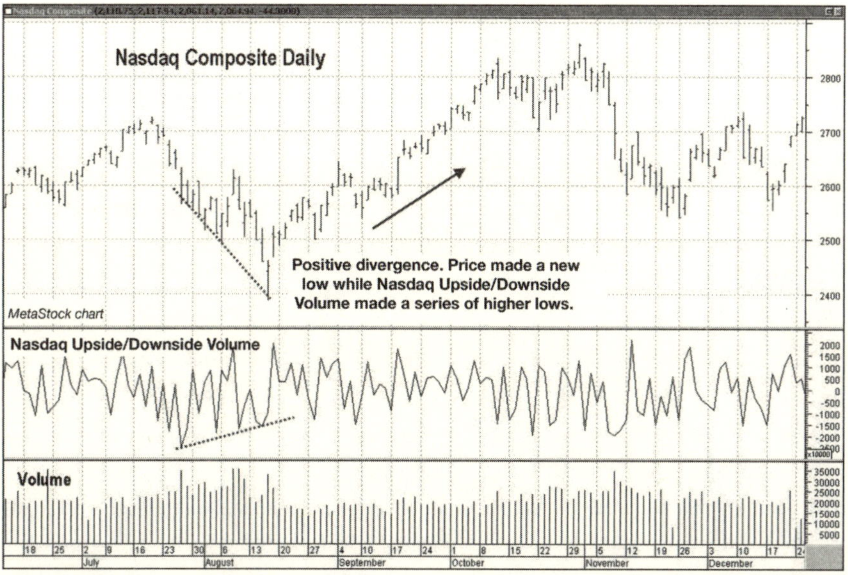

Chart 8.87 Upside/Downside Volume Oscillator, Positive Divergence, Nasdaq Composite Daily

Source: MetaStock

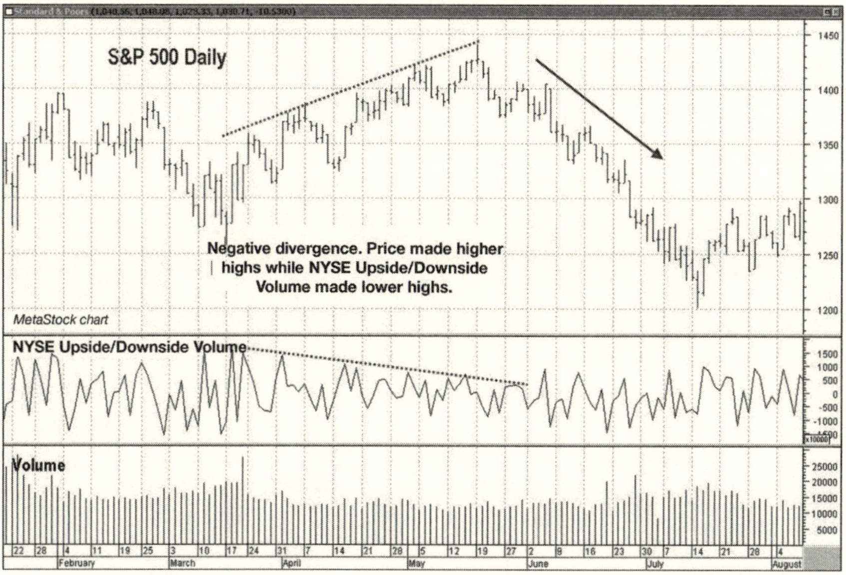

Chart 8.88 Upside/Downside Volume Oscillator, Negative Divergence, S&P 500 Daily

Source: MetaStock

Trends and Market Signals

The Upside/Downside Volume Oscillator is also a great tool when smoothed with a 20-day simple moving average. This allows the indicator to better show trends and also give great positive and negative market signals when it crosses the zero line. The Nasdaq Composite in Chart 8.89 shows a 20-day simple moving average of the oscillator with positive market signals (i.e., the MA crosses above the zero line) and negative ones (i.e., the MA crosses below the zero line), which signal times to buy and sell, respectively.

The 20-day moving average of the oscillator can also be plotted as a histogram, which better shows its characteristics during uptrends and downtrends. Note in the Nasdaq Composite as shown in Chart 8.90 how the oscillator made lower highs and lower lows during the down market of 2008. It then made a series of higher highs and higher lows during the up market of 2009. Plotting the oscillator as a histogram can give an at-a-glance look at the market, showing whether buyers or sellers are in control.

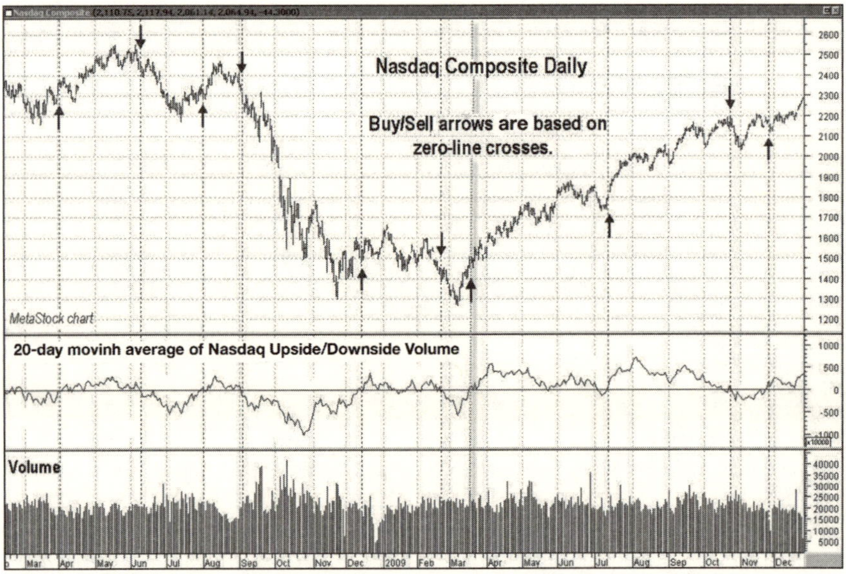

Chart 8.89 Upside/Downside Volume Oscillator, 20-Day Moving Average, Zero-Line Crosses, Nasdaq Composite Daily

Source: MetaStock

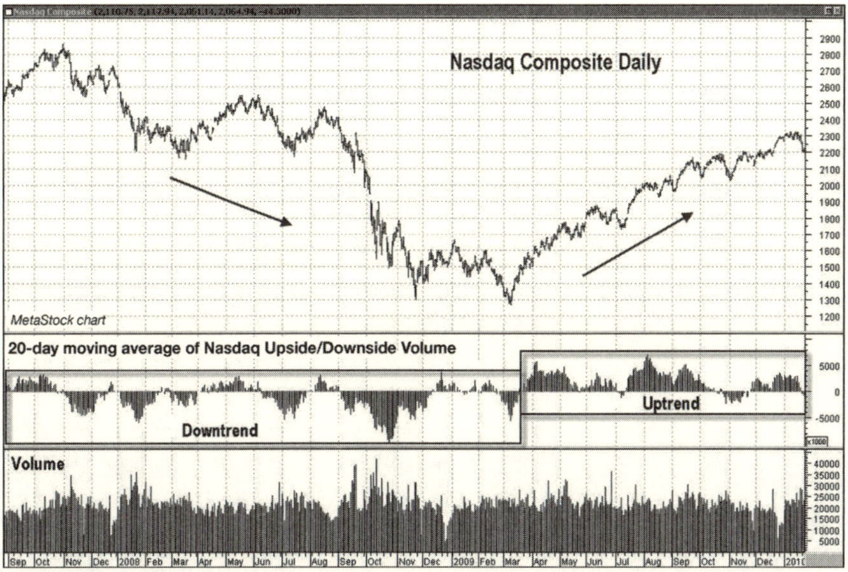

Chart 8.90 Upside/Downside Volume Oscillator, 20-Day Moving Average with Histogram, Nasdaq Composite Daily

Source: MetaStock

Trade Setup

The following example uses the 20-day moving average of the Nasdaq Upside/Downside Volume Oscillator in conjunction with price movements to generate a trade setup and entry. Note in Chart 8.91 that price had been declining into July 2006, while the 20-day moving average of the Nasdaq Upside/Downside Volume Oscillator had been making higher lows, showing a positive divergence. Prices stabilized throughout the remainder of July and into August, showing a drop in selling pressure. A downsloping resistance line could be drawn that connects the high points of the decline, which will be part of our trade entry trigger, along with a cross upward through the zero line in the oscillator.

Trade Entry

Remember, the positive divergence is one piece of the puzzle. In order to enter a trade, price needs to confirm that a trend change is likely to be underway. This happens when price closes above the resistance line along with the 20-day moving average of the Nasdaq Upside/Downside Volume

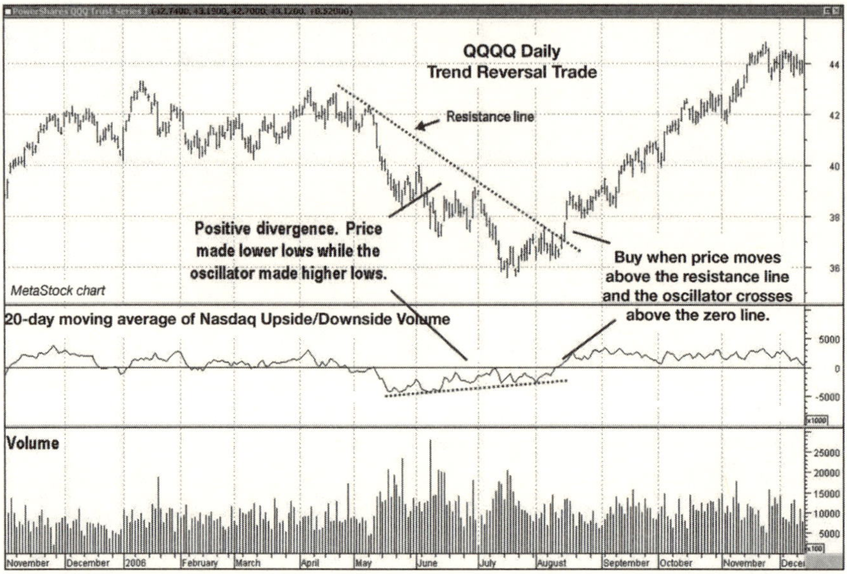

Chart 8.91 Upside/Downside Volume Oscillator, Positive Divergence Trade Setup, Nasdaq Composite Daily

Source: MetaStock

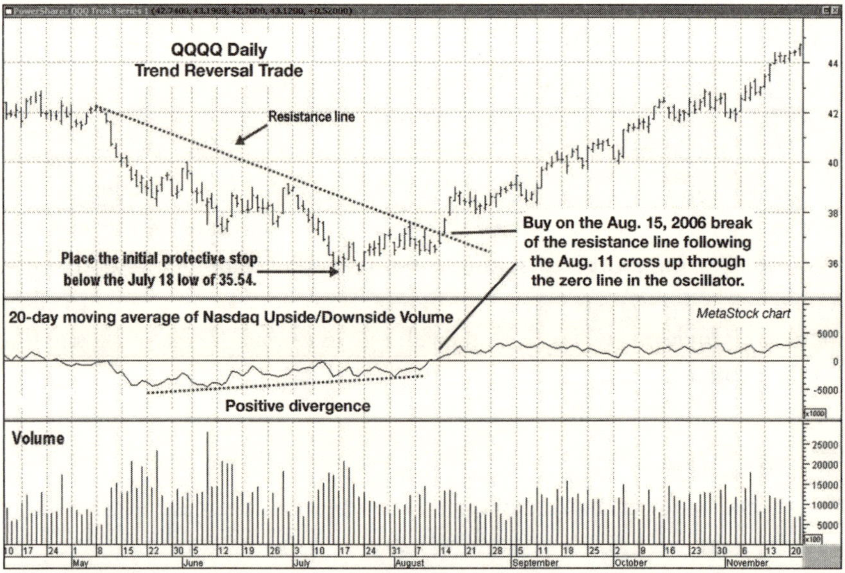

Chart 8.92 Upside/Downside Volume Oscillator, Positive Divergence Trade Entry, Nasdaq Composite Daily

Source: MetaStock

Oscillator crossing up through the zero line (see Chart 8.92). This shows positive price momentum confirmed by a breakup through resistance, both necessary ingredients to start a trend change.

On August 15, 2006, the price of the Nasdaq 100 Trust ETF (QQQQ) closed above its downsloping resistance line, following the August 11 cross up through the zero line in the 20-day moving average of the Nasdaq Upside/Downside Volume Oscillator. This gave two confirming signals that the trend was in the process of reversing. An initial protective stop should have been placed below the July 18 low of 35.54.

Trader Tips

The Upside/Downside Volume Oscillator is computed the same way as the Cumulative Volume Index, except that daily values are not added to a running total. This versatile oscillator can be used for doing the following:

- Identifying overbought and oversold market conditions
- Showing trend divergences that lead to trend corrections or reversals
- Spotting good positive or negative market signals on zero-line crossovers
- Identifying the market trend based on volume patterns

Volume patterns in the market give valuable clues as to whether buyers or sellers are in control and whether or not market psychology is changing. The Upside/Downside Volume Oscillator can allow traders to identify and exploit those patterns.

Yo-Yo Indicator

The catch phrase Yo-Yo indicator was developed by Richard Arms Jr., the creator of the ARMS Index, and was explained in an article he penned for *Barron's* in 1998. It combines the daily spread of a stock or index and divides daily volume by that number to figure out how many shares it takes to move a stock or index through one point of its spread (daily range).

On a historical basis, more volume is required to generate a wider price swing at tops, while the opposite is true at bottoms. This may be explained by the emotions of greed and fear. At tops there is complacency, which requires increased volume to get prices to swing in wider ranges. At bottoms there is fear, which causes prices to swing more widely, thus providing extra "juice" to lower-volume numbers.

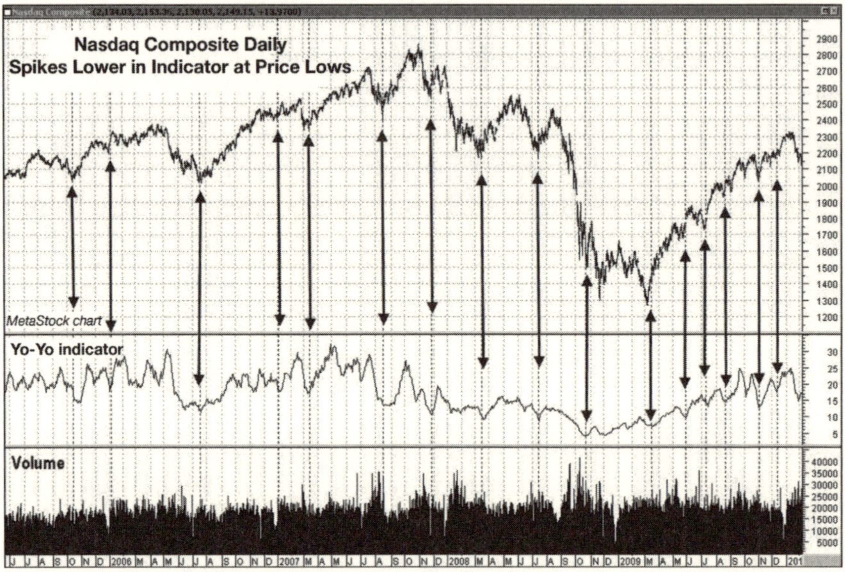

Chart 8.93 Yo-Yo Indicator, Nasdaq Composite Daily

Source: MetaStock

Formulation

This is the formula for the Yo-Yo indicator:

$$\frac{\text{10-day sum of }\{(\text{volume} / 1000) / [(\text{high} - \text{low}) / \text{high}]\}}{10}$$

While the Yo-Yo indicator was developed to exploit the emotions of greed and fear, we have found it to be a versatile tool that can actually trend with price as well as show divergences between price and the indicator, which alerts traders that a change in direction is due. The Nasdaq Composite plot in Chart 8.93 shows how lows in the Yo-Yo indicator coincide with short-term market lows.

Trend Confirmation

The Yo-Yo indicator is also good at confirming trends and typically coincides with market low points. In an uptrending market, the indicator tends to make higher lows, mirroring the price movement. This shows that the level of panic on sell-offs subsides as uptrends develop, demonstrating

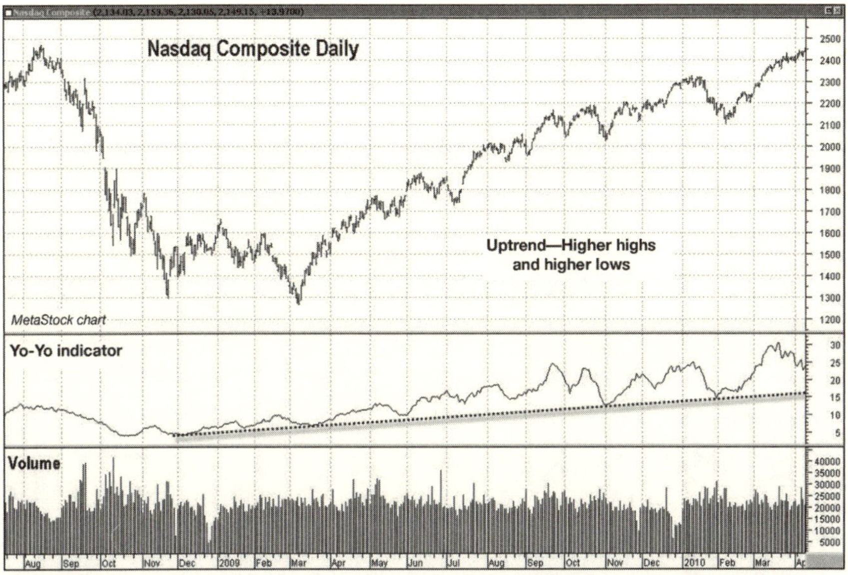

Chart 8.94 Yo-Yo Indicator, Uptrend Confirmation, Nasdaq Composite Daily

Source: MetaStock

positive sentiment among traders. The Nasdaq Composite view in Chart 8.94 shows how the Yo-Yo indicator trends right along with the index. Note the positive divergence (lower lows on prices, higher lows on the indicator) at the March 2009 low.

The plot of the Nasdaq Composite in Chart 8.95 shows how the Yo-Yo indicator trended lower with prices from October 2007 through December 2008.

Divergences

Chart 8.96 gives a closer look at the positive divergence that developed in the Nasdaq Composite preceding the March 2009 low. Note how the indicator bottomed a full two months before price did. That is continued evidence that divergences should not be traded until price confirms a change in trend direction.

The Yo-Yo indicator is also useful across multiple time frames. The weekly chart of the S&P 500 in Chart 8.97 shows a very large negative divergence beginning in early 2007. Notice how prices continued higher for weeks while the indicator began trending lower. This was a full 10 months before the fall top, but it was an indication that there was real trouble ahead.

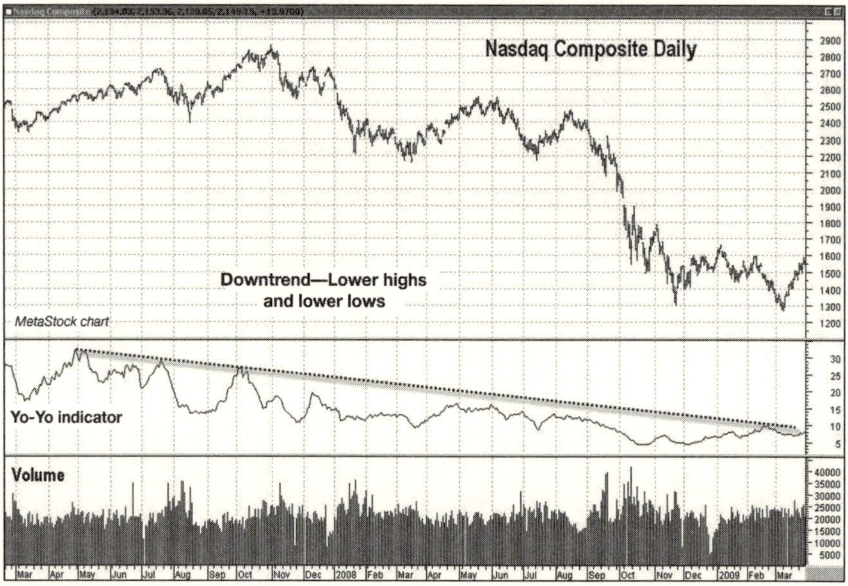

Chart 8.95 Yo-Yo Indicator, Downtrend Confirmation, Nasdaq Composite Daily

Source: MetaStock

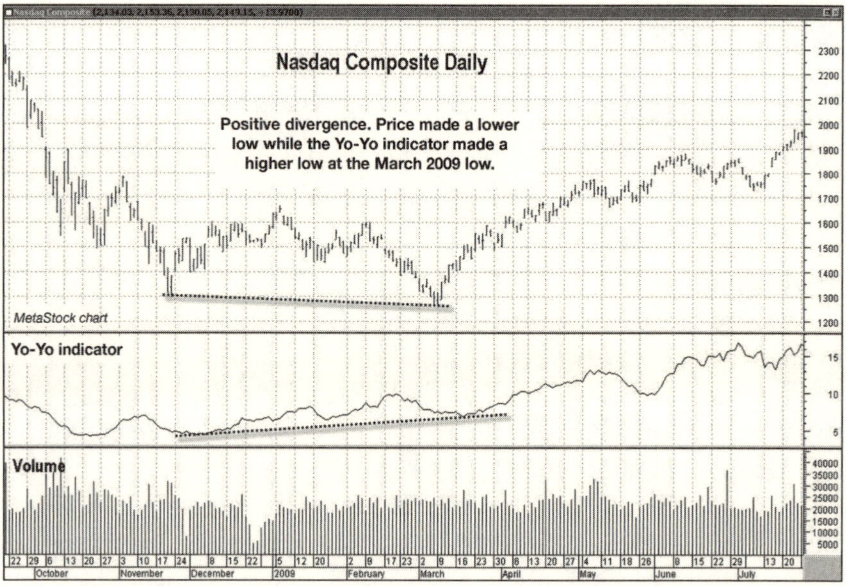

Chart 8.96 Yo-Yo Indicator, Positive Divergence, Nasdaq Composite Daily

Source: MetaStock

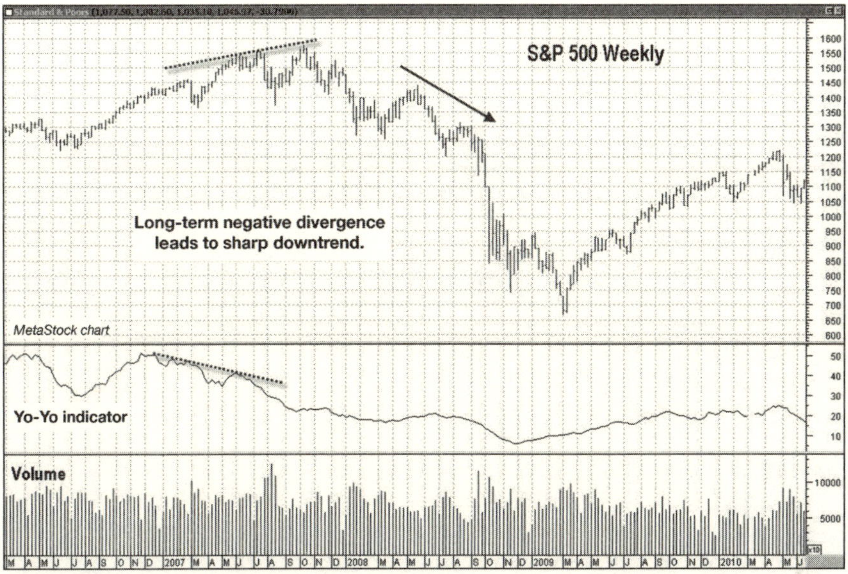

Chart 8.97 Yo-Yo Indicator, Negative Divergence, Nasdaq Composite Daily

Source: MetaStock

Trade Setup

The Yo-Yo indicator is an effective tool to spot a change in sentiment that can tip traders that a change in direction is due. In the example in Chart 8.98, the Yo-Yo indicator is plotted below a price chart of the DJ Diamonds Trust ETF (DIA). Note how the Yo-Yo indicator made slightly lower lows as the selling progressed from February 2004 to August 2004. Notice on the final corrective low in October 2004 how the Yo-Yo indicator made a much higher low, showing a divergence between trader sentiment and price action. The divergence was a clue that the trend was about to change. Confirmation by price action in the form of an upside break of the downsloping resistance line connecting the September 2004 and October 2004 highs would signal a trade entry.

Trade Entry

As Chart 8.98 reveals, price declined during 2004, making lower highs and lower lows; the Yo-Yo indicator confirmed each low by making a slightly lower low each time until the month of October. As price declined into what turned out to be the final low for the move on October 25, 2004,

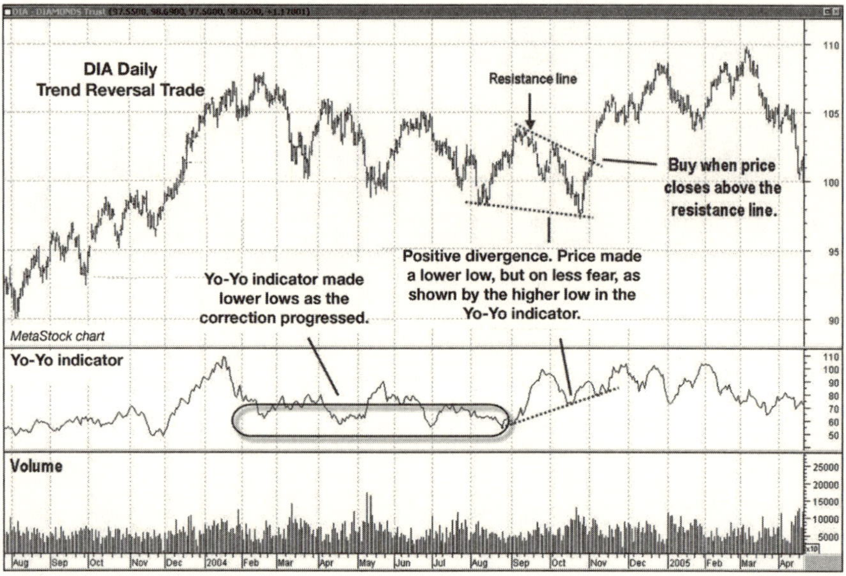

Chart 8.98 Yo-Yo Indicator, Positive Divergence Trade Setup, DJ Diamonds Trust ETF

Source: MetaStock

the Yo-Yo indicator had already begun to make higher lows, displaying a reduced level of fear. The only piece of the puzzle left was for price to confirm a trend reversal by taking out the resistance line drawn over the September–October highs (see Chart 8.99). On November 3, 2004, price closed above the downsloping resistance line, which was the signal that the trend was ready to reverse. An initial protective stop should have been placed below the October 25 low of 97.27.

Trader Tips

The Yo-Yo indicator was developed to track and exploit the emotions of fear and greed. It is also a versatile tool that can do the following:

- Confirm market trends
- Show divergences that lead to short-term changes in direction
- Be used over longer time frames to give a big-picture look at market trends

While the Yo-Yo indicator was developed with a single purpose in mind, it is a versatile analysis tool that can perform multiple functions.

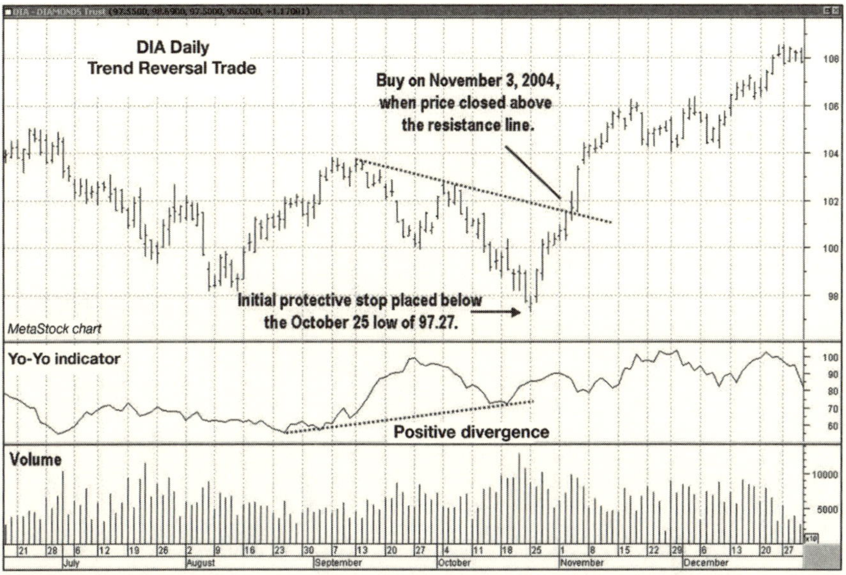

Chart 8.99 Yo-Yo Indicator, Positive Divergence Trade Entry, DJ Diamonds Trust ETF

Source: MetaStock

Summary

Indicator	Description	Uses and Time Frame
Advance/Decline Volume Ratio	Shows whether buyers or sellers are in control of the market through differences between the two bodies of volume	–Confirms price trends and shows trend divergences. It should be smoothed with a moving average to be used effectively. –Shorter term
ARMS/TRIN Index	A contrarian indicator used to detect overbought and oversold periods in the market	–Used to identify short-term overbought and oversold conditions. Its inverse relationship to the market can make it challenging for a new trader to interpret. –Shorter term
10-Day and 30-Day Open ARMS/TRIN	A smoothed version of the ARMS that is useful for short- to intermediate-term market analysis.	–Confirms price trends and shows trend divergences. It can be inverted for easier, more intuitive interpretation. –Shorter to intermediate term
Cumulative Volume Index	Accumulates the daily difference of up vs. down volume to gauge buying and selling pressure in the market	–Confirms price trends and shows trend divergences. It can lag the market at important turning points. –Longer term

(Continued)

Indicator	Description	Uses and Time Frame
Exchange Volume	The daily total of shares traded on a given exchange (NYSE, Nasdaq, etc.)	–Shows the conviction of traders. It needs to be combined with price for meaningful analysis. –Shorter to intermediate term
5-Day Up/Down Volume Oscillator	Used to measure the strength and weakness of market trends by combining advancing and declining volume totals over a 5-day period	–Confirms price trends, shows trend divergences, and provides buy and sell signals on zero-line crossovers. It can be volatile, however, which leaves it prone to whipsaw signals. –Shorter term
Index Volume	The daily total of shares traded in a given index (S&P 500, DJIA, etc.)	–Shows the conviction of traders. It needs to be combined with price for meaningful analysis. –Shorter to intermediate term
Nasdaq/NYSE Volume Ratio	Attempts to measure the speculative tone of the market by comparing Nasdaq to NYSE volume	–Worked well in the past to confirm market tops and bottoms. But Nasdaq volume has continually grown in contrast to the NYSE, which tends to distort the indicator and reduce its effectiveness. –Shorter to intermediate term
10-Day Up/Down Volume Oscillator	Used to measure the strength and weakness of market trends by combining advancing and declining volume totals over a 10-day period	–Confirms price trends, shows trend divergences, and provides buy and sell signals on zero-line crossovers. It is a shorter-term tool that should not be used for long-term market analysis. –Shorter to intermediate term
Upside/Downside Volume	Used to identify market trend and turning points	–Confirms price trends and shows trend divergences. It is best applied to short-term broad market analysis. –Shorter term
Upside/Downside Volume Oscillator	Combines Upside/ and Downside Volume into a single oscillator	–Confirms price trends, shows trend divergences, and provides buy and sell signals on zero-line crossovers when smoothed. It can be volatile and choppy at times. –Shorter to intermediate term
Yo-Yo indicator	Combines the daily spread/range of a stock or index and divides daily volume by that number to figure out how many shares it takes to move the stock or index through 1 point of its spread	–Confirms price trends and shows trend divergences. This indicator is extremely versatile across multiple time frames. –Shorter to intermediate term

Chapter 9

THE VOLUME INDICATORS

We now move forward from broad market indicators and oscillators to focus on volume-based indicators used in analyzing and trading specific securities.

We have categorized these indicators as volume indicators because each has a volume component in its formulation. Although no compilation is ever complete, we have attempted to include those volume indicators most widely used by traders. Chapter 9 lays out 10 specific volume indicators:

1. Accumulation/Distribution
2. Equivolume
3. Intraday Intensity
4. Leibovit Volume Reversal
5. Negative Volume Index
6. Positive Volume Index
7. On-Balance Volume
8. Open Interest
9. Volume Price Trend
10. Volume Rate of Change

Each indicator is described, and accompanied with chart examples and examples of various uses of the indicator or variations of that indicator. To help explain how these tools are put into practice, there is a sample trade setup and execution for each indicator, followed by an assessment of the strengths, weaknesses, and overall applicability of each indicator.

At the end of the chapter, you will find some techniques to make these indicators even more user friendly for Volume Analysis.

When reading through these discussions, you may find it useful to focus on the indicator chart, the volume bar chart, and the relationship between the two. This dual observation will allow you to discern how the volume component acts within the indicator, and offers assistance in timing your trading strategy. Once you have familiarized yourself with this relationship, you will be better able to assess the pattern of behavior of each individual indicator under varying market conditions. Specifically, the chart examples are designed to give you a view of how the indicator appears in bullish and bearish market scenarios, how it behaves with regard to positive and negative divergences, and other useful analytic setups.

Know Your Indicator

When looking at the examples below, it is essential to understand what the indicator is measuring. In reality there are two types of volume indicators. The first type is computed using a combination of price and volume data (e.g., Accumulation/Distribution, Leibovit Volume Reversal, and On-Balance Volume). The second type is computed using only volume data (e.g., Volume Rate of Change). When you begin to use your indicator, notice which type of tool you are using and what it is actually measuring. Some indicators will behave differently for different securities, and some indicators will be easier or more difficult for you to use. Note how successfully the indicator diverges from the price trend, more slowly or more quickly, in a more subtle or more pronounced way. And are there shifts in the ranges of the indicator? In these examples, you will see the volume indicators paired with other technical non-volume-based tools. Often we have chosen price momentum indicators or overbought/oversold indicators in an effort to capture the most data on a trading chart with the least overlapping or redundancy of information for trade setups or entries. This should serve as food for thought in regard to how volume indicators can be used with other non-volume-based indicators in your own trading system.

Tradeworthy Trend or Not?

In Chapters 8, 9, and 10, we suggest trade setup and entry positions. We are in no way advocating a trading system. However, we want you to note that almost all technical-analysis-based trading systems do work to identify trends and provide confirmation of, or spot, divergences. The solution we present here is how to best enhance your current trading system using volume indicators. If we were to take a simplistic view, most trading systems are based upon trading in the direction of the trend, including consolidations and continuations, or against the trend, recognizing divergences and reversal patterns. In our previous discussions, we discussed how to identify the trend and how to confirm the health and strength of a trend, and we looked at different trading patterns that might signal setups for us. Now we view the indicators in different trading environments so that you can get a feel for how they might actually look in your trading system. Many of the trading examples use divergences as an illustration. However, as we all know, there are as many ways to trade as there are traders.

Accumulation/Distribution

The Accumulation/Distribution line measures whether traders are *accumulating* (i.e., buying, on a net basis) or *distributing* (i.e., selling, on a net basis) shares by combining price momentum with volume. This indicator is most effective before turning points, as *volume precedes price*. In many cases, volume patterns change before price turns, which shows a change in trader sentiment. Volume-based indicators catch these changes in sentiment, suggesting that a change in trend could be imminent. This line should not be confused with the accumulation/distribution index originally developed by Larry Williams.

The Accumulation/Distribution line was taken several steps further when the innovative market technician Marc Chaikin set out to improve upon the very popular On-Balance Volume indicator (OBV). Whereas OBV accumulated volume based on the relationship from one day's closing price to the next, Chaikin wanted to quantify the close as to whether the period's action was positive or negative. His methodology compared the close to the midpoint of the range in order to determine whether the period's action was positive or negative.

Formulation

The Accumulation/Distribution line is actually computed in two parts. First, the formula finds the *close location value*, or CLV:

$$\text{CLV} = [(\text{close} - \text{low}) - (\text{high} - \text{close})] \,/\, (\text{high} - \text{low})$$

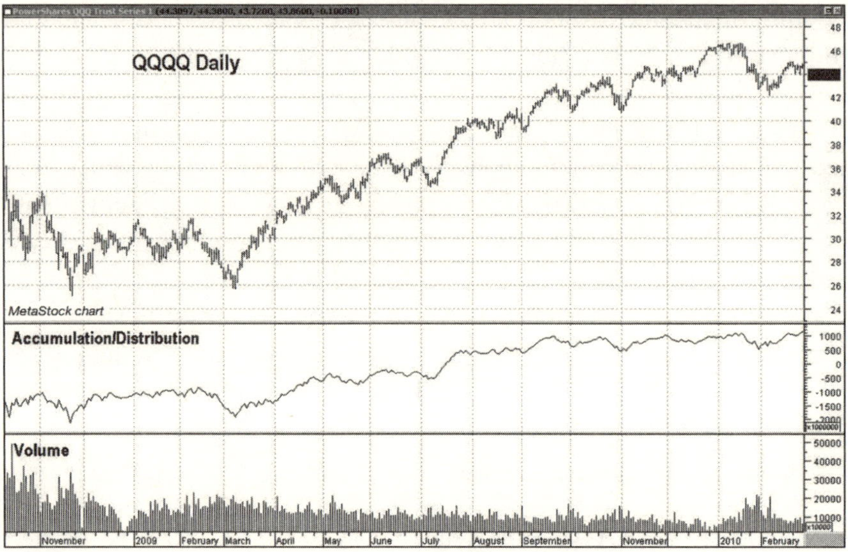

Chart 9.1 Accumulation/Distribution, Nasdaq 100 Trust ETF (QQQQ)

Source: MetaStock

The CLV can have a maximum value of 1 if price closes at its high for the period, and it can have a minimum value of −1 if price closes at its low for the period. Any close above the midpoint of the period will have a value greater than zero, and any close below the midpoint of the period will have a value less than zero. If price closes at the exact midpoint of the period, the value will be zero

Next, the formula calculates the Accumulation/Distribution (A/D) value for the period as follows:

$$\text{A/D line} = \text{yesterday's A/D value} + (\text{CLV} \times \text{period volume})$$

The Accumulation/Distribution indicator is a cumulative indicator, meaning that each day's reading is simply added to or subtracted from the previous day's total. This running total methodology allows a trader to spot systematic accumulation or distribution of shares and is most useful for spotting divergences. Chart 9.1 shows a plot of Accumulation/Distribution for the Nasdaq 100 Trust ETF (QQQQ).

Accumulation

In Chart 9.2, notice the range-bound trade of Amazon.com (AMZN) from June through September 2009 as depicted by the horizontal lines.

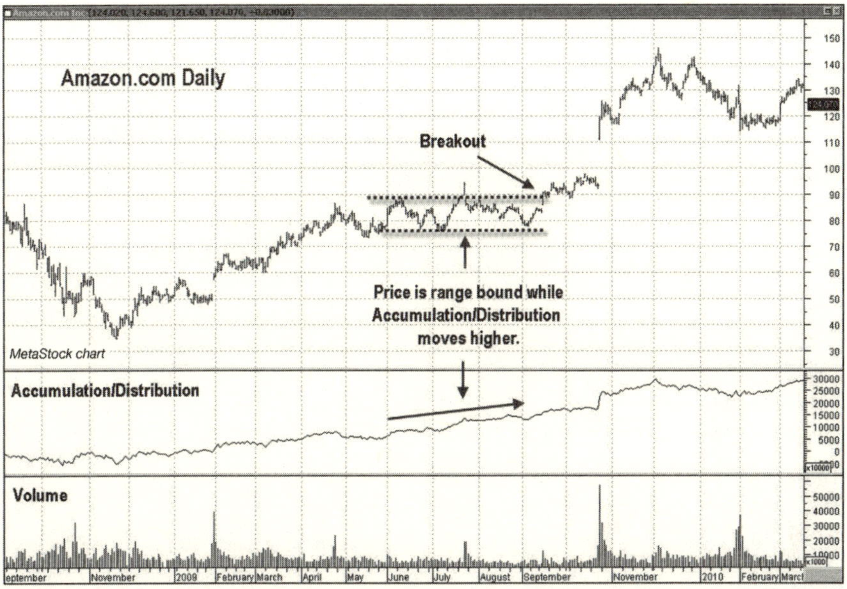

Chart 9.2 Accumulation/Distribution, Positive Accumulation, Amazon.com

Source: MetaStock

Next, look in the lower frame, which shows Accumulation/Distribution rising during the same time period. That shows accumulation of shares, which ultimately resulted in an upside breakout in September.

Distribution

In Chart 9.3, note how the price of Microsoft (MSFT) rallied to a high in April 2008, then began to move lower. Price declined into July, where it consolidated until August. Note that while price was in its two-month range, Accumulation/Distribution was still moving lower, indicating distribution. The downside break that followed in September and October 2008 continued into March 2009.

Trend Confirmation

The Accumulation/Distribution indicator is an excellent tool for revealing and confirming the strength of a move in price. In Chart 9.4, the iShares High Yield Corporate Bond ETF (HYG) put in a significant bottom in March 2009. Following that bottom, HYG rallied 47 percent into early 2010. The Accumulation/Distribution indicator showed that volume was indeed supporting the price action as HYG pushed higher throughout 2009.

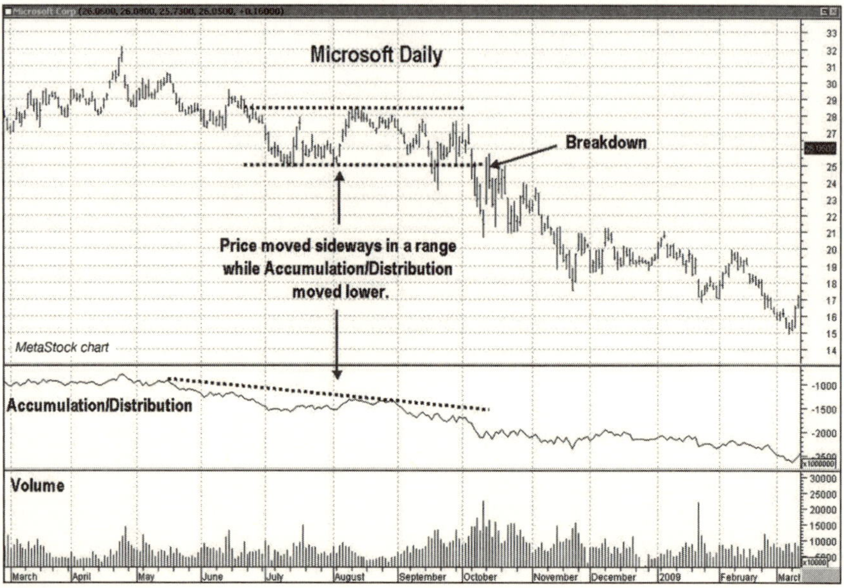

Chart 9.3 Accumulation/Distribution, Negative Distribution, Microsoft Corp.

Source: MetaStock

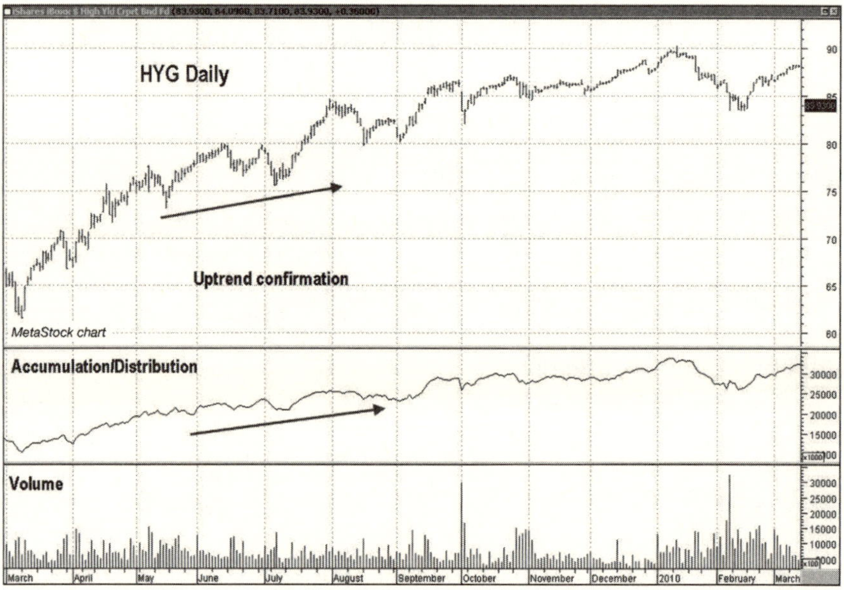

Chart 9.4 Accumulation/Distribution, Uptrend Confirmation, iShares High Yield Corporate Bond ETF

Source: MetaStock

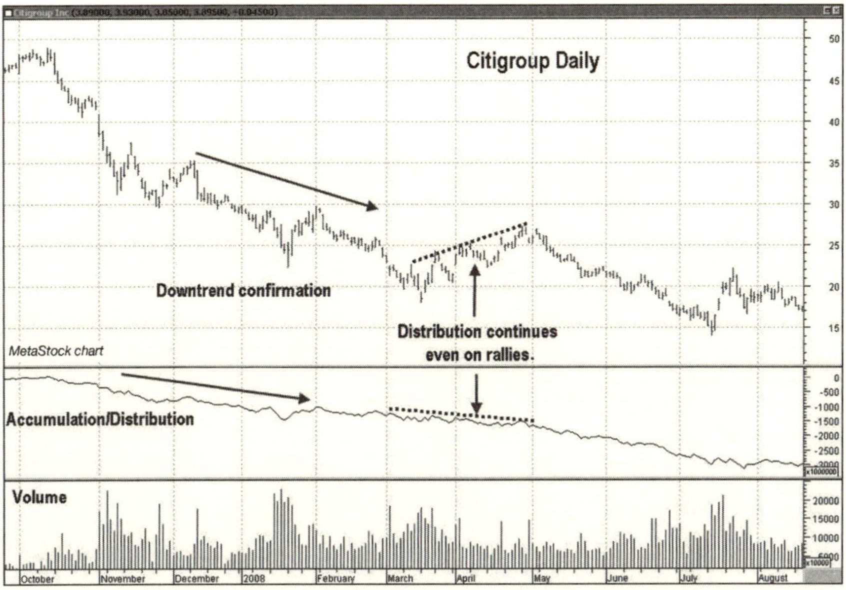

Chart 9.5 Accumulation/Distribution, Downtrend Confirmation, Citigroup

Source: MetaStock

The market top in the fall of 2007 was caused in large part by problems in the financial sector. In Chart 9.5, Citigroup (C) saw intense distribution following that top. Citigroup had actually topped in December 2006 (not shown), but real selling pressure did not develop until October 2007, when the broader market headed south. Note how Accumulation/Distribution confirmed Citigroup's downtrend, continuing to make lower highs even as Citigroup's price rallied from March to May 2008. This is a great example to show how Accumulation/Distribution can keep a trader from buying into false corrections.

Trade Setup

Up until now, all of the examples shown using Accumulation/Distribution have been using a daily time frame. The trade example in the following paragraphs will illustrate the usefulness and versatility of the Accumulation/Distribution indicator in an intraday time frame.

The example of the E-Mini S&P 500 futures contract in Chart 9.6 shows the use of Accumulation/Distribution in a 60-minute time frame from May 31 through June 20, 2010. When spotting divergences with the indicator, it is wise to be patient and wait for price confirmation before entering a trade.

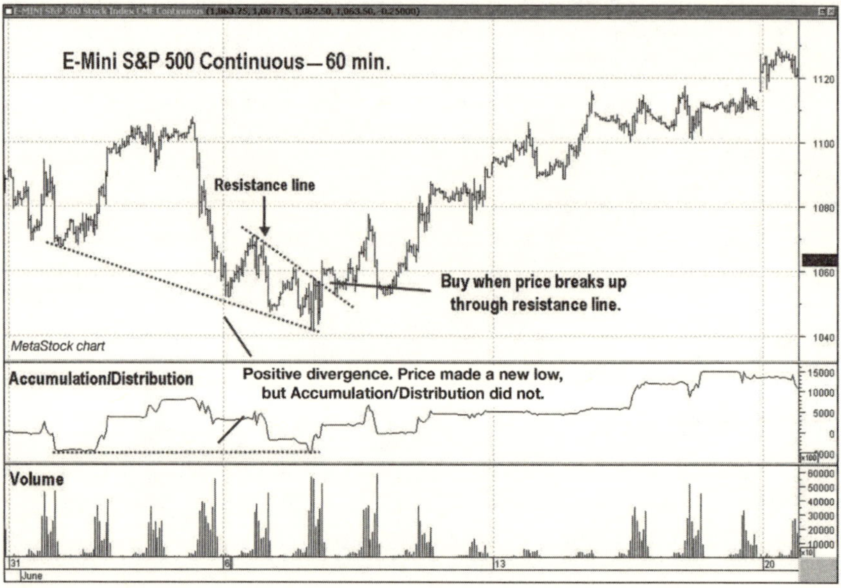

Chart 9.6 Accumulation/Distribution, Positive Divergence Trade Setup, E-Mini S&P 500 Contract

Source: MetaStock

The trade setup takes the form of a positive divergence between price and the Accumulation/Distribution indicator. Note how price makes a series of new lows into June 8, while the indicator holds its previous low. That is a sign of latent buying pressure, which should provide good fuel for the next rally. A buy could have been executed when price broke up through the downsloping resistance line drawn across the high prices made on June 6 to 8.

Trade Entry

As price declined into its June 8, 2010, low, Accumulation/Distribution was holding its prior low made on June 1. Also note that price action became choppy and volatile coming into the low. That was a sign that buyers were coming in to absorb the selling. The choppiness of the trade made it possible to draw a shorter-term resistance line, which would provide more timely entry on a resistance line break. Chart 9.7 shows that the downsloping resistance line was penetrated on June 8, giving a clear buy signal. The initial protective stop should have been placed below the June 8 low of 1041.25.

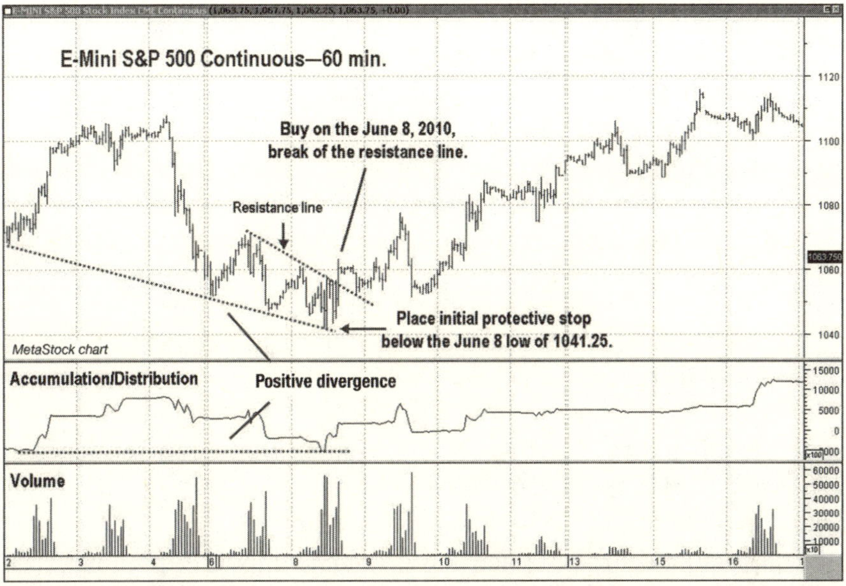

Chart 9.7 Accumulation/Distribution, Positive Divergence Trade Entry, E-Mini S&P 500 Contract

Source: MetaStock

Trader Tips

Accumulation/Distribution is an indicator that tracks trends well. It is effective for the following:

- Providing confirmation in trending situations, showing that price and volume are in sync
- Alerting traders to potential trend changes when price trend and the indicator diverge
- Showing the general flow of money into or out of a security and monitoring whether volume is increasing as the trend moves higher on increased buying pressure or lower on increased selling pressure, demonstrating whether buyers or sellers are in control

The following are some disadvantages of using Accumulation/Distribution:

- The Accumulation/Distribution indicator does not address gaps. As it focuses on the closing price in relation to its own range for the period, it does not consider the relationship of closing prices from one period to the next. For example, if price gaps higher but closes poorly in its range, a negative reading for that period in the indicator would be produced.

- Since price is the predominant value in computing Accumulation/Distribution, good price closes on tepid volume may not show a slowing trend as readily as poor price closes in the period's range. For this reason, it is more difficult to detect smaller changes in the trend.

Equivolume

Equivolume is an indicator system that compares price and volume and plots them together as one piece of data. Equivolume was developed by renowned market technician Richard W. Arms Jr., creator of the ARMS Index, and is discussed in his book *Volume Cycles in the Stock Market.*

Equivolume combines price and volume and plots it in a single box. Instead of plotting volume separately at the bottom of the chart, its inclusion in the price plot gives a trader both the price and volume action of the time period in a single box. It displays the importance of volume in its relationship to price. The height of the box represents the high and low of the time period plotted. The width of the box represents the volume relative to the total shares traded over that time period. The heavier the volume, the wider the box. Typically, wider boxes that penetrate support or resistance are very important, as the width of those boxes shows how much conviction was behind the breakout or price move.

Box width is calculated using what Arms refers to as a normalized value of volume. It is achieved by dividing the actual volume for the period by the total of all volume displayed on the chart. The width of each box plotted is based on a percentage of total volume, with 100 equaling the total of all percentages.

Equivolume is a great tool for identifying breakouts and broad market reversals. Figure 9.1 shows some common Equivolume shapes and their meanings. Chart 9.8 shows an actual plot of Equivolume for the Nasdaq 100 Trust ETF (QQQQ).

Trend Reversals

Equivolume is also a great tool for recognizing individual stock trend reversals. The shape of the box stands out clearly when there is a change in sentiment. Chart 9.9 shows by the width of the box how volume for Cisco Systems (CSCO) increased off the February 2008 low.

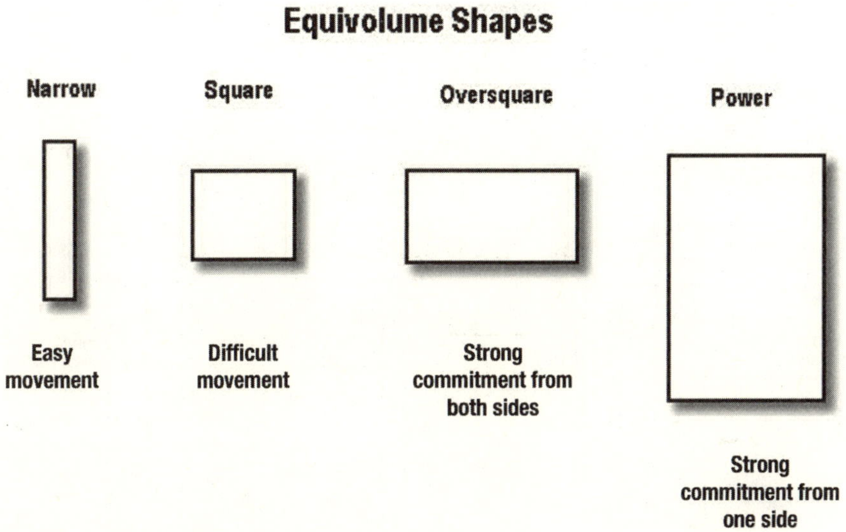

Figure 9.1 Equivolume Box Shapes

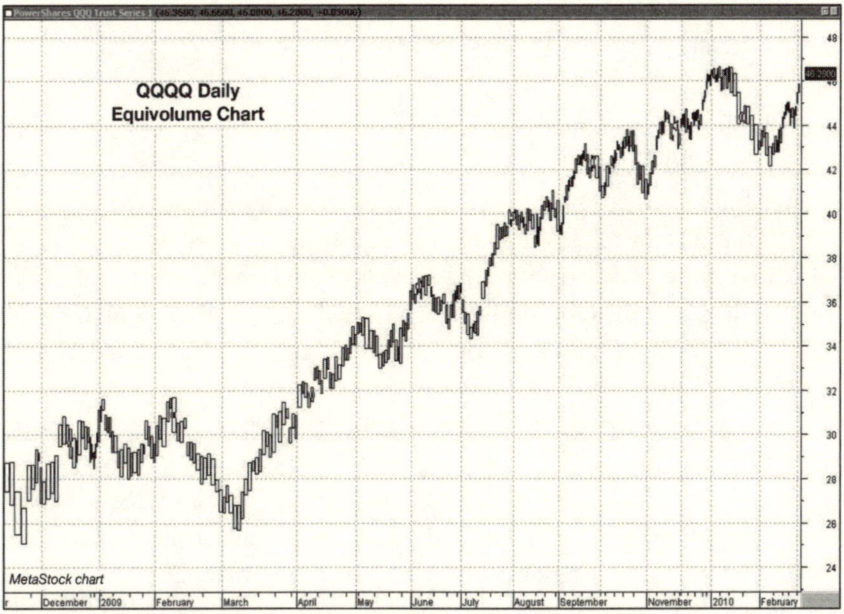

Chart 9.8 Equivolume Diagram, Nasdaq 100 Trust ETF (QQQQ)

Source: MetaStock

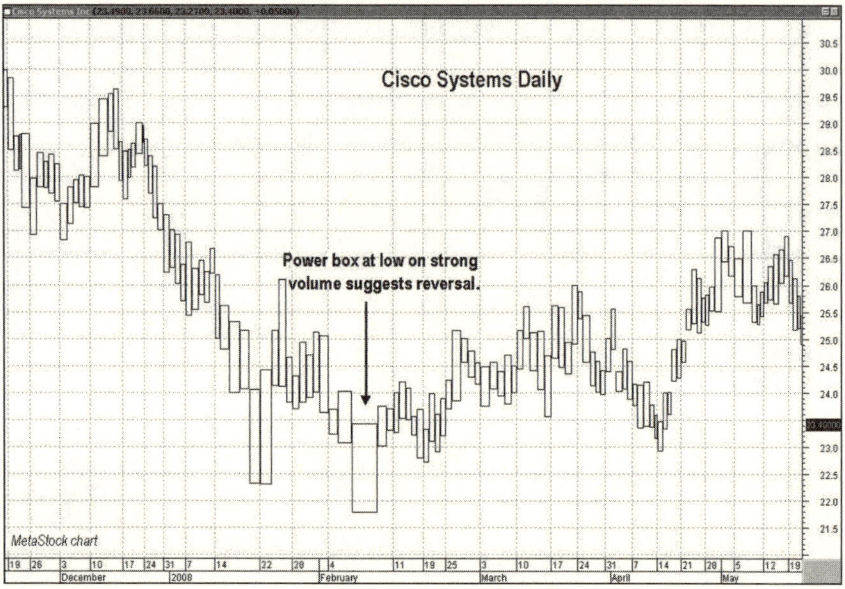

Chart 9.9 Equivolume Power Box at Low, Cisco Systems

Source: MetaStock

The psychology at market tops is different from the panicked, emotional mood at market bottoms. In Chart 9.10, a daily chart of the SPDR Gold Trust ETF (GLD), note the small size of the boxes as GLD goes into its December 2009 high. That shows the complacency and low volatility in a typical uptrend. Next, note the very large box following just off the price high. That torrent of selling marked a significant reversal.

Equivolume can also show changes in market characteristics that can alert traders to a developing trend change. In Chart 9.11, which shows 3M, note how the boxes increase in both height and width heading into the October 2008 low. The increase in the box sizes shows that volatility and volume are increasing, both of which were clues that a bottom was near.

Chart 9.12, a daily chart of the S&P 500 SPDR Trust ETF (SPY), shows how Equivolume can expose a weakening trend that is ripe for a reversal. Notice how narrow the boxes became near the January 2010 high. That was a clue that there was not enough volume to continue to push the market higher. The expansion of box size following the high showed that sellers were assuming control.

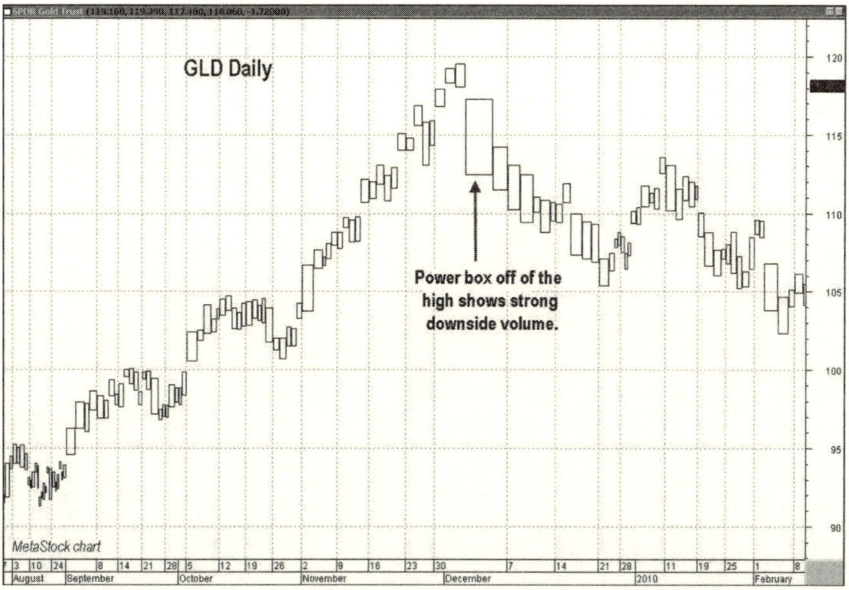

Chart 9.10 Equivolume Chart, Power Box off of High, SPDR Gold Trust ETF

Source: MetaStock

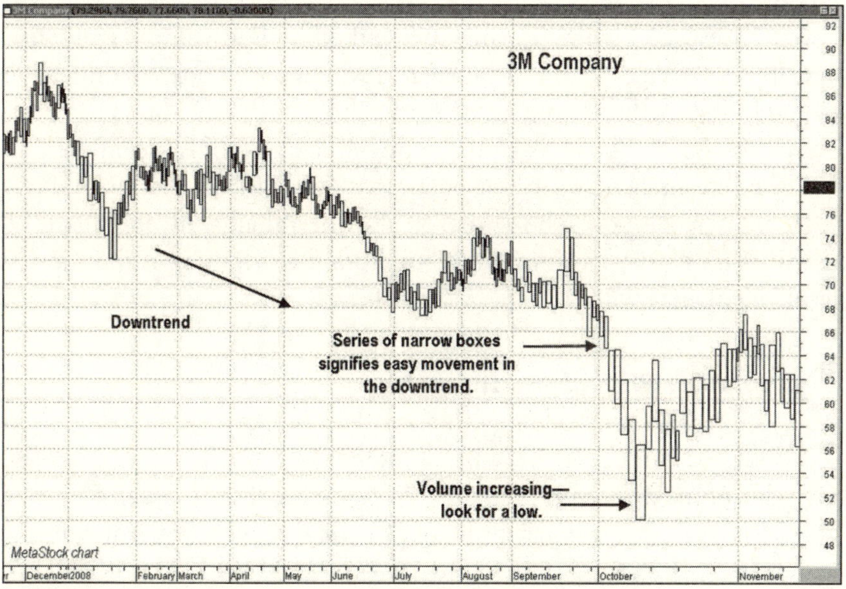

Chart 9.11 Equivolume Chart, Narrow Box Downtrend, 3M Corp.

Source: MetaStock

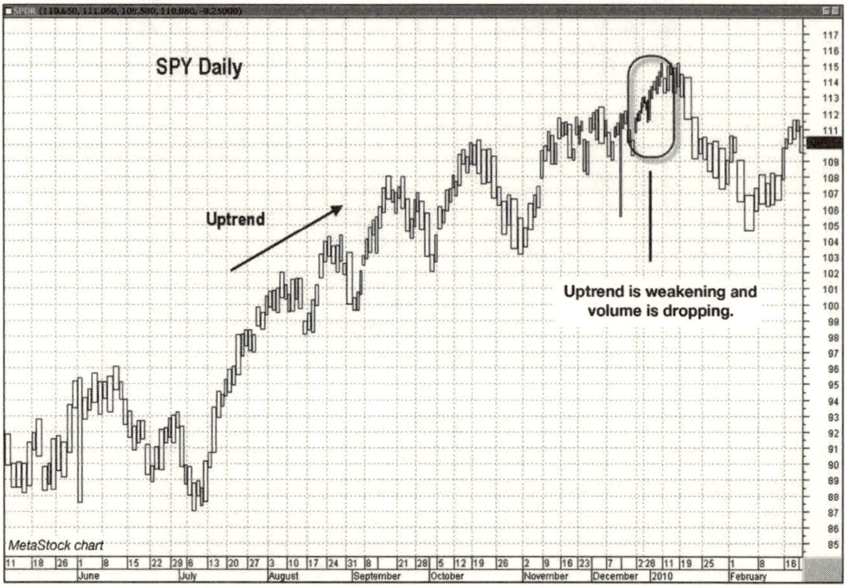

Chart 9.12 Equivolume Diagram, Weakening Trend, S&P 500 SPDR Trust ETF

Source: MetaStock

Breakouts

Power boxes (see Figure 9.1) are a big part of the Equivolume methodology. If price overcomes a resistance area with a power box, that increases the odds that the breakout will be successful. Chart 9.13 shows two great examples of power box breakouts on the same chart for Amazon.com.

Power box breakouts can also occur to the downside. Chart 9.14 shows such a downside power box breakout for the iShares Silver Trust ETF (SLV). Note the expansion of the box from the prior day as the support level is broken.

Equivolume with Other Indicators

Equivolume is a methodology that can be used quite effectively on its own, but combining it with a price momentum oscillator can increase the odds of making winning trades. Note in Chart 9.15, a daily chart of the S&P 500 SPDR Trust ETF (SPY), how combining Equivolume with a 14-day Relative Strength Index (RSI) would work. The 14-day RSI was in oversold territory when the power box was formed off the March 2009 low. Using power box reversals off overbought and oversold conditions can ensure that the trade is entered at a favorable level.

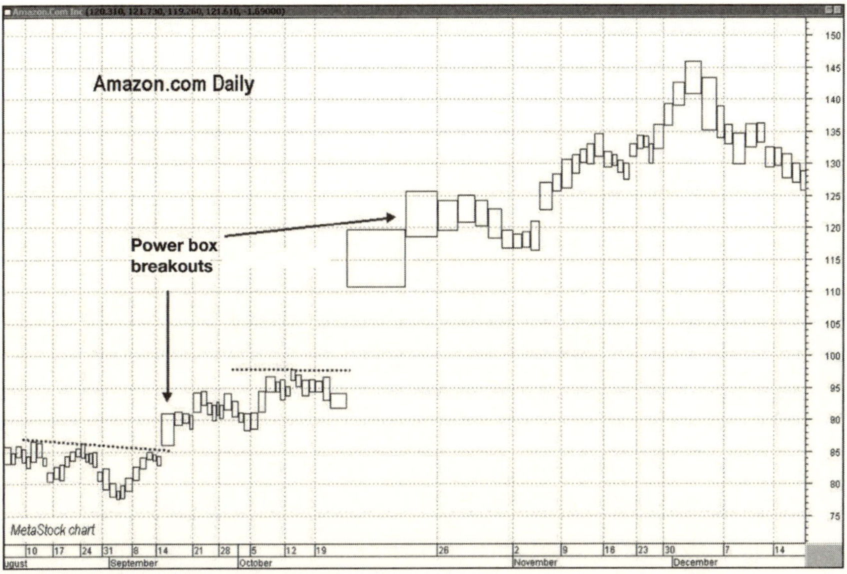

Chart 9.13 Equivolume Diagram, Power Box Upside Breakouts, Amazon.com

Source: MetaStock

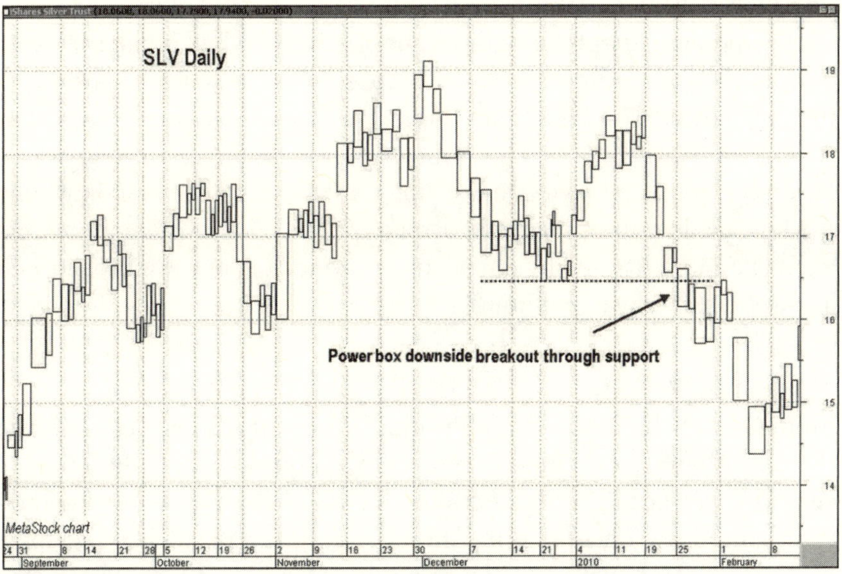

Chart 9.14 Equivolume Diagram, Power Box Downside Breakout, iShares Silver Trust ETF

Source: MetaStock

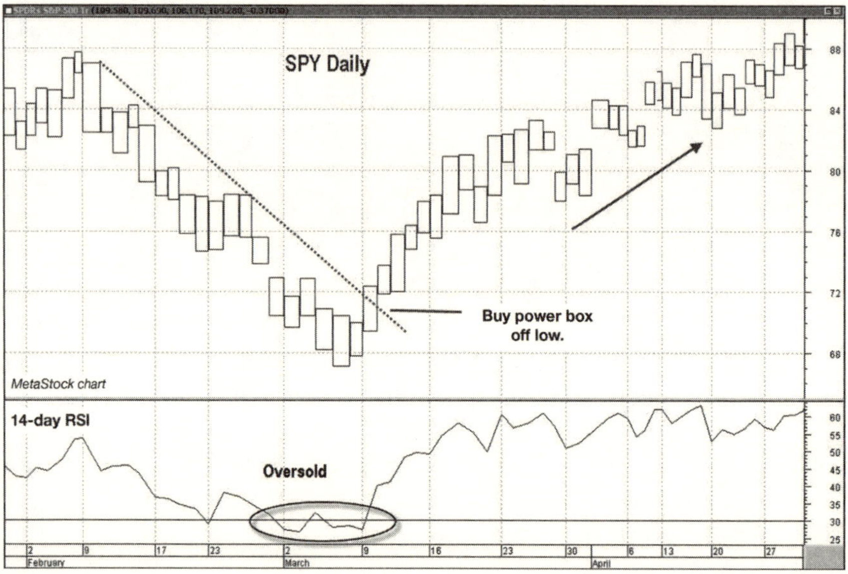

Chart 9.15 Equivolume Diagram with 14-Day RSI, Upside Reversal, S&P 500 SPDR Trust ETF

Source: MetaStock

Trade Setup

One of the strengths of the Equivolume charting method is that breakouts on volume tend to almost jump off the page at the technician. The example in Chart 9.16 shows a trend reversal in Cisco Systems (CSCO) at its August 2006 low. Price had been moving lower from May into August on lackluster volume, showing that selling pressure was abating. Connecting the tops made during the price descent produced a resistance line that would be a trade trigger for a long entry provided the line was broken with a power box (on heavy volume).

Trade Entry

From Chart 9.16 and its "amplification" in Chart 9.17, we can see that the downsloping resistance line was broken on August 9, 2006, with a very wide power box, which signifies that there was a lot of buying pressure behind the one-day price move. Also note the volume bar spike below price. An initial protective stop should have been placed below the August 4 low of 17.10. This was a very strong buy signal. Plotting charts using the Equivolume method makes it much easier for a trader's eyes to spot price moves on high volume.

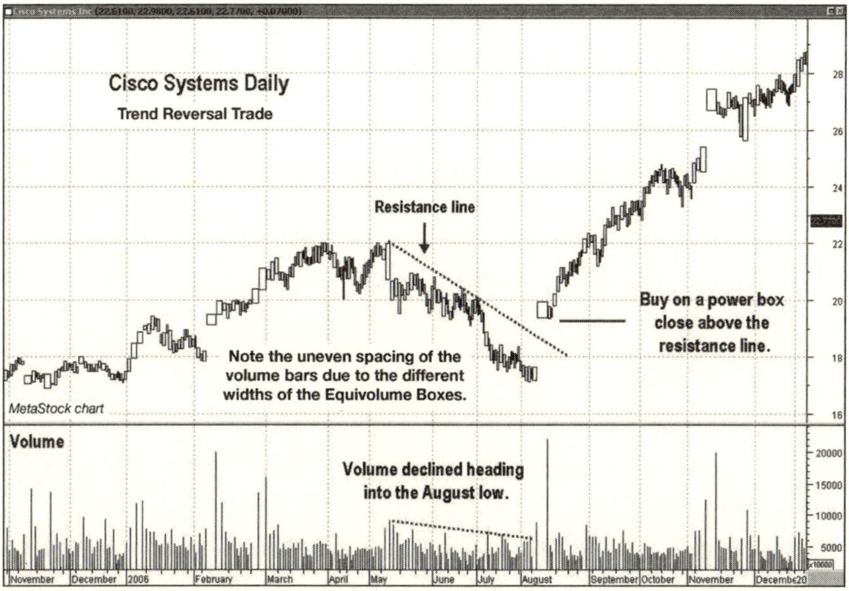

Chart 9.16 Equivolume Diagram, Volume Breakout Trade Setup, Cisco Systems

Source: MetaStock

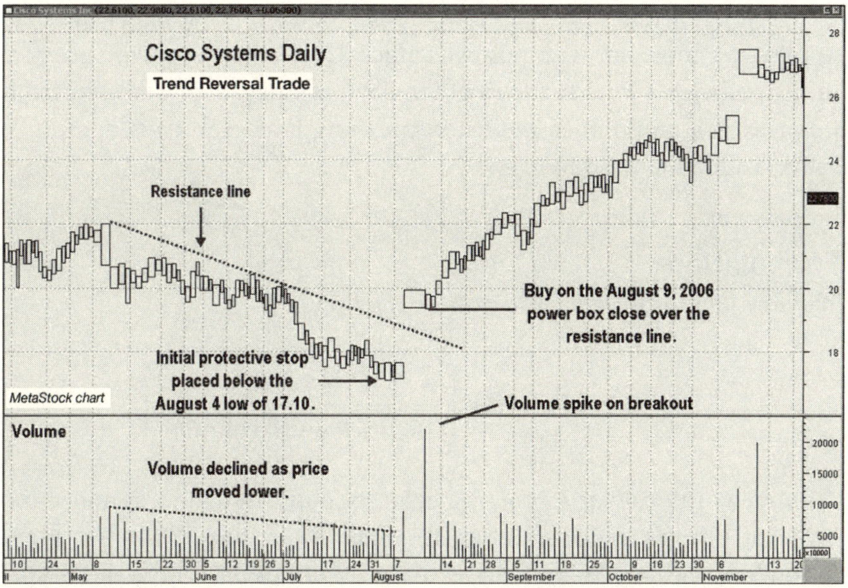

Chart 9.17 Equivolume Diagram, Volume Breakout Trade Entry, Cisco Systems

Source: MetaStock

Trader Tips

Equivolume is a great indicator for the following:

- Identifying trend reversals
- Showing clear pictures of breakouts
- Alerting traders that a change in trend may be near

For more information on the Equivolume methodology, see Arms Insider.com.

Intraday Intensity

Intraday Intensity (II) is a volume indicator that shows the flow of funds for a security based on where it closes in its high and low range. It was developed by the economist David Bostian to track the activity of institutional block traders. The theory behind Intraday Intensity is that institutional traders need to complete their trades by the end of the day, and this need becomes more urgent as the close of trading nears.

As traders move to get their orders filled late in the session, their actions cause prices to rise or fall, which gives a glimpse of their late-day activity via the relationship of the close to the day's range. Closes near the high result in an indicator with positive values. Closes in the middle are zero value, and closes near the lows of the day have negative values. Intraday Intensity is a cumulative indicator, meaning that each day's computed value is added to a running total.

Formulation

The formula for Intraday Intensity is as follows:

$$\text{II} = \text{yesterday's II} + \left[\frac{(2 \times \text{close} - \text{high} - \text{low})}{(\text{high} - \text{low}) \times \text{volume}}\right]$$

Intraday Intensity is a good indicator for confirming trends and showing trend divergences. Because of its cumulative nature, it trends to move in tandem with the higher-degree trend. We present it here in an indicator format; what counts here is the sustained direction of the indicator rather than the position relative to zero. The example of the Nasdaq 100 Trust ETF (QQQQ) in Chart 9.18 shows a plot of Intraday Intensity.

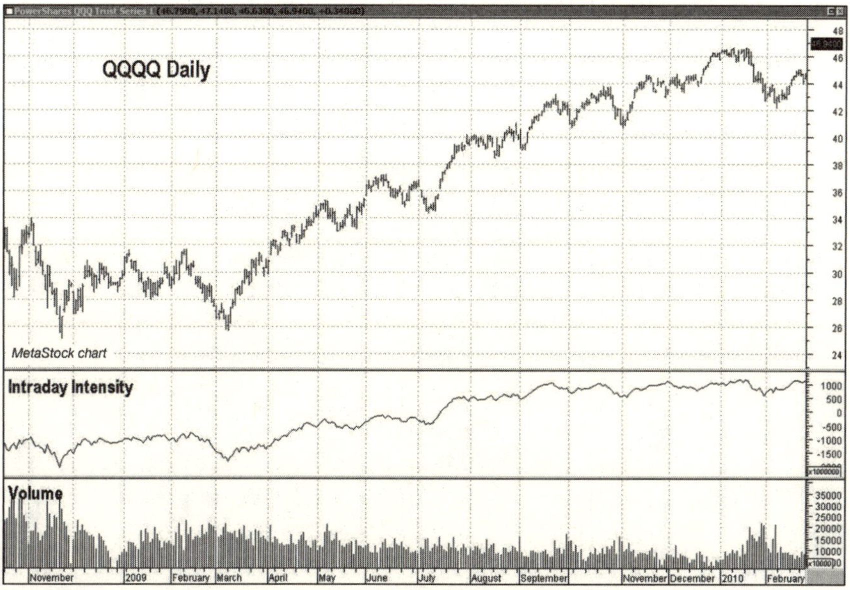

Chart 9.18 Intraday Intensity in Uptrend, Nasdaq 100 Trust ETF

Source: MetaStock

Trend Confirmation

As Intraday Intensity is a cumulative indicator, it has as its main strength trend confirmation. Note in Chart 9.19, a daily chart of IBM, how well it confirms the price uptrend.

Intraday Intensity can also make lower highs and lower lows along with price to confirm downtrends, as Chart 9.20 of the Market Vectors Gold Miners ETF (GDX) demonstrates.

Divergences

Since Intraday Intensity is a cumulative indicator that trends well with price, divergences don't occur very often, but when they do, they should be heeded. The example of the Nasdaq Composite in Chart 9.21 shows the positive divergence at the March 2009 low. Note how price made a lower low in March than in November, yet Intraday Intensity made a higher low.

Negative divergences carry the same significance as positive divergences, signaling that the price trend is ready to correct or even reverse. The example of the Market Vectors Gold Miners ETF (GDX) in Chart 9.22 shows how Intraday Intensity did not confirm the price high in May to June 2009. A sharp sell-off followed.

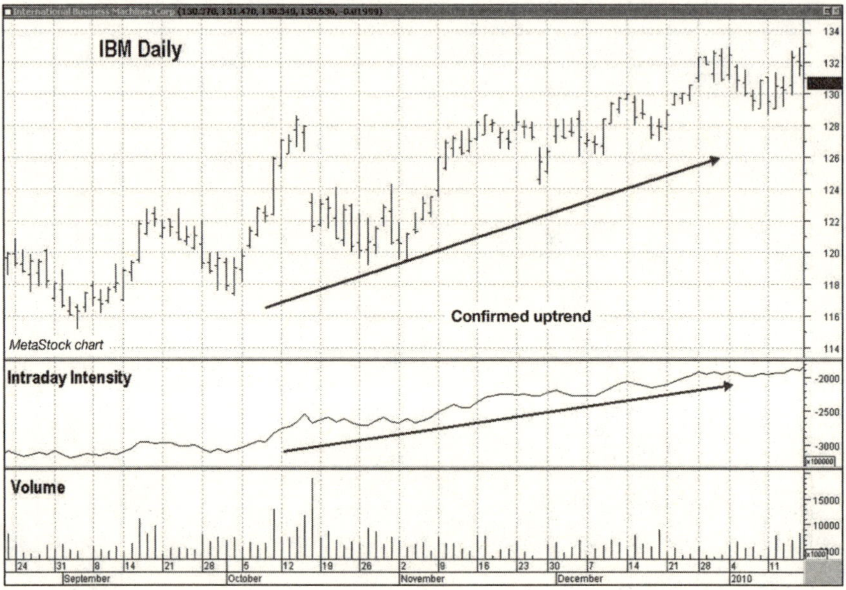

Chart 9.19 Intraday Intensity Confirming Uptrend, IBM Corp.

Source: MetaStock

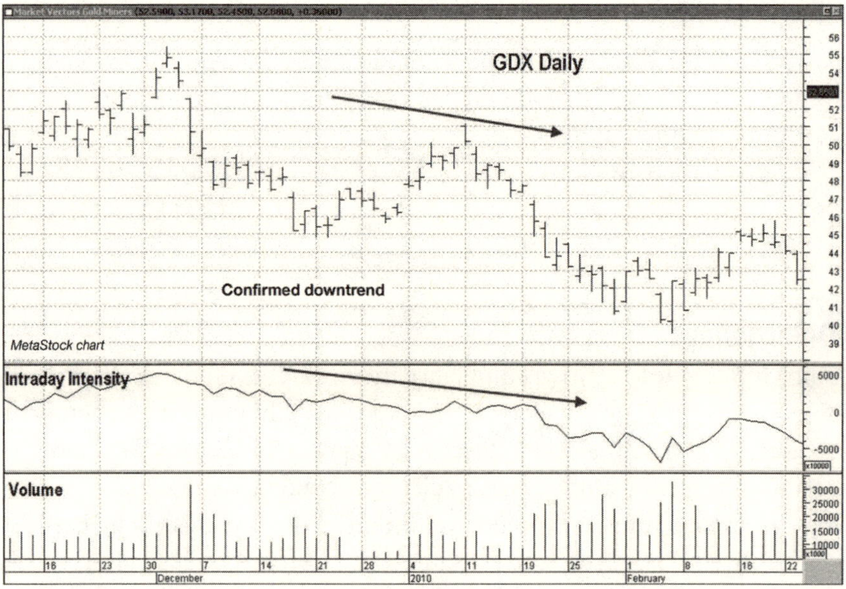

Chart 9.20 Intraday Intensity Confirming Downtrend, Market Vectors Gold Miners ETF

Source: MetaStock

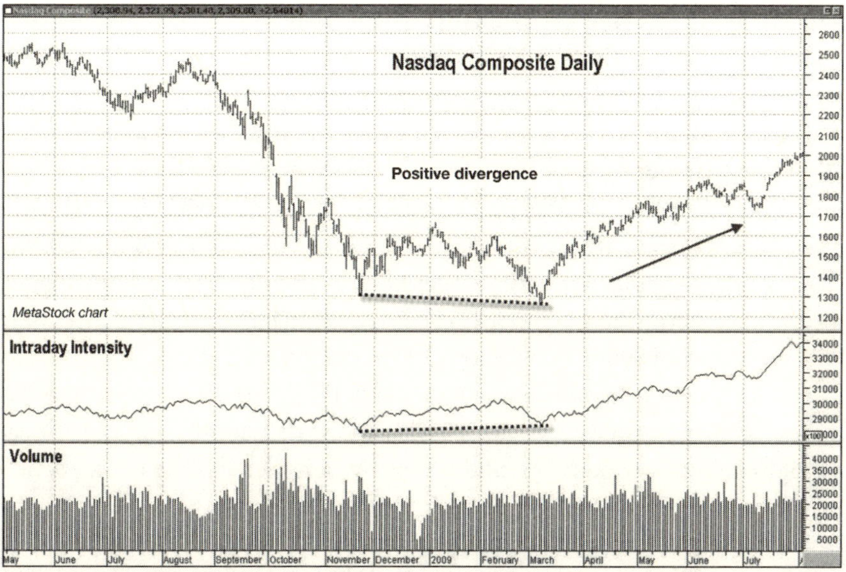

Chart 9.21 Intraday Intensity, Positive Divergence, Nasdaq Composite Daily

Source: MetaStock

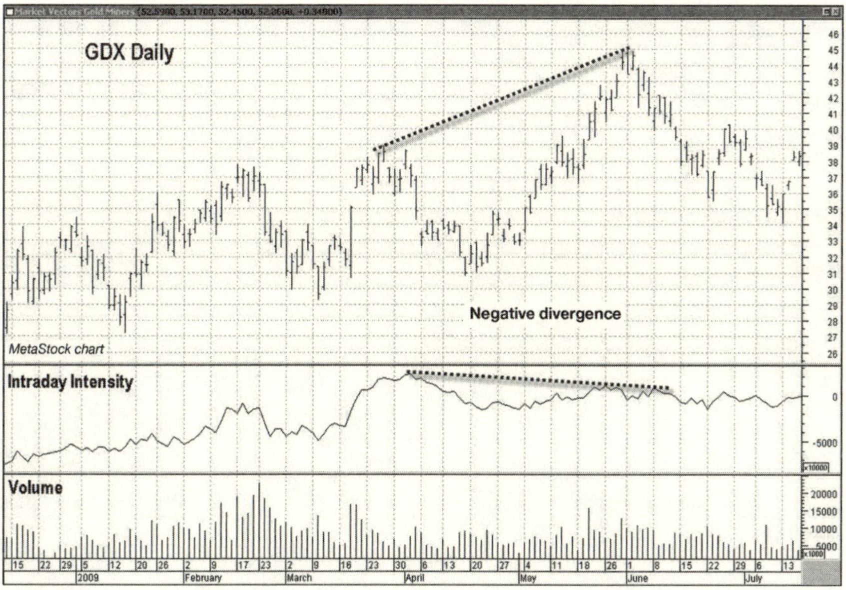

Chart 9.22 Intraday Intensity, Negative Divergence, Market Vectors Gold Miners ETF

Source: MetaStock

Intraday Intensity with Other Indicators

Since Intraday Intensity is such a good trending indicator, it lends itself well to pairing with a price momentum indicator that shows overbought and oversold levels. In such cases, Intraday Intensity acts as a trend filter, dictating whether buys or sells should be further analyzed.

In the example of the iShares High Yield Corporate Bond ETF (HYG) in Chart 9.23, since Intraday Intensity is trending higher, buys will be considered with a 10-period Williams %R used for the trade setup and buy trigger. If you have never used Williams %R, it is a price-based stochastic momentum indicator, meaning that it shows the close in relation to the high and low over a specific period of time. On a scale of 0 to −100, closes near the low of the range get values close to −100, and closes near the high read near zero. Readings between −80 and −100 are considered to be oversold, and readings between zero and −20 are considered to be overbought.

In each case, the trade is set up when the Williams %R indicator dips below −80. The buy is executed when Williams %R moves above −80. Pairing Intraday Intensity to confirm the trend with overbought and oversold readings can produce specific buy points with some solid trades in the direction of the trend.

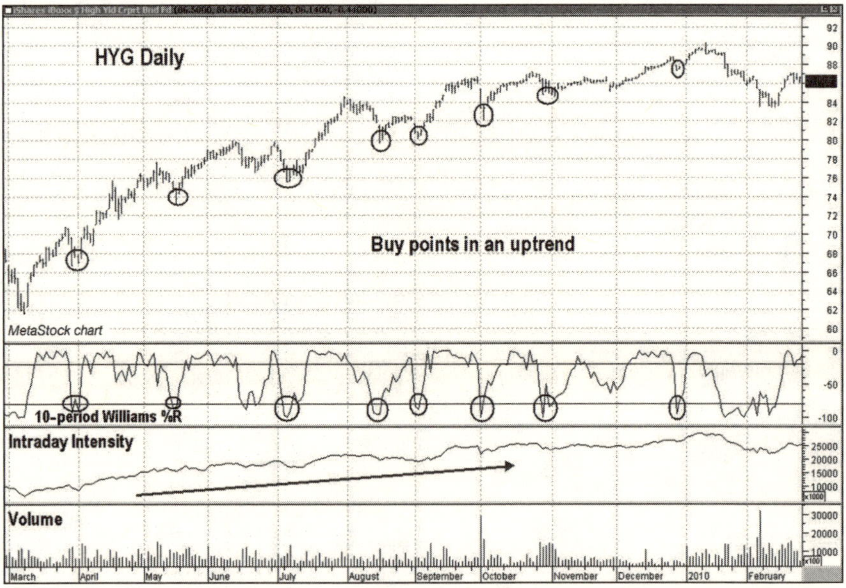

Chart 9.23 Intraday Intensity with 18-Period Williams %R, iShares High Yield Corporate Bond ETF

Source: MetaStock

Trade Setup

In most of the trade examples to this point, the broad market indicators and the cumulative trending indicators have been used to show divergences, which alert traders to an imminent trend change. In the following example of Intraday Intensity, we will show how this indicator can actually show a trend reversal (not a weakening of the existing trend) before price does.

In Chart 9.24, note how price has been in a downtrend from February 2007 into August 2007. Intraday Intensity declined with price into the low, which allowed for a resistance line to be drawn over each high from its June high to its August low. Intraday Intensity broke upward through its resistance line on September 11, 2007, a week before price broke through its own resistance line. That upside break in Intraday Intensity showed latent buying strength.

Trade Entry

Once Intraday Intensity broke through its downsloping resistance line, it signaled that price would likely do the same. Again, it is not wise to enter a trade based solely on an indicator reading. Price should confirm an indicator's movements.

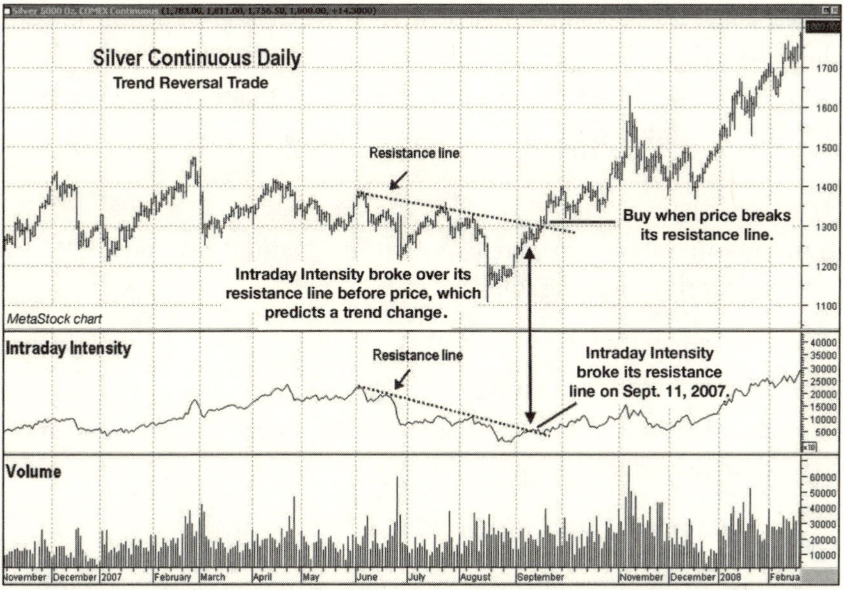

Chart 9.24 Intraday Intensity, Breakthrough for Trade Setup, Silver Continuous Daily

Source: MetaStock

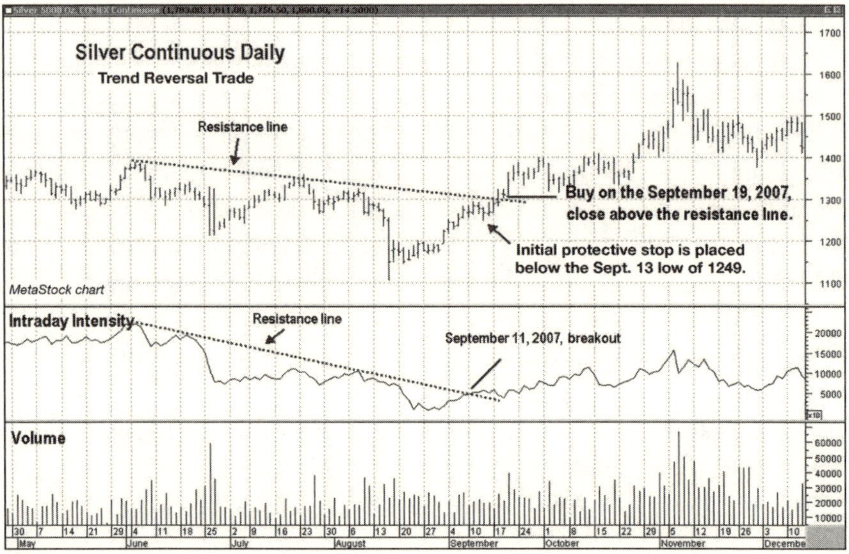

Chart 9.25 Intraday Intensity, Trade Entry, Silver Continuous Daily

Source: MetaStock

Price closed above its resistance line over a week later, on September 19, 2007; that was the clear signal, as price had confirmed the Intraday Intensity breakout, which triggered the buy. An initial protective stop should have been placed below the September 13 low of 1249. The reason for placing the stop there instead of below the August 16 low of 1106 is that if price moved back below its resistance line, that would have signaled a false breakout, negating the reason for the trade. Chart 9.25 gives an up-close view.

Trader Tips

Intraday Intensity is a cumulative indicator that tracks trends well. It is effective for the following things:

- Confirming trends
- Showing long-term divergences
- Pairing with short-term price momentum oscillators for generating short-term trading signals

The following are weaknesses of Intraday Intensity:

- It is not always as reliable at revealing divergences as at confirming trends.
- Reactions to changes in market direction can lag.

Leibovit Volume Reversal

The Leibovit Volume Reversal indicator (also known as the Leibovit VR or simply Volume Reversal) was developed in 1974 by Mark Leibovit, publisher and chief market strategist of the *Volume Reversal* newsletters and author of this book. Volume Reversal first became widely recognized during the author's seven-year tenure as a consulting technical analyst with Louis Rukeyser's *Wall Street Week* and as a market monitor on PBS's *Nightly Business Report*. It has served the financial community well for more than 30 years, having alerted traders to major market reversals as well as to short- and midterm trends in stocks, futures, and indexes.

The Leibovit VR is a volume-based technical indicator, the formulation of which remains proprietary as of this book's publication. The indicator signals a trader to a potential reversal in short-term market control from buyers to sellers, and vice versa. In many cases, these short-term shifts give birth to much larger market trends. Since not all volume spikes coincide with market turning points, the Volume Reversal has its own set of rules that attempt to weed out random volume noise to zero in on the most meaningful reversal patterns.

As the centerpiece of my Volume Analysis, the VR is relied upon heavily for timing and tactical volume overlays. It can be an extremely versatile indicator. Depending on the time frame that is being analyzed, traders can use the VR as a leading market breadth indicator as well as a signal for intraday and short- and midterm trading strategies. Many traders have found that the VR complements their own trading methodology. For more on the VR methodology, the VR newsletters can be accessed at VRTrader.com and VRGoldletter.com. Currently, Leibovit VR software can be accessed as an add-on feature for MetaStock charting software users.

Trend Confirmation

The Volume Reversal is a solid tool for alerting traders that volume is shifting from negative (i.e., selling pressure) to positive (i.e., buying pressure), as shown in the daily chart of the SDPR Gold Trust ETF (GLD) in Chart 9.26. The chart covers the time frame between January 14 and February 23, 2009. GLD had staged a sharp rally from November 13 through December 31, 2008, and had since pulled back to its January 14 low. Any Positive VR formed here would be a good indication that the uptrend started back in November was ready to resume. The Leibovit

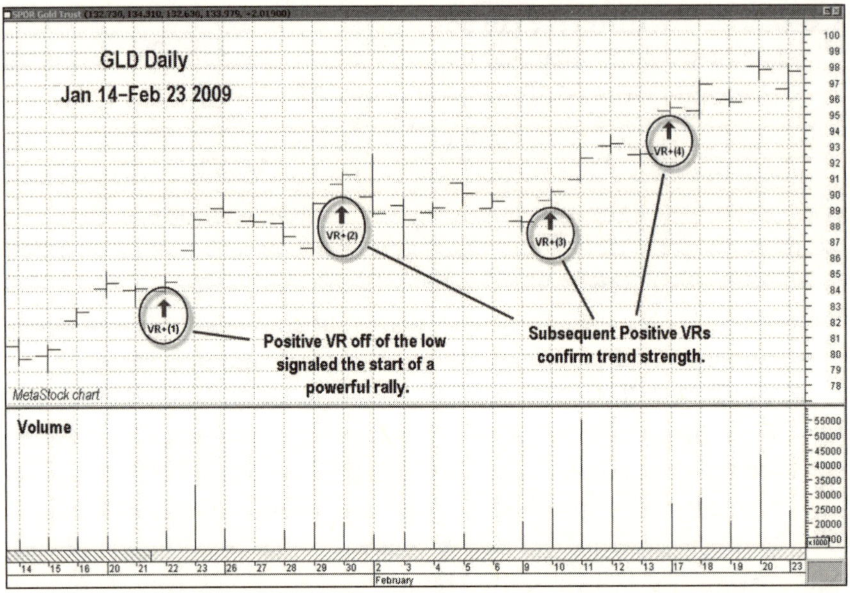

Chart 9.26 Positive Volume Reversals in an Uptrend, SPDR Gold Trust ETF

Source: MetaStock

VR confirmed that buyers were regaining control of the market, as a Positive Volume Reversal (herein shown as VR+) was generated off the January 22, 2009 low. Subsequent Positive Volume Reversals posted on January 30, February 10, and February 17 reinforced the case that buyers were in control and that GLD was ready to move higher.

Chart 9.27 shows how the VR was an alert to a negative change in trend, also using the SDPR Gold Trust ETF (GLD) between December 2009 and February 2010. A Negative Volume Reversal [shown as VR– (1)] on December 3, 2009, signaled the beginning of a strong downtrend, as sellers were gaining control of the market. A second Negative VR [VR– (2)] posted on December 17 confirmed the change in trend. A third Negative VR [VR– (3)] was posted on December 29. These three consecutive Negative VRs warned us that GLD was being distributed in anticipation of lower prices ahead. Another Negative VR [VR– (4)] was posted on January 12, 2010, following a three-week recovery rally, which showed that sellers were once again taking control.

Using the Volume Reversal for Short-Term Trading

The Leibovit VR can be applied to any trading market that uses price and volume data, including the commodities markets. Chart 9.28 shows the

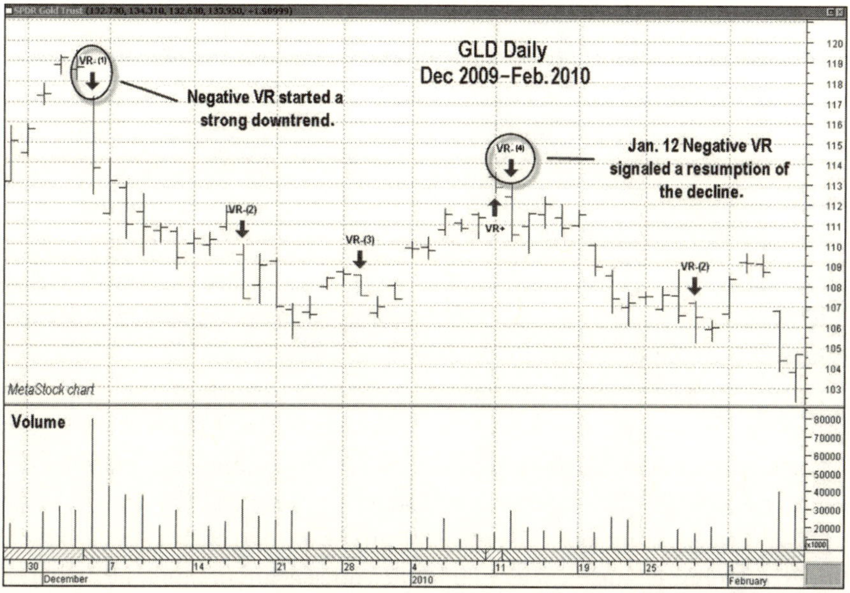

Chart 9.27 Negative Volume Reversals in a Downtrend, SPDR Gold Trust ETF

Source: MetaStock

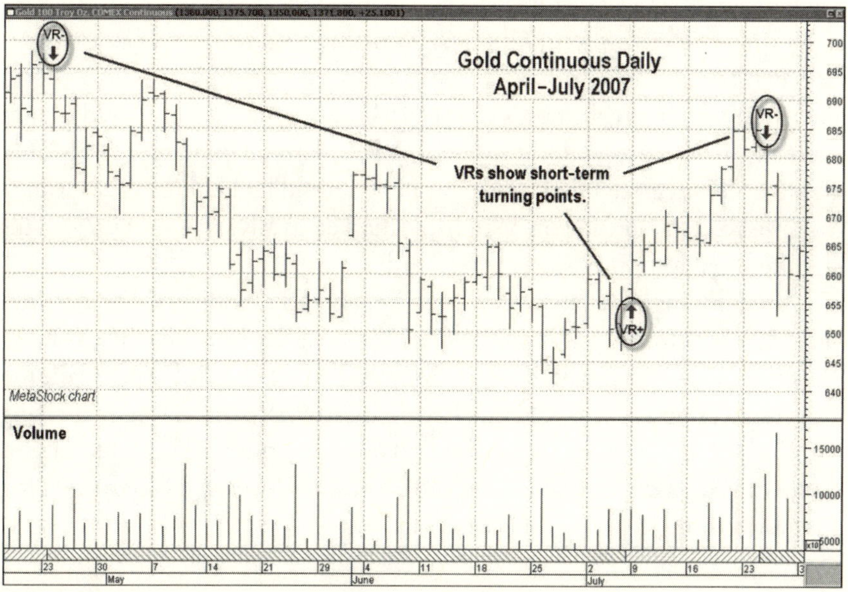

Chart 9.28 Volume Reversals Showing Turning Points, Gold Futures Continuous Daily

Source: MetaStock

VR as applied to the Gold Futures Continuous Daily Contract between April and July 2007. A Negative Volume Reversal (shown on the chart as a VR–) was generated on April 24 and revealed that sellers were trying to take control in the gold futures.

In VR methodology, we anticipate that a Negative Volume Reversal alerts us to the initial formation of a short-term reversal as sellers show increased conviction through heightened volume activity. Following the formation of a Negative VR, the expectation is to see further weakness and follow-through to the downside. Following the Negative VR, gold futures trended lower and eventually bottomed on June 27, 2007.

Conversely, we expect the opposite upon the formation of a VR+. On July 9, a Positive Volume Reversal (shown in Chart 9.28 as a VR+) was generated for a trade to the upside. Gold futures continued to trend higher through July 25, 2007, when a subsequent Negative Volume Reversal (VR–) signaled that sellers were reentering the market. Note how nicely the trend followed through, as gold futures once again began to move lower. The Leibovit VR indicator is quite sensitive to short-term shifts and is able to capture these trends effectively. Traders can find the VR quite versatile, as it works in multiple time frames, from intraday to monthly. More about pairing the VR with other complementary indicators will be discussed in Chapter 11.

In our next example in Chart 9.29 for the iShares Silver Trust (SLV) between January and April 2010, we examine a series of intermediate-term trades. A Negative Volume Reversal (VR–) on January 15 triggered a short trade until a Positive Volume Reversal (VR+) formed on February 11. That Positive VR suggested that a long position should be held until a Negative Volume Reversal formed on March 18 (marked as VR– in Chart 9.29). This signified that a short position was in order.

Three trading days later, on March 23, an early Positive Volume Reversal (VR+) occurred, but it was negated the next day by a Negative Volume Reversal (VR–). Two days later, on March 26, however, a Positive Volume Reversal was posted (marked as VR+ in Chart 9.29), indicating that a long position should be taken in anticipation of higher prices. This trade carried all the way to April 13, when a Negative Volume Reversal formed, signaling that it was time to close the trade.

Trade Setup

The Volume Reversal gives an immediate signal that short-term market sentiment is shifting from buyers to sellers, and vice versa. Since this

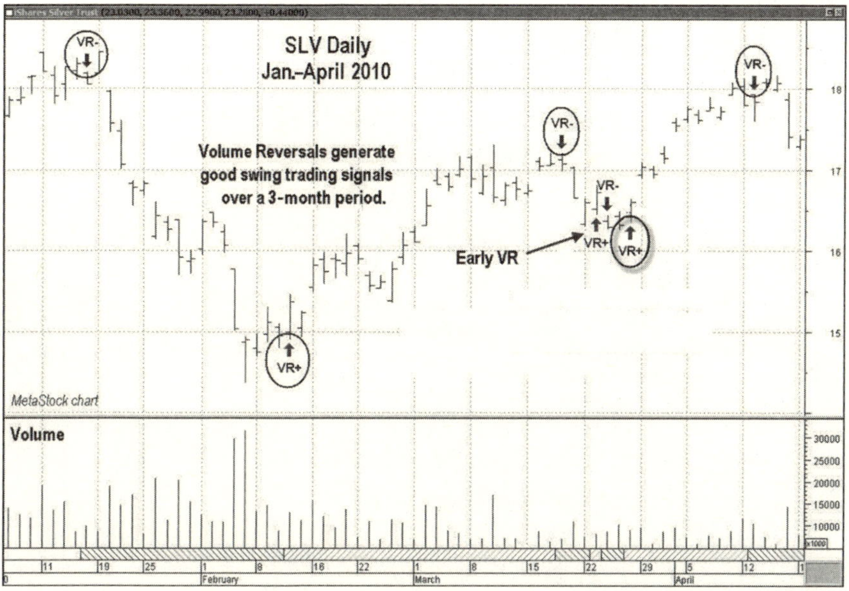

Chart 9.29 Volume Reversals Showing Swing Points, iShares Silver Trust (SLV)

Source: MetaStock

differs from other indicators that use days (in some cases, weeks) of data in their computations, there is no divergence with price or early warning trade setup of any type with the signal itself. Some great clues can be gleaned from the simple relationship between price and volume, and it can make sense to give more weight to volume reversals when they occur. The other differentiating quality about the VR is that its signals are very concise and, as an indicator, it can stand alone. Put more succinctly: Either you have a VR or you don't.

In the example of continuous contract silver futures in Chart 9.30, the relationship between price and volume presented a clear setup that a reversal was due. Volume was not supporting the sharp rise to the December 2006 highs. Note how volume was stable during the month of November as price chopped sideways with an upward bias. Once price definitively broke higher, however, volume began to decrease as price continued its push higher. That set up a negative divergence between price and volume and was a clue to look for a possible change in direction, as the conviction among traders pushing the price higher was lagging.

The final push higher came on December 4, 2006, with silver closing high as volume decreased, presenting an opportunity to draw a short-term support line connecting four of the bottoms in November and December.

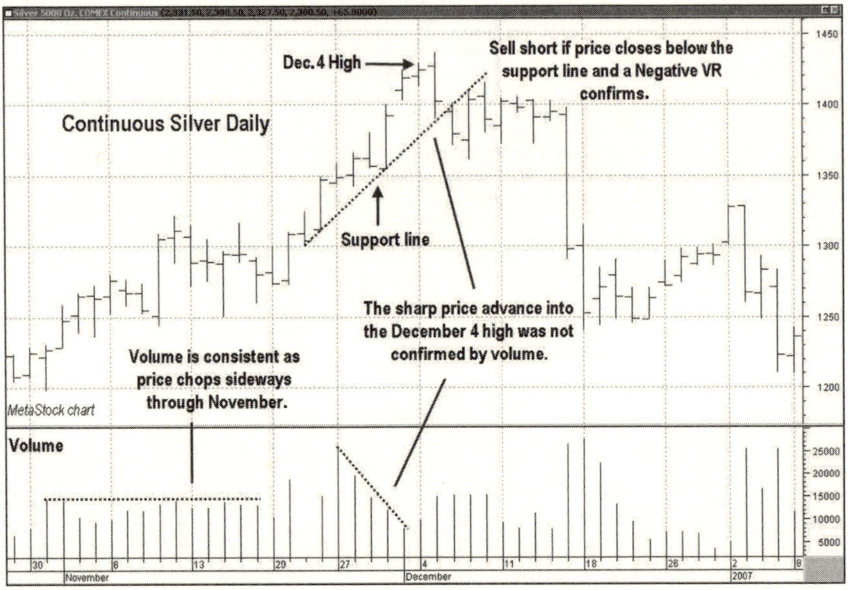

Chart 9.30 Volume Reversal, Negative Divergence, and Trade Setup, Silver Continuous Daily

Source: MetaStock

A Negative VR combined with a close below that support line would be a strong signal that sellers were assuming control of the silver market.

Trade Entry

A Negative VR formed on December 6, 2006 (see Chart 9.31), which also coincided with a close below the support line that connected the lows. That was the definitive signal that the recent push higher was over and that sellers were entering the futures market. An initial protective stop should have been placed over the December 5 high of 1437 in the silver contract. Note how price chopped sideways for six trading days following the VR signal before selling pressure overwhelmed the market and the price of silver collapsed on December 15 (as the middle of Chart 9.31 shows).

The confirmation of a support line break with a Negative VR was a very powerful combination, as the price of silver dropped $2.00 per ounce (a nearly 13 percent gain in the cash market) into early January 2007. Leveraged returns would have been far greater.

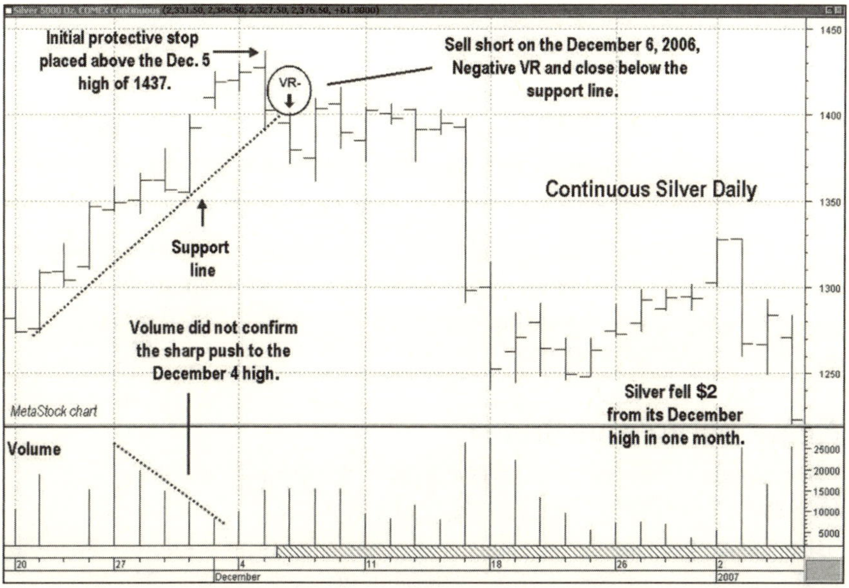

Chart 9.31 Volume Reversal, Negative Divergence, and Trade Entry, Silver Continuous Daily

Source: MetaStock

Trader Tips

The Volume Reversal is a resilient indicator that functions across multiple time frames. It has great utility in tactical and timing strategies, relying heavily on its volume component, and is the quintessential indicator for the trader's mantra: *Volume precedes price*. It is advantageous for the following reasons:

- The VR indicator is sensitive to the early initiations of trend reversals, making it useful for intraday and short-term traders.
- The indicator is quite versatile and can be used in conjunction with other indicators. It may serve as both a leading indicator and a confirmatory indicator in a trading strategy.
- It provides an early-warning alert to shifts in sentiment and the activities of larger institutional players. As such, the Leibovit VR can serve as a signal for larger changes in broad market trends.
- It provides concise trading stops defined by a subsequent VR in an opposite direction.

Some drawbacks:

- Closing price is not necessarily related to the validity of the Volume Reversal. In others words, a Positive Volume Reversal can and does occur even with a down close, and vice versa for a Negative Volume Reversal, where an up close can occur.
- The VR strategy works well for short-term traders, as it is highly sensitive to volume action, but it may need confirmatory or complementary indicators for longer-term trading strategies.

Negative Volume Index

The Negative Volume Index (NVI) was developed by technician Paul Dysart Sr. in the 1940s. It was originally created for broad market trends using advance/decline data. Investing and trading strategist Norman Fosback reintroduced it in the 1970s with a variation that was able to include data from any market index. The Negative Volume Index assumes that so-called smart money is traded on quiet, low-volume days and that the so-called uninformed crowd trades on very active days. For this reason, the Negative Volume Index uses only days when the volume is lower than on the previous day. Fosback believed this revealed what the smart money was doing, in effect leaving its footprints in the sand.

Formulation

The NVI is a cumulative indicator, which means that each day's value is added to a running total. The following formula is used to compute the Negative Volume Index:

Yesterday's NVI + [(today's close – yesterday's close) / yesterday's close]
(if today's volume is lower than yesterday, adding zero otherwise)

The computation is done only if today's volume is less than the previous day's. If today's volume is higher than yesterday's, add zero to yesterday's NVI value; in effect, the NVI is simply carried forward. Fosback created his sell signals based upon whether the NVI was above or below its one-year moving average. Although the indicator's greatest strength is in broad market calculations, it can be used to analyze individual stocks, which is why it is included in this section.

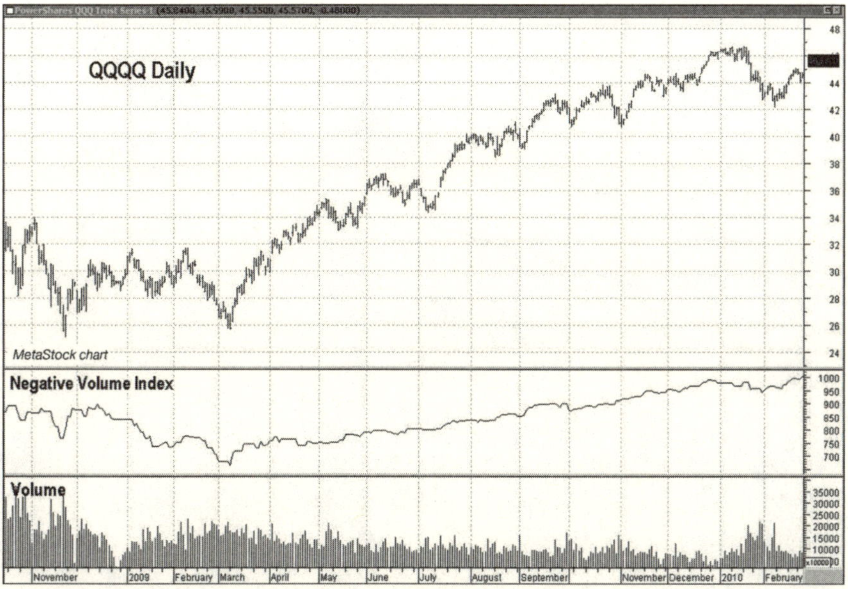

Chart 9.32 Negative Volume Index, Nasdaq 100 Trust ETF

Source: MetaStock

Probably in part because institutions are employing more sophisticated algorithms to make their trades, the NVI is not as effective as it once was, and it is not widely used. It still does confirm trend and show divergences, however, and that will be examined here. The example of the Nasdaq 100 Trust ETF (QQQQ) in Chart 9.32 shows a plot of the NVI.

Confirming Trends

Since the Negative Volume Index is a cumulative indicator, it does have trend confirmation qualities. Chart 9.33 shows how the NVI trends along with price for IBM. This indicator rising with price does not necessarily mean that the price trend is rising on lower volume. The indicator is really tracking the smart money, which trades on lower-volume days. In other words, it is a measure not of volume per se but of the direction on low-volume days, the smart-money days.

The NVI is also good for confirming downtrends. In the example of the iShares Dow Jones U.S. Home Construction ETF (ITB) in Chart 9.34, note how the NVI drops along with price. That means that the smart money is likely to be selling into the downtrend as well.

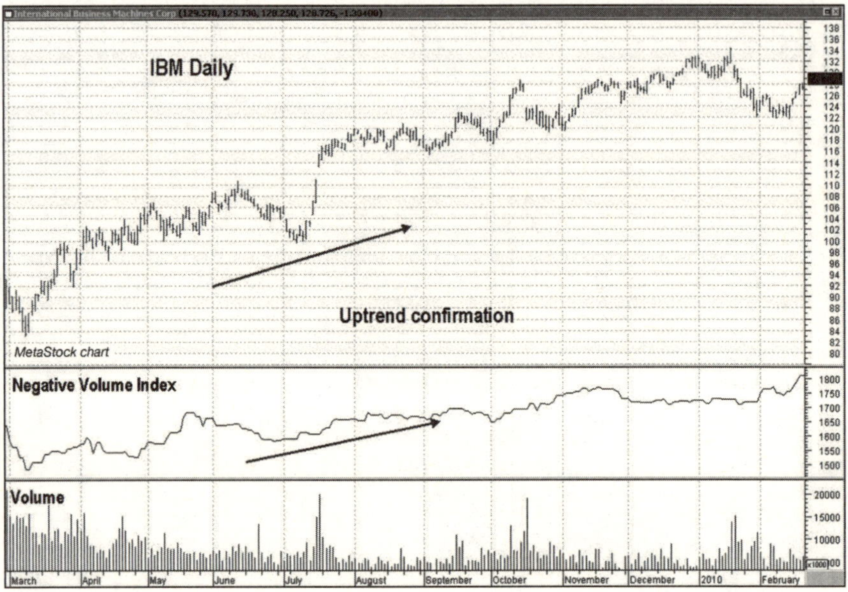

Chart 9.33 Negative Volume Index Confirming Price Trend, IBM

Source: MetaStock

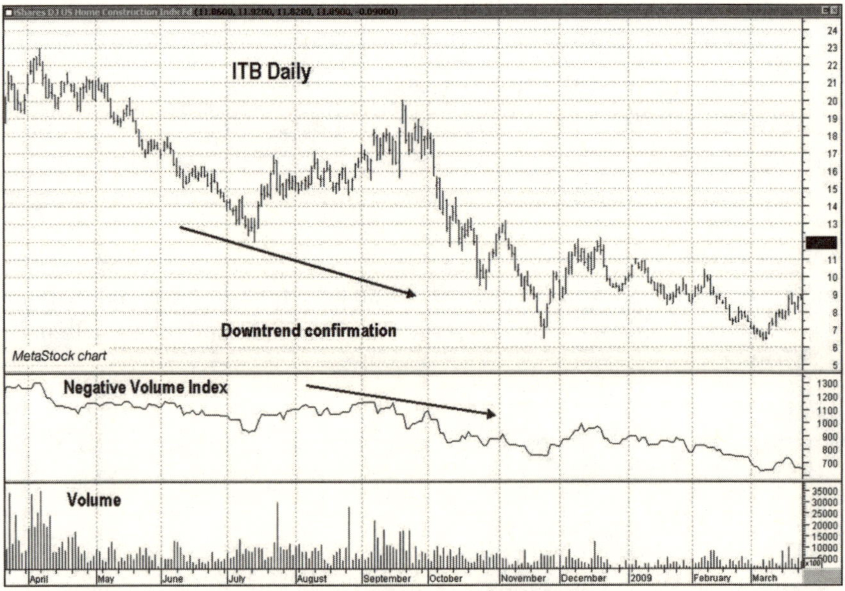

Chart 9.34 Negative Volume Index Confirming Price Downtrend, Dow Jones U.S. Home Construction ETF

Source: MetaStock

Divergences

The NVI can show divergences at key turning points that tip the hand of the smart money to reveal what they are up to. In the example of the Consumer Discretionary SPDR ETF (XLY) in Chart 9.35, note how price made a lower low from March to July 2008. The NVI held its prior low, which was an indication that the smart money was buying shares on the way down, creating the positive divergence. Note how price bounced higher after the positive divergence.

The NVI also shows when the smart money is exiting the market (i.e., when the NVI is moving lower). A negative divergence occurs when price moves higher while the NVI is moving lower. In Chart 9.36, note how the price for Amazon.com (AMZN) made a final high in August 2008 while the NVI was already in an established downtrend. This divergence had been going on for some time, ending in the sharp correction that followed.

NVI with Other Indicators

One effective way to use the NVI for long-term market analysis is to plot its 9-day and 255-day exponential moving averages together. Norman Fosback stated that when the NVI is above its 1-year (255-day) moving

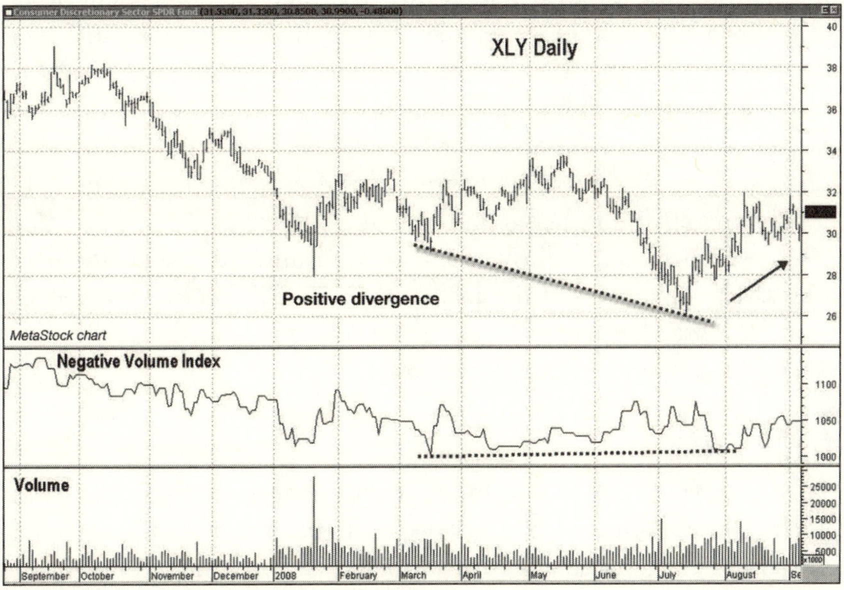

Chart 9.35 Negative Volume Index, Positive Divergence, Consumer Discretionary SPDR ETF

Source: MetaStock

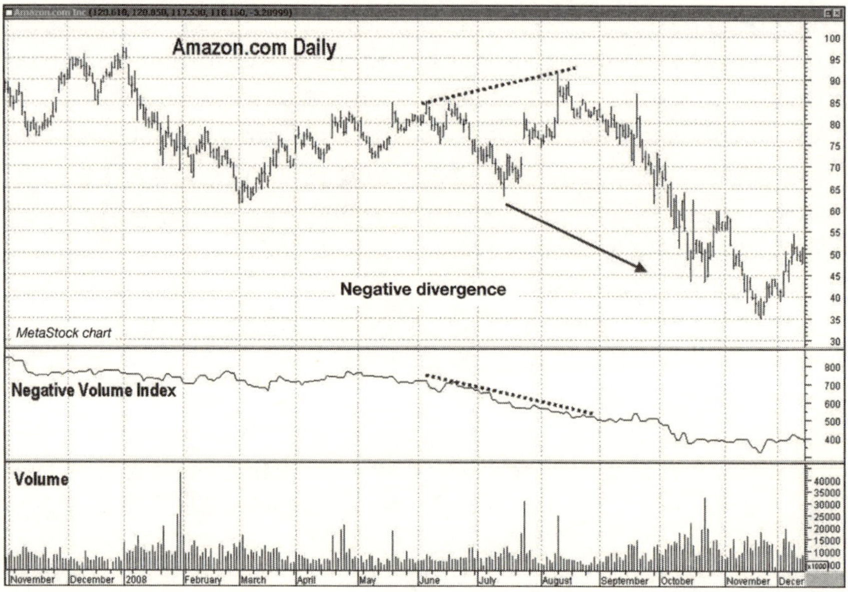

Chart 9.36 Negative Volume Index, Negative Divergence, Amazon.com

Source: MetaStock

average, the odds of a bull market are a 96 percent probability, but when the NVI is below its 1-year moving average, there is a 53 percent probability that a bear market is in place. Pairing the 9-day exponential moving average with the 255-day exponential moving average makes for smoother, more reliable signals. Signals are generated when the 9-day moving average crosses above or below the 255-day moving average. Chart 9.37 shows a healthy buy signal for Microsoft (MSFT) generated in February 2009, just before the March 2009 low.

Chart 9.38 shows a sell signal for the Consumer Discretionary SPDR ETF (XLY) generated in the late summer of 2007, a full two months before the broader market topped. The signal suggested that the smart money was already heading for the exits.

Trade Setup

Since the Negative Volume Index was developed to track the market behavior of smart-money participants, it can be used to show divergences on rallies or sell-offs that are driven merely by uninformed money, for example, herd mentality. Although herd mentality can cause powerful moves in the market, those moves are based more on emotion than on sustainable buying or selling strength.

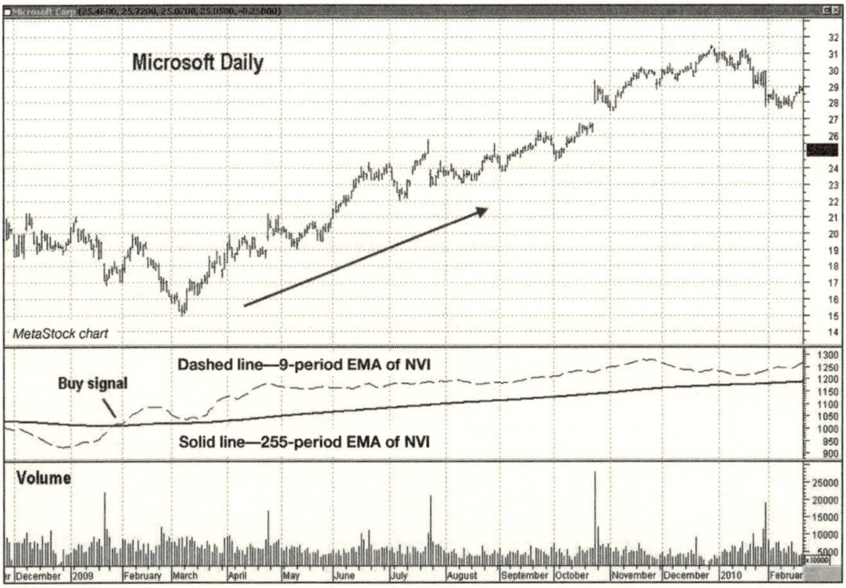

Chart 9.37 Negative Volume Index, 9-Period and 225-Period Exponential Moving Averages, Buy Signal at Crossover, Microsoft Corp.

Source: MetaStock

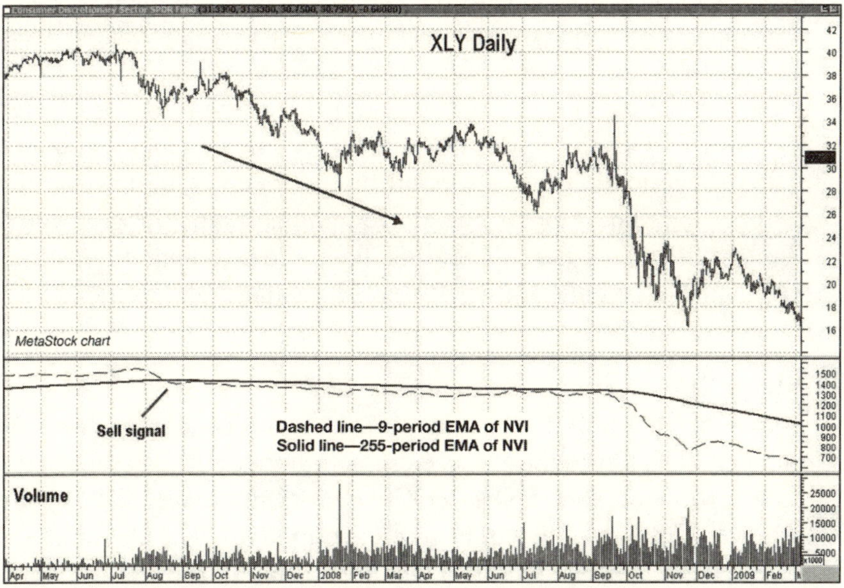

Chart 9.38 Negative Volume Index, 9-Period and 225-Period Exponential Moving Averages, Sell Signal at Crossover, Consumer Discretionary SPDR ETF

Source: MetaStock

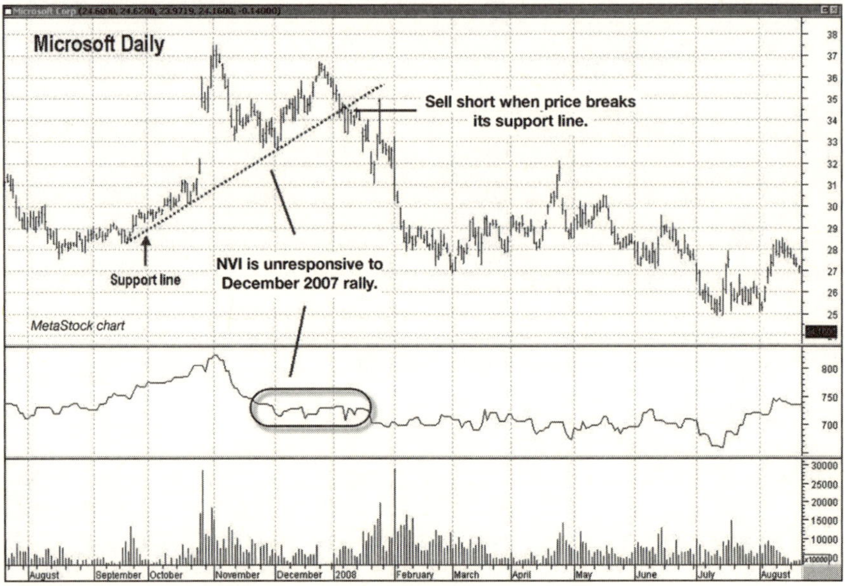

Chart 9.39 Negative Volume Index, Trade Setup, Microsoft Corp.

Source: MetaStock

Spotting those periods in market behavior can lead to profitable trades. The example of Microsoft (MSFT) in Chart 9.39 shows such a setup. Note in the chart how unresponsive NVI is to the December 2007 rally. It shows that the rally was either short covering or one last gasp by the uninformed money that didn't want to miss the next move. The development of this situation suggested drawing a support line to connect the lows off the September low. The support line at five months is quite long; as you'll remember, the longer the support line, the more meaningful it is. Price should confirm the indicator signal before a position can be entered.

Trade Entry

The price of Microsoft managed to push up to a secondary high in late December 2007. Given the absence of smart-money buying, as indicated by the flat configuration of NVI (see Chart 9.40), this looked to be a solid shorting opportunity. The only thing required in the situation was patience, as price needed to break its support line to confirm the divergence. On January 8, 2008, price broke its support line, giving the signal to enter a short position. An initial protective stop should have been placed above the December 24, 2007 high of 36.72.

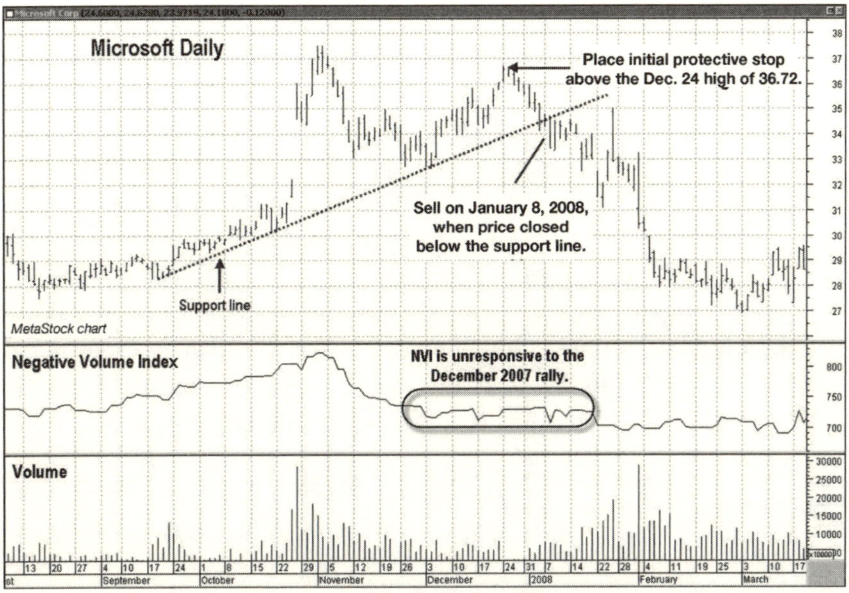

Chart 9.40 Negative Volume Index, Trade Entry, Microsoft Corp.

Source: MetaStock

Trader Tips

The Negative Volume Index is good for the following:

- Tracking the smart money
- Confirming primary market trends
- Showing divergences

The main drawback in using NVI is that it is less reliable than it once was, and it has fallen out of favor. But the examples shown in this section should be enough for you to at least give it consideration as a valuable tool for market analysis. It has been used on individual securities, although that application is not as popular as the broad market application.

Institutional Trading the VWAP Way

The Negative Volume Index has fallen out of favor somewhat because institutions and buy-side dealers who work trades for those institutions have learned to use algorithms and other tools to spread their trades through the day. With that in mind, it makes sense to discuss one of the new tools of the day, albeit one that is better positioned for use by institutional traders: VWAP.

VWAP stands for *Volume Weighted Average Price*; it is a tool used as a benchmark by traders to execute large block orders in line with market volume. Use of this tool allows large block orders to be executed periodically throughout the day, which can act to conceal large purchases and also minimize the market movement that large orders can sometimes cause.

In order to compute VWAP, a time-and-sales data stream is needed to capture individual trades along with a specified time horizon over which VWAP is to be computed (e.g., intraday).

$$\text{VWAP} = \frac{\Sigma(\text{Number of shares traded} \times \text{share price during the period})}{\text{Total shares traded during the period}}$$

Many large institutions use a daily VWAP as a measure against a price target as they accumulate shares throughout the day. VWAP helps to avoid trading at the extreme high or low for the day. VWAP also allows institutions to compute transaction costs by comparing the average realized transaction price against a benchmark price. VWAP is a topic that can be very complicated; many trade execution strategies can be developed that are beyond the scope of this book.

Smaller traders can also use a variation of VWAP to determine whether or not a market is gaining strength or weakening. For example, if an intraday trader is using a 15-minute time horizon and price breaks above the 15-minute VWAP and continues to move higher, it is a sign of strength. Conversely, if price should price break below the 15-minute VWAP and continue to head lower, it would be a sign of weakness. VWAP plots just like a conventional moving average, so it is simple to use. The problem for smaller traders in computing their own VWAP is the sheer volume of data needed, as each transaction throughout the day needs to be processed. Some charting services compute VWAP for you, which makes plotting very convenient.

Whether or not traders use VWAP, they should be aware of the concept and how institutions use it to spread trades through a given time period.

Positive Volume Index

The Positive Volume Index (PVI) was introduced by Paul Dysart Jr., the son of the creator of the NVI, and is based on the same theory as the Negative Volume Index. The PVI is theoretically the inverse of the NVI; it simply tracks the days when volume increases in the market and is based on the idea that on days when volume increases, the unsophisticated crowd has joined in, which means that the trend may be in its latter stages. The theory follows that if a day has decreased volume, then the smart money is moving into position to take advantage of the crowd.

Formulation

The formula for computing the Positive Volume Index is as follows:

Yesterday's PVI + [(today's close – yesterday's close) / yesterday's close]

Importantly, the computation is carried out only if today's volume is greater than yesterday's. If today's volume is lower than yesterday's, add a zero, and yesterday's PVI value is simply carried forward.

Like the Negative Volume Index, the PVI is not as effective as it once was, in part because of more sophisticated trading algorithms being deployed by large traders, and it is not that widely used. It does still confirm trend and show divergences, however, and these will be examined here. Chart 9.41 shows a plot of the PVI for the Nasdaq 100 Trust ETF (QQQQ).

Trend Confirmation

Since the Positive Volume Index is a cumulative indicator, it does have trend analysis and confirmation capabilities. The example of the S&P SPDR Financial ETF (XLF) in Chart 9.42 shows how the PVI rises with price. Again, the PVI tracks unsophisticated money, and that money is flowing into the market, so it is apparent that this crowd (the "herd") is what keeps the trend going.

The PVI also moves with price in downtrends. The S&P SPDR Financial ETF also provides an example in Chart 9.43 of how the herd is driving prices lower during most of 2008.

Divergences

The Positive Volume Index was developed to measure the activity of the herd that causes the market price movement. Being on the wrong side of the herd can be a painful experience, whether or not its reasons are

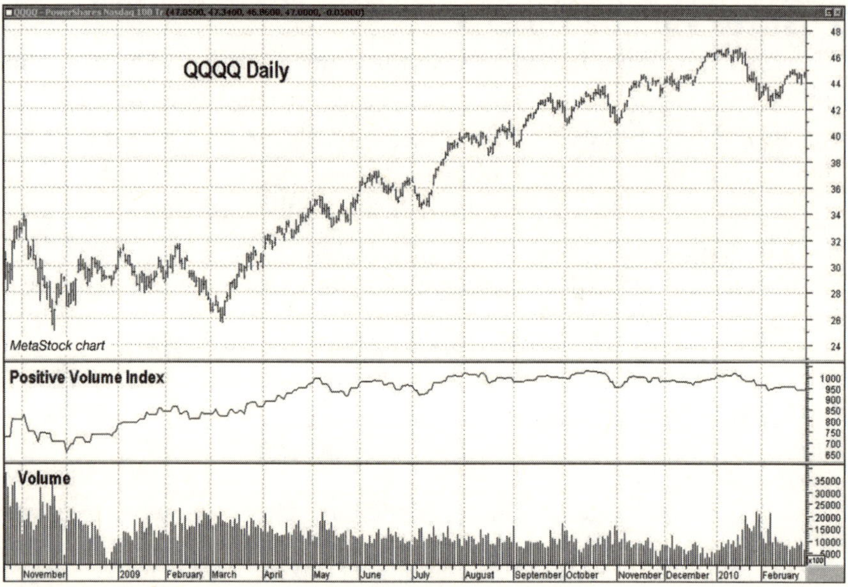

Chart 9.41 Positive Volume Index, Nasdaq 100 Trust ETF

Source: MetaStock

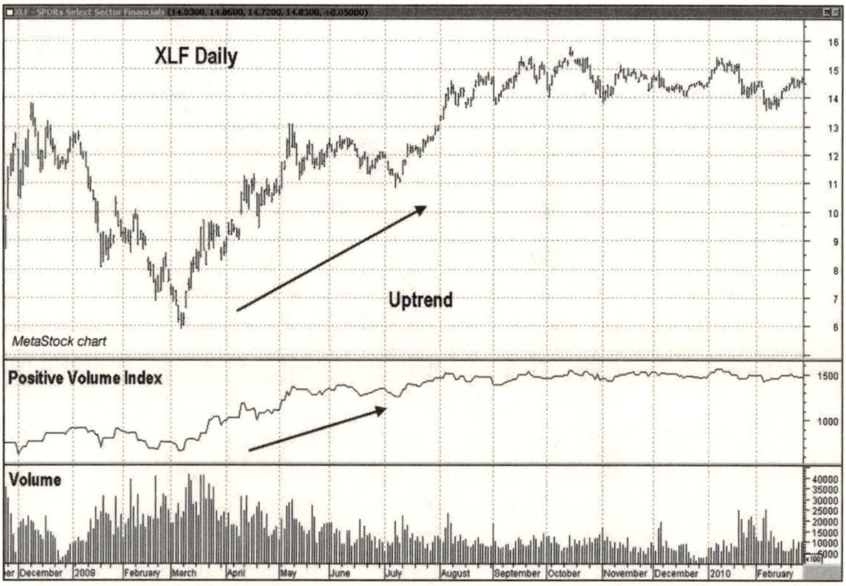

Chart 9.42 Positive Volume Index, Uptrend Confirmation, S&P SPDR Financial ETF

Source: MetaStock

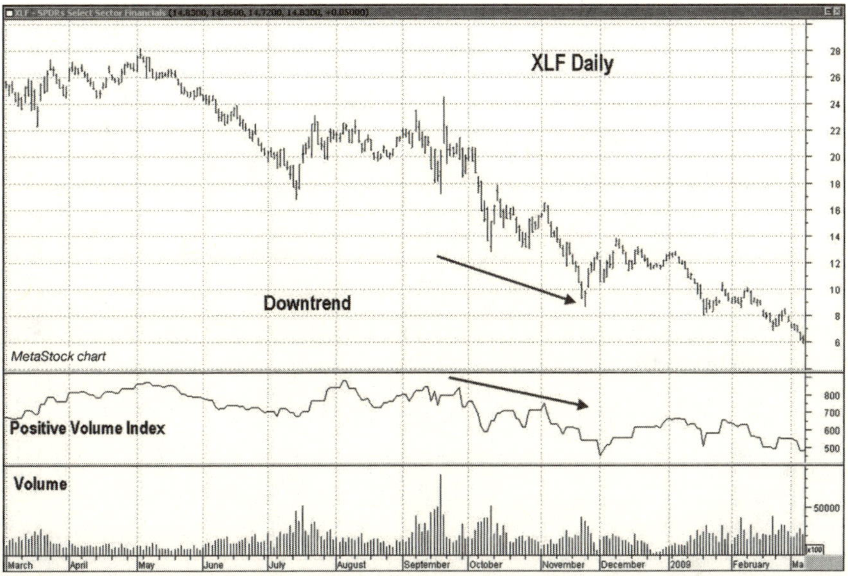

Chart 9.43 Positive Volume Index, Downtrend Confirmation, S&P SPDR Financial ETF

Source: MetaStock

sophisticated. Cisco (CSCO) in Chart 9.44 shows a positive divergence (a lower low in price with a higher low in the indicator) in March 2009. That divergence preceded a major turning point for the overall market.

The PVI also shows negative divergences occurring when price moves higher while the PVI moves lower, showing that the herd is not behind the move. The S&P SPDR Energy ETF (XLE) in Chart 9.45 shows such a divergence. Notice how price made a double top in January 2010 while the PVI made a lower high. A sharp correction followed.

Positive Volume Index with Other Indicators

The theory behind the development of the PVI was to track the unsophisticated money and to use the PVI as a contrarian indicator, that is, to observe the crowd and trade against the prevailing trends before they change. In spite of the intention, the PVI tracks very well with trends because effectively the volume increases are the trend drivers.

To get a better look at the strength and dynamics of a market, it can help to combine the PVI with another indicator or oscillator. Since the PVI

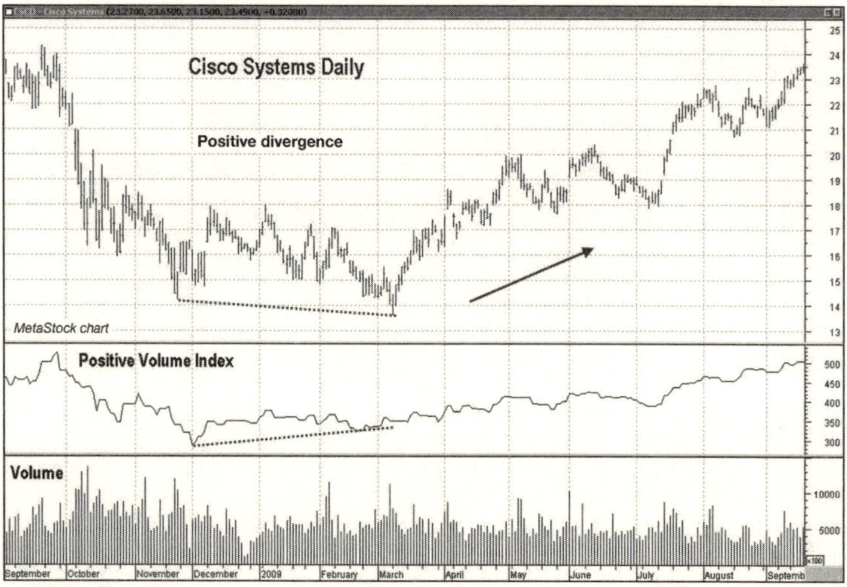

Chart 9.44 Positive Volume Index, Positive Divergence, Cisco Systems

Source: MetaStock

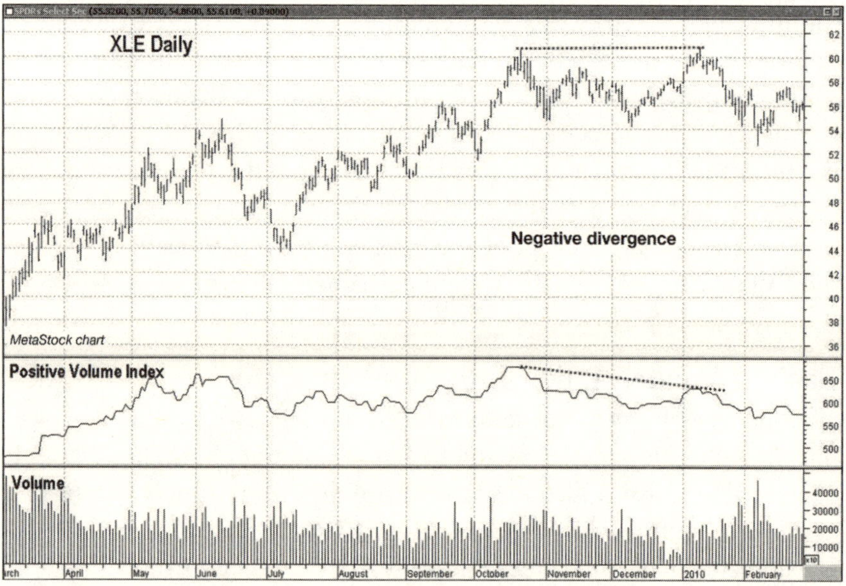

Chart 9.45 Positive Volume Index, Negative Divergence, S&P SPDR Energy ETF

Source: MetaStock

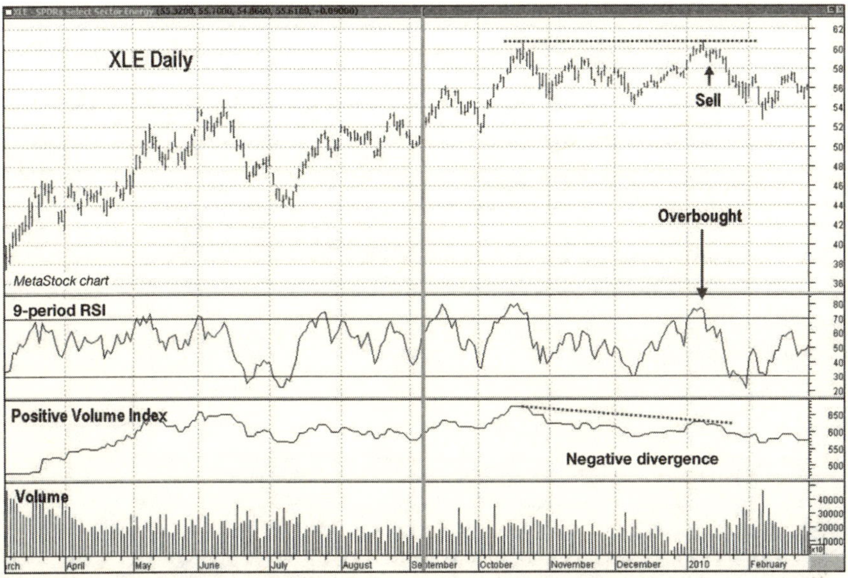

Chart 9.46 Positive Volume Index with 9-Period RSI, Negative Divergence with Overbought Signal, S&P SPDR Energy ETF

Source: MetaStock

is a cumulative indicator, it makes sense, for instance, to pair it with a price-based Overbought/Oversold Oscillator. Chart 9.46 shows how to exploit divergences in the PVI by pairing it with a 9-period Relative Strength Index (RSI).

Chart 9.46 is actually the same as Chart 9.45, which shows the negative divergence in the PVI. Now that the 9-period Relative Strength Index has been added, it gives a clearer look at the condition of the S&P SPDR Energy ETF (XLE) at this juncture. XLE has resistance in the form of the prior high, a negative divergence in the PVI, and an overbought 9-period RSI (a reading over 70). This was a great setup. The sell trade was triggered when the 9-period RSI crossed below the 70 level. Buy setups would be executed on positive divergences (lower price/higher indicator) and an oversold 9-period RSI (below 30). The buy would be executed when the 9-period RSI crosses back above 30.

Trade Setup

While there are still some issues with the validity of the Positive Volume Index today—it doesn't work as well as it once did—it is still possible to use it as a trending indicator that can also show divergences against the

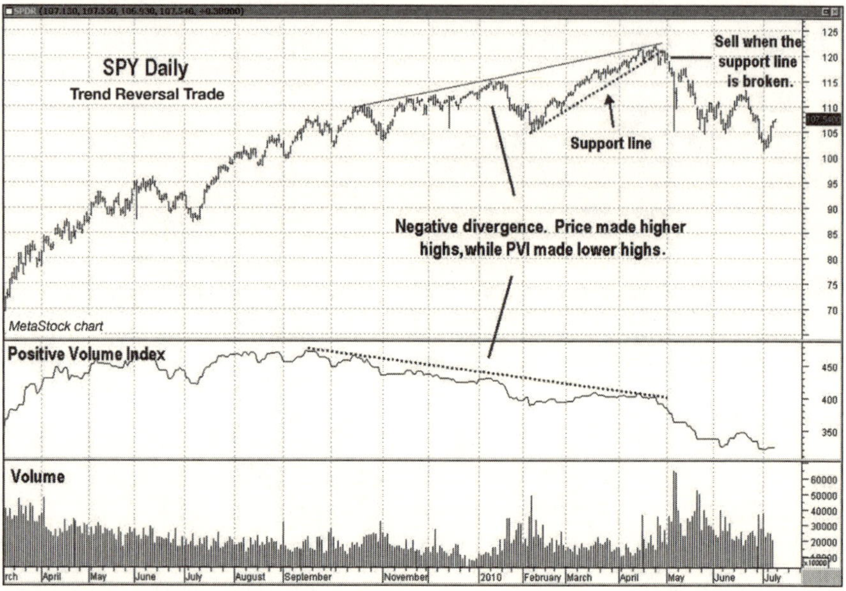

Chart 9.47 Positive Volume Index, Negative Divergence Trade Setup, S&P 500 Trust ETF

Source: MetaStock

trend. The example of the S&P 500 Trust ETF (SPY) in Chart 9.47 shows the entire rally phase off the March 2009 low. Notice how the PVI rises along with price, making higher highs and higher lows until the fall of 2009. The PVI then began to diverge from price action, showing that price action on higher-volume days was weakening relative to earlier in the trend.

While the divergences that appeared could have resulted in a profitable short trade in January 2010, there is also a later negative divergence that would have given the opportunity to enter a short position before the May 6 flash crash. A support line could have been drawn off the February low, connecting the lows through April. A short position should have been entered when price closed below this line.

Trade Entry

Patience paid off in waiting for the February–April 2010 price support line to be broken, as a short trade could have been entered one day after the April 26 high. It is also important to make sure that price closes below the support line to ensure that a short trade is not entered prematurely on daily market noise. As shown in Chart 9.48, the S&P 500 Trust ETF

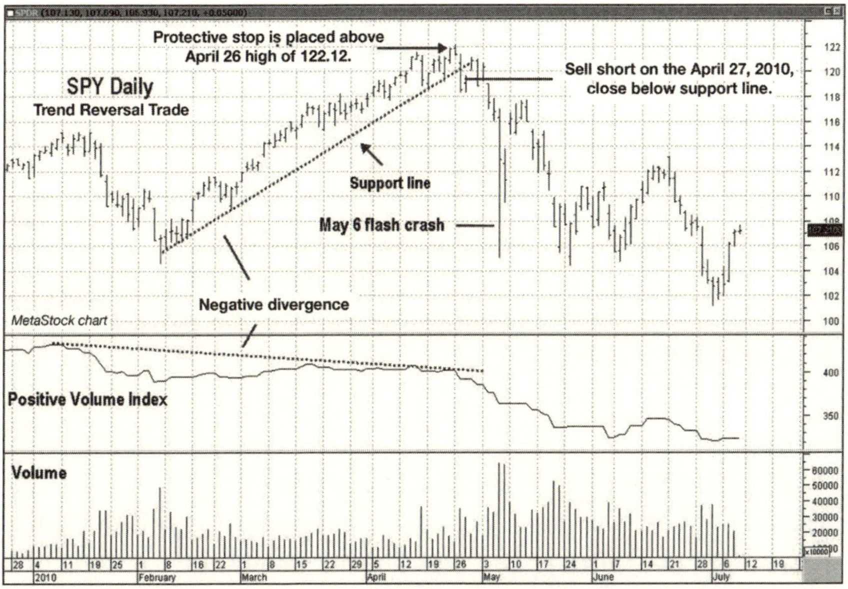

Chart 9.48 Positive Volume Index, Negative Divergence Trade Entry, S&P 500 Trust ETF

Source: MetaStock

(SPY) attempted to rally over the next two days, but the stop price was safely above the April 26 high, keeping the trade intact. This is an example of how even a little-used indicator sent negative signals well before the May 6, 2010 flash crash.

Trader Tips

While the Positive Volume Index was developed to track the activity of unsophisticated traders, the volume increases it tracks can drive meaningful trends. For that reason, the PVI can be used for the following:

- Confirming trends
- Showing divergences
- Generating buy and sell signals when paired with an Overbought/Oversold Oscillator

On-Balance Volume

On-Balance Volume (OBV) is an indicator that combines volume and price change to show the trend of the market. The technique was originally called "cumulative volume" by Woods and Vignolia; renowned market technician Joe Granville refined the indicator as "On-Balance Volume" in 1946. It was not until the release of Mr. Granville's 1963 book *Granville's New Key to Stock Market Profits* that On-Balance Volume became widely known and used.

OBV is still as versatile and solid today as it was when it was first introduced. The indicator can be applied to the broad market using broad market advance/decline data or to individual issues based upon their daily up or down price close. It is a cumulative indicator, meaning that a daily running total is maintained.

Formulation

The math is simple: Total volume for each day is assigned a positive or negative value, depending on price closing higher or lower than the previous day's close. A higher close results in the volume for that day getting a positive value, while a lower close results in a negative value. Each day's volume value (positive or negative) is added to a running total. A rising OBV indicator shows that money is flowing into a security or market, and a falling OBV indicator shows that money is leaving that security or market. OBV is used to show trend confirmation, divergences, and breakouts. The formulas for OBV are as follows:

- If today's close is higher than yesterday's close:

$$\text{OBV} = \text{yesterday's OBV} + \text{today's volume}$$

- If today's close is lower than yesterday's close:

$$\text{OBV} = \text{yesterday's OBV} - \text{today's volume}$$

- If today's close is equal to yesterday's close:

$$\text{OBV} = \text{yesterday's OBV} + 0$$

OBV is expected to trend with price, so when prices rise, OBV should be rising as well. A failure to trend to a new high with price would be a negative divergence, suggesting trend weakness and nonconfirmation.

Chart 9.49 shows a plot of On-Balance Volume for the Nasdaq 100 Trust ETF (QQQQ). Notice how OBV trends higher with the QQQQ price.

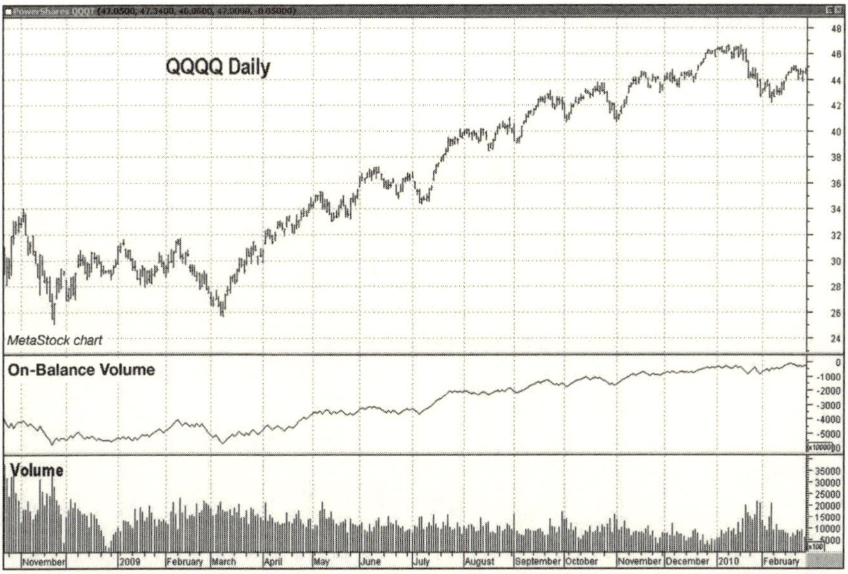

Chart 9.49 On-Balance Volume, Nasdaq 100 Trust ETF

Source: MetaStock

Trend Confirmation

One of OBV's major strengths is to confirm trends. When OBV is trending higher with price, it shows the healthy inflows necessary to support the trend. Chart 9.50 shows a strong price uptrend for the S&P Technology Select SPDR ETF (XLK) confirmed by the upsloping OBV. Note the pattern of higher highs and higher lows on both price and OBV. OBV is also good for confirming downtrends. A downsloping OBV shows that money is flowing out of the market or security being analyzed. Note in Chart 9.51 how the prices of Morgan Stanley and the OBV were each making lower highs and lower lows. That showed that sellers were in control.

Breakouts

On-Balance Volume is also a great tool for confirming breakouts and in many cases even predicting them. Chart 9.52 shows how OBV broke out well before the actual price of Freeport McMoRan (FCX) did. The early breakout verified that buyers were indeed accumulating shares off the November 2008 low. OBV is also good at confirming coincident breakouts. The example of the S&P SPDR Retail ETF (XRT) in Chart 9.53

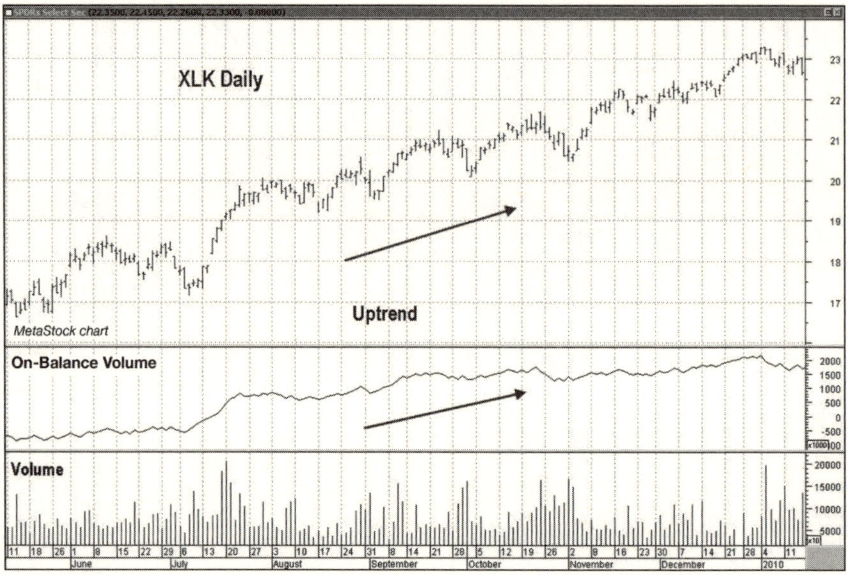

Chart 9.50 On-Balance Volume, Uptrend Confirmation, S&P Technology Select Sector SPDR ETF

Source: MetaStock

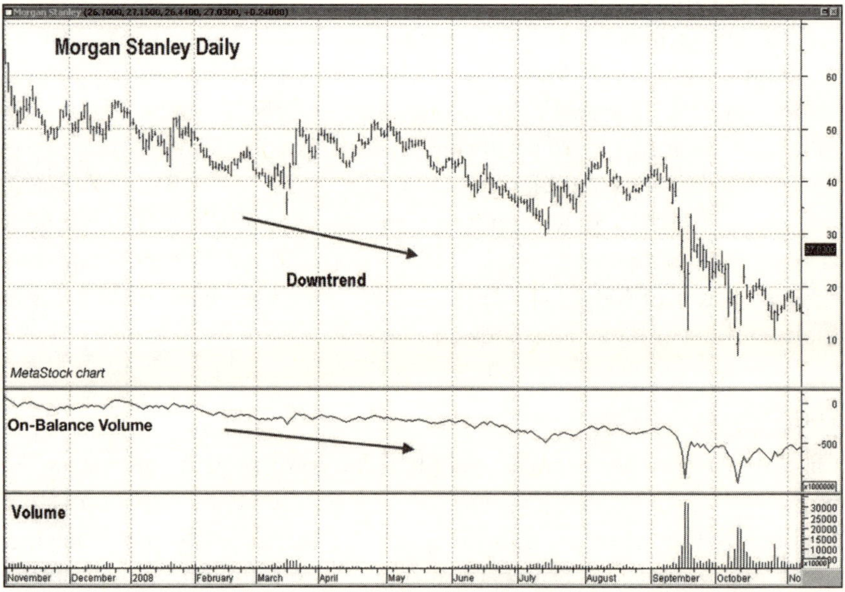

Chart 9.51 On-Balance Volume, Downtrend Confirmation, Morgan Stanley

Source: MetaStock

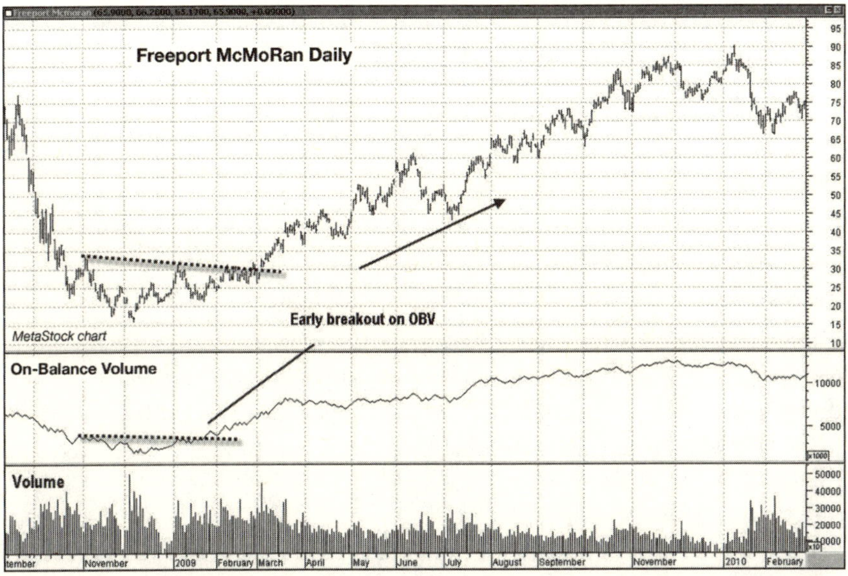

Chart 9.52 On-Balance Volume, Upside Breakout Confirmation, Freeport McMoRan

Source: MetaStock

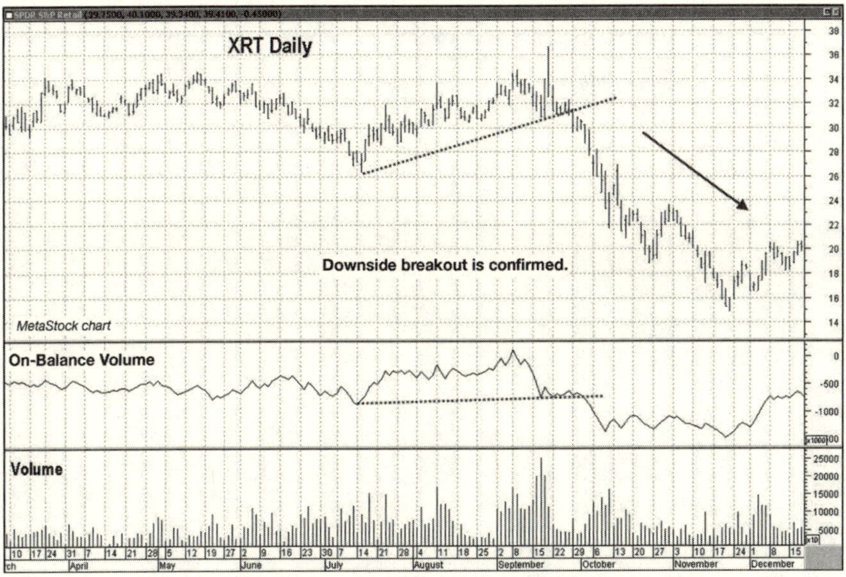

Chart 9.53 On-Balance Volume, Downside Breakout Confirmation, S&P SPDR Retail ETF

Source: MetaStock

shows how OBV broke lower at the same time as XRT in September 2008. That confirmed the breakdown, which showed that sellers were assuming control, starting a sharp decline.

Divergences

Beyond trend and breakout confirmation, On-Balance Volume is also good for showing divergences. A positive divergence is made when price moves lower but OBV moves higher. That shows latent strength not yet reflected in price. Since gains are being made on higher-volume days, it causes OBV to show strength before price. Chart 9.54 shows a positive divergence at the March 2009 low for the iShares Russell 2000 Index ETF (IWM). Note how price broke to a new low while OBV made a higher low.

Negative divergences (i.e., a higher price with a lower OBV) are also valuable indicators of a possible trend change. Chart 9.55 shows how price for Morgan Stanley made a higher high from June to August 2008 while OBV made a lower high, meaning that the August high in price was not confirmed by OBV. Note how selling intensified after price broke below the July low.

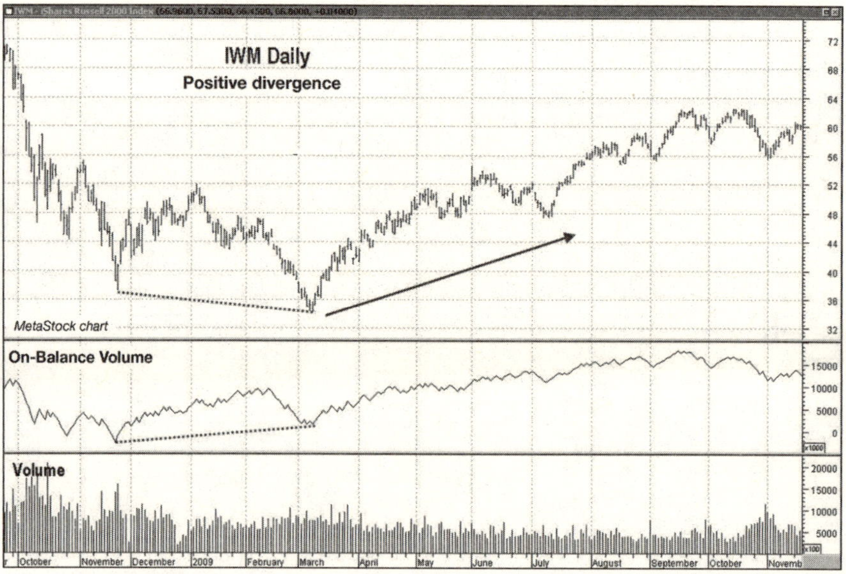

Chart 9.54 On-Balance Volume, Positive Divergence, iShares Russell 2000 Index ETF

Source: MetaStock

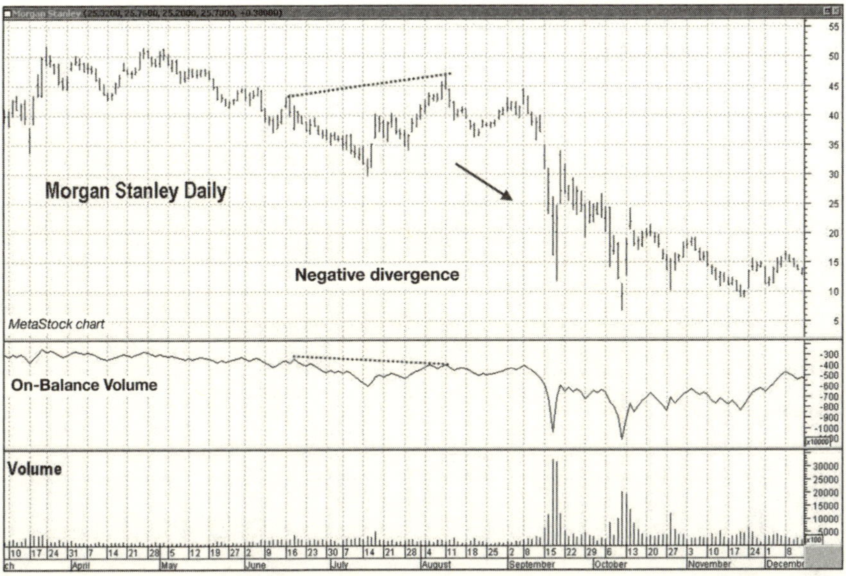

Chart 9.55 On-Balance Volume, Negative Divergence, Morgan Stanley

Source: MetaStock

On-Balance Volume with Other Indicators

OBV's trending qualities make it a superior indicator to pair with a price-based stochastic oscillator. In the example of IBM in Chart 9.56, OBV has been paired with a 10-period slow Stochastic Oscillator (10, 3, 3). OBV generally reflects the market trend and will act as a filter on trade setups. When the OBV confirms the trend; the oscillator helps to time the trade to the trend.

A buy setup occurs when OBV is trending higher (higher lows) and the 10-period Stochastic is oversold (below 20). The buy is executed when the 10-period Stochastic crosses above 20. A short sale setup occurs when OBV is trending lower (lower highs) and the 10-period Stochastic is overbought (above 80). The short sale is executed when the 10-period Stochastic crosses below 80. The up arrows show buys in the fall of 2009, and the down arrow shows a short sale in early 2010.

Trade Setup

The real value of On-Balance Volume is either in confirming a trend or in revealing divergences. This example, once again examines the March 2009 low and the behavior of a reliable trending indicator.

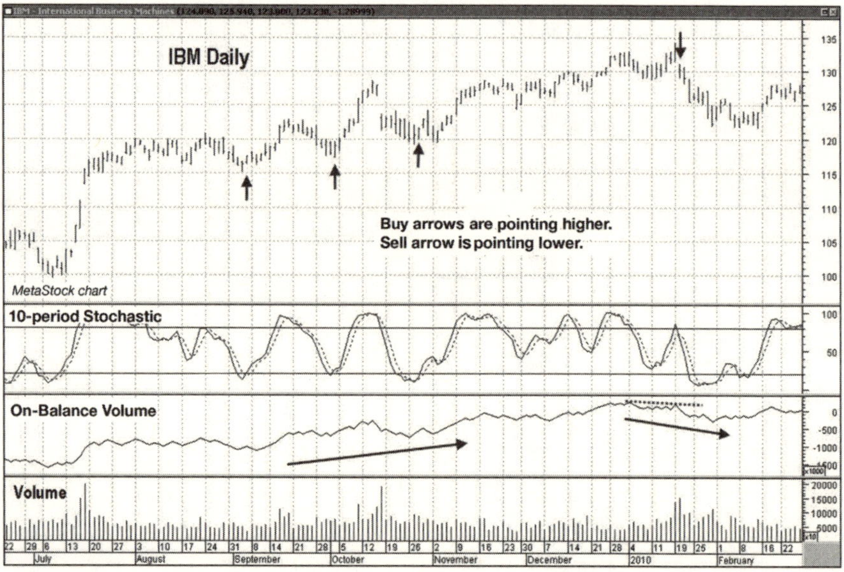

Chart 9.56 On-Balance Volume and 10-Period Slow Stochastic, IBM Corp.

Source: MetaStock

It has been said many times that the March 2009 low caught many by surprise, but a trader looking at his or her trusted indicators would have been able to see that a trend shift was on the way. Chart 9.57 makes it evident that there was a positive divergence between price and OBV in Microsoft (MSFT), as price made lower lows and OBV made slightly higher lows between November 2008 and March 2009. Jumping on this trade prematurely could have resulted in more than one losing trade. Patience was the key as the brutal decline of 2008 slowly ran out of steam. The divergence became very apparent as price plunged down to its March 2009 low. Also notice that a definitive resistance line could have been drawn from the January 2009 high, which gave a clear idea of what resistance level price would need to break through in order for a long position to be entered with confidence.

Trade Entry

As Chart 9.58 shows, a trade could have been entered on the March 18, 2009, close above the resistance line. Price broke back below the resistance line two days later but quickly recovered. Since the initial protective stop was below the March 6 low, price had plenty of room to correct before the new uptrend resumed.

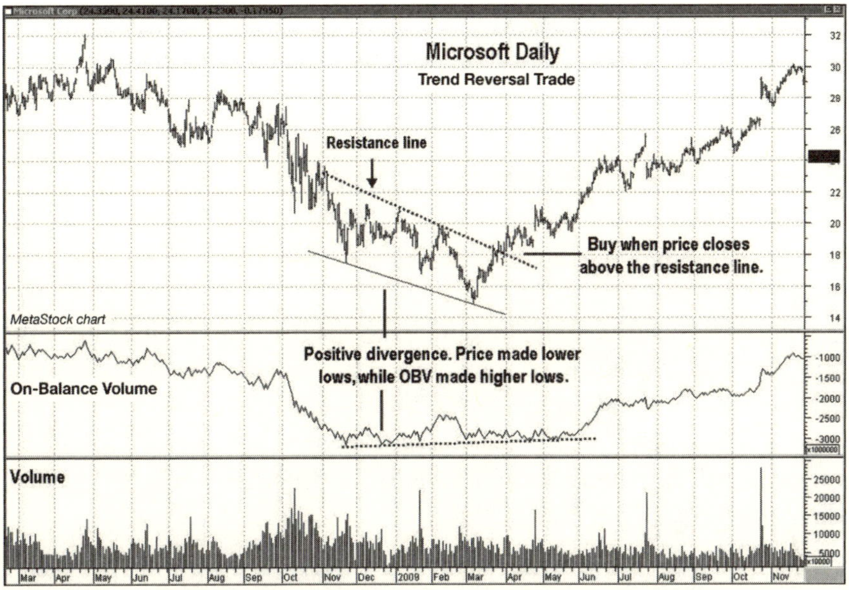

Chart 9.57 On-Balance Volume Trade Setup, Microsoft Corp.

Source: MetaStock

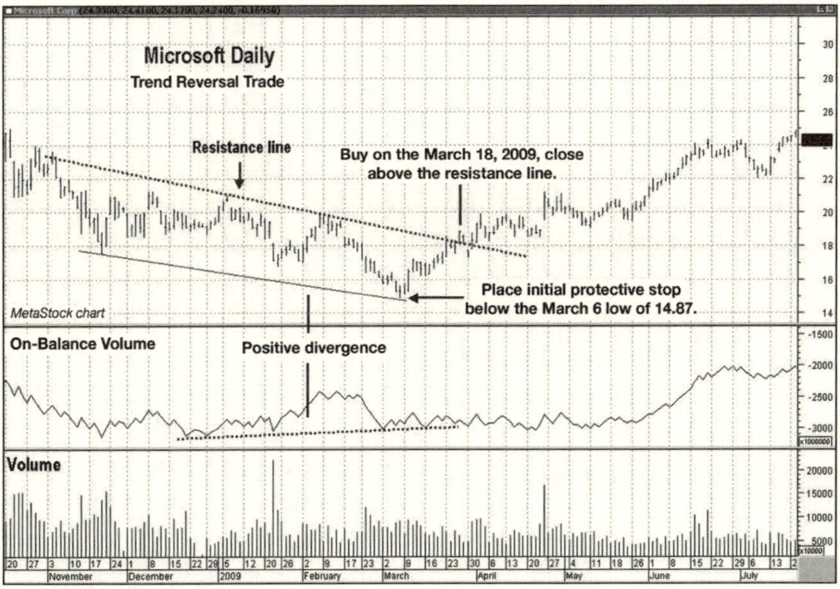

Chart 9.58 On-Balance Volume Trade Entry, Microsoft Corp.

Source: MetaStock

Trader Tips

On-Balance Volume is a versatile indicator that can be used for doing the following:

- Confirming price trends
- Showing trend divergences
- Confirming price breakouts

One drawback of OBV is that, regardless of the day's trading range, the volume measurement is accumulated in the indicator calculation based only on the close. This means that a strong intraday rally with a down close will be accumulated as a negative and a strong intraday decline with an up close will be accumulated as a positive. In other words, the trading direction intraday is ignored.

Open Interest

Volume and Open Interest are not the same. Open Interest is calculated in the futures and options market, where there are contracts, not shares. Open Interest is the total number of open contracts at the end of a given trading day, that is, the net amount of long and short in any particular commodity or option market. Its primary use is to measure the flow of money into a given futures or options contract.

For each buyer of a futures contract, there must be a seller; the combination of a buyer and seller constitutes a contract. That contract remains open until the counterparty closes it. For example, if trader A buys three contracts from trader B (the seller), then Open Interest rises by three contracts. When A decides to exit the market, he needs to sell his contracts. If he sells the contracts and trader B buys them back, then Open Interest drops by 3 because the original contracts are now closed. If, however, trader A sells to trader C (a new participant), then Open Interest remains unchanged because the original three contracts are still open.

Rising Open Interest confirms the market trend, whether up or down. Falling Open Interest indicates a weakening trend, whether trending up or trending down. Sideways Open Interest indicates that a consolidation phase is unfolding. During periods of consolidation, rising Open Interest acts as a confirmation of the eventual breakout, showing that new players coming into the market forced the move.

Volume is analyzed the same way in the futures market as it is in the equity market. The difference is that volume represents the number of contracts that have changed hands instead of the number of shares changing hands, as in the equity market.

Combining Open Interest and volume can give traders an extra layer of analysis that helps determine whether a trend is likely to continue or reverse. The following basic combinations of volume and Open Interest give valid measures of the futures:

- Rising price with rising Open Interest and rising volume shows a strong uptrend.
- Rising price with falling Open Interest and falling volume indicates that the uptrend is weakening.
- Falling price with rising Open Interest and rising volume indicates a strong downtrend.
- Falling price with falling Open Interest and falling volume indicates that the downtrend is weakening.

Open Interest and Volume in Uptrends

Rising volume and Open Interest are signs of positive trader sentiment, as they indicate that new buyers are coming into the market in force. The rising volume shows that there is good value seen by market participants at current price levels and that higher prices are expected. Rising Open Interest shows that the traders entering the market are willing to take on and hold new positions as the price of the underlying instrument rises. Chart 9.59 shows how rising volume and Open Interest validate a healthy uptrend in price for silver.

Another bullish characteristic of a healthy uptrend occurs when price pulls back on a *decrease* in volume and Open Interest. That shows a decrease in selling pressure along with long positions being liquidated, similar to normal profit taking in stocks. This behavior shows that underlying bullish sentiment toward the commodity or derivative has not changed, which means that higher prices can be expected on the resumption of the trend. Chart 9.60 illustrates an orderly pullback for copper in an uptrend.

If price moves in an established uptrend, but Open Interest begins to diverge, it is an indication that a trend change may be imminent. Chart 9.61 shows how Open Interest began to decline as price made a new high for

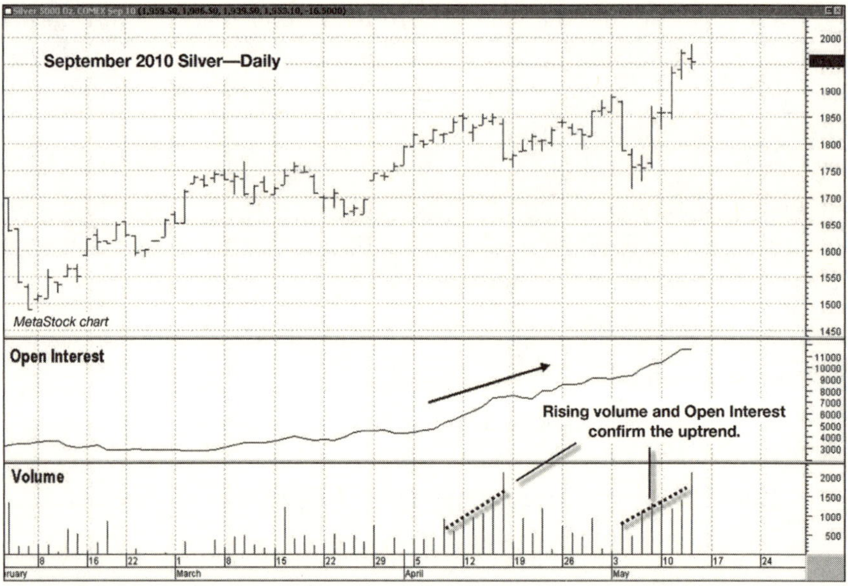

Chart 9.59 Rising Open Interest in Uptrend, September 2010 Silver Daily

Source: MetaStock

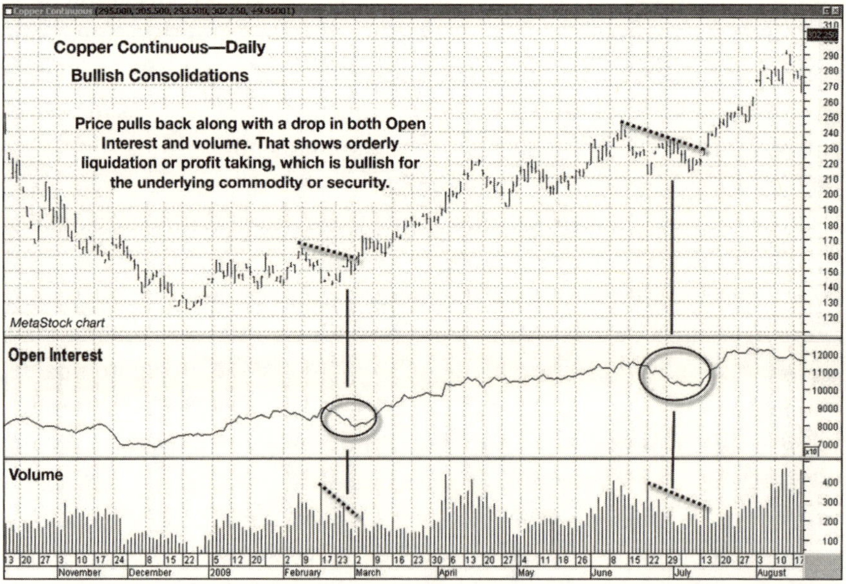

Chart 9.60 Open Interest, Short-Term Pullback in Bullish Consolidation, Copper Daily

Source: MetaStock

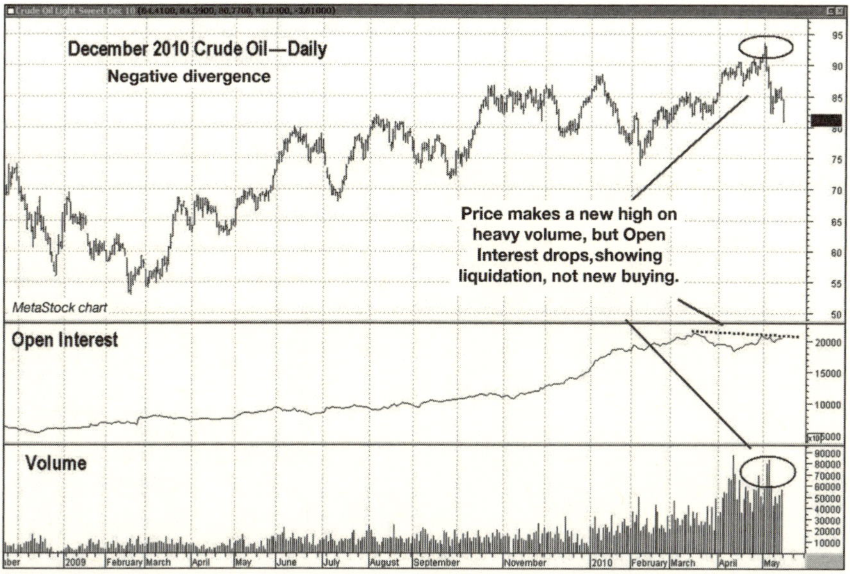

Chart 9.61 Open Interest, Negative Divergence, Crude Oil Daily

Source: MetaStock

crude oil. This was a sign of contract liquidation, meaning that traders were not as confident in the future prospects for crude oil going forward. Note the volume spikes near the high, which also warned that a change in direction was imminent.

Open Interest and Volume in Downtrends

Open Interest and volume can be used to confirm downtrends just as they do uptrends. When price is falling while Open Interest and volume are rising, it indicates that new players are entering the market (rising open interest) with conviction (rising volume). Such activity is a sure sign that selling pressure and lower prices are expected. Chart 9.62 shows falling prices with rising Open Interest and rising volume for wheat. Note how prices continued to decline until the pattern was broken at the end of the decline. At that point, Open Interest and volume began to decline along with price, signaling that selling pressure was abating.

Chart 9.63 is an example of a downtrend in corn caused by long positions being liquidated. Note how Open Interest and volume fell along with price. The decline of Open Interest and volume with price showed that the decline was most likely due to long traders liquidating their positions

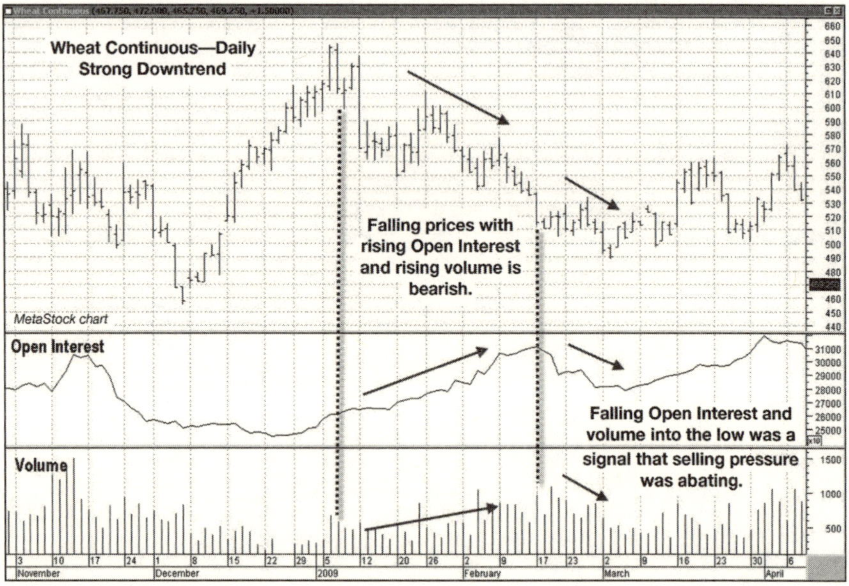

Chart 9.62 Open Interest Confirms Falling Prices, Then Reverses, Wheat Daily

Source: MetaStock

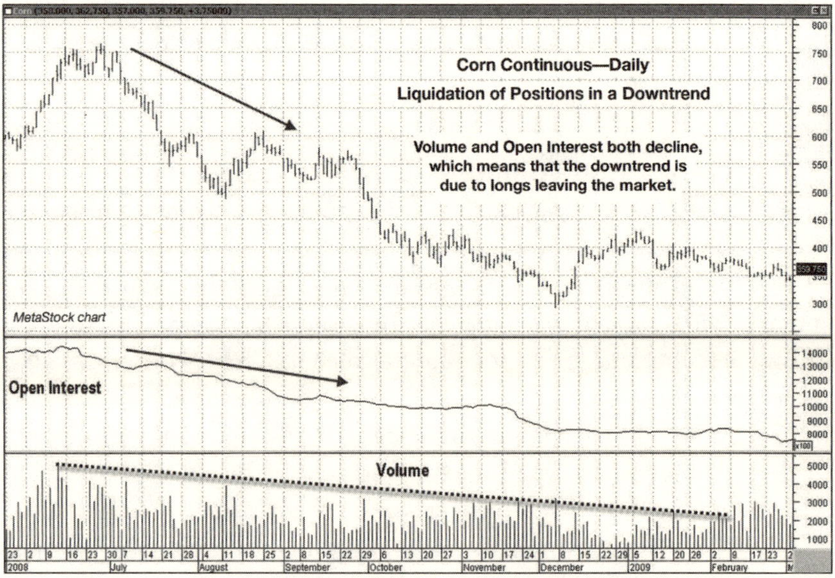

Chart 9.63 Open Interest Confirming Longs Exiting Market, Corn Daily

Source: MetaStock

and not to increased short-selling activity, which would have increased Open Interest and volume. Disillusioned longs were leaving the market, causing price to fall because of the increased supply of contracts for sale.

Open Interest in Accumulation Phases

One clue in a sideways market that contracts are being accumulated is the combination of rising Open Interest with lower overall volume. This situation indicates that traders are willing to acquire new positions in the current trading range. Upside breakouts following these periods have a greater chance of success, as a strong base has been built to sustain the move. Chart 9.64 shows a breakout in gold following an accumulation phase.

A single chart can capture multiple phases of trader sentiment. Changes in price, volume, and Open Interest can alert a trader to short-term sentiment changes. The example of copper in Chart 9.65 shows the different phases as they might unfold.

Trade Setup

Open Interest is a great tool to measure the conviction of traders in the support of price moves. The following example shows how Open Interest could have been used to help identify the July 2008 top in crude oil prices.

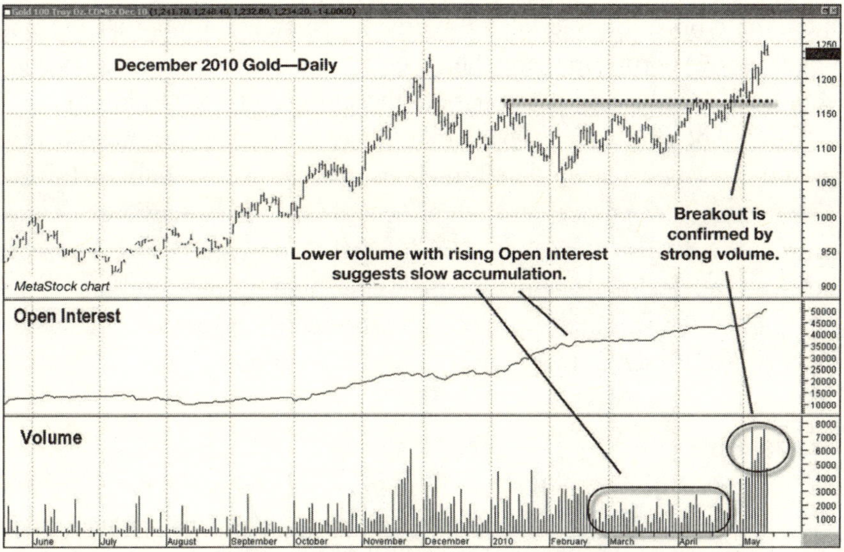

Chart 9.64 Open Interest, Upside Breakout after Accumulation, Gold Daily

Source: MetaStock

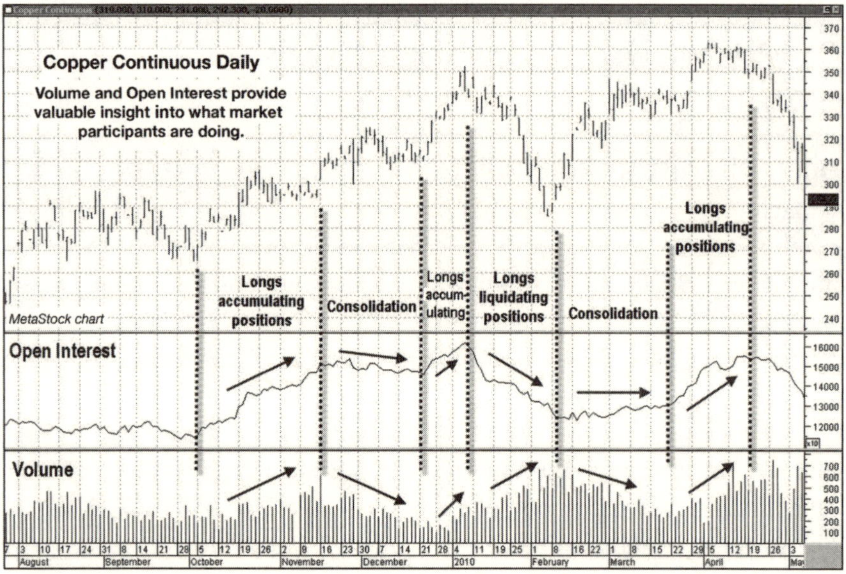

Chart 9.65 Open Interest, Capturing Changes in Sentiment, Copper Daily

Source: MetaStock

As the price of crude moved higher throughout 2008, speculation ran rampant. The cause of the rise was pinned on speculators; there was great debate as to whether the spike higher in crude oil prices was justified. When the bubble burst in the crude oil market, it created a substantial shorting opportunity. Shorting too soon, however, could have led to disaster, as price continued to grind higher throughout the spring and into the summer.

Chart 9.66 shows how Open Interest gave clues that speculators were leaving the market as crude oil made its push to its final high of 147.27. The negative divergence between price and Open Interest was evident as price made higher highs and Open Interest made lower highs. Also note how volume declined as price made higher highs in June and July. Connecting the lows off the April 2008 low showed a support line that, when violated, would signal that a short trade was in order.

Trade Entry

Price reversed sharply off the July 11 high and closed below the April–July support line on July 17, 2008, as Chart 9.67 shows. The initial protective stop should have been placed over the July 11 high of 147.27. Notice how Open Interest continued to decline as price moved lower, showing that traders were continuing to leave the market as more positions were liquidated.

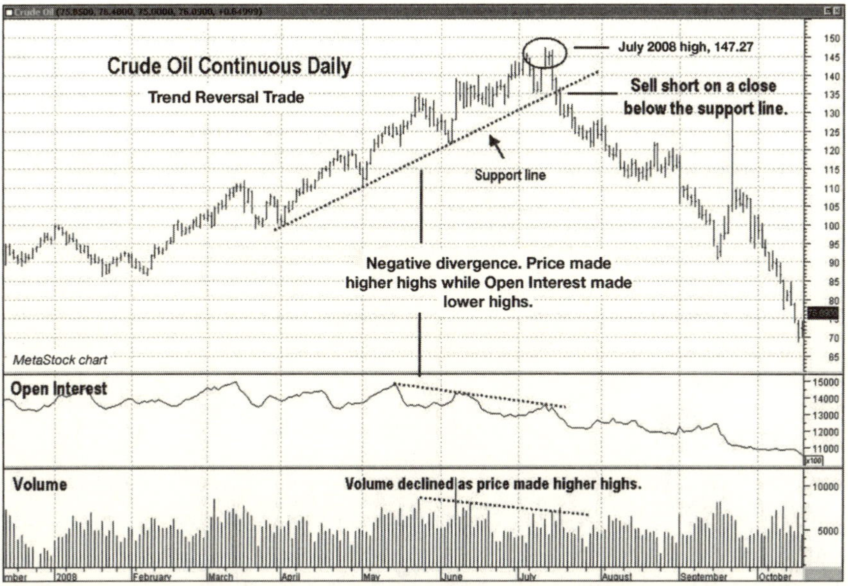

Chart 9.66 Open Interest, Trend Reversal Trade, Crude Oil Daily

Source: MetaStock

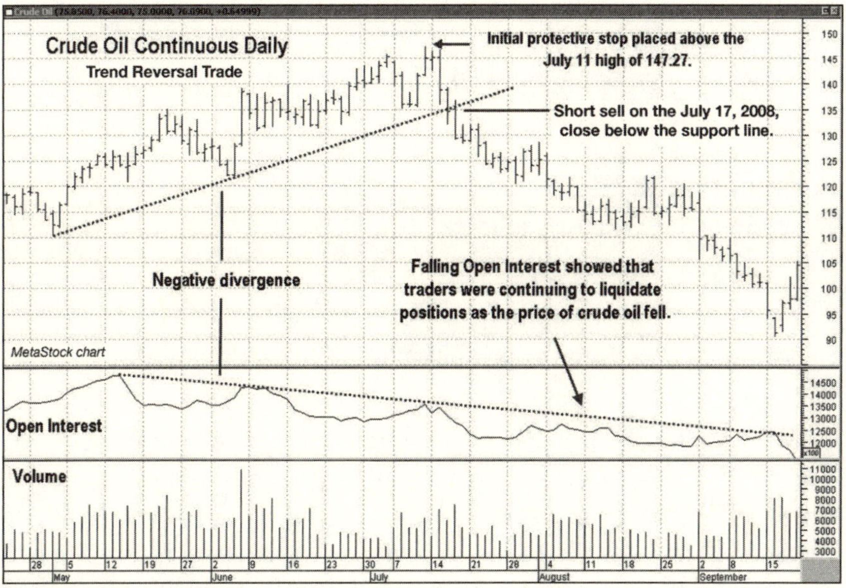

Chart 9.67 Open Interest, Negative Divergence and Trade Entry at Support Line Break, Crude Oil Daily

Source: MetaStock

Trader Tips

Much as share volume tells a lot about share price movements, Open Interest is an effective way to monitor true market conviction behind commodity futures contract trading. Monitoring Open Interest provides information about trend continuation and reversals through divergences, and gives important clues to traders' behavior behind the scenes, such as accumulation or sale of long positions. The downside: It works only for commodities or other securities with Open Interest data, and it may not work as well for thinly traded contracts.

Volume Price Trend

Volume Price Trend (VPT) was developed by David L. Markstein in 1966 in *How to Chart Your Way to Stock Market Profits.* It is among many indicators used to determine the relationship between a stock's price and volume. VPT takes the percentage gain or loss on the day and multiplies that by the day's volume, thus considering the amount of force (volume) behind the move. VPT is similar to On-Balance Volume in that it is a cumulative trending indicator, but while On-Balance Volume simply adds or subtracts all of the day's volume to or from the running total, depending on the direction of the close, VPT takes into account the size of the day's gain or loss and multiplies that number by the day's volume.

Formulation

The formula for VPT is as follows:

$$\text{VPT} = \text{yesterday's VPT} + \{\text{volume} \times [(\text{close today} - \text{previous close}) / \text{previous close}]\}$$

When VPT rises, money is flowing into the market or security being tracked. When VPT falls, money is flowing out of the market or security. If VPT flattens out, it is an early warning sign of a possible trend change. Volume Price Trend is good for confirming trends, showing positive and negative divergences, and confirming breakouts. Chart 9.68 shows a basic plot of Volume Price Trend for the Nasdaq 100 Trust ETF (QQQQ).

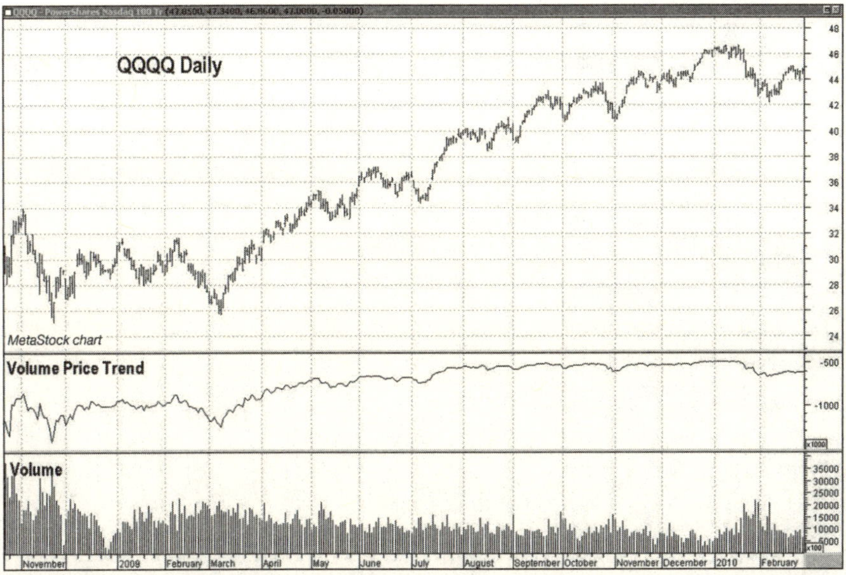

Chart 9.68 Volume Price Trend, Nasdaq 100 Trust ETF

Source: MetaStock

Trend Confirmation

Volume Price Trend is a trending indicator that is good for confirming trends or showing divergences. In the example of 3M (MMM) in Chart 9.69, note how VPT confirms the uptrend by making a series of higher highs and higher lows along with price. This showed that buyers were in control, thus confirming the uptrend. Downtrends are also confirmed by the VPT indicator. The example of Intel (INTC) in Chart 9.70 shows how VPT made lower highs and lower lows along with downtrending price, revealing that sellers were in control. A strong downtrending market like this should tell any prospective buyers that it is not a good time to buy until price and VPT stabilize.

Divergences

Volume Price Trend can show when a trend is weakening and getting ready to reverse. The example of JPMorgan Chase (JPM) in Chart 9.71 shows a positive divergence (i.e., a new price low with a higher low in the indicator) that occurred right at the March 2009 bottom. That divergence showed that buyers were stepping up and that the long, sharp downtrend was ready for a reversal higher.

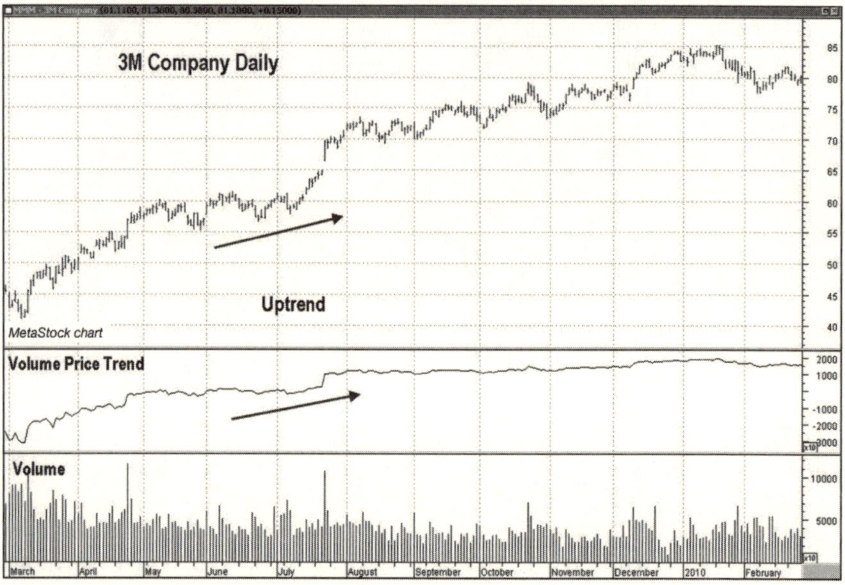

Chart 9.69 Volume Price Trend Confirming Uptrend, 3M Company

Source: MetaStock

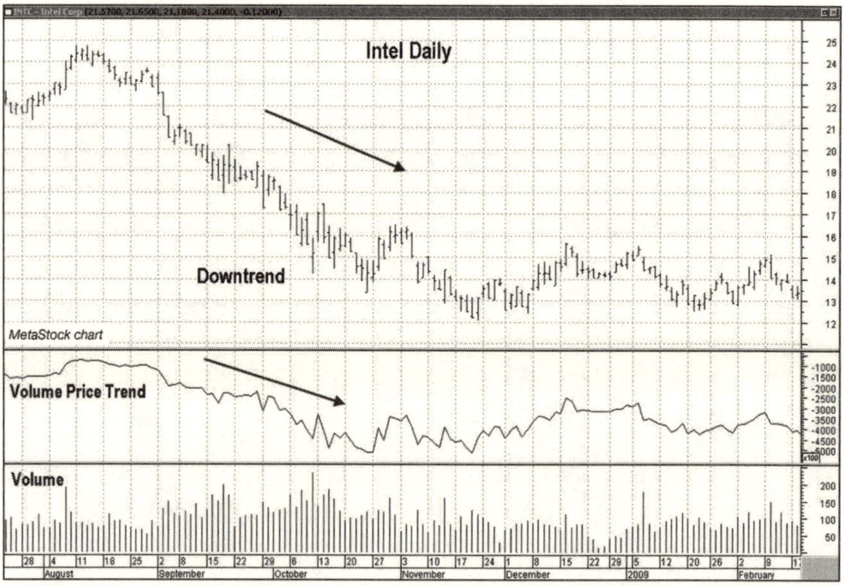

Chart 9.70 Volume Price Trend Confirming Downtrend, Intel Corp.

Source: MetaStock

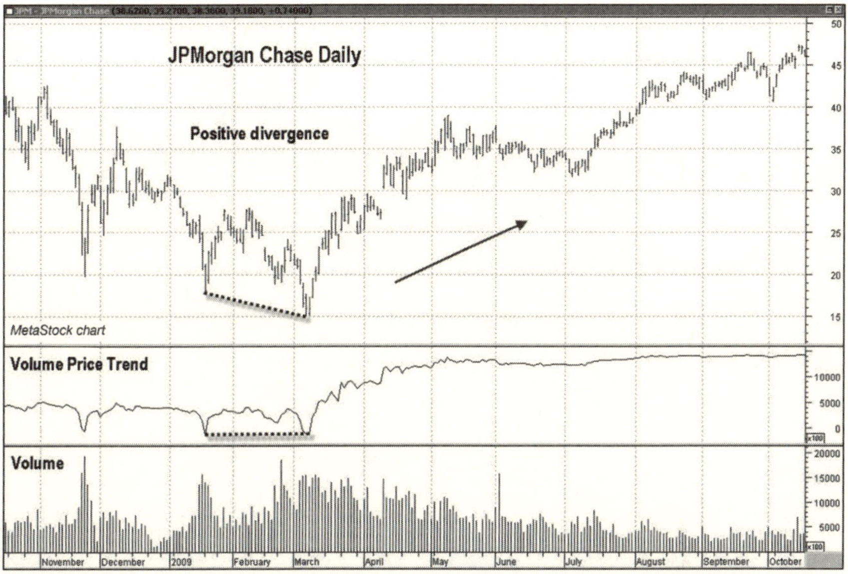

Chart 9.71 Volume Price Trend, Positive Divergence and Reversal, JPMorgan Chase

Source: MetaStock

Chart 9.72 shows a negative divergence for the iShares Barclays 7–10 Year Treasury Trust ETF (IEF); IEF rocketed out to a new price high in December 2008, while VPT did not. VPT's inability to make a new high with price showed latent selling, which demonstrated that sellers were dumping IEF on the final break to its December 2008 high.

Confirming Breakouts

Another strength of Volume Price Trend is its ability to confirm price breakouts. If price overcomes a resistance level and moves higher, or if it moves lower through a support level, VPT should confirm the breakout or breakdown by doing the same. If it does not, the breakout or breakdown is suspect. The example of iShares High Yield Corporate Bond ETF (HYG) in Chart 9.73 shows how VPT confirmed the break higher. Confirmation came after the breakout, but the late move higher in VPT validated the price movement.

Downside price breakdowns are also validated by VPT. Notice in Chart 9.74 (the S&P SPDR Financial ETF, or XLF) how VPT confirmed the downside breakout in XLF as the downtrend resumed in September 2008.

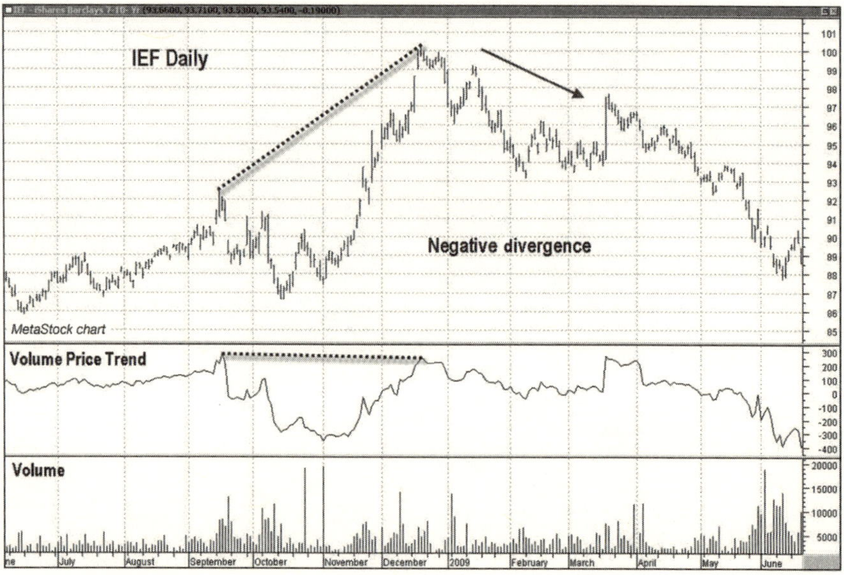

Chart 9.72 Volume Price Trend, Negative Divergence and Reversal, iShares Barclays 7–10 Year Treasury Trust ETF

Source: MetaStock

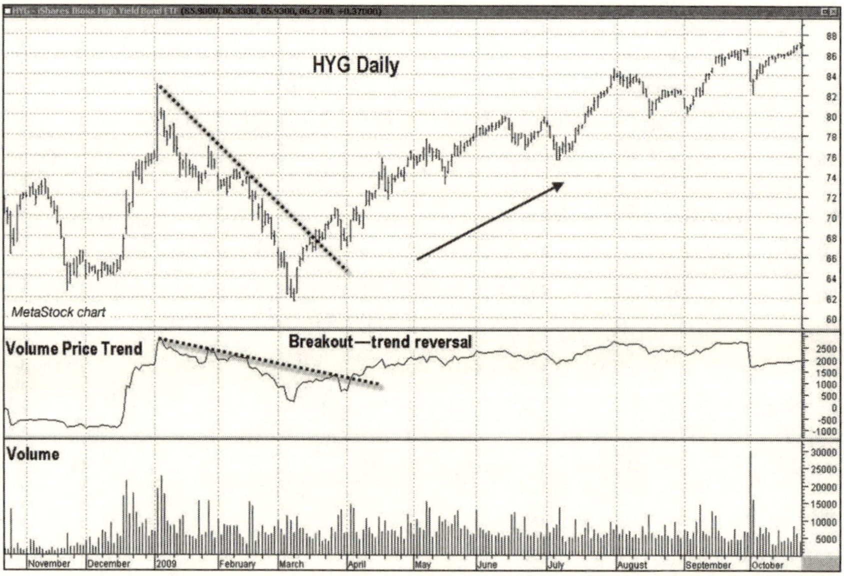

Chart 9.73 Volume Price Trend Confirming Breakout, iShares High Yield Corporate Bond ETF

Source: MetaStock

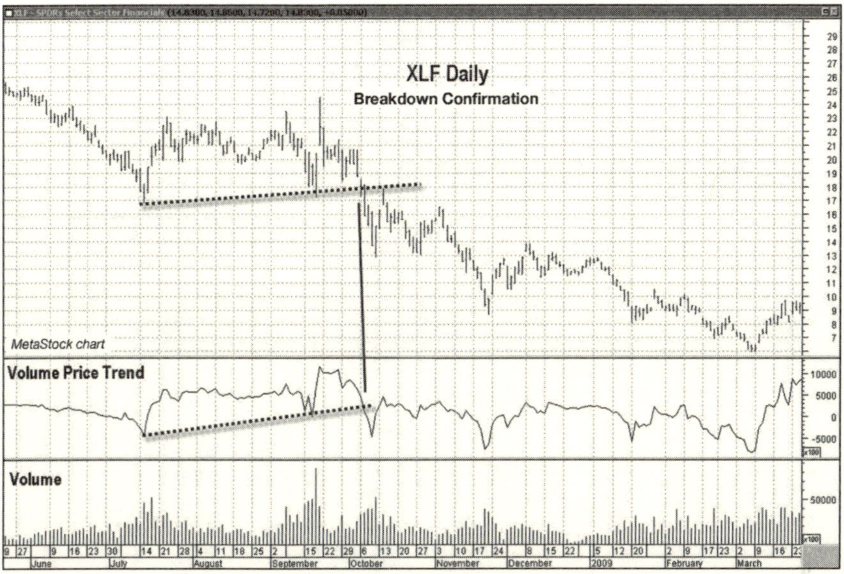

Chart 9.74 Volume Price Trend Confirming Breakdown, S&P SPDR Financial ETF

Source: MetaStock

Volume Price Trend with Other Indicators

Since Volume Price Trend is a cumulative trending indicator, it is best paired with an Overbought/Oversold Oscillator to spot buying or selling opportunities within the larger trend.

In Chart 9.75, VPT is paired with a 14-period slow Stochastic (14, 3, 3) for the 3M Corp. (MMM). As with the other trending indicators, VPT will be used as a trade filter, dictating whether buy or sell setups are to be taken. In an uptrend, a buy setup occurs when the VPT is trending higher and the 14-period Stochastic is below 20 (oversold). A buy is executed once the Stochastic crosses above 20 following the setup. In a downtrend, a sell setup occurs when the VPT is trending lower and the 14-period Stochastic is above 80 (overbought). A short sell is executed when the Stochastic crosses below 80. Chart 9.75 contains buy arrows (pointing higher) and a sell arrow (pointing lower) to designate each trade.

Trade Setup

In the example that follows, we will use VPT to look for a sign that an uptrend is ready to resume. Chart 9.76 shows the powerful uptrend that began for the iShares Russell 2000 Index ETF (IWM) in October 2006

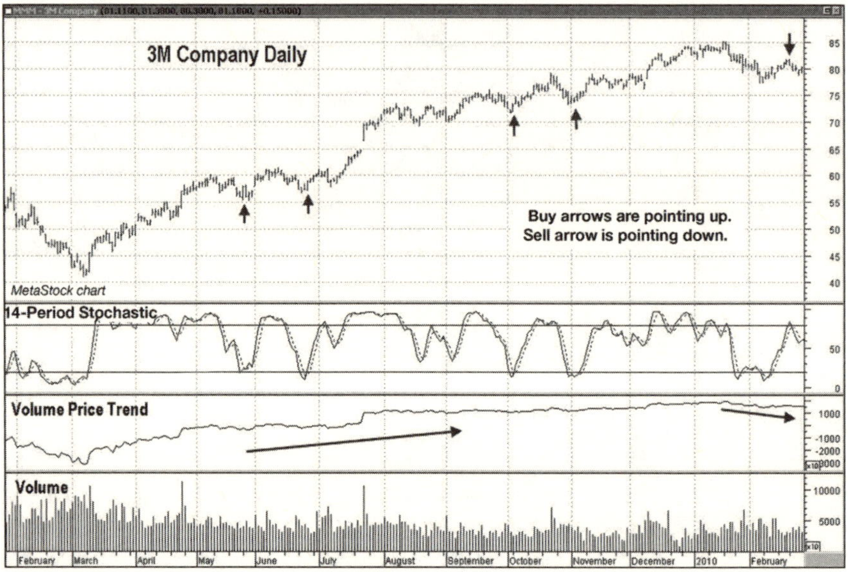

Chart 9.75 Volume Price Trend Paired with 14-Day Slow Stochastic, 3M Corp.

Source: MetaStock

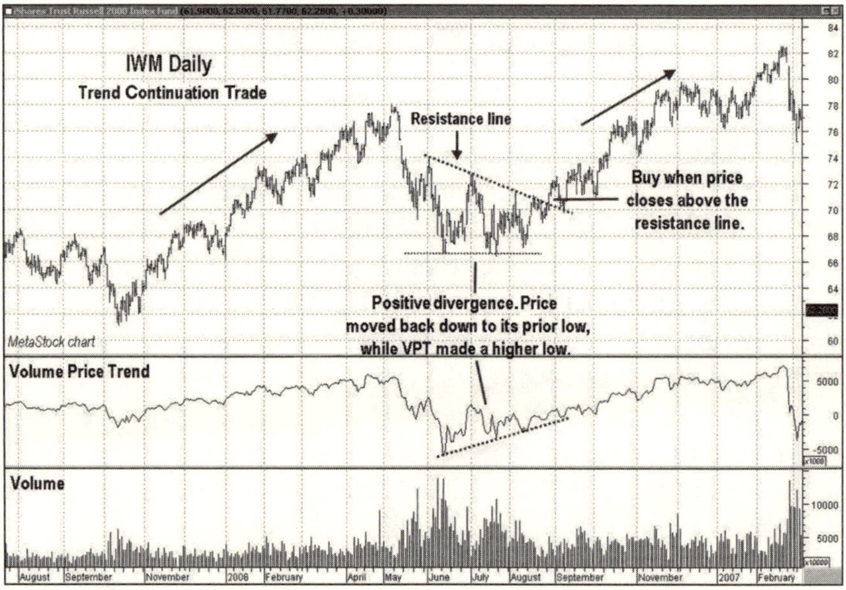

Chart 9.76 Volume Price Trend, Positive Divergence and Trade Setup, iShares Russell 2000 Index ETF

Source: MetaStock

and continued through May 2007. Price then reversed and corrected into July 2007, giving rise to the positive divergence. Note how price came back down to its mid-June low as VPT made a higher low. That indicated weaker selling pressure on the test of the June low. A resistance line could be drawn across the June–August tops. Price closing above this line gave a signal to enter a long position.

Trade Entry

As Chart 9.77 shows, price closed above the resistance line on August 29, 2006, giving a buy signal. The two higher reactionary lows after the July 21 low allowed an opportunity to use a stop closer to the trade entry point. If the low of August 24 had been penetrated, that would have been a sign that another trip down near the June–July lows would be in order, thus signaling that the close above the resistance line was a false breakout. The moral of the story: Never take any signal for granted on any trade, no matter how great a setup looks.

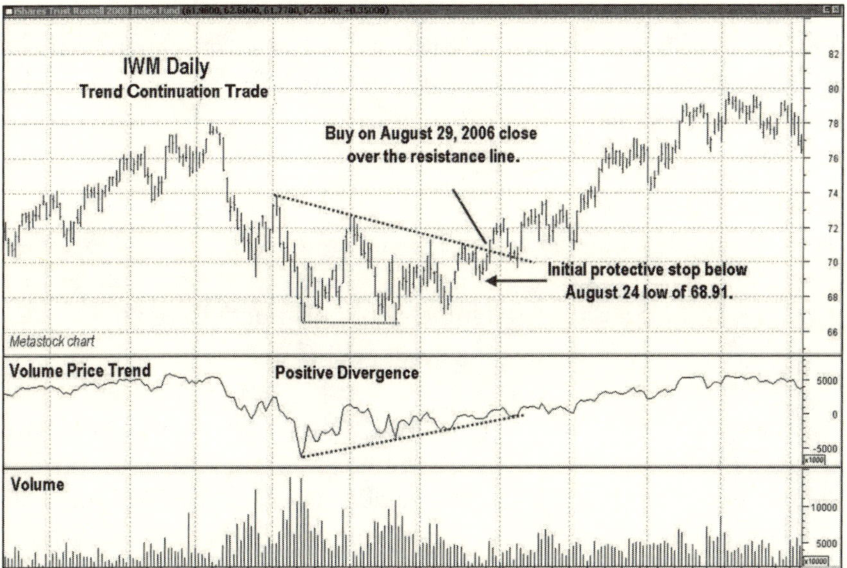

Chart 9.77 Volume Price Trend, Positive Divergence and Trade Entry, iShares Russell 2000 Index ETF

Source: MetaStock

Trader Tips

Volume Price Trend is an indicator that can show when buyers or sellers are in control or if control is shifting from one group to the other. VPT is commonly used for the following:

- Confirming price trends
- Showing divergences
- Confirming price breakouts

One drawback to VPT is that it does not take into account the quality of the close of each trading day. For example, a close below the open and at the bottom of its daily range is counted as all positive as long as the close is above the previous day's closing value.

Volume Rate of Change

The Volume Rate of Change (VROC) is a technical indicator used to gauge the volatility in a security's volume. The higher the volatility, the stronger the conviction of the side that is moving the market (either buyers or sellers). VROC can give an indication as to whether resistance or support levels are likely to be broken. It can also provide information as to whether a trend is developing or resuming.

Formulation

The Volume Rate of Change is calculated as follows:

$$\text{Volume ROC} = [(\text{volume} - \text{volume } n \text{ periods ago}) / \text{volume } n \text{ periods ago}] \times 100$$

Volume Rate of Change is most commonly used to identify short-term trend changes in the market, trend continuation, and breakouts. Anytime volume characteristics change, traders need to take notice. Volume Rate of Change illustrates these changes. Essentially, the indicator reveals the percentage change in the volume over the last n periods. If the volume is higher than the previous period, then the rate of change is positive; conversely, if it is less than its previous period, then the rate of change is negative. This indicator can thus reveal the speed or momentum of the change in volume and, in many ways, the strength of the volume trend.

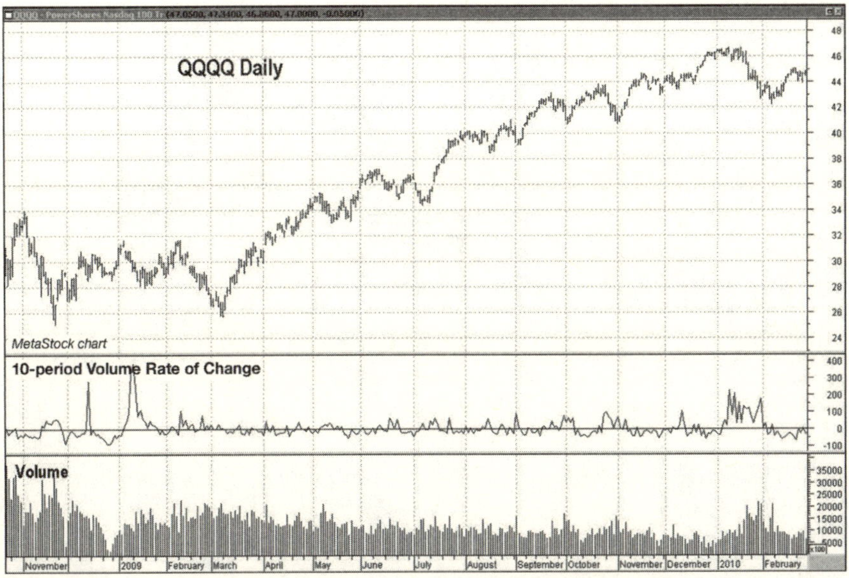

Chart 9.78 The 10-Period Volume Rate of Change, Nasdaq 100 Trust ETF

Source: MetaStock

One of the issues with the indicator is how to set parameters for its use. For short-term traders, periods of 10 to 15 days, much like the volume moving average, are useful. However, at the same time, the jagged and irregular nature of the indicator can often give a false signal, so care must be taken in its translation. Using intermediate time frames of 25 to 50 gives a more robust and smoothed look to the data. Chart 9.78 shows a plot of a 10-day Volume Rate of Change for the Nasdaq 100 Trust ETF (QQQQ).

Price Change of Direction

Volume Rate of Change can be used for spotting short-term buying climaxes that tend to give way to periods of consolidation and profit taking. There is no indication of how long these periods of consolidation will last, but VROC can alert short-term traders when a pullback may be due. Chart 9.79 shows how spikes in the 10-period VROC for Microsoft (MSFT) coincide with short-term tops in an uptrend. Note how volume spiked at a short-term low in early 2010. That was a change in character for volume that was an early indication that the sellers were gaining control. A decent sell-off followed.

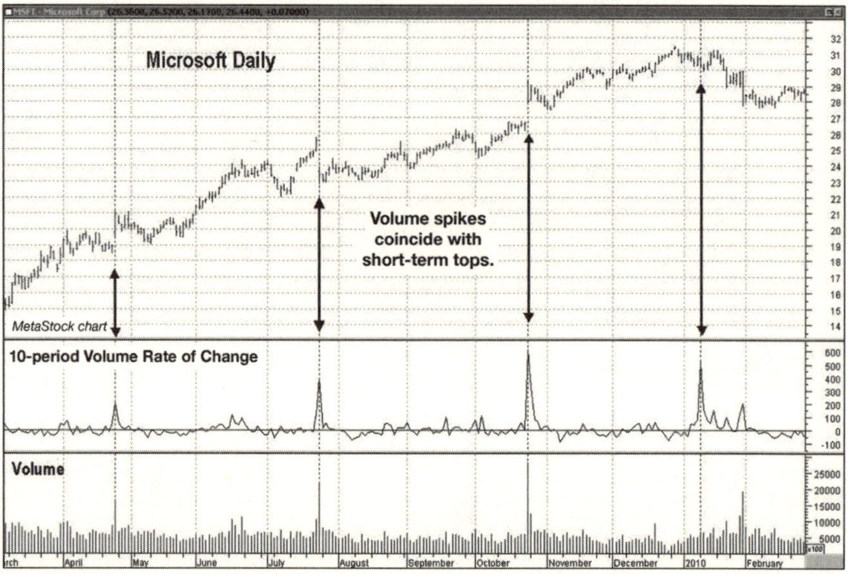

Chart 9.79 The 10-Period Volume Rate of Change, Volume Spikes, and Short-Term Tops, Microsoft Corp.

Source: MetaStock

S&P SPDR Financial ETF (XLF) in Chart 9.80 shows how a 25-day VROC identified short-term change points, in this case both short-term highs and short-term lows. Note how the longer period of 25 days causes a smoother plot in VROC. The spikes on the VROC can indicate that change—one way or another—is near. VROC can also be used to spot longer-term changes in trend. In the S&P 500 Trust ETF (SPY) in Chart 9.81, note how the 50-period VROC (an even longer, more smoothed form of the indicator) nailed the March 2009 bottom with a tremendous spike. That spike showed a change in character in the volume pattern, giving a clue that change was imminent.

Chart 9.82 provides another look at the SPY chart and the March 2009 low, which shows how a shorter-term VROC divergence also gave a clue that a price change was near. As price broke lower to the March 2009 low, the VROC was surprisingly tame compared to the October–November 2008 period. That did not confirm the break lower, giving a clue that the breakdown needed to be watched for signs of a reversal.

Confirming Breakouts

Spikes in the VROC can be used to confirm breakouts. As price enters a resistance area, a new flood of volume is usually necessary to push higher through these areas. The VROC is a great indicator to show a significant

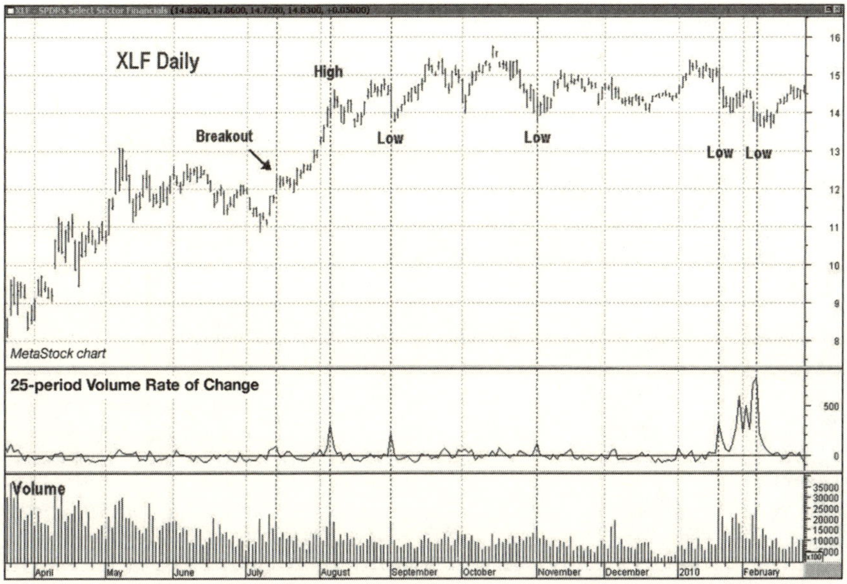

Chart 9.80 The 25-Period Volume Rate of Change, Volume Spikes and Inflection Points, S&P SPDR Financial ETF

Source: MetaStock

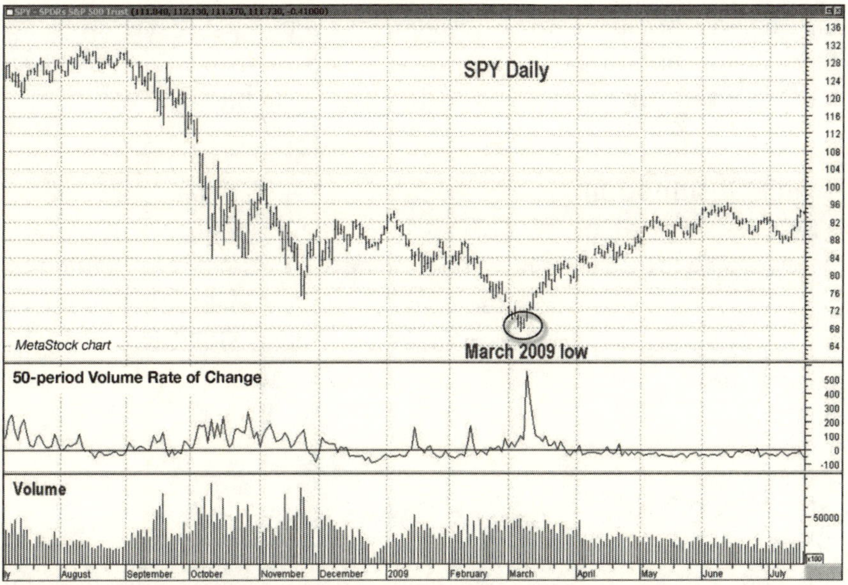

Chart 9.81 The 50-Period Volume Rate of Change, Volume Spike Confirmation of Major Low, S&P 500 Trust ETF

Source: MetaStock

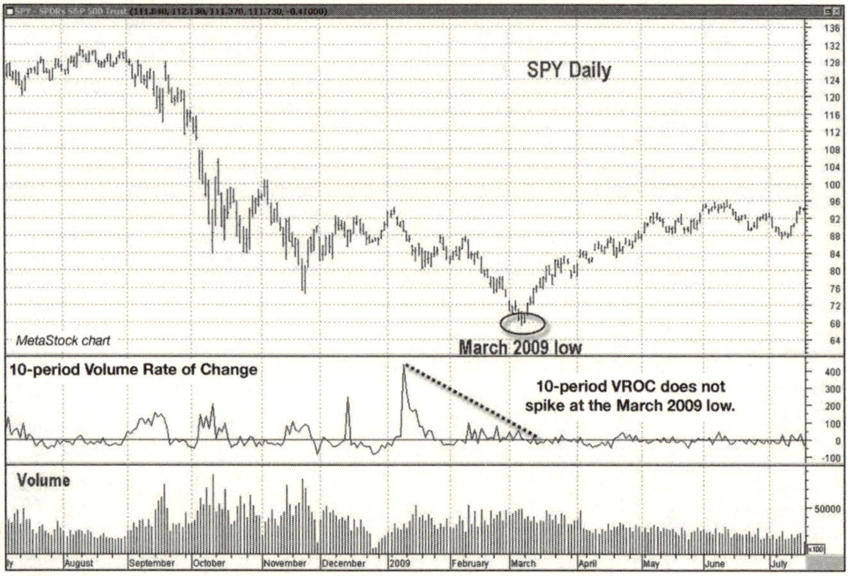

Chart 9.82 The 10-Period Volume Rate of Change, Failure to Confirm Further Breakdown, S&P 500 Trust ETF

Source: MetaStock

volume spike to push prices higher or to drive them lower, depending on the situation. Recall Chart 9.82, which showed how the 10-day VROC for SPY did not confirm the breakdown. In Chart 9.83, note how the 10-day VROC spiked as Intel broke through resistance to higher levels.

Trend Resumption

VROC is also good for identifying when a trend is resuming its previous course. Such a scenario gives good buying opportunities in uptrends as buyers are coming back into the market to drive it higher after corrective phases. Note in the S&P Consumer Select Staples SPDR ETF (XLP) in Chart 9.84 how spikes in the 10-period VROC coincide with short-term bottoms.

Smoothing VROC

To take away some of the volatility and to make peaks and troughs stand out more, VROC can be smoothed into a moving average. Smoothing the VROC can also show zero-line crossovers as an oscillator, showing periods of building or declining momentum.

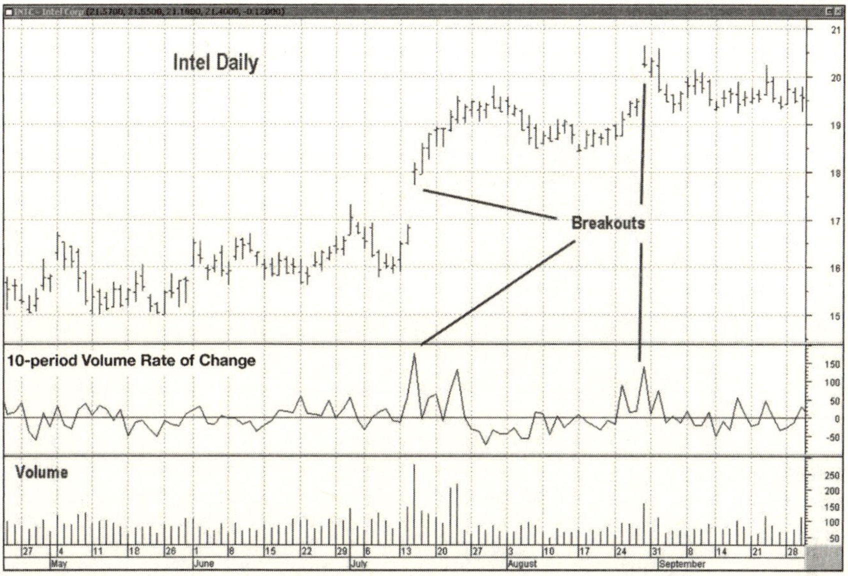

Chart 9.83 The 10-Period Volume Rate of Change, Confirming Breakouts, Intel Corp.

Source: MetaStock

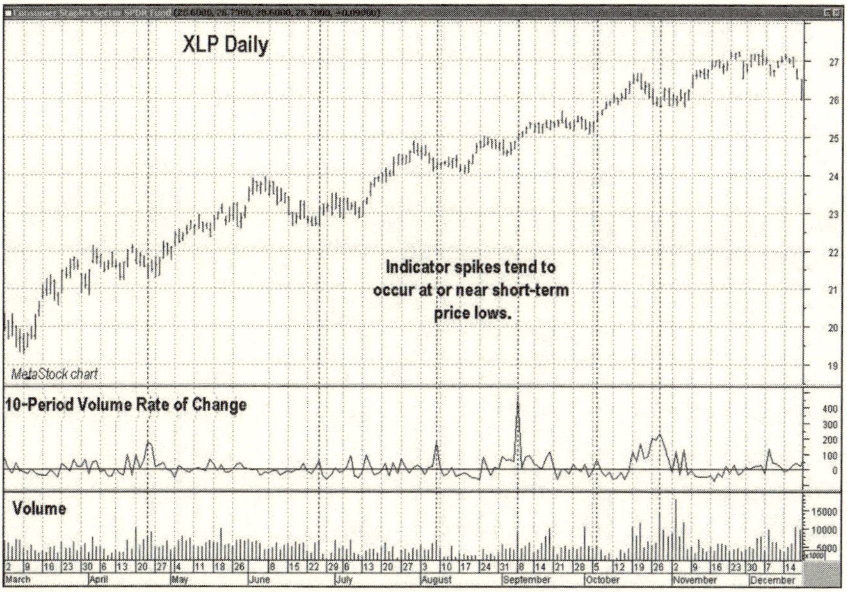

Chart 9.84 The 10-Period Volume Rate of Change Confirming Trend Resumption, S&P Consumer Select Staples SPDR ETF

Source: MetaStock

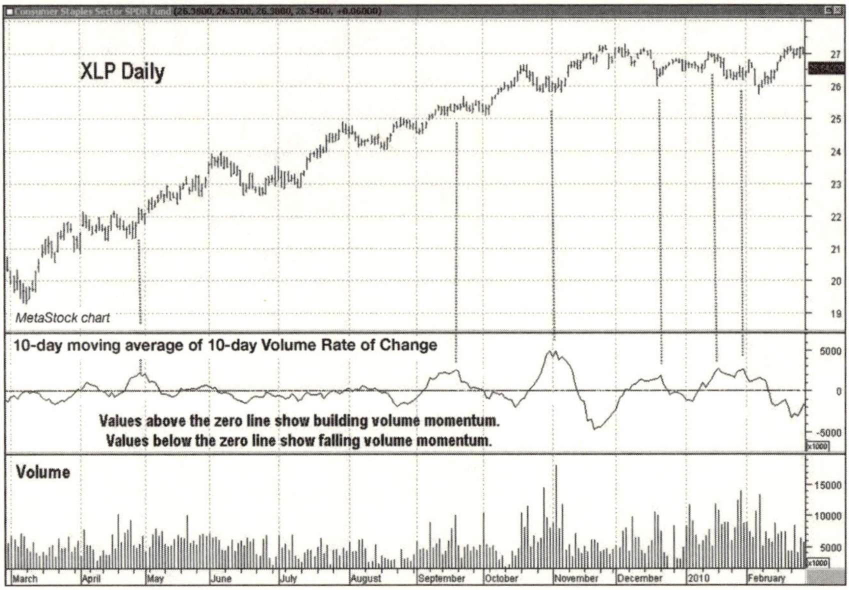

Chart 9.85 Volume Rate of Change, 10-Day Moving Average, Confirming Volume Momentum, S&P Consumer Select Staples SPDR ETF

Source: MetaStock

The reason that VROC isn't classified as an oscillator, however, is that center-line crossovers rarely give clear-cut signals. Also, zero-line crossovers in the VROC have nothing to do with price direction, only the momentum of volume itself. Chart 9.85 is the same time frame of the S&P Consumer Select Staples SPDR ETF (XLP) as Chart 9.84, but this time VROC is smoothed into a 10-day moving average. Note how the peaks and troughs stand out a bit more and also how there are fewer zero-line crosses compared to the raw (unsmoothed) version.

Volume Rate of Change with Other Indicators

Because VROC is a great indicator for marking turning points, a good pairing would be with an Overbought/Oversold Oscillator. As price enters overbought or oversold territory, spikes in the VROC can be used to show that the short-term extreme in price is ready to reverse.

Chart 9.86 shows a 25-day VROC paired with a 10-day Williams %R. As stated earlier, Williams %R is simply a raw Stochastic plotted on an inverse scale. A buy setup occurs when Williams %R enters the oversold zone (less than −80) and VROC spikes higher in relation to its recent

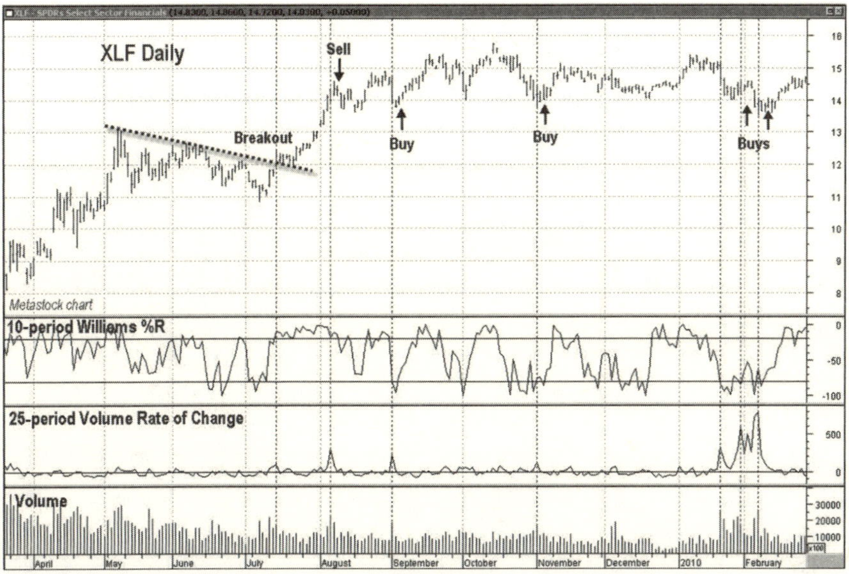

Chart 9.86 The 25-Day Volume Rate of Change with Williams %R Oscillator, S&P SPDR Financial ETF

Source: MetaStock

values. A buy is triggered when the Williams %R crosses up out of the oversold zone (greater than −80). A short-sell setup occurs when Williams %R enters the overbought zone (greater than −20) and VROC spikes in relation to its recent values. A short sell is triggered when Williams %R reverses lower out of overbought territory (less than −20). The S&P SPDR Financial ETF (XLF) in Chart 9.86 shows a breakout on the left-hand side of the chart followed by an assortment of buy and sell signals.

Trade Setup

VROC can give a longer-term look at volume trends when it is set to look at longer time frames. Chart 9.87 shows a divergence between price and volume in the U.S. Dollar Index in the fall of 2008. Note that as price moved higher off its September low, VROC was making lower highs. The decrease in volume is also visible in the plot of volume in the bottom pane of Chart 9.87. With the lack of supportive volume, it was just a matter of patience in waiting for price to violate its uptrend support line and reverse lower.

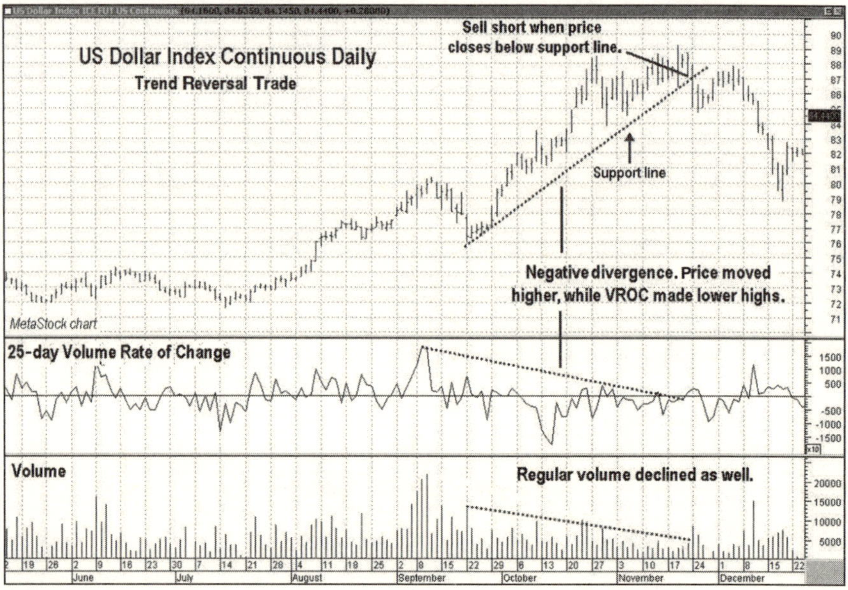

Chart 9.87 The 25-Day Volume Rate of Change, Negative Divergence Trade Setup, U.S .Dollar Index

Source: MetaStock

Trade Entry

Looking at the same chart in more detail in Chart 9.88, we see that both VROC and volume showed that supportive volume was not present on the move higher off the September 2008 lows; it was just a matter of time before the trend reversed. The violation of the upsloping support line would be the signal that the uptrend was at an end. On November 24, 2008, price closed below its support line, which would have triggered a short trade. The initial protective stop should have been placed over the November 19 high of 89.25. Even more patience was required after applying the trade, however, as price consolidated for nine more trading days before beginning its descent in earnest. Also note how VROC spiked once the selling resumed after the nine-day consolidation period.

Trader Tips

Volume Rate of Change is an indicator that alerts traders to changes in volume characteristics that can indicate imminent changes in price. The VROC can be used for the following:

- Showing when a short-term change of direction is likely

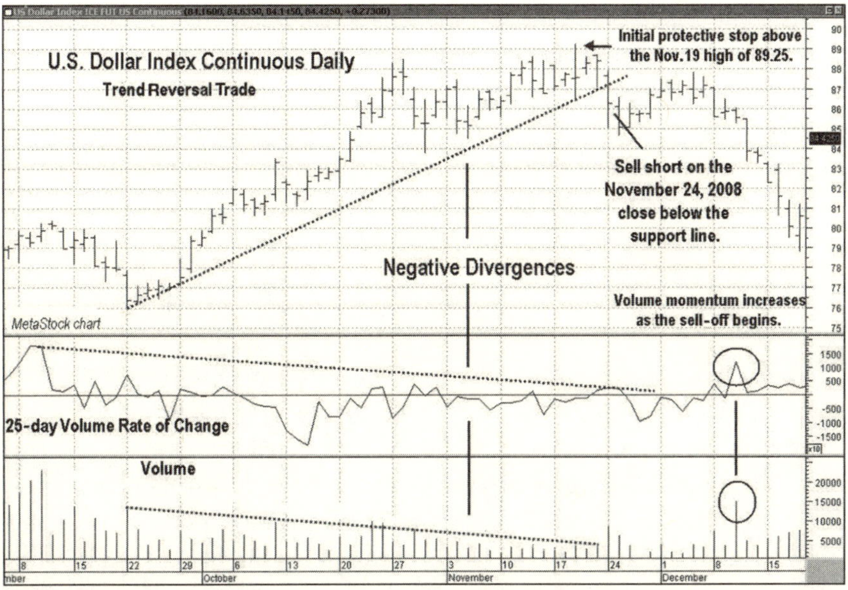

Chart 9.88 The 25-Day Volume Rate of Change, Negative Divergence Trade Entry, U.S. Dollar Index

Source: MetaStock

- Confirming breakouts over resistance or breakdowns below support
- Showing when trend resumption out of a pullback is likely

One drawback of VROC, especially in raw or unsmoothed form, is that its volatile nature sometimes can make it misleading.

Additional Techniques for Assessing Trends Using Indicators

There are several techniques that we have found useful as applied to volume indicators to assess trends. Here we discuss detrending an indicator, normalizing volume by translating volume in comparison to a chosen baseline, normalizing an indicator, and using volume indicators to confirm candlestick patterns.

Detrending an Indicator

Another way we like to display a volume trending indicator is by detrending it. Centered detrending, refined by market technician Steven Achilles, is often used as an alternative format to display price and price-based indicators. Here we apply this technique to cumulative volume indicators.

Detrending converts an indicator into an oscillator format (see Chapter 10) and can be used to create companion oscillators for those indicators that tend to trend closely with price. This technique allows for easier identification of shorter-term high- and low-cycle points than does the trending indicator format. In an oscillator format, overbought and oversold areas and price divergences can also be more easily observed. The detrending of an indicator is accomplished by the following expression:

Indicator close value – simple moving average ($n/2+1$ days ago)

In using the detrending formula, select a time frame (n) that you wish to use and calculate a simple moving average for that time frame. Take the indicator close value and subtract from it the simple moving average $n/2+1$ days ago. We chose a 20-day moving average in our example, since financial market cycles often fluctuate within a 20-day trading range. Longer- or shorter-term traders can set their moving averages accordingly. Note that, when plotted, the centered detrended oscillator will be shifted to the left $n/2+1$, and there will always be an empty or undefined space on the right side of the chart where the indicator plot ends. Chart 9.89 is an example of a detrended Accumulation/Distribution Line using a 20-day moving average. In our example, 11 trading day bars are missing. Notice also how the

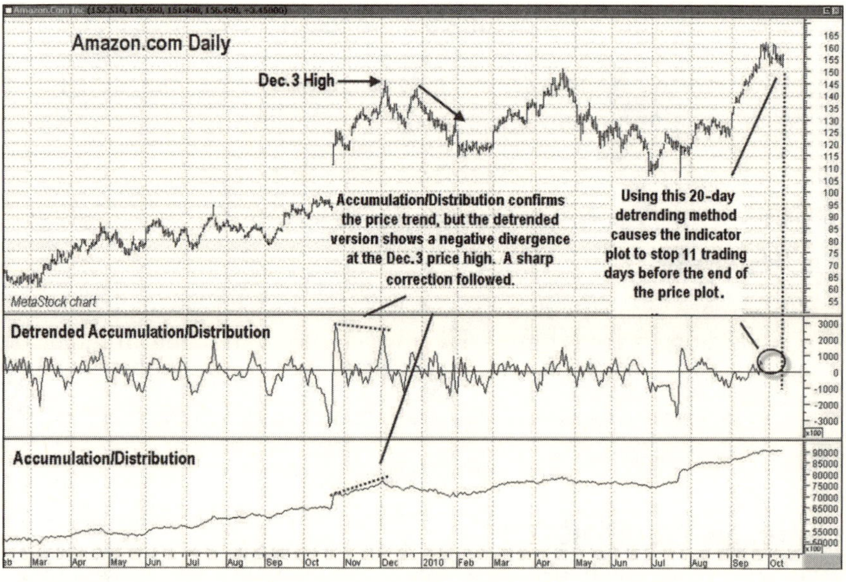

Chart 9.89 Accumulation/Distribution, Raw and Detrended 20-Day Version, Amazon.com

Source: MetaStock

same indicator displayed in a different format can capture different subsets of information. Detrending removed the trending characteristics of the indicator, making it more sensitive to the conditions within a 20-day trading cycle. Where the Accumulation/Distribution Line continued to trend, the detrended oscillator displayed the momentum cycle of shorter-term tops and bottoms, which often coincide with highs and lows in price. This can allow traders to glean important characteristics of both the higher- and lower-degree trend. The detrended oscillator, unlike the trending indicator, generated a negative divergence from the price high in our example, which was an important signal for the decline that followed. This technique lends itself well to Volume Analysis in the futures market, where patterns are by their nature historical and cyclical. When detrending an indicator, take time to familiarize yourself with its characteristics. Some cumulative volume indicators discussed in this chapter will be more adaptive to displaying different subsets of information with greater or lesser degrees of accuracy. Displaying the indicator and its companion detrended oscillator on the same chart with volume is a preferred format for this process. As we have seen, by identifying cyclical tops and bottoms within the higher- and lower-degree trend, traders can anticipate where the next trend reversal may occur and trade accordingly.

Normalizing Volume

Normalized volume is simply a way of displaying volume so that the scale is consistent from security to security or sector to sector. If your trading strategy requires a specific level of volume in order to initiate a trade and you are comparing securities or sectors, this will allow an apples-to-apples comparison. This particular approach was suggested by veteran technician John Bollinger. Here a standard normalization of trading volume gets its own examination.

Normalization allows for easier comparison between issues on the same relative scale to quickly compare volume totals relative to their own average. Divide today's volume by whatever moving average of volume values your trading requires, multiplying by 100. For example, Volume Analysis is often done by comparing daily volume totals across issues using a 20-day or 50-day moving average

Formulation

This is the formula for normalizing volume: (Replace *n* with the moving average length of your choice.)

$$NV = (\text{today's volume} \,/\, n \text{ period moving average of volume}) \times 100$$

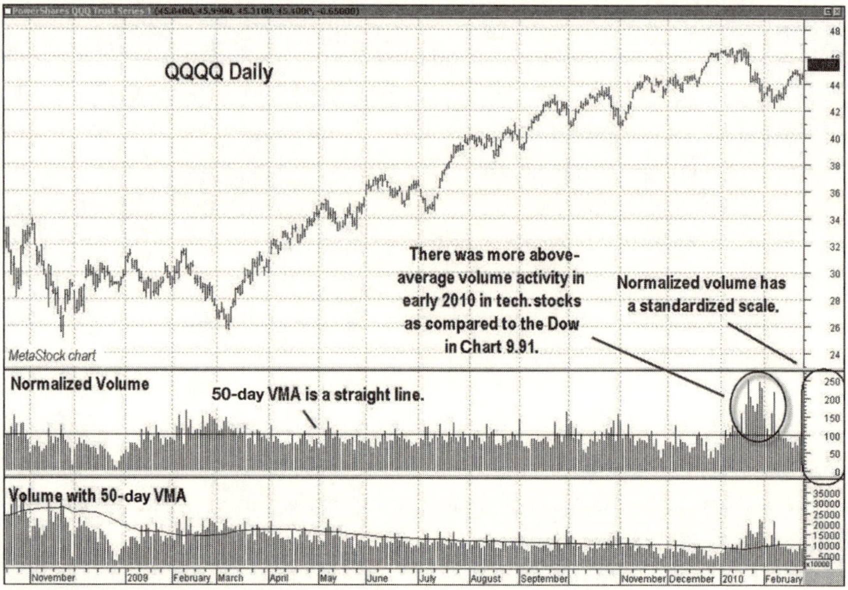

Chart 9.90 Normalized Volume with 50-Day VMA at 100 Baseline, Nasdaq 100 Trust ETF

Source: MetaStock

Translating Volume in Comparison to Its Normalized Volume Baseline

Chart 9.90 gives a plot of the Nasdaq 100 Trust ETF (QQQQ) with Normalized Volume with a separate plot of volume with a simple 50-day volume moving average. Note how the 50-day VMA is plotted across the Normalized Volume chart as a straight line at the 100 level; this is the normalized base level for the indicator, as described below.

On an NV chart, if volume comes in for the day under the *n* average, the reading will be less than 100. If it comes in above average, the reading will exceed 100. If volume comes in at 10 percent above average, the daily volume reading will be 110 (110 percent of the 50-day average); if it is 10 percent below average, the reading will be 90 (90 percent of the 50-day average); and so forth. The example of the DJIA in Chart 9.91 shows how much easier it is to compare the daily relationship between volume and its 50-day moving average with such an indicator/oscillator.

It's also worth looking at the Normalized Volume plotted alongside raw volume at a shorter 10-day moving average of that volume. The result is a more sensitive read on volume behavior. Chart 9.92 shows the DJIA over the same period as before. Underneath the price plot are two volume plots:

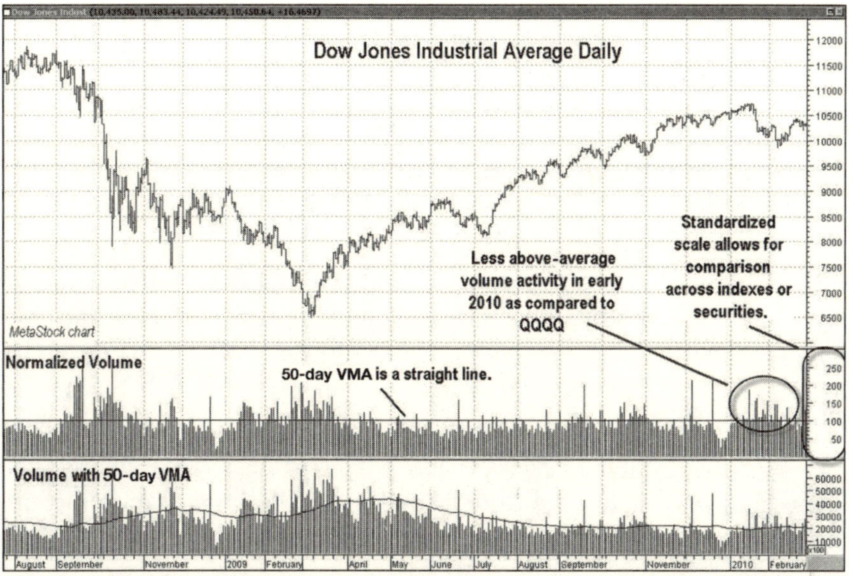

Chart 9.91 Normalized Volume Sector Comparison with 50-Day VMA at 100 Baseline, DJIA Daily

Source: MetaStock

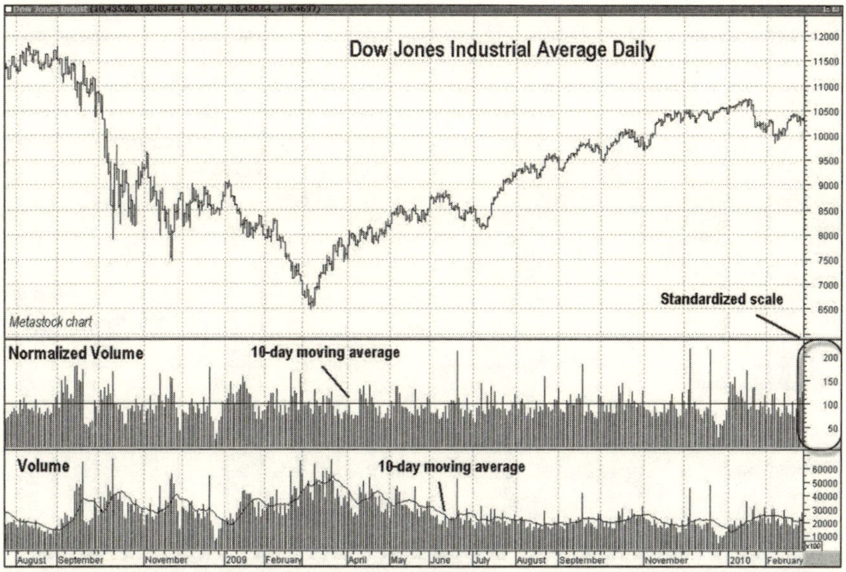

Chart 9.92 Normalized Volume with 10-Day VMA at 100 Baseline, DJIA Daily

Source: MetaStock

One is a plot of daily volume with its 10-day simple moving average, and the other is 10-day Normalized Volume.

When examining volume relative to its moving average it is necessary to know not only whether or not volume was above average but also by how much or how little it varied from that average. While the plot of volume with its 10-day VMA shows volume compared to its average, it isn't easy to figure out by how much it exceeded or trailed the average just by looking at the chart. The plot of Normalized Volume in Chart 9.92, on the other hand, clearly displays in easily quantifiable terms how that day's volume exceeded the average. It is like converting raw data to percentage terms. Was the value over 100? If so, it exceeded average: If the day's value was 105, it was 5 percent above average; if 110, it was 10 percent above average; and so on. If a 10-day average is too volatile, a 20-day average can be used. An example of the same period for the DJIA as the previous charts is shown in Chart 9.93. This time it has a 20-day simple moving average on volume along with a plot of 20-day normalized volume.

An Apples-to-Apples Comparison

Normalization allows for quicker comparisons between potential trades. For example, suppose a trader watching sectors A and B wanted to buy the

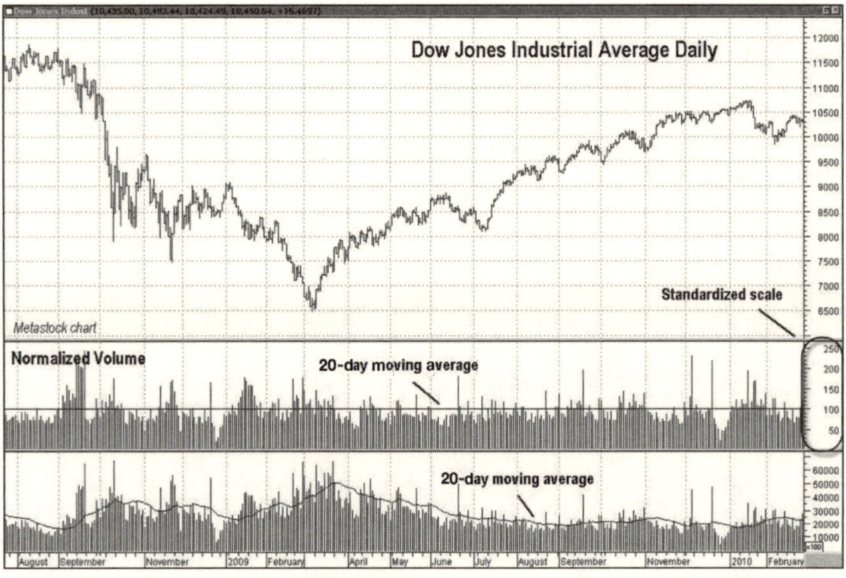

Chart 9.93 Normalized Volume with 20-Day VMA at 100 Baseline, DJIA Daily

Source: MetaStock

sector that showed daily volume more consistently over its 50-day moving average of volume over the past week (or 5 trading days). The trader wouldn't need to compute the 50-day moving average of each and compare that average to the daily raw values. Instead, the trader could simply compare their last five days' Normalized Volume readings, since they are both plotted on the same scale relative to their own moving averages.

So if sector A came in with a 5-day average of 130 and sector B had a 5-day average of 112, sector A would be the choice based on a volume-driven trading scenario. The example just given is rather simplistic, but it should help illustrate how much easier comparisons are when the volume scale is uniform for each index or security.

Trader Tips

Normalized Volume is a different way of plotting volume that does the following:

- Uses a uniform scale regardless of actual daily volume totals
- Shows at a glance whether volume was over or under average and by how much
- Allows for volume comparisons between securities because of the uniform scale

Normalized Volume is a great tool to speed up analysis and give a clearer understanding of daily volume totals.

Normalizing an Indicator

In this section, we examine a technique for normalizing volume indicators. As with normalizing volume, one of the strengths of normalizing an indicator is to give like values for security and index comparisons by plotting it on a common scale. This technique and concept has been suggested and refined by veteran market technician John Bollinger. It is used to display a moving sum and essentially give oscillatorlike properties to longer-trending volume indicators. The formula for normalization of a volume-based indicator is

$$\frac{\text{Sum of the last } n \text{ days of the indicator values}}{\text{Sum of the last } n \text{ days of volume}} \times 100$$

One of the most successful examples of a normalized indicator is 21-day Intraday Intensity as developed by market technician Marc Chaikin. A 21-day normalized Intraday Intensity can be used in shorter time frames

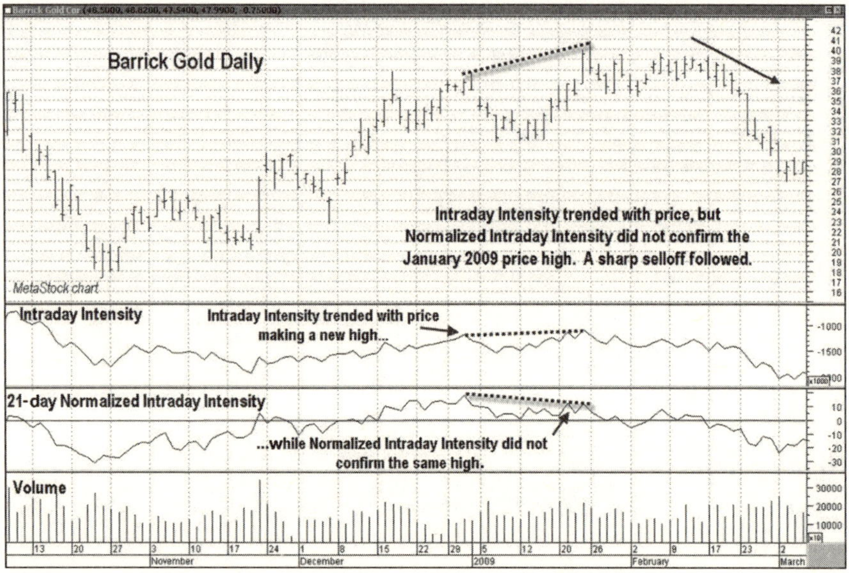

Chart 9.94 21-Day Normalized Intraday Intensity, Negative Divergence, Barrick Gold

Source: MetaStock

than the Intraday Intensity indicator and is sensitive to overbought and oversold conditions as well as price divergences that can lead to trend corrections and reversals. An example of differences in behavior between the raw and normalized versions is shown in Chart 9.94, of Barrick Gold daily. Note that, while Intraday Intensity was trending upward, the normalized version was more sensitive to the trend change, displaying a negative divergence that led to a sharp sell-off. In our next example, the trending nature of the cumulative volume indicator is compared to the normalized version as it displays a divergence from a new price low in Chart 9.95, of JPMorgan Chase daily. A comparison of indicator plots displays shorter-term turning points using the normalized version, as shown in Chart 9.96 of DIA daily. Notice how Intraday Intensity trends well with price, but the normalized version displays peaks and troughs in conjunction with short-term turning points in the price of the DIA, confirming its action along the Bollinger Bands. Using a normalized indicator allows for examination of range-bound behavior and zero crossover interpretations, as well as some scale comparisons. Each volume trending indicator that we have examined will adapt differently to the technique, and as such its properties should be studied over time.

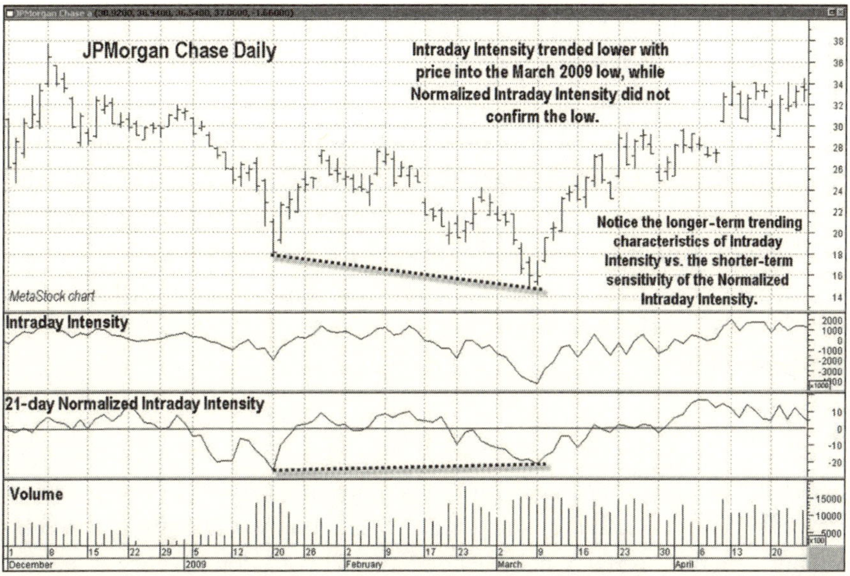

Chart 9.95 Intraday Intensity, Normalized with 21-Day Volume, Positive Divergence, JPMorgan Chase

Source: MetaStock

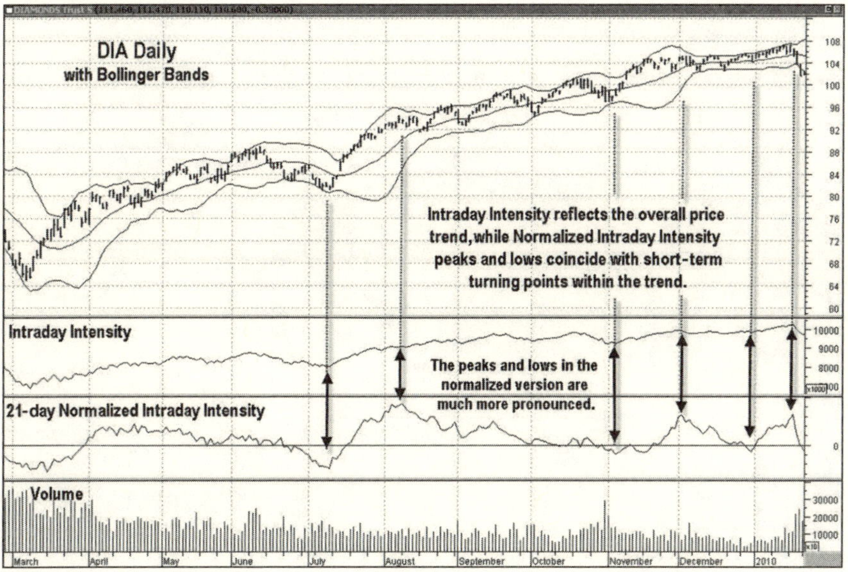

Chart 9.96 Bollinger Bands with 21-Day Normalized Intraday Intensity Comparison, DIA (SPDR Dow Jones Industrial Average)

Source: MetaStock

Volume Indicator/Oscillators as Confirmation for Candlestick Patterns

Candlestick charts give a much more vivid representation of the mindset of traders because of their graphical representation of the closing price and that period's opening price. The extra insight given by using candlesticks can be enhanced when candlestick patterns, indicators, and volume analysis are combined. We will briefly discuss two of the more common candlestick reversal patterns and show how the addition of the Money Flow Index oscillator along with a bar plot of volume can help increase the probability of making a successful trade.

Doji

A doji is a candle pattern that occurs when the opening and closing prices are very close to one another, if not identical. This shows that the strength of buyers and sellers is evenly matched. The formation of a doji signifies indecision and/or uncertainty. The formation of a doji in a sideways moving market has no meaning, but the appearance of a doji in a trending market is a warning that change may be ready to occur in price direction. Chart 9.97 for JPMorgan Chase shows how the formation of a doji on October 14, 2009, was a warning that the prevailing uptrend may have been ending, meriting closer analysis.

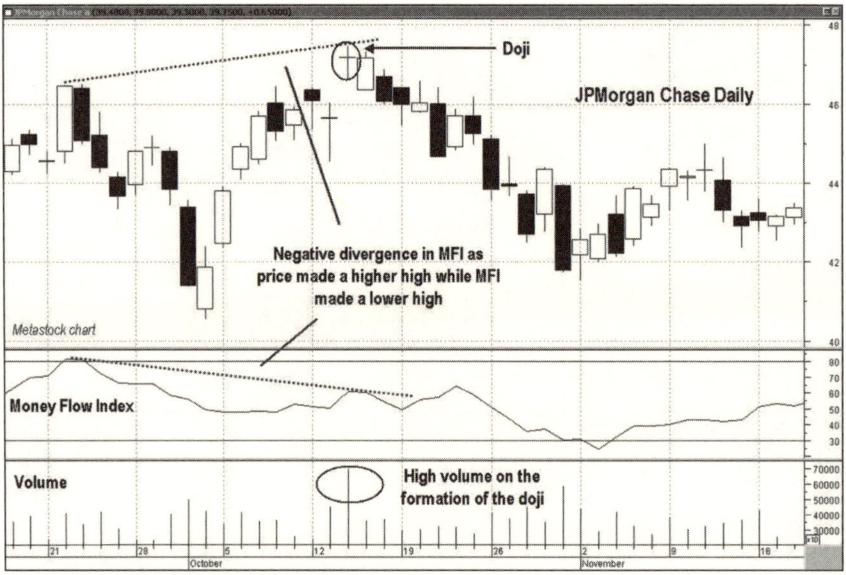

Chart 9.97 Doji Candlestick Reversal from a High, JPMorgan Chase

Source: MetaStock

For this example we have added a 14-day Money Flow Index (MFI) along with a bar plot of volume. Notice how as price formed the doji at the October 14 high, the MFI was already showing a negative divergence in relation to its September high. Volume is also a critical piece of this analysis. Notice how volume jumped sharply higher as the doji was formed. The day's action swung in a wide range, but the open and close were almost identical. This meant that buyers were trying to continue the stock's run, but the activity of sellers increased to the point that caused price to close right where it opened. Shorting this market based on a doji pattern alone was risky, so waiting for price to confirm the doji by reversing lower would have been prudent before entering a short position.

Hammer

The hammer is a reversal pattern that typically has a small real body (the difference between its opening and closing price) with a much longer shadow, or lower line. Hammer patterns form in an established downtrend as price opens and moves sharply lower during the session. As the selling pressure lessens, buyers begin to step in to push the price higher, which causes it to close at or near the high of the day. Hammers formed in sideways markets are not very meaningful, but hammers formed during downtrends merit close attention.

In Chart 9.98 for JPMorgan Chase, price had been in a sharp downtrend until the hammer formed at the November 21 low. By once again adding a 14-day MFI along with a volume plot, we can look a little deeper to see if this hammer pattern has a higher chance for a successful reversal. Notice how as price fell into its November 21 low, MFI reached the oversold level below 20. That was an indication that a bounce of some sort was due. The next piece of analysis shows that volume peaked on the hammer formation day. The high volume as the hammer was formed showed that buyers were entering the market, as they saw good value at the $20 level for JPMorgan Chase.

Even though this hammer pattern was backed up by solid volume and an oversold MFI, it is still not advised to take a long position based on that analysis alone. We prefer to wait for price confirmation that buyers are continuing to enter the market before taking a long position on a reversal. The very next day a long white candle formed, signifying that buyers were entering the market and bidding shares higher, giving our signal to enter a long position.

These are just two examples of how adding volume and volume-based indicators to candlesticks can increase the probability of making a successful

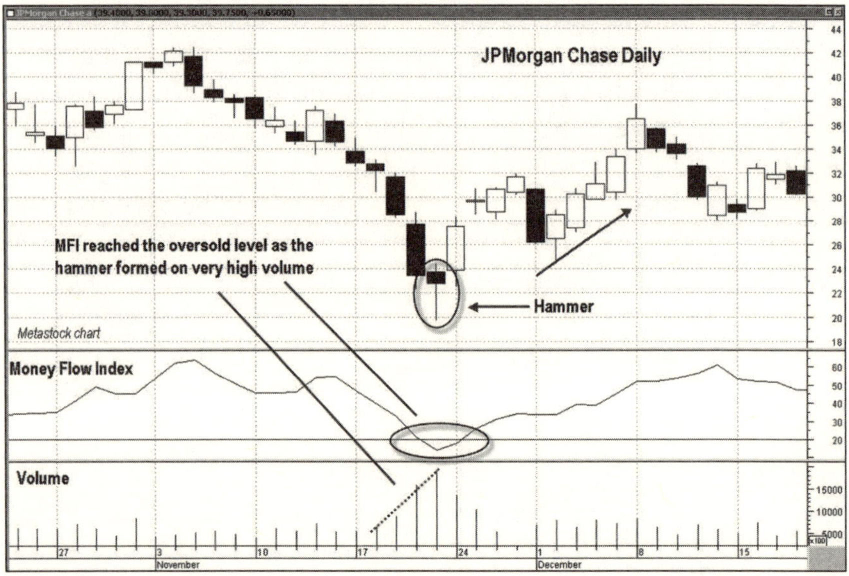

Chart 9.98 Hammer Candlestick Reversal from a Low, JPMorgan Chase

Source: MetaStock

trade. The construction of candlestick charts shows the psychology of traders from a price standpoint. When candlesticks are paired with a volume indicator, additional information relating to the conviction behind the candlestick pattern is displayed. The synergy of the two methodologies expands a trader's information set and can increase a trader's confidence in the trade

Summary

Indicator	Description	Uses and Time Frames
Accumulation/Distribution	Measures the cumulative flow of money into and out of a security	—A/D confirms price trends and shows trend divergences. It does not address price gaps. —It is an intermediate- to long-term indicator.
Equivolume	Combines price and volume into a single plot	—It is a great tool for identifying breakouts and trend reversals. But less data is visible for longer-term traders due to box width. —It is a short-term to intermediate-term indicator.

Indicator	Description	Uses and Time Frames
Intraday Intensity	Shows fund flows into or out of a security based on the position of its close in its daily range	—II confirms price trends and shows trend divergences. It does not address price gaps or day-to-day percentage gains or losses. —It is an intermediate-term to long-term indicator.
Leibovit Volume Reversal	Catches short- to intermediate-term trend reversals showing sentiment shifts from buyers to sellers, and vice versa	—VR provides a concise trading stop on every trade. It is an early-warning system regarding sentiment changes. The VR does not work as well in tight trading ranges as it does when it occurs at intermediate-term highs and lows. —It is an intermediate- to short-term indicator.
Negative Volume Index	An indicator meant to track the so-called smart money by measuring activity on days when volume decreases in relation to the prior day	—NVI confirms price trends and shows trend divergences. It is not as effective as it once was due to changes in market conditions and the advent of high-frequency trading. —It is an intermediate-term to long-term indicator.
Normalized Volume	A technique for plotting volume that uses a uniform scale, which allows for valid comparisons between securities	—NV allows a trader to very quickly see that day's volume in relation to its average. It is difficult to tell, however, if the overall volume trend is rising or falling. —This technique can help to refocus long-term indicators to a shorter time frame.
Positive Volume Index	An indicator meant to track the so-called unsophisticated money by measuring activity on days when volume increases in relation to the prior day	—PVI confirms price trends and shows trend divergences. It is not as effective as it once was due to changes in market conditions and the advent of high-frequency trading. —It is an intermediate- to long-term indicator.
On-Balance Volume	Developed to determine whether a security is under accumulation or distribution	—OBV confirms price trends and shows trend divergences. The strength of price gains or losses and the quality of the closing price are ignored. —It is an intermediate- to long-term indicator.

(Continued)

Indicator	Description	Uses and Time Frames
Open Interest	Shows the number of "open" contracts at the end of each trading day in the futures market	—It confirms price trends and shows trend divergences. Depending on your data service, contract expiration can sometimes distort the Open Interest line. It is available only on futures contracts, which limits the scope of its use. —It is a short-term to intermediate-term indicator.
Volume Price Trend	Measures the amount of force behind a market move by combining price change with volume	—VPT confirms price trends and shows trend divergences. But calculation of VPT does not take into account the quality of the price close in its daily range. —It is an intermediate- to long-term indicator.
Volume Rate of Change	Measures the strength of volume changes over a specified time period	—VROC shows potential change of direction points and confirms breakouts. But it must be used with caution because at times VROC can be a jagged and misleading indicator. —It is a short - to intermediate-term indicator.

Chapter 10

THE VOLUME OSCILLATORS

We are often asked, "How do volume oscillators differ from volume indicators?" The answer is, quite simply, that volume oscillators display market information in either a banded or center-line format. Centered oscillators are usually set up as a formulaic time series crossing above or below a zero centerline. Banded oscillators display information as they move toward or away from upper and lower band ranges, which signal overbought or oversold thresholds.

We find volume oscillators to be invaluable tools, extremely efficient at revealing accumulation and distribution patterns and overbought and oversold conditions that would not be visible otherwise without their volume component. Volume oscillators are versatile and work well alone or as a complement with other indicators in a trading strategy. They can be used to assess the health of a trend and, through divergences from price, measure changes in market sentiment and conviction. Many find there is an increased ease of use with oscillators over time, as crossover trading signals are clearly identified. This chapter presents, explains, and offers examples of 10 different volume oscillators:

1. Chaikin A/D Oscillator
2. Chaikin Money Flow
3. Demand Index
4. Ease of Movement
5. Force Index
6. Herrick Payoff Index
7. Klinger Oscillator

8. Money Flow Index
9. Volume Accumulation Oscillator
10. Percentage Volume Oscillator

Chaikin A/D Oscillator

The Chaikin Accumulation/Distribution (A/D) Oscillator was created by veteran market technician Marc Chaikin to monitor the flow of money into and out of the market with the intent of identifying tops and bottoms in short and intermediate cycles.

Formulation

Computationally, the Chaikin A/D Oscillator is the difference between a 3-day exponential moving average and a 10-day exponential moving average of the Accumulation/Distribution indicator (see Chapter 9). The Chaikin A/D Oscillator is most often used to show overbought/oversold conditions and to spot trend divergences that could lead to a change in price direction. Chart 10.1 shows a basic plot of the Chaikin A/D Oscillator for the Nasdaq 100 Trust ETF (QQQQ).

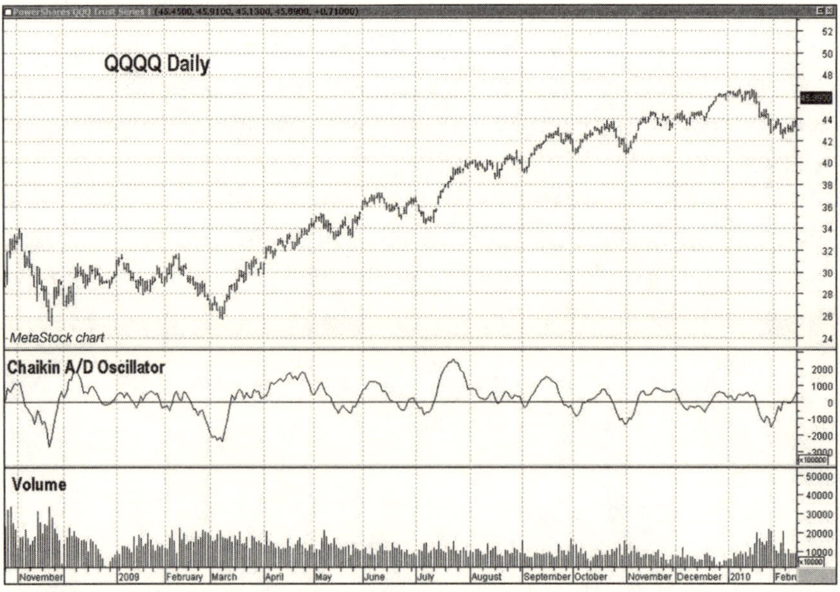

Chart 10.1 Chaikin A/D Oscillator, Nasdaq 100 Trust ETF

Source: MetaStock

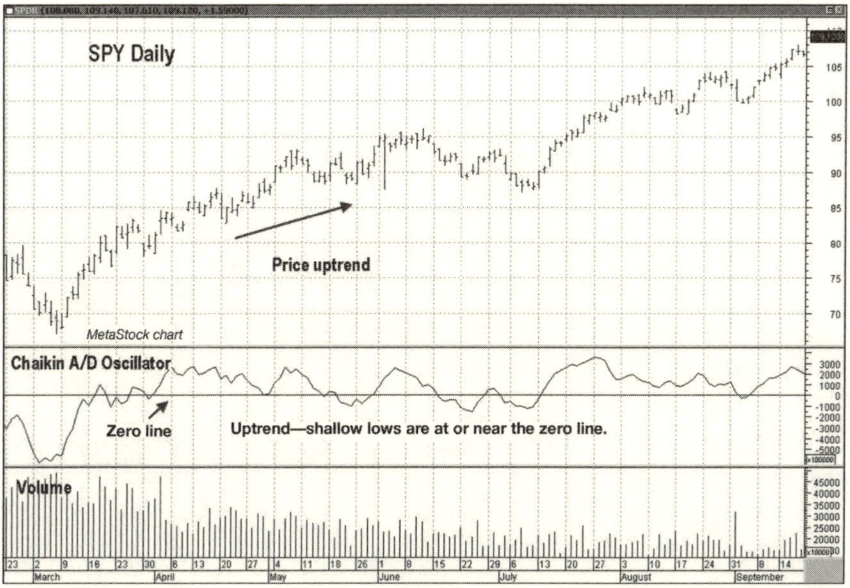

Chart 10.2 Chaikin A/D Oscillator, Higher Lows during Uptrend, S&P 500 SPDR ETF

Source: MetaStock

Trend Confirmation

The Chaikin A/D Oscillator can show discernible characteristics during trending markets. The oscillator tends to make shallower lows with relatively higher highs during uptrends while making deeper lows with relatively lower highs in downtrends. Chart 10.2 shows the Chaikin A/D Oscillator for the S&P 500 SPDR ETF (SPY) during an uptrend from March to August 2009.

Next is a look at the Chaikin A/D Oscillator during downtrends. Chart 10.3 shows how the oscillator makes deeper lows and lower highs for Microsoft (MSFT) as the downtrend continues. The oscillator shows that most of the energy was to the downside during this period.

Divergences

The Chaikin A/D Oscillator is well suited for spotting divergences, for example, when price makes a new high but the oscillator makes lower highs (a negative divergence) or price makes a lower low but the oscillator makes higher lows (a positive divergence). Chart 10.4 shows a negative divergence for Microsoft in December 2009. Note how price continued higher, while the oscillator turned lower and made lower highs. That negative divergence preceded a strong move lower that lasted into February 2010.

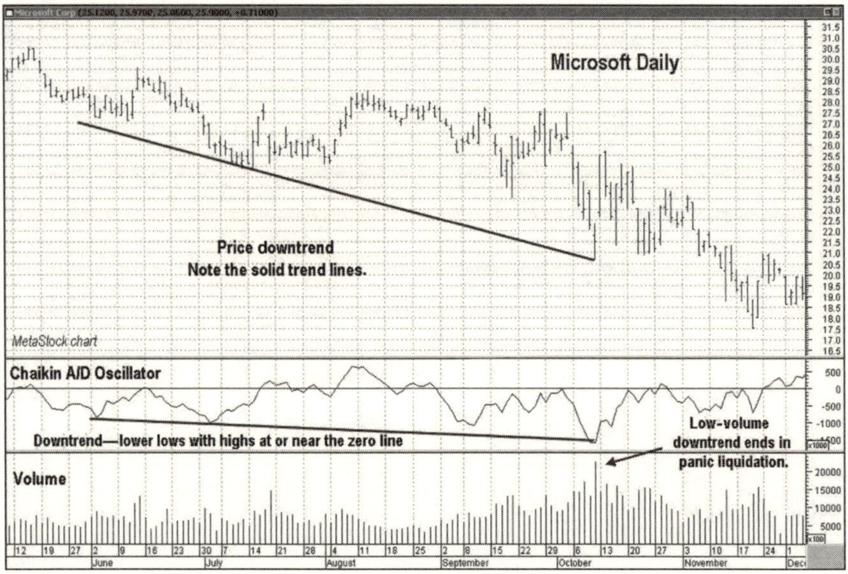

Chart 10.3 Chaikin A/D Oscillator, Lower Highs/Deeper Lows during Downtrend, Microsoft Corp.

Source: MetaStock

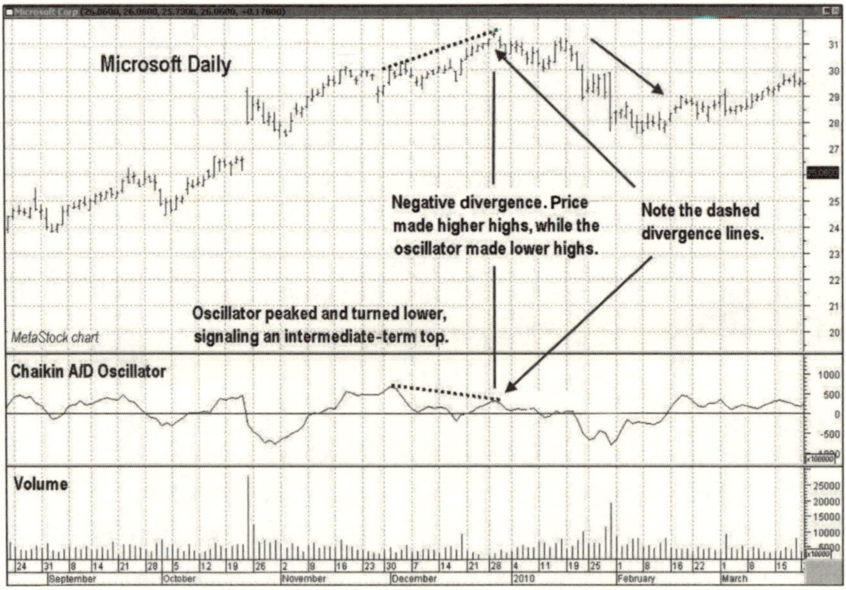

Chart 10.4 Chaikin A/D Oscillator, Negative Divergence, Microsoft Corp.

Source: MetaStock

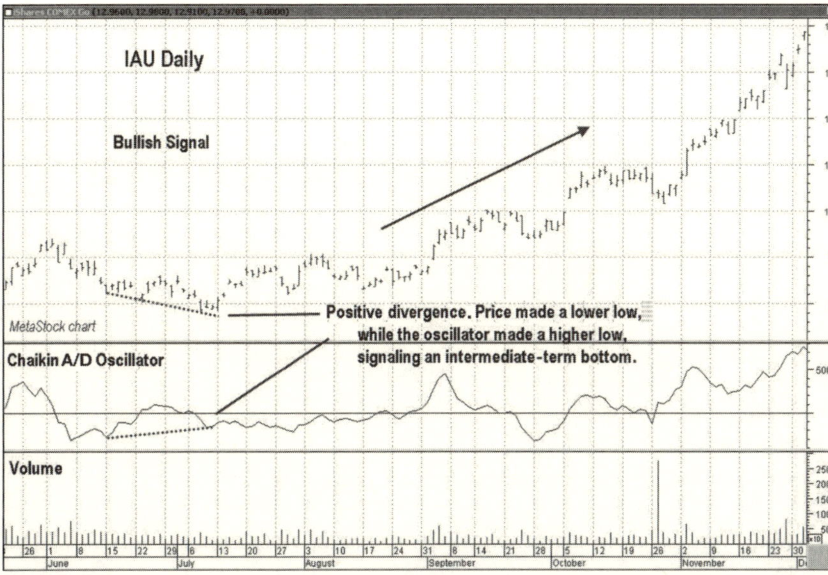

Chart 10.5 Chaikin A/D Oscillator, Positive Divergence, iShares COMEX Gold Trust ETF

Source: MetaStock

Chart 10.5 shows a positive divergence in October 2008 for the iShares COMEX Gold Trust ETF (IAU). Note how price made a lower low while the oscillator held its prior low. That preceded a strong rally that lasted into February 2009. A brief reminder: It is wise not to trade off divergences until price confirms a change in trend direction, usually with a breakthrough at support or resistance.

Zero-Line Crossovers

The Chaikin A/D Oscillator is a centered oscillator, which means that it oscillates around a center (or zero) line. Crosses above the zero line from below are seen as buy signals in an uptrend, and crosses below the zero line from above are seen as sell signals in a downtrend. Signals against the trend (i.e., crosses down in an uptrend, and vice versa) should not be viewed as significant.

The iShares High Yield Corporate Bond ETF (HYG) in Chart 10.6 shows how effective the Chaikin A/D Oscillator is at generating buy signals in an uptrend. Note how crosses below the zero line in the uptrend led to fairly shallow pullbacks.

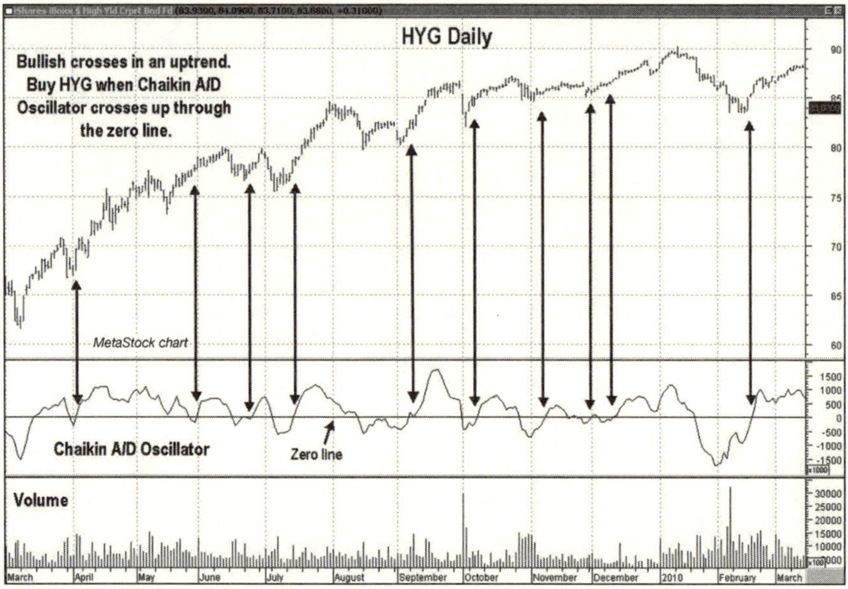

Chart 10.6 Chaikin A/D Oscillator, Buy Signals in Uptrend, iShares High Yield Corporate Bond ETF

Source: MetaStock

The Chakin A/D Oscillator also gives useful sell signals on crosses below the zero line in downtrends. In the July 2007–July 2008 chart of Citigroup (C) (see Chart 10.7), note how downside crosses occurred just before sharp moves lower. Again, these crossovers on the downside were considered significant only because Citigroup was in a strong downtrend during this period.

Combining the Chaikin A/D Oscillator with Other Indicators

The Chakin A/D Oscillator can also be very effective when grouped with other technical indicators. Chaikin recommends that his oscillator be used in conjunction with a 21-day moving average envelope of price. The example that follows also includes a 14-period Relative Strength Index, or RSI. This combination combines the divergence analysis of the Chaikin A/D Oscillator with the overbought/oversold signaling of the RSI.

In Chart 10.8, note how in early January 2007 the Chaikin A/D Oscillator was showing a negative divergence for Microsoft. Additionally, the

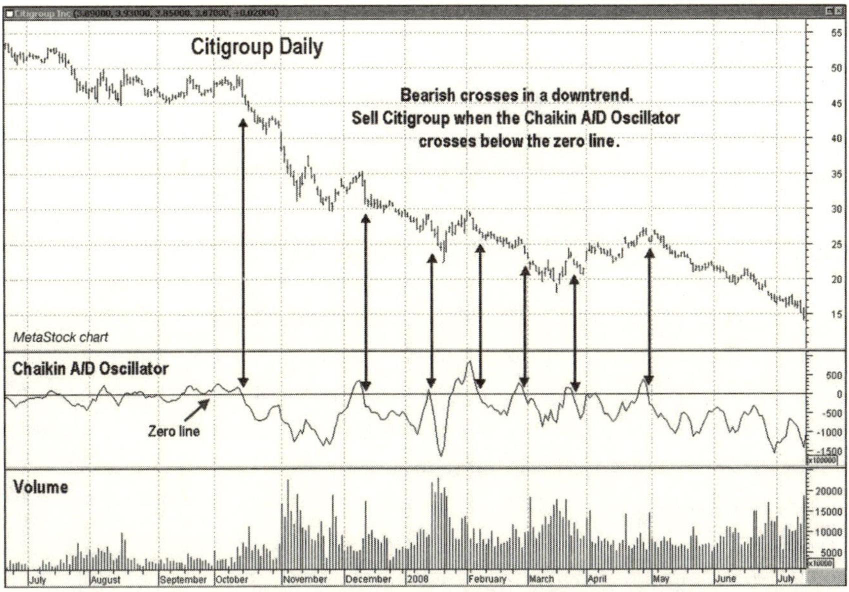

Chart 10.7 Chaikin A/D Oscillator, Sell Signals in Downtrend, Citigroup

Source: MetaStock

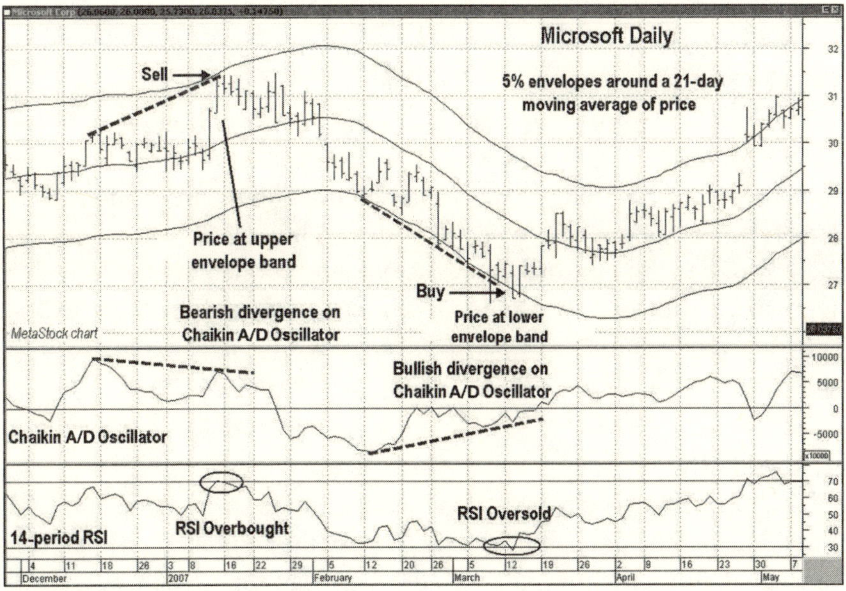

Chart 10.8 Chaikin A/D Oscillator Combined with 14-Day RSI and 21-Day Price Band, Microsoft Corp.

Source: MetaStock

14-period RSI was also in overbought territory, while price was bumping up against the top price envelope, which indicated that a reversal lower was likely. That gave a good sell signal setup. The next setup was for a buy signal in March 2007, as the Chaikin A/D Oscillator showed a positive divergence, making a higher low while price continued lower. The 14-period RSI was in oversold territory, while price was in contact with the lower band of the 21-day moving average envelope. A strong rally followed.

This is just one example of the many other indicators that may be combined with the Chakin A/D Oscillator. A good pairing for a zero-line price- and volume-based oscillator such as the Chaikin A/D Oscillator might be with a price-based momentum indicator such as the 14-day RSI, which gives definite overbought and oversold signals. When pairing, it is important to avoid indicator or oscillator redundancy.

Trade Setup

As demonstrated previously, the Chaikin A/D Oscillator is a great tool for showing divergences between price and momentum. The example that follows shows how a positive divergence can alert a trader that a correction against the larger-degree trend is ending and that the larger-degree trend is ready to resume.

Chart 10.9 shows that price was in an uptrend for IBM from March to June 2009. A corrective pullback unfolded at that point and carried into July. The Chaikin A/D Oscillator showed a positive divergence in July 2009, as it made a higher low while price made a lower low. That was an indication that the pullback was running out of momentum and that the larger-degree uptrend was ready to resume. A buy signal would be generated by price closing above the resistance line connecting the June–July highs along with the Chaikin A/D Oscillator crossing above the zero line. Also note how volume decreased on balance as the sell-off developed. That was another indication that the selling pressure was not very strong.

Trade Entry

Chart 10.10 shows a closer view of the time frame of our trade entry. On July 15, 2009, the price of IBM closed above the resistance line that connected the June and July highs. On the same day, the Chaikin A/D Oscillator also crossed above its zero line, which provided confirmation of the price breakout. An initial protective stop is placed below the July 8, 2009, low of 99.50. Also note how volume exploded higher on the breakout, which provided further confirmation of the price breakout.

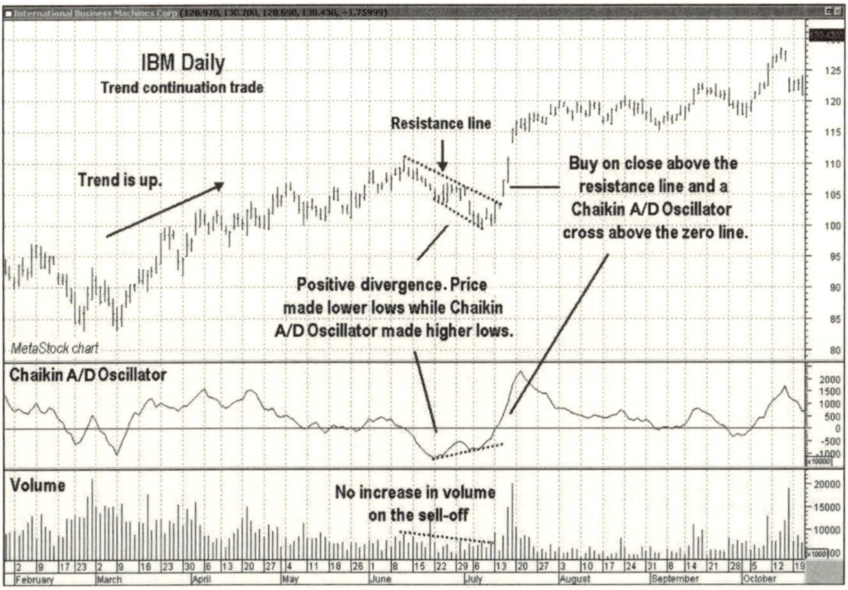

Chart 10.9 Chaikin A/D Oscillator, Trade Setup on Positive Divergence, IBM Corp.

Source: MetaStock

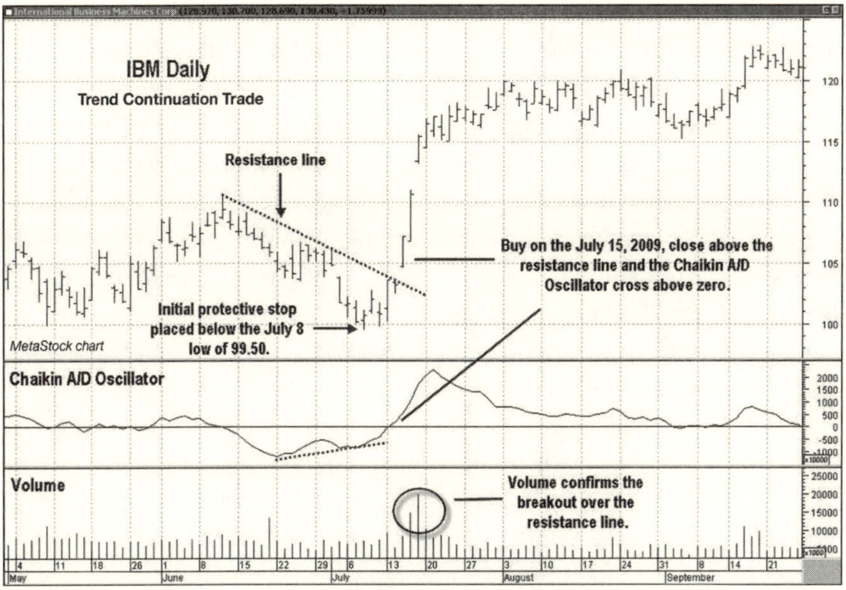

Chart 10.10 Chaikin A/D Oscillator, Trade Entry on Confirming Positive Divergence, IBM Corp.

Source: MetaStock

Trader Tips

The Chaikin A/D Oscillator is useful for the following:

- Showing trend divergences
- Generating buy and sell signals with the trend on zero-line crossovers
- Confirming market trends, accumulation, and distribution
- Combining with other indicators to develop solid trading systems

The many uses for the Chaikin A/D Oscillator make it an invaluable Volume Analysis tool that can be used alone or in combination with other indicators.

Chaikin Money Flow

Like the Chaikin A/D Oscillator presented previously, the Chaikin Money Flow (CMF) Oscillator also was developed by market technician Marc Chaikin. Its values are calculated using the daily values of the Accumulation/Distribution line that was presented at the beginning of Chapter 9 to determine if money is flowing into or out of an issue or market.

Formulation

The CMF indicator is based on the assumption that market strength is indicated by the strength and pattern of daily market closes. More specifically, closes in the upper half of the daily range on increasing volume are positive, and closes in the bottom end of the range on increasing volume are negative. CMF is a centered oscillator using a zero line, which means that readings above zero show market strength and readings below zero show market weakness. CMF is normally plotted using a 21-day period to show trading activity for the last month of data. The value of a 21-period CMF is computed by adding the values of the Accumulation/Distribution line over the last 21 days, then dividing that total by the cumulative sum of volume over the last 21 days.

The CMF Oscillator is used to confirm market trends, spot divergences, and give buy or sell signals in the same direction as the overall trend. The CMF can also be an effective tool for longer-term market analysis when it is constructed over longer data periods. It can be used to analyze individual securities or market indexes that report volume. Chart 10.11 gives a basic chart of the CMF Oscillator for the Nasdaq 100 Trust ETF (QQQQ).

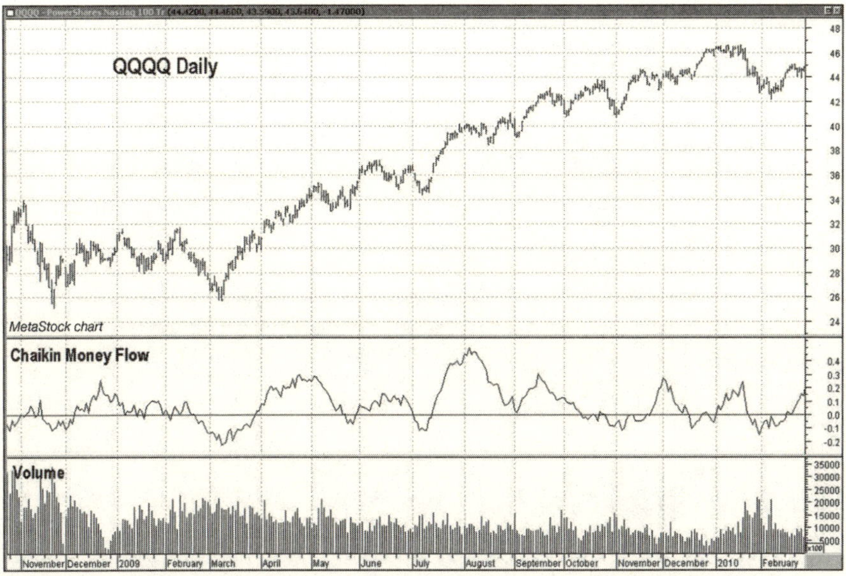

Chart 10.11 Chaikin Money Flow Oscillator, Nasdaq 100 Trust ETF

Source: MetaStock

Trend Confirmation

The CMF Oscillator shows different characteristics in uptrends from what it does in downtrends. The example of the Nasdaq Composite in Chart 10.12 shows how CMF tends to top and bottom in a consistent range above the zero line as the trend unfolds. If the CMF makes a low at a markedly lower point than it has throughout the trend, that signals that a trend change may be imminent. Chart 10.13 shows the characteristics of CMF in a downtrend (in this case, for Citigroup). Note again how it moves in a range with a top at the zero line or just above it, with bottoms well below zero.

Divergences

The CMF Oscillator is a great tool for spotting divergences. Positive divergences are created when price makes a lower low, but CMF makes a higher low. This shows that buyers are accumulating shares, as prices are closing better in their daily ranges as the bottom is formed. Chart 10.14 shows a positive divergence for IBM at the March 2009 low.

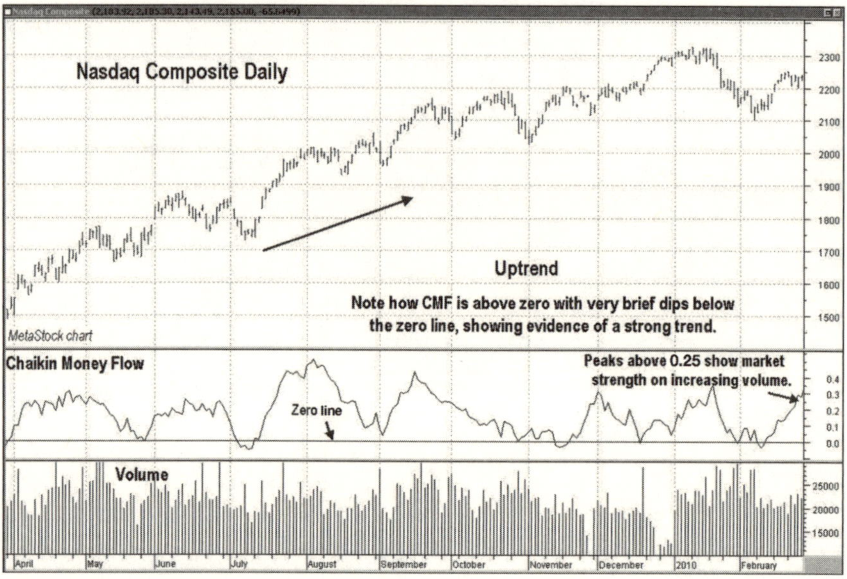

Chart 10.12 Chaikin Money Flow Oscillator Confirming Uptrend, Nasdaq Composite Daily

Source: MetaStock

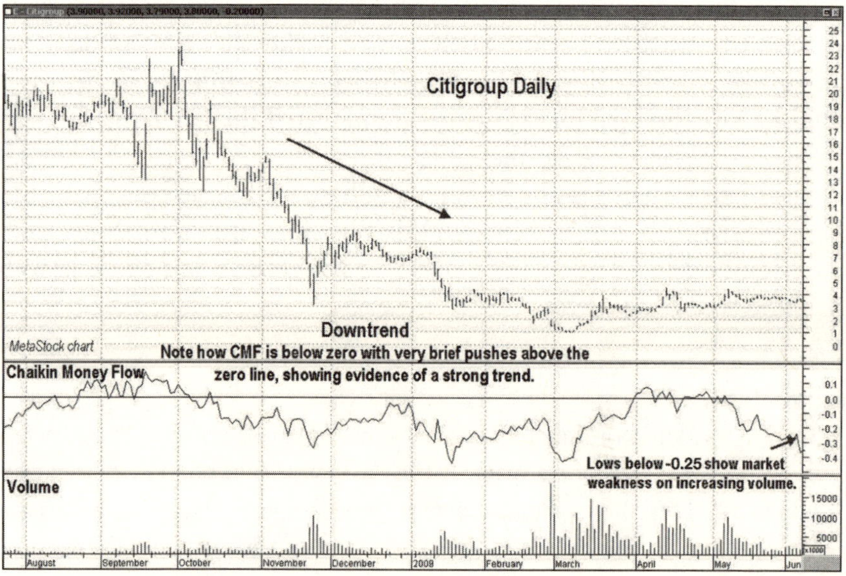

Chart 10.13 Chaikin Money Flow Oscillator Confirming Downtrend, Citigroup

Source: MetaStock

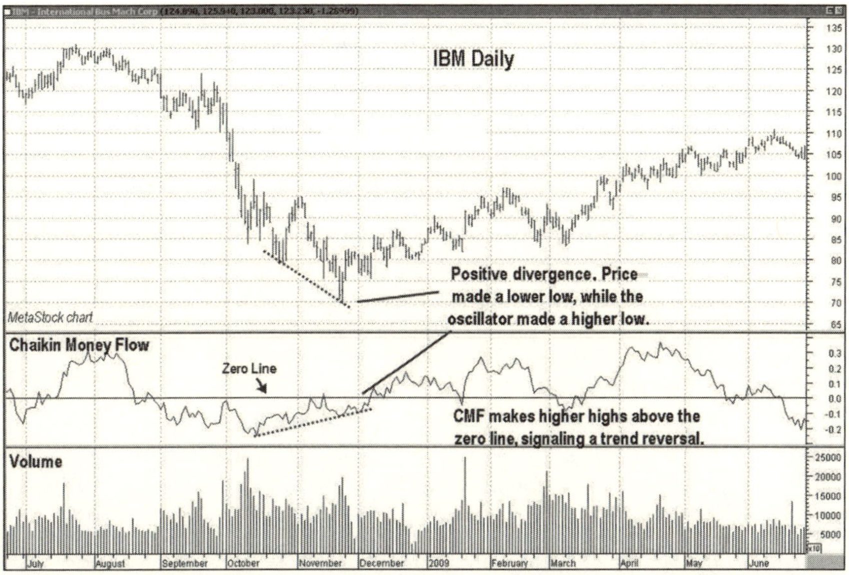

Chart 10.14 Chaikin Money Flow Oscillator, Positive Divergence, IBM Corp.

Source: MetaStock

CMF is also good for showing negative divergences (i.e., a new high for price with a lower high in CMF). Negative divergences show latent weakness, as money is leaving the market. Price closing poorly in its daily range is an indication that sellers are beginning to apply more pressure. The Consumer Staples Select SPDR ETF (XLP) in Chart 10.15 shows a negative divergence appearing in the fall of 2008, just before prices collapsed.

Chaikin Money Flow as a Histogram

Since CMF is viewed as bullish or bearish according to its position relative to the zero line, plotting the indicator as a histogram can sometimes give a clearer perspective than displaying it as a single line. The Nasdaq 100 Trust ETF (QQQQ) in Chart 10.16 shows CMF as a histogram. Note how comparison between highs and lows is easier as well as the visual clarity for CMF's position relative to the zero line. Readings above 0.25 and below –0.25 indicate strong trends, and positions may be added on corrections.

CMF as a Longer-Term Indicator

CMF is also a good indicator when looked at from a longer-term perspective. Chart 10.17 shows a 60-day CMF for the Nasdaq 100 Trust ETF (QQQQ). Note how it trends forward with price off the November 2008 low. CMF also showed a notable positive divergence at the March 2009 low.

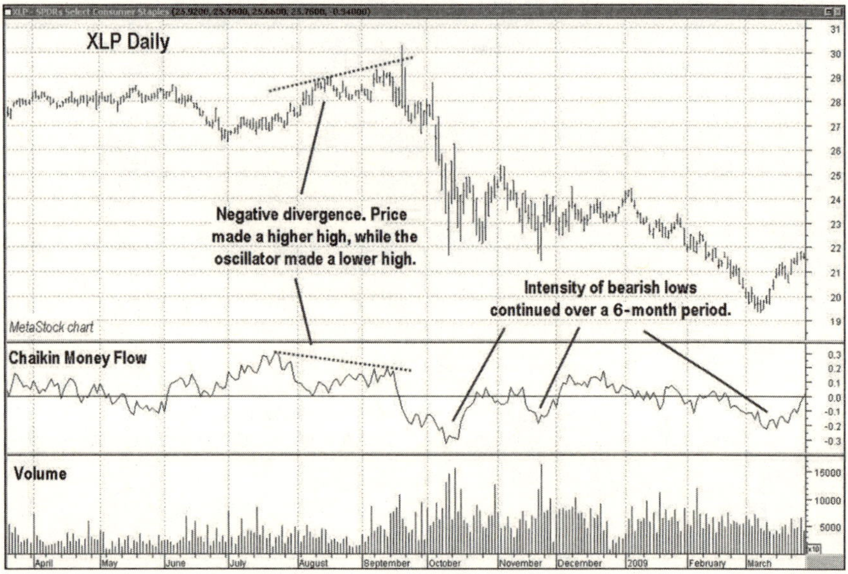

Chart 10.15 Chaikin Money Flow Oscillator, Negative Divergence, Consumer Staples Select SPDR ETF

Source: MetaStock

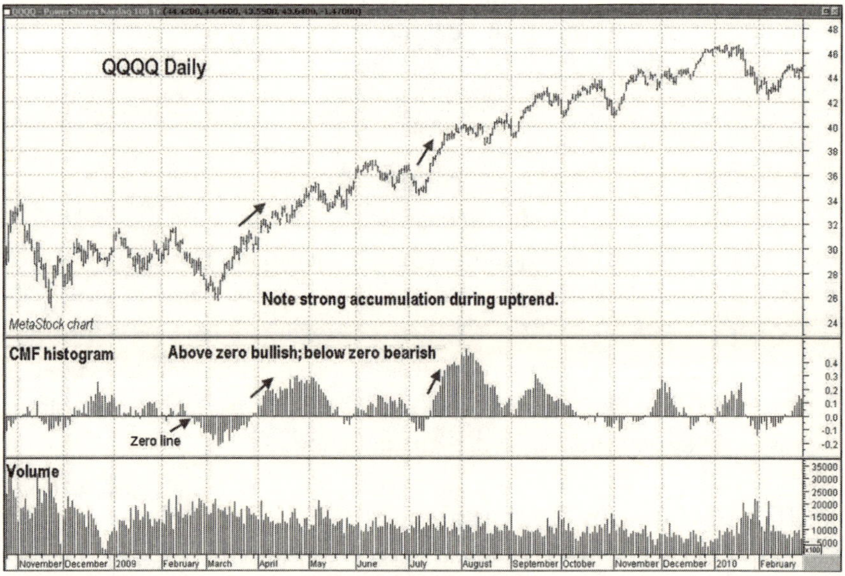

Chart 10.16 Chaikin Money Flow Oscillator, Histogram Display, Nasdaq 100 Trust ETF

Source: MetaStock

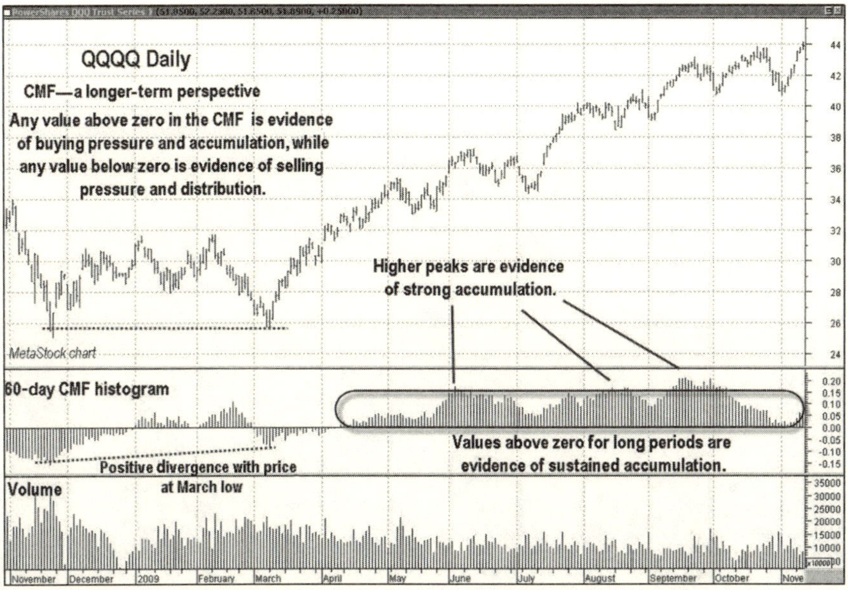

Chart 10.17 Chaikin Money Flow Oscillator, Longer-Term Positive Divergence, Nasdaq 100 Trust ETF

Source: MetaStock

Combining CMF with Other Indicators

Since Chaikin Money Flow is a centered oscillator, it is well paired with an overbought/oversold indicator in order to get a feel for the health of the overall prevailing trend. The indicator acts as a filter to ensure that only oscillator signals in the direction of the larger-degree trend are taken, increasing the chances of trading success.

In the Nasdaq 100 Trust ETF (QQQQ) in Chart 10.18, CMF is paired with RSI. CMF will be used as a trend filter, which means that when CMF is bullish above zero, only long trades will be considered. Conversely, when CMF is bearish below zero, only short trades will be considered. Trades will be entered when the CMF is above zero and the RSI crosses above 40 from oversold territory. Chart 10.18 shows buy signals when the CMF is in bullish territory above zero.

Trade Setup

The Chaikin Money Flow is a centered oscillator; as such, it gives warnings in the form of divergences as well as trading signals on zero-line crossovers. Chart 10.19 shows how negative divergences with price for Cisco Systems (CSCO) warned that a trend change was near, and how a zero-line crossover was part of the trade entry strategy.

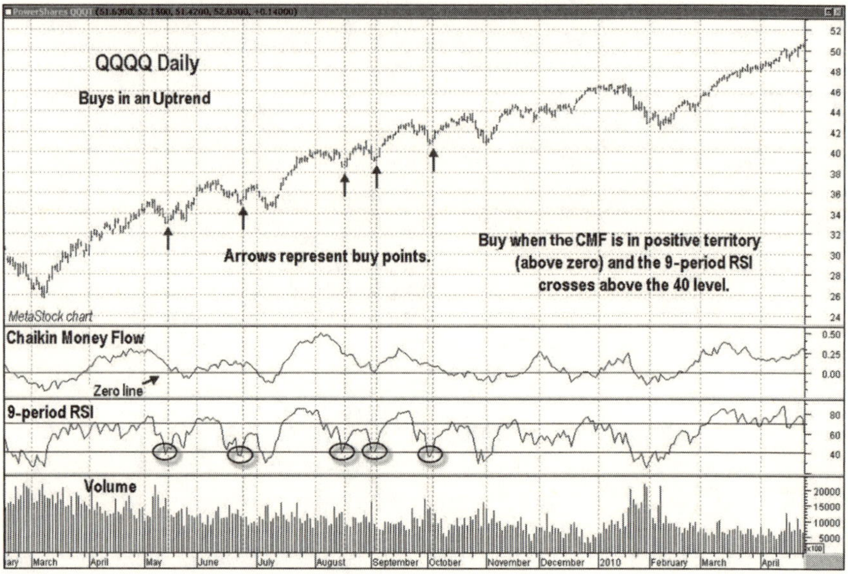

Chart 10.18 Chaikin Money Flow Oscillator with RSI, Bullish above Zero Line, Nasdaq 100 Trust ETF

Source: MetaStock

Chart 10.19 shows how price for Cisco made higher highs while the 21-day CMF made lower highs from September to November 2007. Looking back, this was a major top, but at the time there were merely indications that a change in trend was likely, which would have been a great trading opportunity for active traders. As always, some sort of confirmation was needed to verify that the negative divergence was coming to fruition.

The trade trigger for a short entry in this case would be a close below the support line drawn off of the May–June lows along with the CMF crossing below the zero line.

Trade Entry

Chart 10.20 gives a slightly closer view of the November 2007 trade for Cisco Systems. Price broke down through support on the same day that the 21-day CMF crossed down through the zero line, which generated a sell signal. Note how volume also confirmed the price breakdown with

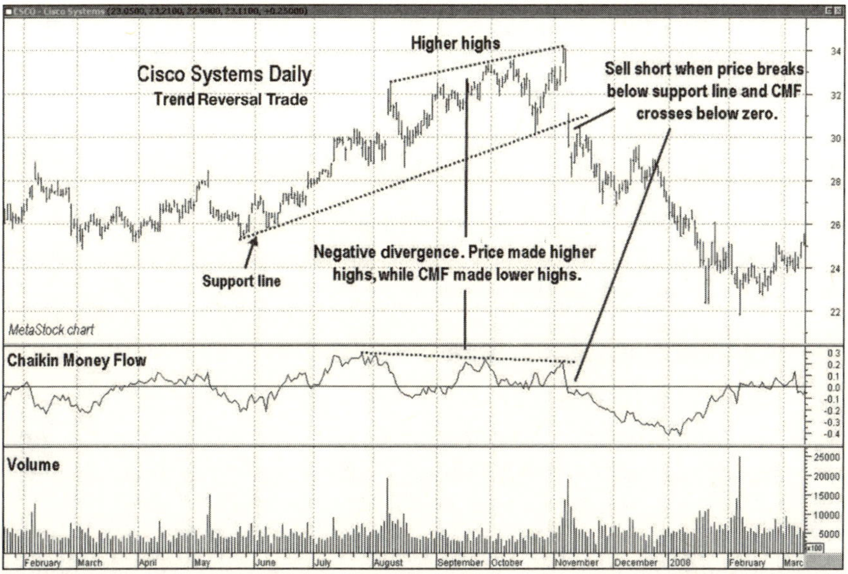

Chart 10.19 Chaikin Money Flow Oscillator, Trade Setup on Negative Divergence, Cisco Systems

Source: MetaStock

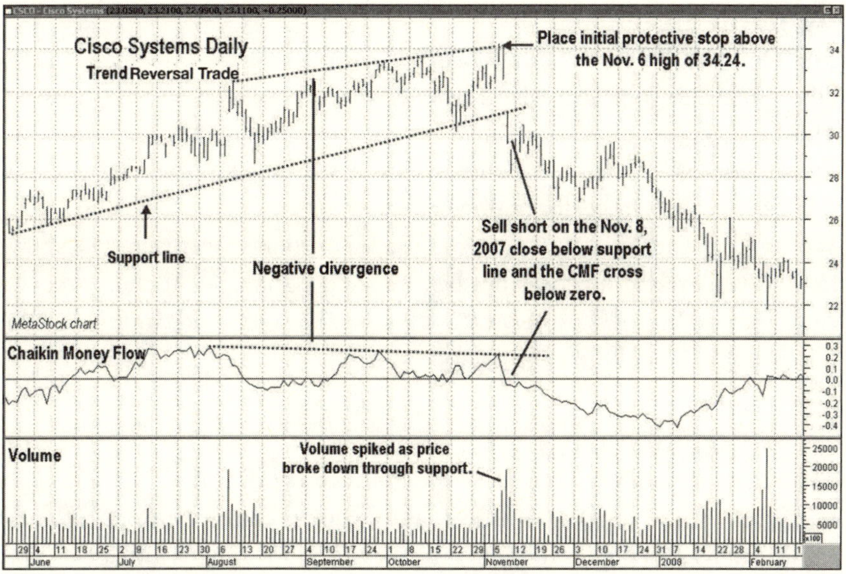

Chart 10.20 Chaikin Money Flow Oscillator, Trade Entry on Confirming Negative Divergence, Cisco Systems

Source: MetaStock

a spike on November 8. That was a sign that the tide had definitely turned and sellers were now in control. An initial protective stop should have been placed over the November 6 high of 34.24.

Trader Tips

Chaikin Money Flow is constructed using the Accumulation/Distribution indicator and volume data. It is most commonly displayed over a 21-day period. CMF is used for the following:

- Identifying bullish and bearish trends relative to zero line
- Spotting trend divergences
- Showing buying opportunities in the direction of the larger-degree trend, especially when combined with another trending indicator

CMF can also be used as a longer-term indicator when the number of days used in its computation is increased; however, gaps can be problematic. Much of its value in market analysis hinges on its ability to show buying and selling pressure.

Demand Index

The Demand Index was developed by technician James Sibbet and combines price and volume to give a ratio of buying pressure to selling pressure. The Demand Index calculations are very complex and require 21 spreadsheet columns to calculate manually. It is constructed in such a way that it is often a leading indicator of price change.

The Demand Index is a centered oscillator that confirms trends, shows trend divergences, and provides buy and sell signals by crossing over the zero line. Chart 10.21 shows a plot of the Demand Index for the Nasdaq 100 Trust ETF (QQQQ).

Trend Confirmation

The Demand Index is a great tool for confirming price trends in both daily and weekly time frames. The Demand Index moves with price, making higher highs and higher lows in uptrends, and lower highs and lower lows in downtrends. In the weekly chart of the S&P SPDR Energy ETF (XLE) (see Chart 10.22), note how the Demand Index trended with price before breaking its downtrend line in early 2010, giving notice that a change in trend may be at hand.

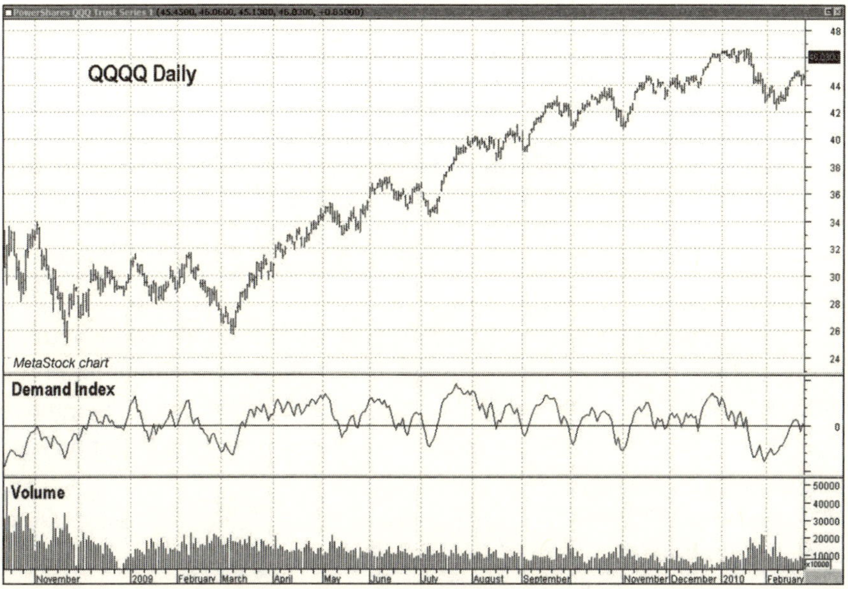

Chart 10.21 Demand Index Oscillator, Nasdaq 100 Trust ETF

Source: MetaStock

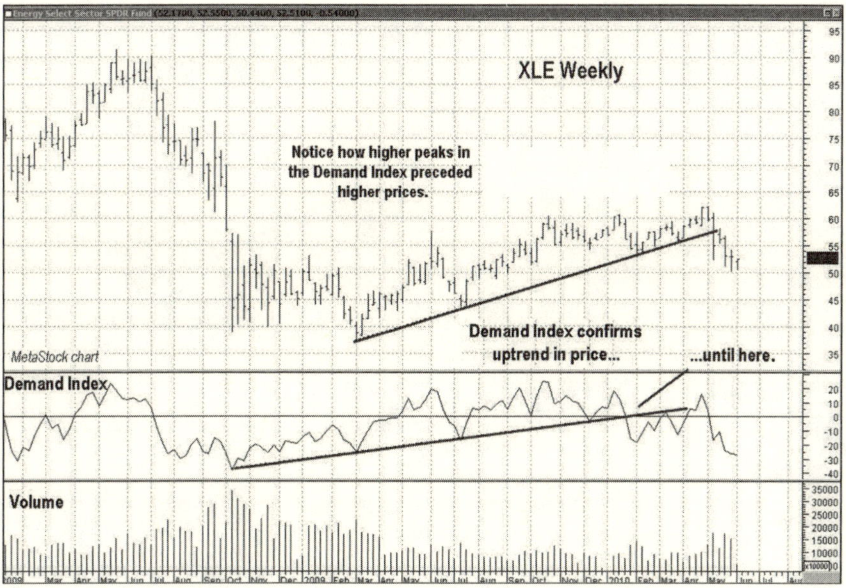

Chart 10.22 Demand Index Oscillator Confirming Uptrend, S&P SPDR Energy ETF

Source: MetaStock

Chart 10.23, a weekly chart of Morgan Stanley, shows the Demand Index in a downtrend. Note how the Demand Index began breaking down 9 months before price actually topped. This was a sign that the uptrend was in its final push. The Demand Index also broke its subsequent downtrend line before price broke its downtrend line, providing early clues that a major bottom was in the making.

Divergences

The Demand Index shows divergences, which indicates that a trend correction or reversal is imminent. Chart 10.24 shows a daily plot of the S&P SPDR Select Financial ETF (XLF); here the positive divergence (i.e., lower prices with a rising indicator) gave a strong clue that a bounce higher in price was due.

Negative divergences (i.e., rising prices with a falling indicator) show that a correction or reversal of an uptrend is due. There are two interesting parts to Chart 10.25. First, notice how the Demand Index broke out to a new high in April 2008, which signaled that a new push higher in price was due. The subsequent push higher also caused a negative divergence to

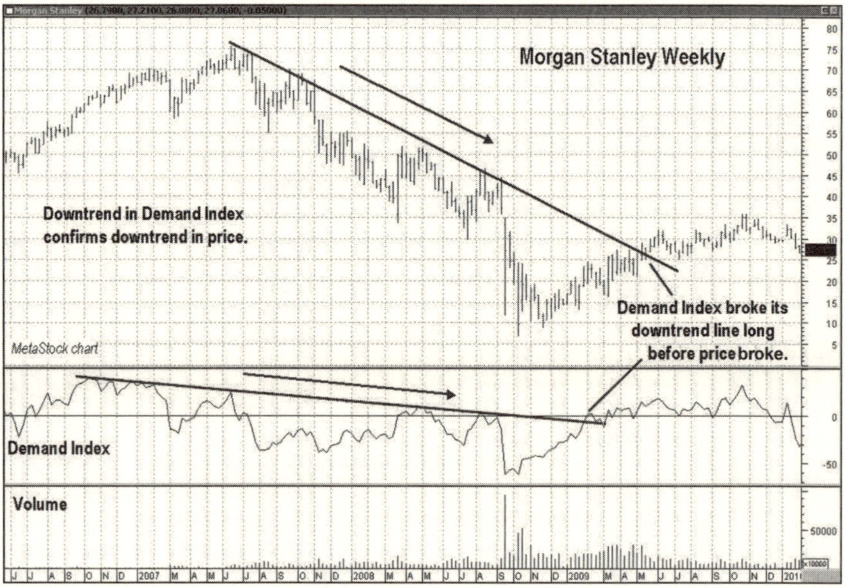

Chart 10.23 Demand Index Oscillator Confirming Downtrend, Morgan Stanley

Source: MetaStock

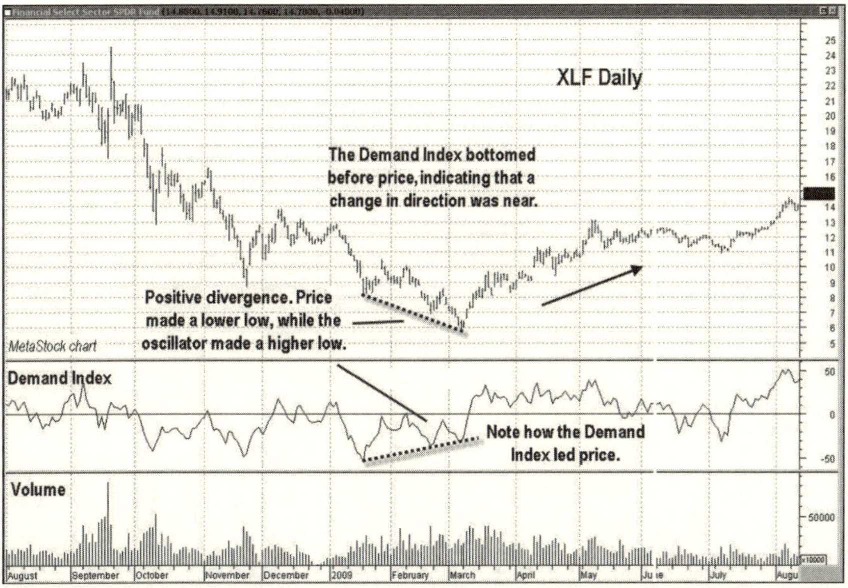

Chart 10.24 Demand Index Oscillator, Positive Divergence, S&P SPDR Select Financial ETF

Source: MetaStock

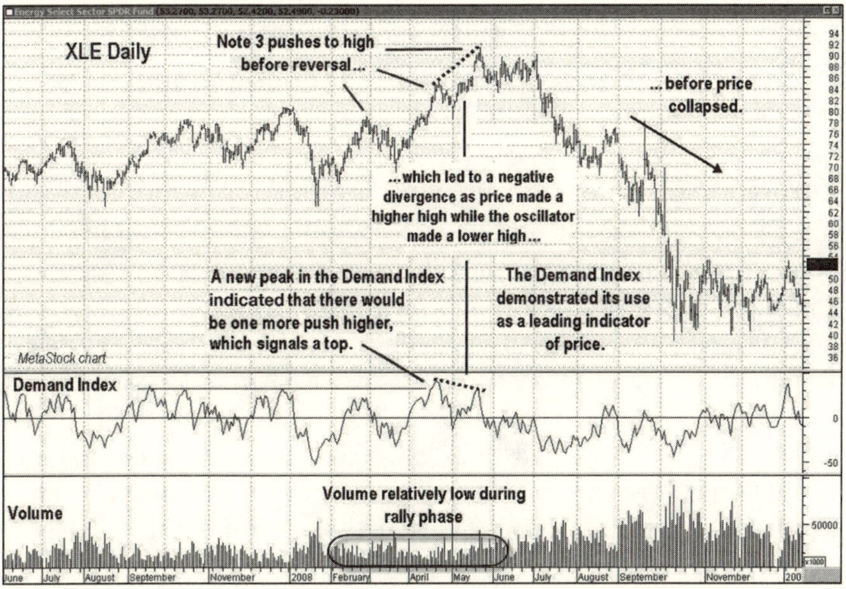

Chart 10.25 Demand Index Oscillator, Negative Divergence, S&P SPDR Select Energy ETF

Source: MetaStock

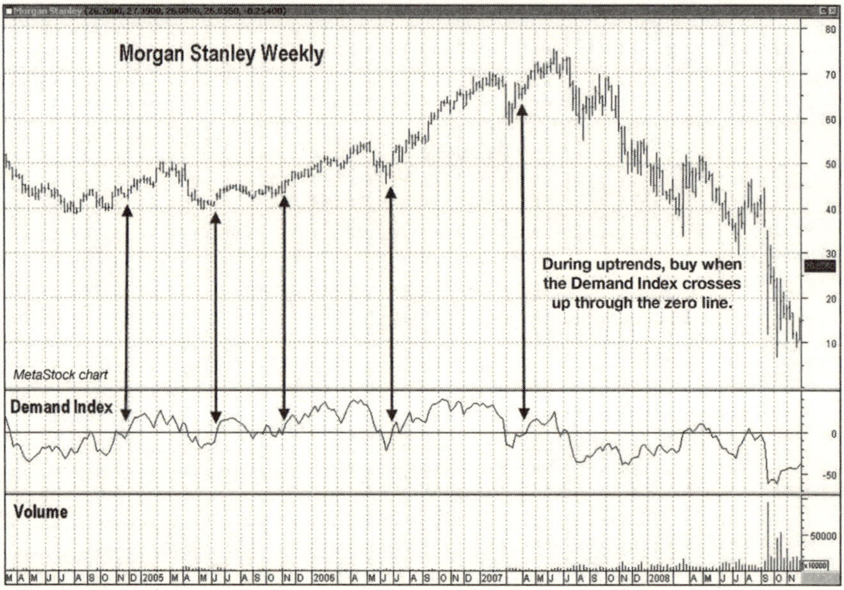

Chart 10.26 Demand Index Oscillator, Zero-Line Cross Buy Signals, Morgan Stanley

Source: MetaStock

form in the Demand Index. Following that divergence, the S&P SPDR Select Energy ETF (XLE) lost more than 50 percent of its value over the next three months.

Zero-Line Crossovers

The Demand Index also provides good buy and sell signals in the direction of the prevailing trend when it crosses above or below its zero line. Crosses above the zero line from below provide reliable buy signals in an uptrend, and crosses below the zero line from above provide reliable sell signals in a downtrend. Chart 10.26, a weekly chart of Morgan Stanley, shows the buy signals that were generated during the uptrend from late 2004 to the 2007 top. Chart 10.27, a weekly chart of the Semiconductor HOLDRs ETF (SMH), shows how crosses below the zero line in a downtrend provide good sell signals, although they lag somewhat.

The Demand Index with Other Indicators

The Demand Index is well suited to trend with price and provide buy and sell signals at zero-line crossovers, but perhaps its best use is in revealing divergences with price and the potential for price corrections or trend reversals.

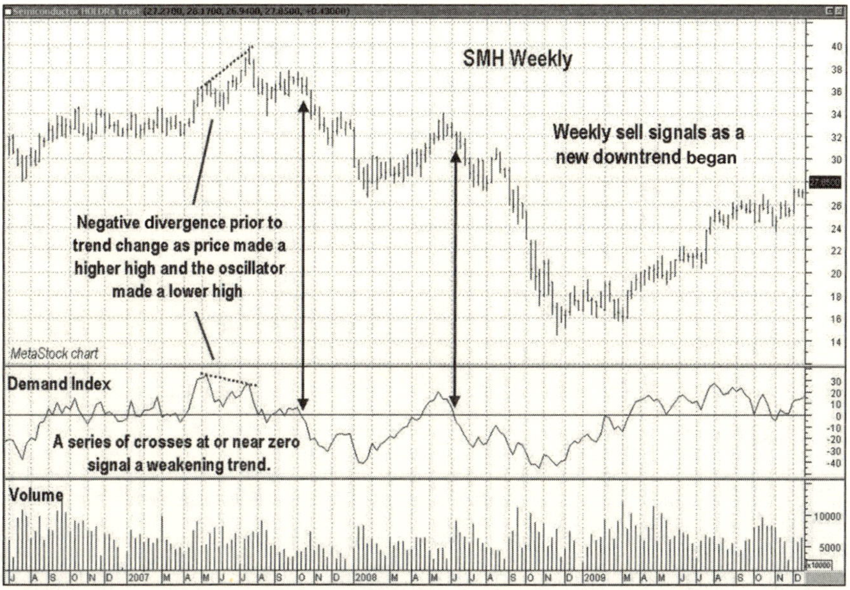

Chart 10.27 Demand Index Oscillator, Zero-Line Cross Sell Signals, Semiconductor HOLDRs

Source: MetaStock

Chart 10.28, a daily chart of Barrick Gold (ABX), shows how pairing the Demand Index with a 9-period Relative Strength Index can produce reliable trading signals. The pairing combines the divergence indication capability of the Demand Index with the overbought/oversold metrics of the 9-period RSI. Note in the chart how this indicator pairing catches intermediate turning points. The initial sell in July 2008 was generated by the setup of a negative divergence in the Demand Index along with an overbought reading in the 9-period RSI. The sell is executed when the 9-period RSI breaks below 70 (which is the boundary for an overbought reading). The September 2008 buy was set up with a positive divergence in the Demand Index (lower price with a rising Demand Index) and the 9-period RSI being below 30 (which is the boundary for oversold status). The buy was executed when the 9-period RSI broke above 30. The remaining buys and sells can be seen in Chart 10.28.

Trade Setup

The trade example described here will use the Demand Index in a weekly time frame. Trading on a weekly time frame can be more challenging because of the increased difficulty in setting useful stops. However, the

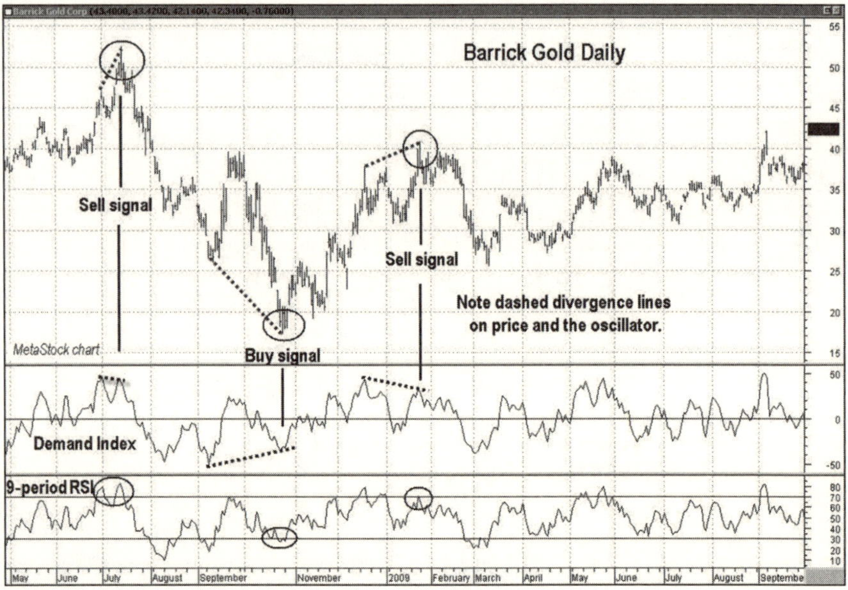

Chart 10.28 Demand Index Oscillator with 9-Period RSI, Combined Buy and Sell Signals, Barrick Gold

Source: MetaStock

Demand Index tends to give less frequent and more reliable signals when weekly charts are used. This signal can also be used by long-only traders as an indication to exit long positions and step aside in anticipation of increased selling pressure.

In Chart 10.29, a weekly chart, notice how the U.S. Dollar Index was in an uptrend from July 2008 through November 2008. After a rather sharp sell-off into December 2008, price once again climbed back up near its November high. This rally and push back up to the November high caused a negative divergence in the Demand Index. Just as with most other types of trades, with the Demand Index it is unwise to enter a position solely because of a divergence between an indicator and the price. In Chart 10.29, also notice the weak volume on what turned out to be the final push to the February 2009 high. The configuration of the rally allowed for a good support line to be drawn, which connected the lows from July 2008 through February 2009. A short trade could have been entered when price closed down through its support line and the Demand Index crossed down through the zero line.

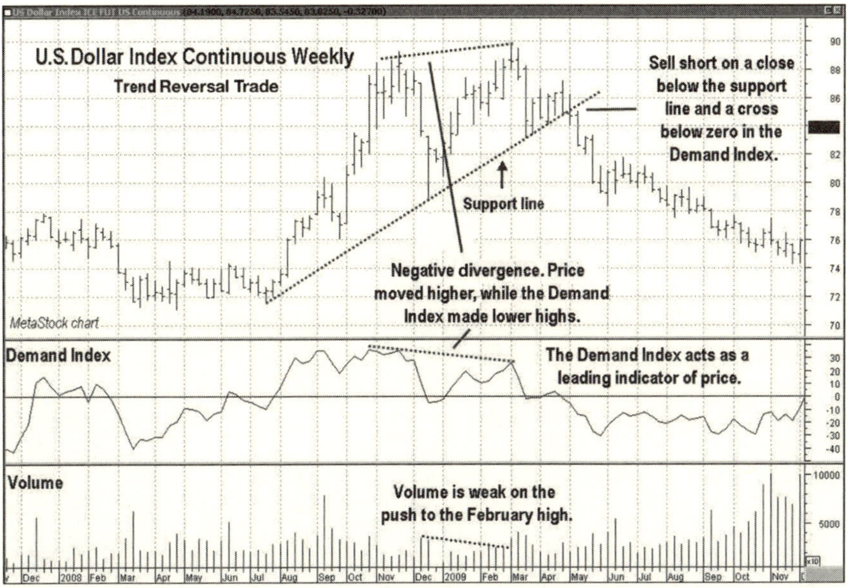

Chart 10.29 Demand Index Oscillator, Trade Setup, U.S. Dollar Index

Source: MetaStock

Trade Entry

In Chart 10.30, price closed below the support line the week of May 2, 2009. The Demand Index actually broke below its zero line the week before, but waiting for price to confirm is always the safest way to go. An initial protective stop should have been placed above the 87.22 high made the week of April 25, 2009. The reactionary high posted that week before price once again moved lower and provided an opportunity to place the stop closer to the entry point, thus lowering exposure. Also notice how volume increased once price began to move lower—a sure sign that sellers were in control.

Trader Tips

The Demand Index is a versatile tool that can be used effectively for the following:

- Acting as a leading oscillator, identifying and confirming trends
- Showing trend divergences that lead to corrections or trend reversals
- Providing buy and sell signals with zero-line crossovers, especially when paired with an Overbought/Oversold Oscillator

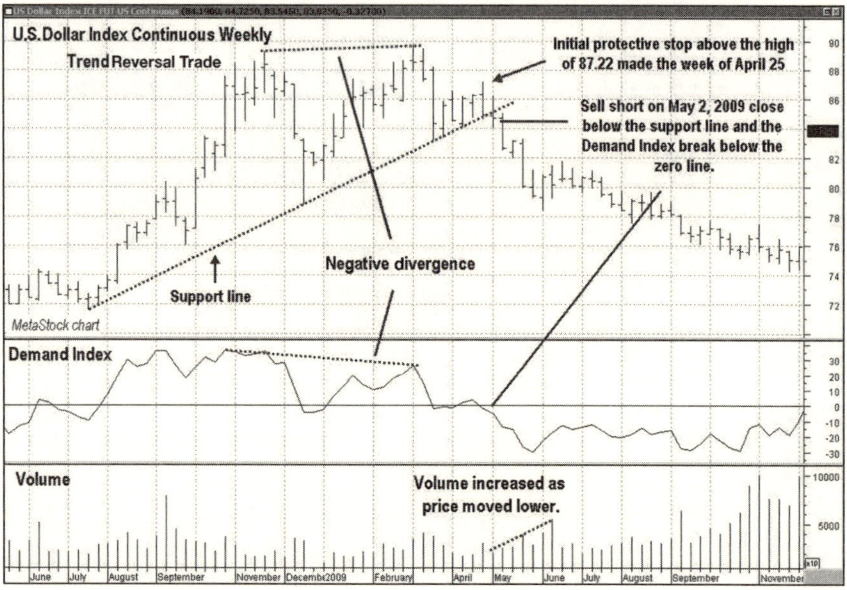

Chart 10.30 Demand Index Oscillator, Trade Entry, U.S. Dollar Index

Source: MetaStock

One drawback to the Demand Index is its choppy, volatile behavior in daily time frames when used for zero-line crossovers. Weekly time frames are less volatile and give more reliable crossover signals.

Ease of Movement

Ease of Movement (EOM) is one of many oscillators developed by Richard Arms Jr., whose innovative ARMS Index was presented in Chapter 8. Through its unique method of relating price and volume, EOM is used to calculate how much volume is required to move prices, or, put another way, the ease with which prices are moving.

Formulation

Ease of Movement is a centered oscillator, which means that readings over the center line (in this case, a zero line) are interpreted as positive, and readings below the center line (or zero) are interpreted as negative. A value greater than zero indicates that the stock is being accumulated, while negative values reflect increased selling pressure. A high positive value appears when price moves up easily on low volume. Strong negative numbers show that price is moving downward easily on low volume. When there is small price movement on heavy volume, the Ease of Movement Oscillator is zero. The Ease of Movement Oscillator is a product of the Equivolume charting method examined in Chapter 9 and is calculated as follows:

$$\text{EOM} = \text{midpoint move} / \text{box ratio}$$

where

$$\text{Midpoint move} = [(\text{high} + \text{low})/2] - [(\text{previous high} + \text{previous low})/2]$$

$$\text{Box ratio} = \text{volume (in 10,000s)} / (\text{high} - \text{low})$$

The raw value of EOM is usually smoothed with a moving average. Most charting software allows you to pick a moving average to smooth the raw EOM; the examples that follow use a 21-period moving average. EOM is used to confirm trends, show divergences, and provide buy and sell signals with zero-line crossovers in the direction of the trend. Chart 10.31 shows a basic plot of EOM for the Nasdaq 100 Trust ETF (QQQQ).

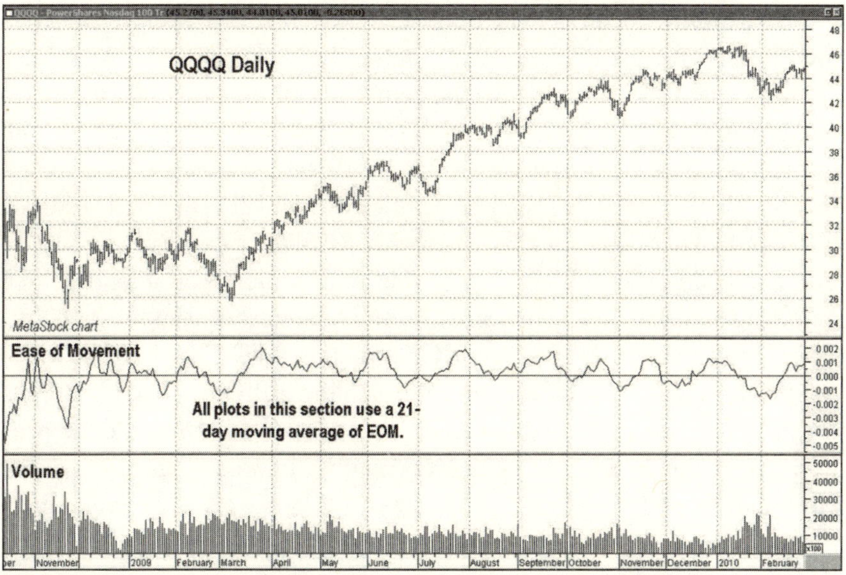

Chart 10.31 Ease of Movement Oscillator, Nasdaq 100 Trust ETF

Source: MetaStock

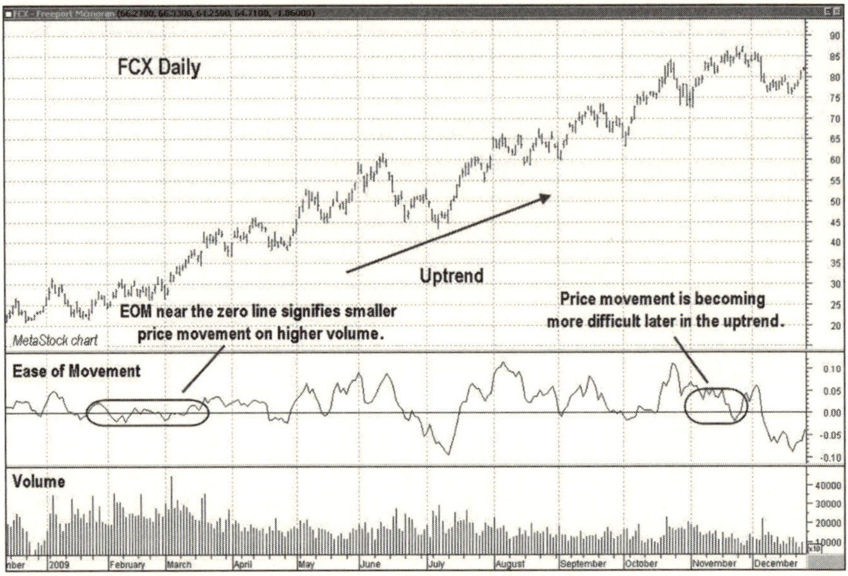

Chart 10.32 Ease of Movement Oscillator, Confirmation of Uptrend, Freeport McMoRan

Source: MetaStock

Trend Confirmation

Ease of Movement can help identify the trend of a security simply based on the zones from which it reverses. An uptrend usually causes EOM to form oscillator highs in a range above the zero line and lows at or slightly below the zero line. Freeport McMoRan (FCX) in Chart 10.32 shows just that, with the exception of the deeper low in July 2009, which signaled a sharp correction. Prices recovered after that, however, and the uptrend resumed through the fall of 2009 as reflected in the behavior of the EOM Oscillator.

Ease of Movement shows a range shift in downtrends, as it tends to bottom in a range well below the zero line and top out at or near the zero line. The iShares Dow Jones U.S. Home Construction ETF (ITB) in Chart 10.33 shows the depth below the zero line at which the EOM Oscillator bottomed before recovering as the March 2009 low approached. Also note the positive divergence (a higher low in EOM with a lower low in price) at the November 2008 low.

Divergences

Ease of Movement is a great indicator for showing divergences. Note in Chart 10.34 for the Dow Jones Diamonds Trust ETF (DIA) that EOM held its prior low and did not make a new low in March as price fell to a

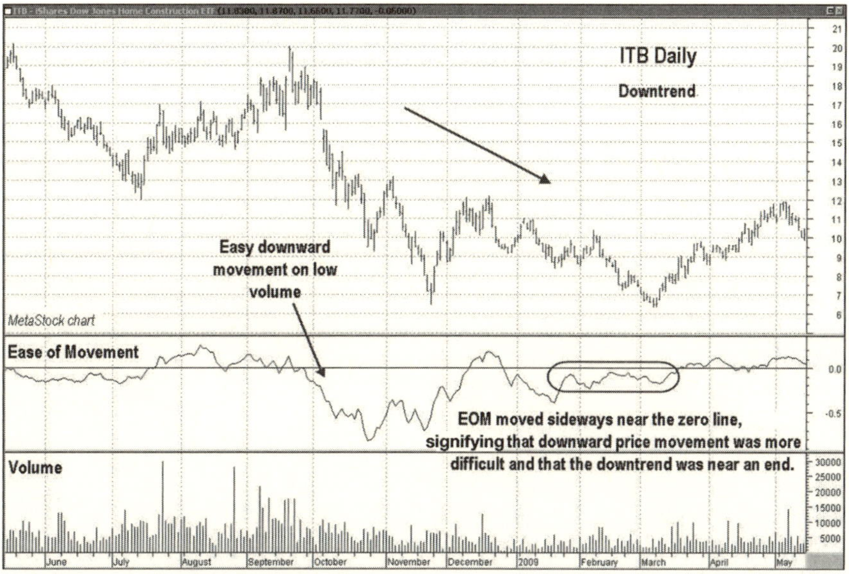

Chart 10.33 Ease of Movement Oscillator, Confirmation of Downtrend, iShares Dow Jones U.S. Home Construction ETF

Source: MetaStock

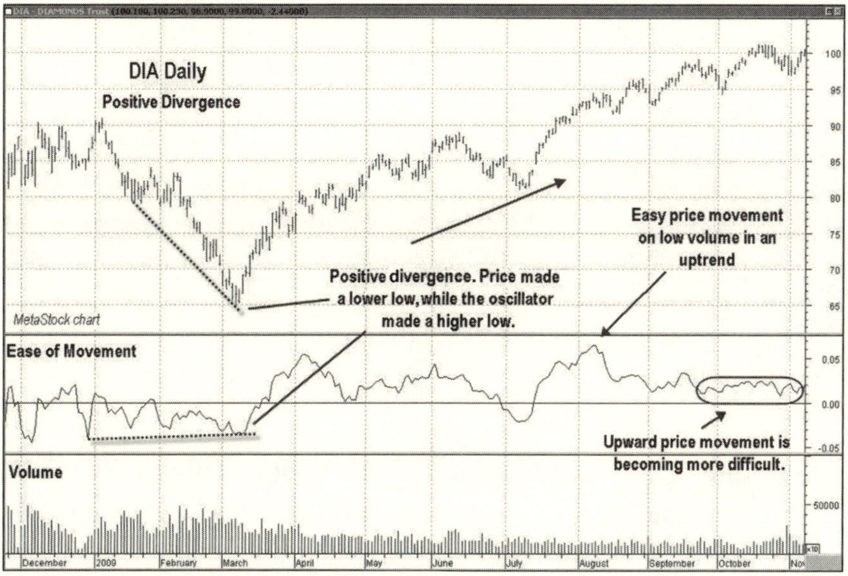

Chart 10.34 Ease of Movement Oscillator, Positive Divergence, Dow Jones Diamonds Trust ETF

Source: MetaStock

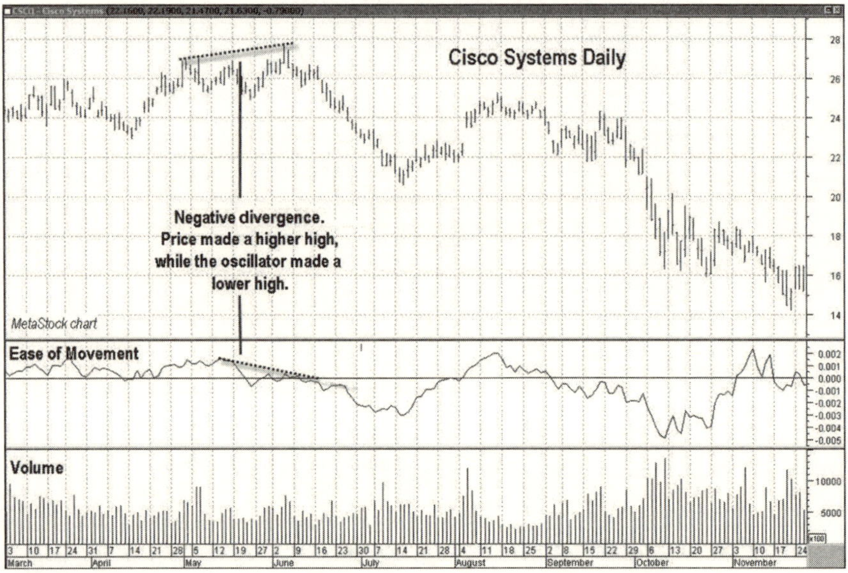

Chart 10.35 Ease of Movement Oscillator, Negative Divergence, Cisco Systems

Source: MetaStock

new low. This positive divergence revealed that the price-downward movement was more difficult, suggesting that the price action would begin to take on a more bullish tone.

Negative divergences appear when price makes a higher high and the EOM Oscillator makes a lower high. That shows latent weakness, as sellers are distributing shares even as price advances. Note in Chart 10.35 how Cisco Systems made a new short-term price high in June 2008, but the EOM Oscillator was already beginning to break down. Also note the characteristics of EOM following the June 2008 divergence. The oscillator began making lows well below the zero line and topping out right around the zero line. Those are characteristics of a downtrend.

Combining Ease of Movement with Other Indicators

In this example, Ease of Movement is paired with the MACD indicator. MACD moves with the market being analyzed and provides a filter for long or short trades. If MACD is in bullish territory above its zero line, only buys are considered when EOM crosses up through its zero line. If MACD is

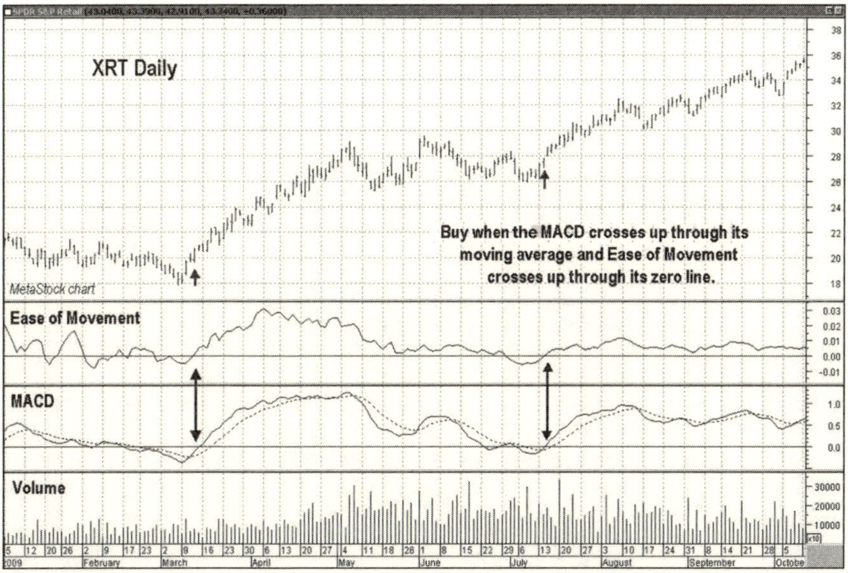

Chart 10.36 Ease of Movement Oscillator Combined with Volume Price Trend, Buy Points on Uptrend, S&P SPDR Retail ETF

Source: MetaStock

in bearish territory below its zero line, only short sells are considered when EOM crosses down through its zero line.

In the example of the S&P SPDR Retail ETF (XRT) in Chart 10.36, XRT is in an uptrend, meaning that only buys should be considered. The arrows on the chart represent buy points based on the uptrend and the Ease of Movement Oscillator crossing up through the zero line.

Trade Setup

Ease of Movement is a great tool for showing divergences with price action, alerting traders that a change in direction could be near. Chart 10.37 shows how the price of Yum! Brands (YUM) bottomed in November 2008. Price then rallied to a high in January 2009 before pulling back into its March 2009 low. Since November 2008 was the actual low and a higher low was made in March, this trade is labeled as a trend continuation trade. As price continued lower from January into March 2009, note how Ease of Movement made a higher low. This formed a positive divergence, which indicated that price was not moving downward as easily on low volume.

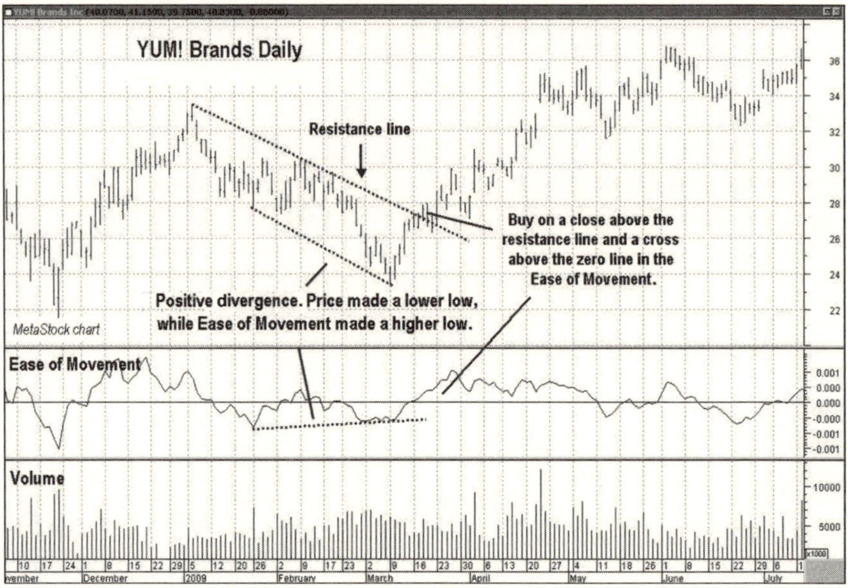

Chart 10.37 Ease of Movement Oscillator, Trade Setup on Positive Divergence, Yum! Brands

Source: MetaStock

A downsloping resistance line could be drawn across the January–March highs. A close above this line along with Ease of Movement crossing above zero would be a signal to initiate a long trade.

Trade Entry

On March 18, 2009, the price of Yum! Brands closed above its downsloping resistance line. Note in Chart 10.38 how Ease of Movement actually crossed above its zero line two days prior to the resistance line break. It was wise to wait for confirmation from price action before entering the trade, thus increasing its odds for success. An initial protective stop should have been placed at the March 9 low of 23.37.

Trader Tips

Ease of Movement is an oscillator that can be used for the following:

- Showing higher positive and lower negative values on light volume, confirming a trend

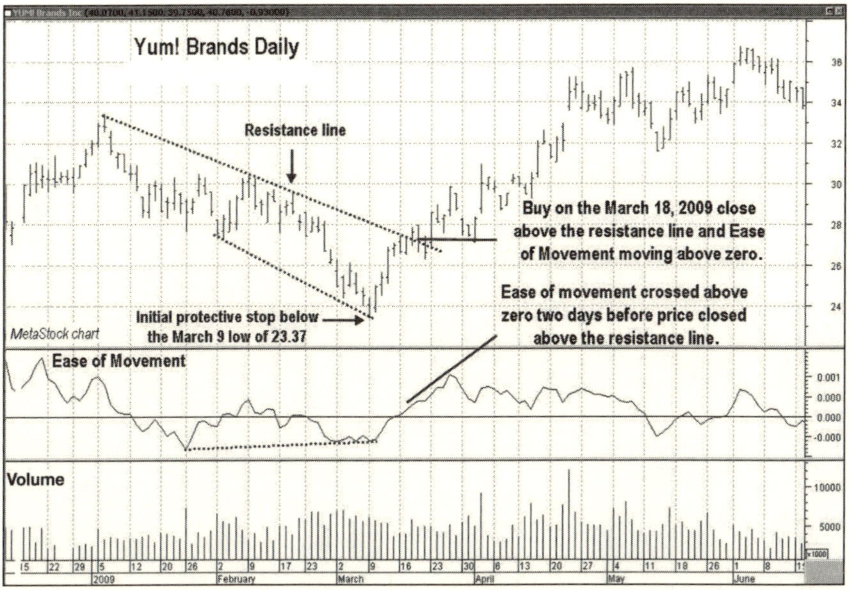

Chart 10.38 Ease of Movement Oscillator, Trade Entry on Positive Divergence and Confirmation, Yum! Brands

Source: MetaStock

- Identifying trend divergences as price movement becomes more difficult
- Indicating buy or sell opportunities in the direction of the larger-degree trend

The Ease of Movement Oscillator has a tendency to be volatile. Use a 21-period moving average to smooth.

Force Index

The Force Index (FI) was developed by successful trader and market technician Dr. Alexander Elder to provide a measurement of the force or power of the bulls behind rallies or of the bears behind declines. The Force Index is a centered oscillator; that is, readings above zero are considered positive, and readings below zero are considered negative.

Formulation

The Force Index is calculated as follows:

(Today's close − yesterday's close) × today's volume

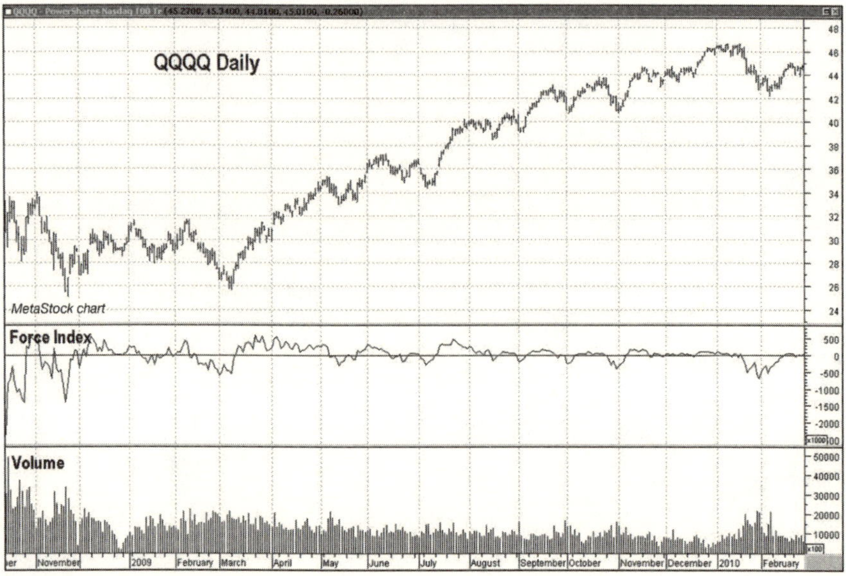

Chart 10.39 Force Index Oscillator, Nasdaq 100 Trust ETF

Source: MetaStock

The Force Index is not as good at trend confirmation as some other oscillators, but it is quite effective when used to detect trend divergences or when paired with a trending indicator for trading purposes. Since the Force Index produces a choppy data line, it is usually presented in a smoothed format. The most common method of presentation is a 13-period exponential moving average for intermediate-term analysis. A 2-day exponential moving average is suggested for short-term trading.

The Nasdaq 100 Trust ETF (QQQQ) in Chart 10.39 shows a basic plot of the 13-day exponential moving average of the Force Index. All Force Index charts that follow will employ the 13-day exponential moving average.

Trend Confirmation

The Force Index, unlike many other oscillators, is very volatile, and traders should be aware that at times it does not show clear indications of uptrends or downtrends. Its choppy, volatile nature can cause it to make deep lows in uptrends, as demonstrated by the iShares High Yield Corporate Bond ETF (HYG) in Chart 10.40. It did, however, make lower highs in December 2009 and January 2010 as compared with the spring and summer of 2009, which showed that a correction was near.

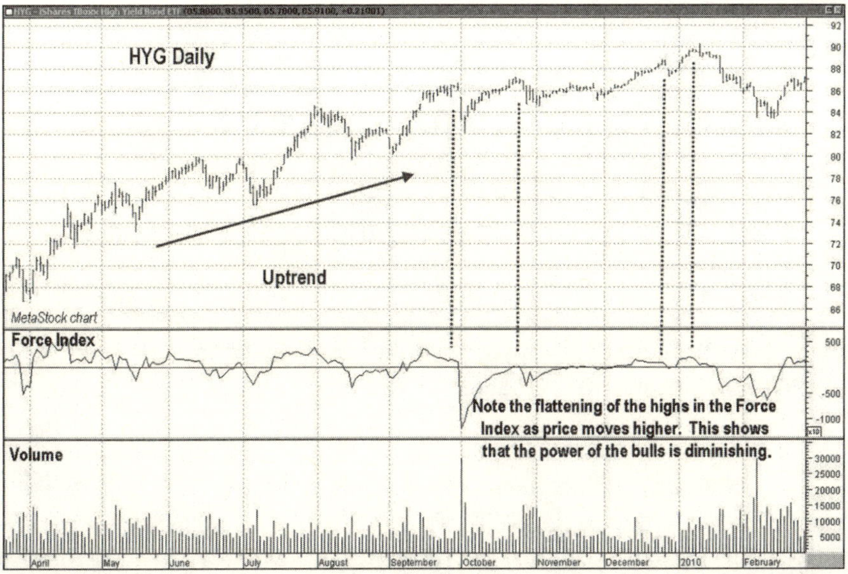

Chart 10.40 Force Index Oscillator, Uptrend Reading, iShares High Yield Corporate Bond ETF

Source: MetaStock

Downtrends also tend to show mixed characteristics in a Force Index plot; the Force Index is more heavily influenced by the magnitude of the most recent price movements. The S&P SPDR Select Financial ETF (XLF) in Chart 10.41 shows how the Force Index was very volatile in the fall of 2008 before settling down and tracking closer to the zero line into 2009.

Divergences

The Force Index is a highly effective tool when used to look for divergences between price action and the indicator. Positive divergences occur when price makes a new low but the Force Index makes a higher low. Chart 10.42 shows a very large positive divergence at the November 2008 low for the S&P SPDR Select Retail ETF (XRT). The Force Index began a series of higher lows in October 2008, which gave an indication that the push lower was running out of gas.

The Force Index also spots negative divergences that form when price makes a higher high and the Force Index makes a lower high. Chart 10.43 shows a pronounced negative divergence for the Market Vectors Gold Miners ETF (GDX), which gave an early warning before selling unfolded in early 2010.

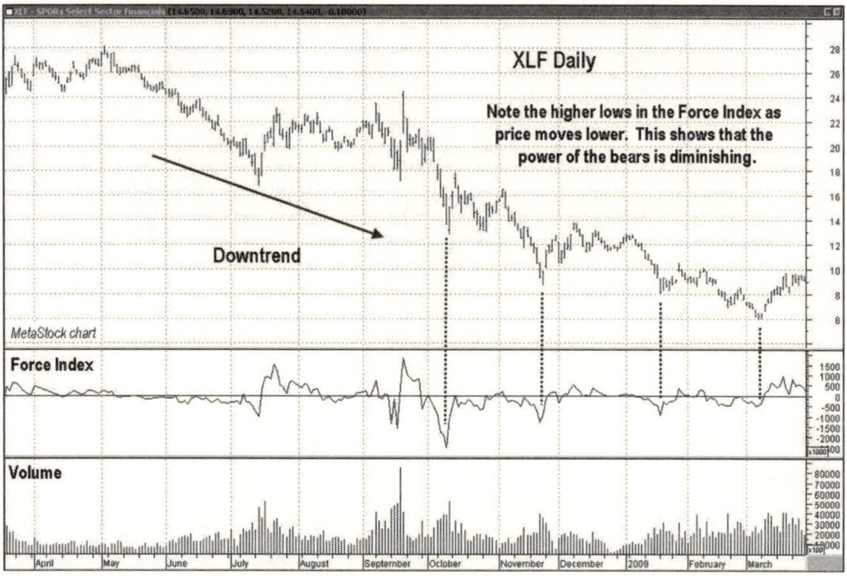

Chart 10.41 Force Index Oscillator, Downtrend Reading, S&P SPDR Select Financial ETF

Source: MetaStock

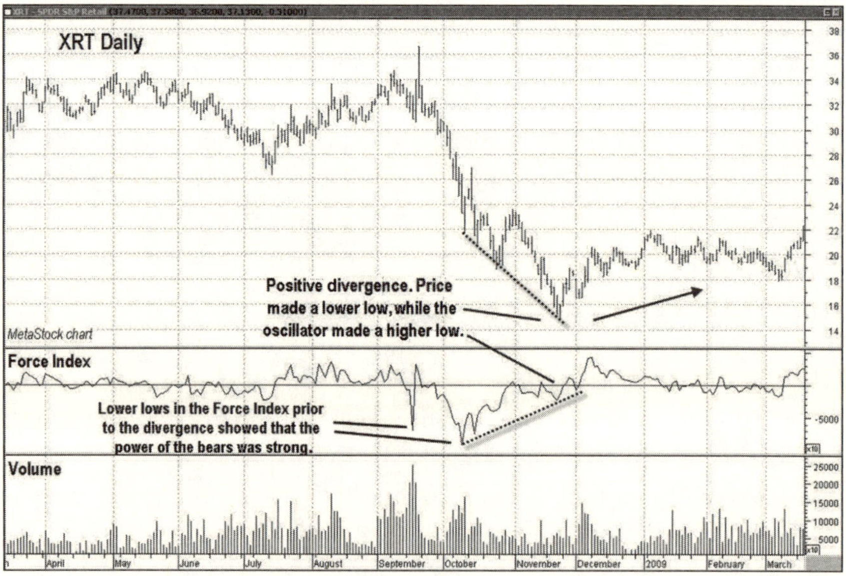

Chart 10.42 Force Index Oscillator, Positive Divergence, S&P SPDR Select Retail ETF

Source: MetaStock

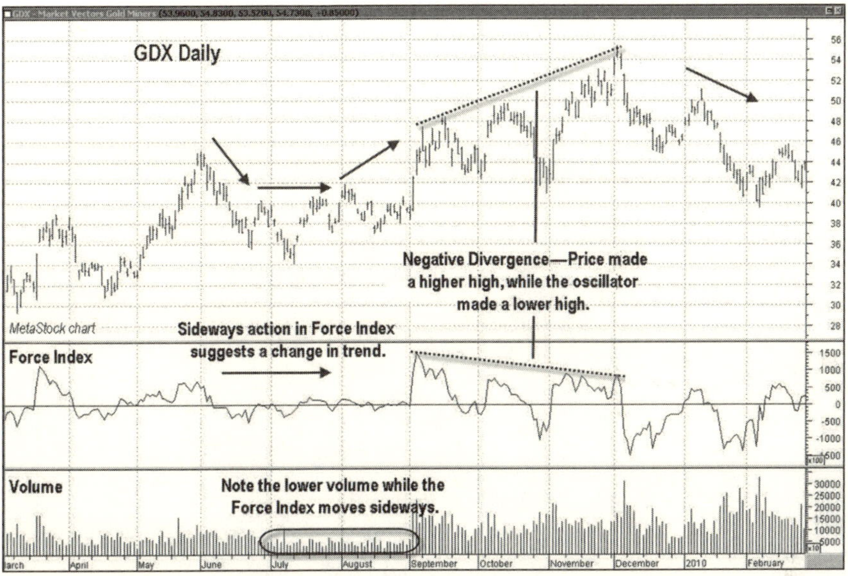

Chart 10.43 Force Index Oscillator, Negative Divergence, Market Vectors Gold Miners ETF

Source: MetaStock

Combining Force Index with Other Indicators

Since the Force Index is a relatively sensitive short- to intermediate-term indicator, it works well when paired with a cumulative trending indicator. In Chart 10.44, the Force Index is paired with the Volume Price Trend indicator. Volume Price Trend in this case acts as a filter for trading signals provided by the Force Index. When Volume Price Trend is in an uptrend (i.e., making higher highs and higher lows), buys will be considered on Force Index crosses up through the zero line, while a downtrending Volume Price Trend (i.e., lower highs and lower lows) indicates short sells, but only when the Force Index crosses down through the zero line.

For the Consumer Discretionary Select Sector SPDR ETF (XLY) in Chart 10.44, note the uptrend on Volume Price Trend (the trend filter), which indicates that only buys should be considered. The arrows show buy signals generated on crosses above the zero line. Note that the volatile nature of the Force Index generates some less-than-optimal signal entry points, but trading along the trend and using the Volume Price Trend indicator helps to reduce the risk of a bad trade.

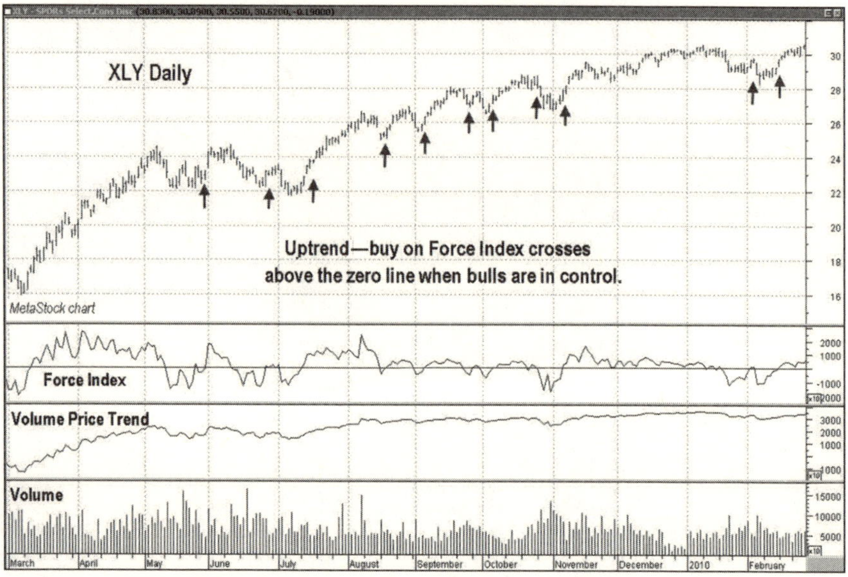

Chart 10.44 Force Index Oscillator Combined with Volume Price Trend, Buy Signals, Consumer Discretionary Select Sector SPDR ETF

Source: MetaStock

Trade Setup

The Force Index is very good at helping traders spot short-term divergences that can lead to effective trades. In Chart 10.45, note how price for the Market Vectors Steel ETF (SLX) bottomed in October 2009 before advancing into January 2010. As the price of SLX pulled back to its February low, the Force Index showed a positive divergence, while price decreased as volume moved lower. Both were signs that selling momentum was drying up and that the uptrend was ready to resume. A downsloping resistance line could have been drawn to connect the January and February highs. A buy order could have been placed when price closed above the resistance line and the Force Index crossed above the zero line.

Trade Entry

In Chart 10.46, the positive divergence in the Force Index was substantiated on February 16, 2010, as the price of SLX closed above the downsloping resistance line. The Force Index did not cross above zero until February 16, however, so a patient trader would have had to wait a couple of days before entering a long position. An initial protective stop should have been placed

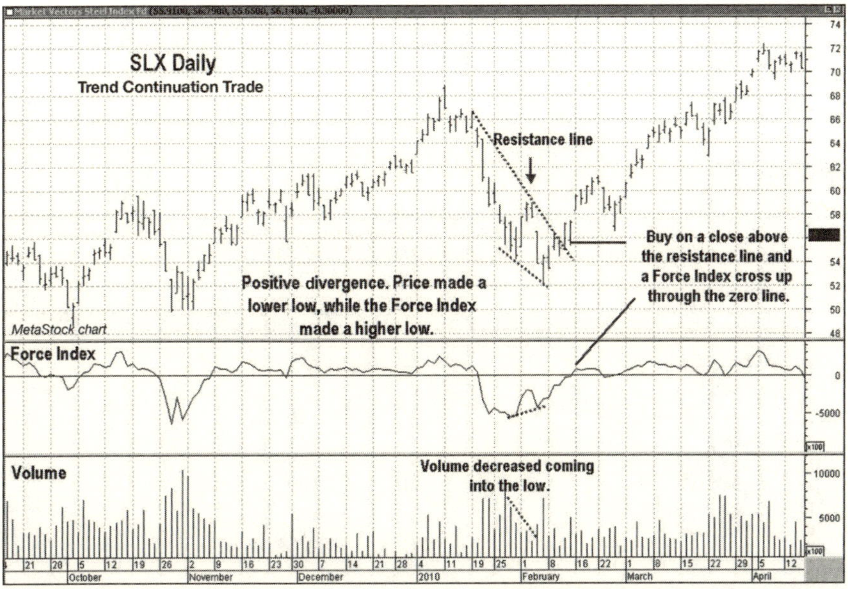

Chart 10.45 Force Index Oscillator, Trade Setup on Positive Divergence, Market Vectors Steel ETF

Source: MetaStock

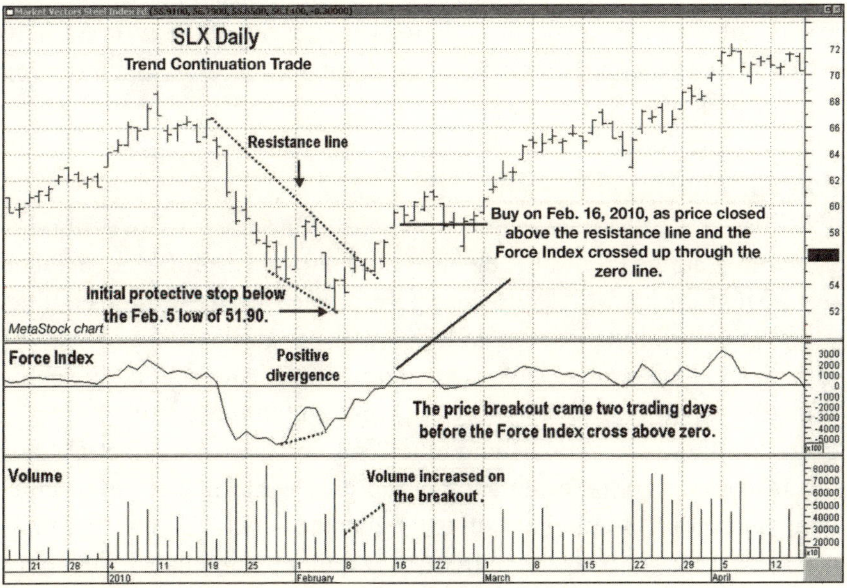

Chart 10.46 Force Index Oscillator, Trade Entry on Positive Divergence, Market Vectors Steel ETF

Source: MetaStock

below the February 5 low of 51.90. The extra time it took for the Force Index to confirm the price action was well worth it, as price advanced roughly 20 percent from that entry point.

Trader Tips

The Force Index is normally smoothed with a 2- or 13-period exponential moving average to make it easier to use for the following:

- Spotting trend divergences and generating buy and sell signals in the direction of the larger-degree trend
- Giving a quick, short-term read on bullish or bearish control of the market
- Signaling that price direction will continue

Herrick Payoff Index

The Herrick Payoff Index (HPI) analyzes price, volume, and Open Interest to determine the amount of money flowing into and out of a futures contract. The HPI uses the mean or average price for each day as its starting point and then includes volume and Open Interest in its calculations to measure the amount of money flowing into or out of the contract. This oscillator can be applied only to futures contracts because Open Interest is a component in its calculation.

Formulation

The Herrick Payoff Index is rather complex in its calculation. A number of charting applications already have the Herrick Payoff Index included (e.g., MetaStock), which provides ease of use on any futures contract where price, volume, and open-interest data are available.

As a direct consequence of using volume in the calculation, one of the strengths of the HPI is its ability to give a trader an early warning of a change in the price trend. (Remember: Volume precedes price!) Adding Open Interest into the calculation also provides information on whether or not traders are entering or exiting the market, which helps to determine whether a trend is likely to continue or whether it will change direction.

The HPI is a centered oscillator with values above the zero line that signal a bullish money flow into a futures contract and values below the zero line that signal a bearish outflow. Chart 10.47 shows a basic plot of the Herrick Payoff Index for crude oil.

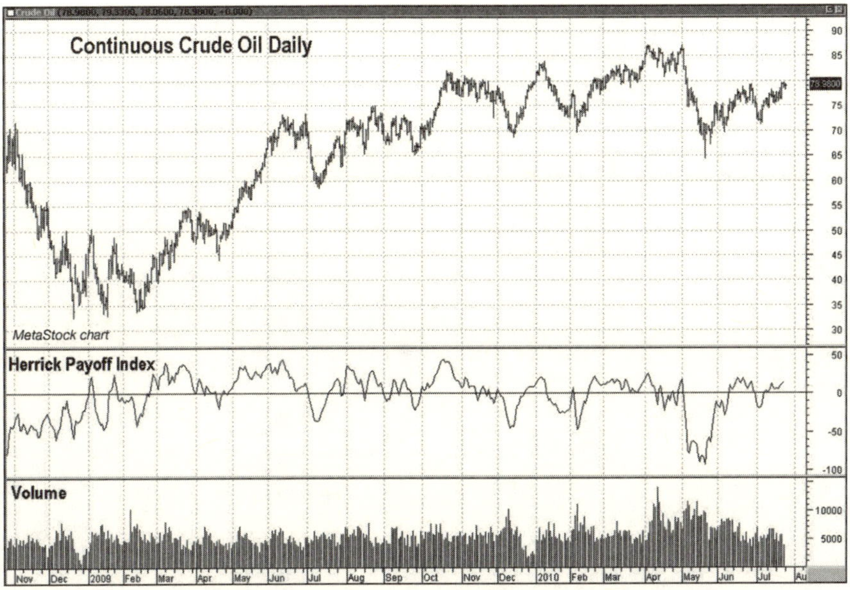

Chart 10.47 Herrick Payoff Index, Crude Oil Continuous Daily

Source: MetaStock

Trend Confirmation

Just as with many other oscillators and indicators, the HPI tends to peak and trough at different ranges in uptrends and downtrends. Chart 10.48 shows how the HPI for continuous copper makes shallow bottoms just below the zero line and peaks well above the zero line in its 2009 uptrend. The opposite is true during downtrends, as the HPI peaks at or just above the zero line while making troughs well below the zero line. Chart 10.49 shows these characteristics during the 2008 downtrend for continuous copper.

Divergences

The HPI is a great oscillator for alerting traders to the current health of a trend. A bullish divergence occurs when price makes a new low and the HPI does not. A bearish divergence occurs when price makes a higher high and the HPI does not. Chart 10.50 shows a bearish divergence for continuous contract gold, as price made a higher high in December 2009, but the HPI did not. This nonconfirmation alerted traders that a near-term pullback was developing.

A bullish divergence occurs when price makes a new low, but the HPI does not. Chart 10.51 shows how traders of continuous soybeans would have been alerted to a pending change of direction at the December 2009

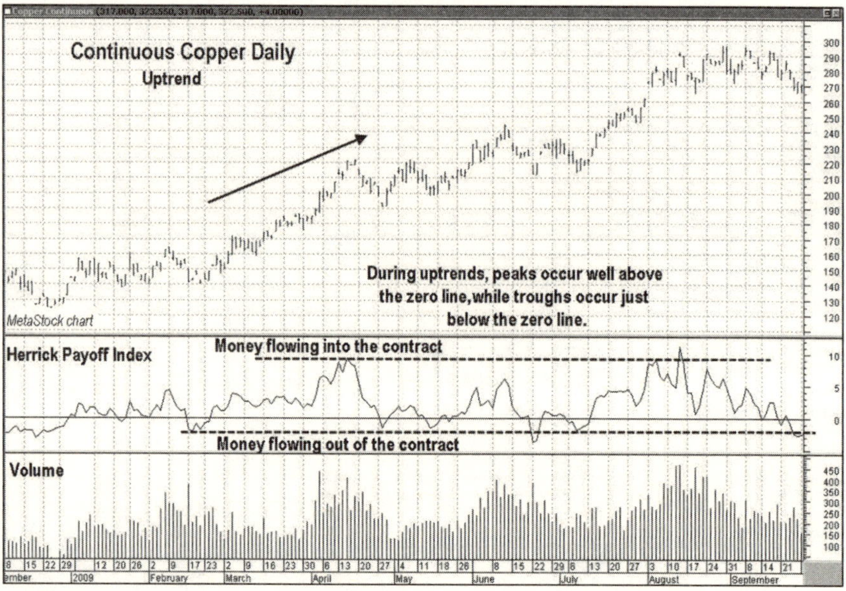

Chart 10.48 Herrick Payoff Index, Positive Range during Uptrend, Copper Continuous Daily

Source: MetaStock

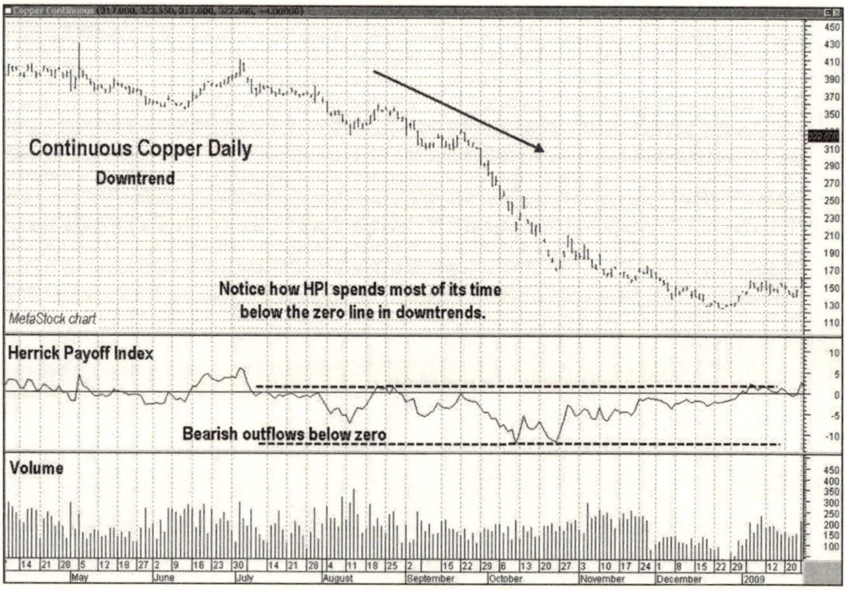

Chart 10.49 Herrick Payoff Index, Negative Range Confirms Downtrend, Copper Continuous Daily

Source: MetaStock

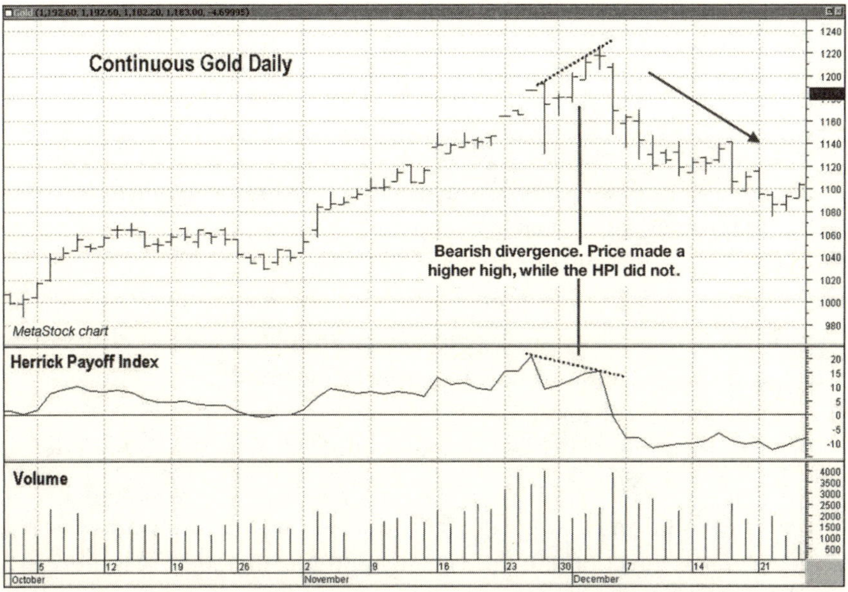

Chart 10.50 Herrick Payoff Index, Negative Divergence, Gold Continuous Daily

Source: MetaStock

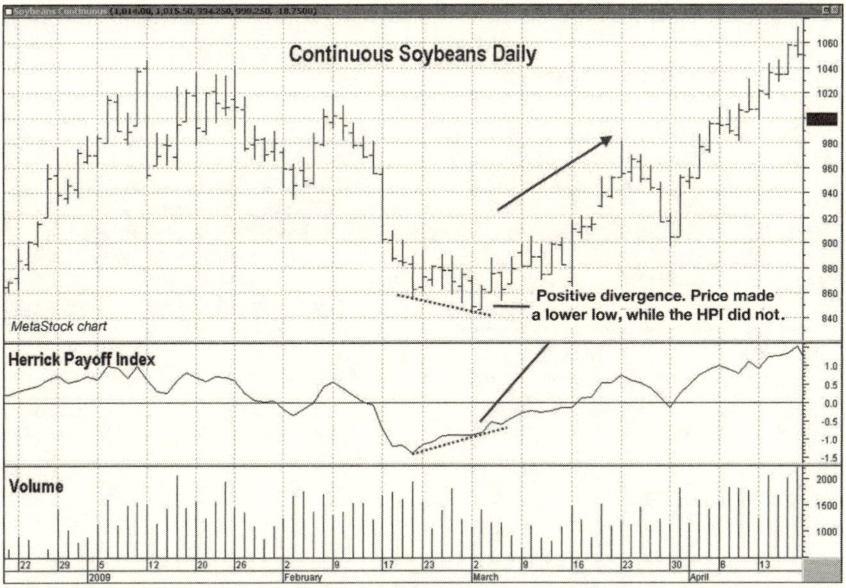

Chart 10.51 Herrick Payoff Index, Positive Divergence, Soybeans Continuous Daily

Source: MetaStock

low. Note how price made a new low, while the HPI actually began to move higher. This divergence preceded a powerful rally.

Using HPI with Other Indicators

Since HPI is a centered oscillator usually good for short-term to intermediate-term signals, it pairs well with a long-term trending indicator. In the example of continuous silver in Chart 10.52, HPI is paired with the Accumulation/Distribution indicator. Accumulation/Distribution will give a sense of the prevailing trend and its strength, and the HPI can be used to show the trader when the prevailing trend is ready to resume following price pullbacks.

Note in the chart how the Accumulation/Distribution line held its low while price entered a deep correction. That showed that overall selling pressure was not very strong. The HPI then showed a positive divergence as silver made a reactionary low in July 2009, which alerted traders that the larger-degree uptrend was ready to resume. This is another example of how pairing a short-term to intermediate-term oscillator with a long-term trending indicator can be very effective.

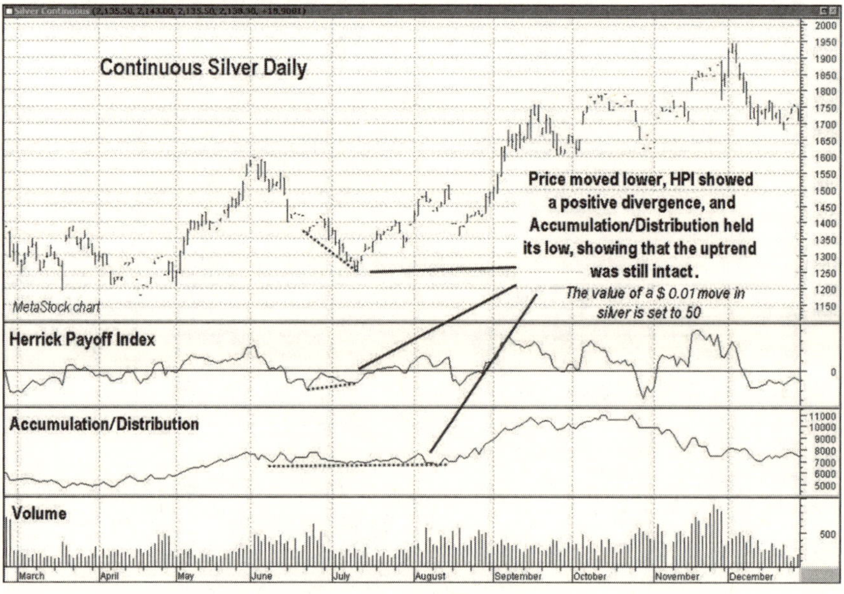

Chart 10.52 Herrick Payoff Index Combined with Accumulation/Distribution, Positive Divergence, Silver Continuous Daily

Source: MetaStock

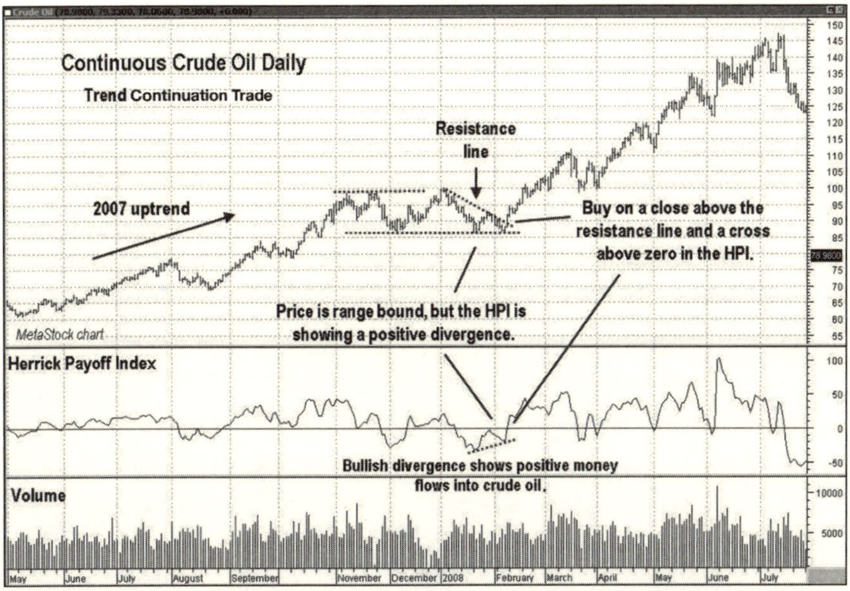

Chart 10.53 Herrick Payoff Index, Positive Divergence Trade Setup, Crude Oil Continuous Daily

Source: MetaStock

Trade Setup

One aspect of the HPI we have not yet examined is its ability to be used as a trade trigger, with crosses above the zero line showing bullish money flows while crosses below the zero line show bearish money flows. In Chart 10.53, note how crude oil had been in an uptrend throughout 2007 before pausing in a three-month consolidation that lasted into February 2008. As price traded back down to the bottom of the range in early February, note how the HPI formed a positive divergence, making a higher low while price touched the bottom of its consolidation range.

That was a very good setup, allowing a trader to take a chance on a long trade while using a tight stop just below the consolidation pattern. If price had broken through the bottom of the consolidation pattern, the trade would have been stopped out. A downsloping resistance line was drawn to connect the tops of January and February. A long position would be entered on a close above that line and a cross above the zero line in the HPI. This would provide confirmation between price and the HPI.

Trade Entry

Chart 10.54 zooms in on the time frame in which the buy for continuous crude oil was triggered. Price broke above its resistance line along with a cross

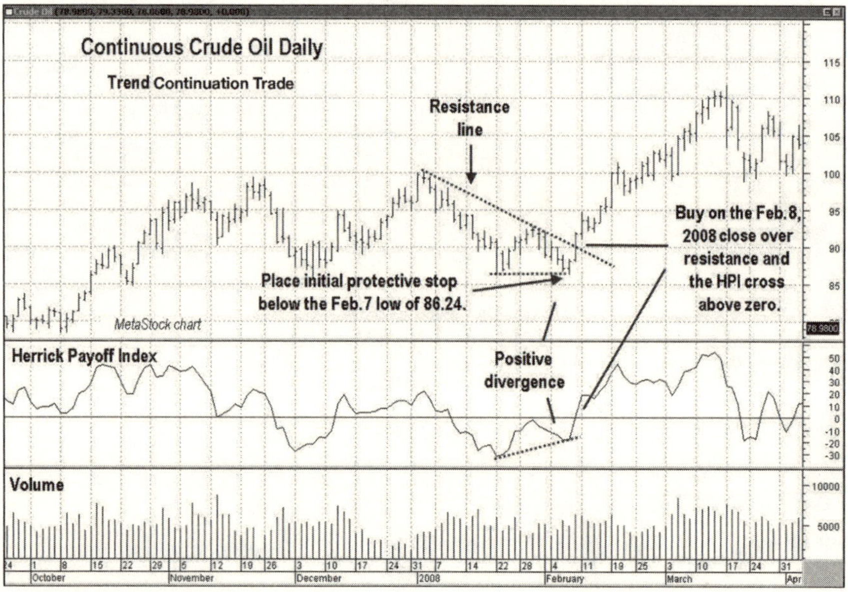

Chart 10.54 Herrick Payoff Index, Positive Divergence Trade Entry, Crude Oil Continuous Daily

Source: MetaStock

above the zero line in the HPI on February 8, 2009. This showed a price break through resistance accompanied by positive money flows into crude oil. Price actually had not broken out of its 3-month consolidation range; however, a trade like this has tremendous upside with minimal risk, as the initial protective stop was placed just below the bottom of the trading range. Should price break lower out of the range, the trade would be stopped out. If price were to break higher on a resumption of the uptrend, it would be a great trade. Price did continue higher up to 110 from the February 8 close of 91.77.

Trader Tips

The HPI is an oscillator that is specifically applicable to futures contracts and that is used for the following:

- Showing bullish and bearish divergences with price
- Giving buy and sell signals on crosses above and below its zero line
- Showing trending money flow characteristics as it peaks and troughs in different ranges

One drawback of the HPI is that it requires Open Interest in its calculation, which limits its use to futures contracts.

Klinger Oscillator

The Klinger Oscillator (KO) was developed by Stephen J. Klinger. The goal in developing this oscillator was to formulate a volume-based indicator that would be useful in both short- and long-term analysis. Klinger wanted an indicator sensitive enough to signal short-term turning points and also able to reflect longer-term trends in money flows into and out of a security.

Formulation

The Klinger Oscillator is based on the premise that the daily difference between accumulation and distribution can be qualified to create a *volume force* measurement behind price movement. When the daily high, low, and close are added together, a trend can be defined. Accumulation occurs when the current day's sum is greater than the prior day's. Distribution occurs when the current day's sum is less than the prior day's. In the rare occurrence that the sums are identical, the existing trend remains in effect. The steps are as follows:

1. Find the average price of the day by summing the high, low, and close and then dividing by three.
2. If today's average price is greater than the previous day's average price, assign a plus sign to today's volume.
3. If today's average price is less than the previous day's average price, assign a minus sign to today's volume.
4. Calculate a 34-period exponential moving average of the signed volume from steps 2 and 3.
5. Calculate a 55-period exponential moving average of the signed volume from steps 2 and 3.
6. Subtract the 55-period exponential moving average from the 34-period exponential moving average and plot the difference.
7. Calculate and plot a 13-period exponential moving average of the daily differences from step 6.

According to Klinger, volume combined with intraday changes in price reveals buying and selling pressure. Volume Force is the difference

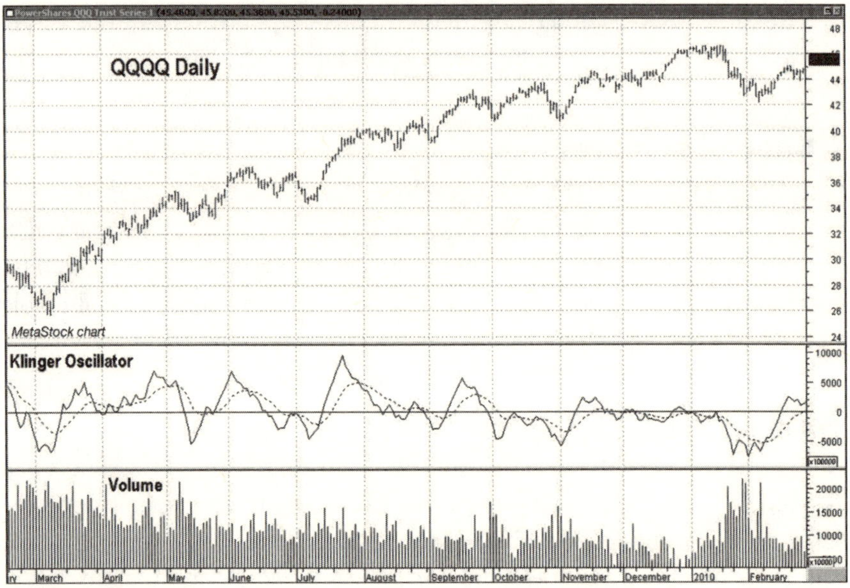

Chart 10.55 Klinger Oscillator, Nasdaq 100 Trust ETF

Source: MetaStock

between the number of shares being accumulated or distributed each trading day. Volume Force should confirm uptrends by rising along with price until the trend matures. At that point the Volume Force will contract, alerting the trader to a potential change in trend. The Klinger Oscillator is also meant to show positive divergences at bottoms as it begins to rise, which reveals accumulation before the trend actually changes.

The Klinger Oscillator is a centered oscillator, which means that buy and sell signals are generated when the oscillator crosses above or below a midpoint or zero line. It is not advised to follow signals against the trend in every case. For example, crosses above the zero line in a downtrend should not be blindly treated as buys, and crosses below the zero line in an uptrend should not be blindly treaded as sells. Chart 10.55 shows a basic plot of the Klinger Oscillator for the Nasdaq 100 Trust ETF (QQQQ).

Trend Confirmation

The Klinger Oscillator displays a different range during a downtrend as compared to an uptrend, demonstrating the characteristic of range shift. In the example of the continuous contract of the U.S. Dollar Index in

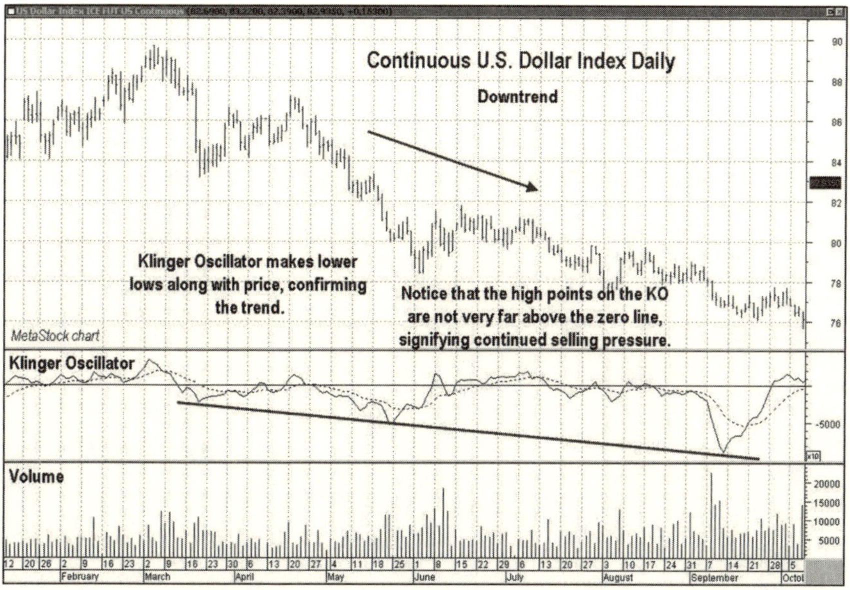

Chart 10.56 Klinger Oscillator, Downtrend, U.S. Dollar Index Continuous Contract

Source: MetaStock

Chart 10.56, notice how the KO makes lower lows as price trends lower. Also note the range of the KO and how it peaks at points at or just above the zero line, which shows persistent selling pressure.

Next is a look at the daily chart of the S&P SPDR Select Retail ETF (XRT) (see Chart 10.57) as an example of the behavior of the KO in an uptrend. Notice how the oscillator stays in a range mostly above the zero line, making higher lows along with price while the oscillator also forms peaks well above the zero line, which signifies continued buying pressure.

Divergences

One of the strengths of the Klinger Oscillator is its ability to show divergences as trends mature. The KO shows evidence of weakening buying pressure in an uptrend by making lower highs as the trend continues. The KO also shows latent buying pressure as downtrends mature. In each case, the KO gives an early warning that the current trend is weakening and that a change in direction may be imminent. The S&P SPDR Select Retail ETF (XRT) in Chart 10.58 shows how the Klinger Oscillator revealed a pronounced negative divergence with price before prices reversed in early May 2010.

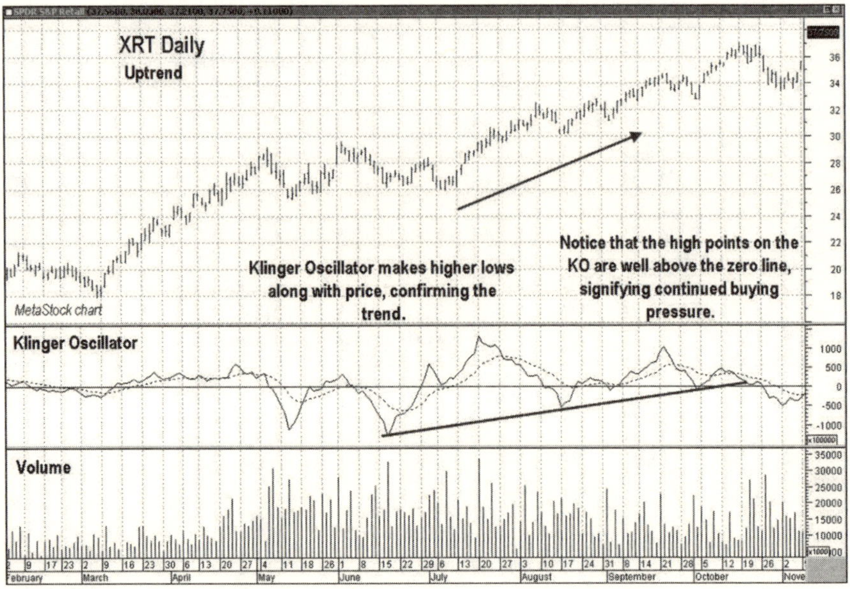

Chart 10.57 Klinger Oscillator during Uptrend, S&P SPDR Select Retail ETF

Source: MetaStock

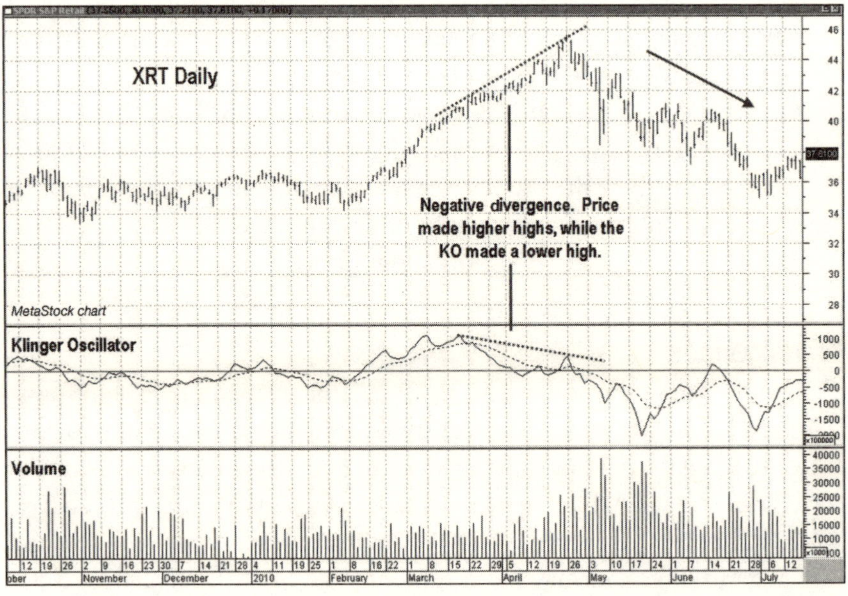

Chart 10.58 Klinger Oscillator, Negative Divergence, S&P SPDR Select Retail ETF

Source: MetaStock

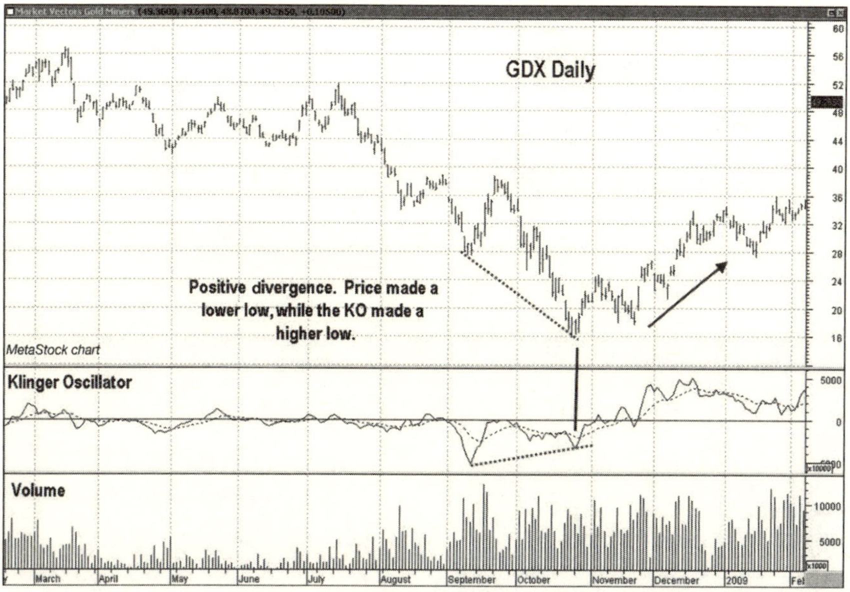

Chart 10.59 Klinger Oscillator, Positive Divergence, Market Vectors Gold Miners ETF

Source: MetaStock

The KO is also a valuable tool to spot divergences at bottoms, alerting traders that buyers are beginning to enter the market. Notice in the example of the Market Vectors Gold Miners ETF (GDX) in Chart 10.59 how the KO detected the appearance of buyers as price made its final low in October 2008.

Cumulative Klinger Oscillator

Klinger also recommends a cumulative version of his KO. The idea is to accumulate the daily values by adding each day's value to a running total and to plot the result as a cumulative trending indicator. He also recommends a 13-day exponential moving average of the indicator, which is useful as a trigger line to enter and exit trades. The culmulative configuration gives the oscillator a completely different look.

Chart 10.60 is another snapshot of the Nasdaq 100 Trust ETF (QQQQ) shown earlier in the chapter, only this time with the Cumulative KO and trigger line. Note how stable the KO appears in showing its trends, but there is a significant lag factor. The Cumulative KO is good for showing long-term divergences, but its zero-line crosses come much too late to be used for short-term trading signals.

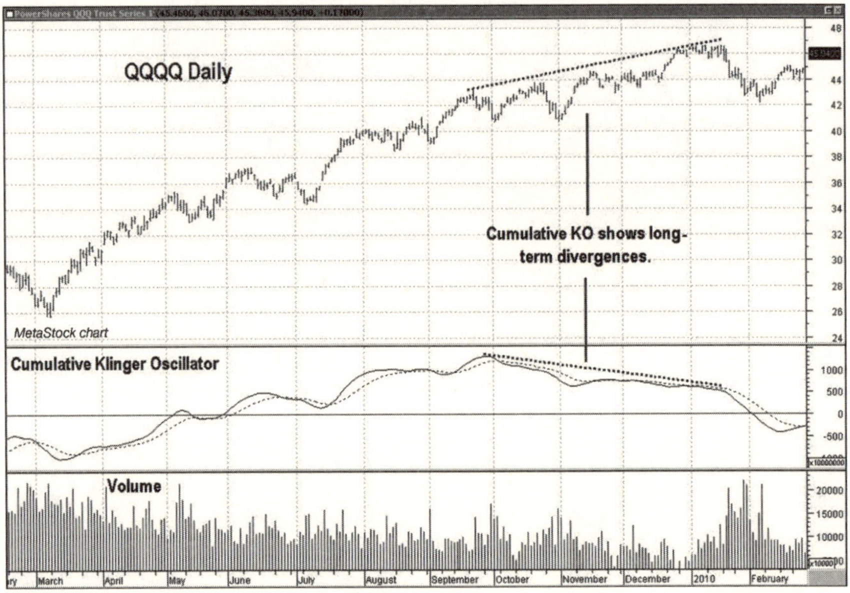

Chart 10.60 Cumulative Klinger Oscillator, 13-Day Exponential Moving Average, Long-Term Negative Divergence, Nasdaq 100 Trust ETF

Source: MetaStock

Klinger Oscillator with Other Indicators

Since the Klinger Oscillator is a short- to intermediate-term oscillator, it is well paired with a short- to intermediate-term price momentum indicator. In this example, the KO will be paired with the MACD line. This shows which direction price and volume are moving, so it acts as a guide as to whether to either buy crosses up through the zero line or sell crosses down through the zero line.

In the example of the Industrial Select SPDR ETF (XLI) in Chart 10.61, the MACD line is making higher highs and higher lows, trending above its zero line in an uptrend. This suggests that crosses up through the zero line in the KO should be treated as buys. Chart 10.61 shows the buy points in the XLI uptrend from August 2009 to April 2010. Note how once XLI topped in April 2010, the next cross up signal in the KO and MACD came well after the correction.

Trade Setup

One of the Klinger Oscillator's greatest strengths is in its ability to show divergences against the trend. This trade example demonstrates that

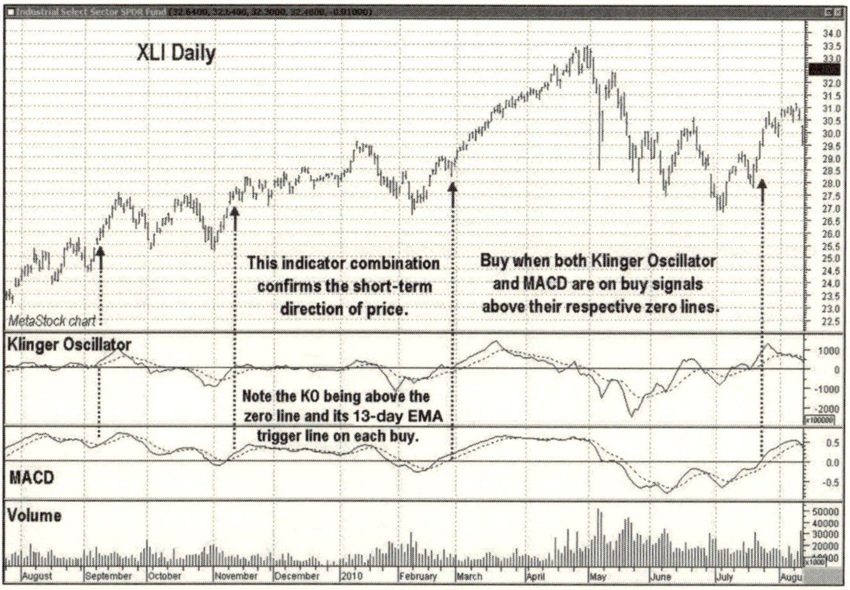

Chart 10.61 Klinger with MACD Indicator, Buy Points, Industrial Select SPDR ETF

Source: MetaStock

feature along with its ability to act as a trade trigger by crossing its midpoint line or zero line.

Note in Chart 10.62 how the price of Freeport McMoRan (FCX) pushed higher from January through early April 2010. During that time frame, buying pressure was on the decline, as depicted by the negative divergence in the KO. Note how the KO made lower highs as price made higher highs. A support line was drawn that connected the lows from January through March. A close below this support line along with the KO crossing below zero would be the trigger for a short trade.

Trade Entry

Chart 10.63 is a closeup of the same February–June time frame from the Freeport McMoRan example above. It shows that a trade could have been entered on April 16, 2010, as price closed below the support line, since KO had broken below zero 4 days earlier, on April 12. Remember, it is always wise to wait for price to confirm an oscillator signal of a change in direction by breaking either a support or a resistance line. An initial protective stop should have been placed above the April 6 high of 88.30.

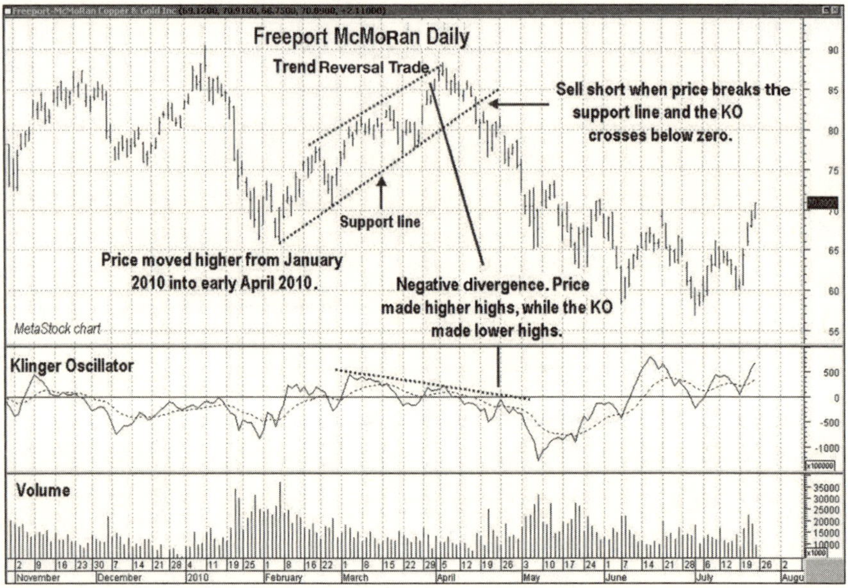

Chart 10.62 Cumulative Klinger Oscillator, Negative Divergence Trade Setup, Freeport McMoRan

Source: MetaStock

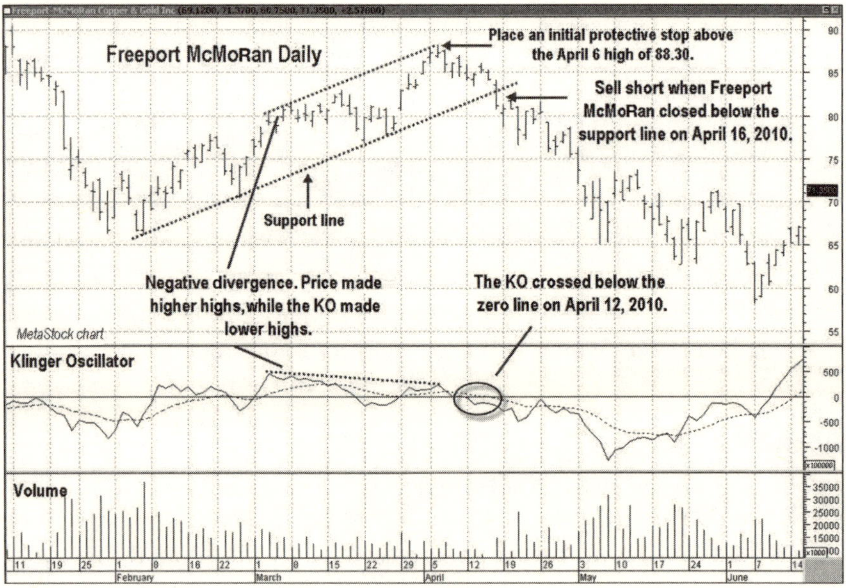

Chart 10.63 Cumulative Klinger Oscillator, Negative Divergence Trade Entry, Freeport McMoRan

Source: MetaStock

Trader Tips

The Klinger Oscillator, a centered oscillator designed to provide short-, intermediate-, and long-term analysis in one indicator, is best used for the following:

- Confirming the price trend
- Showing divergences against the price trend on new highs or lows
- Generating buy and sell signals with zero-line crossovers
- Functioning in a cumulative form for long-term looks at the market

A drawback of the Klinger Oscillator is that frequent short-term crossovers of the zero line can provide whipsaw trading signals.

Money Flow Index

The Money Flow Index (MFI) is a volume oscillator combining price momentum with volume; it is similar in calculation to the price-based Relative Strength Index (RSI). The incorporation of volume in MFI calculations, however, makes it a good measure of the strength of money flowing into and out of a security.

MFI compares positive money flow to negative money flow to create an oscillator that can be plotted with price. While most of the other volume oscillators presented have been zero-based, MFI is a banded oscillator, which means that it is plotted on a scale with clear overbought and oversold areas. The MFI is measured on a scale from 0 to 100 and is most commonly calculated using a 14-day period.

Formulation

The formula for computing MFI is a multistep process:

Typical price = (day high + day low + day close) / 3
Raw money flow = (typical price) × (volume)
Positive money flow = sum of raw money flow for the specified number of periods where typical price increased

Negative money flow = sum of raw money flow for the specified number of periods where typical price decreased

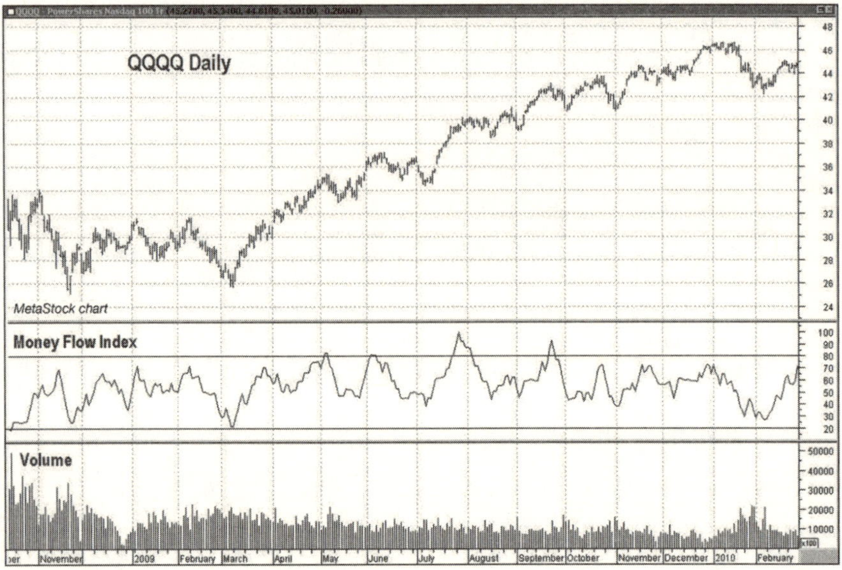

Chart 10.64 Money Flow Index, Nasdaq 100 Trust ETF

Source: MetaStock

$$\text{Money ratio} = \text{positive money flow} / \text{negative money flow}$$

$$\text{MFI} = 100 \times \frac{\text{positive money flow}}{\text{positive} + \text{negative money flow}}$$

The Money Flow Index is one of the most widely used volume-based indicators. Its computation over a 14-day period means that the price component has 14 data points to consider, making it a very robust indicator.

MFI is a great tool for identifying trends, overbought and oversold conditions, and divergences. All charts shown below use a 14-period Money Flow Index. Chart 10.64 shows a basic plot of the Money Flow Index for the Nasdaq 100 Trust ETF (QQQQ).

Trend Confirmation

As is common with many oscillators, the Money Flow Index shows different ranges in uptrends in comparison to downtrends. In uptrends, generally the MFI tends to make highs between 70 and 80 and lows between 35 and 45. The range shifts in downtrends, with highs between 60 and 70 and lows between 20 and 30. Chart 10.65 shows the MFI in an uptrend for the S&P 500 SPDR ETF (SPY). Note how the MFI tends to top at

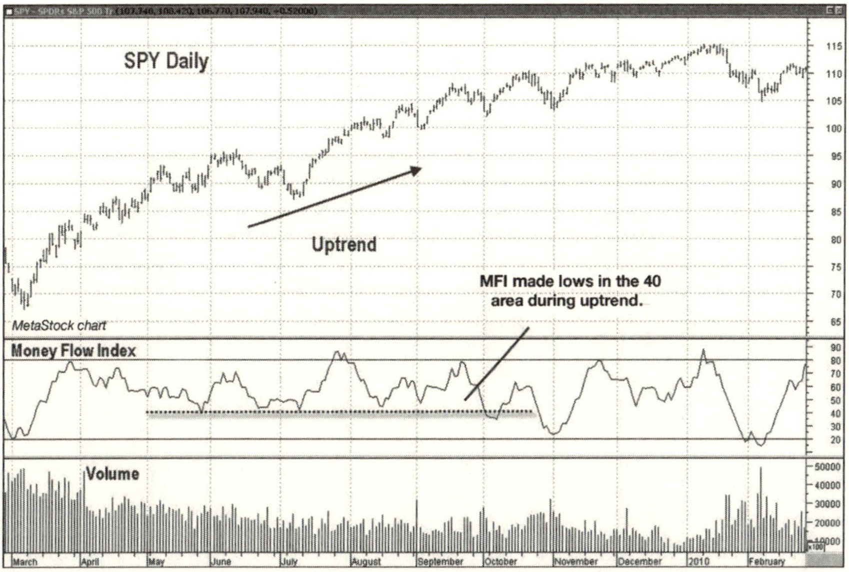

Chart 10.65 Money Flow Index during Uptrend, S&P 500 SPDR ETF

Source: MetaStock

around 80 and bottom at around 40. The different range characteristics of the MFI in a downtrend are illustrated in Chart 10.66 of the same ETF, SPY. Note how during 2008 the MFI topped in the 60 to 70 range and regularly hit the 20 area at oscillator lows.

Detecting Overbought and Oversold Conditions

The MFI is widely used for evaluating overbought and oversold conditions in a stock, index, or commodity as long as price and volume data can be provided. The security being analyzed is considered overbought when the MFI reaches levels of 80 or above, suggesting that a price correction is due. Conversely, when the MFI falls to levels of 20 or below, the security is considered oversold and due for a bounce higher in price. With zero-based oscillators, buy and sell signals are generated by crosses of the zero line, but with a banded oscillator, buy signals are generated when the oscillator crosses up from oversold territory (in this case, below 20), and sell signals are generated when the oscillator crosses down from overbought territory (in this case, 80). Chart 10.67 shows the overbought and oversold default zones for the MFI for Cisco Systems (CSCO).

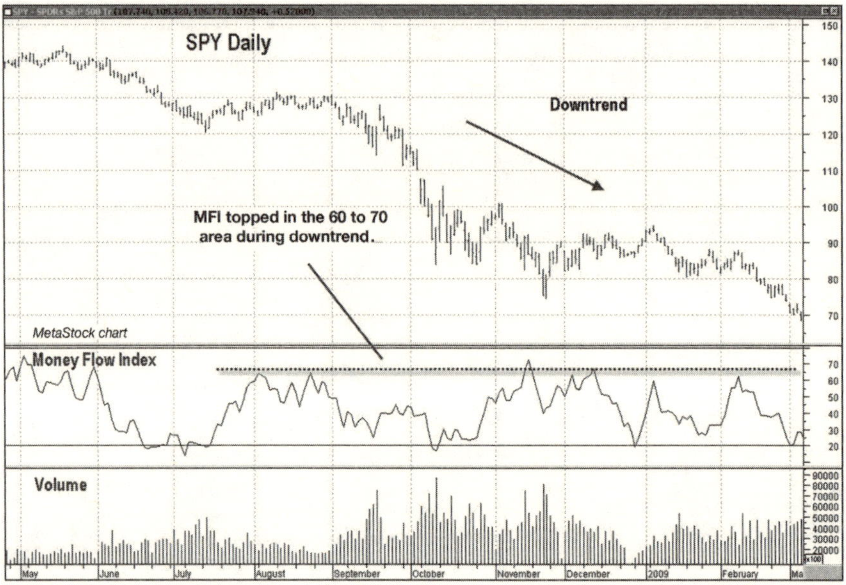

Chart 10.66 Money Flow Index during Downtrend, S&P 500 SPDR ETF

Source: MetaStock

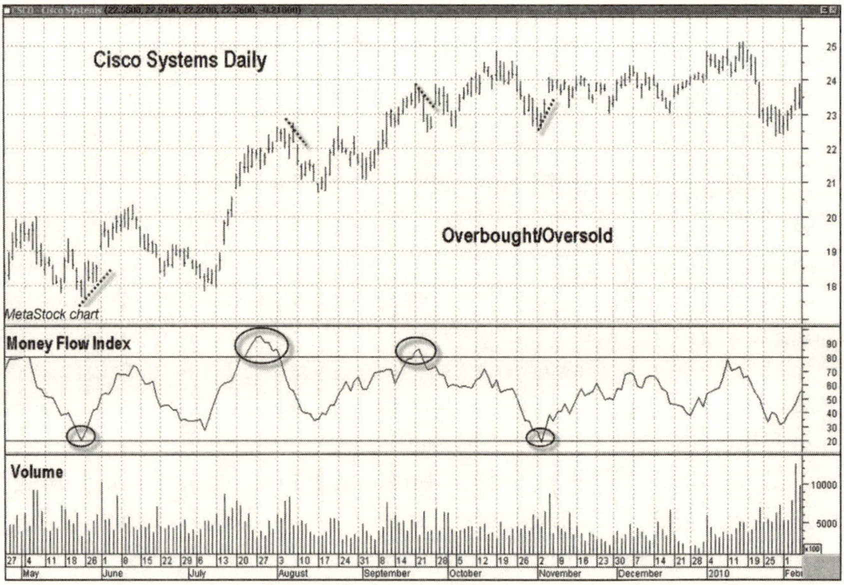

Chart 10.67 Money Flow Index, Overbought and Oversold Zones, Cisco Systems

Source: MetaStock

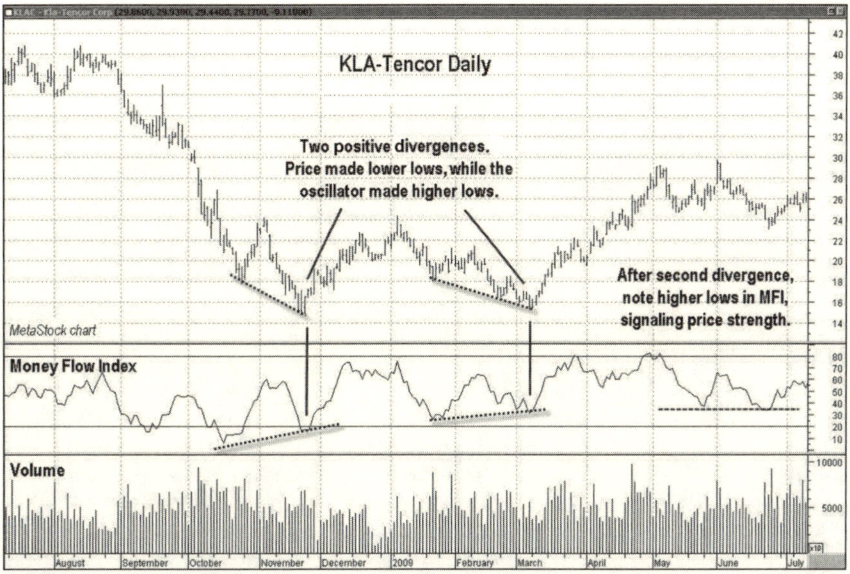

Chart 10.68 Money Flow Index, Positive Divergences, KLA-Tencor

Source: MetaStock

Divergences

The MFI is a great indicator for showing trend divergences. Positive divergences occur when price makes a new low while the MFI makes a higher low. The chart of KLA-Tencor (see Chart 10.68) shows two positive divergences on the same chart. Each divergence resulted in a strong rally. The second divergence occurred right at the March 2009 low.

The Money Flow Index also shows when a move higher may be near its end, alerting traders to take action if they so choose. Negative divergences occur when price makes a higher high but the MFI makes a lower high. Chart 10.69 shows a pair of negative divergences for the iShares Dow Jones U.S. Real Estate ETF (IYR), each followed by a sharp sell-off.

Money Flow Index with Other Indicators

Since the Money Flow Index is a banded oscillator, it is best paired with a cumulative trending indicator. In this example, MFI is paired with the Volume Price Trend indicator to identify the predominant trend. When Volume Price Trend is in an uptrend (i.e., with higher highs and higher lows), only buys will be considered. When Volume Price Trend is

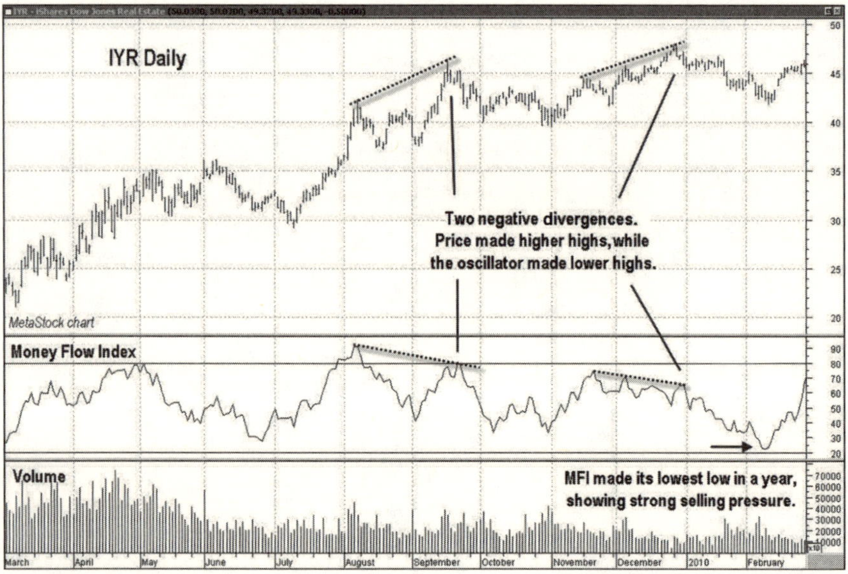

Chart 10.69 Money Flow Index, Negative Divergences, iShares Dow Jones U.S. Real Estate ETF

Source: MetaStock

in a downtrend (i.e., with lower highs and lower lows), only short sells will be considered.

A setup for a buy trade occurs when the Volume Price Trend is in an uptrend and the MFI pulls back below 30 (i.e., it is oversold). Chart 10.70 shows buys in the 2009 uptrend in the S&P SPDR Select Retail ETF (XRT). In this case, the bottom (oversold) boundary on the chart example has been increased from 20 to 30, as it has been our experience that the MFI tends to make higher bottoms in an uptrend. Some good buying opportunities on pullbacks are missed by leaving the bottom (oversold) boundary at 20 in an uptrending market. The buy would then be executed when the MFI crosses back above 30, or out of oversold territory. This allows traders to effectively buy the dips as prices pull back in an uptrend. The sell setup would be just the opposite of the buy, using crosses down from overbought territory in a downtrend.

Trade Setup

The MFI can be used to time trade entry either by using its overbought/oversold readings or by looking at divergences confirmed by price action. In the following example, we will look at the latter situation. The example

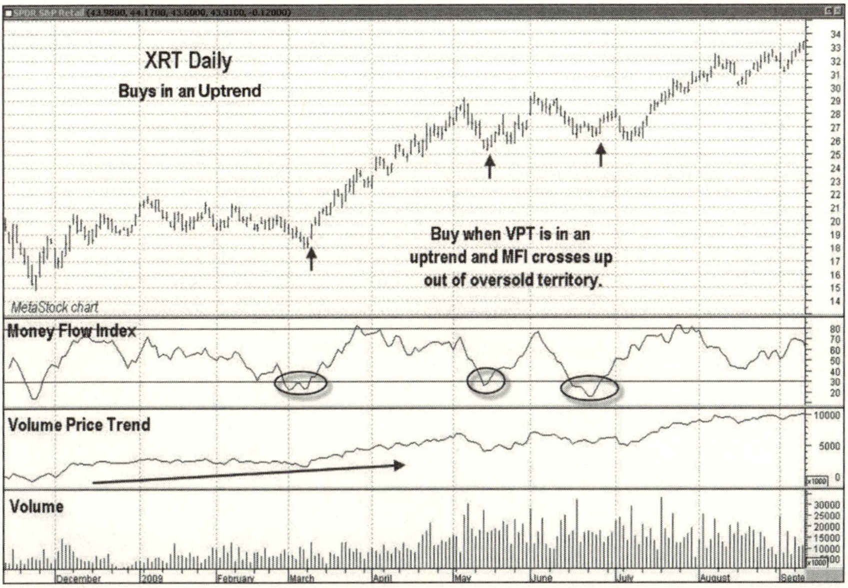

Chart 10.70 Money Flow Index Combined with Volume Price Trend, Buy Signals in Uptrend, S&P SPDR Select Retail ETF

Source: MetaStock

of continuous gold in Chart 10.71 shows how gold began an uptrend off its October 24, 2008, low. Price rallied up to a February 2009 high, after which a corrective pullback began. As the pullback developed, volume was not confirming the move lower; it decreased as price continued to fall. As price made its way down to its April 2009 low, volume decreased and the MFI made a higher low, forming a positive divergence. A downsloping resistance line was drawn that connected the highs from February to April. A close above that line would be a signal to execute a long trade and jump aboard the trend.

Trade Entry

The orderly pullback into the April 2009 low in the gold example, highlighted in Chart 10.72, showed that buyers were still in control and that the uptrend would resume once profit taking had run its course. Price closed above the downsloping resistance line on May 6, 2009. An initial protective stop should have been placed below the April 17 low of 865.60. In Chart 10.72, note how volume increased as price moved higher off its April low. This was yet another piece of evidence that buyers were in control of the gold market at that time.

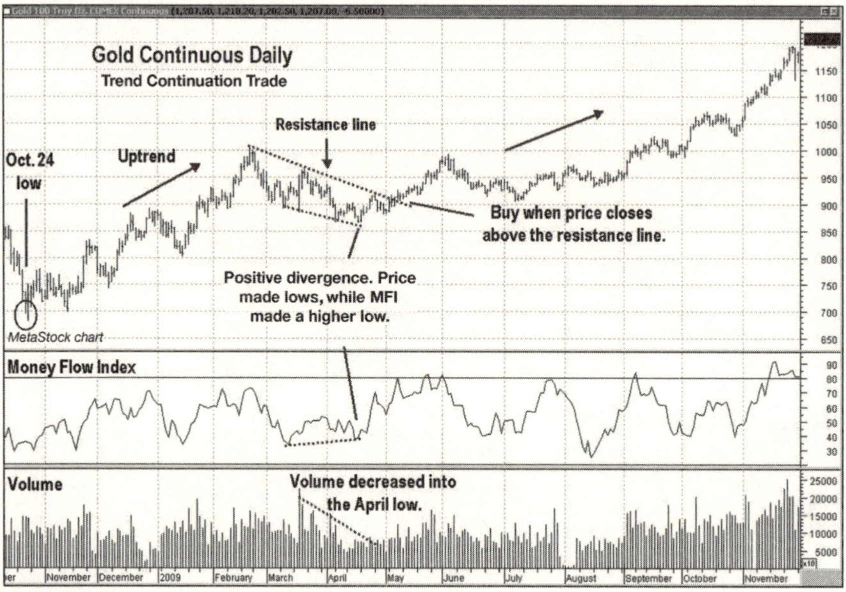

Chart 10.71 Money Flow Index, Trade Setup with Positive Divergence, Gold Continuous Daily

Source: MetaStock

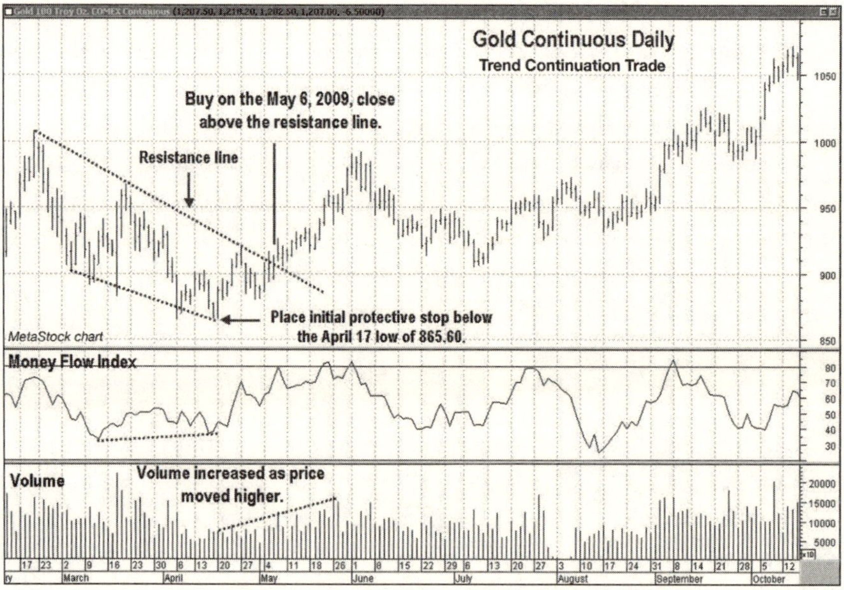

Chart 10.72 Money Flow Index, Trade Entry, Gold Continuous Daily

Source: MetaStock

Trader Tips

The Money Flow Index is one of the most widely used of the volume-based oscillators. Its robust price component complements its volume component to provide a greater depth of analysis than most price/volume oscillators. The Money Flow Index is used for the following:

- Confirming buying or selling pressure in a trend
- Showing trend divergences leading to potential reversals
- Indicating overbought and oversold market conditions
- Giving reliable buy and sell signals in the direction of the larger-degree trend

A drawback of the Money Flow Index is that it takes time to learn its characteristics in uptrends versus downtrends. The overbought/oversold levels often change, depending on the market trend. Traders should make sure to learn the tendencies of the MFI to top or bottom at certain levels, depending on the issue, market, and trend.

Volume Accumulation Oscillator

The Volume Accumulation Oscillator (VAO) is a trending oscillator that accumulates daily volume totals based on the day's close relative to the midpoint of the day's range. The VAO was developed by Marc Chaikin to address some of the shortcomings of On-Balance Volume and is a more sensitive indicator. While it is technically an oscillator, it is cumulative and thus exhibits many of the characteristics of an indicator.

Where On-Balance Volume assigns the entire volume for the day as positive or negative, depending on the close relative to the prior day's close, Chaikin wanted to see the position of the close each day in relation to the midpoint of the day's range. Closes below the midpoint of the daily range assign a negative value to the day's volume, and closes above the midpoint assign a positive value. How much of the volume is added to or subtracted from the running total depends on where the closing price is in relation to the day's midpoint. The only time the whole day's volume is given a positive value is when the close is at the day's high. The opposite is true for a close at the day's low.

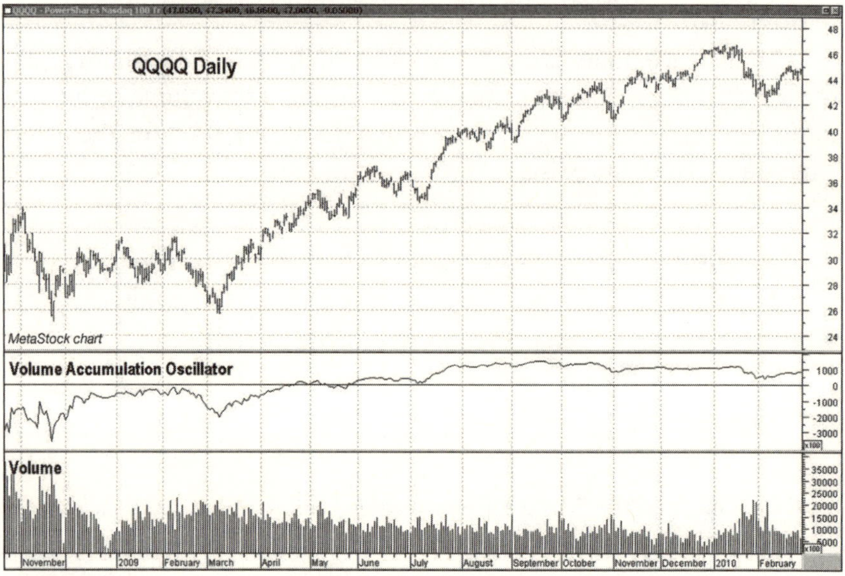

Chart 10.73 Volume Accumulation Oscillator, Nasdaq 100 Trust ETF

Source: MetaStock

Formulation

The formula for the VAO is as follows:

VAO = yesterday's VAO + (volume × {close – [(high + low) / 2]})

As with On-Balance Volume, the VAO is used for confirming market trends, showing divergences, and showing breakouts. Chart 10.73 shows a plot of the VAO for the Nasdaq 100 Trust ETF (QQQQ).

Trend Confirmation

VAO is primarily used as a trend confirmation oscillator. If the VAO is making higher highs and higher lows along with price, the VAO is confirming the uptrend. If the VAO is making lower highs and lower lows along with price, the VAO is confirming the downtrend. Chart 10.74 shows an uptrend of KLA-Tencor, confirmed by VAO.

VAO is also used to confirm downtrends and does so when it makes lower highs and lower lows along with price. Chart 10.75 shows a confirmed downtrend for Newmont Mining, with sellers firmly in control.

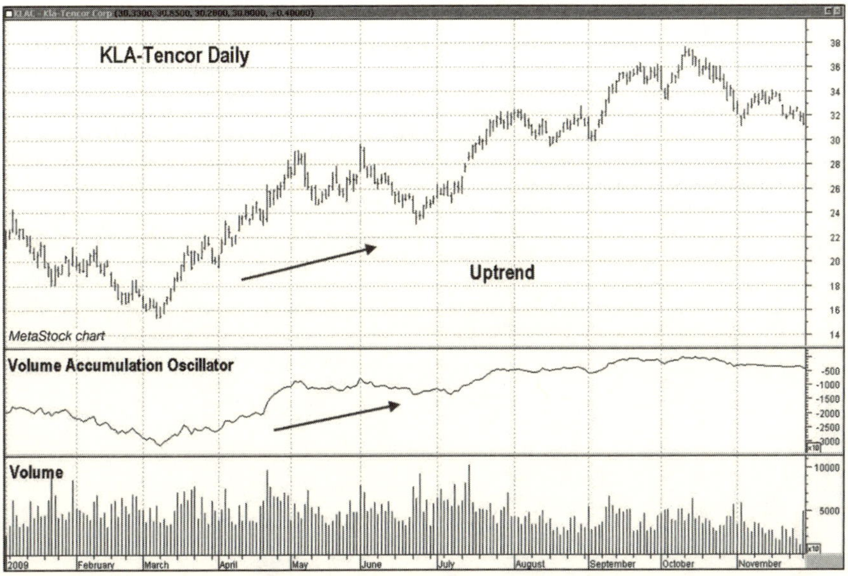

Chart 10.74 Volume Accumulation Oscillator Confirming Uptrend, KLA-Tencor

Source: MetaStock

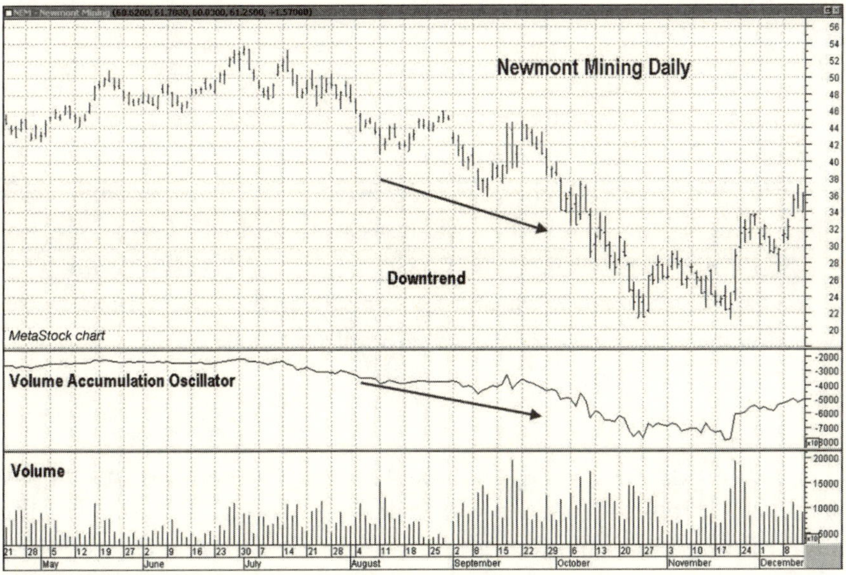

Chart 10.75 Volume Accumulation Oscillator Confirming Downtrend, Newmont Mining

Source: MetaStock

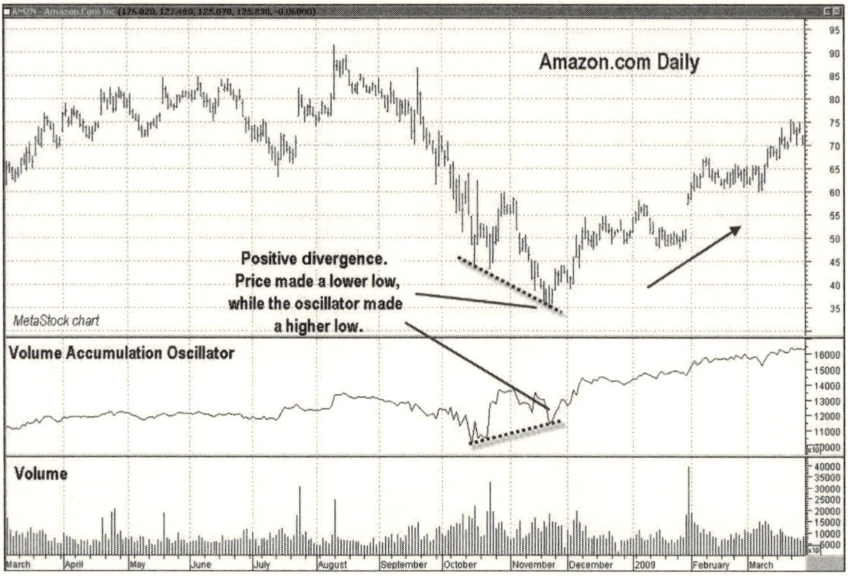

Chart 10.76 Volume Accumulation Oscillator, Positive Divergence, Amazon.com

Source: MetaStock

Divergences

The Volume Accumulation Oscillator also shows positive and negative divergences that can alert the trader when a change in price direction is due. Chart 10.76 shows a positive divergence for Amazon.com at the November 2009 low. Note how price made a lower low in November, while the VAO made a higher low. Negative divergences occur when price makes a higher high while the VAO makes a lower high. The example of the S&P SPDR Select Energy ETF (XLE) in Chart 10.77 shows how XLE made a slightly higher high from October 2009 to January 2010, while the VAO made a much lower high. A sharp sell-off followed.

Breakouts

The Volume Accumulation Oscillator is also a good tool to confirm price breakouts through resistance or breakdowns through support. For the S&P SPDR Select Financial ETF (XLF) in Chart 10.78, note how the VAO broke higher through overhead resistance (the dashed line) with XLF following the March 2009 low, which signaled a buyer push and a sharp rise in price. VAO also confirms downward breakdowns through support. Chart 10.79 shows how Cisco (CSCO) and the VAO both broke

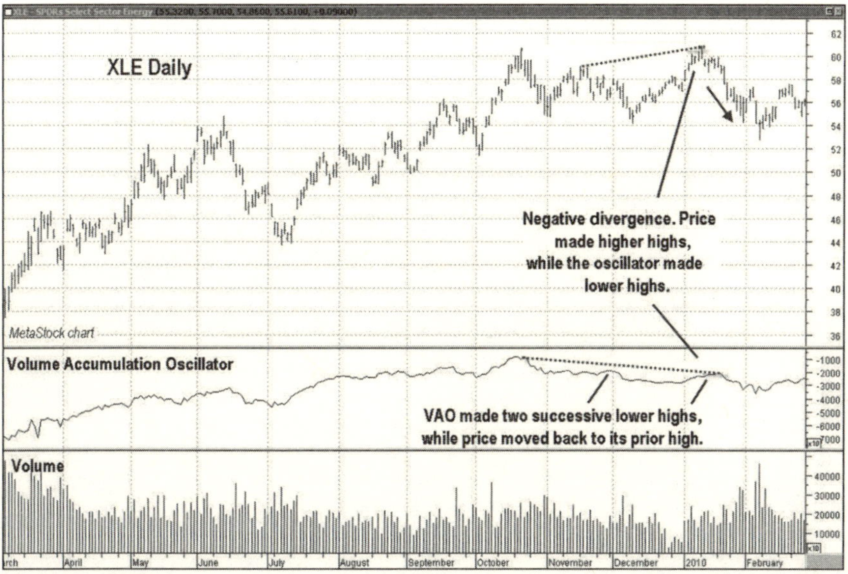

Chart 10.77 Volume Accumulation Oscillator, Negative Divergence, S&P SPDR Select Energy ETF

Source: MetaStock

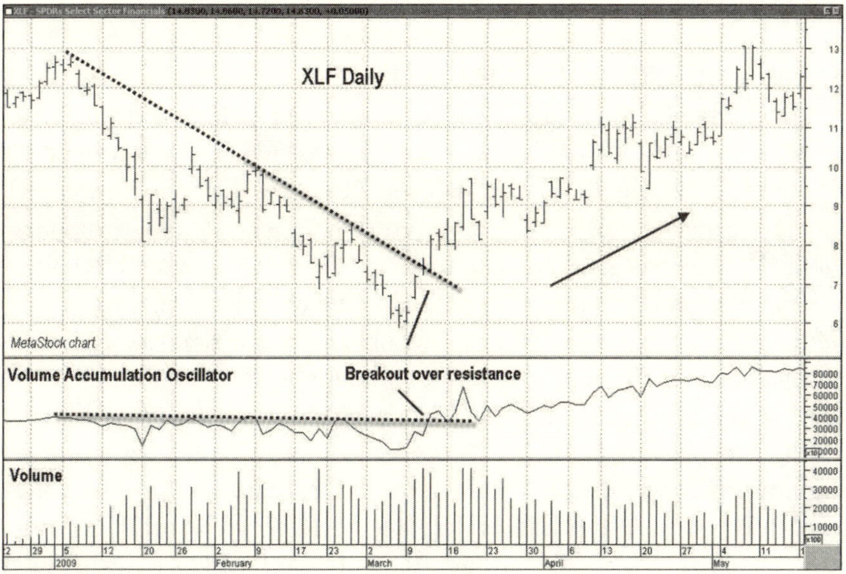

Chart 10.78 Volume Accumulation Oscillator, Upside Breakout, S&P SPDR Select Financial ETF

Source: MetaStock

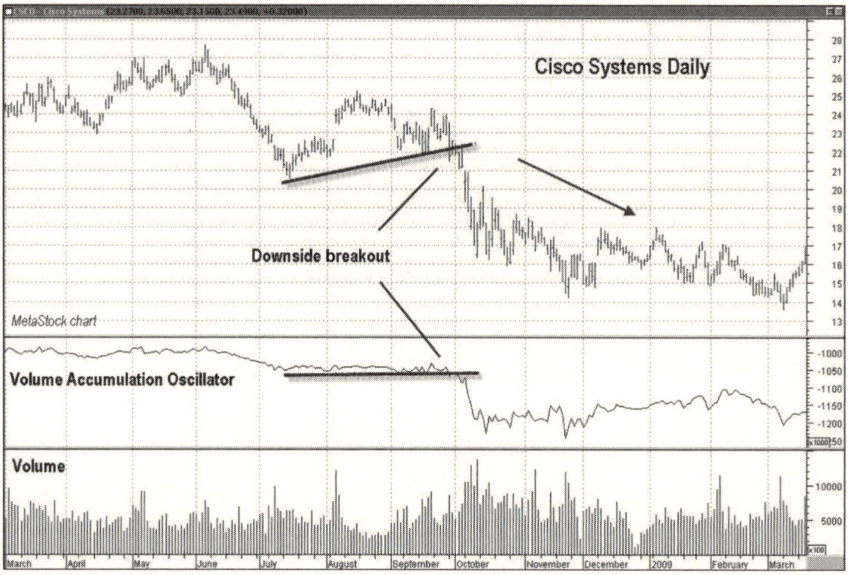

Chart 10.79 Volume Accumulation Oscillator, Downside Breakout, Cisco Systems

Source: MetaStock

their own support levels at the same time, providing confirmation of the downside break.

Combining VAO with Other Indicators

VAO is another trending oscillator that is best paired with an Overbought/Oversold Oscillator. In this case, the VAO is paired with a 10-period Williams %R, which is a price-based 10-period raw (not smoothed) stochastic oscillator plotted on an inverted scale. The volume component of the VAO gives a good read on trend health, which allows for its pairing with a price-based oscillator. As with all trending indicators, the direction of the VAO is used as a filter for buy or sell setups. A buy setup occurs when the VAO is trending higher (i.e., with higher lows) and the Williams %R is oversold (i.e., below −80). A buy is executed when the Williams %R crosses above −80. A short sell setup occurs when the VAO is trending lower (i.e., with lower highs) and the Williams %R is overbought (i.e., over −20). A short sale is executed when the Williams %R crosses below −20. The arrows on Chart 10.80, the S&P SPDR Select Energy ETF (XLE), show the buys (upward-pointing arrows) and short sales (downward-pointing arrows).

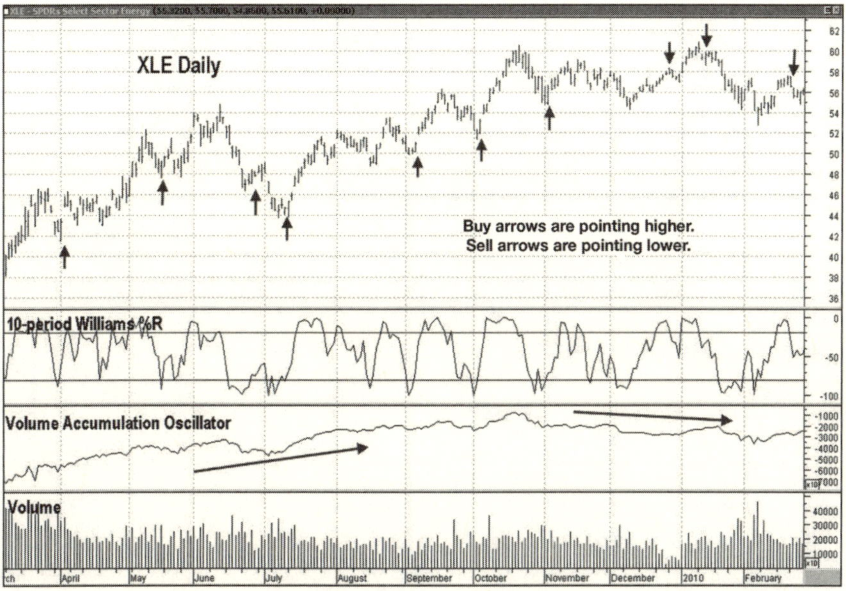

Chart 10.80 Volume Accumulation Oscillator Combined with Williams %R Stochastic, Buy Points, S&P SPDR Select Energy ETF

Source: MetaStock

Trade Setup

The VAO gives great clues that a trend is weakening and may be ready to reverse. In the JPMorgan Chase example in Chart 10.81, note how price moved higher into its April 15, 2010, high while the VAO made a much lower high, producing a glaring negative divergence. The volume bars plotted in the lower pane of the chart also provided confirmation that the buying pressure behind the advance was not very strong. A support line was drawn connecting the February–April lows, which would be the trigger line for a short trade on a price close below the line.

Trade Entry

The price of JPMorgan Chase closed below the support line on April 16, 2010 (see Chart 10.82). Note how volume spiked on April 16 as price broke below the support line. This provided additional confirmation that sellers had taken control at that point. An initial protective stop on the short sale should have been placed over the April 15 high of 48.20.

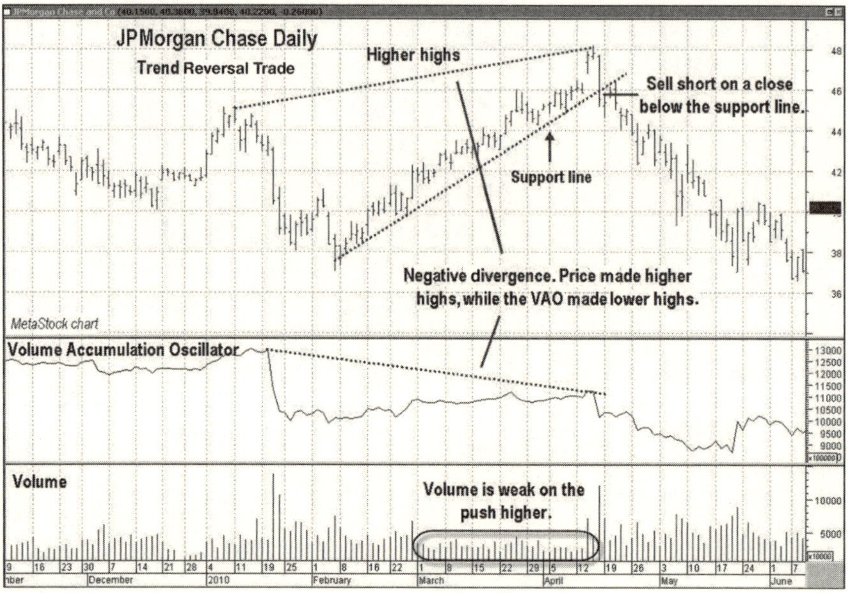

Chart 10.81 Volume Accumulation Oscillator, Trade Setup on Negative Divergence, JPMorgan Chase

Source: MetaStock

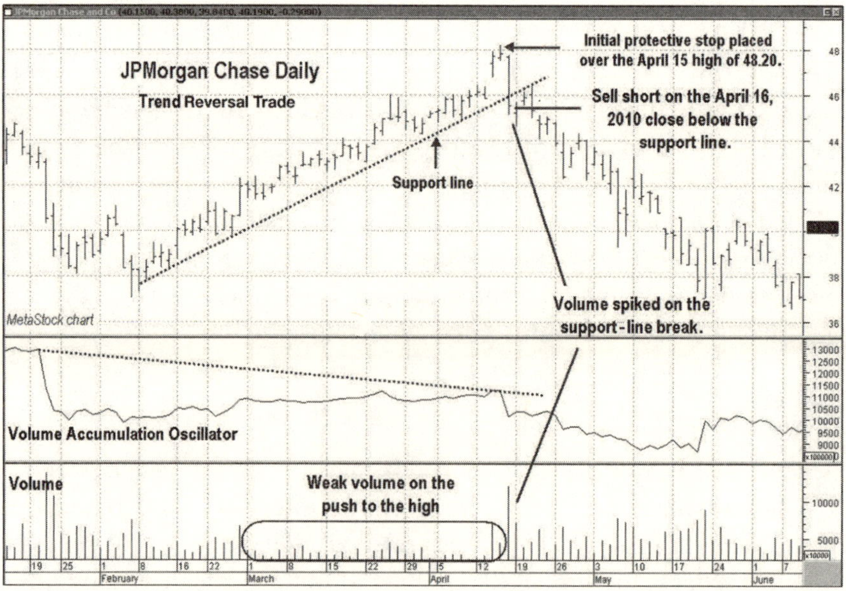

Chart 10.82 Volume Accumulation Oscillator, Trade Entry on Negative Divergence and Support-Line Break, JPMorgan Chase

Source: MetaStock

Trader Tips

The Volume Accumulation Oscillator is a versatile tool that is often used for the following:

- Confirming price trends with a sensitive read on accumulation and distribution
- Showing trend divergences
- Confirming price breakouts through resistance and support levels

Even though the VAO is classified as a centered oscillator, its cumulative nature causes zero-line crossovers to be much too late for use for the timing of market entries and exits. The scale can also be affected by the starting date of the data plot.

Percentage Volume Oscillator

The Percentage Volume Oscillator (PVO) measures the relationship between a shorter and longer EMA of volume.

Formulation

The PVO calculates a fast and slow EMA of volume, with the difference between the two moving averages divided by the slower plotted as a percentage on a single line. The oscillator scale includes a zero line, which is used to measure volume strength. Values above the zero line are believed to be strong enough to keep the current trend in force, while values below the zero line show a weakening trend on below-average volume.

$$\text{PVO} = \left[\frac{(\text{shorter EMA of volume} - \text{longer EMA of volume})}{\text{longer EMA of volume}}\right] \times 100$$

When the market is trending (either up or down), the PVO should be rising. When the PVO peaks and turns lower, a short-term change of direction is imminent. The PVO is used to confirm price trends and show divergences. The Nasdaq 100 Trust ETF (QQQQ) in Chart 10.83 shows a plot of the PVO. This example uses a 10-day period for the short moving average and a 25-day period for the longer-term moving average.

Trend Confirmation

The PVO confirms trends and is best for analyzing trends during their natural ebbs and flows in volume. The key in using the oscillator is to watch

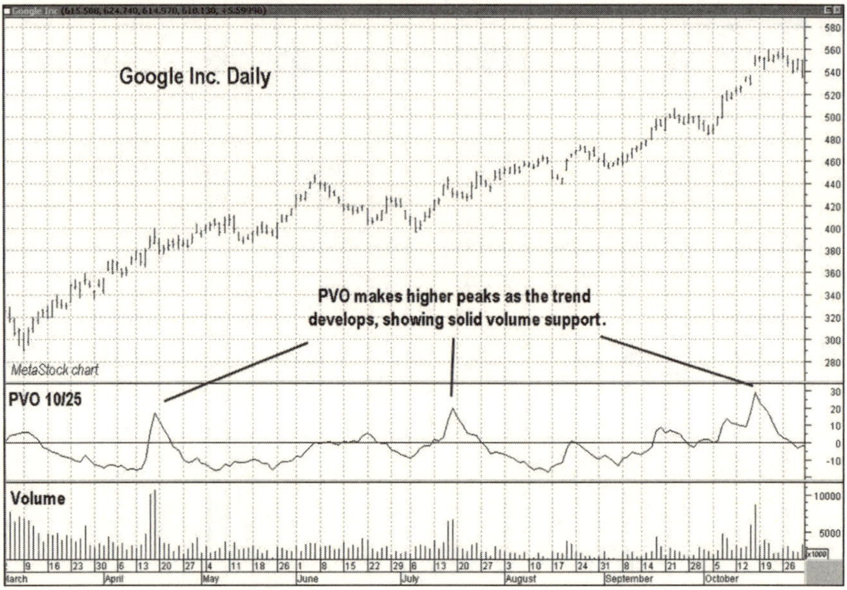

Chart 10.83 Percentage Volume Oscillator, Nasdaq 100 Trust ETF

Source: MetaStock

its behavior when price moves higher out of a pullback in an uptrend or breaks lower after a corrective phase in a downtrend. In either case, as the trend resumes, the oscillator should move higher, as the short-term burst in volume (the short-term moving average) comes in at a higher pace than the longer-term average.

Amazon.com in Chart 10.84 illustrates this concept. Note how the oscillator moves higher on up moves and pulls back on down moves. For this example, the pair of volume moving averages used in the oscillator are a 10-period, short-term moving average and a 25-period, longer-term moving average. Chart 10.85 is the same chart of Amazon.com, except that we now use shorter-term volume moving averages, which result in higher volatility. In this example, the short-term moving average is a 5-period average, and the longer-term moving average is a 15-period average. Notice how much more volatile and sensitive this oscillator is using short-time-frame parameters and showing more pronounced highs during the uptrend.

Divergences

The PVO shows divergences between price and volume momentum. Positive divergences occur when price makes a lower low accompanied by the Volume Oscillator, showing decreased selling pressure. Chart 10.86 shows a

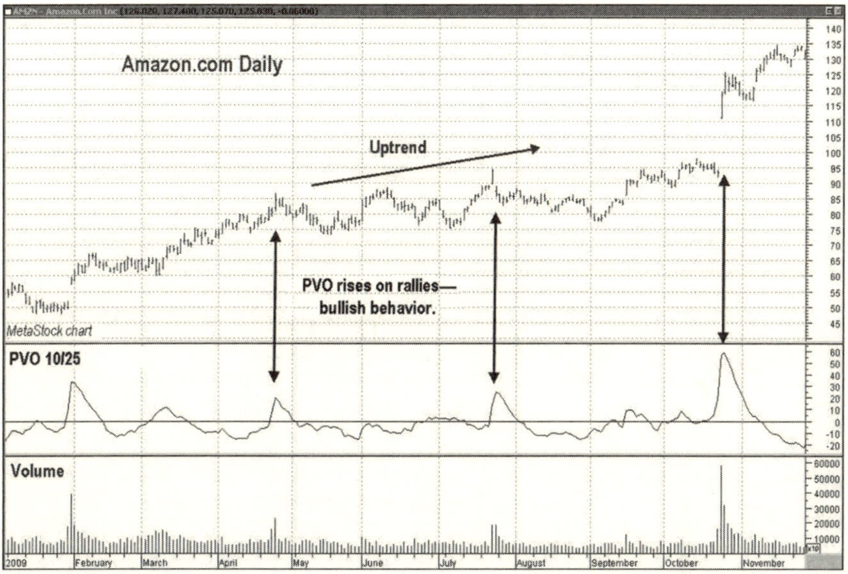

Chart 10.84 Percentage Volume Oscillator Confirming Uptrend, Amazon.com

Source: MetaStock

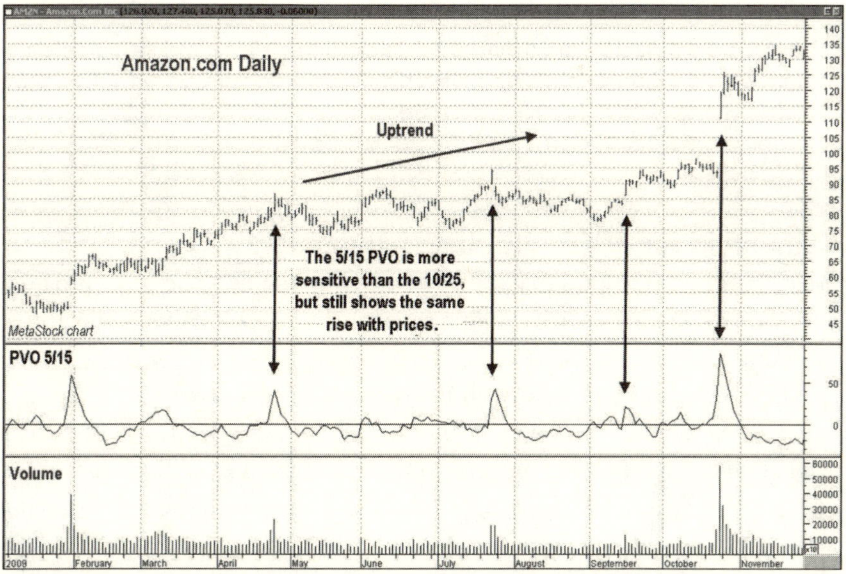

Chart 10.85 Percentage Volume Oscillator with 5-Day and 15-Day Moving Averages Confirming Uptrend, Amazon.com

Source: MetaStock

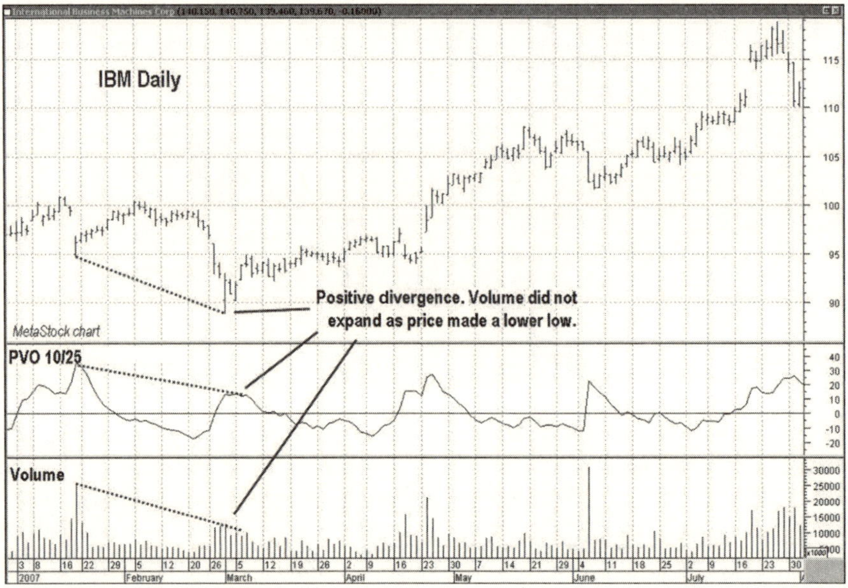

Chart 10.86 Percentage Volume Oscillator, Positive Divergence, IBM Corp.

Source: MetaStock

positive divergence for IBM at its November 2008 low. Note how selling pressure dried up as the volume push was not as great as it was at the October low.

This shows that buying support has weakened as price makes the new high and can warn that a correction is imminent. The PVO can also show a negative divergence with price highs when price makes a higher high but the PVO does not. Chart 10.87 shows a negative divergence for Microsoft (MSFT) in December 2009. A sharp sell-off followed.

Combining the PVO with Other Indicators

We discuss two examples of pairing the PVO: in the first, the PVO is paired with its own moving average; in the second, the PVO is paired with a price momentum oscillator.

The PVO can be plotted with its own moving average (i.e., 5-day simple moving average) to give a trader an additional signal that there is a change in the short-term volume trend. Note, however, in the chart of the Nasdaq 100 Trust ETF (QQQQ; Chart 10.88) how well the 5-day moving average trends with the oscillator, usually crossing over only when the oscillator appears ready to change direction. By using these crossovers and the position of prices, a trader can get a good read on whether buying pressure or selling pressure is developing.

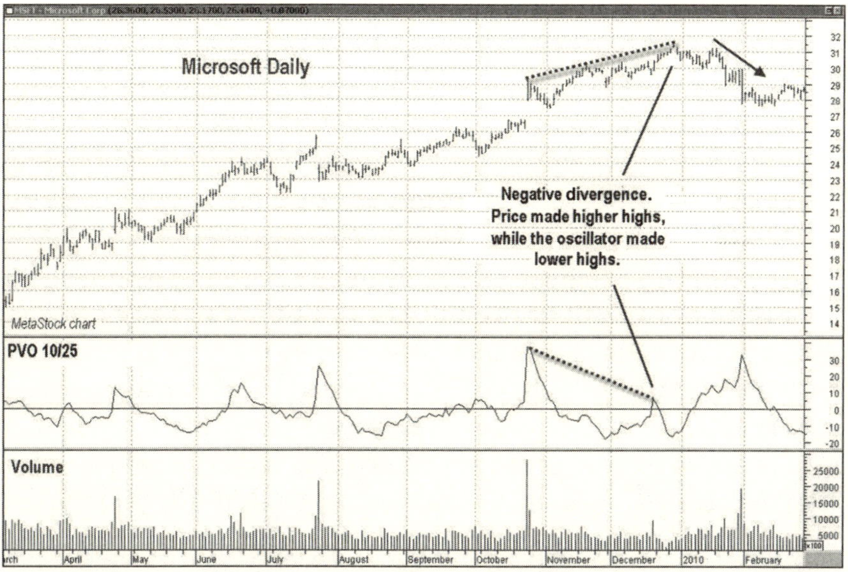

Chart 10.87 Percentage Volume Oscillator, Negative Divergence, Microsoft Corp.

Source: MetaStock

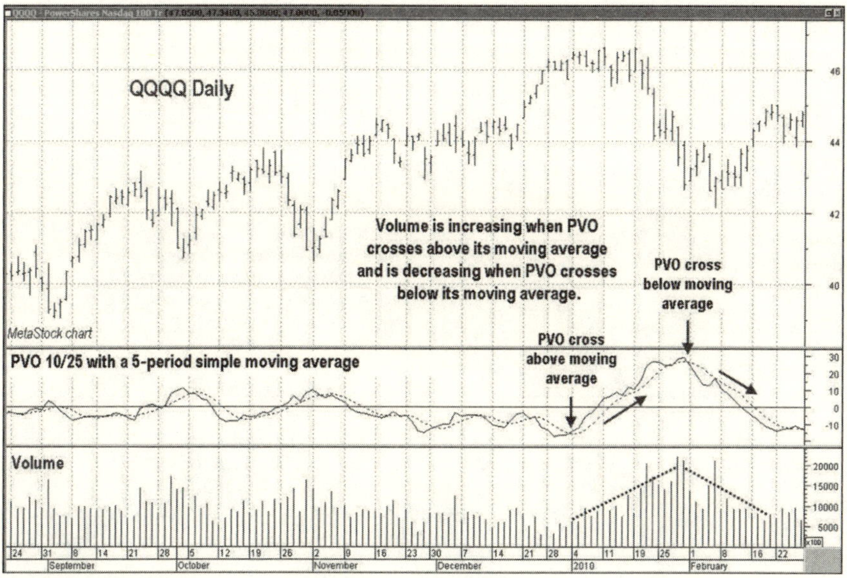

Chart 10.88 Percentage Volume Oscillator with Its Own 5-Day Moving Average, Nasdaq 100 Trust ETF

Source: MetaStock

The PVO also gives buy and sell signals when paired with a price momentum oscillator. The volume spikes that usually accompany sell-offs in uptrends can provide great buying opportunities when price rebounds and the uptrend resumes. In Chart 10.89, again for the Nasdaq 100 Trust ETF (QQQQ), the PVO is paired with a 9-period Relative Strength Index (RSI), which is a price momentum oscillator. The RSI will be used to define a trade setup and act as a trigger. In the chart, QQQQ is in an uptrend in late 2009. Since QQQQ is in an uptrend, waiting for a 9-period RSI to cross below 30 for a setup may be a fruitless endeavor, as this momentum oscillator is also one that experiences a range shift between uptrends and downtrends. The RSI tends to bottom at 40 in uptrends, so the oversold level was reset to 40 from the more common setting of 30. As expected, the PVO spiked higher on sell-offs. A buy setup is achieved when the PVO spikes and the RSI falls below the 40 level (oversold). A buy is executed when the PVO begins to turn lower and RSI crosses back above 40.

Note the setups and buy trades as marked in Chart 10.89. Remember, it is very important to know if an oscillator is subject to range shift and

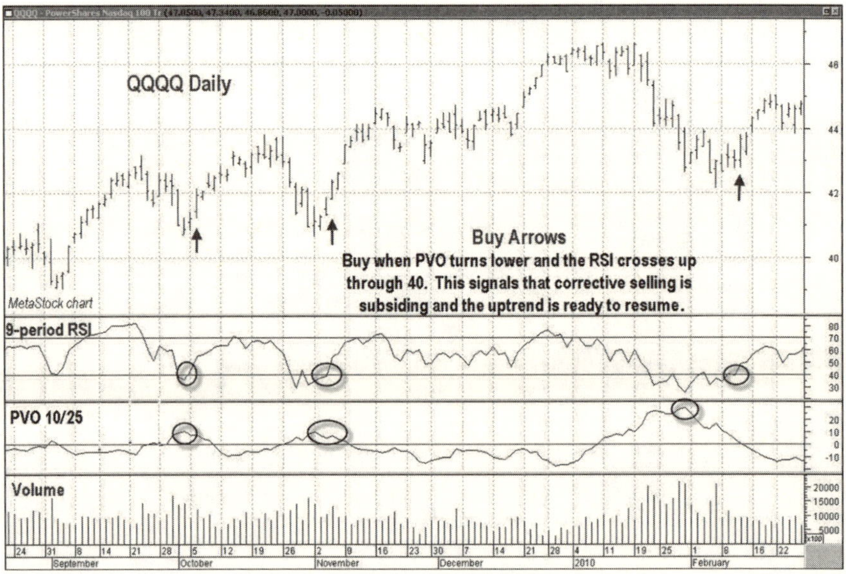

Chart 10.89 Percentage Volume Oscillator with 9-Period RSI, Buy Signals, Nasdaq 100 Trust ETF

Source: MetaStock

what are its parameters in an uptrend or downtrend. This allows a trader to reset overbought and oversold ranges to existing market conditions.

Trade Setup

One of the best uses for the PVO is to detect volume and price divergences. The PVO can act as a leading signal in short-term moves.

In Chart 10.90, the PVO was used to display a very strong divergence between price and volume for Google as it moved toward its January 2010 high. The PVO calculation in this example used a combination of a 10-day and a 25-day exponential moving average. Note how it made a much lower peak in December 2009 as compared to its October high. This was a sure sign that buying pressure was weakening. That fact was reinforced further when the oscillator slipped below its zero line as price made its final peak. The volume plot in the bottom frame also confirmed weakening buying pressure, as volume totals were very low during the final rally phase into the January high. A support line could have been drawn connecting the lows of the final leg higher from October 2009 into January 2010. A short sell could have been initiated once price confirmed this weakness by closing below its upsloping support line.

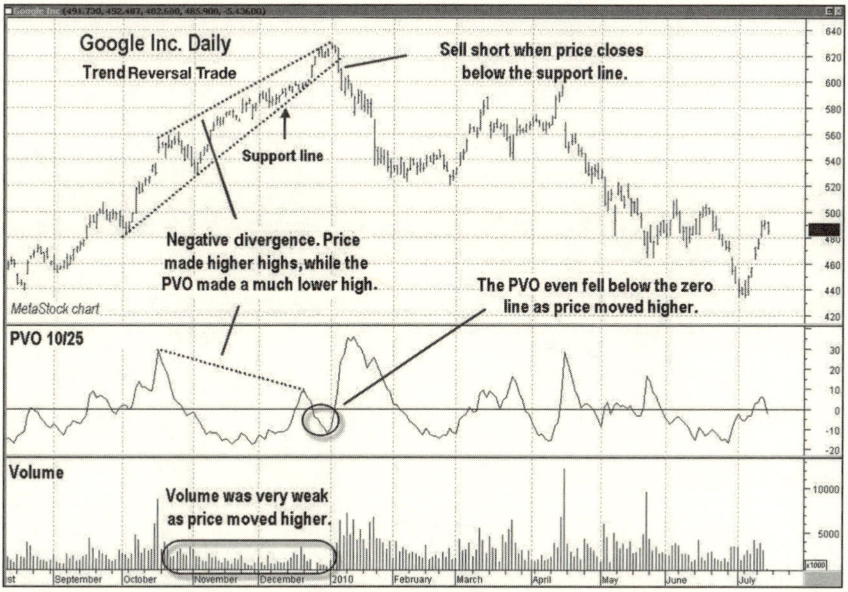

Chart 10.90 Percentage Volume Oscillator, Trend Reversal Trade Setup, Google Inc.

Source: MetaStock

Trade Entry

As the price of Google continued higher throughout December, it was obvious that buying pressure was lagging (see Chart 10.91). That would have been a great setup for aggressive traders. The only thing to do at this point was to wait for price action to give a signal that a trend change was imminent.

Using the support line that connected the October–January lows gives us a clear-cut line that when crossed signals an entry point. On January 6, 2010, price closed below the support line, giving a signal to enter a short position. An initial protective stop should have been placed over the January 4 high of 629.51. Note in Chart 10.91 how volume increased (shown by both volume and the PVO) as price moved lower, a sure sign that the trend was changing and sellers were in control.

Trader Tips

The Percentage Volume Oscillator is used for the following:

- Verifying trends based on the PVO pattern
- Confirming trends
- Showing trend divergences
- Alerting to a change of direction

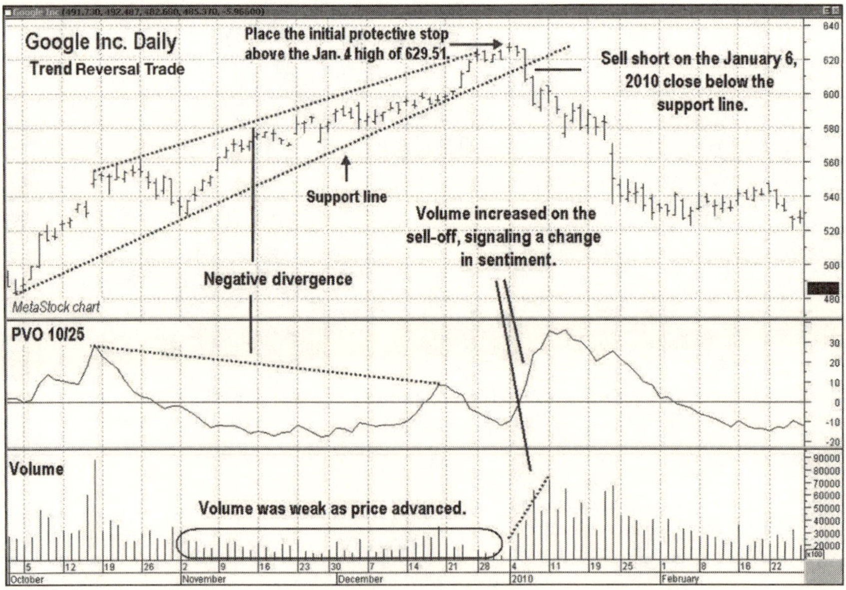

Chart 10.91 Percentage Volume Oscillator, Trend Reversal Trade Entry, Google Inc.

Source: MetaStock

The Percentage Volume Oscillator may at times be volatile and choppy, giving false or whipsaw signals.

Summary

Indicator	Description	Uses and Time Frames
Chaikin Accumulation/ Distribution Oscillator	An oscillator formed by using the difference between exponential moving averages of the Accumulation/ Distribution line	—Confirms the price trend, shows trend divergences, and generates buy and sell signals on zero-line crossovers. It can sometimes cause whipsaw trades with frequent zero-line crossovers. Also, it does not account for price gaps. —It is a short- to intermediate-term oscillator.
Chaikin Money Flow	The total of the Accumulation/Distribution line over *n* periods divided by the volume over *n* periods (*n* is usually defaulted to 21 periods)	—Confirms the price trend, shows trend divergences, and generates buy and sell signals on zero-line crossovers. It does not account for price gaps. —It is a short- to intermediate-term oscillator.
Demand Index	Combines price and volume in such a way that it is thought to be a leading indicator of price action	—Confirms the price trend, shows trend divergences, and generates buy and sell signals on zero-line crossovers. Its calculation is very complex. It can also be very choppy in shorter time frames, causing whipsaw signals. —It is a short- to intermediate-term oscillator.

(Continued)

Indicator	Description	Uses and Time Frames
Ease of Movement	Shows the relationship between a security's price change and its volume	—Confirms the price trend, shows trend divergences, and generates buy and sell signals on zero-line crossovers. It needs smoothing. —It is a short- to intermediate-term oscillator.
Force Index	Measures the force of buying pressure behind advances and the force of selling pressure behind declines	—Shows trend divergences and generates buy and sell signals on zero-line crossovers. It does not show trend characteristics as well as most oscillators. —It is a short- to intermediate-term oscillator.
Herrick Payoff Index	Measures the flow of money into or out of futures contracts	—Confirms the price trend, shows trend divergences, and generates buy and sell signals on zero-line crossovers. It needs Open Interest in its calculation, which limits the scope of its use to futures. —It is a short- to intermediate-term oscillator.
Klinger Oscillator	Developed to provide both short-term and long-term analysis of price and volume trends	—Confirms the price trend, shows trend divergences, and generates buy and sell signals on zero-line crossovers. It can cause whipsaw signals with frequent zero-line crossovers. —It is a short- to long-term oscillator.

Indicator	Description	Uses and Time Frames
Money Flow Index	Measures the force of buying pressure behind advances and the force of selling pressure behind declines	—Confirms the price trend, shows trend divergences, and shows overbought and oversold conditions in the market. It doesn't always reach default overbought or oversold levels (80/20), depending on the price trend. —It is a short- to intermediate-term oscillator.
Volume Accumulation Oscillator	Attempts to show price trend based on the price close in its daily range combined with volume	—Confirms the price trend, shows trend divergences, and confirms price breakouts. —It is an intermediate- to long-term oscillator.
Percentage Volume Oscillator	Uses the percent difference between two exponential volume moving averages to show periods of strong or weak volume	—Confirms the price trend and shows trend divergences. It can be volatile and choppy at times, which can reduce its reliability. —It is a short-term oscillator.

Chapter 11

DEVELOPING TACTICAL VOLUME OVERLAYS

The volume indicators and oscillators we examined in Chapters 8 through 10 each offered its unique perspective toward identifying trend direction, strength, and market conviction. In Chapter 7 we explained various parameters that might influence indicator selection for our Volume Analysis. In this chapter, we discuss how traders and active fund managers can develop these volume-based tools to create *tactical volume* overlays to assist in trend identification, timing, and short-term trading.

Whether trading positions are rebalanced quarterly or taken intraday, identifying the current trend direction and robustness is crucial to risk assessment and ultimately to profitability. It is difficult to overlook the importance of volume in this equation. This chapter will describe the utility of volume overlay systems in trend identification, short-term trading, and timing and suggest parameters and guidance for designing them as complementary components of your preferred trading strategy.

The Importance of Tactical Overlay Systems

A good tactical trading overlay runs on its own, without interfering in the selection process or trading style of a trader or fund manager. The purpose of a tactical overlay is not to catch every twist and turn in the market but to keep traders on the right side of market trends. Having a trustworthy overlay serves as a barometer of prevailing general market conditions and tells a trader when to increase risk exposure or when to reduce it.

Combining volume indicators is a good place to begin to view the synergies used in these components. Our first set of indicator combinations serves to identify a prevailing trend using longer-term indicators and time frames useful to both traders and fund managers.

Trend Identification Overlays

When selecting an indicator to use in a basic intermediate- to longer-term Trend Identification Overlay, it is best to start with a cumulative indicator that trends well with price but can also reveal trend strength. Pairing a trending indicator with a moving average to generate signals is the beginning of a very basic overlay structure. For this example, we will combine Accumulation/Distribution (see Chapter 9) with a simple moving average that generates signals as the indicator crosses above and below its own moving average. When choosing a moving average, select one that does not move in exact symmetry with your chosen indicators, but at the same time does not lag or fail to generate strong crossover signals when the market shifts. There are many techniques for selecting moving average lengths, including using the Fibonacci numbers. For this example, we will keep it simple and use a 40-week SMA as an equivalent to a 200-day SMA, which many portfolio managers and intermediate- and longer-term traders rely upon.

Although Accumulation/Distribution trends well with price, it can appear choppy at times, giving brief, false crossover signals when paired with its 40-week SMA. Chart 11.1 displays the minor whipsaw signals produced by the A/D line in 2008. To help reduce these whipsaw periods, we will add a 40-week SMA to price. Buy signals are generated when the A/D line and price both close above their 40-week moving average. This provides price confirmation for indicator signals, a core idea that we have discussed throughout our Volume Analysis.

Chart 11.2 shows how this simple Trend Identification Volume Overlay works. Traders should reduce risk when both the A/D crosses and price closes below the 40-week moving average. Risk should be increased when the A/D and price cross above their 40-week moving average. Our example using the S&P 500 displays how even managers and traders who select positions based purely on fundamentals can benefit from a simple tactical volume-trend-following system to keep them on the right side of market trends. An overlay component such as this works independently and acts as a "risk guide" to alert traders to shifts in trend direction.

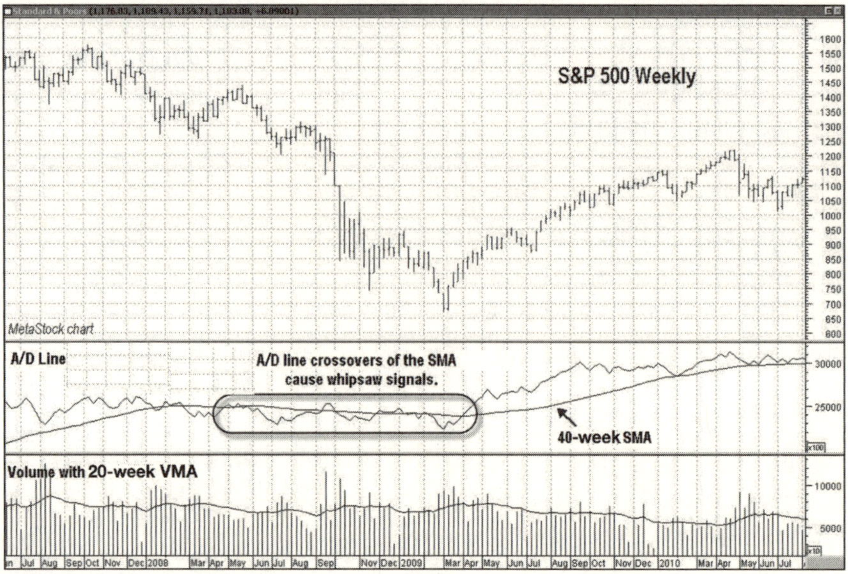

Chart 11.1 Trend Identification Overlay A/D Line with its 40-Week SMA, S&P 500 Index

Source: MetaStock

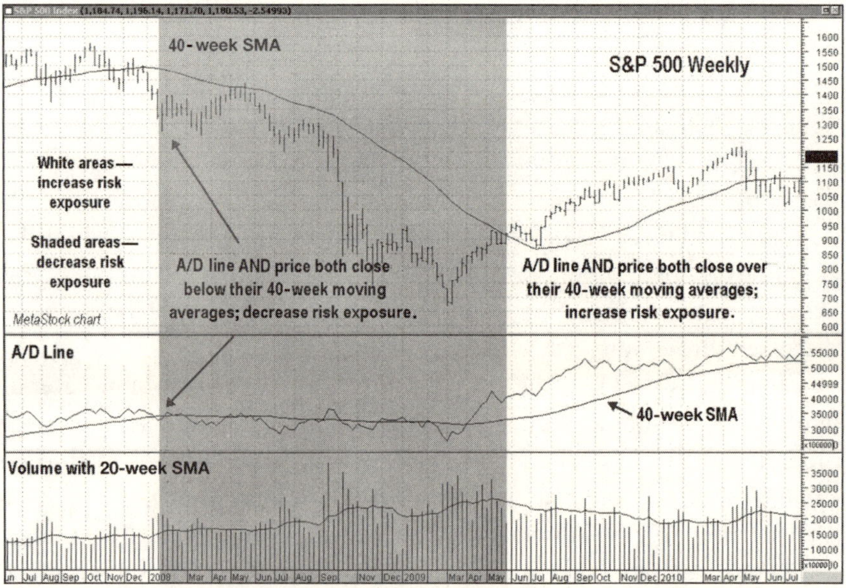

Chart 11.2 Trend Identification Volume Overlay A/D, Price, and 40-week SMA, S&P 500 Index

Source: MetaStock

Adding Additional Overlays Features

The beauty of tactical volume overlays lies in their flexibility. More indicators can be added to create additional opportunities within the macro trend. For example, a second, faster indicator could be added to the A/D line in the chart for the S&P 500 to try to exploit trading opportunities within macro trends.

Chart 11.3 covers the same time frame for the S&P 500 as the one in Chart 11.2, only this time the Klinger Oscillator (KO; see Chapter 10) has been added as a second volume overlay indicator. The Klinger Oscillator is a "faster" short- to intermediate-term indicator that generates more signals, showing more active traders when it may be a good time to add risk exposure or attempt to catch countertrend rallies. The Klinger Oscillator gives a positive signal (meaning that it is ok to add risk) when it crosses above its center or zero line. Although the darker-shaded areas in May 2008 and January 2009 seem very narrow, remember it is a weekly time frame, which means that the narrow bands are actually periods lasting two to three weeks.

The combination of the Accumulation/Distribution line along with price continues to act as the overall trend determinant. In this new synergy, however,

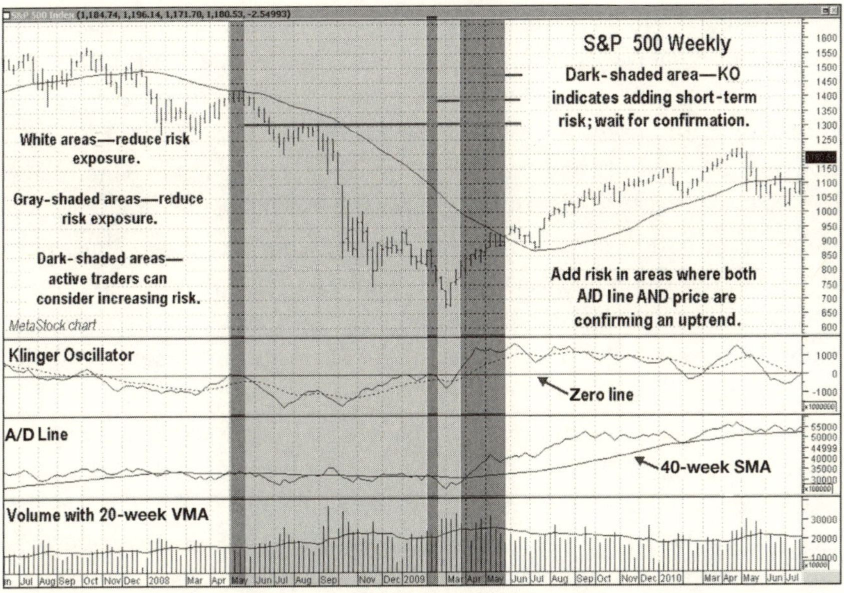

Chart 11.3 Overlay of Indicators across Multiple Time Frame Signals, S&P 500 Index

Source: MetaStock

when A/D and price are below their respective moving averages, positive signals from the Klinger Oscillator can be viewed as short-term opportunities to increase risk exposure. The understanding is that short-term risk will be reduced once the Klinger Oscillator returns to a negative signal as long as A/D and price remain below their moving averages.

The lightly shaded areas in Chart 11.3 show when the A/D and price are on a negative signal (i.e., below their 40-week SMA). The darker-shaded areas represent time periods during the downtrend in which the Klinger Oscillator moved above its zero line, indicating that adding more short-term risk exposure at this time would have been appropriate. The unshaded areas represent the time periods when A/D and price were above their 40-week SMA, signaling an uptrend.

Pairing Accumulation/Distribution with the Klinger Oscillator in this example allows more active traders to try to exploit countertrend moves. Notice in Chart 11.3 how the positive signal generated by the Klinger Oscillator in May 2008 was rather short lived before the downtrend resumed, while the positive signal given in March 2009 was actually the beginning of a major trend reversal. What clues would the market have given that a real trend reversal was underway rather than a rollover and resumption of the previous downtrend? For the answer to that question, we turn to our Volume Analysis. Chart 11.4 includes a plot of volume that displays the sentiment and conviction of traders at the time of each signal. The positive May 2008 signal was accompanied by weak volume that was mostly flat, if not declining, as price moved higher. This was a signal that there was very little conviction behind the price movement and that the larger-degree downtrend would likely resume. The signal generated at the March 2009 low, however, was a different story. Notice how volume had really picked up as price bottomed and reversed higher. This was a sign that trader sentiment was changing and that this signal was more powerful. Ten weeks after the Klinger Oscillator signal (the end of the shaded area), Accumulation/Distribution and price crossed above their moving averages, signaling that the trend had indeed reversed.

Although development and use of tactical volume overlays can help preserve capital and increase returns, the development of more customized parameters will require a period of back testing and trial and error. For example, in the previous charts, why not use a 21- or 55-week moving average with Accumulation/Distribution? Why use the Klinger Oscillator and not the Money Flow Index? These types of decisions are typical ones a trader must consider when customizing a tactical volume overlay. While the beauty of tactical overlay systems lies in their versatility, their development

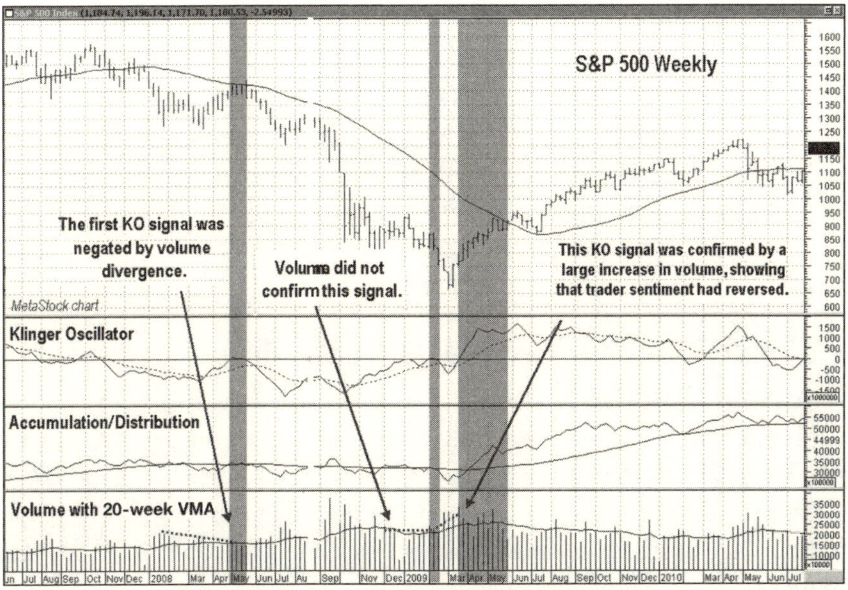

Chart 11.4 Trend Identification Overlay with Volume, S&P 500 Index

Source: MetaStock

requires structural planning and effort. Most trading and charting programs will facilitate the development of an overlay; the rewards are worth the effort.

Time-Frame Considerations

As a starting point in developing a basic overlay structure with multiple volume indicators, consider pairing indicators across multiple time frames to identify the direction and strength of a tradeworthy trend.

1. *Use a longer-term cumulative type of volume-based indicator to measure the strength and sustainability of the overall trend.* Examples of such indicators are On-Balance Volume, Volume Price Trend, Intraday Intensity, and Accumulation/Distribution. Broad market indicators such as the Cumulative Volume Index are great to measure the volume patterns for the overall health of the broad market.
2. *Use an intermediate-term price/volume indicator to capture shorter-term price movements that can alert the trader when to expect "bumps in the road" (i.e., trend corrections or reversals).* Examples of such indicators are Money Flow Index, Force Index, Demand Index, Chaikin Money Flow, and Ease of Movement.

3. *Use a short-term indicator to identify when the time is right to either enter a position in the direction of the overall trend or attempt a trade against the trend.* Because of their time-frame versatility, the Leibovit Volume Reversal indicator, Klinger Oscillator, and Percentage Volume Oscillator are well suited for this purpose.
4. *Set the volume moving average to a preferred time frame to alert to change points in market direction.*

Leibovit Volume Reversal, a Versatile Tactical Volume Overlay

One methodology used frequently in our tactical volume overlays is the Leibovit Volume Reversal indicator. The Volume Reversal is an easy indicator overlay to implement in that it has no look-back periods to set, has no moving averages to cross, and works across multiple time frames. Basically, either you have a Volume Reversal—or you don't.

In the example that follows, we present a basic overlay structure using the VR as it is applied to a sector proxy such as the iShares Dow Jones Real Estate Index Fund ETF (IYR). A Positive VR signals the appropriate time to add exposure in the real-estate REIT space, while a Negative VR signals a trader or manager to consider reducing risk exposure. Note that a basic VR overlay allows for VR signals to appear on the chart as they are generated.

Chart 11.5 of IYR covers the same 3-year period as the broader market example of the S&P 500 Index in Chart 11.3, only in this case we analyze it in a monthly time frame. Note that there were only three signals in over three years on this chart. A Negative VR formed in May 2007, a Positive VR posted in April 2009, and a Negative VR was again generated in May 2010. Each of these signals served as an alert to take a position or increase, reduce, or hedge portfolio risk.

Another structural possibility for a trend identification overlay might utilize the Leibovit VR alone or in a combination with other longer-time-frame indicators to create a simple and easy-to-use alert.

Trading Overlays

In this section we will examine a few volume indicator/oscillator combinations that are used to create overlays for the purpose of identifying active trading opportunities. We encourage your exploration of synergies among multiple combinations that can then be applied to your current trading strategy.

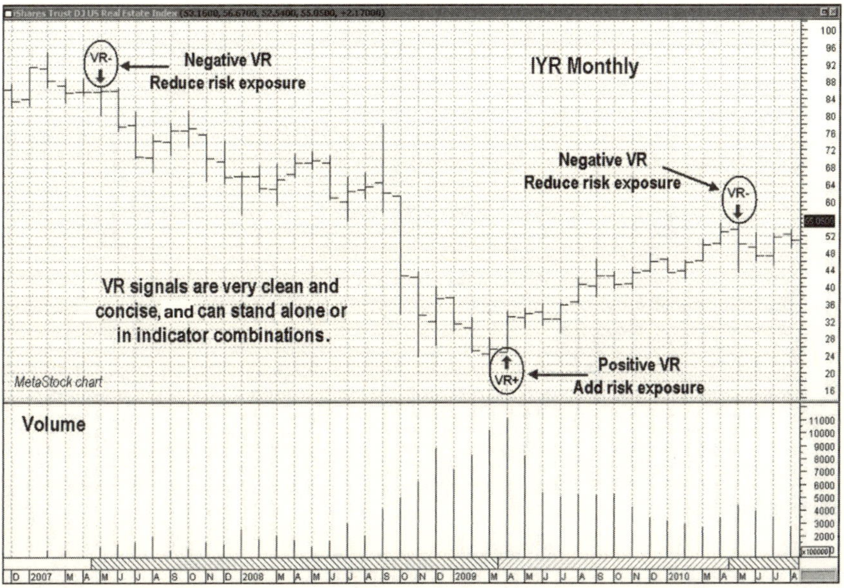

Chart 11.5 Leibovit VR Overlay, iShares Dow Jones Real Estate Index Fund

Source: MetaStock

In the tactical volume overlay example that follows, we begin with the 2008 crash/correction and follow its early warning signals leading up to the flash crash in May 2010. In Chart 11.6, a daily chart of the Nasdaq 100 Trust ETF (QQQQ), three indicators are plotted. The first frame below price displays the Volume Price Trend (VPT). VPT is a long-term trending indicator in that it uses a cumulative running total of the magnitude of daily gains or losses multiplied by that day's volume. Generally, VPT confirms price trends, but when it fails to confirm, it serves as an early-warning system that a trend may be lagging or approaching a reversal.

The second frame includes the Money Flow Indicator (MFI). MFI is normally calculated with the previous 14 periods, and that setting is used in this example to demonstrate MFI's ability to reveal market shifts over a 3-week time frame. Using MFI in conjunction with a long-term trending indicator can assist traders in identifying the correct trend and avoiding incorrect countertrend signals (i.e., selling short in an uptrend or going long in a downtrend).

Displayed in the third frame in Chart 11.6 is the volume moving average, or VMA. Chapter 4 discussed several different styles of volume overlays that can be used for Volume Analysis. Any one of those discussed in the previous chapters can be utilized. Our preference is to include the

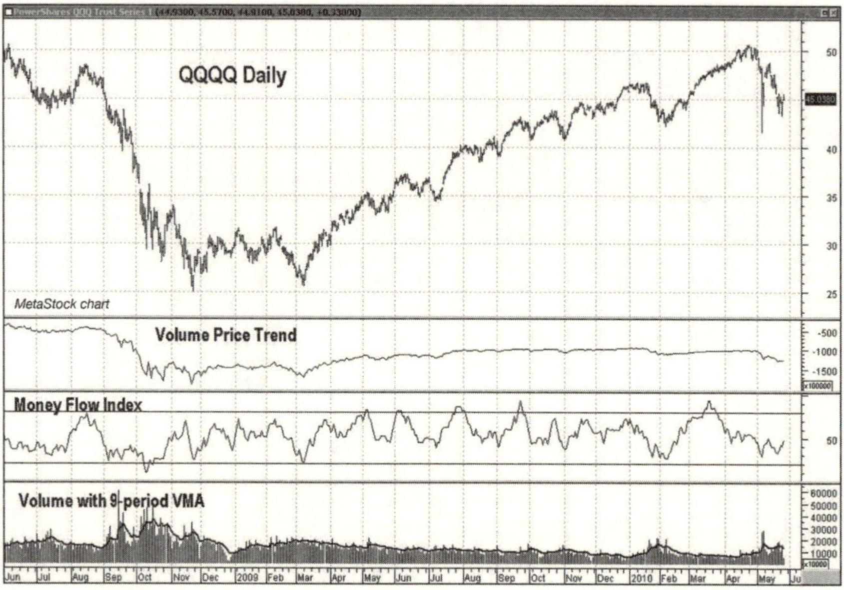

Chart 11.6 Short-Term Trading Overlay with VMA, Nasdaq 100 Trust ETF

Source: MetaStock

VMA to pinpoint short-term swings in the market. The current example uses a 9-period exponential moving average of volume.

Recall our trader's mantra: *When the VMA peaks and heads lower, it is a signal that a near-term change of direction is imminent.* In the current example, short-term countertrend selling has run its course, and the larger-degree uptrend is ready to resume.

One of our preferred methodologies in tactical overlays is to combine a trending indicator with a shorter-term oscillator and the VMA (a volume overlay), as we have done here. Doing so gives a trader a broader perspective of the health and direction of the market, allowing for the exploitation of shorter-term trading opportunities as they develop.

Again, the Volume Price Trend (VPT) indicator, shown in the first frame, was chosen because of its strengths in relation to trend confirmation. Market trends are more correctly identified when a clear pattern of higher highs and higher lows (i.e., an uptrend) or lower highs and lower lows (i.e., a downtrend) are displayed on the chart. When the VPT confirms an uptrend (i.e., it doesn't make lower highs while the market advances), long trades should be considered. When the VPT shows a divergence in making

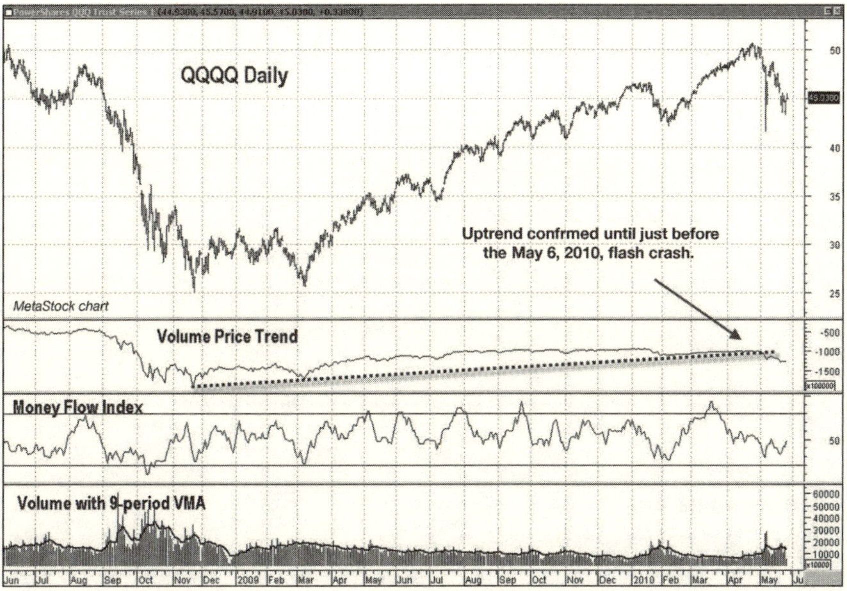

Chart 11.7 Trading Overlay, with VMA, MFI and Volume Price Trend Divergence, Nasdaq 100 Trust ETF

Source: MetaStock

a lower high while price continues its uptrend to a new high, it is a red flag that the trend may be ready to reverse. This action casts doubt on any subsequent trading signals in the direction of the trend until the situation is resolved, either by the trend reversing (which is likely) or by the indicator working itself out of its divergent state (which is a rare outcome). In Chart 11.7, which shows the Nasdaq 100 Trust ETF (QQQQ) uptrend, notice how VPT confirms the trend until it diverges just before the May 6, 2010, flash crash.

When you are choosing a volume indicator for a tactical overlay, we recommend observing it under different trading conditions and becoming knowledgeable about its behavior in specific environments. For example, the MFI is often displayed as an Overbought/Oversold Oscillator. It is generally recommended that a trader sell when the oscillator moves above the 80 level and then crosses back down through the 80 level; buys are recommended when the oscillator moves below the 20 level and crosses back up through the 20 level. The MFI is also widely used as an early-warning signal, as divergences from price often forecast changes in trend.

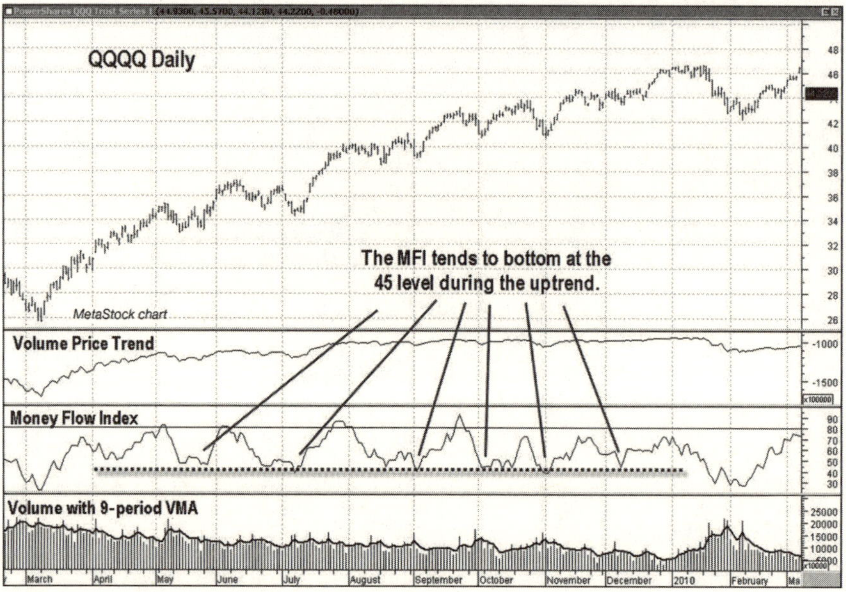

Chart 11.8 Trading Overlay, Money Flow Index Range Bottoms, Nasdaq 100 Trust ETF

Source: MetaStock

Another useful attribute of MFI (as with most oscillators) is to identify at what levels it tends to form tops and bottoms, especially in trending markets. Noticing where MFI forms its turning points allows a trader the opportunity to get great entry points following countertrend moves. Chart 11.8, which applies to the Nasdaq 100 Trust ETF (QQQQ), shows the uptrend off the March 2009 low. A dashed line has been added to the MFI plot to show how the MFI tends to bottom in the 45 area during this uptrend. The MFI bottoming at the 45 level as opposed to the conventional lower boundary of 20 shows solid price and volume momentum. In trending markets, not every twist and turn in the MFI or any other indicator or oscillator is as important as noting the levels at which it tends to reverse. Changes in these levels can alert the trader that the strength of the trend may be changing. This is valuable information to have when looking to initiate new positions in the direction of the trend.

The final structural piece included in this shorter-term trading overlay is a volume overlay, and for this example we have included the versatile VMA again. The VMA, as you may remember from our discussion on Volume Analysis and volume overlays in Chapter 4, is a useful tool to identify turning points in the market. In our example, it is used to confirm trade setups given

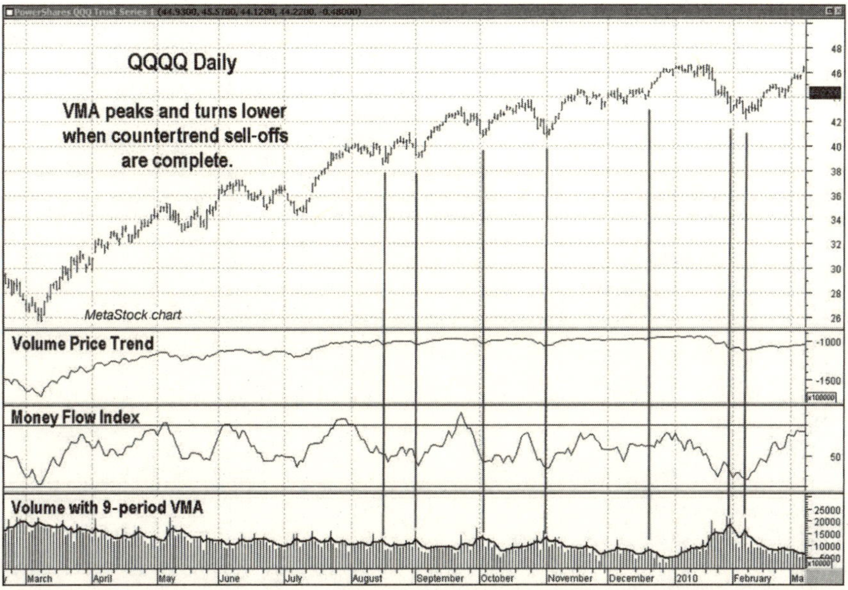

Chart 11.9 Trading Overlay with Volume Moving Average Peaks, Nasdaq 100 Trust ETF

Source: MetaStock

by an oscillator, MFI in this case. The VMA typically works better for detecting these points during market lows than during market highs. (Remember: Volume spikes tend to be more prevalent at lows than at highs because of the more emotional mindset of traders in downtrends as compared to uptrends.) Trading at highs tends to be more subdued, as traders are likely to be more complacent, while volume tends to build more at market lows because a change in sentiment is required to push the market higher again.

The VMA shows when volume peaks have been reached, which usually signals that the short-term trend is about to change. If that volume change signal coincides with a larger-degree trend signal on the MFI, then the odds of making a profitable trade are enhanced. Note in Chart 11.9 (the Nasdaq 100 Trust ETF; QQQQ) how the 9-period VMA shows short-term turning points in the QQQQ.

Loud and Clear: How a Short-Term Trading Overlay with the VMA Generates Stronger Signals

In our example, combining volume indicators across multiple time frames increased the robustness of our trading overlay. In looking at Chart 11.10,

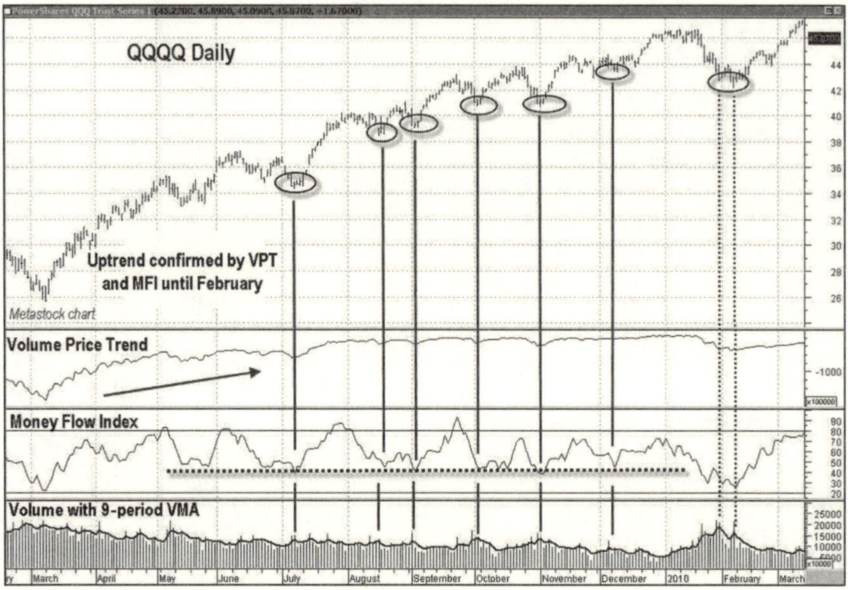

Chart 11.10 Combined Buy Signals Generated by Shorter-Term Trading Overlay during Uptrend, Nasdaq 100 Trust ETF

Source: MetaStock

which shows the Nasdaq 100 Trust ETF (QQQQ) with the Volume Price Trend (VPT), we see clearly that the trend had been higher since the March 2009 low. That would encourage a trader to look at trades on the long side and to buy on pullbacks. From there, we look to the mid- to shorter-term indicators (i.e., MFI and VMA) to identify desirable entry points.

Since we have previously identified the 45 area as a likely bottoming zone for MFI, we can now pair it with a 9-period VMA to spot short-term turning points and more easily identify trade entries. Note in Chart 11.10 how six valid long-side trade entries were identified with this combination of indicators: VPT, MFI, and VMA. In each case, the MFI came down to the 45 level and found support as the 9-period VMA made a small peak and turned lower. The synergy of these two indicators along with the verified uptrend in the VPT provided consistent trade entry signals in the direction of the major trend.

Going further, note on the right side of Chart 11.10 (in January–February 2010) how the MFI broke down below the 45 level during that correction, a sign that the uptrend was weakening. Since MFI is computed using a combination of price momentum and volume, it showed that this pullback was longer and more intense than previous pullbacks during the uptrend. The VPT was still holding its uptrend line off the November 2008 low, which signaled that the uptrend was still intact, but the MFI signaled that trader sentiment was beginning to change.

In Chart 11.11, note how in January 2010, not only did the MFI violate its previous bull market support level, but there was also a higher level of volume associated with the sell-off than in past sell-offs, as displayed in the VMA. Indeed, a valid buy signal was given at the February 2010 low, as the trend was still up and the VMA made a peak and turned lower. The change in the volume pattern and MFI, however, signaled that this movement may have been the final push higher in the uptrend before a healthy correction unfolded. Indeed, that was the case.

While the buy signal at the February 2010 low would have resulted in a profitable trade, there were separate, distinct warnings from MFI and VPT, showing that the uptrend was weakening. First, note in Chart 11.11 how the MFI showed a pronounced negative divergence as the price of QQQQ made a higher high in April, while MFI was nowhere near its previous high. Second, note how VPT began to break down, violating the

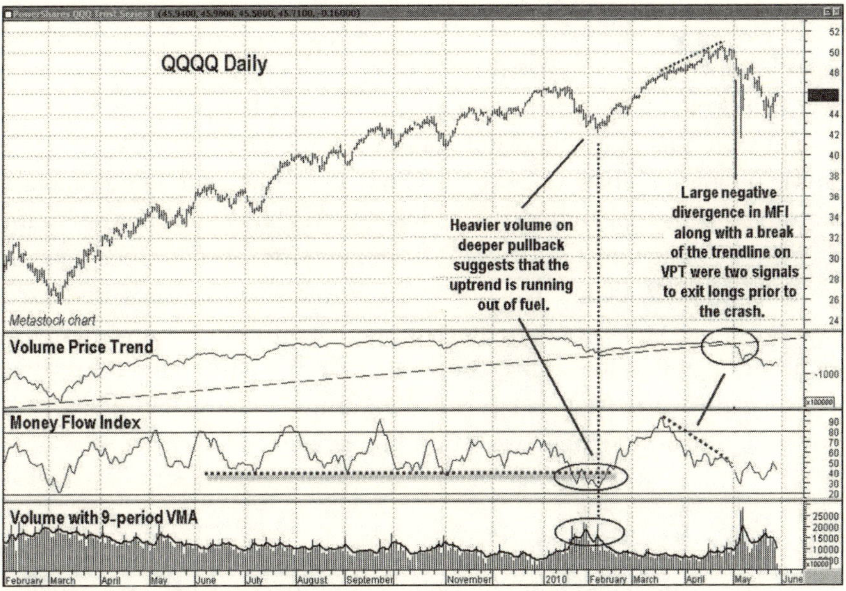

Chart 11.11 Short-Term Trading Overlay, Divergences Signaled, Nasdaq 100 Trust ETF

Source: MetaStock

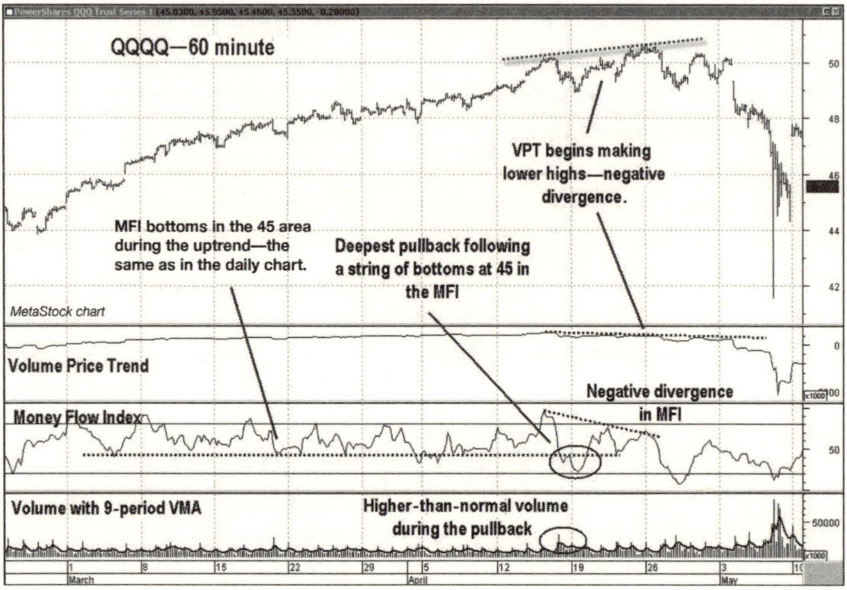

Chart 11.12 Short-Term Trading Volume Overlay, 60-Minute Time Frame, Nasdaq 100 Trust ETF

Source: MetaStock

uptrend line (which began in late 2008 off a November low). These were two signs to lighten up on long positions or move to cash.

This combination of indicators can work in different time frames. Note in the 60-minute chart of QQQQ (Chart 11.12) how the same precrash warning signals appeared. First, see how the MFI tended to bottom in the 45 area the same way it did in the daily time frame. Second, note how the low on April 19, 2010, had higher-than-usual volume and was much deeper on the MFI than the others during the rally phase shown. Finally, notice the same negative divergences in VPT and MFI that were present on the daily chart. That also provided a warning to those trading in intraday time frames that there was a trend reversal ahead.

Creating Timing Overlays

When using combinations of indicators for overlays, we like to use indicators that can show the health of the long-term trend while displaying short- to intermediate-term shifts in trends as they occur. Combining volume indicators creates synergy in an overlay that can help active managers and traders better time market entries and exits as well.

In the previous example, we established that the long-term indicator (VPT) and intermediate-term oscillator (MFI) were breaking down. To that we can add the Leibovit Volume Reversal to develop a *timing overlay*. In the earlier explanation of the Leibovit Volume Reversal in Chapter 9, we observed the ability of this indicator to capture short-term changes in direction as control changed from buyers to sellers. It also has kept traders out of trouble with respect to sharp downside corrections and crashes, which can prove to be very useful when more conventional long-term indicators are flashing warning signs without giving clear-cut signals.

Note at the top of Chart 11.13, which shows the 60-minute Nasdaq 100 Trust ETF (QQQQ), how *four* Negative Volume Reversals posted over a two-week period from April 15 to April 30, 2010, as price stalled above 50. That showed a classic distribution pattern and gave another signal that the smart money was unloading shares prior to the flash crash on May 6.

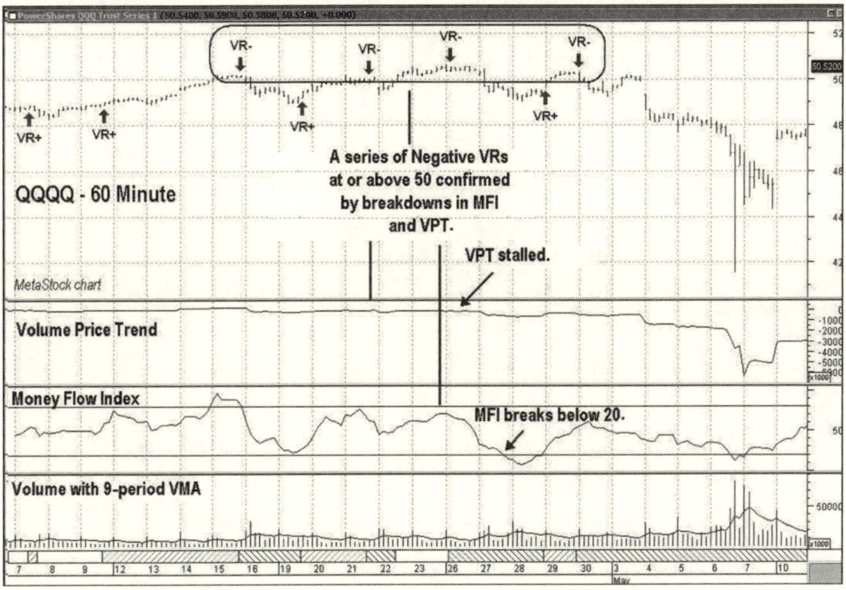

Chart 11.13 Tactical Timing Overlay with Volume Reversal, 60-Minute Intervals, Nasdaq 100 Trust ETF

Source: MetaStock

The Volume Reversal was a true example of a "canary in the coal mine" warning of pending danger.

The Leibovit Volume Reversal can be combined with other volume indicators in any market or sector. The following example of the iShares Dow Jones Real Estate Index Fund ETF (IYR) shows how the VR can act as a leading indicator in an overlay of other indicators using crossovers to generate buy and sell signals.

Chart 11.14 (the iShares Dow Jones Real Estate Index Fund ETF, or IYR) shows On-Balance Volume (OBV; described in Chapter 9) as our long-term trending indicator. That was paired with Ease of Movement (described in Chapter 10) as the short-term to intermediate-term oscillator. Ease of Movement generates buy signals on crosses up through the zero line and sell signals on crosses down through the zero line. Note how OBV is trending higher through the period (i.e., with higher highs and higher lows), yet there are a couple of good trading opportunities against the trend for more active traders.

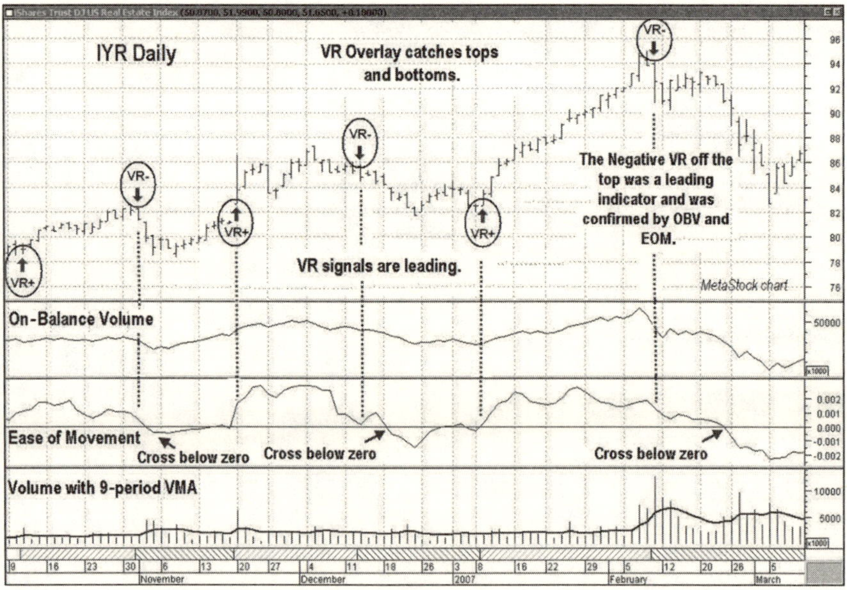

Chart 11.14 Timing Overlay Using Leading Leibovit VR Signals, iShares Dow Jones Real Estate Index ETF

Source: MetaStock

The Leibovit VR gave earlier warnings that pullbacks were due; it also provided timely alerts to stand aside during volatile shifts. Note on the right side of Chart 11.14 how in February 2007 a leading Negative VR was formed off the top, but if one waited to either get short or take profits on longs, much profit would have been lost. That top in February 2007 turned out to be a major top in that market, and utilizing the Volume Reversal would have prevented unnecessary losses.

The final example shows how a string of six straight Negative VRs signaled the trouble brewing before the May 6, 2010, flash crash. In Chart 11.15 (the E-Mini S&P 500), we pair OBV as our long-time-frame indicator with Ease of Movement as the short-term/intermediate-term indicator. Note how no fewer than six Negative VR warnings were posted in a 5-week period preceding the flash crash, while OBV and Ease of Movement displayed suspicious behavior.

As we've seen, the Leibovit Volume Reversal is versatile and works well as a leading indicator to provide synergy when combined with other indicators for a superior timing overlay.

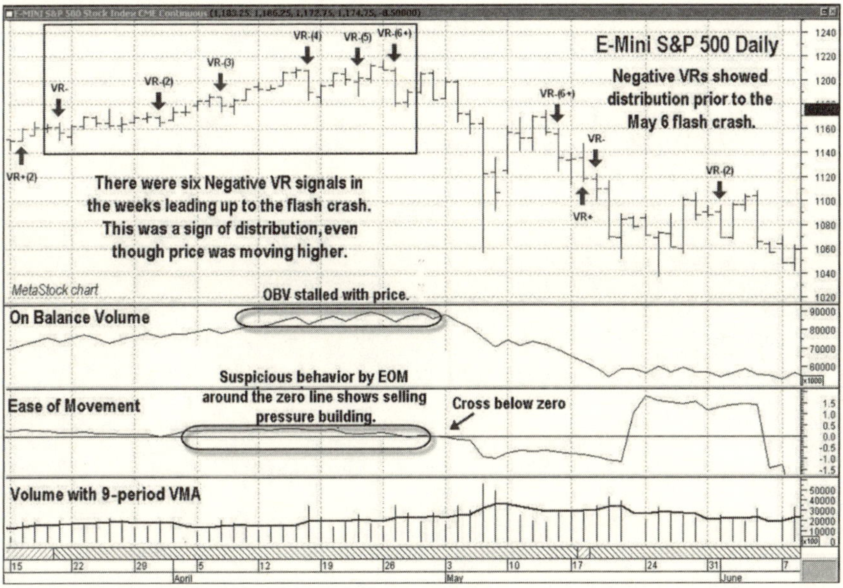

Chart 11.15 Timing Overlay Using Leading Leibovit VR Signals, E-Mini S&P 500 Daily

Source: MetaStock

Summary

- The use of tactical volume overlays can greatly enhance the ability of a trader to recognize and/or confirm market direction.
- Overlays help traders and managers confirm long-term trends as well as identify short-term trading opportunities and the timing of broad market shifts in trend.
- Different volume indicators and oscillators can be utilized for tactical overlays, with particular emphasis on the synergy that develops between multiple volume indicators across differing time frames.

CONCLUSION: KEEPING A TRADER'S EYE ON VOLUME

Together we've ventured off-road through the pages of *The Trader's Book of Volume*, taking a detour from traditional price-based technical analysis to explore the less-traveled roads through Volume Analysis.

Today the terrain is changing; with electronic trading and exchanges, the size of our markets is growing exponentially and internationally to include economic booms in the natural-resource-based economies of Australia, Brazil, Canada, India, and Russia. Despite the globalization of our marketplace, the conviction of a move in any market continues to be a function of the pressures of supply and demand, with volume inextricably linked to price movements. Although these "normal" movements are part of doing business, Volume Analysis helps the trader see how "the crowd" has perceived the price move and subsequently identify the direction and strength of the current trend or the next potential reversal.

We look to volume as a determination of the conviction of a price move, for embedded within volume data is the sentiment of the market itself. Volume allows us to follow the footprints of buyers and sellers in the marketplace. It shows us how and where the larger market participants are playing, and it doesn't lie. I would be so bold as to say that Volume Analysis essentially hinges on the premise that "smart institutional money" moves ahead of news, ignores noise, and leaves a relatively clear trail for us to follow.

Volume patterns not only precede and record an event as it occurs but help a trader to profitably forecast the end result. As such, Volume Analysis analyzes what is happening *today* in the market and contains a prediction for the future. In my opinion, Volume Analysis is the closest thing we have to a real working "crystal ball." The fears, hopes, expectations, and privileged information represented by volume are all rolled up right there right in front of you.

The adage "Volume precedes price" truly tells the story of the marketplace. It's the power of money at work, and the resulting force is volume. You can read and analyze all the news and fundamentals you wish; you can choose or not choose to listen to CNBC. But the bottom line is that trader conviction is what makes and moves markets.

In our exploration, we have examined volume and Volume Analysis from multiple perspectives. We've observed the behavior of volume in simple and complex charting patterns; looked at volume overlays, news, and noise; and finally examined trading techniques using volume indicators and oscillators. We've kept our eyes on the road, with the end goal being the development of tactical volume overlays for timing the broad market and short-term trading.

Developing a professional trading strategy takes time and diligent effort. However, at some point I encourage every trader to select and refine those volume indicators that best suit his or her time frame and trading preferences. I cannot stress enough that volume should be a necessary component of every trading strategy. It is complementary to almost any trading approach and is well worth the effort in financial returns.

Arming yourself with the indicators, oscillators, and techniques presented herein will give you an advantage over those who ignore volume altogether or simply give it a passing glance. In trading, as in life, practice makes perfect. Incorporating new Volume Analysis techniques into your trading plan may take some getting used to, but the skills acquired will forever change the way you view the market.

My ability to forecast and sidestep every major crash from 1987 through the flash crash of 2010 should be reason enough for you to begin using volume as an integral component of your strategy. Remember, successful traders not only make profitable trades but also excel at keeping their losses to a minimum. Toward that end, I hope I've succeeded in convincing you that the trader's mantra, "Volume precedes price," is as much a truth today as it was when I first heard it. Volume continues to be a living, breathing warning signal of potential market trends and reversals—heed it as it sounds. The door is generally way too small to exit when markets are in meltdown mode.

All said and done, the best preparation is in the planning. Begin by using the various volume technical tools presented. They will add an additional dimension to your trading and empower you to be a better and more profitable trader. How do I know? Over the past 35 years, the practice of Volume Analysis has provided me the opportunity to call the shots ahead of the crowd and in a sense become that proverbial "one-eyed man in the land of the blind." It can do the same for you. So keep your eye on the Volume!

SOURCES

Richard W. Arms, Jr., **Volume Cycles in the Stock Market**, Salt Lake City, Utah: Equis International, Inc., 1994

Richard W. Arms, Jr., **Profits in Volume**, Larchmont, NY: Larchmont Investors Intelligence, Inc., 1971

Joseph E. Granville, **A Strategy of Daily Stock Market Timing for Maximum Profit**, Englewood Cliffs, N.J.: Prentice-Hall, Inc., 1970

Robert D. Edwards and John Magee, **Technical Analysis of Stock Trends, 9th Edition**, Boca Raton, Fla.: CRC Press, Taylor & Francis Group, 2007

Gerald Appel, **The Moving Average Convergence-Divergence Trading Method**, Toronto: Scientific Information Systems, 1985

Jake Bernstein, **The Compleat Day-Trader**, New York: McGraw-Hill, 1995

Yale Hirsch, **The Stock Trader's Almanac**, Old Tappan, N.J.: Hirsch Organization, 1997.

Edwin LeFevre, **Reminiscences of a Stock Operator**, New York: G. H. Doran, 1923. Reprint, New York: John Wiley & Sons, 1993

Larry Williams, **The Secret of Selecting Stocks for Immediate and Substantial Gains**, Brightwaters, N.Y.: Windsor Books, 1986.

Gregory L. Morris, **Candlestick Charting Explained: Timeless Techniques for Trading Stocks and Futures,** 3rd Edition, New York: McGraw-Hill, 2006.

John Bollinger, **Bollinger on Bollinger Bands**, New York: McGraw-Hill, 2002

Steve B. Achelis, **Technical Analysis from A to Z**, 2nd Edition, New York: McGraw-Hill, 2001

Charles D. Kirkpatrick and Julie R. Dahlquist, **Technical Analysis: The Complete Resource for Financial Market Technicians**, Upper Saddle River, N.J.: Pearson Education, Inc., 2006

Martin J. Pring, **Technical Analysis Explained,** 4th Edition, New York: McGraw Hill, 2001

Perry J. Kaufman, **New Trading Systems and Methods,** 4th Edition, New York: John Wiley & Sons, 1998

Stan Weinstein, **Secrets for Profiting in Bull and Bear Markets**, New York: McGraw-Hill, 1988

MetaStock: http://www.equis.com

http://www.investopedia.com

http://wikipedia.org

INDEX

ABOUT THE AUTHOR

Mark Leibovit (Sedona, AZ) is the Chief Market Strategist for VRTrader.com. Previously, Mr. Leibovit was a member of the Midwest Options Exchange and the Chicago Board Options Exchange, where he became a market maker in 1976. In 1979, after being a consultant for several regional brokerage firms, Mr. Leibovit left the floor and began publishing his newsletter *The Volume Reversal Survey*, now VRTrader.com. His Annual Forecast Model (available at VRTrader.com) has gained increasing notoriety on Wall Street as a predictor of future market movement. Released each year in early February, it has accurately pinpointed market highs and lows. Its claim to fame began back in 1987, when it predicted the ominous stock market crash nine months in advance. It also forecast the 2000 bear market in the February 1, 2000, report entitled: "It Looks Like an Honest to Goodness Bear Market."

Mr. Leibovit, who holds CIMA and AIF designations and is a member of the Market Technicians Association (MTA) and the CFA Institute, was one of the ten "Elves" on Louis Rukeyser's *Wall Street Week* television program, where he served as a weekly consultant for seven years. Now, he appears as a regular Market Monitor guest with Paul Kangas on PBS's *The Nightly Business Report*. He is a frequent guest on several radio and television financial programs, including CNBC, CNN, Bloomberg, and CBS in Chicago. He has been interviewed by *Barron's, BusinessWeek, The Wall Street Journal, Forbes*, CBS.Marketwatch.com, and *DTN Wall Street*, among others.